How to Prepare for the

CPA

Certified Public Accountant Examination

How to Prepare for the

CPA

Certified Public Accountant Examination

Fifth Edition

by Person/Wolinsky CPA Review Courses

SAMUEL PERSON, MS, CPA

NICKY DAUBER, MS, CPA

BARRON'S

The authors are indebted to the American Institute of Certified Public Accountants, Inc., for permission to use the following copyright © materials:

1. *Information for CPA Candidates,* Eleventh Edition, 1993. An abridged version of the Content Specification Outline, copyright © 1993 by the American Institute of Certified Public Accountants, Inc., is reprinted with permission.

2. *Uniform CPA Examinations*
   a. For the May 1994 Examination, questions from the Uniform CPA Examination, copyright © 1994 by the American Institute of Certified Public Accountants, Inc., are reprinted with permission.
   b. For the Simulated CPA Examination, questions from the Uniform CPA Examination, copyright © 1992 and 1993 by the American Institute of Certified Public Accountants, Inc., are reprinted with permission.
   c. For the preliminary readiness tests, selected past four-option, multiple-choice questions were used.

All inquiries should be addressed to:
Barron's Educational Series, Inc.
250 Wireless Boulevard
Hauppauge, New York 11788

Library of Congress Catalog Card No. 94-40500
International Standard Book No. 0-8120-2865-1

Library of Congress Cataloging in Publication Data
Person, Samuel.
   How to prepare for the certified public accountant examination,
CPA / by Person/Wolinsky CPA Review Courses, Samuel Person, Nicky A.
Dauber.—5th ed.
       p.   cm.
   Rev. ed. of : Barron's how to prepare for the certified public accountant examination,
CPA / by Person/Wolinsky CPA Review Courses, Samuel Person, Andrew N. Gusman.
4th ed. c1992.
   Includes bibliographical references.
   ISBN 0-8120-2865-1
   1. Accounting—Examinations, questions, etc. I. Dauber, Nicky A. II. Person/Wolinsky
CPA Review Courses (Firm) III. Person, Samuel. How to prepare for the certified public
accountant examination, CPA. IV. Title. V. Title: CPA.
HF5661.P48 1995
657'.076—dc20
                                                                94-40500
                                                                CIP

PRINTED IN THE UNITED STATES OF AMERICA

5678   100   987654321

Contents

Abbreviations

Term	Meaning
Aa	Designation used by *Moody's* and *Standard & Poor's* to indicate bond quality. "Aa" is considered high quality, having very strong capacity to pay interest and repay principal.
ACRS	Accelerated Cost Recovery System
AICPA	American Institute of Certified Public Accountants
APB	Accounting Principles Board
ARE	Accounting & Reporting
AUDIT	Auditing
CPI	Consumer Price Index
CS	Consulting Services
DSE	Development-Stage Enterprise
EDP	Electronic Data Processing
EOQ	Economic Order Quantity
EPS	Earnings Per Share
EU	Equivalent Units (of production)
FAC	Financial Accounting Concept
FARE	Financial Accounting & Reporting
FAS	Financial Accounting Standard
FASB	Financial Accounting Standards Board
FIFO	First-In, First-Out (inventory method)
FOB	Free On Board
GAAP	Generally Accepted Accounting Principle
GAAS	Generally Accepted Auditing Standard
GASB	Governmental Accounting Standards Board
LIFO	Last-In, First-Out (inventory method)
LPR	Business Law and Professional Responsibilities
NASBA	National Association of State Boards of Accountancy
R & D	Research and Development
SAS	Statement on Auditing Standards
SEC	Securities and Exchange Commission
SSAE	Statement on Standards for Attestation Engagements
SSARS	Statement on Standards for Accounting and Review Services
SYD	Sum-of-the-Years' Digits (inventory method)
UCC	Uniform Commercial Code

Preface

Objectives of this Book

This book has three goals:

1. To provide CPA candidates with an overall study plan, time-saving techniques, and attributes necessary for success on the CPA exam.
2. To acquaint future CPA candidates with the form and content of the CPA examination.
3. To provide CPA candidates with the information they need in order to make an informed choice among review program alternatives.

This book is not intended as a comprehensive review of subject matter tested on the CPA exam; rather, it is a guide to the preparation process that must precede the examination. That process is one that extends over a period of months, and that requires of the candidate a level of insight and discipline experienced in few other situations in life. How a candidate goes about preparing for the exam is the primary determinant of his or her success on it. This book provides the candidate with the basis for feeling confident about passing the CPA exam. It contains information about the form and content of the exam, a detailed discussion of how to prepare for the exam, and two CPA exams with answers fully explained.

In instances where the pronouns *he* and *him* appear, they have been used to conform with standard business prose. It should be understood that, in every case except where specifically stated, these references apply to both men and women.

About Person/Wolinsky

Person/Wolinsky has been in the business of preparing candidates for the CPA exam since 1967. It offers a national CPA review course with over 170,000 alumni and 50 locations across the United States.

The firm's founders, Sam Person and Dan Wolinsky, are both CPAs with many years of experience in business, academic, and professional circles. Mr. Person is a former Professor of Accounting, School of Professional Accountancy, C.W. Post Campus, Long Island University. He has been a member of the AICPA Council, the Board of Directors of the New York State Society of CPAs and a trustee of the Society's Foundation for Accounting Education. Mr. Wolinsky is a charter holder of the CMA awarded by the Institute of Management Accountants. He is also Professor Emeritus, School of Professional Accountancy, C.W. Post Campus, Long Island University.

The Person/Wolinsky course is presented in a variety of formats in an effort to meet the differing needs of individual candidates. Options include classroom courses, self-study courses, and in-house training courses for CPA firms. Computer software is available. The ideas presented in this book reflect the wisdom achieved during Person/Wolinsky's many years of training CPA candidates.

The authors would like to thank Joan Fitzgerald for her singular efforts in the coordination of this publication. Her dedication, attention to detail, and high sense of order are deeply appreciated.

How To Use This Guide

This book contains three types of informational material. The background chapters (Chapters 1, 2, 10) describe the form and content of the CPA examination. The test-efficiency technique chapters (Chapters 3 through 6) develop an overall study plan and provide test strategies for the various question types. The practice examination chapters (Chapters 7 through 9) include two examinations with explained answers and readiness tests.

Success on the CPA examination depends, in part, on familiarity with past test questions and, in part, on test-taking efficiency (since all questions must be answered in order to do well). This book will help you gain familiarity and efficiency on the exam. The overall study plan will help you determine your weaknesses and decide on the best course of action. The test tactics will help you make the best use of your allotted time. The test questions included will provide you with an opportunity to become familiar with actual CPA examination questions. Nothing should faze you when you get to the examination.

The best way of using this book is as follows:

Step 1: Get an Overview of the Exam

Read Chapters 1 and 2. These will provide you with information on content, conditioning requirements, and where to seek information and application forms. They will also provide you with an *abridged AICPA Content Specification Outline*, which you should read carefully in order to get an overview of the material covered on the exam.

Step 2: Organize Your Strategy

In order to plan your course of action, you should read Chapters 3 through 6 very carefully.

Chapter 3 provides you with an insight into the kind of commitment that is necessary in order to pass this examination. *Your 7-Stage Study Program* is outlined, along with guidelines as to whether you should plan a self-study program or seek help in a review course.

Chapter 4 provides you with a detailed summary of the subject matter covered on the exam and bibliographies by exam section.

Chapter 5 provides you with test tactics for each type of question found on the examination: four-option multiple-choice, other objective formats, computational, and essay. Sample questions and solutions are also included in order to show you how to apply your knowledge.

Chapter 6 shows you *how to chart your progress and plan your course of action*. Once you have taken any of the preliminary readiness tests and the sample examinations, you will score your work and analyze your weak areas.

Step 3: Begin Your Review

Now, begin your practice. Take each section of the preliminary readiness tests (a typical sampling of AICPA questions) according to the instructions given in Chapter 7. Be sure to practice the test tactics outlined in Chapter 5. When you have completed these tests, turn to Chapter 6 to plan your course of action.

Step 4: Two Sample Examinations— Practice Your Strategy

Chapters 8 and 9 provide you with two practice examinations: (1) a Simulated CPA Examination, consisting of questions from former Accounting Practice, Accounting Theory, Business Law, and Auditing examinations, and (2) the May 1994 CPA Examination, which is the first examination to reflect (a) the realignment of the topical areas on the examination, and (b) the renaming of all examination sections other than Auditing.

First, take the Simulated CPA Examination. Analyze your weaknesses and look at the Content Specification Outline to determine the relative importance of a topic area, and then review using one of the recommended methods described in Chapter 3. Chapter 6 will guide your study plan.

Then, take the May 1994 Examination, following the guidelines outlined in the previous paragraph.

Step 5: A Final Word

Don't forget to read Chapter 10 just before taking the examination. The two days of test-taking during the CPA examination are an extremely pressured time, so you should do the most to thoroughly prepare yourself for it. This chapter will help you do this. And be sure to read the *Instructions for the Uniform Certified Public Accountant Examination*. Not following instructions can cause you to fail. Be sure to read them carefully.

The use of this book along with the guidelines outlined will provide you with a clear understanding of what you must do in order to prepare effectively for the CPA examination.

Best of luck!

1. An Introduction to the CPA Examination

GENERAL PURPOSE AND CHARACTER

One function, historically, of the CPA exam has been to identify persons able to demonstrate a certain level of accounting competence. That level, as established by the exam, becomes the standard by which all accountants are judged. One either is a CPA or is not a CPA and, rightly or wrongly, is subject to a variety of value judgments regarding one's professional credentials. For someone planning a career in accounting, it is not a question of *whether* to take the CPA exam, but of *when* to take it, and of *how to prepare* for it.

Passing the CPA exam is, for the aspiring accountant, the achievement of professional stature. As an occupational standard, the exam provides a means of ensuring that those who offer their services to the public as professional accountants possess the degree of competence called for in such engagements. To succeed on the exam, one must know not only the subject matter tested but also the nature of the test itself: how it is constructed, how it is graded, what is likely to appear, etc.

The CPA exam does not presuppose extensive work experience in public accounting. Having a general familiarity with business situations is certainly an advantage when dealing with question situations, but it is not essential. The CPA exam is textbook oriented. It presents questions having a difficulty level suitable for an entry-level accountant recently graduated from college. Ideally, the candidate should sit for the examination during the semester before graduation (if allowed by state law), or as soon as possible after completing college.

The exam is prepared by the Board of Examiners of the American Institute of Certified Public Accountants (AICPA), a private, professional organization made up of CPAs and CPA firms across the country. The test is administered by individual state boards of accountancy and the National Association of State Boards of Accountancy (NASBA). Each state, through its board of accountancy, establishes its own licensing requirements for CPAs. Each state, however, has adopted the Uniform CPA Examination as its measure of academic preparation. Further licensing requirements regarding work experience and educational background differ slightly from state to state. Grading of the exam is done by the AICPA's Advisory Grading Service. This ensures uniformity of evaluation without regard to where the exam was taken. After grading, papers are returned to the body that administered the exam for reporting results to candidates.

STRUCTURE AND GENERAL CONTENT

The Uniform CPA Examination is divided into four sections: Business Law & Professional Responsibilities (LPR), Auditing (AUDIT), Accounting & Reporting—Taxation, Managerial, and Governmental and Not-for-Profit Organizations (ARE), and Financial Accounting & Reporting—Business Enterprises (FARE). The following schedule indicates the length of each section and when it is administered:

Section	Hours	Day	Time
LPR	3.0	Wed.	9:00—12:00 Noon
AUDIT	4.5	Wed.	1:30—6:00 P.M.
ARE	3.5	Thurs.	8:30—12:00 Noon
FARE	4.5	Thurs.	1:30—6:00 P.M.
Total	15.5		

The exam is given twice yearly in early May and November. Some 50 to 60 percent of each section is made up of four-option multiple-choice questions; 20 to 30 percent is in the form of essay or computational questions (none in the case of ARE), and 20 to 30 percent is in the form of other objective formats questions (40 to 50 percent in the case of ARE).

The *LPR* section deals with legal concepts rather than with the practice of law. The examiners presume that a CPA should be able to recognize the legal implications of situations that arise in the practice of accounting or auditing. Essay and objective questions present hypothetical situations in which the candidate must decide how a legal dispute should be resolved and, in essay questions, support conclusions with reasons. The focus is on federal or widely adopted laws such as the Uniform Commercial Code, Model Business Corporation Act, Uniform Partnership Act, etc. The LPR section also focuses on professional ethics. In particular, candidates must be familiar with the AICPA "Code of Professional Conduct."

The *AUDIT* section tests candidates' knowledge of generally accepted auditing standards and procedures. In answering the essay and objective questions presented, the candidate must demonstrate an ability to apply an understanding of auditing concepts and procedures to specific fact situations. Candidates are expected to have a general knowledge of EDP and statistical sampling. As with ARE and FARE, candidates are not expected to be familiar with auditing pronouncements issued within the six months preceding the examination.

The focus of the *ARE* section is on federal taxation, managerial accounting, and accounting for governmental and not-for-profit organizations. The underlying computations are not difficult since testing computational dexterity is not the aim of the ARE section. Rather, its aim is to test underlying theory and the reasoning involved in its application.

The concern of the *FARE* section is with the conceptual underpinnings and applications of generally accepted accounting principles for business enterprises. The candidate's grasp of accounting concepts is tested in essay, computational, and objective questions that ask him to define, explain, evaluate, or discuss accounting procedures appropriate for particular situations. In both the ARE and FARE sections, the candidate is *not* expected to be familiar with technical pronouncements (or tax law changes, in the case of the ARE section) issued within the six months preceding the examination.

ABRIDGED AICPA CONTENT SPECIFICATION OUTLINE

The AICPA has promulgated its "Content Specification Outlines" to formally and officially communicate to exam preparers, accounting educators, and candidates what can be tested on the CPA exam.

Obviously, such a document is helpful for anyone seeking to organize his study effort. The body of knowledge encompassed by the exam is so enormous that a candidate needs to be able to select for study not only the right topics, but those aspects of a topic that are likely to be tested.

Following is an abridged version of the AICPA's "Content Specification Outlines" for each exam section. The relative emphasis each topical area receives on the exam is indicated in parentheses next to each Roman-numeraled item:

Business Law & Professional Responsibilities

The Business Law & Professional Responsibilities section tests candidates' knowledge of the CPA's professional responsibilities and of the legal implications of business transactions, particularly as they relate to accounting and auditing. This section includes the CPA's professional responsibilities, business organizations, contracts, debtor-creditor relationships, government regulation of business, Uniform Commercial Code, and property. The subjects in this section normally are covered in standard textbooks on business law, auditing, taxation, and accounting, and in the following publications: AICPA *Code of Professional Conduct*, Statements on Auditing Standards, Statements on Standards for Consulting Services, and Statements on Responsibilities in Tax Practice.

The Business Law & Professional Responsibilities section is chiefly conceptual. It is not intended to test competence to practice law or expertise in legal matters, but to determine that candidates (1) recognize relevant legal issues, (2) recognize the legal implications of business situations, (3) can apply the underlying principles of law to accounting and auditing situations, and (4) understand the CPA's professional standards and responsibilities.

This section deals with federal and widely adopted uniform laws. Where there is no federal or uniform law on a subject, the questions are intended to test knowledge of the majority rules. Federal taxation may be covered where appropriate in the overall context of a question. Professional ethics questions are based on the AICPA *Code of Professional Conduct* because it is national in its application, whereas codes of other organizations and jurisdictions may be limited in their application.

Selected essay responses will be graded for writing skills.

LPR Section

I. Professional Responsibilities (15 percent).

    A. Code of Conduct and Other Responsibilities
       1. Code of Professional Conduct
       2. Proficiency, Independence, and Due Care
       3. Responsibilities in Consulting Services
       4. Responsibilities in Tax Practice
    B. The CPA and the Law
       1. Common Law Liability to Clients and Third Parties
       2. Federal Statutory Liability
       3. Working Papers, Privileged Communication, and Confidentiality

II. Business Organizations (20 percent).

    A. Agency
       1. Formation and Termination
       2. Principal's Liabilities
       3. Disclosed and Undisclosed Principals
       4. Agent's Authority and Liability
    B. Partnerships and Joint Ventures
       1. Formation and Existence
       2. Liabilities and Authority of Partners and Joint Owners
       3. Allocation of Profit or Loss
       4. Transfer of Interest
       5. Termination and Dissolution
    C. Corporations
       1. Formation, Purposes, and Powers
       2. Stockholders, Directors, and Officers
       3. Financial Structure, Capital, and Distributions
       4. Merger, Consolidation, and Dissolution
    D. Estates and Trusts
       1. Formation and Purposes
       2. Allocation Between Principal and Income
       3. Fiduciary Responsibilities
       4. Distributions and Termination

III. Contracts (10 percent).

    A. Formation
    B. Performance
    C. Third-Party Assignments
    D. Discharge, Breach, and Remedies

IV. Debtor-Creditor Relationships (10 percent).

    A. Rights and Duties—Debtors and Creditors
       1. Liabilities and Defenses
       2. Release of Parties
       3. Remedies of Parties

    B. Rights and Duties—Guarantors
       1. Liabilities and Defenses
       2. Release of Parties
       3. Remedies of Parties
    C. Bankruptcy
       1. Voluntary and Involuntary Bankruptcy
       2. Effects of Bankruptcy on Debtors and Creditors
       3. Reorganizations

V. Government Regulation of Business (15 percent).

    A. Regulation of Employment
       1. Payroll Taxes
       2. Employee Safety
       3. Employment Discrimination
       4. Wage and Hour
       5. Pension and Other Fringe Benefits
    B. Federal Securities Acts
       1. Securities Registration
       2. Reporting Requirements
       3. Exempt Securities and Transactions

VI. Uniform Commercial Code (20 percent).

    A. Commercial Paper
       1. Types of Negotiable Instruments
       2. Requisites of Negotiability
       3. Transfer and Negotiation
       4. Holders and Holders in Due Course
       5. Liabilities, Defenses, and Rights
       6. Discharge
    B. Sales
       1. Contracts Covering Goods
       2. Warranties
       3. Product Liability
       4. Risk of Loss
       5. Performance and Obligations
       6. Remedies and Defenses
    C. Secured Transactions
       1. Attachment of Security Interests
       2. Perfection of Security Interests
       3. Priorities
       4. Rights of Debtors, Creditors, and Third Parties

VII. Property (10 percent).

    A. Real Property
       1. Types of Ownership
       2. Lessor-Lessee
       3. Deeds, Recording, Title Defects, and Title Insurance
       4. Mortgages and Other Liens

5. Fixtures
6. Environmental Liability
B. Personal Property
1. Types of Ownership
2. Bailments
C. Fire and Casualty Insurance
1. Coinsurance
2. Multiple Insurance Coverage
3. Insurable Interest

Auditing

The Auditing section tests candidates' knowledge of generally accepted auditing standards and procedures. This section includes engagement planning, the control structure, evidence and procedures, and reporting. In preparing for this section, candidates should study publications such as the following:

- Statements on Auditing Standards
- Statements on Standards for Accounting and Review Services
- Statements on Quality Control Standards
- Statements on Standards for Attestation Engagements
- Statement on Standards for Accountants' Services on Prospective Financial Statements
- U.S. General Accounting Office Government Auditing Standards
- AICPA Audit and Accounting Guides
- AICPA Audit and Accounting Manual
- AICPA Auditing Procedure Studies
- Auditing textbooks

AUDIT Section

I. Planning the Engagement (20 percent).

A. Pre-engagement Acceptance Activities
B. Staffing and Supervision Requirements
C. Understanding the Entity's Business and Its Industry
D. Analytical Procedures
E. Audit Risk and Materiality
F. Errors, Irregularities, and Illegal Acts
G. Documentation and Audit Programs
H. Engagement Responsibilities
1. Attestation
2. Audit
3. Review
4. Compilation
5. Prospective Financial Statements
I. Quality Control Considerations

II. Considering the Internal Control Structure (25 percent).

A. Definitions and Basic Concepts
B. Understanding and Documenting the Structure
1. Control Environment
2. Accounting System
3. Control Procedures
C. Assessing Control Risk
D. Testing Controls
E. Other Considerations
1. Reportable Conditions
2. Reports on Internal Control
3. Special-Purpose Reports on Internal Control Structure of Service Organizations

III. Obtaining Evidence and Applying Procedures (35 percent).

A. Audit Evidence
1. Nature, Competence, and Sufficiency of Evidential Matter
2. Evidential Matter for Financial Statement Assertions and Objectives
3. Confirmations
4. Analytical Procedures and Related Inquiries
5. Audit Sampling
6. Accounting Estimates
B. Tests of Details of Transactions and Balances
1. Sales, Receivables, and Cash Receipts
2. Purchases, Payables, and Cash Disbursements
3. Inventories and Production
4. Personnel and Payroll
5. Financing and Investing
6. Other
C. Other Specific Audit Topics
1. Substantive Tests Prior to the Balance Sheet Date
2. Effect of the Internal Audit Function
3. Using the Work of a Specialist
4. Inquiry of a Client's Lawyer
5. Subsequent Events
6. Client Representations
7. Related Parties and Related-Party Transactions
8. Using the Computer in Performing the Audit
9. Going Concern
10. Working Papers

D. Review and Compilation Procedures
1. Understanding the Accounting Principles and Practices of the Industry
2. Inquiry and Analytical Procedures
3. Other Procedures

IV. Preparing Reports (20 percent).

A. Reports on Audited Financial Statements
1. Reporting Responsibilities
2. Presentation in Conformity with Generally Accepted Accounting Principles
3. Standard Report
4. Departures from Unqualified Opinions
5. Explanatory Language Added to the Standard Report
6. Uncertainties
7. Going Concern
8. Consistency
9. Comparative Financial Statements
10. Part of Audit Performed by Other Independent Auditors
11. Dating and Addressing the Auditor's Report
B. Reports on Reviewed and Compiled Financial Statements
C. Other Reporting Considerations
1. Attestation Engagements
2. Prospective Financial Statements
3. Special Reports
4. Review of Interim Financial Information
5. Compliance with Laws and Regulations
6. Subsequent Discovery of Facts Existing at the Date of the Auditor's Report
7. Consideration of Omitted Procedures After the Report Date
8. Letters for Underwriters
9. Filings Under Federal Securities Statutes
10. Other Information in Documents Containing Audited Financial Statements
11. Required Supplementary Information
12. Reporting on Information Accompanying the Basic Financial Statements
13. Reporting on Condensed Financial Statements
14. Reporting on Financial Statements Prepared for Use in Other Countries
15. Reports on the Application of Accounting Principles
16. Communication with Audit Committees
17. Governmental Reporting Responsibilities

Accounting & Reporting—Taxation, Managerial, and Governmental and Not-for-Profit Organizations

The ARE section tests candidates' knowledge of federal taxation, managerial accounting, and accounting for governmental and not-for-profit organizations. This section includes the underlying theory and its application in practice to federal taxation, managerial accounting and governmental and not-for-profit accounting. In preparing for this section, candidates should study publications such as the following:

- Internal Revenue Code and Income Tax Regulations
- Income tax textbooks
- Managerial and cost accounting textbooks
- Pronouncements of the Governmental Accounting Standards Board
- Pronouncements of the Financial Accounting Standards Board and its predecessors
- AICPA Audit and Accounting Guides
- Governmental and not-for-profit accounting textbooks and chapters of accounting textbooks pertaining to this area

ARE Section

I. Federal Taxation—Individuals (20 percent).

A. Inclusions in Gross Income
B. Exclusions and Adjustments to Arrive at Adjusted Gross Income
C. Deductions from Adjusted Gross Income
D. Filing Status and Exemptions
E. Tax Accounting Methods
F. Tax Computations, Credits, and Penalties
G. Other
1. Tax Procedures
2. Preparers' Responsibilities

II. Federal Taxation—Corporations (25 percent).

A. Determination of Taxable Income or Loss
B. Tax Accounting Methods
C. S Corporations
D. Personal Holding Companies
E. Consolidated Returns
F. Tax Computations, Credits, and Penalties
G. Other
1. Distributions
2. Incorporation, Reorganization, Liquidation, and Dissolution
3. Tax Procedures
4. Preparers' Responsibilities

III. Federal Taxation—Partnerships, Estates and Trusts, and Exempt Organizations (10 percent).

A. Partnerships
1. Basis of Partner's Interest
2. Determination of Partner's Taxable Income and Partner's Elections
3. Partner Dealing with Own Partnership
4. Treatment of Partnership Liabilities
5. Distribution of Partnership Assets
6. Termination of Partnership
B. Estates and Trusts
1. Income Taxation
2. Determination of Beneficiary's Taxable Income
3. Estate and Gift Taxation
C. Exempt Organizations
1. Types of Organization
2. Requirements for Exemption
3. Unrelated Business Income Tax

IV. Managerial Accounting (15 percent).

A. Cost Estimates
B. Budgeting
C. Capital Budgeting
D. Cost-Volume-Profit Analysis
E. Process and Job Order Costing
F. Standard Costing
G. Joint and By-Product Costing
H. Cost Allocation
I. Performance Measurement
J. Inventory Control Techniques
K. Analytical Methods and Procedures
1. Regression and Correlation Analysis
2. Probability Analysis
3. Differential Cost Analysis
4. Product and Service Pricing
5. Ratio Analysis

V. Accounting for Governmental and Not-for-Profit Organizations (30 percent).

A. Conceptual Reporting Issues
1. Measurement Focus and Basis of Accounting
2. Objectives of Financial Reporting
3. Use of Fund Accounting
4. Budgetary Process
5. Financial Reporting Entity
6. Elements of Financial Statements

B. Accounting and Financial Reporting for Governmental Organizations
1. Governmental-Type Funds and Account Groups
2. Proprietary-Type Funds
3. Fiduciary-Type Funds
C. Accounting and Financial Reporting for Not-for-Profit Organizations

Financial Accounting & Reporting—Business Enterprises

The FARE section tests candidates' knowledge of generally accepted accounting principles. This section includes coverage of financial accounting theory and its application in practice to assets, liabilities, equity, income statement items, and other financial accounting and reporting issues. In preparing for this section, candidates should study publications such as the following:

- Pronouncements of the Financial Accounting Standards Board and its predecessors
- AICPA Audit and Accounting Guides
- Accounting textbooks

FARE Section

I. Concepts, Standards, and Financial Statements (15 percent).

A. Conceptual Framework
B. Basic Concepts and Accounting Standards
C. Nature and Purpose of Financial Statements
D. Financial Statement Presentation and Disclosure

II. Recognition, Measurement, Valuation, and Presentation of Assets in Conformity with Generally Accepted Accounting Principles (15 percent).

A. Cash, Cash Equivalents, and Marketable Securities
B. Receivables, Accruals, and Related Contra Accounts
C. Inventories
D. Property, Plant, and Equipment Owned or Leased and Related Contra Accounts
E. Investments
F. Intangibles and Other Assets

III. Recognition, Measurement, Valuation, and Presentation of Liabilities in Conformity with Generally Accepted Accounting Principles (15 percent).

    A. Payables and Accruals
    B. Deferred Revenues
    C. Deferred Income Tax Liabilities
    D. Capitalized Lease Liability
    E. Employee Benefits
    F. Notes and Bonds Payable
    G. Other Liabilities
    H. Contingent Liabilities and Commitments

IV. Recognition, Measurement, Valuation and Presentation of Equity Accounts in Conformity with Generally Accepted Accounting Principles (10 percent).

    A. Corporations
       1. Preferred and Common Stock and Additional Paid-In Capital
       2. Distributions and Retained Earnings
       3. Treasury Stock
       4. Stock Options, Warrants, and Rights
       5. Other Equity Accounts
    B. Partnerships
    C. Proprietorships
    D. Reorganizations and Changes in Entity

V. Recognition, Measurement, and Presentation of Revenues and Expenses in Conformity with Generally Accepted Accounting Principles (30 percent).

    A. Revenues and Gains
    B. Expenses and Losses
    C. Provision for Income Taxes
    D. Other Items
       1. Discontinued Operations
       2. Extraordinary Items
       3. Accounting Changes
       4. Earnings Per Share

VI. Other Financial Accounting and Reporting Issues (15 percent).

    A. Statement of Cash Flows
    B. Consolidated and Combined Financial Statements
    C. Business Combinations
    D. Personal Financial Statements
    E. Financial Statements Prepared on Other Comprehensive Bases
    F. Financial Statement Disclosures
    G. Constant Dollar, Current Cost, and Current-Value Accounting
    H. Analysis of Financial Statements

The preceding outline goes a long way toward identifying topical coverage, but ultimately a candidate must develop an insight into what concepts within a particular APB Opinion, FASB Statement, or AICPA Statement on Auditing Standards the examiners expect an entry-level accountant to know. The text of FAS #52, for example, which deals with foreign currency translation, is 78 pages long. The relevant parts for CPA exam purposes can probably be covered in less than four pages. In the preceding outline, the topic would appear as one of many encompassed by "Recognition, Measurement, and Presentation of Revenues and Expenses in Conformity with Generally Accepted Accounting Principles."

GRADING

As noted previously, grading the CPA exam is the responsibility of the AICPA Advisory Grading Service. Actual grading of essay and computational answers is performed mainly by CPAs and attorneys who serve as graders on a per-diem basis during the grading period.

Graders work from "grading guides" that contain the AICPA "unofficial answers." Also listed in the guides are key words, concepts, or check figures, along with point values assigned to each.

The grading guides for some questions may contain more points of available credit than are actually necessary to get a perfect score. A grading guide for a ten-point essay question, for example, may contain as many as fourteen or fifteen one-point gradable concepts for which credit will be given until the maximum of ten is reached. A "perfect" answer would include every gradable concept, but obviously a perfect answer is not necessary in order to receive a perfect score. Indeed, the examiners are well aware that it would be unreasonable to expect perfection under the timed, pressure situation of the CPA exam. For most questions, however, candidates need to correctly identify all concepts in the grading guide to receive the maximum number of technical points.

Answers to selected essay responses on the LPR, AUDIT, and FARE sections are used to assess candidates' writing skills. Five percent of the total points available on these sections will be allocated to writing skills. The characteristics of writing skills include (1) coherent organization, (2) conciseness, (3) clarity, (4) use of standard English, (5) responsiveness to the requirements of the question, and (6) appropriateness for the reader.

It should be noted that the assignment of credit for writing skills will be positive credit, and not a penalty deducted from the candidate's grade. The extent of the testing will be *two responses* per section, which may be in one or more questions. Further, the grading of writing skills will be performed by the same individuals who grade for substance; there will *not* be a separate grading. The candidate should keep in mind that the AICPA is looking for "comprehensiveness and control" of the English language. Accordingly, if the candidate's paper meets these criteria on the first reading by the grader, maximum writing skills credit will probably be awarded.

The minimum passing score for the CPA exam is 75. As you might expect, no grades between 69 and 75 are given. Those that fall within that range are adjusted either up or down. Further adjustment may be made to grades of all candidates on a particular section. If the overall passing percentage for a particular section is unacceptably low, the Board of Examiners will "curve" the results by awarding "bonus points" to the final grade a candidate receives. Individual questions are neither curved nor "thrown out."

Each section is graded horizontally, which is to say, each grader sees only one question. Each section, therefore, is graded by multiple graders (including an optical scanner for objective-type questions), none of whom knows how the candidate is performing on other questions. When all questions on a section have been graded, they are reassembled and a total score is computed.

Objectivity is further enhanced by the anonymity given to each candidate's answer papers. The only identifying information is a preassigned candidate number and the state in which the exam is being given. Thus, the grader knows nothing about the candidate's name, age, race, sex, or number of times sitting for the exam.

An elaborate system of pretest and post-test analysis and review has been established by the AICPA. During the grading process, papers are placed into one of three groups: obvious pass, marginal, and obvious failure. Papers are then subjected to as many as three reviews.

The first review subjects obvious passes and obvious failures to a cursory review, while marginal papers receive an intensive review.

The second review is performed by a supervisor or a reviewer not involved in the initial review. Papers receiving grades of 68 through 74 receive a second review. Papers meeting the "passing" requirements are awarded an advisory grade of 75; otherwise, a maximum advisory grade of 69 is assigned. Minimum grade requirements for certain jurisdictions are also considered at this point.

In the third review, the Director considers failing papers of candidates receiving high scores on all sections except one. At this point, the reviewer considers whether the overall presentation in the candidate's paper demonstrates that the candidate possesses the technical competence to function effectively as a CPA. If the reviewer is satisfied, the candidate is passed.

Indeed, the AICPA does everything that fairness and reasonableness will allow to help candidates pass the CPA exam.

2. Apply for the CPA Examination

HOW TO APPLY FOR THE CPA EXAMINATION

After an accounting student has decided to become a CPA, one of the first things to do is to ascertain the application deadline to sit for the exam. The deadline varies from state to state. Usually it falls around the first of April or September, but in some states it can be as many as ninety days or as few as thirty before the date of the exam. Also, the deadline can differ depending upon whether the candidate is sitting for the first time or applying for re-examination. Incredibly, many candidates are lax about attending to such mundane details, and end up taking the CPA exam six months later than they should have only because they didn't apply on time.

When applying for the exam, an application fee and/or an examination fee must be paid to the board administering the exam. For the first sitting, fees range from $35 to $220. This out-of-pocket cost represents one more reason why the CPA exam should be approached with every intention of passing it the first time through.

CONDITIONING REQUIREMENTS

State accountancy boards also establish what are called "conditioning requirements." That is, conditions that must be met in order for a candidate to receive credit for individual CPA exam sections passed, even though all four sections have not been passed. Typically, credit will be granted when a candidate first succeeds in passing at least two sections.

In general, the conditioning requirement pertains to the number of sections to be passed initially. Once a candidate is "conditioned," he may thereafter be credited for sections passed individually. For example: candidate Andrews sits for all four sections, passes ARE and FARE, but fails AUDIT and LPR. If Andrews is conditioned (see additional considerations following), and at the next exam he passes only one of the two remaining sections, he will nevertheless receive credit for it because he has "conditioned" at his first sitting.

Many states impose a time limit on the conditional credit given by stipulating an upper limit stated in either years or examinations beyond which conditional credit earned will be lost unless the entire exam is passed. The next five or six exams is the most common limit imposed.

Further variations from state to state are found in other conditions established. Some states set minimum failing scores on sections not passed in order for a candidate to receive credit for the section(s) he did pass. Some states require candidates for re-examination to continue to sit for all sections for which conditional credit has not been granted. Some states require candidates who fail the entire exam to wait one full year before sitting again. As noted in Chapter 1, the CPA examination is designed and graded by the AICPA, but it is the state boards of accountancy that determine how exam results will be evaluated and used as part of the licensing process.

STATE REQUIREMENTS

The CPA examination requirements vary from state to state. The candidate should check with his particular state board at the time of decision to become a CPA. A listing of state board addresses follows later in this chapter.

WHERE TO SEEK INFORMATION AND APPLICATION FORMS

As noted previously, entry into the accountancy profession is controlled by the individual state boards of accountancy. Accordingly, one of the first things a prospective CPA candidate should do is to ascertain the various requirements for becoming a CPA by contacting the state board of accountancy. Following is a list of the addresses and phone numbers for each of the boards within the United States and its territories.

The State Boards of Accountancy of the United States

ALABAMA STATE BOARD OF PUBLIC ACCOUNTANCY
RSA Plaza
770 Washington Avenue
Montgomery, AL 36130
Tel: (205) 242-5700
Fax: (205) 242-2711

ALASKA STATE BOARD OF PUBLIC ACCOUNTANCY
Department of Commerce and Economic Development
Div. of Occupational Licensing
Box 110806
Juneau, AK 99811-0806
Tel: (907) 465-2580
Fax: (907) 465-2974

ARIZONA STATE BOARD OF ACCOUNTANCY
3110 North 19th Avenue, Suite 140
Phoenix, AZ 85015-6038
Tel: (602) 255-3648
Fax: (602) 255-1283

ARKANSAS STATE BOARD OF ACCOUNTANCY
101 East Capitol, Suite 430
Little Rock, AR 72201
Tel: (501) 682-1520
Fax: (501) 682-5538

CALIFORNIA STATE BOARD OF ACCOUNTANCY
2000 Evergreen Street, Suite 250
Sacramento, CA 95815-3832
Tel: (916) 263-3680
Fax: (916) 263-3675

COLORADO STATE BOARD OF ACCOUNTANCY
1560 Broadway, Suite 1370
Denver, CO 80202
Tel: (303) 894-7800
Fax: (303) 894-7790

CONNECTICUT STATE BOARD OF ACCOUNTANCY
Secretary of the State
30 Trinity Street
Hartford, CT 06106
Tel: (203) 566-7835
Fax: (203) 566-5757

DELAWARE STATE BOARD OF ACCOUNTANCY
Cannon Building, Suite 203
P.O. Box 1401
Dover, DE 19903
Tel: (302) 739-4522
Fax: (302) 739-2711

DISTRICT OF COLUMBIA BOARD OF ACCOUNTANCY
Dept. of Consumer and Regulatory Affairs, Room 923
614 H Street, N.W., c/o P.O. Box 37200
Washington, DC 20013-7200
Tel: (202) 727-7468
Fax: (202) 727-8030

FLORIDA BOARD OF ACCOUNTANCY
2610 N.W. 43rd Street, Suite 1A
Gainesville, FL 32606
Tel: (904) 955-2165
Fax: (904) 955-2164

GEORGIA STATE BOARD OF ACCOUNTANCY
166 Pryor Street, S.W.
Atlanta, GA 30303
Tel: (404) 656-3941 .
Fax: (404) 651-9532

GUAM TERRITORIAL BOARD OF PUBLIC ACCOUNTANCY
c/o Camacho & Duenas, P.C.
P.O. Box 2789
Agana, GU 96910
Tel: (671) 472-7011
Fax: (671) 472-7012

HAWAII BOARD OF PUBLIC ACCOUNTANCY
   Department of Commerce and Consumer Affairs
   P.O. Box 3469
   Honolulu, HI 96801-3469
   Tel: (808) 586-2694
   Fax: (808) 586-2689

IDAHO STATE BOARD OF ACCOUNTANCY
   Owyhee Plaza, Suite 470
   1109 Main Street, Statehouse Mail
   Boise, ID 83720
   Tel: (208) 334-2490
   Fax: (208) 334-2615

ILLINOIS BOARD OF EXAMINERS
   University of Illinois-Urbana Champaign
   10 Henry Administration Building
   506 S. Wright Street
   Urbana, IL 61801-3260
   Tel: (217) 333-1565
   Fax: (217) 333-3126

ILLINOIS DEPARTMENT OF PROFESSIONAL
REGULATION
   Public Accountancy Section
   320 W. Washington Street, 3rd Floor
   Springfield, IL 62786-0001
   Tel: (217) 785-0800
   Fax: (217) 782-7645

INDIANA STATE BOARD OF PUBLIC
ACCOUNTANCY
   Professional Licensing Agency, Indiana
   Government Center S.
   302 West Washington Street, Room E034
   Indianapolis, IN 46204-2246
   Tel: (317) 232-5987
   Fax: (317) 232-2312

IOWA ACCOUNTANCY EXAMINING BOARD
   1918 S.E. Hulsizer Avenue
   Ankeny, IA 50021-3941
   Tel: (515) 281-4126
   Fax: (515) 281-7372

KANSAS BOARD OF ACCOUNTANCY
   Landon State Office Building
   900 S.W. Jackson, Suite 556
   Topeka, KS 66612-1239
   Tel: (913) 296-2162

KENTUCKY STATE BOARD OF ACCOUNTANCY
   332 West Broadway, Suite 310
   Louisville, KY 40202-2115
   Tel: (502) 595-3037
   Fax: (502) 595-4281

STATE BOARD OF CPAs OF LOUISIANA
   1515 World Trade Center
   2 Canal Street
   New Orleans, LA 70130
   Tel: (504) 566-1244
   Fax: (504) 566-6314

MAINE STATE BOARD OF ACCOUNTANCY
   Department of Professional and Financial
   Regulation, Division of Licensing and Enforcement,
   State House Station 35
   Augusta, ME 04333
   Tel: (207) 582-8723
   Fax: (207) 582-5415

MARYLAND STATE BOARD OF PUBLIC
ACCOUNTANCY
   501 St. Paul Place, 9th Floor
   Baltimore, MD 21202-2272
   Tel: (410) 333-6322
   Fax: (410) 333-6314

MASSACHUSETTS BOARD OF PUBLIC
ACCOUNTANCY
   Saltonstall Building, Room 1315
   100 Cambridge Street
   Boston, MA 02202-0001
   Tel: (617) 727-1806
   Fax: (617) 727-7378

MICHIGAN BOARD OF ACCOUNTANCY
   Department of Commerce—BOPR
   P.O. Box 30018
   Lansing, MI 48909-7518
   Tel: (517) 373-0682
   Fax: (517) 373-2795

MINNESOTA STATE BOARD OF ACCOUNTANCY
   85 East 7th Place, Suite 125
   St. Paul, MN 55101
   Tel: (612) 296-7937
   Fax: (612) 282-2644

MISSISSIPPI STATE BOARD OF PUBLIC
ACCOUNTANCY
961 Highway 80 East, Suite A
Clinton, MS 39056-5246
Tel: (601) 924-8457

MISSOURI STATE BOARD OF ACCOUNTANCY
P.O. Box 613
Jefferson City, MO 65102-0613
Tel: (314) 751-0012
Fax: (314) 751-0890

MONTANA STATE BOARD OF PUBLIC
ACCOUNTANTS
Arcade Building, Lower Level
111 North Jackson, P.O. Box 200513
Helena, MT 59620-0513
Tel: (406) 444-3739
Fax: (406) 444-1667

NEBRASKA STATE BOARD OF PUBLIC
ACCOUNTANCY
P.O. Box 94725
Lincoln, NE 68509-4725
Tel: (402) 471-3595
Fax: (402) 471-4484

NEVADA STATE BOARD OF ACCOUNTANCY
200 South Virginia Street, Suite 670
Reno, NV 89501-2408
Tel: (702) 786-0231
Fax: (702) 786-0234

NEW HAMPSHIRE BOARD OF ACCOUNTANCY
57 Regional Drive
Concord, NH 03301
Tel: (603) 271-3286

NEW JERSEY STATE BOARD OF ACCOUNTANCY
P.O. Box 45000
Newark, NJ 07101
Tel: (201) 504-6380
Fax: (201) 648-3536

NEW MEXICO STATE BOARD OF PUBLIC
ACCOUNTANCY
1650 University N.E., Suite 400-A
Albuquerque, NM 87102
Tel: (505) 841-9109
Fax: (505) 841-9113

NEW YORK STATE BOARD FOR PUBLIC
ACCOUNTANCY
State Education Department
Cultural Education Center, Room 3013
Albany, NY 12230-0001
Tel: (518) 474-3836
Fax: (518) 473-6995

NORTH CAROLINA STATE BOARD OF CPA
EXAMINERS
1101 Oberlin Road, Suite 104
P.O. Box 12827
Raleigh, NC 27605-2827
Tel: (919) 733-4222
Fax: (919) 733-4209

NORTH DAKOTA STATE BOARD OF
ACCOUNTANCY
2701 S. Columbia Road
Grand Forks, ND 58201
Tel: (701) 775-7100
Fax: (701) 775-7430

ACCOUNTANCY BOARD OF OHIO
77 South High Street, 18th Floor
Columbus, OH 43266-0301
Tel: (614) 466-4135
Fax: (614) 466-2628

OKLAHOMA ACCOUNTANCY BOARD
4545 Lincoln Boulevard, Suite 165
Oklahoma City, OK 73105-3413
Tel: (405) 521-2397
Fax: (405) 521-3118

OREGON STATE BOARD OF ACCOUNTANCY
3218 Pringle Road, S.E. #1B
Salem, OR 97302-6307
Tel: (503) 378-4181
Fax: (503) 378-3575

PENNSYLVANIA STATE BOARD OF
ACCOUNTANCY
613 Transportation and Safety Building
P.O. Box 2649
Harrisburg, PA 17105-2649
Tel: (717) 783-1404
Fax: (717) 787-7769

PUERTO RICO BOARD OF ACCOUNTANCY
Box 3271
Old San Juan Station
San Juan, PR 00904-3271
Tel: (809) 722-2122
Fax: (809) 721-8399

RHODE ISLAND BOARD OF ACCOUNTANCY
Department of Business Regulation
233 Richmond Street, Suite 236
Providence, RI 02903-4236
Tel: (401) 277-3185
Fax: (401) 277-6654

SOUTH CAROLINA BOARD OF ACCOUNTANCY
Dutch Plaza, Suite 260
800 Dutch Square Blvd.
Columbia, SC 29210
Tel: (803) 731-1677
Fax: (803) 731-1680

SOUTH DAKOTA BOARD OF ACCOUNTANCY
301 East 14th Street, Suite 200
Sioux Falls, SD 57104
Tel: (605) 339-6746

TENNESSEE STATE BOARD OF ACCOUNTANCY
500 James Robertson Parkway
2nd Floor
Nashville, TN 37243-1141
Tel: (615) 741-2550
Fax: (615) 741-6470

TEXAS STATE BOARD OF PUBLIC
ACCOUNTANCY
333 Guadalupe Tower III
Suite 900
Austin, TX 78701-3942
Tel: (512) 505-5500
Fax: (512) 505-5575

UTAH BOARD OF ACCOUNTANCY
160 East 300 South
P.O. Box 45802
Salt Lake City, UT 84145-0802
Tel: (801) 530-6456
Fax: (801) 530-6511

Prospective candidates wishing information from the American Institute of Certified Public Accountants may contact them at 1211 Avenue of the Americas, New York, NY 10036-8775, telephone (212) 596-6200. Of particular interest is their booklet entitled, "Information for CPA Candidates."

VERMONT BOARD OF PUBLIC ACCOUNTANCY
Pavillion Office Building
Montpelier, VT 05609-1106
Tel: (802) 828-2837
Fax: (802) 828-2496

VIRGINIA BOARD FOR ACCOUNTANCY
3600 West Broad Street
Richmond, VA 23230-4917
Tel: (804) 367-8590
Fax: (804) 367-2474

VIRGIN ISLANDS BOARD OF PUBLIC
ACCOUNTANCY
P.O. Box 3016
Christiansted
St. Croix, VI 00822
Tel: (809) 773-4305
Fax: (809) 773-9850

WASHINGTON STATE BOARD OF
ACCOUNTANCY
210 East Union, Suite H
P.O. Box 9131
Olympia, WA 98507-9131
Tel: (206) 753-2585
Fax: (206) 664-9190

WEST VIRGINIA BOARD OF ACCOUNTANCY
201 L & S Building
812 Quarrier Street
Charleston, WV 25301-2617
Tel: (304) 558-3557
Fax: (304) 558-1325

WISCONSIN ACCOUNTING EXAMINING BOARD
1400 E. Washington Avenue
P.O. Box 8935
Madison, WI 53708-8935
Tel: (608) 266-1397
Fax: (608) 267-0644

WYOMING BOARD OF CERTIFIED PUBLIC
ACCOUNTANTS
Barrett Building, 2nd Floor
Room 217-218
Cheyenne, WY 82002
Tel: (307) 777-7551
Fax: (307) 777-6005

Candidates will also find organizations sponsoring CPA review courses to be helpful in providing information concerning necessary steps to follow in becoming a CPA.

3. Develop Your Study Program

Each year well over 125,000 candidates sit for the CPA examination. Most don't make it. The passing statistics are well known: only about 20 percent of first-time candidates sitting for all four sections pass; only about 30 percent of the papers in each of the four sections are rated as passing. Typically, many of the candidates are sitting for fewer than all four sections, usually because they failed to pass every section at an earlier sitting.

Leaving aside anxiety that causes some people to freeze up in test situations, there are generally *two reasons for poor performance on the CPA exam: (1) inadequate preparation, and (2) lack of "examsmanship" skills.* Learning "examsmanship" skills is ultimately part of a sound preparation program, but it is useful to speak of the two separately.

The more a candidate knows about the ingredients for success on the CPA exam, the better able he will be to do what he must to assure success. One of the first things he must do is to approach the exam with a positive attitude about his prospects for passing. From the first day of preparation to the days of the exam, confidence is crucial. Similarly, he must approach the task of studying for the exam with enthusiasm and with a willingness to work harder than he has ever worked before. Attitude and motivation are ultimately as important as subject mastery.

The CPA exam is a very passable exam. The overall difficulty level of questions is seldom more than that experienced in Intermediate Accounting (or a comparable level for nonaccounting topics on the exam). The average student who works hard *can* pass the CPA exam. It is the *approach* to passing the exam that is more important than a candidate's academic record. This is borne out by the fact that ultimately eighty to ninety percent of *serious* candidates do pass the CPA exam within three years of their first sitting. Some people, it appears, have to fall on their faces once or twice before they are ready to make a commitment to becoming a serious candidate.

MAKE A COMMITMENT

Like most things of value in life, becoming a professional by passing a rigorous licensing examination is a matter of wanting it badly enough—badly enough to undergo a review program that must extend over a period of months and that will require all of the self-discipline, maturity, and commitment that the candidate can muster. It is far from impossible to pass the CPA exam, but it cannot be accomplished without a systematic, efficient, on-target review program.

Young candidates, fresh out of undergraduate accounting programs, often do not realize this. Having never experienced a situation like the CPA examination, they assume that the study habits that got them through college will transfer effectively to the CPA exam. Their approach is understandable but potentially self-defeating. As seen in Chapter 1, the scope of the CPA exam is far greater than anything experienced in college. The CPA exam is drawing from an entire accounting curriculum, not just topics studied within the previous fifteen weeks. The CPA exam is fifteen and one-half hours over two days, not three or four final exams spread over a week. The first-time candidate who fails to appreciate the special demands of the CPA exam will almost surely become a second- or a third-time candidate.

The successful candidate's achievement is directly proportional to the extent to which his review program has been an organized, systematic effort. That requires hard work and commitment. Space must be created in an already busy life to accomplish a successful review. Certain obligations, such as job and family responsibilities, cannot be ignored, but optional social activities must often be suspended for the duration of the review period. It is a matter of setting priorities. Passing the CPA exam must be the paramount objective, fixed in the mind's eye, during the months preceding the examination.

The ability to set such priorities and to stick with decisions made is a mark of a candidate's maturity.

While it may be disagreeable to forego the pleasures of a weekend off, it must be done if one is to accomplish the sustained, coherent study necessary. One must resist the temptation to become involved in idle recreation when the result will be to further delay one's progress. Such pleasures will still be there after one becomes a CPA and, in any event, the review period, in the long run, is a brief interlude in a larger continuum. Whatever sacrifices must be made will be only temporary and ultimately offset by the benefits of becoming a CPA.

At least that is the frame of mind with which one should approach the review period: with firm resolve and established goals. Very likely one *will* take a weekend off or "waste" an evening watching television, but the resulting pangs of conscience will send one back to the books with renewed fervor. The resolutions we make at the start of review serve as ideals that ultimately may be beyond our reach, but nevertheless they continue to motivate us during the long hours of drudgery that any such effort must inevitably entail.

YOUR 7-STAGE STUDY PROGRAM

Stage 1—Apply to sit for the exam. Secure necessary forms, etc., from your state board of accountancy and/or NASBA. Complete and return as instructed.

Stage 2—Self-appraisal. Take stock of yourself, your academic preparation, as well as your work habits and other strengths and weaknesses. Use the abridged AICPA Content Specification Outlines in Chapter 1 as a checklist of subject mastery. Working through the outlines, determine how familiar you are with each topic listed, keeping in mind the percentage indicator of relative emphasis given to each topical area. As you might expect, your familiarity will range from "knowledgeable" to "no prior learning." That variability will have implications for how you review. (After you take the Preliminary Readiness Tests in Chapter 7, you will have a rough indicator of your readiness for the CPA exam.)

Stage 3—Decide what kind of review program to undertake. Your options range from self-designed self-study to a formal review course. Selecting the right option is a matter of making an honest self-appraisal and deciding which approach is most likely to produce the desired result. You must consider how up-to-date your knowledge is, how much new learning will be necessary, how much you know about the CPA exam itself, how much time you have to devote to review, how

inclined you are to procrastinate, and how well you can study on your own. The chief concern at this stage is to decide on the best possible game plan *for you.* Success will depend on the choice you make and how well you stick to it.

Stage 4—Arrange your life to accommodate the necessities of review. You must plan on setting aside a minimum of two to three hours per day for either classroom attendance or self-study. This represents a sizeable chunk of time that will force dislocations in other areas of your life. That in turn may adversely affect friends and family. Since their cooperation and support can make your task much more manageable, and since your ties to them should endure long after you become a CPA, you should seek their understanding and share with them the sense of purpose you feel. If they are made to feel a part of your hopes and plans, they will forgive your irritability and unsociability during the review period.

At the office, your supervisors and co-workers are not likely to be as sympathetic. Your efforts to become a CPA are viewed as a worthy endeavor by your employer, but not one that should affect your availability for overtime, business travel, or other job requirements. In other words, there will be little opportunity for you to find much flexibility in your job responsibilities to accommodate your review program. You are expected to show that you can become a CPA even while you are giving your full effort to job performance. The arrangements necessary to allow for the hours that must be set aside are usually made by forgoing participation in all nonessential personal and social activities during the review period.

In many ways, your life off the job during the two to three months of review may come to resemble that of a recluse. If, however, you keep your focus on the long-term benefits of whatever temporary sacrifices you have to endure, the inevitable tedium will seem more bearable. The worst part of failing the CPA exam is having to gear up for and go through the review process all over again. It should be done right the first time.

Stage 5—Take the plunge. After the necessary decisions have been made about your strengths and weaknesses, after you have decided what kind of review program to undertake, and after you have arranged your life to allow for review time, go to it! Procrastination is the thief of time, and time is the candidate's scarcest resource.

Usually, the hardest part of any large undertaking is getting started. Some people procrastinate by busying themselves with preparatory details, telling themselves that everything must be arranged and in place before they can start. Other people simply postpone: "First thing Monday morning," they'll say, or "As soon as I clear up a few things at work...," etc.

The point to remember is that things in your life will never be exactly as you would like them to be; once a decision is made, action should follow. Natural inertia must be overcome.

Stage 6—Maintain momentum. As you might expect, it is not easy to sustain an intense and tedious effort over a long period of time. As one encounters setbacks or obstacles, it is easy to become discouraged. Self-doubt is a natural human reaction. Expect it and deal with it. But recognize it as nothing more than a passing mood. If you have the self-discipline and motivation that characterizes successful candidates, you will not lose the momentum of effort that you have established.

There are certain things a candidate can do during the review period that will help maintain momentum:

1. *Set daily goals.* Decide which topics will be studied, which set of questions will be answered, which deficiencies will be corrected, etc. Specific goals give purpose and direction to a review session.

2. *Maintain a progress record of your study.* Since the mass of information that must be assimilated is so vast, and the review period so long, a perpetual record of work done and work to be done helps the candidate control his time and effort better.

3. *Monitor performance of questions answered.* This is really part of "2," preceding, but deserves special mention, nevertheless. Since your ability to answer questions is ultimately what counts, your performance with practice questions from past exams should be noted carefully. Maintain answer sheets that highlight incorrect responses. You will want to review those items in the final days before the exam.

4. *Keep fit—both physically and mentally.* Believe it or not, sitting for the CPA exam is almost as grueling physically as it is mentally. Imagine sitting hunched over a writing surface that may or may not be at a comfortable height for periods of three to four and one-half hours at a stretch, four times in two days! It will help if, during the review period, you can prepare for that eventuality by maintaining a modest regimen of daily exercise.

Actually, you will need such exercise during the review period as well, since some physical counterbalance will be necessary for the periods during which you must remain relatively immobile while in class or studying at home. Beyond that, it is well established that physical fitness and mental alertness are at least causally connected.

To reduce mental fatigue, it helps to "walk away from it" periodically when you feel, during study sessions, that your brain has become overloaded with information. A brief respite will usually help to clear the neurological circuitry.

Stage 7—Final readiness review. Ideally, the entire review program should be completed at least four or five days before the exam begins. If that is accomplished, there will be no last-minute panic because of material not covered. At that point a relatively leisurely final readiness review can be undertaken that will round out the overall effort. You will want to review study aids for those topics about which you still feel unsure or that you are almost certain will appear on your exam. You will also want to review any past questions that were answered incorrectly, since they indicate potential gaps in your understanding.

You will want to refresh your memory of key formulas, definitions, concepts, acronyms, etc., one last time. Likewise, you will want to mentally rehearse your handling of the test situation itself (i.e., exam-day reminders and the question-answering techniques discussed in Chapter 5). Finally, on the eve of the examination, you will want to relax. You will be too apprehensive to study, anyway, but your apprehensiveness will be allayed by the knowledge that you have done all that you could to get ready and that you stand as good a chance of passing as anybody else.

SELECT THE RIGHT PREPARATION APPROACH

How a candidate reviews is something he will have to decide for himself based upon an honest appraisal of his strengths and weaknesses. No one knows better than he the quality of his academic preparation, the extent of his familiarity with the CPA exam, or the capacity he has for establishing a regimen and sticking to it. One of the most discouraging feelings that a candidate can have is knowing that he failed because he didn't do the job he could have done and should have done in reviewing the material tested. However one prepares, the primary concern should be to do it right.

Of course, preparation really begins with the first accounting course a candidate takes. *Preparation is a two-stage process. Stage one* consists of building a solid academic foundation during one's college years; *stage two* is the formal review program undergone immediately prior to the examination. A review program should be precisely that: a review of things previously learned, not an initial learning experience. Invariably there will be topics on the CPA exam that were not studied in college. Those gaps will have to be filled, and a well-designed review program will anticipate that necessity, but the primary activity should be review. The candidate who, as an accounting major, had his sights aimed toward passing the CPA exam is in a position to be confident about his prospects for passing. The candidate who only lately has arrived at a decision to become a CPA, and who therefore may not have an exam-directed accounting background, will have to work extra hard during his review program.

A solid, exam-directed academic background (STAGE ONE) implies that a candidate as an accounting major was involved in genuine learning, as opposed to the intellectual chicanery that will often allow one to pass courses but come away with little real understanding. At one time or another we all do what has to be done to get through a course that we are taking only because we must. Our primary goal is to get it over with, get a respectable grade, and satisfy requirements. Obviously, if CPA exam-related courses are handled this way, a candidate is ill-prepared to take the CPA exam despite his nominal status as a graduate accountant. He may have retained some of the information crammed in during "all-nighters." He may be fairly proficient at parroting textbook solutions—even without the help of his friends—but he will probably lack the overall grasp of the body of knowledge that, in its coherent entirety, comprises his accounting curriculum and the CPA exam. The successful CPA candidate must be adept at problem-solving in a pressure situation. The exam tests reasoning ability, which is predicated on genuine understanding rather than temporary familiarity.

One point to note regarding adequacy of undergraduate preparation: the most successful candidates are not necessarily those with the highest grade-point averages. Super achievers in terms of grades are often overly thorough perfectionists. Such an inclination is more of a hindrance than an advantage. Perfect answers to questions are not needed. And the candidate who gets hung up trying to write perfect answers will often fail to budget time wisely and end up turning in a paper with some perfect answers and some incomplete answers. The idea is to get the job done within the constraints of the CPA exam format, not self-imposed constraints that demand perfection. Satisfying the grader is a matter of giving the grader what he is looking for—no more, no less. The average student whose knowledge and test-taking skills are sound, and whose attitude is pragmatic, will often outperform a colleague with a higher academic standing.

Your Review Program

STAGE TWO of the preparation process is the formal review program undertaken in the final months before the examination. It should be a formal review in terms of having a well-thought-out sequence of study that takes into account the relative coverage each topic receives on the CPA exam. It follows that such a program, given the scope of the CPA exam, can only be carried out over a period of months.

That necessity can be a stumbling block for many candidates, particularly first-timers. Never before (and probably never again) has the typical first-time candidate been required to sustain a months-long study effort aimed toward passing a single exam. The challenge is formidable but certainly not unreasonable. As a gateway to professional status, the CPA exam should be a test of character as well as intellect.

One of the first decisions a candidate faces after resolving to sit for the exam is what type of review program to follow. There are basically *two ways to go: (1) self-designed self-study, and (2) a commercial review or "coach" course.* Often, a candidate right out of college will have had some sort of exam-directed course work during his final semester which may or may not have been adequate preparation. Often such courses concentrate on certain segments of the exam, such as accounting problems or business law, but, because of time constraints, cannot provide coverage comprehensive enough to ensure success. Commercial courses include both private, proprietary types, and university-operated, non-credit courses offered to the public.

THE COMMERCIAL REVIEW COURSE

A high-quality commercial review course makes use of the talents and backgrounds of its staff in developing a professionally designed, experience-tested program of study. Like college, a good review course should be viewed as an investment for the future: by enabling one to pass sooner than later, it pays for itself. What is purchased is the knowledge and skill of CPAs who have not only been through the exam but who have made a special study of its form and content. Through study aids, lectures, and demonstration, they pass their wisdom along to others. The ability of a professional review course to increase a candidate's chances for success has been attested to by several independent studies.

Such courses are presented in a variety of modes: (1) live classroom, (2) audio classroom, and (3) home-study. A *live classroom format* is the conventional arrangement in which an instructor presents to students, in lecture fashion, selected topics for that particular session. The length of a session is usually three hours. An *audio classroom mode* involves the use of audio cassette recordings of previously presented live lectures. In a well-run audio classroom, an instructor uses the tapes as a teaching aid. If it is well-run, an audio classroom format can be just as effective as a completely live arrangement. In fact, it can be even better if the instructor on tape is superior to the one in the classroom. A *home-study review course* usually contains a combination of cassette lectures and printed materials. Such courses may or may not be classroom-based. Those that are have the benefit of containing classroom-tested materials and instructional techniques.

There are many ways to achieve the same end, of course, and this is nowhere better illustrated than in the descriptive brochures distributed by commercial review courses. The greatest variable seems to be course length: some courses run five or six months; some less than one month. Usually those of five or six months spend a lot of time reviewing elementary material. Often, they will devote a portion of class time to in-class problem solving. Those of less than a month usually are presented as "intensive," "live-in" crash courses designed to provide a candidate with a final refresher before exam day.

Selecting a particular review course is not easy. The candidate is, to a large extent, entrusting his immediate professional future to the organization involved. His tuition becomes a sound investment only if it achieves its expected return. As with any investment decision, one should choose the option that best meets one's needs and objectives. In CPA review, a candidate has to consider which arrangement will be most effective for him. He must take into account the quality of his academic preparation, his present knowledge, and his psychological strengths and weaknesses.

Certain features distinguish a superior review course. It should have an established track record of turning out successful candidates. Its faculty should consist of experienced, dynamic instructors who not only impart knowledge effectively, but also instill the confidence crucial to success. The course must be flexible enough to accommodate the individual needs of its students. Students typically are forced to miss an occasional lecture because of job or personal requirements.

Provision for convenient make-up opportunities should be available. Instructional materials should be streamlined yet comprehensive. They should contain cogent summaries that illuminate core information and maximize memory retention. They should contain past question-and-answer material that trains candidates to write passing answers to future questions. They should not require the use of supplemental textbooks or pronouncements, nor should they require extensive supplemental note-taking. A questionnaire for selecting a good review course follows.

CPA REVIEW COURSE QUESTIONNAIRE

1. **Reputation**
   Does the course have the recommendation of people whose opinions you respect?

2. **Faculty**
   Are faculty members experienced CPA *review* instructors?

3. **Materials**
   Are materials comprehensive? They must strike the proper balance between giving a candidate more than is necessary and giving the candidate too little.
   Are materials up-to-date?
   Are materials organized for maximum usability?
   Are materials complete, or must they be supplemented by textbooks, pronouncements, etc.?
   Are materials well-written?
   Is computer software available for supplemental study?

4. **Convenience**
   In terms of geographic location and class meeting times, is the course compatible with your work schedule?

5. **Class size**
   Is class size so large as to be an impediment to effective learning?

6. **Make-up and review**
   What provisions does the course make for reviewing a lecture already presented? What provisions are made for make-up of lectures missed because of absence?

7. **Course structure**
   Is the course organized into four subcourses directed at individual examination sections (i.e., LPR, AUDIT, ARE, and FARE)? Can you enroll in individual subcourses or must you enroll in some combination?

8. **Course schedules**

Are the sessions for individual courses (i.e., LPR, AUDIT, ARE, and FARE) evenly distributed over the length of the review period so as to enhance learning effectiveness and memory retention?

9. **Organizational strength**

Is the sponsoring organization a solid, well-established entity? What is its reputation in the business and academic community?

10. **Cost**

Is the course fairly and competitively priced? Is the price all-inclusive? What discounts are available? What payment terms are available?

Most candidates, therefore, in order to ensure an organized, successful review effort, should enroll in a professional review course. A recent survey of candidates by NASBA disclosed that more than half of the candidates sitting for the exam had taken some type of coaching course that had contributed to examination success. Additional hours of independent study were also cited as factors accounting for success.

THE SELF-DESIGNED STUDY PROGRAM

The biggest advantage of a self-designed, self-study program is that it is inexpensive, at least in terms of initial out-of-pocket costs. In such a program, the individual candidate performs his own research into the requirements of the CPA exam and then designs for himself a program of study that takes into account his relative strengths and weaknesses. Such a program usually would be built around relevant textbooks, FASB and AICPA pronouncements, AICPA Unofficial Questions and Answers, etc. It might also include one of the numerous review manuals that attempt to capture all of the necessary information a candidate needs within the confines of 2,000 or so pages.

The biggest disadvantage of a self-designed self-study program is that the candidate may unwittingly become his own worst enemy. He may fail to get an accurate picture of examination form and content. He may fail to be objective about his strengths and weaknesses. Operating on his own, he may fail to structure his activity in the most efficient way. In the end, what looked to be the cheapest, easiest way turns out to be the most costly. The exam will have to be repeated, salary increases that follow exam success will have to be forgone, and additional review costs will have to be incurred. Psychologically, the candidate must deal with

the knowledge of having wasted a significant block of valuable time. Even worse, he must face the depressing prospect of having to repeat the review process all over again. A self-designed, self-study review program *can* work, but it requires an uncommon degree of insight, confidence, and self-discipline.

Review Manuals

There are several CPA review manuals that provide assistance to candidates in the form of study outlines and past exam questions and answers. Some of them, in an effort to be "comprehensive," overwhelm the reader with more than 2,000 pages of material that the candidate is expected to assimilate. Someone working on his own can easily feel intimidated by the task ahead if he has not yet worked out an organized plan of study. Such manuals are most useful when they are supplemental to, or part of, a classroom CPA review course. Printed materials generally need an instructor to illuminate them and to guide the candidate through.

GUIDELINES FOR SELECTING A CPA REVIEW MANUAL

1. **Comprehensiveness.** This is difficult for the inexperienced candidate to judge since a clear understanding of the nature of exam coverage is not usually possible until *after* the review program has begun. Nevertheless, comprehensive coverage is a must.

   Many authors err on the side of including *too* much, of giving the reader more than he actually needs for efficient exam preparation. That approach does the candidate as much a disservice as giving him insufficient material. A good manual must demonstrate the exercising of editorial selectivity. The authors should provide the candidate with only what he needs to know to pass the exam. To do otherwise will clutter his mind with nonessential information.

2. **Convenience.** A two-volume, 2,000 page, 8½ × 11 manual weighs about 9½ pounds. Carrying such a mass can be a nuisance. Portability is a consideration since a candidate will often want to study "on the run"; i.e., on the way to work, during lunch hour, while away on business, etc. A multivolume work can help overcome the problem of bulky materials.

3. **Coherence.** Coherence is a matter of parts relating smoothly to one another. In order to be coherent, a manual must be "user-friendly." The internal structure of parts, chapters, etc., must be logi-

cally sequenced. Layout and typeface should enhance readability. Internal cross-references should be clear. The overall impression should be one of a unified whole rather than a fragmented assemblage of parts.

4. **Currency.** It is essential to use only up-to-date materials when preparing for the CPA exam. The AICPA Board of Examiners expects candidates to have a knowledge of accounting and auditing pronouncements six months after a pronouncement's effective date unless early application is permitted, in which case candidates are responsible for knowledge of the new pronouncement six months after the date of issue. With respect to federal taxation, candidates are expected to be familiar with the Internal Revenue Code and Federal Tax Regulations in effect six months prior to the exam.

5. **Completeness.** A determination must be made of the extent to which the manual can stand alone as a self-sustaining review vehicle. Will additional books or tutoring be necessary? Obviously, a manual that purports to provide a complete review must contain more than outlines of pronouncements and past exam questions. It must also meet the candidate's need for developing examsmanship skills. It must help the candidate set up a carefully planned, intensive review program. It must provide the candidate with the confidence to pass.

Computer Software

Those who enjoy working with computers may find this type of study tool useful—particularly as a supplemental study aid.

Original Source Material

Another way to prepare for the CPA exam, of course, is to use neither a professional review course nor a review manual but, rather, to go directly to the source publications embodying the knowledge tested by the exam. Such an approach presupposes that the candidate (1) has unhampered access to those publications, and (2) has the necessary knowledge to select the right information for review.

If one were to assemble the published body of information tested by the AICPA, the following would be included:

1. Current textbooks for intermediate accounting, advanced accounting, auditing, cost accounting, managerial accounting, governmental and not-for-profit accounting, federal income taxes, and business law.

2. FASB and GASB pronouncements.
3. AICPA Statements on Auditing Standards.
4. AICPA publications such as *Code of Professional Conduct, Statements on Standards for Accounting and Review Services, Statements on Quality Control Standards, Statements on Standards for Attestation Engagements, Statements on Standards for Accountants' Services on Prospective Financial Statements, Standards for Consulting Services, Statements on Responsibilities in Tax Practice, and Industry Audit Guides.*
5. A standard tax service.
6. U.S. General Accounting Office Government Auditing Standards
7. Federal statutes and uniform acts: Securities Act of 1933, Securities Exchange Act of 1934, Federal Bankruptcy Act, Uniform Commercial Code, Uniform Partnership Act, Uniform Limited Partnership Act, and Model Business Corporation Act.
8. AICPA *Questions and Unofficial Answers for the Uniform CPA Examination* for the most recent three to five years.

The sheer mass of paper represented by such a list is enough to frighten all but the most masochistic of candidates. After considering the cost of such publications and the long hours of solitary review ahead, the average, sensible candidate is likely to opt for a more efficient, less burdensome approach.

DEVELOP "EXAMSMANSHIP"

One of the things a quality review course does best is to teach examsmanship. "Examsmanship" can be defined as skillful test-taking (i.e., the ability to deal effectively with a test situation and the demands of a particular test). Certain examsmanship skills are almost universal while others relate only to particular examinations. On the CPA exam, examsmanship consists of five elements:

1. Familiarity with exam format.
2. Anticipating exam content.
3. Dealing with the unexpected.
4. Budgeting time.
5. Working efficiently.

To become a successful candidate, it is not enough just to know accounting, auditing, taxes, or business law. One must also know how that material will be tested. A candidate must be familiar with the format of the exam so that there are no surprises when he opens his test booklet and surveys the task in front of him. The questions appearing—at least in terms of format—should look like old friends that the candidate has seen many times before during his review program.

The best way of developing a comfortable familiarity with exam format is through practice with past questions. After weeks of working through recent objective, essay, and computational questions, a candidate develops a feel for their idiosyncrasies. Patterns of structure and style emerge. Narratives unfold in certain ways; requirements are set up in familiar patterns. The candidate, although anxious about answering specific points of content, is not distracted by format. He knows what to expect.

The same type of assurance should exist when a candidate contemplates the general content of the exam. Of course, the AICPA Content Specification Outlines go a long way toward telling a candidate what to expect. It is the candidate's responsibility to familiarize himself with the contents of these outlines, and to see to it that his final review program focuses on them—both in terms of overall content and of relative emphasis allotted to individual areas. As is the case with exam format, an ability to anticipate exam content distinguishes the successful candidates from the unsuccessful.

So much of examination success is dependent on psychological factors. The first thing a candidate usually does when he receives his examination booklet is to leaf through it quickly to see what his task will be—which topics appear, what the essay, computational, and other objective formats questions deal with, etc. The fewer surprises there are, the more confident the candidate will be. Obviously, the sort of familiarity and resulting confidence necessary for success is something that can be achieved by thorough preparation. There are enough obstacles to overcome in formulating answers to questions without the testing instrument itself being an impediment.

As with many situations in life, however, there will usually be one or two surprises in each of the examination sections: a topic appearing for the first time, a topic reappearing after an absence that suggested it was to be honored more in the breach than the observance, an aspect of a topic heretofore not tested, etc. The successful candidate will be able to deal with such surprises without falling to pieces. He may be taken aback momentarily. He may feel an unaccustomed twinge of anxiety, but it will pass and he will be able to get on with answering the question. Even if the question at hand deals with a topic unfamiliar to the candidate, he knows certain things:

1. If the topic is appearing for the first time on the CPA exam, the question is probably very easy. Closer analysis will reveal this.
2. If he is experiencing difficulty handling it, so are all of his fellow candidates.
3. His own instincts as a well-prepared candidate are probably his truest guide. He should resist the urge to second-guess himself.

The successful candidate under such circumstances remains cool and does not allow his concentration to be interrupted or his confidence shaken. Indeed, that is the *essence of examsmanship—the ability to deal with the pressures of the examination experience.*

Time-Saving Techniques Are Essential

A CPA candidate's biggest challenge, both before and during the CPA exam, is to use the time well. During the review period, procrastination will be a candidate's undoing. During the exam, an inability to establish a time budget for each question and stick to it at all costs will almost guarantee a return trip to next May or November's exam. An inability to work within the time constraints created by the exam ranks with poor reading ability, poor communication skills, and careless work habits as one of the primary reasons for failure.

The CPA exam is a very passable exam—but only for those who have done their homework. Candidates walking into the test site must know their information cold. They must be able to recall and apply it almost automatically. They must be like a highly complex, fine-tuned mechanism that can work through the exam with a minimum of wasted time or motion. A candidate who is well-prepared—both in terms of content review and examsmanship skills—should have no difficulty working within the time parameters of each question. The candidate who is not will find that even fifteen and one-half hours for the entire exam is inadequate.

One of the best ways of developing time-management skills is through practice with past questions. During the review program, the candidate should devote about half of his study effort to answering past questions. Such questions should be answered under simulated exam conditions. At the least, this means spending no more time with the question than would be available on the exam itself. The candidate will find, in the beginning at least, that budgeted time has expired before he has finished his answer. With practice, and by learning the test tactics in Chapter 5, he will be able to compose a point-winning answer within the time allotted.

Efficient use of time is a cornerstone of overall efficient work habits. Working efficiently is necessitated by the scarcity of time. The candidate must consciously learn systematic question-answering techniques that, when combined with his knowledge of content, will enable him to get the job done. Such talents will be a necessary part of his success as a CPA, so it is not inappropriate that they be requirements of the certification process.

Becoming a CPA *is* within the grasp of the average accounting graduate. As noted at the beginning of this chapter, most candidates do make it eventually. It's mainly a matter of making up their minds that they want it badly enough. The discouraging passing rates are more a function of poor preparation than they are of inherent difficulty. And therein lies the crucial point for candidates. The CPA exam requires study skills, test-taking skills, and attributes of character that they have never had to practice before. If they are not up to it, they will fail until they are. Successful candidates are prepared, confident, self-disciplined, and motivated.

4. Review Examination Content

WHAT YOU SHOULD STUDY: A SUMMARY

The subject areas reviewed herein are those categorized in the AICPA *Content Specification Outlines for the Uniform Certified Public Accountant Examination*, which are presented in abridged form in Chapter 1. An indication of the relative weight given to each subject may be determined by examining the outline for each section.

Following is a review of the subject areas that are unique to each section. It should be noted that the nature of the examination is such that the subject matter covered might appear in four-option multiple-choice questions, other objective formats questions, and essay or computational questions (none in the case of the ARE exam). This is accomplished by the construction of questions. In many instances, objective-type questions that require computations are smaller versions of computational-type questions, in that isolated computations are required.

Business Law and Professional Responsibilities (LPR): Subject Matter Covered

As noted previously, the LPR section tests an overview level of knowledge about selected areas of professional responsibilities and of law encountered in business situations. The emphasis is on testing a candidate's grasp of general concepts, legal principles, and ethical considerations. Candidates are not expected to be familiar with the practice of law, but rather with textbook information. They must demonstrate an ability to recall and apply such information to hypothetical situations contained in examination questions. Following are the areas tested. The candidate's background for these topics will usually come from a college-level course in business law. Certain topics, however, are not covered in a college course—or are covered too superficially—and therefore require extracurricular study.

RULES OF CONDUCT (SUMMARY OF AICPA CODE OF PROFESSIONAL CONDUCT)

Independence

Specific relationships prohibited:
> Direct and certain indirect financial relationships with clients, officers, directors, or principal stockholders.
> Relationships in which the CPA can be considered part of management.

Integrity and Objectivity

A member should not knowingly misrepresent facts or subordinate his judgment to others.

General Standards

The CPA should not undertake any engagement that he cannot reasonably expect to complete with professional competence. The CPA shall adequately plan, supervise, and exercise due professional care in the performance of professional services. He must obtain sufficient relevant data to afford a basis for conclusions or recommendations in relation to any services performed.

Compliance with Standards

A member who performs professional services must comply with the appropriate standards (GAAS, GAAP, etc.).

Confidential Client Information

A CPA should not disclose any confidential client information without the consent of the client, unless required to do so by law, or AICPA regulations.

Contingent Fees

A member in public practice should not, except for certain tax-related matters, perform professional services for a contingent fee.

Acts Discreditable

A CPA should not commit an act that is discreditable to the profession.

Advertising

A CPA may advertise as long as it is not done in a false, misleading, or deceptive manner.

Commissions and Referral Fees

A CPA may accept a commission for recommending or referring to a client a product or service if the CPA does not also perform certain attest services. In situations where commissions are permitted, disclosure to certain parties is required.

Form of Practice and Name

Public accounting may be practiced in a form of organization permitted by a state law or regulation (i.e., proprietorship, partnership, professional corporation, and, in some states, limited liability companies and limited liability corporations). Misleading names should not be used.

STANDARDS FOR CONSULTING SERVICES

Consulting services provided by CPAs have evolved from advice on accounting-related matters to a wide range of services involving technical disciplines, industry knowledge, and consulting skills.

Consulting services include consultations, advisory services, implementation services, transaction services, staff and other supporting services, and product services.

The practice standards to be followed consist of general standards (appropriate competence, due care, adequate planning and supervision, and gathering sufficient relevant data as a basis for conclusions or recommendations) and compliance standards (integrity and objectivity, arriving at an understanding with the client about the engagement, etc.).

RESPONSIBILITIES IN TAX PRACTICE

The CPA should apply the same standards of professional conduct in performing tax work for a client as are applied in an audit and other professional activities. The CPA should not knowingly perform any act or prepare any return or related document that he has reason to believe is false or misleading or for which he does not have sufficient competence to handle.

THE CPA AND THE LAW

The liability of the CPA to clients and third parties for breach of contract, negligence, and fraud is the basis for questions on this topic. The CPA is liable under both common law and statutory law. The candidate is expected to be familiar with relevant court decisions as well as with liability under federal securities statutes and the Internal Revenue Code. Also tested are concepts concerning work papers and accountant/client privilege.

AGENCY

Agency law deals with the rights and obligations that principals and agents have toward each other and toward third parties. Candidates are expected to know the nature of agency authority as well as the responsibilities of parties when an agency relationship is terminated. Particular attention is given to distinction between actual and apparent authority.

PARTNERSHIPS AND JOINT VENTURES

CPA exam questions test the major provisions of the Uniform Partnership Act and Uniform Limited Partnership Act. Candidates should be familiar with the rights, duties, and liabilities of partners during partnership operation, as well as allocation of profit or loss during partnership dissolution.

CORPORATIONS

The Model Business Corporation Act is the basis for CPA exam questions on this subject. Questions focus on the legal aspects of corporate stock, the fiduciary responsibility of corporate officers and directors, rights of shareholders, and federal income tax implications of the corporate form of business. The candidate must also be familiar with the legal implications of merger, consolidation, and dissolution.

ESTATES AND TRUSTS

Questions deal with the creation and administration of estates and trusts. This involves knowing the elements of valid trusts and the rules for allocation of trust principal and income. Further considerations involve fiduciary responsibilities as well as distributions and termination.

CONTRACTS

The primary focus of this fundamental topic is the enforceability of a contract as determined by the presence of certain requisite legal elements. In analyzing a question situation, the candidate must determine whether offer and acceptance have taken place; whether consent is mutual; whether subject matter is legal; whether the parties have capacity to contract, have given consideration, and have complied with the Statute of Frauds. Candidates must also be familiar with the rights of third parties, standards of performance, discharge of obligation, and remedies for breach.

SURETYSHIP AND CREDITOR'S RIGHTS

Suretyship and guarantee are based on common law and deal with promises of one party to be responsible for the debt of another. The candidate must know the rights of a surety upon default by the debtor and payment by the surety, including the computation of prorata share in a co-surety situation. He must also be familiar with the defenses a surety has against a creditor and certain exceptions to those defenses.

BANKRUPTCY

Questions are based on the Bankruptcy Reform Act of 1978. Candidates must be familiar with voluntary and involuntary petitions, management of a debtor's estate, voidable preferences, priority of claims, and discharge of debts. Also tested is an awareness of the general provisions governing corporate reorganizations. Questions often focus on the powers of trustees and priorities of claims in bankruptcy proceedings.

EMPLOYMENT REGULATIONS

Mastery of this subject is a matter of having a passing familiarity with the broad provisions of the Federal Insurance Contributions Act (social security), the Federal Unemployment Tax Act, employee safety laws including the various workers' compensation laws and the Federal Occupational and Safety Health Act (OSHA), wage and hour laws, and relevant employment discrimination laws. Question situations typically reflect the impact of these statutes on the employer/employee relationship.

FEDERAL SECURITIES ACTS

The Securities Act of 1933 and the Securities Exchange Act of 1934 are the two sources of questions on this topic. Candidates must know the 1933 Act provi-

sions regarding registration, exemptions to registration, and parties' bases for liability. For the 1934 Act, they must know the periodic reporting and registration requirements. The 1934 Act's antifraud provisions are tested chiefly through their impact on CPAs associated with reports filed with the SEC.

COMMERCIAL PAPER

The candidate is tested on the major provisions of Articles 3 and 4 of the Uniform Commercial Code (UCC). Article 3 deals with the various types of commercial paper, the concept and requisites of negotiability, transfer of commercial paper, holders in due course, and liabilities of parties to commercial paper. Article 4 pertains to banking. The candidate is expected to be familiar with concepts relating to the bank/depositor and bank/third-party relationships.

The candidate is also expected to be somewhat familiar with two other types of negotiable instruments: documents of title and investment securities. Documents of title are governed by Article 7 of the UCC, and investment securities by Article 8. Both are similar in form and function to commercial paper instruments. An understanding of Article 3 will enable candidates to grasp concepts contained in Articles 7 and 8 very quickly.

SALES

This topic is concerned with Article 2 of the Uniform Commercial Code. Questions deal with modifications of common law contract rules governing contracts for the sale of goods. Additional Article 2 provisions concerning warranties, product liability rights of parties upon breach and passage of title, and risk of loss are also tested. A solid understanding of contract fundamentals will be most helpful here.

SECURED TRANSACTIONS

Secured transactions are governed by Article 9 of the Uniform Commercial Code. The candidate must be familiar with the characteristics of a secured credit sale and a secured loan transaction. Also required is knowledge of the mechanics and implications of attachment and perfection of security interest. Questions often deal with conflicting security interests and the rights of parties upon disposition of collateral.

PROPERTY

The primary focus of questions for this topic is on real property: types of ownership, transfer of real property, tenancies and leases, and mortgages. The candidate is expected to distinguish between realty and personalty, joint tenancy and tenancy in common, and reversionary and remainder interests. The liabilities associated with assuming a mortgage as opposed to purchasing subject to a mortgage, and the recording of deeds and mortgages are also tested. Questions also focus on bailments, types of ownership relating to personal property, as well as environmental liability.

INSURANCE

Fundamentals of fire and casualty insurance as they relate to business situations are tested for this topic. Familiarity with terminology is important as well as with concepts of insurable interest, multiple insurance coverage, and co-insurance. Frequent questions require the candidate to compute recovery in a partial loss situation using the co-insurance formula.

Auditing (AUDIT): Subject Matter Covered

Pronouncements issued by the American Institute of CPAs are tested extensively on the CPA examination. As such, this section has been prepared and organized to acquaint CPA candidates with those pronouncements that have particular applicability to the CPA exam.

The pronouncement summaries reflect the impact of any subsequent amendments and interpretations likely to be of significance to the CPA candidate. Pronouncements that have been omitted are either obsolete or not relevant for the CPA exam.

The abbreviated references to the pronouncements relevant to the Auditing exam are as follows:

FAS—Financial Accounting Standards Board Statement
SAS—Statement on Auditing Standards
SSAE—Statement on Standards for Attestation Engagements
SSARS—Statement on Standards for Accounting and Review Services

AUDITING PRONOUNCEMENTS

Generally Accepted Auditing Standards— Extracted from SAS #1

General Standards
1. Adequate technical training and proficiency.
2. Independence in mental attitude.
3. Due professional care in performance.

Field Work Standards
1. Adequately planned work and a properly supervised staff.
2. Sufficient understanding of internal control structure.
3. Gathering of sufficient competent evidential matter to form a basis for an opinion.

Reporting Standards
1. Use of generally accepted accounting principles.
2. Identify inconsistent application of such principles.
3. Informative disclosures.
4. Expression of an opinion on financial statements taken as a whole or an explanation as to why one cannot be given.

Audit Planning

1. **SAS #7—Communications Between Predecessor and Successor Auditors**
   Utilized before acceptance to obtain information from the predecessor that will assist in determining whether to accept the engagement. The prospective client should be requested to authorize the predecessor to respond fully. Inquiries should be specific, and reasonable response should be prompt and full, subject to specific reasons for limiting the reply.

   Utilized after acceptance to facilitate the successor's procedures about matters that he believes may affect the audit. The client should be requested to authorize the predecessor to allow the review of working papers. If the successor comes to believe that financial statements prepared by the predecessor may require revisions, he should request that the client arrange a meeting among the three parties to discuss and attempt to resolve the matter.

2. **SAS #22—Planning and Supervision**
   The auditor should learn enough about the client's business to permit the planning and performance of the audit in accordance with GAAS. Planning should consider such things as business and industry background, accounting policies and procedures, assessed level of control risk, etc.

   Planning procedures should involve the auditor in such items as review of his work papers, discussions with other personnel of his firm, and discussions with client personnel. Efforts should culminate with the preparation of a written audit program.

Supervision should include such matters as instructing assistants, keeping informed of significant problems in progress, reviewing work performed, etc.

3. SAS #41—Working Papers
Working papers provide the main documentation supporting the auditor's report. They are the property of the auditor. They may take many different forms including written documents, tapes, films, etc.

4. SAS #47—Audit Risk and Materiality in Conducting an Audit
Audit risk is the risk that the auditor may unknowingly fail to modify an opinion on financial statements that are materially misstated. The constituent parts of audit risk are inherent, control, and detection risks. Materiality, which relates to the financial importance of an item, is a matter of the auditor's professional judgment.

5. SAS #56—Analytical Procedures
Analytical procedures involve the study and comparison of relationships among financial and nonfinancial data. These include such procedures as comparison of financial information with prior periods, budgets, industry patterns, etc. Analytical procedures should be used in the planning and overall review stages of the audit and may be used in substantive testing.

6. SAS #65—The Auditor's Consideration of the Internal Audit Function in an Audit of Financial Statements
When an internal audit staff exists, the independent auditor must obtain an understanding of the internal audit function and decide if its activities are relevant to the audit. If the auditor decides that they are, and it is efficient to consider their work, then their competence and objectivity must be assessed. If the auditor concludes that they are competent and objective, then the effect and extent of their work on the audit must be considered, as well as evaluating and testing its effectiveness. The auditor may also use internal auditors to provide direct assistance during the audit.

7. SAS #73—Using the Work of a Specialist
The work done by an outside specialist and the auditor's understanding of that work should be documented. The auditor should be able to understand the methods and assumptions used and should know whether the findings support the representations of the client.

Internal Control Structure

1. SAS #48—The Effects of Computer Processing on the Examination of Financial Statements
Classifying controls into general and application controls has no effect on the objectives of an internal control structure, since assets still need to be safeguarded and financial records must be reliable for the preparation of financial statements.

Computer processing characteristics that may be distinguished from manual processing relate to transactions trails, uniform processing of transactions, segregation of functions, potential for errors and irregularities, potential for increased management supervision, and initiation or subsequent authorization of transactions.

2. SAS #55—Consideration of the Internal Control Structure in a Financial Statement Audit
To properly plan an audit, the auditor should obtain sufficient knowledge of the entity's internal control structure. The internal control structure consists of three elements: the control environment, the accounting system, and the control procedures.

a. *Control environment*—The overall attitude of the board of directors, management, and others concerning the importance of control and its emphasis in the entity.

b. *Accounting system*—Consists of the methods and records established to identify, assemble, classify, record, and report an entity's transactions and to maintain accountability for assets and liabilities.

c. *Control procedures*—Those procedures in addition to the control environment and accounting system that management has established to provide assurance that objectives will be achieved.

The auditor will first obtain an understanding of the internal control structure. Next, the auditor will assess control risk. If the auditor desires to seek a reduction in the assessed level of control risk below the maximum level, he will perform tests of controls. The auditor will use the knowledge obtained in the above steps to determine the nature, timing, and extent of substantive tests to be performed.

3. **SAS #60—Communication of Internal Control Structure Related Matters Noted in an Audit**

The independent auditor must communicate to the audit committee or the board of directors any reportable conditions in the internal control structure the auditor discovers while performing an audit under GAAS. While a written report is preferable, an oral report documented in the audit work papers is also acceptable.

4. **SAS #61—Communication with Audit Committees**

Requires the auditor to determine that certain significant items related to the conduct of the audit are communicated to the audit committee. The communication can be made orally, or in writing.

5. **SAS #70—Reports on the Processing of Transactions by Service Organizations**

If an entity uses services of other organizations to process significant transactions (e.g., EDP service centers) or to handle significant assets or liabilities (e.g., bank trust departments), the internal control structure of the service organization may be considered part of the user organization's internal control structure and thus be subject to audit planning and control risk assessment considerations by the user organization auditor.

The user organization auditor should consider obtaining, from the service organization auditor, a report on policies and procedures placed in operation at the service organization and related tests of operating effectiveness.

6. **SSAE #2—Reporting on an Entity's Internal Control Structure Over Financial Reporting**

The purpose and scope of an engagement to examine and report on management's written assertion about the effectiveness of an entity's internal control structure over financial reporting are different from the purpose and scope of the auditor's consideration of the internal control structure during an audit of financial statements. The content of the report would include an appropriate title, identification of the assertion in an introductory paragraph, a scope paragraph, a paragraph referring to inherent limitations, and, in a final paragraph, an opinion as to whether management's assertion is fairly stated in all material respects, based upon stated or established criteria.

Audit Evidence and Procedures

1. **SAS #12—Inquiry of a Client's Lawyer Concerning Litigation, Claims, and Assessments**

Matters that should be covered in an audit inquiry letter include a description and evaluation of pending or threatened litigation, unasserted claims, etc., for which the lawyer has been engaged and a request for the lawyer's comment on those matters with which the auditor differs with management.

The lawyer's response may be limited to matters to which he has given substantial attention and/or which he considered material. The lawyer's refusal to furnish the information requested is a limitation of the scope of the audit precluding an unqualified opinion. Further, the lawyer's inability to furnish information due to uncertainties would result in an unqualified opinion, although modified.

2. **SAS #19—Client Representations**

The auditor must obtain certain written representations from management as part of an audit under GAAS. These representations include such matters as management's responsibility for fair presentation of financial statements, availability and completeness of records, subsequent events, etc.

3. **SAS #31—Evidential Matter**

Evidence gathered should form an internally consistent pattern. It should be competent and sufficient. Competence is determined by validity and relevance, with the greatest assurance coming from evidence obtained in an environment with a good internal control structure and from independent external sources. Regarding sufficiency, the auditor must judge the relative risk and the relationship between the cost of obtaining evidence and its usefulness.

4. **SAS #39—Audit Sampling**

Sampling may be performed either through the use of nonstatistical or statistical methodology. Statistical sampling involves the sampling risk that the sample chosen may not be representative of the population. It also requires the establishment of a tolerable misstatement and rate under which deviation may exist without causing material misstatement of financial statements. In general, statistical sampling allows for (a) design of an efficient sample, (b) measurement of the sufficiency of evidential matter, and (c) objective evaluation of sample results.

Sampling may be used for both tests of controls and substantive testing. However, in the former, it should not be used for procedures that depend primarily on segregation of duties for effectiveness. In the latter, the more reliable the internal control structure, the smaller the sample required, but critical items should be examined in full (100 percent) and not sampled.

5. **Extracted from SAS #45 and FAS #57— Related-Party Transactions**
A related party is any one with which the reporting entity may deal when one party directly or indirectly has the ability to significantly influence the management or operating policies of the other, to the extent that one of the parties might be prevented from fully pursuing its own separate interest. Examples that may indicate related-party matters are such things as interest-free or low-rate loans, real estate sold well below appraised value, etc.

The auditor should review for the presence of an environment that might motivate related-party transactions; e.g., insufficient working capital or credit, etc. He should evaluate the client's procedures for identifying and accounting for related-party transactions.

6. **SAS #53—The Auditor's Responsibility to Detect and Report Errors and Irregularities**
Errors refer to unintentional mistakes; irregularities refer to intentional misstatements. The auditor should design the audit to provide reasonable assurance of detecting errors and irregularities that are material to the financial statements.

Irregularities should be communicated to the audit committee or the board of directors. If the financial statements are materially affected by an irregularity, they should be revised. If they are not revised, a qualified or adverse opinion should be issued. If the auditor is unable to conclude whether possible irregularities may materially affect the financial statements, the auditor should issue a qualified opinion or disclaim an opinion. If the client refuses to accept the modified report, the auditor should withdraw from the engagement.

7. **SAS #54—Illegal Acts by Clients**
Illegal acts refer to violations of laws or governmental regulations. The auditor's responsibility to detect and report misstatements resulting from illegal acts having a direct and material effect on the financial statements is the same as that for material errors and irregularities as described in SAS #53. The auditor should also be aware of the possibility of illegal acts having an indirect financial statement effect.

When the auditor becomes aware of information about a possible illegal act, the auditor should inquire of management at a level above those involved. If the auditor concludes that an illegal act has or is likely to have occurred, the audit committee should be informed.

The auditor should express a qualified or adverse opinion if an illegal act having a material effect on the financial statements has not been accounted for or disclosed, and disclaim an opinion if he is precluded by the client from obtaining the evidential matter needed to determine whether such an act has occurred. If the client refuses to accept the modified report, the auditor should withdraw from the engagement.

8. **SAS #57—Auditing Accounting Estimates**
The auditor is responsible for evaluating the reasonableness of accounting estimates. When evaluating such estimates, the auditor should obtain sufficient evidential matter to provide reasonable assurance that all estimates that could be material have been developed, are reasonable, are presented in conformity with GAAP, and are properly disclosed.

9. **SAS #59—The Auditor's Consideration of an Entity's Ability to Continue as a Going Concern (as amended)**
The auditor must consider if there is substantial doubt about an entity's ability to continue as a going concern for a reasonable period of time. In making the evaluation, the auditor considers certain negative conditions and events, and the mitigating plans of management. If the auditor concludes that substantial doubt remains, the unqualified auditor's report will include an explanatory paragraph.

10. **SAS #67—The Confirmation Process**
Confirmation of accounts receivable is considered to be a generally accepted auditing procedure. The auditor should consider whether the positive or negative form of confirmations should be utilized. Throughout the confirmation process, the auditor should adopt an attitude of professional skepticism.

Reporting Standards and Types of Reports

1. **SAS #32—Adequacy of Disclosure in Financial Statements**

   The auditor should express a qualified or adverse opinion if management omits information from financial statements that is required by GAAP. If practicable, the information should be provided in the auditor's report.

2. **SAS #58—Reports on Audited Financial Statements (as amended)**

   The standard report consists of an introductory paragraph, a scope paragraph, and an opinion paragraph. These may be modified, depending upon the nature of the opinion.

   The following opinions may be rendered:

   a. *Unqualified*—Financial statements are presented fairly, in conformity with GAAP. May under certain circumstances include an explanatory paragraph.

   b. *Qualified*—Adds an explanatory paragraph and, in the opinion paragraph, states "except for" (insufficient evidence, scope restrictions, departure from GAAP), the financial statements are presented fairly.

   c. *Adverse*—The financial statements are not presented fairly, in conformity with GAAP; a separate paragraph discloses reasons and principal effects.

   d. *Disclaimer*—No opinion expressed; a separate paragraph states why.

   A continuing auditor should update his report on prior periods presented on a comparative basis with the current period.

   The auditor should disclose all the substantive reasons for a changed opinion, using a separate explanatory paragraph. He may modify or disclaim an opinion for one period while expressing an unqualified opinion on financial statements of another period presented.

   A predecessor auditor may reissue his report for a prior period at the client's request if he performs certain additional procedures, such as obtaining a letter from the successor auditor stating whether the successor's audit revealed any matters that might affect the predecessor auditor's report. If the successor's audit did, the predecessor must perform other needed procedures. The reissued report bears the date of the previous report; if the report is revised, he should dual-date it.

   A successor auditor, when not presenting the predecessor's audit report, should include in the introductory paragraph the fact that another auditor audited that period, giving the type of opinion and reasons if other than an unqualified opinion.

   For unaudited reports, pages must be clearly marked "unaudited" and be accompanied by a disclaimer of opinion.

3. **SAS #62—Special Reports**

   a. *Financial statements not using GAAP*

   Such statements must offer a comprehensive basis of accounting other than GAAP such as that used to comply with requirements of a government agency, or cash, or modified cash basis, etc. The auditor's report should contain a title that includes the word "independent" and the following paragraphs: (1) financial statements were audited and are the responsibility of management, (2) audit was conducted in accordance with GAAS, (3) the basis of presentation, and (4) either an expression or disclaimer of an opinion on the presentation in conformity with the accounting basis described.

   b. *Reports expressing an opinion on elements of financial statements*

   GAAP does not have to apply. The auditor's report should contain a title that includes the word "independent" and the following paragraphs: (1) the specific elements were audited and are the responsibility of management, (2) the audit was conducted in accordance with GAAS, (3) the basis on which the items are presented, and (4) either an expression or disclaimer of opinion in conformity with the basis of accounting described.

   c. *Reports on compliance with agreements/regulations*

   The auditor can provide negative assurance relating to applicable covenants of an agreement, provided the auditor has audited the financial statements to which they relate. The assurance can be given in the auditor's report accompanying the financial statements or given separately.

   d. *Reports in prescribed form*

   When a printed form requires an auditor's assertion the auditor believes is not justified, he should reword it or attach a separate report.

4. **SAS #68—Compliance Auditing Applicable to Governmental Entities and Other Recipients of Governmental Financial Assistance**

The purpose of this SAS is to provide guidance for compliance audits conducted under GAAS and the Single Audit Act of 1984. The auditor should be concerned with the effects of laws and regulations that have a direct and material effect on the entity's financial statements. The auditor's assessment of control risk may be affected by compliance with laws and regulations. The auditor's report should include, among other things, references to GAAS and Government Auditing Standards, tests of compliance, positive assurance with respect to items tested, and negative assurance for those not tested.

5. **SAS #69—The Meaning of "Present Fairly in Conformity with Generally Accepted Accounting Principles" in the Independent Auditor's Report**

Fairness requires presentation under GAAP; conformity with GAAP requires general acceptance of principles applied that reflect the substance of transactions and offer informative, classified financial statements within limits that are reasonable.

6. **SAS #71—Interim Financial Information**

The objective of a review of interim financial information is to provide the accountant, through inquiries and analytical procedures, with a basis for reporting whether material modifications should be made for such information to conform to GAAP. Procedures include inquiries, analyses, reviews, and obtaining written representations from management. To perform a review of interim financial information, sufficient knowledge of the client's internal control structure policies and procedures, as they relate to both annual and interim financial information, is also needed.

If the accountant believes that financial information is misstated as a result of a GAAP departure, and certain conditions are met, the matter should be discussed with the appropriate level of management and, if management does not appropriately respond, with the audit committee. If the audit committee does not respond within a reasonable time, the accountant may consider withdrawing.

The accountant's report, among other things, indicates that a review is not an audit; gives any material modifications required under GAAP;

and states that, subject to exceptions noted, the reviewer is not aware of any modifications to make the statements conform to GAAP. Each page of information must bear the "unaudited" label.

7. **SSARS #1—Compilation and Review of Financial Statements (as amended)**

This pronouncement relates to unaudited statements of nonpublic entities. A "compilation" pertains to preparation of financial statements from management-supplied data, without the expression of any assurance concerning them. A "review" involves inquiry and analytical procedures to provide a basis for expressing limited assurance that the financial statements conform to GAAP or another comprehensive accounting basis.

The report accompanying a compilation, among other matters, identifies the performance of a compilation in accordance with Statements on Standards for Accounting and Review Services issued by the AICPA, and is limited to statement preparation, with no audit or review involved. Each page of the compiled financial statements should be marked "See Accountant's Compilation Report."

The report accompanying a review, among other matters, identifies the performance of a review in accordance with Statements on Standards for Accounting and Review Services issued by the AICPA and what it is and is not, and states that subject to exceptions noted, the accountant is not aware of any material modifications to make the financial statements conform to GAAP. Each page of the financial statements should be marked "See Accountant's Review Report." An accountant who is not independent cannot issue a review report.

8. **SSARS #2—Reporting on Comparative Financial Statements**

If the same level of service (e.g., compilation in both periods) is used for each period, utilize the SSARS #1 type of accountant's report. If the level of service is stepped up or down, then the report must be modified following specific guidelines.

In the case of a predecessor's report, the predecessor is not required to reissue his report but may do so at the client's request. When reissuing, the previous report date is used unless a revision is made. Then, a dual-dated report for the revised aspect is used.

9. **SSARS #3—Compilation Reports on Financial Statements Included in Certain Prescribed Forms**

The compilation report, among other things, should identify the statements and that they have been compiled. No audit or review was performed and no opinion or other form of assurance is expressed. The presentation differs from GAAP but conforms to the prescribed form.

10. **SSARS #4—Communication Between Predecessor and Successor Accountants**

A successor may, but is not required to, communicate with a predecessor about acceptance of a compilation or review engagement. The client should be requested to permit the successor to inquire and to authorize the predecessor to respond. The predecessor should respond promptly and fully unless, because of circumstances, he must place limits on such response.

11. **SSARS #6—Reporting on Personal Financial Statements Included in Written Personal Financial Plans**

This statement provides that under certain conditions, the accountant may submit a written personal financial plan containing unaudited personal financial statements without complying with the requirements of SSARS #1.

Other Reporting Considerations

1. **Extracted from SAS #1—Subsequent Events**

Subsequent events are those that have a material effect and occur after the balance sheet date but before the issuance of financial statements and the auditor's report. One type provides additional information about conditions that actually existed at the balance sheet date; this type requires adjustment of the financial statements. A second type provides information about conditions that did not exist at the balance sheet date but arose thereafter; here, financial statements should not be adjusted but disclosure may be required.

2. **Extracted from SAS #1—Subsequent Discovery of Facts**

Subsequent discovery of facts arises when the auditor becomes aware of facts that may have existed at the date of the report that might have affected it had he been aware of them. The auditor must undertake to determine reliability of the facts and their existence at the date of the auditor's report. Action must be taken if the audit report would have been affected had the auditor known of the facts at the date of the report and if it is believed persons in possession of the financial statements would attach importance to the facts.

3. **SAS #8—Other Information in Documents Containing Audited Financial Statements**

The auditor has no obligation to corroborate other information contained in the document. However, the auditor should read it and judge whether it is materially inconsistent with the financial statements. If it is inconsistent, revision must take place.

4. **SAS #21—Segment Information**

The auditor is not required to apply special audit procedures or express a separate opinion on segment information. The auditor should, however, evaluate and test the methods of determining segment information. If the segment information is not disclosed, the auditor is not required to provide it, but he should comment on its absence.

5. **SAS #26—Association with Financial Statements**

The accountant's association arises when (a) he consents to the use of his name in a written communication containing audited or unaudited financial statements, or (b) the auditor has prepared or assisted in the preparation of such statements even though his name does not appear.

A disclaimer on unaudited statements should be issued indicating that no audit has been made and no opinion is expressed. Each page of the financial statements should be marked "unaudited."

If the information is presented in a document containing financial statements of a public entity that have not been audited or reviewed, the accountant's name should be excluded or the statements marked "unaudited," and a notation included that the accountant expressed no opinion on them.

6. **SAS #29—Reporting on Information Accompanying the Basic Financial Statements in Auditor-Submitted Documents**

When the auditor submits to a client a document containing financial statements and other information, he must report on all of the client representations in that document; e.g., schedules, summaries, etc.

7. **SAS #37—Filings Under the Federal Securities Statutes**

The accountant's responsibility is that of an expert when his report is included in a registration statement and his standard of reasonableness therefore is "that required of a prudent man in the management of his or her own property."

In connection with a prospectus, the accountant should not allow his name to be used in any way to indicate greater responsibility than he intends to undertake.

8. **SAS #42—Reporting on Condensed Financial Statements and Selected Financial Data**

Condensed financial statements should be so marked but do not constitute fair presentation under GAAP. The auditor's report, among other things, should state whether they are fairly stated in relation to the complete statements. The naming of the auditor in a client-prepared document does not, in itself, require the auditor to report on condensed statements, provided these statements are included with audited statements or are incorporated by reference.

Entity management determines the specific selected financial data to be presented. The auditor, in reporting, should limit the report to data derived from audited statements.

9. **SAS #46—Consideration of Omitted Procedures After the Report Date**

If the auditor concludes, subsequent to the audit report date, that he omitted one or more audit procedures, the auditor must determine if the omission impairs the present ability to support the original opinion. If necessary, the CPA should arrange either to apply the omitted procedures or to apply alternate ones.

10. **SAS #50—Reports on the Application of Accounting Principles**

When an accountant (i.e., reporting accountant) is asked to evaluate accounting principles or is requested to render an opinion on the application of accounting principles by an entity that is audited by another CPA (i.e., continuing accountant), the reporting accountant, after accepting the engagement, should consult with the continuing accountant to ascertain all the available facts relevant to forming a professional judgment.

11. **SAS #52—Required Supplementary Information**

If supplementary information is required by the FASB or the GASB, it is not a required part of the basic financial statements and is not audited. The auditor need not refer in the report to the supplementary information or the limited procedures unless (a) the information is omitted, (b) it departs from guidelines, or (c) prescribed audit procedures cannot be accomplished. If supplementary information is omitted, the auditor need not present it.

12. **SAS #72—Letters for Underwriters and Other Requesting Parties**

The types of services that CPAs perform include examination of financial statements and schedules included in registration statements filed with the SEC. As such, CPAs confer with various parties with respect to certain aspects of the Securities Act of 1933, and of the SEC, as well as perform other services. Issuance of letters for underwriters (comfort letters) is one of them.

A typical letter includes, among other things (a) a statement regarding the independence of the accountants, (b) an opinion regarding the audited financial statements and schedules included in the registration statement and whether they are in compliance in all material respects with the applicable requirements of the 1933 Act, and related published rules and regulations, (c) negative assurance with respect to unaudited condensed interim financial statements, and changes in certain account balances during a specified period.

13. **Statement on Standards for Accountants' Services on Prospective Financial Information**

A CPA may compile, examine, or apply agreed-upon procedures to prospective financial statements (i.e., financial forecasts and financial projections).

A financial forecast is an entity's expected financial position, results of operations, and changes in cash flows, based on assumptions reflecting conditions expected to exist and the course of action expected to be taken. A financial projection, on the other hand, is based on one or more hypothetical assumptions which are not necessarily expected to occur.

14. **SSAE #1—Statement on Standards for Attestation Engagements**

Attestation engagements involve the issuance of a written communication containing the expression of a conclusion as to the reliability of a written assertion (e.g., the investment performance of a mutual fund) that is the responsibility of another party. A CPA may examine, review, or apply agreed-upon procedures to an assertion.

15. SSAE #3—Compliance Attestation

A practitioner may accept an engagement to examine or apply agreed-upon procedures to management's assertion about (a) compliance with requirements of specified laws, regulations, rules, contracts, or grants (referred to as compliance with specified requirements) and (b) the effectiveness of an entity's internal control structure over compliance with specified requirements (referred to as internal control structure over compliance).

An examination engagement leads to the expression of an opinion about whether management's assertion is fairly stated in all material respects based on established or agreed-upon criteria.

The objective of an agreed-upon procedures engagement is to present specific findings about an entity's compliance with specified requirements or about the effectiveness of an entity's internal control structure over compliance based on procedures agreed upon by the users of the report; no opinion or negative assurance is provided about whether the assertion is presented fairly.

U.S. GENERAL ACCOUNTING OFFICE GOVERNMENT AUDITING STANDARDS

General Standards

1. *Qualifications*—Adequate professional proficiency for the tasks required.
2. *Independence*—Free from personal and external impairments to independence, organizationally independent, and maintain an independent attitude and appearance.
3. *Due professional care* should be exercised in conducting the audit and in preparing related reports.
4. *Quality control*—Have an internal quality control system and an external quality control review program.

Field Work Standards for Financial Audits

1. Generally Accepted Government Auditing Standards (GAGAS) incorporate GAAS standards of field work for financial audits and prescribe supplemental standards for the unique needs of governmental financial audits.
2. Supplemental planning
   (a) Include consideration of the audit requirements of all levels of government.
   (b) Compliance with legal and regulatory requirements should be tested to provide reasonable assurance of detecting errors, irregularities, and illegal acts that could have a direct and material effect on the financial statements or the results of financial-related audits.
   (c) The auditor should also be aware of the possibility of illegal acts that could have an indirect and material effect on the financial statements or results of financial-related audits.
3. Supplemental evidence (working papers)
   (a) Both GAAS and GAGAS require retention of the auditor's work in working papers.
   (b) Supplemental GAGAS requirements for working papers are that:
      (1) A written audit program is cross-referenced to the working papers.
      (2) There is documentation as to the objective, scope, methodology, and audit results.
      (3) Sufficient information is contained so that supplementary oral explanations are not required.
      (4) Papers are legible, with adequate indexing and cross-referencing, and include summaries and lead schedules, as appropriate.
      (5) Information included is restricted to matters that are materially important and relevant to the objectives of the audit.
      (6) Evidence of supervisory reviews of the work conducted is contained.
4. Internal control
   Both GAAS and GAGAS require that a sufficient understanding of the internal control structure is to be obtained to plan the audit and to determine the nature, timing, and extent of tests to be performed.

Reporting Standards for Financial Audits

1. GAGAS incorporate the GAAS standards of reporting for financial audits, and prescribe sup-

plemental standards of reporting needed to satisfy the unique needs of governmental financial audits.

2. Supplemental reporting standards
    (a) A statement that the audit was made in accordance with generally accepted government auditing standards.
    (b) *Report on compliance*—A written report that contains a statement of positive assurance on items tested for compliance and negative assurance on those items not tested. It should include all material instances of noncompliance, and all instances or indications of illegal acts that could result in criminal prosecution.
    (c) *Report on internal controls*—A written report on the understanding of the entity's internal control structure and the assessment of control risk made. Include, as a minimum, a description of the scope of the work performed, significant controls, and any reportable conditions noted, including those considered to be material weaknesses.
    (d) Written audit reports of the results of each financial-related audit.
    (e) *Privileged and confidential information*—If certain information is prohibited from general disclosure, report the nature of the omitted information and the requirement that makes the omission necessary.
    (f) *Report distribution*—Submit written audit reports to the appropriate officials both within and outside the organization that was audited. Unless restricted by law or regulation, copies should be made available for public inspection.

Accounting & Reporting— Taxation, Managerial, and Governmental and Not-for-Profit Organizations (ARE): Subject Matter Covered

Federal Income Taxation

Material dealing with federal income taxation does not require extensive arithmetic computations.

There are many specific areas relative to federal taxation that appear on the examination. An overview of these may be seen by reference to the "Content Specification Outline" (pages 2–7).

In general terms, exam coverage focuses on the taxation of individuals, corporations, partnerships, estates and trusts, and exempt organizations. The material tested has not significantly emphasized the calculation of tax liability and/or tax credits.

For the past several years, there has been great frequency of change in the Internal Revenue Code. Candidates are responsible for knowledge of the Internal Revenue Code and Tax Regulations in effect six months before the examination date.

The major considerations in this area are:

1. An awareness of basic gross income inclusions for individual taxpayers, including business income, interest, rents and royalties, dividends, and capital gains and losses.
2. An awareness of exclusions and adjustments in arriving at adjusted gross income of individuals.
3. An awareness of the determination of capital gains and losses, including the recognition of gains and losses and holding period.
4. An awareness of itemized deductions for individuals, including interest, taxes, contributions, medical expenses, casualty losses, and miscellaneous deductions.
5. An awareness of filing status and exemptions for individuals.
6. An awareness of tax accounting methods, tax computations, penalties, and other administrative tax procedures applicable to individuals.
7. An awareness of the determination of taxable income or loss for corporations.
8. An awareness of special considerations for corporations, including background on incorporation, S corporations, personal holding companies, consolidated returns, distributions to stockholders, and the area of reorganization and liquidation.
9. An awareness of tax accounting methods, tax computations, penalties, and other administrative tax procedures applicable to corporations.
10. An awareness of the background of partnership taxation, including the formation of a partnership, the basis of a partner's interest and how it is determined, the basis of property contributed to a partnership, the determination of a partner's taxable income, transactions between a partner and the partnership, the distribution of partnership assets, and the termination of a partnership.
11. An awareness of relevant tax credits with respect to all types of taxpayers.
12. An awareness of the broad aspects of exempt organizations, including types of organizations,

requirements for exemption, and the tax on unrelated business income.

13. An awareness of the broad aspects relative to the taxation of estates and trusts, including gift taxation.
14. An awareness of preparers' responsibilities applicable to tax returns of individuals and corporations.

On a philosophical note, the candidate should realize that due to the very nature of the subject, examination questions in this area can occasionally be very specific and narrow. It is the authors' belief that a more meaningful method of testing candidates in this area must evolve; indeed, open-book examinations would be appropriate. The type of material appearing on examination questions over the past several years does not seem to mesh with the profile of the CPA candidate as an entry-level accountant.

However, it is probable that all candidates taking the examination face the same problem, and it must be assumed that this is taken into consideration during the grading process.

Managerial Accounting

As indicated in the "Content Specification Outline" (pages 2–7), this is a rather broad subject area that encompasses a number of subtopics.

The subject area includes material on *quantitative techniques*, which are highly mathematically oriented. However, on balance, exam coverage of such material over the past decade has not been extremely deep in concept, difficult in application, or regular in appearance.

The major considerations in this area are:

1. An awareness of the various elements that enter into the components of a product; i.e., material, labor, and overhead (both actual and applied).
2. An awareness of the various cost accounting methods and systems, with particular emphasis on job order costing, process costing, standard costing, joint and by-product costing.
3. An awareness of the various techniques for planning and control, including budgeting, breakeven and cost-volume-profit analysis, capital budgeting techniques, and other quantitative techniques.
4. An awareness of analytical methods and procedures including, but not limited to, regression and correlation analysis, probability analysis, and ratio analysis.

5. The ability to make the calculations and computations that are essential to this subject area. Included in this category are items such as the determination of equivalent units of production in process costing, variance analysis in standard costing, and the allocation of costs in joint costing.

The background for this area is provided by a college-level course in cost accounting or its equivalent.

Accounting for Governmental and Not-for-Profit Organizations

This subject area requires familiarity with *fund accounting, types of funds and account groups, types of not-for-profit and governmental organizations, and the presentation of financial statements for various not-for-profit and governmental organizations.*

The major considerations in this area are:

1. An awareness of the essentials of fund accounting and the nuances that make it unique, as well as such conceptual reporting issues as the budgetary process.
2. An awareness of the types of funds and the rationale for establishing each fund.
3. An awareness of the various types of not-for-profit and governmental organizations.
4. While the ARE exam does not require the preparation of journal entries and financial statements for various types of not-for-profit entities, it is essential to have an understanding of the underlying logic and terminology.

The background for this area is provided in either a special college-level course or in a course in advanced accounting.

OFFICIAL ACCOUNTING PRONOUNCEMENTS

While professional pronouncements issued by the Financial Accounting Standards Board are tested extensively on the FARE section of the exam, the following Financial Accounting Standards Board Statements are relevant to the topic of accounting for not-for-profit organizations (other than governmental units) tested on the ARE exam:

1. **FAS #93—Recognition of Depreciation by Not-for-Profit Organizations**
   Depreciation must be recognized as an expense by all not-for-profit organizations other than governmental units. (It should also be noted that proprietary funds and nonexpendable trust funds of governmental units will recognize depreciation as an expense.)

Works of art and similar items are likely to have estimated useful lives that are extraordinarily long. Accordingly, depreciation of these items is generally not recognized.

2. **FAS #116—Accounting for Contributions Received and Contributions Made**
In general, all unconditional contributions of assets, donated services, or liability reductions should be recorded at fair market value on the date of receipt. Further, gain or revenue should be recorded.

3. **FAS #117—Financial Statements of Not-for-Profit Organizations**
This statement establishes standards for general-purpose external financial statements. All not-for-profit organizations are required to present a statement of financial position, a statement of activities, and a statement of cash flows:

a. The statement of financial position requires reporting of total amounts for assets (that are presented in the order of relative liquidity, or by classifying them as current or noncurrent), liabilities (that are presented according to their nearness to maturity or use of cash, or by classifying them as current or noncurrent), and net assets (i.e., equity, classified as unrestricted, temporarily restricted, or permanently restricted).

b. The statement of activities is required to report the amount of change in permanently, temporarily restricted, and unrestricted net assets for the period. Generally, reporting of gross revenues and expenses is required.

c. The statement of cash flows will generally be prepared in accordance with FAS #95, "Statement of Cash Flows." It should be noted that changes in terminology may be necessary. For example, "changes in net assets" and "statement of activities" are used in place of "net income" and "income statement," respectively.

It should be noted that while the Governmental Accounting Standards Board issues pronouncements relative to governmental accounting, no summaries are contained herein since none to date have had any significant impact on the CPA examination.

Financial Accounting & Reporting—Business Enterprises (FARE): Subject Matter Covered

Concepts, Standards, and Financial Statements

Questions in this subject area include:
1. Definitions of accounting terms and objectives of financial statement presentation and disclosure.
2. Review of environmental factors behind generally accepted accounting concepts.
3. Explanation of drawbacks and/or seeming contradictions between or among two or more concepts, principles, or methods.
4. Defending or explaining theoretical positions that are and are not generally accepted.
5. Problem situations presented in that the proper concepts, principles, or methods must be applied and defended.

The background for this area is provided by a college-level course in accounting theory.

Recognition, Measurement, Valuation, and Presentation of Assets in Conformity with Generally Accepted Accounting Principles

In this subject area, the candidate must be familiar with *cash, marketable securities and investments, receivables and accruals, inventories, property, plant and equipment, capitalized lease assets, intangibles, and prepaid expenses and deferred charges.*

The major considerations in this area include:
1. An awareness of professional pronouncements relative to such matters as investments in debt and equity securities, lease transactions, capitalization of interest, intangible assets, accounting for income taxes (but not federal income taxes *per se*), and accounting for pension costs.
2. The ability to prepare appropriate schedules and computations relative to the assets involved, including schedules of inventories, presentation of investments in the balance sheet, etc.
3. The ability to determine allowance items for such assets as accounts receivable, property, plant and equipment, and intangible assets, along with the related expense charges.
4. An awareness of inventory methods of all types, including the retail inventory method and dollar-value LIFO techniques.

The candidate's background for this area will come from college-level courses in elementary and intermediate accounting or their equivalents.

Recognition, Measurement, Valuation, and Presentation of Liabilities in Conformity with Generally Accepted Accounting Principles

This subject area requires familiarity with *payables and accruals, deferred revenue, deferred income tax liabilities, capitalized lease liability, bonds payable, long-term notes payable, and contingent liabilities and commitments.*

The major considerations in this area are:

1. An awareness of professional pronouncements relative to such matters as accounting for income taxes (but not federal income taxes *per se*), lease transactions, accounting for transactions in bonds, contingent liabilities, and accounting for pension costs.
2. The ability to prepare appropriate schedules and computations, including determination of capitalized leases, guarantees and warranties, and the book (carrying) value of bonds outstanding.
3. The ability to determine expense charges associated with these liabilities.
4. An awareness of the types of temporary differences with respect to accounting for income taxes.
5. An awareness of different methods for amortizing bond discount or premium, with particular emphasis on the "effective interest" method.

A candidate's preparation in intermediate accounting or its equivalent will provide the necessary background.

Recognition, Measurement, Valuation, and Presentation of Equity Accounts in Conformity with Generally Accepted Accounting Principles

Subjects that will be tested in this area include *preferred and common stock, additional paid-in capital, retained earnings and dividends, treasury stock and other contra accounts, stock options, warrants and rights, change in entity, as well as partnerships and proprietorships.*

The major considerations in this area are:

1. An awareness of the appropriate accounting treatment of various classes of capital stock, including the issuance and retirement of stock and the determination of book value per share.
2. An awareness of the various elements of additional paid-in capital.
3. An awareness of retained earnings, including prior-period adjustments and dividend payments of various types.
4. An awareness of accounting for treasury stock based on the par value and cost methods.

5. An awareness of the treatment of stock options, warrants, and rights.
6. An awareness of reorganization and change in entity and bankruptcy.
7. An awareness of accounting for partnerships, including admission of partners, withdrawal of partners, dissolution, and liquidation.

This particular subject area is one in which the ability to make computations is not an overwhelming concern.

The background for this area is provided in college-level courses in intermediate accounting and advanced accounting or their equivalents.

Recognition, Measurement, and Presentation of Revenues and Expenses in Conformity with Generally Accepted Accounting Principles

This area includes coverage of *revenues and gains, cost of goods sold, expenses, provision for income tax, recurring vs. nonrecurring transactions and events, accounting changes, and earnings per share.*

Obviously, in many instances, the measurement of revenue and expense items is directly associated with the valuation of assets and liabilities. To this extent, there is an overlap between the material in this subject area and that in subject areas previously reviewed. By the same token, there is necessary duplication of coverage. For example, a knowledge of the equity method of accounting for investments in common stock is categorized both with respect to valuation of the asset and recognition of income.

The major considerations in this area are:

1. An awareness of professional pronouncements relative to such matters as investments in common stock, accounting for intangible assets, foreign currency transactions, reporting the results of operations, accounting for income taxes, accounting changes, and reporting earnings per share.
2. An awareness of various revenue recognition methods, including the installment sales method, the cost recovery method, the percentage of completion method, and the equity method of accounting for investments in common stock.
3. An awareness of the components and nature of the cost of goods sold.
4. An awareness of expenses of all types, including general and administrative expenses, selling expenses, etc.
5. An awareness of the determination and components of the provision for income tax.
6. An awareness of the treatment of discontinued operations, extraordinary items, and accounting changes.

7. The ability to make computations relative to the various income and expense items that form part of an income statement, including earnings-per-share computations.

The background for this area is generally provided in college-level courses in intermediate accounting and advanced accounting or their equivalents.

Other Financial Accounting and Reporting Issues

For this area also, it should be noted that there are overlaps and/or duplications. *For an indication of the items included in this subject area, see the details in the "Content Specification Outline" (see page 2).*

The major considerations in this area are:

1. An awareness of professional pronouncements relative to such matters as the statement of cash flows, consolidated and combined financial statements, business combinations, accounting policies, nonmonetary transactions, interim financial statements, inflation accounting, segment reporting, development stage enterprises, personal financial statements, and loss contingencies.
2. The ability to make appropriate determinations relative to the subject matter involved.

The background for the various areas involved is provided in college-level courses in intermediate accounting and advanced accounting or their equivalents.

OFFICIAL ACCOUNTING PRONOUNCEMENTS

Professional pronouncements issued by the Financial Accounting Standards Board and the American Institute of CPAs are tested extensively on the CPA examination. As such, this section has been prepared and organized to acquaint CPA candidates with those pronouncements that have particular applicability to the FARE section of the exam. Its organization reflects the "Content Specification Outline" in Chapter 1.

The pronouncement summaries reflect the impact of any subsequent amendments and interpretations likely to be of significance to the CPA candidate. Pronouncements that have been omitted are either obsolete or not relevant for the CPA examination.

The abbreviated references to the accounting pronouncements below are for the following:

FAC—Statement of Financial Accounting Concepts
APB—Accounting Principles Board Opinion (The Accounting Principles Board was a predecessor to the Financial Accounting Standards Board.)
FAS—Financial Accounting Standards Board Statement

General Concepts and Standards

1. **FAC #1—Objectives of Financial Statements**
Objectives include the providing of information that is useful in making economic decisions, particularly those related to investment and credit granting. However, financial accounting alone is not meant to measure directly the value of an enterprise.

2. **FAC #2—Qualitative Characteristics Making Accounting Information Useful**
Primary qualities include both relevance (timeliness, predictive value, and feedback value) and reliability (verifiability, representational faithfulness, and neutrality). Other qualities include comparability, understandability, and favorable cost/benefit relationship.

3. **FAC #4—Objectives of Financial Reporting by Nonbusiness Organizations**
Objectives include information about allocation of resources, assessment of both current entity and managerial performance, and assessment of the ability to continue such performance. Information is directed toward the needs of governing bodies, resource providers, managers, and constituents.

4. **FAC #5—Recognition and Measurement in Financial Statements of Business Enterprises**
Recognition involves incorporating an item into the financial statements as an asset, liability, revenue, and expense, etc. The item should be expressed in both words and dollars, with the amount included in the totals of the financial statements. Recognition of an asset or liability not only involves recognizing it initially, but also recognizing later changes such as disposition, liquidation, etc.

Recognition of an item should satisfy the following four criteria subject to materiality and cost/benefit:
a. *Definition*—The item conforms to the definition of a financial statement element.
b. *Measurability*—Reliable measurement exists.
c. *Relevance*—It affects a user's decision.
d. *Reliability*—Information is verifiable and neutral.

5. **FAC #6—Elements of Financial Statements**
The statement replaces FAC #3 ("Elements of Financial Statements of Business Enterprises") and amends FAC #2 to apply to not-for-profit as well as to for-profit entities.

Financial statements reflect in numbers and words resources, claims to resources, and transactional effects and other events causing a change in resources and claims.

Similarities exist between for-profit and not-for-profit entities; however, the elements of *investments by owners, distributions to owners,* and *comprehensive income* are not applicable to not-for-profit entities.

There are ten interrelated elements in measuring entity financial position and performance:

a. *Assets*—Possible future economic benefits occurring because of past events. (A valuation account is part of the related asset.)

b. *Liabilities*—Possible future sacrifices of economic benefits as a result of past transactions. (A valuation account is part of the related liability.)

c. *Equity (net assets)*—Represents residual interest.

   (1) As to a *for-profit* organization, equity is the ownership interest.

   (2) As to a *not-for-profit* organization, there is no equity *per se*. Rather, *net assets* are of three classes: permanently donor-restricted, temporarily donor-restricted, and unrestricted.

d. *Investments by owners*—May be the form of assets or represent services or conversion of liabilities of the entity.

e. *Distributions to owners*—Decreases in equity resulting from transferring assets, performing services, or incurring debt to owners.

f. *Comprehensive income*—The equity change arising from transactions and other events with nonowners. (Over an entity's life, comprehensive income equals the excess of cash receipts over cash outlays, excluding cash invested or disinvested by owners.)

   Comprehensive income consists not only of its basic components—revenues, expenses, gains and losses, but all intermediate components that result from combining the basic components; i.e., gross margin.

g. *Revenues*—Increases in assets or reductions in liabilities from manufacturing goods or performing services related to major operational activities.

h. *Expenses*—Reductions in assets or increases in liabilities from manufacturing goods or performing services related to major operational activities.

i. *Gains*—Increases in equity arising from incidental transactions.

j. *Losses*—Decreases in equity arising from incidental transactions.

6. **APB #22—Disclosure of Accounting Policies**
Accounting policies are the specific policies determined for use by the entity's management. Every financial statement, whether presented singly or in combination, should present a description of all such material policies used (e.g., depreciation methods, inventory pricing, etc.) in a separate section preceding footnotes or as the first such note.

7. **APB #29—Accounting for Nonmonetary Transactions**

a. *Dissimilar assets*—Utilize fair value of the asset given up or asset received if the latter is not ascertainable, recognizing gain or loss.

b. *Similar assets*—For transactions not resulting in a culmination of the earning process, utilize net book value of the asset given up. Gain is not recognized, but a loss is recognized if the asset received has a lower fair value than the book value of the asset given up.

Assets

1. **APB #17—Intangible Assets**
An intangible, whether of limited life or indeterminable useful life, shall be amortized over the period of benefit using the straight-line method unless some other method is more appropriate. Such period should be the lesser of legal life, useful life, or forty years.

2. **APB #18—The Equity Method of Accounting for Investments in Common Stock (as amended)**
The equity method should be used to account for investments in common stock on consolidated and parent company financial statements, and financial statements of companies owning at least 20 percent but not more than 50 percent of the common stock and/or where the investor is able to exercise significant influence over the operations of the investee.

   The equity method adds to the initial cost of the investment, the investor's share of the investee's post acquisition net income/loss on an accrual basis; dividends reduce the investment's carrying value.

For changes in the valuation account of current asset securities, losses will be included in determination of net income; recoveries in subsequent periods will be included as gains. For noncurrent asset securities, such changes will be shown as a separate reduction of owners' equity on the balance sheet. However, if a decline is judged to be other than temporary, the write-down is accounted for as a realized loss in determination of net income.

3. **FAS #13—Accounting for Leases (as amended)**
Leases that transfer substantially all the economic benefits and risks of ownership should be accounted for by:
a. Lessee as the present value of an asset acquired and liability incurred.
b. Lessor as a sale or transfer.
All other leases are considered operating leases.
Criteria for lessee capitalization require the presence of any one of the following:
a. Ownership transfer at end of lease.
b. Bargain price option to buy at end of lease.
c. Lease term of 75 percent or more of property economic life.
d. Present value of minimum lease payments is 90 percent or more of the fair value of leased property.
Criteria for lessor capitalization require existence of criteria for lessee capitalization and that both of the following conditions exist:
a. Reasonable predictability as to collection of minimum lease payments.
b. Absence of uncertainties regarding the amount of reimbursable costs not yet incurred by the lessor.

4. **FAS #34—Capitalization of Interest Cost (as amended)**
Interest incurred during the building period of the following must be capitalized as part of their cost:
a. Assets built for the entity's own use.
b. Assets built as identifiable projects for sale or lease; e.g., ships, real estate developments.

5. **FAS #115—Accounting for Certain Investments in Debt and Equity Securities**
This statement establishes standards of financial accounting and reporting for investments in equity securities that have readily determinable fair (market) values, and for all investments in debt securities.

At acquisition, an enterprise shall classify debt and equity securities into one of three categories; namely, trading securities, held-to-maturity securities, and available-for-sale securities.

The statement provides that trading securities be presented at fair value on the statement date, with unrealized gains and losses included in earnings. Held-to-maturity securities are to be presented at amortized cost on the statement date, with unrealized gains and losses not recognized. Available-for-sale securities should be presented at fair value on the statement date, with unrealized gains and losses reported as a separate component of stockholders' equity.

Further, in a classified statement of financial position, trading securities are classified as current assets, and securities in the other categories are classified as either current or noncurrent under the normal one-year or operating cycle rule.

Liabilities

1. **APB #14—Accounting for Convertible Debt and Debt Issued with Stock Purchase Warrants**
When the warrants are detachable from the bonds, the portion of the proceeds allocable to the warrants should be accounted for as paid-in capital. When the warrants are not detachable, no allocation of proceeds to the conversion feature is needed.

2. **APB #21—Interest on Receivables and Payables**
The difference between the present value, using an imputed interest rate, and the face amount of a note should be treated as premium or discount, and amortized, using the interest method, as interest expense or income so as to produce a constant rate of interest. Presentation of discount/premium on the balance sheet should be as additions/deductions to/from the items with which they are associated. This pronouncement does not relate to trade receivables/payables.

3. **APB #26 and FAS #4—Early Extinguishment of Debt**
All extinguishments before maturity are basically the same. A gain or a loss resulting therefrom is treated as extraordinary, whether resulting from early extinguishment, at scheduled maturity, or later.

4. **FAS #5—Accounting for Contingencies**

Accrue a loss from a contingency by a charge to income if:

a. Information prior to issuance of financial statements indicates that it is probable that an asset has been impaired or a liability incurred at the statement date.

b. The amount of loss can be reasonably estimated.

5. **FAS #6—Classification of Short-Term Obligations Expected to be Refinanced**

Short-term obligations (other than trade payables) should be excluded from current liabilities only if the entity intends to refinance them on a long-term basis and if such intent is supported by appropriate written documentation.

6. **FAS #15—Accounting by Debtors and Creditors for Troubled Debt Restructuring**

Restructuring takes place if the creditor grants a concession to the debtor for economic or legal reasons related to the latter's financial difficulties. A debtor recognizes gain on restructuring of payables. A creditor recognizes loss between fair market value of assets received and his book value of the investment.

7. **FAS #43—Accounting for Compensated Absences**

Accrue a liability for employees' compensation for future absences if all the following conditions exist:

a. Employees' rights to such compensation are attributable to services already rendered.

b. Such rights are not contingent upon continued employment.

c. Payment is probable.

d. The amount can be reasonably estimated.

8. **FAS #47—Disclosure of Long-Term Obligations**

All unconditional purchase obligations not otherwise recognized should be disclosed on the balance sheet, provided they:

a. Are noncancellable in form or in substance.

b. Were negotiated as part of arranging financing for facilities that will provide the contracted goods/services.

c. Have a remaining term in excess of one year.

9. **FAS #49—Accounting for Product Financing Arrangements**

A product financing arrangement is one that involves a sponsor controlling disposition of a product. When the sponsor must purchase the inventory at specified prices, and payments are set, with adjustment added for purchasing and holding costs of the other entity, then the sponsor must reflect a liability rather than a sale when proceeds come in and the sponsor does not remove the item from its inventory.

10. **FAS #109—Accounting for Income Taxes**

The objectives of accounting for income taxes are to (a) recognize the amount of taxes payable or refundable for the current year, and (b) recognize deferred tax assets and liabilities for the future consequences of events that have been recognized in the financial statements or tax returns.

The statement requires comprehensive allocation of income taxes among financial periods in accounting for temporary differences. A temporary difference is the difference between the tax basis of an asset or liability and its basis as reported in the financial statements (i.e., book basis).

The year-end deferred item is determined by applying tax rates expected to be in effect in future years (based on existing tax laws) to reversals of temporary differences expected to occur in such future years.

11. **FAS #112—Employers' Accounting for Post-employment Benefits**

An employer who provides benefits to former or inactive employees after employment, but before retirement, should account for such benefits following the conditions of FAS #43 (reviewed above), or FAS #5 (also reviewed in the above section), if FAS #43 conditions cannot be met, but a liability nevertheless exists (i.e., the event is probable and can be reasonably estimated).

Ownership

1. **APB #16—Business Combinations**

The purchase method of accounting for a business combination should be used when cash and other assets are distributed or liabilities incurred to effect a combination. Recording should be at fair market value of net assets acquired, recognizing goodwill for any difference between these net assets and the purchase price.

The pooling method applies only if voting stock (at least 90 percent) is issued to effect the combination of common stock interests, and certain other conditions are fulfilled. Recording is made at the book value of net assets acquired. No goodwill results.

2. APB #25—Accounting for Stock Issued to Employees

Stock issued under noncompensatory plans is accounted for as with any other issuance of stock to nonemployees. For compensatory plans, accounting differs. Measurement of compensation is equal to the difference between market value at the measurement date and the option price. Measurement date is the first date on which both the number of shares and the option price are known.

3. FAS #16—Prior-Period Adjustments

All items of profit and loss from a period are to be included in arriving at net income, except for items specified as prior-period adjustments. The latter are defined as either corrections of errors and/or realized income tax benefits of pre-acquisition operating loss carry-forwards of purchased subsidiaries. Prior-period adjustments are reflected as adjustments to opening retained earnings for the year in which determined or realized.

4. FAS #52—Foreign Currency Translation

Translation gains/losses from translated financial statements into reporting currency should *not* be included in period net income. The accumulated sum should be disclosed as a separate component of equity until sale/liquidation of the investment in the foreign entity.

Transaction gains/losses (arising from specific transactions) *are* considered part of period net income for the period in that exchange rates change.

Income and Expense

1. APB #15—Earnings Per Share (as amended)

Earnings per share (E.P.S.) is to be shown on the income statement for all periods presented. For simple capital structures, a single E.P.S. presentation is sufficient; for complex structures, both primary and fully diluted E.P.S. must be shown.

Primary E.P.S. is based on weighted-average common shares outstanding, as adjusted for common stock equivalents having a dilutive effect (defined as 3 percent or more).

Fully diluted E.P.S. reflects all the factors in the primary computation, plus adding all other dilutive effects that could have occurred if contingently issuable shares were to be issued; e.g., effect of convertible securities that are not considered common stock equivalents.

Common stock equivalents represent securities containing provisions enabling the holder to become a common stockholder through conversion; e.g., options, warrants, and certain convertible securities that at the time of issuance had an effective yield to holders of less than 66⅔ percent of the then average Aa corporate bond yield.

In arriving at E.P.S., antidilutive factors must be excluded. Their effect would be to increase the E.P.S. over the amount it would have been by excluding them.

2. APB #30—Reporting the Results of Operations

Net income should reflect all items of profit/loss with the single exception of prior-period adjustments. In determination of net income, separate discontinued operations of a segment of a business (net of tax effect) and extraordinary gains/losses (net of tax effect) from and following income from continuing operations.

As to ascertaining when a segment fits into the discontinued category, the measurement date is the date on which management commits itself to a formal plan to dispose. Gains/losses to be reflected include the operating results of the segment for the year, anticipated operating losses during phase-out, and anticipated and actual losses on asset disposals.

Extraordinary items to be so categorized for the entity must be material, unusual in nature, and occur infrequently. Generally these involve events caused by major catastrophes, governmental expropriation, and/or prohibition.

3. FAS #2—Accounting for Research and Development Costs

R & D costs are charged to expense when incurred. For materials, equipment, and facilities applicable to R & D projects, but with no alternative uses, cost capitalization and depreciation to R & D is the appropriate accounting.

4. FAS #45—Accounting for Franchise Fee Revenue

The franchisor recognizes franchise fee revenue from the initial sale of a franchise only when he has substantially performed all material services/conditions. Start of operations by a franchisee sets the earliest date at which substantial performance takes place unless an earlier date can be justified.

5. **FAS #48—Revenue Recognition When Right of Return Exists**

If the buyer has the right of return, revenue should be recognized at the time of sale only if certain conditions exist. These include: (a) sales price is determinable, (b) obligation to pay is not contingent on merchandise resale, (c) loss/damage does not change the obligation, (d) seller is not required to make additional performance, (e) returns can be reasonably estimated, etc.

Other Financial Topics

1. **APB #20—Accounting Changes**
   a. *Accounting principle change*—Use of a generally accepted accounting method different from one used previously in financial statements. The cumulative effect of the change, net of taxes, must be presented on the income statement between extraordinary items and net income. Disclosure should include the nature and justification for change, explaining why the new method is preferred.
   b. *Accounting estimate change*—Estimates change as new information becomes available. This affects only current and future periods, and its impact is included in arriving at income from continuing operations. Footnote disclosure should be employed for material changes.
   c. *Reporting entity change*—Occurs when components of the accounting entity change; e.g., consolidated statements instead of individual statements. Financial statements of all prior periods presented must be restated as to income only from continuing operations, extraordinary items, net income, and E.P.S. Disclosure of the reason for change must also be made.

2. **APB #28—Interim Financial Reporting**

An interim period should be viewed as an integral part of an annual period. Its objective is to achieve a fair measure of both the annual operating results and the ending balance sheet. Reporting should be for current quarter, current year-to-date, or the past twelve-months-to-date, along with comparable data for the preceding year.

3. **FAS #7—Accounting and Reporting by Development Stage Enterprises**

A development stage enterprise (D.S.E.) is one devoting substantially all of its efforts to establishing a new business, and either of the following conditions exist:
   a. Planned principal operations have not started.
   b. Principal operations have started but there has been no significant revenue therefrom.

Financial statements of such enterprises must disclose cumulative deficit on the balance sheet, cumulative revenue, expense from inception on the operating statement, and cumulative sources and uses on the changes statement. The first year in which a D.S.E. is no longer considered as such, it must disclose that in prior years it had been a D.S.E.

4. **FAS #14—Financial Reporting for Segments of a Business Enterprise**

Segment information must be presented for significant segments. To be significant, a segment must satisfy one or more of the following separate annual tests:
   a. Revenue is 10 percent or more of combined revenue.
   b. Operating profit/loss is 10 percent or more of the greater of either combined operating profit (excluding segments with operating losses) or combined operating loss of all segments that did have a loss.
   c. Identifiable assets are 10 percent or more of combined identifiable assets.

Segment information should be presented either within the body of the financial statements, in footnotes, or in a separate schedule. As a matter of practicality, reportable segments should not exceed ten.

5. **FAS #87—Employers' Accounting for Pensions**

This statement establishes standards for pension plans. The two broad types of pension plans are:
   a. *Defined-contribution*—A pension plan that specifies an amount to be contributed annually by an employer, rather than the benefits to be paid. (This type of plan operates simply.)
   b. *Defined-benefit*—A pension plan that specifies a determinable pension benefit, usually based on factors such as age, years of service, and salary.

For defined benefit plans, the components of pension expense are:

a. *Service (normal) cost*—Based on the actuarial present value of benefits attributed by the pension plan formula to employee service during the current period.
b. *Prior service cost*—The cost of retroactive benefits allocated to future years of service.
c. *Expected return on plan assets*—A reduction of the pension expense based on investment income.
d. *Interest cost*—The increase in the projected benefit obligation due to the passage of time.
e. *Actuarial gains and losses*—Changes resulting from experience that differs from assumptions that have been made.

6. **FAS #88—Employers' Accounting for Settlements and Curtailments of Defined Benefit Pension Plans and for Termination of Benefits**
This statement requires the immediate recognition of gain or loss from a settlement upon plan termination. A settlement occurs when there is a discharge of all or a portion of an employer's pension benefit obligation. Immediate recognition of gain or loss is also required upon curtailment, which is an event materially reducing future expected years of service of current employees or eliminating (for a substantial number of employees) the accrual of defined benefits for future services. Under certain circumstances, termination of benefits may result in the recognition of a liability and a loss.

7. **FAS #95—Statement of Cash Flows**
This pronouncement requires a statement of cash flows as part of a full set of financial statements. The statement provides that cash receipts and cash payments be classified according to whether they stem from operating, investing, or financing activities. Operating activities include the cash effects of all transactions and other events that generally involve producing and delivering goods and providing services. Investing activities include making and collecting loans, and acquiring and disposing of debt or equity instruments and property, plant, and equipment and other productive assets (other than inventories). Financing activities include (a) obtaining resources from owners and providing them with a return on, and a return of, their investment, (b) borrowing money and repaying amounts involved, or otherwise settling the obligation, and (c) obtaining and paying for other resources obtained from creditors on long-term credit.

The statement encourages use of the direct method, but permits use of the indirect method.

8. **FAS #106—Employers' Accounting for Postretirement Benefits Other Than Pension Costs**
This statement establishes standards for employers' accounting for postretirement benefits other than pensions. Specifically, it applies to postretirement life insurance plans, health care plans, and/or welfare benefits plans.
It significantly changes the current practice of accounting for such benefits on a pay-as-you-go basis by requiring accrual, during the years the employee renders the necessary service, of the expected cost of providing those benefits to the employee, his or her dependents, and/or designated beneficiaries.

BIBLIOGRAPHIES BY EXAM SECTIONS

The CPA examination is largely a test of the information contained in the following publications. Additionally, however, candidates are expected to be familiar with provisions of the Internal Revenue Code, federal securities regulations, and professional pronouncements of the FASB, AICPA, and GASB not covered by textbooks.

Business Law and Professional Responsibilities (LPR)

AICPA, Professional Standards; Code of Professional Conduct; U.S. Auditing Standards; Tax Practice; Consulting Services.
Clarkson, Miller, Jentz, and Cross, *West's Business Law*, 5th ed. St. Paul Minn.: West Publishing Co., 1991.
Federal Bankruptcy Code.
Mann and Roberts, *Smith and Roberson's Business Law*, 8th ed. St. Paul Minn.: West Publishing Co., 1991.
Metzger, Mallor, Barnes, Bowers, and Phillips, *Business Law and the Regulatory Environment*, 8th ed. Homewood, Ill.: Richard D. Irwin, 1992.
Schantz and Jackson, *Business Law*, 2d ed. St. Paul, Minn.: West Publishing Co., 1987.
Uniform Commercial Code—Commercial Paper Article; Sales Article; Secured Transactions Article.

Auditing (AUDIT)

AICPA, *Audit and Accounting Guide, Audit Sampling*, AICPA, 1983.

AICPA, *Audit and Accounting Manual, Non-authoritative Practice Aids*, Chicago: Commerce Clearing House, 1992.

AICPA, *Audit Guide, Consideration of the Internal Control Structure in a Financial Statement Audit*, AICPA, 1990.

AICPA, Auditing Procedure Study, *Auditors' Use of Microcomputers*, AICPA, 1986.

AICPA, Auditing Procedure Study, *Audit of Inventories*, AICPA, 1986.

AICPA, Auditing Procedure Study, *Confirmation of Accounts Receivable*, AICPA, 1984.

AICPA, Auditing Procedure Study, *The Independent Auditor's Consideration of the Work of Internal Auditors*, AICPA, 1989.

AICPA, *Codification of Statements on Auditing Standards*, nos. 1 to 73. Chicago: Commerce Clearing House, 1994.

AICPA, *Codification of Statements on Standards for Accounting and Review Services*, nos. 1 to 7, Chicago: Commerce Clearing House, 1993.

AICPA, *Codification of Statements on Standards for Attestation Engagements*, Chicago: Commerce Clearing House, 1993.

AICPA, *Professional Standards*, vols. 1 & 2. Chicago: Commerce Clearing House, 1994.

Arens and Loebbecke, *Auditing: An Integrated Approach*, 6th ed. Englewood Cliffs, N.J.: Prentice-Hall, 1994.

Cushing and Romney, *Accounting Information Systems*, 5th ed. Redding, Mass.: Addison Wesley, 1990.

Dauber, Siegel, and Shim, *The Vest Pocket CPA*. Englewood Cliffs, N.J.: Prentice-Hall, 1988.

Defliese, Jaenicke, O'Reilly, and Hirsch, *Montgomery's Auditing*, 11th ed. College Version. New York: John Wiley & Sons, 1990.

General Accounting Office, *Government Auditing Standards*, U.S. Government Printing Office, 1994.

Guy, Alderman, and Winters, *Auditing*, 3d ed. San Diego: Harcourt Brace Jovanovich, 1993.

Guy and Carmichael, *Audit Sampling*, 2d ed. New York: John Wiley & Sons, 1986.

Hermanson, Strawser, and Strawser, *Auditing Theory and Practice*, 5th ed. Homewood, Ill.: Richard D. Irwin, 1989.

Kell and Boynton, *Modern Auditing*, 5th ed. New York: John Wiley & Sons, 1992.

Robertson, *Auditing*, 6th ed. Homewood, Ill.: Richard D. Irwin, 1990.

Taylor and Glezen, *Auditing: Integrated Concepts and Procedures*, 5th ed. New York: John Wiley & Sons, 1991.

Wallace, *Auditing*, 2d ed. Boston: PWS-Kent, 1991.

Watne and Turney, *Auditing, EDP Systems*, 2d ed. Englewood Cliffs, N.J.: Prentice-Hall, 1990.

Weber, *EDP Auditing*, 2d ed. New York: McGraw-Hill, 1988.

Whittington, Pany, Meigs, and Meigs, *Principles of Auditing*, 10th ed. Homewood, Ill.: Richard D. Irwin, 1992.

Accounting & Reporting— Taxation, Managerial, and Governmental and Not-for-Profit Organizations (ARE)

Afterman and Jones, Governmental Accounting and Auditing Disclosure Manual. Boston: Warren, Gorham, and Lamont, 1992.

AICPA, Audit and Accounting Guide, *Audits of State and Local Governmental Units*, AICPA, 1992.

AICPA, Industry Audit Guide, *Audits of Colleges and Universities*, AICPA, 1992.

AICPA, Audit and Accounting Guide, *Audits of Providers of Health Care Services*, AICPA, 1992.

Anderson, Needles, and Caldwell, *Managerial Accounting*, Boston: Houghton Mifflin, 1989.

Dauber, Siegel, and Shim, *The Vest Pocket CPA*. Englewood Cliffs, N.J.: Prentice-Hall, 1988.

Federal Tax Course 1994. Chicago: Commerce Clearing House.

Fischer, Taylor, and Leer, *Advanced Accounting*, 4th ed. Cincinnati: South-Western, 1990.

GASB, *Codification of Governmental Accounting and Financial Reporting Standards*. Norwalk Conn.: GASB.

Hay and Wilson, *Accounting for Governmental and Nonprofit Entities*, 9th ed. Homewood, Ill.: Richard D. Irwin, 1992.

Horngren, Foster, and Datar, *Cost Accounting: A Managerial Emphasis*, 8th ed. Englewood Cliffs, N.J.: Prentice-Hall, 1994.

Larsen, *Modern Advanced Accounting*, 5th ed. New York: McGraw-Hill, 1991.

Pahler and Mori, *Advanced Accounting: Concepts and Practices*, 4th ed. San Diego: Harcourt Brace Jovanovich, 1991.

Polimeni, Fabozzi, and Adelberg, *Cost Accounting: Concepts and Applications for Managerial Decision Making*, 3d ed. New York: McGraw-Hill, 1991.

U.S. Master Tax Guide. Chicago: Commerce Clearing House.

Usry and Hammer, *Cost Accounting: Planning and Control*, 10th ed. Cincinnati: South-Western, 1991.

A standard tax service, the Internal Revenue Code, and Income Tax Regulations.

Financial Accounting & Reporting—Business Enterprises (FARE)

AICPA, *Personal Financial Statements Guide*, AICPA, 1991.

AICPA, *Technical Practice Aids*, AICPA, 1991.

Beams, *Advanced Accounting*, 4th ed. Englewood Cliffs, N.J.: Prentice-Hall, 1988.

Chasteen, Flaherty, O'Connor, *Intermediate Accounting*, 4th ed. New York: Random House, 1992.

Dauber, Siegel, and Shim, *The Vest Pocket CPA*, Englewood Cliffs, N.J.: Prentice-Hall, 1988.

FASB, *Current Text, Accounting Standards,* Norwalk, Conn.: FASB.

FASB, *Original Pronouncements, Accounting Standards,* Norwalk, Conn.: FASB.

Kieso & Weygandt, *Intermediate Accounting*, 7th ed. New York: John D. Wiley & Sons, 1992.

Nikolai & Bazley, *Intermediate Accounting,* 5th ed. Boston: PWS-Kent, 1991.

Pahler, Mori, *Advanced Accounting: Concepts and Practice*, 4th ed. San Diego: Harcourt Brace Jovanovich, 1991.

Smith, Skousen, *Intermediate Accounting*, 10th ed. Cincinnati: South-Western, 1990.

Welsch, Zlatkovich, *Intermediate Accounting*, 8th ed. Homewood, Ill.: Richard D. Irwin, 1989.

Williams, Stanga, Holder, *Intermediate Accounting*, 4th ed. San Diego: Harcourt Brace Jovanovich, 1992.

5. How to Approach CPA Examination Questions

One of the first things a successful CPA candidate learns is that questions on the CPA exam cannot be approached as if they were college homework or quiz questions. They are significantly different and require the learning of new skills in order to answer them successfully under examination conditions.

The first difference is that they must be answered within a specified time period. The examiners do not tell candidates when to start and stop answering individual questions. They merely recommend time estimates within which questions should be answered. It is up to the candidate to establish a time budget and stick to it. He must resist the temptation to spend more than the allotted time on a question despite the fact that an answer can be developed further. Stealing time allotted for a question yet to be answered increases the risk that the test will be over with questions still unanswered. Ultimately, the absence of an answer will fail a candidate more surely than a poor answer to a question. As noted in Chapter 1, a candidate does not need a perfect answer to receive maximum credit. Candidates who were perfectionists as accounting students must resist the impulse to try to write perfect answers to CPA exam questions. It is more important to get the whole job done than to get it partly perfect.

Another important difference, particularly with the essay and computational questions, is that the solution requirements are often more precise and more rigidly graded than, say, a college midterm or final exam. Graders work from highly structured grading guides that are keyed to the set of requirements given in each question. One grader sees only one question's solutions. The hundreds, perhaps thousands, of solutions that he compares to his grading guide are totally anonymous. Unlike the classroom instructor, he is not influenced by subjective factors such as good looks, friendliness, concientious attendance, or participation in class discussion.

Candidates who were sometimes able to bluff their way through college exam questions will find no opportunity for that on the CPA exam. Question requirements must be read, analyzed, and answered in full. An essay or computational solution that evades or ignores some of these requirements, or that tries to work around them, will not contain the key computations or concepts that the grader is looking for. The candidate only receives credit for items that appear in both the answer and on the grading guide.

A further difference between CPA exam and college homework or exam questions is that the former are often broader in scope than the latter. A computational question on financial accounting on the FARE exam may, for example, require the candidate to synthesize his knowledge of fixed asset accounting, interim reporting, income tax deferral, earnings per share, and income recognition all in a single question. Questions encountered in college assignments generally deal with a much narrower body of information. The CPA exam is intended to be a comprehensive test of a candidate's overall mastery. The same breadth of topical coverage appears in essay questions for AUDIT and LPR.

The objective questions are probably the most familiar type of question for the candidate. Currently 50 to 60 percent of the exam consists of four-option, multiple-choice questions. Candidates have been encountering such questions since their grammar school days. Here again, however, CPA exam items have been subject to a rigorous pre-exam analysis and testing. There are very few poorly made or "giveaway"-type objective questions.

In answering CPA exam questions, the candidate must work systematically and efficiently. *Time is his scarcest resource.* He must know what to expect in the way of question format and he must have question-answering skills learned and practiced long before he sits down to take the exam. Indeed, on examination day the last thing that should be on a candidate's mind is *how* to answer a CPA exam question. The time for developing question-answering techniques is *before* the exam. At the exam, the only thing the candidate should be uncertain of is what specific points of substance will be tested.

QUESTION TYPES—AND SPECIFIC TEST TACTICS

Four-Option Multiple-Choice Questions

In format, objective questions on the CPA exam are the familiar four-option multiple-choice variety found on most standardized tests. The advantages—from the AICPA's viewpoint—of using multiple-choice items are two: (1) they can be quickly and uniformly machine-scored, and (2) they enable the examiners to cover a wider range of topics than would be possible with a few long essay or computational questions.

Objective questions, despite their simplicity of construction and ease of grading, can be quite sophisticated in terms of cognitive skills tested. Some questions ask little more than simple recall of rote learning, while most require higher-level reasoning abilities in which the candidate must synthesize and evaluate information, make a decision regarding an answer choice, and move on quickly to the next question.

TYPICAL FARE QUESTION

How would the retained earnings of a subsidiary acquired in a business combination usually be treated in a consolidated balance sheet prepared immediately after the acquisition?
  A. Excluded for both a purchase and a pooling of interests.
  B. Excluded for a pooling of interests but included for a purchase.
  C. Included for both a purchase and a pooling of interests.
  D. Included for a pooling of interests but excluded for a purchase.

The correct answer, "D," would be entered on a machine-scored answer sheet by blackening in a circle containing the letter "D."

TYPICAL ARE QUESTION

The following information pertains to Spruce City's liability for claims and judgments:

Current liability at January 1, 1994	$100,000
Claims paid during 1994	800,000
Current liability at December 31, 1994	140,000
Noncurrent liability at December 31, 1994	200,000

What amount should Spruce report for 1994 claims and judgments expenditures?
  A. $1,040,000
  B. $940,000
  C. $840,000
  D. $800,000

The correct answer choice is "C." The other answer choices represent feasible alternatives resulting from a mishandling of the data given. The candidate, therefore, who is not completely sure of how to account for information presented is deluded into thinking his computation is correct because it corresponds to one of the answer choices given.

The candidate must be careful to note the answer sheet structure before he starts blackening circles. The answer spaces will be arrayed horizontally on some sheets and vertically on others—for the same test! This is done purposely so that candidates in neighboring rows will have differently structured answer sheets and therefore will not be able to copy from one another.

TEST TACTICS

Don't Be Confused by the Phrasing of Questions—Read Carefully!

One point that cannot be overemphasized is the necessity for *careful reading of the questions*. While there are never any deliberate verbal or numerical tricks in the questions, certain techniques of phrasing questions can be confusing.

In particular, the use of qualifying words such as "most," "least," or "best," or of negative terms such as "not," "incorrect," or "inappropriate" can cause the candidate to misinterpret his task. Such words are generally printed in **boldface** type on the exam but even that may not prevent their being overlooked by a careless reading. The mind must remain alert to the shifts in thought patterns that such expressions require.

Throughout the exam, the candidate must *work quickly yet read carefully*. That ability can be developed through practice with past questions.

Move Along Briskly

Decisions regarding answer choices must be made. The candidate cannot afford to get hung up on any particular question. He must move along briskly. He must concentrate on the question at hand and not agonize over past uncertainties or future obstacles. If he finds himself "spinning wheels" on a particular question and unable to attempt an educated guess, he should place a large question mark in the margin and return to it after the others have been completed. A fresh perspective may prove helpful.

Account for All Key Facts

In approaching four-option multiple-choice questions, *make certain that key facts have been noted and accounted for*. When two or more questions relate to a single set of facts, all questions should be scanned and solved as a group. Key words or phrases should be highlighted by underlining or circling.

Remember that wrong answer choices represent feasible alternatives likely to be selected by candidates with only a partial understanding. A combination of knowledge and careful analysis will minimize the chance of selecting wrong answer choices. Generally, concentration is enhanced by ignoring answer choices until the question narrative has been studied and a tentative answer attempted.

Avoid Answer Transcription Errors

Answer choices selected should be *entered directly on the machine-scored answer page*. This reduces the possibility of transcription errors that occur when answers are noted in the test booklet and later transferred en masse to the official answer sheet.

"Guess" Correctly

When logic or memory fails, and an answer must be *guessed* at, certain techniques increase the probability of selecting the right answer. For example, when more than one answer choice seems correct, the one that should be selected is the one that does not require any qualifications in order to make it correct. Often, all but two of the choices can be eliminated. This at least creates a 50 percent probability of being right.

This technique is illustrated by the following example from LPR:

Which of the following employees are exempt from the minimum and maximum hour provisions of the Fair Labor Standards Act?
A. Children.
B. Railroad and airline employees.
C. Members of a union recognized as the bargaining agent by the National Labor Relations Board.
D. Office workers.

This is a question requiring recall of particular facts which usually are either there or not there in a candidate's memory. Nevertheless, common-sense logic should enable the candidate to narrow his choice to two: "B" and "D." Choice "D" would be correct if one views "office workers" as including administrative employees. But that would necessitate qualifying the answer in order to make it correct. (Administrative employees *are* exempt from the minimum and maximum hour provisions of the Fair Labor Standards Act.) The *best* choice, therefore, arrived at by elimination, is answer choice "B."

Inasmuch as no penalties for incorrect answers have been associated with objective questions, *no question should be left blank*. Even a wild guess has a 25 percent probability of being right.

"Other Objective Formats" Questions

These questions, like the four-option multiple-choice questions, are machine-scored, but the questions and answers will be in different formats.

These formats consist of matching questions to answers, questions requiring yes or no responses, and/or numerical answers to questions (i.e., FARE and ARE exams, only).

About twenty to thirty of the available points on the FARE, AUDIT, and LPR sections and forty to fifty of the available points on the ARE section will be allocated to these types of questions.

Recording Answers

All answers are recorded using a "blackening-in-the-oval" answer sheet, as used for four-option multiple-choice questions.

Answer sheets may vary from examination to examination. It is important to pay strict attention to the manner in which the answer sheet is structured. As you proceed, be absolutely certain that the space in which you have indicated your answer corresponds directly in number with the item in your question booklet.

It should be noted that a matching question may have many answers from which to choose (perhaps ten or more). Furthermore, an answer may or may not be allowed to be used more than once. As such, when an answer may be used only once, it is wise to "check it off" directly on the exam to prevent it from being used a second time.

SAMPLE QUESTIONS AND ANSWERS

The purpose of this illustration is to provide examples of "other objective formats" questions that appear on the examination, and to illustrate how you would record the answers to them on your answer sheets.

Example 1 is an AUDIT question, and the entire Objective Answer Sheet is presented on page 52. This Objective Answer Sheet consists of the answer grid for sixty 4-option multiple-choice questions and the "other objective formats" example (i.e., Question 2).

Example 2 is applicable to the ARE exam. Only the portion of the Objective Answer Sheet related to this question is shown (page 55), and the correct answers have been filled in.

UNIFORM CERTIFIED PUBLIC ACCOUNTANT EXAMINATION

OBJECTIVE ANSWER SHEET
AUDIT

Example 1

Number 2 (Estimated time—15 to 25 minutes)

Instructions

Question Number 2 consists of 10 items. Select the **best** answer for each item. Use a No. 2 pencil to blacken the appropriate ovals on the Objective Answer Sheet to indicate your answers. **Answer all items.** Your grade will be based on the total number of correct answers.

Items 61 through 70 represent generally accepted auditing standards that relate to the auditor's professional qualities and the auditor's judgment exercised in performing the audit. The list on the right represents various auditor requirements or ways in which the auditor might satisfy one of the generally accepted auditing standards.

Required:

For each generally accepted auditing standard, select the auditor requirement that would best satisfy that generally accepted auditing standard and blacken the corresponding oval on the Objective Answer Sheet. Auditor requirements may be selected once, more than once, or not at all.

Items to be Answered:

Generally Accepted Auditing Standards

61. Adequate technical training.
62. Independent mental attitude.
63. Due professional care.
64. Proper supervision of assistants.
65. Understanding of the internal control structure.
66. Sufficient competent evidential matter.
67. Financial statements presented in accordance with GAAP.
68. Consistent application of GAAP.
69. Adequate financial statement disclosure.
70. Expression of an opinion.

Auditor Requirements

A. Judicial impartiality.
B. Review the work performed by assistants.
C. Proper education and experience.
D. Use of statistical sampling.
E. Satisfaction that the financial statements are comparable between periods.
F. Consideration of the types of possible misstatements.
G. Development of specific audit objectives.
H. Proper classification of items in the financial statements.
I. Issuance of an auditor's report.
J. Statement as to the overall fairness of financial statement presentation.

Example 2

Number 2 (Estimated time—15 to 25 minutes)

Instructions

Question Number 2 consists of 8 items. Select the **best** answer for each item. Use a No. 2 pencil to indicate your answers on the Objective Answer Sheet. Items 61 through 68 require numerical answers. Also, Items 63 through 68 require determining whether a variance is favorable (F) or unfavorable (U). For the numerical answers, you are to both write your numerical answer in the boxes and blacken the corresponding oval below each box. **These items cannot be graded if you fail to blacken the ovals.** Write zeros in any blank boxes preceding your numerical answer. If there is a discrepancy between the amount written in the boxes and the amount indicated by the blackened ovals, the amount indicated by the blackened ovals will prevail. **Answer all items.** Your grade will be based on the total number of correct answers.

Webb & Co. prepares income tax returns for individuals. Webb uses the weighted average method and actual costs for financial reporting purposes. However, for internal reporting, Webb uses a standard cost system. The standards, based on equivalent performance, have been established as follows:

| Labor per return | 5 hrs. | @ $20 per hr. |
| Overhead per return | 5 hrs. | @ $10 per hr. |

For March 19X1, budgeted overhead is $490,000 for the standard labor hours allowed. The following additional information pertains to the month of March:

Inventory data

Returns in process, March 1	
(25% complete)	2,000
Returns started in March	8,250
Returns in process, March 31	
(80% complete)	1,250

Actual cost data

Returns in process, March 1:	
Labor	$ 60,000
Overhead	25,000
Cost incurred, March 1–31:	
Labor (40,000 hours)	890,000
Overhead	450,000

In computing equivalent units of performance or cost per return data, Webb uses the weighted average method.

Required:

Items 61 through 68 are questions about Webb's operations for March 19X1. For each item, calculate the numerical answer. To record your answer, write the number in the boxes on the Objective Answer Sheet and blacken the corresponding oval below each box. These items cannot be graded it you fail to blacken the oval. In addition, for Items 63 through 68, determine whether the variance is favorable (F) or unfavorable (U) and blacken the corresponding oval on the Objective Answer Sheet.

Items to be Answered:
61. How many tax returns were completed?
62. What were the equivalent units of performance (equivalent tax returns prepared)?
63. What was the labor rate variance?
64. What was the labor efficiency variance?
65. What was the total labor variance?
66. What was the overhead volume variance?
67. What was the overhead budget variance?
68. What was the total overhead variance?

Example:
The following is an example of the manner in which the answer sheet should be marked. **Zeros have been preprinted on the Objective Answer Sheet for the ones, tens, and hundreds columns.**

Item
What was the total variance from budget?
Answer Sheet

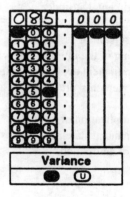

Zeros have been preprinted for the ones, tens, and hundreds columns.

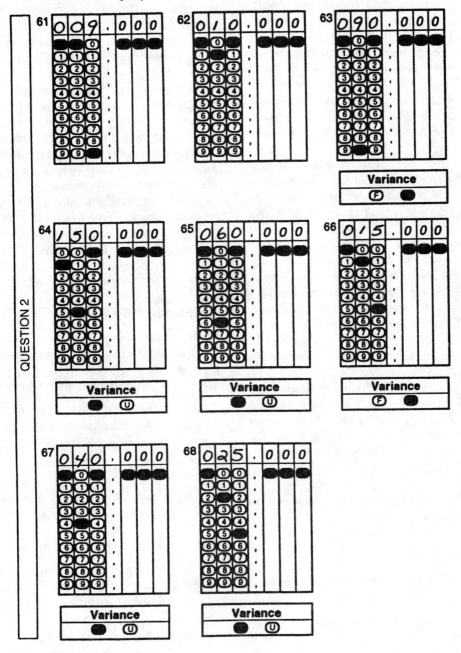

Computational Questions

FARE computational questions must be struggled with and mastered to be truly appreciated. Every accounting student, upon completing a textbook "AICPA-adapted" homework question, has probably despaired of ever being able to answer a similar question under CPA exam conditions within the time frame allowed. There he sits, after having just spent an hour solving a CPA exam problem for homework that should have been answered by a CPA candidate within thirty minutes. Chances of ever passing the CPA exam seem remote.

Fortunately, it's a long road from Intermediate Accounting to the FARE exam, and the accounting student/CPA candidate can learn the examsmanship techniques necessary for solving computational problems more efficiently.

Computational problems are intended to simulate "real-world" accounting situations. Ultimately, they are much too neat and simple to realistically portray real-world situations, but their requirement that candidates analyze and account for a series of sometimes related, sometimes unrelated facts within a question narrative is a valid analogue to real-world accounting situations. In both situations the accountant needs to be able to synthesize data and decide how to best handle it.

On the FARE exam, the approach a candidate takes to solving a computational question is all important. He must work methodically and efficiently. He must resist the urge to rush into beginning a solution before the entire narrative is digested. Otherwise, he is likely to waste time with false starts and poorly presented solutions.

The following section presents an approach to answering computational questions.

TEST TACTICS

Read Questions Twice—for Understanding, for Analysis

Computational questions, like essay questions, must be read very, very carefully. As with essay questions, *two readings are necessary—once for a general understanding and once for a careful analysis*. Techniques of highlighting key facts through underlining, marginal notes, or circling should be used. The requirements section should be studied very carefully, both to ensure that a complete solution is presented and to provide guidance on organizing the solution. Information presented should be interpreted straightforwardly without looking for hidden meanings or tricks.

Use of Calculators

Calculators will be provided at the exam site for the ARE and FARE exams. The purpose is to save time, and should not be taken to mean an increase in the difficulty level of the exams.

A calculator can be ordered through the AICPA Order Department (1-800-862-4272); cost is $5.60 for students and $8 for all others.

Before the start of the ARE and FARE exams, the candidates will be instructed to perform certain test calculations so that they can learn how to operate the calculator and to ensure that it is functioning properly. A replacement calculator will be available in the event of a malfunction. Each candidate must sign, date, and submit the "calculator sign-off record," which is included on page 1 of the Examination Answer Booklet.

Candidates will need to use the calculators for only four primary functions: addition, subtraction, multiplication, and division. However, the calculators will also have function keys for square root, percentage, and memory.

Use Standard Abbreviations

To save time, use abbreviations whenever appropriate. Use only those that have general currency.

Keep Computations Brief for Obvious Answers

It is not essential that answers to exam questions contain laborious computations in support of obvious answers, as unofficial AICPA answers are inclined to do.

Explain Journal Entries

Journal entries should always contain brief explanations unless the requirements state otherwise.

Basic Problem-Solving Techniques

The following problem-solving techniques are useful for ensuring a systematic approach that will produce an organized, coherent answer:

A. Getting Ready for the Answer
1. *Always read the requirements first.*
2. After the first reading for "feel," which should take a minute or so, read the question again slowly and begin to solve.

    In this connection, time devoted to a careful analysis of the facts will be well spent. While reading, underline key points in the statement of fact and cross out information that has no meaning (or seems to have no meaning).

3. If a question has two or more unrelated subparts, answer the easier part(s) first; the order of answering parts of a question is not important.

4. *Do not read into questions.*

   In the *rare case* that an assumption must be made, state the nature of the assumption clearly on the answer, giving reasons, if any.

5. Draw a mental image of the solution format before proceeding.

   In this connection, very often the requirements will specifically indicate the desired format. If this is not the case, there are only two possibilities:

   a. The format will be specific; i.e., an income statement, a balance sheet, etc.

   b. If the format is not indicated or specific, adhere to "real world" rules for working-paper construction; express the answer logically, using good schedule technique.

6. In short, this implies that one should "solve for the efficient solution."

B. Developing the Answer

1. The depth of writing is not essential; getting the key points is.

2. *Organizing the answer.*

   a. Do not copy any more of the question than is essential to the solution; do not prepare unnecessary worksheets or journal entries.

   b. It is perfectly acceptable to abbreviate. For example, "accounts receivable" can be written as "A/R," etc. (The graders are experienced accountants who will understand the abbreviations.)

   c. *With respect to journal entries,* (1) it does not matter how many are made to handle a particular situation, and (2) brief, obvious, abbreviated explanations should be given unless a requirement specially states that explanations are to be omitted.

If in doubt, remember that there is no penalty for too many entries, only for not expressing the facts required. However, journal entries that contradict each other should be avoided.

   d. Always include an appropriate heading with the solution. This can best be accomplished by paraphrasing the requirements.

   e. Do not waste time on minor arithmetic matters. For the most part, arithmetic is simple and reasonable. Therefore, evaluate the reasonableness of computations.

   f. *Don't plug answers.* If an error is discovered, rather than redo the solution, indicate where the correct number should appear with a marginal note.

3. *Handling the facts in a question.*

   In working through a question, as a specific piece of information is handled, it should be "ticked off." In this manner, each question "falls apart" and information to be dealt with is eliminated.

   Thus, where an item is not used in proceeding through a question, it will be handled later or has no bearing, in which event it will disappear.

   It should also be kept in mind that for exam purposes, all facts, unless indicated otherwise, must be assumed to be material.

4. *"Massaging" the facts.*

   On recent exams, questions have appeared that have two or more unrelated parts based on the same facts.

   These questions do not present difficulty with respect to the concepts; indeed, the more difficult part of the question deals with placing the facts in the appropriate portions of the solution. For example, the current portion of a long-term debt would appear in one part, the long-term portion in another, and related expenses in the third.

   With respect to such questions, care should be taken to handle the information appropriately.

SAMPLE QUESTION AND SOLUTION

The preceding advice is illustrated by the following problem and solution:

Question (AICPA Adapted)

(Estimated time—45 to 55 minutes)

The following information pertains to Woodbine Circle Corporation:

Adjusted Trial Balance
December 31, 1994

	Debit	Credit
Cash	$ 500,000	
Accounts receivable, net	1,500,000	
Inventory	2,500,000	
Property, plant, and equipment	15,100,000	
Accumulated depreciation		$ 4,900,000
Accounts payable		1,400,000
Income taxes payable		100,000
Notes payable		1,000,000
Common stock ($1 par value)		1,100,000
Additional paid-in capital		6,100,000
Retained earnings, 1/1/94		3,000,000
Sales—regular		10,000,000
Sales—AL Division		2,000,000
Interest on municipal bonds		100,000
Cost of sales—regular	6,200,000	
Cost of sales—AL Division	900,000	
Administrative expenses— regular	2,000,000	
Administrative expenses— AL Division	300,000	
Interest expense—regular	210,000	
Interest expense— AL Division	140,000	
Loss on disposal of AL Division	250,000	
Gain on repurchase of bonds payable		300,000
Income tax expense	* 400,000	
	$30,000,000	$30,000,000

Other financial data for the year ended December 31, 1994:

Federal income taxes

Paid on Federal Tax Deposit Forms	$ 300,000
Accrued	100,000
Total charged to income tax expense (estimated)	$ 400,000*

*Does not properly reflect current or deferred income tax expense or intraperiod income tax allocation for income statement purposes

Income per tax return	$2,150,000
Tax rate on all types of taxable income	40%

Temporary difference

Depreciation, per financial statements	$ 600,000
Depreciation, per tax return	750,000

Income not taxable

Interest on municipal bonds	100,000

Discontinued operations

On September 30, 1994, Woodbine sold its Auto Leasing (AL) Division for $4,000,000. Book value of this business segment was $4,250,000 at that date. For financial statement purposes, this sale was considered as discontinued operations of a segment of a business. Since there was no phase-out period, the measurement date was September 30, 1994.

Liabilities

On June 30, 1994, Woodbine repurchased $1,000,000 carrying value of its long-term bonds for $700,000. All other liabilities mature in 1994.

Capital Structure

Common stock, par value $1 per share, traded on the New York Stock Exchange:

Number of shares outstanding at 1/1/94	900,000
Number of shares sold for $8 per share on 6/30/94	200,000
Number of shares outstanding at 12/31/94	1,100,000

Required:

Using the multiple-step format, prepare a formal income statement for Woodbine for the year ended December 31, 1994, together with the appropriate supporting schedules. Recurring and nonrecurring items in the income statement should be properly separated. All income taxes should be appropriately shown.

Approach

1. Check estimated time: 45 to 55 minutes.
2. Scan information presented, developing a sense of how it fits together and how it will be used to respond to the requirements. A first reading indicates the following:
   — The trial balance contains items that are explained in the "other financial data."
   — The balance sheet items on the trial balance are not relevant, since the question concerns an income statement. They could be "ticked off" and ignored.
   — The results of the "AL Division" are segregated because they are related to discontinued operations.
   — The gain on repurchase of bonds, further explained under "liabilities" in the "other financial data," is an extraordinary item.
   — Any income from discontinued items (net of taxes) and extraordinary items (net of taxes) must be presented separately.
   — The $400,000 income tax expense on the trial balance, as per the "other financial data," represents an estimated amount that is *not* allocated to the various income statement sections and may therefore be ignored.
   — Income taxes must be appropriately allocated to income from continuing operations, discontinued operations, and extraordinary items.
   — Earnings per share must be disclosed on the face of the income statement.
   — The "income per tax return" is of no consequence, since an income statement must be prepared.
3. As a matter of technique, prior to preparing the statement, the candidate should use initials or some other means to indicate the presentation of the various items; i.e., continuing operations, discontinued operations, etc. This is done by making notations on the question sheet.
4. On the answer sheet, lay out the solution format; i.e., a multiple-step income statement.
   — Remember the heading.

— Leave enough space between line items to insert financial data as it is developed.

Woodbine Circle Corporation
Income Statement
For the Year Ended 12/31/94

Sales	$
Cost of goods sold	
Gross profit on sales	
Operating expenses	
Operating income	
Other revenue and expense items:	
Income from continuing operations before income tax	
Provision for income taxes:	
Net income from continuing operations	
Discontinued operations, net of income taxes	
Extraordinary gain, net of tax	
Net income to retained earnings	$
Earnings per common share	$

5. The first computational step is determination of *income from continuing operations*.
   a. *To arrive at operating income*, the operating items referred to as "regular" are listed (ignoring those items related to the discontinued AL Division). This includes sales of $10,000,000 less cost of sales of $6,200,000. Gross profit is $3,800,000, from which is subtracted the operating (administrative) expenses of $2,000,000, to arrive at *operating income of $1,800,000*. These amounts should be entered directly on the pro forma statement created in step #4 above.
   b. Next, examination of the trial balance indicates, consistent with the "multiple-step format," that there are other revenue and expense items consisting of interest on municipal bonds of $100,000 and interest expense of $210,000, or a reduction of *$110,000*. Income from continuing operations is therefore $1,690,000, which, of course, is subject to a provision for income taxes. Working down the statement being created, these items are entered as line items. (See completed solution following.)
6. There are two portions of the income tax provision related to income from continuing operations—*the taxes currently payable and the deferred portion on temporary differences.*

a. As to temporary differences, there is a depreciation temporary difference of $750,000 less $600,000, or *$150,000*. The interest on municipal bonds will never be taxed and therefore is not a factor in the income tax provision.

b. Since depreciation is higher for tax purposes, taxable income will be lower. Taxable income from continuing operations is therefore $1,690,000 less the $150,000 temporary difference and the $100,000 municipal bond interest, or *$1,440,000*, which requires a tax currently payable at 40 percent, or *$576,000*, as noted on the completed solution following.

c. The *deferred portion* of the tax provision, which is an expense debit (and a balance sheet credit, since taxable income is lower), is 40 percent of the $150,000 temporary difference, or *$60,000*, as noted. The total tax is *$636,000* and *net income from continuing operations* is *$1,054,000*, as noted.

7. The next item to consider is the results of discontinued operations, the details of which appear in *supporting schedule #1*, which should be set up at this time. Here, also, a pro forma skeleton may be created, with computations inserted step by step. The two components of discontinued operations relate to (a) the results of operations, and (b) the gain or loss on disposal, both of which are presented net of taxes.

a. As to the *results of operations*, the figures flow from the trial balance reference to "AL Division." Sales less costs and expenses results in income before taxes of *$660,000*, against which a 40 percent tax provision, or *$264,000*, is made. The net income from discontinued operations is therefore *$396,000*, as noted in schedule #1 of the completed solution following.

b. As to the *loss on disposal*, the amount before taxes, which appears on the trial balance, and which agrees with the "other financial data" of $4,250,000 less $4,000,000, is *$250,000*. Against this loss, there is a "negative" provision for taxes, since the loss reduces the tax by $250,000 × 40 percent, or *$100,000*. The net loss from disposal is *$150,000*. The total results of discontinued operations, net of tax effect, *transferred to the income statement*, are *$246,000*.

8. The next income item appearing on the trial balance is the "gain on repurchase of bonds payable" of *$300,000*, which is substantiated by the "other financial data," indicating a repurchase at $700,000 of $1,000,000 worth of bonds. Gains or losses on the early retirement of bonds are classified as extraordinary items, net of tax effect. This is indicated on the income statement wherein the gain, reduced by the 40 percent tax, is *$180,000*.

9. At this point, net income transferred to retained earnings, in the amount of *$1,480,000*, is computed.

10. The last piece of "other financial data" to be handled concerns the capital structure. It serves as a clue that *earnings-per-share data must be disclosed* on the face of the income statement.

a. Set up *supporting schedule #2*. First, since shares were issued during the year, a weighting is required. From January 1 through June 30, 900,000 shares were outstanding. For six months, this results in a weight of *450,000* shares. Next, there were 1,100,000 shares outstanding from July 1 through December 31, which results in a weight of *550,000*. Accordingly, the weighted-average shares outstanding are *1,000,000* shares.

b. The earnings-per-share computations, based on 1,000,000 weighted-average shares, are presented for continuing operations, $1.054; discontinued operations, $.396; loss on disposal of a segment ($.150); the total before extraordinary items, $1.30; extraordinary items, $.180, and the total earnings per share, *$1.48*. Note also that the numbers are rounded to three decimal places and the total agrees with the income statement bottom line. The total of *schedule #2* is transferred to the income statement.

11. At this point, the solution—a multiple-step income statement with supporting schedules—is complete. A quick review of the question narrative should indicate that all information has been accounted for in one way or another. Irrelevant information has been ignored and relevant information has been used to generate the required solution.

Completed Solution

Woodbine Circle Corporation
Income Statement
For the Year Ended December 31, 1994

Sales		$10,000,000
Cost of goods sold		6,200,000
Gross profit on sales		3,800,000
Operating expenses—		
Administrative expenses		2,000,000
Operating income		1,800,000
Other revenue and expense items:		
Interest on municipal bonds	$ 100,000	
Interest expense	(210,000)	(110,000)
Income from continuing operations before income tax		1,690,000
Provision for income taxes:		
Taxes currently payable	576,000	
Deferred portion on temporary difference	60,000	636,000
Net income from continuing operations		1,054,000
Discontinued operations, net of income taxes (Sch. #1)		246,000
Extraordinary gain (net of $120,000 provision for income taxes)		180,000
Net income to retained earnings		$ 1,480,000
Earnings per common share (Sch. #2)		$1.48

Discontinued Operations

Income from operations of discontinued AL Division:

Sales		$2,000,000	
Less: Cost of sales	$900,000		
Administrative expenses	300,000		
Interest expense	140,000	1,340,000	
Income before taxes		660,000	
Less income taxes		264,000	$ 396,000
Loss on disposal of division:			
Loss on sale		250,000	
Less income tax effect		100,000	(150,000)
Discontinued operations, net of income taxes			$ 246,000

Earnings per Common Share

Weighted-average shares outstanding

January 1, 1994—June 30, 1994;		
900,000 × 6/12	450,000	
July 1, 1994—December 31, 1994;		
1,100,000 × 6/12	550,000	
Total		1,000,000
Earnings per share from continuing operations		$1.054
Earnings per share from operations of discontinued division		.396
Earnings per share (loss) on disposal of discontinued division		(.150)
Earnings per share before extraordinary gain		1.300
Earnings per share on extraordinary gain		.180
Total earnings per share		$1.480

Essay Questions

Essay questions on LPR, AUDIT, and FARE test a candidate's ability to verbalize his conceptual understanding of topics covered in each section. An accomplished writing style is not as important as an ability to package and communicate the key words and phrases looked for by the graders.

Skill in communication, of course, is no mean achievement. It requires organization, clarity, and a sense of the audience. The candidate's main objective is to convey to the grader as effectively as possible his response to the question requirements. In so doing, he is expected to observe the conventions of standard written English and generally to write with the competence of a learned professional.

A "learned professional" does not mean sounding like a university scholar or the author of an accounting pronouncement. The candidate should write in his most natural, businesslike English. It will save him time and it will please the grader.

On the **LPR** section, candidates can expect to encounter three types of essay questions:

1. *Argumentative*. Here, the candidate is placed in the role of judge. He must analyze facts, draw conclusions, and support his conclusions with references to facts in the narrative and appropriate legal principles.

2. *Identification of legal principles or requirements.* The ability of the candidate to recall rote learning is being tested in these types of questions.
3. *Discussion of legal implications or consequences.* Here, the candidate is more of a counselor than a magistrate. He is discussing rather than rendering judgment, theorizing rather than deciding.

Three types of questions also appear on the **FARE** section:

1. *Classification and definition.* For the most part, these require candidates to recall rote learning and to write in clear, precise language. The candidate must remember to not give examples in place of definitions.
2. *Description of accounting procedures.* These are "how to" type questions in which the candidate writes what amounts to a set of directions on how to account for a transaction or situation.
3. *General discussion.* These usually contain the most open-ended type requirements, which in turn place the burden of structuring an adequately developed response on the candidate.

Similar type questions appear on the **AUDIT** section. Additionally, certain auditing questions require candidates to analyze a particular business situation and to present findings or make recommendations.

Two conclusions can be drawn from the above:

1. Several types of questions fall under the heading "essay": straight definitional, directions on "how to" or "what to," presentations of checklist findings, analysis, discussion, argument, and persuasion.
2. A broad range of cognitive and technical skills is tested: simple recall of rote learning, systematic analysis of facts and presentation of conclusions, and the ability to organize and present thoughts.

As with computational problems, the candidate must resist the impulse to plunge right into a written solution. Too often candidates simply write down thoughts as they occur, regardless of sequence or relative importance. The result is often a disconnected, disorganized series of thoughts that needlessly lose points because the grader cannot follow a logical pattern of idea development.

Candidates must not forget the humanity of the grader. Graders work under less than ideal conditions, often after having worked a full day somewhere else. They work on what is essentially a piecework basis. If, in the midst of all this, a grader comes face-to-face with an essay of run-on sentences, without paragraphs, written illegibly in red ink, it is safe to conclude that he will not be disposed to give the candidate any benefit of doubt or charitable consideration.

TEST TACTICS

Communicate Clearly, Using Effective Writing Skills

CPAs are expected to communicate recommendations and conclusions in clear, unequivocal language. The ability of the candidate, therefore, to organize and present what he knows in acceptable written English is considered by the examiners. As previously noted, answers to selected essay responses are used to assess candidates' writing skills. Five percent of the total points available on all exam sections other than ARE will be allocated to writing skills.

Six qualities of good writing are expected in responses to essay questions:

1. *Coherent organization*—Ideas, in order to be communicated effectively, need to be structured in a natural, logical way. A well organized essay requires a certain amount of prior planning. Responses should be organized so that each principal idea is placed in the first sentence of the paragraph, followed by supporting concepts and examples.
2. *Conciseness*—Important points should be conveyed in as few words as possible; i.e., short sentences and simple wording.
3. *Clarity*—The use of precise words linked together in well-formed coherent sentences. Coherence is a matter of words, sentences, and paragraphs fitting together smoothly. Prevent uncertainty; choose words that relay the intended meaning.
4. *Use of standard English*—Include proper punctuation, capitalization, and accurate spelling. While CPAs are not expected to be masters of the essay form, they are expected to have competence in standard written English.
5. *Responsiveness to the requirements of the question*—Answers should address the requirements of the question and not be a broad explanation of the general subject area.
6. *Appropriateness for the reader*—Unless otherwise instructed, candidates should assume that the intended reader is a knowledgeable CPA.

Address Your Answer to the Question

The first and most important stage in developing a good answer to any essay question is to *closely read* the question requirements. The organization of the answer should follow logically from the specified requirements. If the "required" consists of three subparts, organize your answer into three subparts; if the "required" suggests a chart-like answer, make a chart. If the requirements tell you to "set forth reasons for conclusions stated," make sure that you do. Interpret the requirements in a straightforward, common-sense fashion, circling or underlining the key words or phrases and making sure that your answer addresses itself to those items.

Focus on Key Facts

In addition to a careful analysis of the question requirements, *an equally careful reading of the question narrative must be made*. To ensure that key facts are noted as points to address in your answer, highlight those facts by underlining, circling, making marginal notes, tick marks, or checks. Careful reading usually means reading the narrative *twice*—once for general comprehension and once for specific focus on relevant facts.

Outline to Ensure Completeness and Coherence

One of the things that must be guarded against is incompleteness. This happens when *all* of the requirements have not been dealt with. As previously noted, prior planning is necessary to prevent this. The impulse to launch into paragraph one and to develop the essay as you go along must be resisted. Too much time and too many words are wasted that way. Rather, *a brief thumbnail outline of the answer-to-be should be used to collect and organize ideas*. The resulting answer will be concise and complete.

A "thumbnail outline," as the term implies, is a rough, brief sketch of the proposed answer. It need not take more than one or two minutes to write. Its value lies in forcing one to think before writing, in crystallizing key thoughts, and in establishing a framework for essay development. Since it is generally not feasible to write a rough draft *plus* a finished draft of each essay answer, a thumbnail outline also serves as the equivalent of a rough draft. It helps to prevent false starts, poor coherence, or writing oneself into a corner.

Be Concise

After the narrative has been digested, and after the appropriate answer has been thought through and mapped out, the writing itself should be done. Prior analysis and organization have ensured completeness and coherence so that at this point the task becomes primarily one of expressing thoughts in a readable style—not literary, not scintillating perhaps, but readable. Sentences should be short and precise. Paragraphs should be brief and limited to one principal idea.

Use Examples to Support Your Arguments

All good expository writing alternates between the abstract and the concrete, the general and the specific. Your essay answers should do likewise. For exam purposes, a paragraph should start with the statement of a general idea and be followed by supporting facts or arguments. This leads to a formula-like approach to paragraph development that, when combined with the analysis and organization techniques described above, produces a systematic approach to answering essay questions.

Practice—To Increase Your Efficiency

The time constraints of the exam make it imperative to have an efficient, effective, systematic approach. The time to develop such an approach is *before* the exam by practicing with past exam questions. You should practice developing answers through at least an outline stage. Such practice will enable you to walk into the exam with no doubt in your mind about how to approach and develop a response to an essay question.

SAMPLE QUESTION AND SOLUTION

The preceding advice is illustrated by the following question and solution:

Question (AICPA Adapted)

(Note that while this question is applicable to the FARE section, the techniques have equal applicability to LPR and AUDIT.)

(Estimated time—15 to 25 minutes)

Deskin Company purchased a new machine to be used in its operations. The new machine was delivered by the supplier, installed by Deskin, and placed into operation. It was purchased under a long-term payment plan for which the interest charges approximated the prevailing market rates. The estimated useful life of the new machine is ten years, and its estimated residual (salvage) value is significant. Normal maintenance was performed to keep the new machine in usable condition.

Deskin also added a wing to the manufacturing building that it owns. The addition is an integral part of the building. Furthermore, Deskin made significant leasehold improvements to office space used as corporate headquarters.

Required:

a. What costs should Deskin capitalize for the new machine? How should the machine be depreciated? **Do not discuss specific methods of depreciation.**

b. How should Deskin account for the normal maintenance performed on the new machine? Why?

c. How should Deskin account for the wing added to the manufacturing building? Where should the added wing be reported on Deskin's financial statements?

d. How should Deskin account for the leasehold improvements made to its office space? Where should the leasehold improvements be reported on Deskin's financial statements?

Approach

1. Check estimated time (15–25 minutes); allow 4–6 minutes for each part.

2. Study requirements
   a. Read requirements first to develop a sense of what is required overall and in each part.
   b. Understand the requirements. Read carefully. Follow directions; i.e., do not discuss specific methods of depreciation.
   c. Jot down your thoughts relative to the requirements. These notes may be written on a piece of scrap paper or in the margin of the question. The following are sample thoughts:
      (1) *Part a*—What is the general rule for capitalizing? Describe in general terms how the amount of depreciation is determined.
      (2) *Part b*—"Account for" can be answered with a journal entry. "Why" requires explanation of the theoretical rationale.
      (3) *Parts c and d*—"Where reported" refers to the balance sheet and/or income statement effect.
   d. Visualize the answer
      Mentally outline short sentences and paragraphs to respond to *each* part. Remember to label the part you are answering before starting. Following are relevant thoughts.
      Part a—What gets capitalized? Why? Reason. How is a machine depreciated?
      Part b—Accounting treatment for normal maintenance? Why? Reason.

Part c—Accounting treatment—wing. On balance sheet; on income statement.
Part d—Accounting treatment—leasehold improvements. On balance sheet; on income statement.

3. Read and analyze the narrative
   a. Be careful and thorough.
   b. Highlight key facts.
   c. As the narrative is read, jot down pertinent thoughts on a piece of scrap paper or in the margin of the question.
   d. A mental review of concepts, principles, key phrases and/or acronyms should be made at this time; jot these down.
   e. Interpret straightforwardly; do not read into the questions what is not there.

4. Refocus on requirements. Organize key phrases and/or acronyms into a solution outline.

Solution outline

a. *Part a*
   Delivered; freight S/B capitalized.
   Installation S/B capitalized.
   Interest is expensed.
   Concept; capital expenditure vs. revenue expenditure.
   Key phrases; related to a future period, period of benefit, matching.
   Depreciable cost; cost—est. salvage.
   Depreciation; depreciable cost/est. useful life.

b. *Part b*
   Normal maintenance S/B expensed.

c. *Part c*
   Capitalize.
   Depreciate over shorter of remaining life or useful life of addition.
   Balance sheet—cost less accumulated depreciation.

d. *Part d*
   Capitalize and amortize.
   Balance sheet—cost less amortization.
   Income statement—amortization expense based on shorter of remaining lease term or useful life.

5. Write essay
Note that the question has been thought through and visualized. Write essay answers using the preceding as a guide to development.

Completed Solution

Part a

Generally, the capitalizable costs of an asset include all costs necessary to bring an asset to its state of intended end use and to the location of such use.

Specifically, when fixed (plant) assets are purchased under a deferred (long-term) payment plan, they are recorded at the current cash price; interest is not capitalized. In addition, Deskin would capitalize delivery and installation costs.

Depreciation represents the systematic and rational allocation of the capitalizable cost of an asset over its estimated useful life. Depreciable cost is the capitalizable cost less any salvage (residual) value.

Part b

Normal maintenance costs should be expensed as incurred. Such costs do not prolong the life of an asset or make it more useful. Hence, they benefit only the period in which they are incurred.

Part c

The wing added to the building should be capitalized as a building addition. It should be depreciated over the remaining useful life of the building or the useful life of the addition, whichever is shorter.

The wing should be reported on the balance sheet under property, plant, and equipment.

Part d

Leasehold improvements are amortized over the life of the improvement, or the life of the lease, whichever is shorter.

In the balance sheet, the unamortized cost of leasehold improvements may be presented (separately) under either property, plant, and equipment, or intangible assets. The periodic amortization expense is reported in the income statement.

Comments

1. Note how essay and paragraph structure parallel the requirement structure.
2. Note how the question requirements are kept in focus. They provide the stimuli; the essay answer provides the response.
3. Note that the writing style is systematic and precise. Vagueness, ambiguity and wordiness are successfully avoided.
4. The grader, in evaluating an answer, would work from a grading guide that outlines an ideal answer and that lists key words or thoughts to look for in a candidate's answer. A good answer will have most of those words or thoughts listed in the thumbnail outline. The essay itself serves mainly as a vehicle for relating ideas and for communicating them effectively.

GENERAL REMINDERS FOR ESSAY AND COMPUTATIONAL QUESTIONS

Be Prepared

Bring adequate writing supplies. Writing essays or preparing schedules in pencil is permitted. An answer written with a sharp pencil looks better than one in ink with numerous cross-outs.

Budget Your Time

1. For each question, *allocate the budgeted time* among the subparts. Do not exceed the allotted time.
2. If time is running out, *outline*, in sentence form, the remainder of the answer or state how it should be completed. You may return to it after all of the questions have been answered but not before.

Plan Your Answers

1. Spend the first few minutes *scanning* the exam and *planning* the order of question attack.
2. Keep in mind that graders work from *grading guides* that outline specific items to be looked for in evaluating your answer. Your answer must contain a majority of items enumerated in order to earn sufficient credit.
3. *Support conclusions with reasons.* Demonstration of reasoning ability is just as important as arriving at correct conclusions.
4. In essay questions, use phraseology employed by the question but *do not recopy the requirements verbatim.* Such copying is a waste of time and will be construed as unnecessary padding.
5. *Concentrate on the question at hand.* Do not worry about questions already answered or questions to come.
6. *Respond directly to the requirements.* Do not present extraneous material.
7. *Say what you mean and mean what you say.* Don't equivocate or contradict yourself.

Be Legible

1. *Leave plenty of space between answers* to subparts. (Sometimes separate sheets of paper will be appropriate.) This also allows for later additions as necessary.
2. If your penmanship is so poor that legibility is a real problem, skip lines when writing answers.
3. Try to make your answer pages as *visually presentable* as possible under the circumstances. That is, observe adequate margins, use appropriate headings, use a straightedge for charts or lines, skip a line between paragraphs, etc.
4. *Identify and turn in all answer papers.* Question number and part should be clearly indicated at the top of the page.

6. Chart Your Progress and Plan Your Course of Action

HOW TO USE THIS CHAPTER

This chapter is aimed at analyzing your test material in order to help you pinpoint your weak areas, and then providing you with a course of action.

If you have not already done so, you should now read "Chapter 3—Develop Your Study Program." This chapter provides you with insight into the kind of commitment that is necessary in order to pass this examination. *Your 7-Stage Study Program* is outlined, along with guidelines as to whether you should plan a self-study program or seek help in a review course.

In order to plan your course of action, you will be taking tests in the following order:

- *Preliminary Readiness Tests* (Chapter 7)
- *Simulated CPA Examination* (Chapter 8)
- *May 1994 CPA Examination* (Chapter 9)

Be sure to take each test, using the directions provided at the beginning of each chapter. When you have completed each test, you will use the following procedure:

Pinpoint Your Weak Areas for Each Test Section

I. *CHECK YOUR ANSWERS*
   In order to do this, you should refer to the "Answer Key—Four-Option Multiple-Choice Questions" section of the examination chapter to check your answers. For "other objective formats," essay, and computational questions, you should compare your answers with the model answers provided.

II. *SCORE YOURSELF*
   You must figure out the percentage of questions that you answer correctly. For "other objective formats," essay, and computational questions, you must compare your answer to the model answer provided and, based on correspondences between the two, estimate the percentage of

credit you would be likely to achieve under exam conditions. With respect to "writing skills" points, the average candidate is likely to receive three to five points.

III. *EVALUATE YOUR SCORE*
   If you did not get at least 75 percent of the credit available, you should prepare for intensive work.

   In any event, review the section "Solutions and Explained Answers" for *all* questions you answered incorrectly. (This section pertains to the Simulated CPA Examination and the May 1994 CPA Examination.)

IV. *ANALYZE YOUR ERRORS*
   The charts in this chapter will help you determine your specific *Topical Area* weaknesses. You should list the number of correct answers you had (or points you achieved) under each category listed and, based on the percentage answered correctly, determine your strength or weakness in that area.

Determine Your Overall Priorities

I. *ANALYZE YOUR OVERALL SCORE*
   Align your scores for each of the four sections of the test and determine which sections need the most attention. (Place your scores in "A Summary of Your Test Scores" on page 68.) Consider any section in that you did not get at least 75 percent of the credit available to need a great deal of work.

   Now, taking those sections that need the most attention, determine which Topical Areas need the most work.

II. *REVIEW OF TEST TACTICS*
   Review the test tactics in Chapter 5 for each question type. Your time-saving approach in answering questions must become automatic in order for you to do well on the examination.

Begin Your Study Program

Now that you have analyzed your overall score and determined those areas that should be worked on most diligently, you are ready to begin your actual review. Refer to Chapter 3 for guidance in selecting a review program that is best suited to your needs.

Test What You've Learned

When you feel you are stronger in your weak areas, take another test. This procedure should be used for the Preliminary Readiness Tests, as well as for the Simulated CPA Examination and the May 1994 CPA Examination.

Between each test:
- Pinpoint Your Weak Areas
- Determine Your Overall Priorities
- Begin Your Study Program
- Test What You've Learned

To compare your test scores, fill in the spaces below. If you have not improved, you should spend more time in reviewing those Topical Areas in which you have performed poorly and in reviewing the test tactics in Chapter 5.

A SUMMARY OF YOUR TEST SCORES

In the space provided, place the percentage of the items that you answered correctly. Be sure that you add the scores for *four-option multiple-choice* questions, *"other objective formats"* questions, and *essay/computational* questions on both the Simulated and May 1994 examinations.

	PRELIMINARY READINESS TESTS	SIMULATED CPA EXAM	MAY 1994 CPA EXAM
Business Law & Professional Responsibilities (LPR)	_____	_____	_____
Auditing (AUDIT)	_____	_____	_____
Accounting & Reporting—Taxation, Managerial, and Governmental and Not-for-Profit Organizations (ARE)	_____	_____	_____
Financial Accounting & Reporting— Business Enterprises (FARE)	_____	_____	_____

(Minimum Percent Needed = 75 percent)

A RECORD OF YOUR TEST SCORES

Preliminary Readiness Test

BUSINESS LAW & PROFESSIONAL RESPONSIBILITIES (LPR) TEST

I. CHECK YOUR ANSWERS using the Answer Key—Four-Option Multiple-Choice Questions on page 105.

II. SCORE YOURSELF:

    Total Items   __30__

    Number Correct _____

    Percent Correct _____

    (Minimum Percent Needed = 75 percent)

Record your score in "A Summary of Your Test Scores" on page 68.

III. EVALUATE YOUR SCORE: If you did not get at least 75 percent of the questions correct, you should prepare for intensive work.

IV. ANALYZE YOUR ERRORS: To determine your specific weaknesses, list the number of correct answers you had under each of the following categories and, based on the percentage answered correctly, determine your strength or weakness in that area.

FOUR-OPTION MULTIPLE-CHOICE QUESTIONS

TOPICAL AREA	QUESTIONS	NUMBER OF QUESTIONS	NUMBER CORRECT
Accountants' Legal Responsibility	1, 2	2	
Agency	3	1	
Bankruptcy	4, 5	2	
Commercial Paper	6, 7	2	
Contracts	8, 9	2	
Corporations	10, 11	2	
Documents of Title	12	1	
Employment Regulations	13	1	
Estates & Trusts	14, 15	2	
Federal Securities Regulations	16, 17	2	
Insurance	18	1	
Investment Securities	19	1	
Partnerships	20, 21	2	
Professional Responsibilities	22	1	
Property	23, 24	2	
Sales	25, 26	2	
Secured Transactions	27, 28	2	
Suretyship and Creditor's Rights	29, 30	2	

Total: _____

AUDITING (AUDIT) TEST

I. CHECK YOUR ANSWERS using the Answer Key—Four-Option Multiple-Choice Questions on page 105.

II. SCORE YOURSELF:

    Total Items   30

    Number Correct

    Percent Correct

    (Minimum Percent Needed = 75 percent)

Record your score in "A Summary of Your Test Scores" on page 68.

III. EVALUATE YOUR SCORE: If you did not get at least 75 percent of the questions correct, you should prepare for intensive work.

IV. ANALYZE YOUR ERRORS: To determine your specific weaknesses, list the number of correct answers you had under each of the following categories and, based on the percentage answered correctly, determine your strength or weakness in that area.

FOUR-OPTION MULTIPLE-CHOICE QUESTIONS

TOPICAL AREA	QUESTIONS	NUMBER OF QUESTIONS	NUMBER CORRECT
Audit Evidence	1–6	6	
Audit Planning	7–10	4	
Audit Reporting Standards	11–15	5	
Auditing Concepts and Standards	16–18	3	
Electronic Data Processing (EDP)	19, 20	2	
Internal Control	21–25	5	
Other Reporting Areas	26–28	3	
Statistical Sampling	29, 30	2	

Total:

ACCOUNTING & REPORTING—TAXATION, MANAGERIAL, AND GOVERNMENTAL AND NOT-FOR-PROFIT ORGANIZATIONS (ARE) TEST

I. CHECK YOUR ANSWERS using the Answer Key—Four-Option Multiple-Choice Questions on page 106.

II. SCORE YOURSELF:

Total Items   __30__
Number Correct _____
Percent Correct _____
(Minimum Percent Needed = 75 percent)
Record your score in "A Summary of Your Test Scores" on page 68.

III. EVALUATE YOUR SCORE: If you did not get at least 75 percent of the questions correct, you should prepare for intensive work.

IV. ANALYZE YOUR ERRORS: To determine your specific weaknesses, list the number of correct answers you had under each of the following categories and, based on the percentage answered correctly, determine your strength or weakness in that area.

FOUR-OPTION MULTIPLE-CHOICE QUESTIONS

TOPICAL AREA	QUESTIONS	NUMBER OF QUESTIONS	NUMBER CORRECT
Cost Accounting	1–5	5	
Federal Income Taxes— Capital Gains & Losses	6	1	
Federal Income Taxes— Corporations	7–9	3	
Federal Income Taxes— Estates & Trusts	10	1	
Federal Income Taxes— Exempt Organizations	11	1	
Federal Income Taxes— Individuals	12–14	3	
Federal Income Taxes— Partnerships	15	1	
Managerial Accounting & Quantitative Methods	16–20	5	
Not-for-Profit Accounting— Governmental Units	21–25	5	
Not-for-Profit Accounting— Other Than Governmental Units	26–30	5	

Total: _____

FINANCIAL ACCOUNTING & REPORTING—BUSINESS ENTERPRISES (FARE) TEST

I. CHECK YOUR ANSWERS using the Answer Key—Four-Option Multiple-Choice Questions on page 106.
II. SCORE YOURSELF:
Total Items ___30___
Number Correct _____
Percent Correct _____
(Minimum Percent Needed = 75 percent)
Record your score in "A Summary of Your Test Scores" on page 68.

III. EVALUATE YOUR SCORE: If you did not get at least 75 percent of the questions correct, you should prepare for intensive work.
IV. ANALYZE YOUR ERRORS: To determine your specific weaknesses, list the number of correct answers you had under each of the following categories and, based on the percentage answered correctly, determine your strength or weakness in that area.

FOUR-OPTION MULTIPLE-CHOICE QUESTIONS

TOPICAL AREA	QUESTIONS	NUMBER OF QUESTIONS	NUMBER CORRECT
Accounting Concepts	1	1	
Accounting Fundamentals	2, 3	2	
Bonds, Accounting for	4	1	
Cash Flows	5, 6	2	
Consolidation and Business Combination	7, 8	2	
Financial Statement Analysis	9	1	
Financial Statements	10	1	
Fixed Assets	11, 12	2	
Foreign Currency Translation	13	1	
Income Taxes, Accounting for	14	1	
Installment Sales	15	1	
Intangibles	16	1	
Inventories	17	1	
Investments	18, 19	2	
Leases	20, 21	2	
Liabilities	22, 23	2	
Long-Term Contracts	24	1	
Partnerships	25	1	
Pension Costs	26	1	
Receivables	27, 28	2	
Stockholders' Equity	29, 30	2	

Total: _____

Turn to "How To Use This Chapter" (page 67) for guidance in planning your course of action.

Simulated CPA Examination

BUSINESS LAW & PROFESSIONAL RESPONSIBILITIES (LPR) SECTION

I. CHECK YOUR ANSWERS using the Answer Key—Four-Option Multiple-Choice Questions on page 169 and the Solutions and Explained Answers section on page 173.

II. SCORE YOURSELF: To estimate points earned on "*other objective formats*" and *essay questions*, compare your answers to the model answers provided in the section Solutions and Explained Answers (see page 173). Based on correspondences between your answers and model answers, you should be able to get a rough idea of how many points your answers would earn under exam conditions.

	Four-Option Multiple-Choice	Other Objective Formats	Essay
Total Items	60*	2†	2†
Points Earned			

Total Points Earned = _____

* 1 point each
† 10 points each

Record your score in "A Summary of Your Test Scores" on page 68.

III. EVALUATE YOUR SCORE: If you did not get at least 75 percent of the questions correct, you should prepare for intensive work.

In any event, you should begin your study program by reviewing the section "Solutions and Explained Answers" (see page 173) for *all* questions you answered incorrectly.

IV. ANALYZE YOUR ERRORS: To determine your specific weaknesses, list the number of correct answers you had under each of the following categories and, based on the percentage answered correctly, determine your strength or weakness in that area.

FOUR-OPTION MULTIPLE-CHOICE QUESTIONS

TOPICAL AREA	QUESTIONS	NUMBER OF QUESTIONS	NUMBER CORRECT
Accountants' Legal Responsibility	1–9	9	
Agency	11, 13–15	4	
Bankruptcy	27–33, 39	8	
Contracts	21–24, 26	5	
Corporations	17, 19, 20	3	
Documents of Title	46, 47	2	
Employment Regulations	35, 36	2	
Federal Securities Regulations	37, 38, 40–43, 45	7	
Investment Securities	48	1	
Partnerships	12, 16, 18	3	
Professional Responsibilities	10, 34, 44, 54, 55	5	
Sales	49–52, 56, 57	6	
Secured Transactions	53, 58-60	4	
Suretyship and Creditor's Rights	25	1	

Total: _____

"OTHER OBJECTIVE FORMATS" QUESTIONS

TOPICAL AREA	QUESTIONS	POINTS AVAILABLE	POINTS EARNED
Bankruptcy	3	10	
Property	2	10	

Total: _____

ESSAY QUESTIONS

TOPICAL AREA	QUESTIONS	POINTS AVAILABLE	POINTS EARNED
Commercial Paper	5	10	
Estates and Trusts	4	10	

Total: _____

AUDITING (AUDIT) SECTION

I. CHECK YOUR ANSWERS using the Answer Key—Four-Option Multiple-Choice Questions on page 169 and the Solutions and Explained Answers section on page 207.

II. SCORE YOURSELF: To estimate points earned on "*other objective formats*" and *essay questions*, compare your answers to the model answers provided in the section Solutions and Explained Answers (see page 207). Based on correspondences between your answers and model answers, you should be able to get a rough idea of how many points your answers would earn under exam conditions.

	Four-Option Multiple-Choice	Other Objective Formats	Essay
Total Items	90*	2†	2†
Points Earned	_____	_____	_____

Total Points Earned = _____

* 2/3 point each
† 10 points each

Record your score in "A Summary of Your Test Scores" on page 68.

III. EVALUATE YOUR SCORE: If you did not get at least 75 percent of the questions correct, you should prepare for intensive work.

In any event, you should begin your study program by reviewing the section "Solutions and Explained Answers" (see page 207) for *all* questions you answered incorrectly.

IV. ANALYZE YOUR ERRORS: To determine your specific weaknesses, list the number of correct answers you had under each of the following categories and, based on the percentage answered correctly, determine your strength or weakness in that area.

FOUR-OPTION MULTIPLE-CHOICE QUESTIONS

TOPICAL AREA	QUESTIONS	NUMBER OF QUESTIONS	NUMBER CORRECT
Audit Evidence	11, 15, 26, 36, 37, 39–41, 82–86, 88–90	16	
Audit Planning	4–8, 17, 38, 42, 75–80, 87	15	
Audit Reporting Standards	14, 46–49, 51, 55, 59, 61, 62	10	
Auditing Concepts and Standards	2, 52	2	
Electronic Data Processing (EDP)	1, 3, 18, 43	4	
Internal Control	16, 19, 21–25, 27–34, 60, 66–74, 81	26	
Other Reporting Areas	9, 12, 35, 44, 45, 50, 53, 54, 56–58, 63–65	14	
Statistical Sampling	10, 13, 20	3	

Total: _____

"OTHER OBJECTIVE FORMATS" QUESTIONS

TOPICAL AREA	QUESTIONS	POINTS AVAILABLE	POINTS EARNED
Audit Evidence	3	10	
Other Reporting Areas	2	10	

Total: _____

ESSAY QUESTIONS

TOPICAL AREA	QUESTIONS	POINTS AVAILABLE	POINTS EARNED
Audit Evidence	4	10	
Internal Control	5	10	

Total: _____

ACCOUNTING & REPORTING—TAXATION, MANAGERIAL, AND GOVERNMENTAL AND NOT-FOR PROFIT ORGANIZATIONS (ARE) SECTION

I. CHECK YOUR ANSWERS using the Answer Key—Four-Option Multiple-Choice Questions on page 170 and the Solutions and Explained Answers section on page 262.

II. SCORE YOURSELF: To estimate points earned on "*other objective formats*" and *essay questions*, compare your answers to the model answers provided in the section Solutions and Explained Answers (see page 262). Based on correspondences between your answers and model answers, you should be able to get a rough idea of how many points your answers would earn under exam conditions.

	Four-Option Multiple-Choice	Other Objective Formats
Total Items	60*	2†
Points Earned		

Total Points Earned =_____

* 1 point each
† 20 points each

Record your score in "A Summary of Your Test Scores" on page 68.

III. EVALUATE YOUR SCORE: If you did not get at least 75 percent of the questions correct, you should prepare for intensive work.

In any event, you should begin your study program by reviewing the section "Solutions and Explained Answers" (see page 262) for *all* questions you answered incorrectly.

IV. ANALYZE YOUR ERRORS: To determine your specific weaknesses, list the number of correct answers you had under each of the following categories and, based on the percentage answered correctly, determine your strength or weakness in that area.

FOUR-OPTION MULTIPLE-CHOICE QUESTIONS

TOPICAL AREA	QUESTIONS	NUMBER OF QUESTIONS	NUMBER CORRECT
Cost Accounting	48–50	3	
Federal Income Taxes— Corporations	1–25	25	
Federal Income Taxes— Estates & Trust	33, 34	2	
Federal Income Taxes— Exempt Organizations	35	1	
Federal Income Taxes— Partnerships	26–32	7	
Managerial Accounting & Quantitative Methods	36–47	12	
Not-for-Profit Accounting— Governmental Units	51–55	5	
Not-for-Profit Accounting— Other than Governmental Units	56–60	5	

Total: _____

"OTHER OBJECTIVE FORMATS" QUESTIONS

Topical Area	Questions	Points Available	Points Earned
Federal Income Taxes— Individuals	2	20	
Not-for-Profit Accounting— Governmental Units	3	20	

Total: _____

FINANCIAL ACCOUNTING & REPORTING—BUSINESS ENTERPRISES (FARE) SECTION

I. CHECK YOUR ANSWERS using the Answer Key—Four-Option Multiple-Choice Questions on page 172 and the Solutions and Explained Answers section on page 302.

II. SCORE YOURSELF: To estimate points earned on *"other objective formats"* and *essay questions*, compare your answers to the model answers provided in the section Solutions and Explained Answers (see page 302). Based on correspondences between your answers and model answers, you should be able to get a rough idea of how many points your answers would earn under exam conditions.

	Four-Option Multiple-Choice	Other Objective Formats	Essay/ Computational
Total Items	60*	2†	2†
Points Earned			

Total Points Earned = _____

* 1 point each
† 10 points each

Record your score in "A Summary of Your Test Scores" on page 68.

III. EVALUATE YOUR SCORE: If you did not get at least 75 percent of the questions correct, you should prepare for intensive work.

In any event, you should begin your study program by reviewing the sections "Solutions and Explained Answers" (see page 302) for *all* questions you answered incorrectly.

IV. ANALYZE YOUR ERRORS: To determine your specific weaknesses, list the number of correct answers you had under each of the following categories and, based on the percentage answered correctly, determine your strength or weakness in that area.

FOUR-OPTION MULTIPLE-CHOICE QUESTIONS

Topical Area	Questions	Number of Questions	Number Correct
Accounting Concepts	10–13	4	
Accounting Fundamentals	15, 17	2	
Bankruptcy	58	1	
Bonds, Accounting for	51, 52	2	
Cash Flows	36–38	3	
Consolidations and Business Combinations	53–56	4	
Financial Statement Analysis	35, 57	2	
Financial Statements	43–46	4	
Fixed Assets	3–5	3	
Foreign Currency Translations	16	1	
Income Taxes, Accounting for	60	1	
Inflation Accounting	42	1	
Installment Sales	14, 18	2	
Intangibles	6	1	
Inventories	2	1	
Investments	1, 47, 48	3	
Leases	28, 49, 50	3	
Liabilities	19–27	9	
Partnerships	59	1	
Pension Costs	39–41	3	
Receivables	7–9	3	
Stockholders' Equity	29-34	6	

Total: _____

"OTHER OBJECTIVE FORMATS" QUESTIONS

Topical Area	Questions	Points Available	Points Earned
Bonds, Accounting for	2a	5	
Financial Statement Analysis	2b	5	
Fixed Assets	3a	5	
Pension Costs	3b	5	

Total: _____

ESSAY/COMPUTATIONAL QUESTIONS

Topical Area	Questions	Points Available	Points Earned
Accounting Concepts	4a	5	
Long-Term Contracts	4b	5	
Receivables	5a	5	
Stockholders' Equity	5b	5	

Total: _____

May 1994 CPA Examination

BUSINESS LAW & PROFESSIONAL RESPONSIBILITIES (LPR) SECTION

I. CHECK YOUR ANSWERS using the Answer Key—Four-Option Multiple-Choice Questions on page 424 and the Solutions and Explained Answers section on page 428.

II. SCORE YOURSELF: To estimate points earned on *"other objective formats"* and *essay questions*, compare your answers to the model answers provided in the section Solutions and Explained Answers (see page 428). Based on correspondences between your answers and model answers, you should be able to get a rough idea of how many points your answers would earn under exam conditions.

	Four-Option Multiple-Choice	Other Objective Formats	Essay
Total Items	60*	2†	2†
Points Earned			

Total Points Earned =_____

* 1 point each
† 10 points each

Record your score in "A Summary of Your Test Scores" on page 68.

III. EVALUATE YOUR SCORE: If you did not get at least 75 percent of the questions correct, you should prepare for intensive work.

In any event, you should begin your study program by reviewing the section "Solutions and Explained Answers" (see page 428) for *all* questions you answered incorrectly.

IV. ANALYZE YOUR ERRORS: To determine your specific weaknesses, list the number of correct answers you had under each of the following categories and, based on the percentage answered correctly, determine your strength or weakness in that area.

FOUR-OPTION MULTIPLE-CHOICE QUESTIONS

TOPICAL AREA	QUESTIONS	NUMBER OF QUESTIONS	NUMBER CORRECT
Accountants' Legal Responsibility	9, 10	2	
Corporations	11–14	4	
Employment Regulations	26–30	5	
Estates and Trusts	15–20	6	
Federal Securities Regulations	31–40	10	
Professional Responsibilities	1–8	8	
Property	56–60	5	
Sales	41–47	7	
Secured Transactions	48–55	8	
Suretyship and Creditor's Rights	21–25	5	

Total: _____

"OTHER OBJECTIVE FORMATS" QUESTIONS

TOPICAL AREA	QUESTIONS	POINTS AVAILABLE	POINTS EARNED
Accountants' Legal Responsibility	2a	5	
Bankruptcy	2b	5	
Commercial Paper	3a	5	
Insurance	3b	5	

Total: _____

ESSAY QUESTIONS

TOPICAL AREA	QUESTIONS	POINTS AVAILABLE	POINTS EARNED
Partnerships	4	10	
Property and Contracts	5	10	

Total: _____

AUDITING (AUDIT) SECTION

I. CHECK YOUR ANSWERS using the Answer Key—Four-Option Multiple-Choice Questions on page 424 and the Solutions and Explained Answers section on page 462.

II. SCORE YOURSELF: To estimate points earned on "*other objective formats*" and *essay questions*, compare your answers to the model answers provided in the section Solutions and Explained Answers (see page 462). Based on correspondences between your answers and model answers, you should be able to get a rough idea of how many points your answers would earn under exam conditions.

	Four-Option Multiple-Choice	Other Objective Formats	Essay
Total Items	90*	2†	2†
Points Earned			

Total Points Earned = _____

* 2/3 point each
† 10 points each

Record your score in "A Summary of Your Test Scores" on page 68.

III. EVALUATE YOUR SCORE: If you did not get at least 75 percent of the questions correct, you should prepare for intensive work.

In any event, you should begin your study program by reviewing the section "Solutions and Explained Answers" (see page 462) for *all* questions you answered incorrectly.

IV. ANALYZE YOUR ERRORS: To determine your specific weaknesses, list the number of correct answers you had under each of the following categories and, based on the percentage answered correctly, determine your strength or weakness in that area.

FOUR-OPTION MULTIPLE-CHOICE QUESTIONS

TOPICAL AREA	QUESTIONS	NUMBER OF QUESTIONS	NUMBER CORRECT
Audit Evidence	6–8, 11, 38–42, 45, 47–50, 54 55, 57, 58, 62	19	
Audit Planning	1, 2, 3, 4, 5, 24, 51, 52	7	
Audit Reporting Standards	53, 63, 65–67, 69–77, 82, 86–90	20	
Auditing Concepts and Standards	3, 15	2	
Electronic Data Processing (EDP)	16, 31, 56	3	
Internal Control	18–23, 25–30 32–37	18	
Other Reporting Areas	9, 10, 12–14, 46, 59–61, 64, 68, 78–81, 83–85	18	
Statistical Sampling	17, 43, 44	3	

Total: _____

"OTHER OBJECTIVE FORMATS" QUESTIONS

TOPICAL AREA	QUESTIONS	POINTS AVAILABLE	POINTS EARNED
Audit Planning	3	10	
Internal Control	2	10	

Total: _____

ESSAY QUESTIONS

TOPICAL AREA	QUESTIONS	POINTS AVAILABLE	POINTS EARNED
Audit Evidence	5	10	
Audit Planning	4	10	

Total: _____

ACCOUNTING & REPORTING—TAXATION, MANAGERIAL, AND GOVERNMENTAL AND NOT-FOR PROFIT ORGANIZATIONS (ARE) SECTION

I. CHECK YOUR ANSWERS using the Answer Key—Four-Option Multiple-Choice Questions on page 425 and the Solutions and Explained Answers section on page 514.

II. SCORE YOURSELF: To estimate points earned on "*other objective formats*" and *essay questions*, compare your answers to the model answers provided in the section Solutions and Explained Answers (see page 514). Based on correspondences between your answers and model answers, you should be able to get a rough idea of how many points your answers would earn under exam conditions.

	Four-Option Multiple-Choice	Other Objective Formats
Total Items	60*	2†
Points Earned	_____	_____

Total Points Earned = _____

* 1 point each
† 20 points each

Record your score in "A Summary of Your Test Scores" on page 68.

III. EVALUATE YOUR SCORE: If you did not get at least 75 percent of the questions correct, you should prepare for intensive work.

In any event, you should begin your study program by reviewing the section "Solutions and Explained Answers" (see page 514) for *all* questions you answered incorrectly.

IV. ANALYZE YOUR ERRORS: To determine your specific weaknesses, list the number of correct answers you had under each of the following categories and, based on the percentage answered correctly, determine your strength or weakness in that area.

FOUR-OPTION MULTIPLE-CHOICE QUESTIONS

TOPICAL AREA	QUESTIONS	NUMBER OF QUESTIONS	NUMBER CORRECT
Cost Accounting	40, 42	2	
Federal Income Taxes— Capital Gains & Losses	1	1	
Federal Income Taxes— Corporations	21–25	5	
Federal Income Taxes— Estates & Trust	33	1	
Federal Income Taxes— Exempt Organizations	34–35	2	
Federal Income Taxes— Individuals	2–14, 16, 17, 32	16	
Federal Income Taxes— Miscellaneous Topics	15, 18–20	4	
Federal Income Taxes— Partnerships	26–31	6	
Managerial Accounting & Quantitative Methods	36–39, 41, 43–50	13	
Not-for-Profit Accounting— Governmental Units	51–57	7	
Not-for-Profit Accounting— Other than Governmental Units	58–60	3	

Total: _____

"OTHER OBJECTIVE FORMATS" QUESTIONS

TOPICAL AREA	QUESTIONS	POINTS AVAILABLE	POINTS EARNED
Federal Income Taxes— Corporations	2	20	
Not-for-Profit Accounting— Governmental Units	3	20	

Total: _____

FINANCIAL ACCOUNTING & REPORTING—BUSINESS ENTERPRISES (FARE) SECTION

I. CHECK YOUR ANSWERS using the Answer Key—Four-Option Multiple-Choice Questions on page 427 and the Solutions and Explained Answers section on page 561.

II. SCORE YOURSELF: To estimate points earned on "*other objective formats*" and *essay questions*, compare your answers to the model answers provided in the section Solutions and Explained Answers (see page 561). Based on correspondences between your answers and model answers, you should be able to get a rough idea of how many points your answers would earn under exam conditions.

	Four-Option Multiple-Choice	Other Objective Formats	Essay Compu-tational
Total Items	60*	2†	2†
Points Earned			

Total Points Earned = _____

* 1 point each
† 10 points each

Record your score in "A Summary of Your Test Scores" on page 68.

FOUR-OPTION MULTIPLE-CHOICE QUESTIONS

TOPICAL AREA	QUESTIONS	NUMBER OF QUESTIONS	NUMBER CORRECT
Accounting Concepts	1–3, 42, 57	5	
Bonds, Accounting for	29, 34, 43, 46	4	
Cash	12, 13	2	
Cash Flows	5, 50	2	
Consolidation	7, 51, 52, 55, 56	5	
Financial Statement Analysis	60	1	
Financial Statements	4, 6, 9, 10, 38–40, 48, 53, 54	10	
Fixed Assets	17, 18, 45	3	
Income Taxes, Accounting for	24, 47	2	
Inflation Accounting	58, 59	2	
Installment Sales	23, 41	2	
Intangibles	20	1	
Investments	14, 16, 19, 44	4	
Leases	25, 26	2	
Liabilities	11, 21, 22, 30	4	
Partnerships	35–37	3	
Pension Costs	27, 28	2	
Receivables	15	1	
Stockholders' Equity	8, 31–33, 49	5	

Total: _____

III. EVALUATE YOUR SCORE: If you did not get at least 75 percent of the questions correct, you should prepared for intensive work.

In any event, you should begin your study program by reviewing the section "Solutions and Explained Answers" (see page 561) for *all* questions you answered incorrectly.

IV. ANALYZE YOUR ERRORS: To determine your specific weaknesses, list the number of correct answers you had under each of the following categories and, based on the percentage answered correctly, determine your strength or weakness in that area.

"OTHER OBJECTIVE FORMATS" QUESTIONS

TOPICAL AREA	QUESTIONS	POINTS AVAILABLE	POINTS EARNED
Financial Statements	2, 3	20	

Total: _____

ESSAY/COMPUTATIONAL QUESTIONS

TOPICAL AREA	QUESTIONS	POINTS AVAILABLE	POINTS EARNED
Inventories	4	10	
Liabilities, Leases, Corporation Bonds, and Accounting for Income Taxes	5	10	

Total: _____

Answer Sheet

PRELIMINARY READINESS TESTS

LPR	AUDIT	ARE	FARE
1. Ⓐ Ⓑ Ⓒ Ⓓ	1. Ⓐ Ⓑ Ⓒ Ⓓ	1. Ⓐ Ⓑ Ⓒ Ⓓ	1. Ⓐ Ⓑ Ⓒ Ⓓ
2. Ⓐ Ⓑ Ⓒ Ⓓ	2. Ⓐ Ⓑ Ⓒ Ⓓ	2. Ⓐ Ⓑ Ⓒ Ⓓ	2. Ⓐ Ⓑ Ⓒ Ⓓ
3. Ⓐ Ⓑ Ⓒ Ⓓ	3. Ⓐ Ⓑ Ⓒ Ⓓ	3. Ⓐ Ⓑ Ⓒ Ⓓ	3. Ⓐ Ⓑ Ⓒ Ⓓ
4. Ⓐ Ⓑ Ⓒ Ⓓ	4. Ⓐ Ⓑ Ⓒ Ⓓ	4. Ⓐ Ⓑ Ⓒ Ⓓ	4. Ⓐ Ⓑ Ⓒ Ⓓ
5. Ⓐ Ⓑ Ⓒ Ⓓ	5. Ⓐ Ⓑ Ⓒ Ⓓ	5. Ⓐ Ⓑ Ⓒ Ⓓ	5. Ⓐ Ⓑ Ⓒ Ⓓ
6. Ⓐ Ⓑ Ⓒ Ⓓ	6. Ⓐ Ⓑ Ⓒ Ⓓ	6. Ⓐ Ⓑ Ⓒ Ⓓ	6. Ⓐ Ⓑ Ⓒ Ⓓ
7. Ⓐ Ⓑ Ⓒ Ⓓ	7. Ⓐ Ⓑ Ⓒ Ⓓ	7. Ⓐ Ⓑ Ⓒ Ⓓ	7. Ⓐ Ⓑ Ⓒ Ⓓ
8. Ⓐ Ⓑ Ⓒ Ⓓ	8. Ⓐ Ⓑ Ⓒ Ⓓ	8. Ⓐ Ⓑ Ⓒ Ⓓ	8. Ⓐ Ⓑ Ⓒ Ⓓ
9. Ⓐ Ⓑ Ⓒ Ⓓ	9. Ⓐ Ⓑ Ⓒ Ⓓ	9. Ⓐ Ⓑ Ⓒ Ⓓ	9. Ⓐ Ⓑ Ⓒ Ⓓ
10. Ⓐ Ⓑ Ⓒ Ⓓ	10. Ⓐ Ⓑ Ⓒ Ⓓ	10. Ⓐ Ⓑ Ⓒ Ⓓ	10. Ⓐ Ⓑ Ⓒ Ⓓ
11. Ⓐ Ⓑ Ⓒ Ⓓ	11. Ⓐ Ⓑ Ⓒ Ⓓ	11. Ⓐ Ⓑ Ⓒ Ⓓ	11. Ⓐ Ⓑ Ⓒ Ⓓ
12. Ⓐ Ⓑ Ⓒ Ⓓ	12. Ⓐ Ⓑ Ⓒ Ⓓ	12. Ⓐ Ⓑ Ⓒ Ⓓ	12. Ⓐ Ⓑ Ⓒ Ⓓ
13. Ⓐ Ⓑ Ⓒ Ⓓ	13. Ⓐ Ⓑ Ⓒ Ⓓ	13. Ⓐ Ⓑ Ⓒ Ⓓ	13. Ⓐ Ⓑ Ⓒ Ⓓ
14. Ⓐ Ⓑ Ⓒ Ⓓ	14. Ⓐ Ⓑ Ⓒ Ⓓ	14. Ⓐ Ⓑ Ⓒ Ⓓ	14. Ⓐ Ⓑ Ⓒ Ⓓ
15. Ⓐ Ⓑ Ⓒ Ⓓ	15. Ⓐ Ⓑ Ⓒ Ⓓ	15. Ⓐ Ⓑ Ⓒ Ⓓ	15. Ⓐ Ⓑ Ⓒ Ⓓ
16. Ⓐ Ⓑ Ⓒ Ⓓ	16. Ⓐ Ⓑ Ⓒ Ⓓ	16. Ⓐ Ⓑ Ⓒ Ⓓ	16. Ⓐ Ⓑ Ⓒ Ⓓ
17. Ⓐ Ⓑ Ⓒ Ⓓ	17. Ⓐ Ⓑ Ⓒ Ⓓ	17. Ⓐ Ⓑ Ⓒ Ⓓ	17. Ⓐ Ⓑ Ⓒ Ⓓ
18. Ⓐ Ⓑ Ⓒ Ⓓ	18. Ⓐ Ⓑ Ⓒ Ⓓ	18. Ⓐ Ⓑ Ⓒ Ⓓ	18. Ⓐ Ⓑ Ⓒ Ⓓ
19. Ⓐ Ⓑ Ⓒ Ⓓ	19. Ⓐ Ⓑ Ⓒ Ⓓ	19. Ⓐ Ⓑ Ⓒ Ⓓ	19. Ⓐ Ⓑ Ⓒ Ⓓ
20. Ⓐ Ⓑ Ⓒ Ⓓ	20. Ⓐ Ⓑ Ⓒ Ⓓ	20. Ⓐ Ⓑ Ⓒ Ⓓ	20. Ⓐ Ⓑ Ⓒ Ⓓ
21. Ⓐ Ⓑ Ⓒ Ⓓ	21. Ⓐ Ⓑ Ⓒ Ⓓ	21. Ⓐ Ⓑ Ⓒ Ⓓ	21. Ⓐ Ⓑ Ⓒ Ⓓ
22. Ⓐ Ⓑ Ⓒ Ⓓ	22. Ⓐ Ⓑ Ⓒ Ⓓ	22. Ⓐ Ⓑ Ⓒ Ⓓ	22. Ⓐ Ⓑ Ⓒ Ⓓ
23. Ⓐ Ⓑ Ⓒ Ⓓ	23. Ⓐ Ⓑ Ⓒ Ⓓ	23. Ⓐ Ⓑ Ⓒ Ⓓ	23. Ⓐ Ⓑ Ⓒ Ⓓ
24. Ⓐ Ⓑ Ⓒ Ⓓ	24. Ⓐ Ⓑ Ⓒ Ⓓ	24. Ⓐ Ⓑ Ⓒ Ⓓ	24. Ⓐ Ⓑ Ⓒ Ⓓ
25. Ⓐ Ⓑ Ⓒ Ⓓ	25. Ⓐ Ⓑ Ⓒ Ⓓ	25. Ⓐ Ⓑ Ⓒ Ⓓ	25. Ⓐ Ⓑ Ⓒ Ⓓ
26. Ⓐ Ⓑ Ⓒ Ⓓ	26. Ⓐ Ⓑ Ⓒ Ⓓ	26. Ⓐ Ⓑ Ⓒ Ⓓ	26. Ⓐ Ⓑ Ⓒ Ⓓ
27. Ⓐ Ⓑ Ⓒ Ⓓ	27. Ⓐ Ⓑ Ⓒ Ⓓ	27. Ⓐ Ⓑ Ⓒ Ⓓ	27. Ⓐ Ⓑ Ⓒ Ⓓ
28. Ⓐ Ⓑ Ⓒ Ⓓ	28. Ⓐ Ⓑ Ⓒ Ⓓ	28. Ⓐ Ⓑ Ⓒ Ⓓ	28. Ⓐ Ⓑ Ⓒ Ⓓ
29. Ⓐ Ⓑ Ⓒ Ⓓ	29. Ⓐ Ⓑ Ⓒ Ⓓ	29. Ⓐ Ⓑ Ⓒ Ⓓ	29. Ⓐ Ⓑ Ⓒ Ⓓ
30. Ⓐ Ⓑ Ⓒ Ⓓ	30. Ⓐ Ⓑ Ⓒ Ⓓ	30. Ⓐ Ⓑ Ⓒ Ⓓ	30. Ⓐ Ⓑ Ⓒ Ⓓ

7. Preliminary Readiness Tests

Honest self-appraisal is one of the first steps a candidate should take in deciding what sort of review program will work best for him. As noted in Chapter 3, self-appraisal involves an honest assessment of academic preparation as well as individual work habits. Regarding the latter, it is obvious that different people require differing degrees of outside direction. Some candidates function best in a review course that makes no assumptions about their ability to learn independently of the course activities. Other require the structure of a well designed course but have the ability to guide their own efforts within the course framework.

Assessment of academic preparation is best begun by looking at the AICPA's *Content Specification Outlines* (see Chapter 1). They should be used as checklists for the candidate to evaluate the range and depth of his subject mastery. After this procedure is performed, the need for an organized review program becomes apparent. A second procedure is the use of diagnostic readiness tests that present the candidate with representative CPA exam questions. Such tests give the candidate a rough idea of how, given his current state of knowledge, he could expect to do on the CPA exam were he to sit for it immediately.

The following tests comprise a total of 120 four-option multiple-choice questions. These questions have been selected from past questions on actual CPA examinations. They are of average difficulty and were selected to represent the range of topics tested by four-option multiple-choice questions on each examination section. Though no essay, computational, or other objective formats questions have been included, your score on these tests will provide you with a good idea as to your overall preparedness for the CPA examination.

Allow no more than 45 to 55 minutes for the Business Law and Professional Responsibilities (LPR) and Auditing (AUDIT) sections, no more than 60 to 70 minutes for Accounting and Reporting—Taxation, Managerial, and Governmental and Not-for-Profit Organizations (ARE), and no more than 65 to 75 minutes for Financial Accounting and Reporting—Business Enterprises (FARE). Take each section in one sitting.

Before beginning these readiness tests, be sure to review the test tactics outlined in "Chapter 5—How to Approach CPA Examination Questions." After completing the readiness tests, check your answers against the Answer Key on page 105. Then turn to "Chapter 6—Chart Your Progress and Plan Your Course of Action" for guidance in analyzing your score and planning your review program.

Remember: Read directions carefully!

TESTS

Business Law & Professional Responsibilities (LPR)

(Estimated time—45 to 55 minutes)

Directions: Select the **best** answer for each of the following items. Select only one answer for each item. Answer all items.

1. A CPA firm issues an unqualified opinion on financial statements not prepared in accordance with GAAP. The CPA firm will have acted with scienter in all the following circumstances **except** where the firm
   A. Intentionally disregards the truth.
   B. Has actual knowledge of fraud.
   C. Negligently performs auditing procedures.
   D. Intends to gain monetarily by concealing fraud.

2. A CPA partnership may, without being lawfully subpoenaed or without the client's consent, make client workpapers available to
   A. An individual purchasing the entire partnership.
   B. The IRS.
   C. The SEC.
   D. Any surviving partner(s) on the death of a partner.

3. Generally, an agency relationship is terminated by operation of law in all of the following situations **except** the
   A. Principal's death.
   B. Principal's incapacity.
   C. Agent's renunciation of the agency.
   D. Agent's failure to acquire a necessary business license.

4. On June 5, 1989, Gold rented equipment under a four-year lease. On March 8, 1990, Gold was petitioned involuntarily into bankruptcy under the Federal Bankruptcy Code's liquidation provisions. A trustee was appointed. The fair market value of the equipment exceeds the balance of the lease payments due. The trustee
   A. May **not** reject the equipment lease because the fair market value of the equipment exceeds the balance of the lease payments due.
   B. May elect **not** to assume the equipment lease.
   C. Must assume the equipment lease because its term exceeds one year.
   D. Must assume and subsequently assign the equipment lease.

5. A claim will **not** be discharged in a bankruptcy proceeding if it
   A. Is brought by a secured creditor and remains unsatisfied after receipt of the proceeds from the disposition of the collateral.
   B. Is for unintentional torts that resulted in bodily injury to the claimant.
   C. Arises from an extension of credit based upon false representations.
   D. Arises out of the breach of a contract by the debtor.

6. Which of the following negotiable instruments is subject to the provisions of the UCC Commercial Paper Article?
   A. Installment note payable on the first day of each month.
   B. Warehouse receipt.
   C. Bill of lading payable to order.
   D. Corporate bearer bond with a maturity date of January 1, 1999.

7. Bond fraudulently induced Teal to make a note payable to Wilk, to whom Bond was indebted. Bond delivered the note to Wilk. Wilk negotiated the instrument to Monk, who purchased it with knowledge of the fraud and after it was overdue.

If Wilk qualifies as a holder in due course, which of the following statements is correct?
   A. Monk has the standing of a holder in due course through Wilk.
   B. Teal can successfully assert the defense of fraud in the inducement against Monk.
   C. Monk personally qualifies as a holder in due course.
   D. Teal can successfully assert the defense of fraud in the inducement against Wilk.

8. To satisfy the consideration requirement for a valid contract, the consideration exchanged by the parties must be
   A. Legally sufficient.
   B. Payable in legal tender.
   C. Simultaneously paid and received.
   D. Of the same economic value.

9. Payne entered into a written agreement to sell a parcel of land to Stevens. At the time the agreement was executed, Payne had consumed alcoholic beverages. Payne's ability to understand the nature and terms of the contract was not impaired. Stevens did not believe that Payne was intoxicated. The contract is
   A. Void as a matter of law.
   B. Legally binding on both parties.
   C. Voidable at Payne's option.
   D. Voidable at Stevens' option.

10. In general, which of the following must be contained in articles of incorporation?
    A. Names of the initial officers and their terms of office.
    B. Classes of stock authorized for issuance.
    C. Names of states in which the corporation will be doing business.
    D. Name of the state in which the corporation will maintain its principal place of business.

11. Which of the following statements is correct concerning the similarities between a limited partnership and a corporation?
    A. Each is created under a statute and must file a copy of its certificate with the proper state authorities.
    B. All corporate stockholders and all partners in a limited partnership have limited liability.
    C. Both are recognized for federal income tax purposes as taxable entities.
    D. Both are allowed statutorily to have perpetual existence.

12. Under a nonnegotiable bill of lading, a carrier who accepts goods for shipment, must deliver the goods to
    A. Any holder of the bill of lading.
    B. Any party subsequently named by the seller.
    C. The seller who was issued the bill of lading.
    D. The consignee of the bill of lading.

13. Workers' Compensation Acts require an employer to
    A. Provide coverage for all eligible employees.
    B. Withhold employee contributions from the wages of eligible employees.
    C. Pay an employee the difference between disability payments and full salary.
    D. Contribute to a federal insurance fund.

14. Jay properly created an inter vivos trust naming Kroll as trustee. The trust's sole asset is a fully rented office building. Rental receipts exceed expenditures. The trust instrument is silent about the allocation of items between principal and income. Among the items to be allocated by Kroll during the year are insurance proceeds received as a result of fire damage to the building and the mortgage interest payments made during the year. Which of the following items is(are) properly allocable to principal?

	Insurance proceeds on building	Current mortgage interest payments
A.	No	No
B.	No	Yes
C.	Yes	No
D.	Yes	Yes

15. A trustee's fiduciary duty will probably be violated if the trustee
    A. Invests trust property in government bonds.
    B. Performs accounting services for the trust.
    C. Sells unproductive trust property.
    D. Borrows money from the trust.

16. Under the Securities Act of 1933, the registration of an interstate securities offering is
    A. Required only in transactions involving more than $500,000.
    B. Mandatory, unless the cost to the issuer is prohibitive.
    C. Required, unless there is an applicable exemption.
    D. Intended to prevent the marketing of securities, which pose serious financial risks.

17. Corporations that are exempt from registration under the Securities Exchange Act of 1934 are subject to the Act's
    A. Provisions dealing with the filing of annual reports.
    B. Provisions imposing periodic audits.
    C. Antifraud provisions.
    D. Proxy solicitation provisions.

18. Daly tried to collect on a property insurance policy covering a house that was damaged by fire. The insurer denied recovery, alleging that Daly had no insurable interest in the house. In which of the following situations will the insurer prevail?
    A. The house belongs to a corporation of which Daly is a 50 percent stockholder.
    B. Daly is not the owner of the house but a long-term lessee.
    C. The house is held in trust for Daly's mother and, on her death, will pass to Daly.
    D. Daly gave an unsecured loan to the owner of the house to improve the house.

19. A person who loses a stock certificate is entitled to a new certificate to replace the lost one, provided certain requirements are satisfied. Which of the following is **not** such a requirement?
    A. The request for a new certificate is made before the issuer has notice that the lost certificate has been acquired by a bona fide purchaser.
    B. The owner files a sufficient indemnity bond with the issuer.
    C. The owner satisfies any reasonable requirements of the issuer.
    D. The fair market value of the security is placed in escrow with the issuer for six months.

20. Eller, Fort and Owens do business as Venture Associates, a general partnership. Trent Corp. brought a breach of contract suit against Venture and Eller individually. Trent won the suit and filed a judgment against both Venture and Eller. Trent will generally be able to collect the judgment from
    A. Partnership assets only.
    B. The personal assets of Eller, Fort, and Owens only.
    C. Eller's personal assets only after partnership assets are exhausted.
    D. Eller's personal assets only.

21. Lewis, Clark, and Beal entered into a written agreement to form a partnership. The agreement required that the partners make the following capital contributions: Lewis, $40,000; Clark, $30,000; and Beal, $10,000. It was also agreed that in the event the partnership experienced losses in excess of available capital, Beal would contribute additional capital to the extent of the losses. The partnership agreement was otherwise silent about division of profits and losses. Which of the following statements is correct?
    A. Profits are to be divided among the partners in proportion to their relative capital contributions.
    B. Profits are to be divided equally among the partners.
    C. Losses will be allocated in a manner different from the allocation of profits because the partners contributed different amounts of capital.
    D. Beal's obligation to contribute additional capital would have an effect on the allocation of profit or loss to Beal.

22. A violation of the profession's ethical standards most likely would have occurred when a CPA
    A. Compiled the financial statements of a client that employed the CPA's spouse as a bookkeeper.
    B. Received a fee for referring audit clients to a company that sells limited partnership interests.
    C. Purchased the portion of an insurance company that performs actuarial services for employee benefit plans.
    D. Arranged with a financial institution to collect notes issued by a client in payment of fees due.

23. Ivor, Queen, and Lear own a building as joint tenants with the right of survivorship. Ivor donated his interest in the building to Day Charity by executing and delivering a deed to Day. Both Queen and Lear refused to consent to Ivor's transfer to Day. Subsequently, Queen and Lear died. After their deaths, Day's interest in the building consisted of
    A. Total ownership due to the deaths of Queen and Lear.
    B. No interest because Queen and Lear refused to consent to the transfer.
    C. A 1/3 interest as a joint tenant.
    D. A 1/3 interest as a tenant in common.

24. On April 6, Ford purchased a warehouse from Atwood for $150,000. Atwood had executed two mortgages on the property: a purchase money mortgage given to Lang on March 2, which was not recorded; and a mortgage given to Young on March 9, which was recorded the same day. Ford was unaware of the mortgage to Lang. Under the circumstances,
    A. Ford will take title to the warehouse subject only to Lang's mortgage.
    B. Ford will take title to the warehouse free of Lang's mortgage.
    C. Lang's mortgage is superior to Young's mortgage because Lang's mortgage is a purchase money mortgage.
    D. Lang's mortgage is superior to Young's mortgage because Lang's mortgage was given first in time.

25. An important factor in determining if an express warranty has been created is whether the
    A. Statements made by the seller became part of the basis of the bargain.
    B. Sale was made by a merchant in the regular course of business.
    C. Statements made by the seller were in writing.
    D. Seller intended to create a warranty.

26. Under the UCC Sales Article, which of the following statements is correct concerning a contract involving a merchant seller and a nonmerchant buyer?
    A. Only the seller is obligated to perform the contract in good faith.
    B. The contract will be either a sale or return or sale on approval contract.
    C. The contract may **not** involve the sale of personal property with a price of more than $500.
    D. Whether the UCC Sales Article is applicable does **not** depend on the price of the goods involved.

27. Sun, Inc., manufactures and sells household appliances on credit directly to wholesalers, retailers, and consumers. Sun can perfect its security interest in the appliances without having to file a financing statement or take possession of the appliances if the sale is made by Sun to
    A. Consumers.
    B. Wholesalers that sell to buyers in the ordinary course of business.
    C. Retailers.
    D. Wholesalers that sell to distributors for resale.

28. Under the UCC Transactions Article, if a debtor is in default under a payment obligation secured by goods, the secured party has the right to

	Peacefully repossess goods without judicial process	Reduce the claim to a judgment	Sell the goods and apply the proceeds toward the debt
A.	Yes	Yes	Yes
B.	No	Yes	Yes
C.	Yes	Yes	No
D.	Yes	No	Yes

29. Mane Bank lent Eller $120,000 and received securities valued at $30,000 as collateral. At Mane's request, Salem and Rey agreed to act as uncompensated co-sureties on the loan. The agreement provided that Salem's and Rey's maximum liability would be $120,000 each.

Mane released Rey without Salem's consent. Eller later defaulted when the collateral held by Mane was worthless and the loan balance was $90,000. Salem's maximum liability is
   A. $30,000
   B. $45,000
   C. $60,000
   D. $90,000

30. A distinction between a surety and a co-surety is that only a co-surety is entitled to
   A. Reimbursement (Indemnification).
   B. Subrogation.
   C. Contribution.
   D. Exoneration.

Auditing (AUDIT)

(Estimated time—45 to 55 minutes)

Directions: Select the **best** answer for each of the following items. Select only one answer for each item. Answer all items.

1. Tracing bills of lading to sales invoices provides evidence that
   A. Shipments to customers were invoiced.
   B. Shipments to customers were recorded as sales.
   C. Recorded sales were shipped.
   D. Invoiced sales were shipped.

2. Which of the following procedures is **least** likely to be performed before the balance sheet date?
   A. Testing of internal control over cash.
   B. Confirmation of receivables.
   C. Search for unrecorded liabilities.
   D. Observation of inventory.

3. Which of the following statements concerning evidential matter is correct?
   A. Competent evidence supporting management's assertions should be convincing rather than merely persuasive.
   B. An effective internal control structure contributes little to the reliability of the evidence created within the entity.
   C. The cost of obtaining evidence is **not** an important consideration to an auditor in deciding what evidence should be obtained.
   D. A client's accounting data **cannot** be considered sufficient audit evidence to support the financial statements.

4. The negative request form of accounts receivable confirmation is useful particularly when the

	Assessed level of control risk relating to receivables is	Number of small balances is	Consideration by the recipient is
A.	Low	Many	Likely
B.	Low	Few	Unlikely
C.	High	Few	Likely
D.	High	Many	Likely

5. To satisfy the valuation assertion when auditing an investment accounted for by the equity method, an auditor most likely would
   A. Inspect the stock certificates evidencing the investment.
   B. Examine the audited financial statements of the investee company.
   C. Review the broker's advice or canceled check for the investment's acquisition.
   D. Obtain market quotations from financial newspapers or periodicals.

6. Which of the following is not an audit procedure that the independent auditor would perform concerning litigation, claims, and assessments?
   A. Obtain assurance from management that it has disclosed all unasserted claims that the lawyer has advised are probable of assertion and must be disclosed.
   B. Confirm directly with the client's lawyer that all claims have been recorded in the financial statements.

C. Inquire of and discuss with management the policies and procedures adopted for identifying, evaluating, and accounting for litigation, claims, and assessments.

D. Obtain from management a description and evaluation of litigation, claims, and assessments existing at the balance sheet date.

7. As the acceptable level of detection risk decreases, an auditor may change the

A. Timing of substantive tests by performing them at an interim date rather than at year end.

B. Nature of substantive tests from a less effective to a more effective procedure.

C. Timing of tests of controls by performing them at several dates rather than at one time.

D. Assessed level of inherent risk to a higher amount.

8. Analytical procedures used in planning an audit should focus on identifying

A. Material weaknesses in the internal control structure.

B. The predictability of financial data from individual transactions.

C. The various assertions that are embodied in the financial statements.

D. Areas that may represent specific risks relevant to the audit.

9. When considering the objectivity of internal auditors, an independent auditor should

A. Test a sample of the transactions and balances that the internal auditors examined.

B. Determine the organizational level to which the internal auditors report.

C. Evaluate the quality control program in effect for the internal auditors.

D. Examine documentary evidence of the work performed by the internal auditors.

10. Which of the following procedures would an auditor **least** likely perform in planning a financial statement audit?

A. Coordinating the assistance of entity personnel in data preparation.

B. Discussing matters that may affect the audit with firm personnel responsible for non-audit services to the entity.

C. Selecting a sample of vendors' invoices for comparison to receiving reports.

D. Reading the current year's interim financial statements.

11. An explanatory paragraph following the opinion paragraph of an auditor's report describes an uncertainty as follows:

As discussed in Note X to the financial statements, the Company is a defendant in a lawsuit alleging infringement of certain patent rights and claiming damages. Discovery proceedings are in progress. The ultimate outcome of the litigation cannot presently be determined. Accordingly, no provision for any liability that may result upon adjudication has been made in the accompanying financial statements.

What type of opinion should the auditor express under these circumstances?

A. Unqualified.

B. "Subject to" qualified.

C. "Except for" qualified.

D. Disclaimer.

12. If a publicly held company issues financial statements that purport to present its financial position and results of operations but omits the statement of cash flows, the auditor ordinarily will express a(an)

A. Unqualified opinion with a separate explanatory paragraph.

B. Disclaimer of opinion.

C. Adverse opinion.

D. Qualified opinion.

13. An auditor has previously expressed a qualified opinion on the financial statements of a prior period because of a departure from generally accepted accounting principles. The prior-period financial statements are restated in the current period to conform with generally accepted accounting principles. The auditor's updated report on the prior-period financial statements should

A. Express an unqualified opinion concerning the restated financial statements.

B. Be accompanied by the original auditor's report on the prior period.

C. Bear the same date as the original auditor's report on the prior period.

D. Qualify the opinion concerning the restated financial statements because of a change in accounting principle.

14. King, CPA, was engaged to audit the financial statements of Newton Company after its fiscal year had ended. King neither observed the inventory count nor confirmed the receivables by

direct communication with debtors, but was satisfied concerning both after applying alternative procedures. King's auditor's report most likely contained a(an)

A. Qualified opinion.
B. Disclaimer of opinion.
C. Unqualified opinion.
D. Unqualified opinion with an explanatory paragraph.

15. How does an auditor make the following representations when issuing the standard auditor's report on comparative financial statements?

	Examination of evidence on a test basis	Consistent application of accounting principles
A.	Explicitly	Explicitly
B.	Implicitly	Implicitly
C.	Implicitly	Explicitly
D.	Explicitly	Implicitly

16. A CPA firm evaluates its personnel advancement experience to ascertain whether individuals meeting stated criteria are assigned increased degrees of responsibility. This is evidence of the firm's adherence to which of the following prescribed standards?

A. Quality control.
B. Human resources.
C. Supervision and review.
D. Professional development.

17. Which of the following standards requires a critical review of the work done and the judgment exercised by those assisting in an audit at every level of supervision?

A. Proficiency.
B. Audit risk.
C. Inspection.
D. Due care.

18. For an entity's financial statements to be presented fairly in conformity with generally accepted accounting principles, the principles selected should

A. Be applied on a basis consistent with those followed in the prior year.
B. Be approved by the Auditing Standards Board or the appropriate industry subcommittee.
C. Reflect transactions in a manner that presents the financial statements within a range of acceptable limits.
D. Match the principles used by most other entities within the entity's particular industry.

19. When an auditor tests a computerized accounting system, which of the following is true of the test data approach?

A. Test data must consist of all possible valid and invalid conditions.
B. The program tested is different from the program used throughout the year by the client.
C. Several transactions of each type must be tested.
D. Test data are processed by the client's computer program under the auditor's control.

20. An auditor would **least** likely use computer software to

A. Access client data files.
B. Prepare spreadsheets.
C. Assess EDP control risk.
D. Construct parallel simulations.

21. Which of the following statements about internal control structure is correct?

A. A properly maintained internal control structure reasonably ensures that collusion among employees cannot occur.
B. The establishment and maintenance of the internal control structure is an important responsibility of the internal auditor.
C. An exceptionally strong internal control structure is enough for the auditor to eliminate substantive tests on a significant account balance.
D. The cost-benefit relationship is a primary criterion that should be considered in designing an internal control structure.

22. After obtaining an understanding of an entity's internal control structure, an auditor may assess control risk at the maximum level for some assertions because the auditor

A. Believes the internal control policies and procedures are unlikely to be effective.
B. Determines that the pertinent internal control structure elements are **not** well documented.
C. Performs tests of controls to restrict detection risk to an acceptable level.
D. Identifies internal control policies and procedures that are likely to prevent material misstatements.

23. To obtain evidential matter about control risk, an auditor ordinarily selects tests from a variety of techniques, including

A. Analysis.
B. Confirmation.
C. Reperformance.
D. Comparison.

24. When control risk is assessed at the maximum level for all financial statement assertions, an auditor should document the auditor's

	Understanding of the entity's internal control structure elements	Conclusion that control risk is at the maximum level	Basis for concluding that control risk is at the maximum level
A.	Yes	No	No
B.	Yes	Yes	No
C.	No	Yes	Yes
D.	Yes	Yes	Yes

25. Which of the following controls would be most effective in assuring that the proper custody of assets in the investing cycle is maintained?
    A. Direct access to securities in the safety deposit box is limited to only one corporate officer.
    B. Personnel who post investment transactions to the general ledger are not permitted to update the investment subsidiary ledger.
    C. The purchase and sale of investments are executed on the specific authorization of the board of directors.
    D. The recorded balances in the investment subsidiary ledger are periodically compared with the contents of the safety deposit box by independent personnel.

26. An auditor's report would be designated a special report when it is issued in connection with
    A. Interim financial information of a publicly held company that is subject to a limited review.
    B. Compliance with aspects of regulatory requirements related to audited financial statements.
    C. Application of accounting principles to specified transactions.
    D. Limited use prospective financial statements such as a financial projection.

27. Before issuing a report on the compilation of financial statements of a nonpublic entity, the accountant should
    A. Apply analytical procedures to selected financial data to discover any material misstatements.
    B. Corroborate at least a sample of the assertions management has embodied in the financial statements.
    C. Inquire of the client's personnel whether the financial statements omit substantially all disclosures.
    D. Read the financial statements to consider whether the financial statements are free from obvious material errors.

28. Which of the following statements concerning prospective financial statements is correct?
    A. Only a financial forecast would normally be appropriate for limited use.
    B. Only a financial projection would normally be appropriate for general use.
    C. Any type of prospective financial statements would normally be appropriate for limited use.
    D. Any type of prospective financial statements would normally be appropriate for general use.

29. An auditor is testing internal control procedures that are evidenced on an entity's vouchers by matching random numbers with voucher numbers. If a random number matches the number of a voided voucher, that voucher ordinarily should be replaced by another voucher in the random sample if the voucher
    A. Constitutes a deviation.
    B. Has been properly voided.
    C. Cannot be located.
    D. Represents an immaterial dollar amount.

30. The risk of incorrect acceptance and the likelihood of assessing control risk too low relate to the
    A. Effectiveness of the audit.
    B. Efficiency of the audit.
    C. Preliminary estimates of materiality levels.
    D. Allowable risk of tolerable error.

Accounting & Reporting— Taxation, Managerial, and Governmental and Not-for-Profit Organizations (ARE)

(Estimated time—60 to 70 minutes)

Directions: Select the **best** answer for each of the following items. Select only one answer for each item. Answer all items.

1. At the end of Killo Co.'s first year of operations, 1,000 units of inventory remained on hand. Variable and fixed manufacturing costs per unit

were $90 and $20, respectively. If Killo uses absorption costing rather than direct (variable) costing, the result would be a higher pretax income of

A. $0
B. $20,000
C. $70,000
D. $90,000

2. Jones, a department manager, exercises control over the department's costs. Following is selected information relating to the department for July:

Variable factory overhead
  Budgeted based on standard hours
    allowed $80,000
  Actual   85,000

Fixed factory overhead
  Budgeted   25,000
  Actual   27,000

The department's unfavorable spending variance for July was

A. $7,000
B. $5,000
C. $2,000
D. $0

3. Cay Co.'s 1991 fixed manufacturing overhead costs totaled $100,000, and variable selling costs totaled $80,000. Under direct costing, how should these costs be classified?

	Period costs	Product costs
A.	$0	$180,000
B.	$ 80,000	$100,000
C.	$100,000	$ 80,000
D.	$180,000	$0

4. In a traditional job order cost system, the issue of indirect materials to a production department increases

A. Stores control.
B. Work in process control.
C. Factory overhead control.
D. Factory overhead applied.

5. A manufacturing company prepares income statements using both absorption and variable costing methods. At the end of a period actual sales revenues, total gross profit, and total contribution margin approximated budgeted figures; whereas net income was substantially greater than the budgeted amount. There were no beginning or ending inventories. The most likely

explanation of the net income increase is that, compared to budget, actual

A. Manufacturing fixed costs had increased.
B. Selling and administrative fixed expenses had decreased.
C. Sales prices and variable costs had increased proportionately.
D. Sales prices had declined proportionately less than variable costs.

6. On June 1, 1993, Ben Rork sold 500 shares of Kul Corp. stock. Rork had received this stock on May 1, 1993, as a bequest from the estate of his uncle, who died on March 1, 1993. Rork's basis was determined by reference to the stock's fair market value on March 1, 1993. Rork's holding period for this stock was

A. Short-term.
B. Long-term.
C. Short-term if sold at a gain; long-term if sold at a loss.
D. Long-term if sold at a gain; short-term if sold at a loss.

7. With regard to consolidated returns, which one of the following statements is correct?

A. The common parent must directly own 51 percent or more of the total voting power of all corporations included in the consolidated return.
B. Of all intercompany dividends paid by the subsidiaries to the parent, 70 percent are excludible from taxable income on the consolidated return.
C. Only corporations that issue their audited financial statements on a consolidated basis may file consolidated tax returns.
D. Operating losses of one group member may be used to offset operating profits of the other members included in the consolidated return.

8. Ati Corp. has two common stockholders. Ati derives all of its income from investments in stocks and securities, and it regularly distributes 51 percent of its taxable income as dividends to its stockholders. Ati is a

A. Personal holding company.
B. Regulated investment company.
C. Corporation subject to the accumulated earnings tax.
D. Corporation subject to tax only on income not distributed to stockholders.

9. An S corporation may deduct
   A. Charitable contributions within the percentage of income limitation applicable to corporations.
   B. Net operating loss carryovers.
   C. Foreign income taxes.
   D. Compensation of officers.

10. Eng and Lew, both U.S. citizens, died in 1993. Eng made taxable lifetime gifts of $100,000 that are **not** included in Eng's gross estate. Lew made no lifetime gifts. At the dates of death, Eng's gross estate was $300,000, and Lew's gross estate was $400,000. A federal estate tax return must be filed for

	Eng	Lew
A.	No	No
B.	No	Yes
C.	Yes	No
D.	Yes	Yes

11. To qualify as an exempt organization other than an employees' qualified pension or profit-sharing trust, the applicant
    A. Is barred from incorporating and issuing capital stock.
    B. Must file a written application with the Internal Revenue Service.
    C. Cannot operate under the "lodge system" under which payments are made to its members for sick benefits.
    D. Need **not** be specifically identified as one of the classes on which exemption is conferred by the Internal Revenue Code, provided that the organization's purposes and activities are of a nonprofit nature.

12. Ed and Ann Ross were divorced in January 1993. In accordance with the divorce decree, Ed transferred the title in their home to Ann in 1993. The home, which had a fair market value of $150,000, was subject to a $50,000 mortgage that had 20 more years to run. Monthly mortgage payments amount to $1,000. Under the terms of settlement, Ed is obligated to make the mortgage payments on the home for the full remaining 20-year term of the indebtedness, regardless of how long Ann lives. Ed made 12 mortgage payments in 1993. What amount is taxable as alimony in Ann's 1993 return?
    A. $0
    B. $ 12,000
    C. $100,000
    D. $112,000

13. In 1993, Smith paid $6,000 to the tax collector of Wek City for realty taxes on a two-family house owned by Smith's mother. Of this amount, $2,800 covered back taxes for 1992, and $3,200 covered 1993 taxes. Smith resides on the second floor of the house, and his mother resides on the first floor. In Smith's itemized deductions on his 1993 return, what amount was Smith entitled to claim for realty taxes?
    A. $6,000
    B. $3,200
    C. $3,000
    D. $0

14. Which one of the following expenditures qualifies as a deductible medical expense for tax purposes?
    A. Vitamins for general health **not** prescribed by a physician.
    B. Health club dues.
    C. Transportation to physician's office for required medical care.
    D. Mandatory employment taxes for basic coverage under Medicare A.

15. The basis of property (other than money) distributed by a partnership to a partner, in complete liquidation of the partner's interest, shall be an amount equal to the
    A. Fair market value of the property.
    B. Book value of the property.
    C. Adjusted basis of such partner's interest in the partnership, reduced by any money distributed in the same transaction.
    D. Adjusted basis of such partner's interest in the partnership, increased by any money distributed in the same transaction.

16. Kim Co.'s profit center Zee had 1991 operating income of $200,000 before a $50,000 imputed interest charge for using Kim's assets. Kim's aggregate net income from all of its profit centers was $2,000,000. During 1991, Kim declared and paid dividends of $30,000 and $70,000 on its preferred and common stock, respectively. Zee's 1991 residual income was
    A. $140,000
    B. $143,000
    C. $147,000
    D. $150,000

17. The following information pertains to Syl Co.:

Sales $800,000
Variable costs 160,000
Fixed costs 40,000

What is Syl's break-even point in sales dollars?
A. $200,000
B. $160,000
C. $ 50,000
D. $ 40,000

18. Lin Company is buying machinery it expects will increase average annual operating income by $40,000. The initial increase in the required investment is $60,000, and the average increase in required investment is $30,000. To compute the accrual accounting rate of return, what amount should be used as the numerator in the ratio?
A. $20,000
B. $30,000
C. $40,000
D. $60,000

19. Controllable revenue would be included in a performance report for a

	Profit center	Cost center
A.	No	No
B.	No	Yes
C.	Yes	No
D.	Yes	Yes

20. Vince Inc. has developed and patented a new laser disc reading device that will be marketed internationally. Which of the following factors should Vince consider in pricing the device?

I. Quality of the new device.
II. Life of the new device.
III. Customers' relative preference for quality compared to price.

A. I and II only.
B. I and III only.
C. II and III only.
D. I, II, and III.

21. The following information for the year ended June 30, 1988, pertains to a proprietary fund established by Burwood Village in connection with Burwood's public parking facilities:

Receipts from users of parking
   facilities $400,000

Expenditures
  Parking meters 210,000
  Salaries and other cash expenses 90,000
  Depreciation of parking meters 70,000

For the year ended June 30, 1988, this proprietary fund should report net income of
A. $0
B. $ 30,000
C. $100,000
D. $240,000

22. During its fiscal year ended June 30, 1988, Lake County financed the following projects by special assessments:

Capital improvements $2,000,000
Service-type projects 800,000

For financial reporting purposes, what amount should appear in special assessment funds?
A. $2,800,000
B. $2,000,000
C. $ 800,000
D. $0

23. Ridge City issued the following bonds during the year ended July 31, 1988:

General obligation bonds issued for
  the Ridge water and sewer enterprise
  fund that will service the debt $700,000
Revenue bonds to be repaid from admission
  fees collected by the Ridge municipal
  swimming pool enterprise fund 290,000

The amount of these bonds that should be accounted for in Ridge's general long-term debt account group is
A. $990,000.
B. $700,000.
C. $290,000.
D. $0.

24. The fund balance reserved for encumbrances account of a governmental unit is decreased when
A. Supplies previously ordered are received.
B. A purchase order is approved.
C. The vouchers are paid.
D. Appropriations are recorded.

25. The revenues control account of a governmental unit is increased when
A. The budget is recorded.
B. Property taxes are recorded.
C. Appropriations are recorded.
D. The budgetary accounts are closed.

26. In April 1987, Alice Reed donated $100,000 cash to her church, with the stipulation that the income generated from this gift is to be paid to Alice during her lifetime. The conditions of this donation are that, after Alice dies, the principal can be used by the church for any purpose voted on by the church elders. The church received interest of $8,000 on the $100,000 for the year ended March 31, 1988, and the interest was remitted to Alice. In the church's March 31, 1988, financial statements
    A. $8,000 should be reported under support and revenue in the activity statement.
    B. $92,000 should be reported under support and revenue in the activity statement.
    C. $100,000 should be reported as support in the activity statement.
    D. The gift and its terms should be disclosed only in notes to the financial statements.

27. The following information was available from Forest College's accounting records for its current funds for the year ended March 31, 1988:

    Restricted gifts received
Expended	$ 100,000
Temporarily restricted	300,000

    Unrestricted gifts received
Expended	600,000
Not expended	75,000

    What amount should be included in unrestricted current funds revenues for the year ended March 31, 1988?
    A. $ 600,000
    B. $ 700,000
    C. $ 775,000
    D. $1,000,000

28. The following expenditures were among those incurred by Alma University during 1987:

Administrative data processing	$ 50,000
Scholarships and fellowships	100,000
Operation and maintenance of physical plant	200,000

    The amount to be included in the functional classification "Institutional Support" expenditures account is
    A. $ 50,000
    B. $150,000
    C. $250,000
    D. $350,000

29. Which of the following funds are usually encountered in a not-for-profit private university?

	Current funds	Plant funds
A.	No	Yes
B.	No	No
C.	Yes	No
D.	Yes	Yes

30. Revenue of a hospital from grants specified by the grantor for research would normally be included in
    A. Nonoperating gains.
    B. Other operating revenue.
    C. Patient service revenue.
    D. Ancillary service revenue.

Financial Accounting and Reporting—Business Enterprises (FARE)

(Estimated time—65 to 75 minutes)

Directions: Select the **best** answer for each of the following items. Select only one answer for each item. Answer all items.

1. At December 31, 1992, Date Co. awaits judgment on a lawsuit for a competitor's infringement of Date's patent. Legal counsel believes it is probable that Date will win the suit and indicated the most likely award together with a range of possible awards. How should the lawsuit be reported in Date's 1992 financial statements?
    A. In note disclosure only.
    B. By accrual for the most likely award.
    C. By accrual for the lowest amount of the range of possible awards.
    D. Neither in note disclosure nor by accrual.

2. On February 12, 1992, VIP Publishing, Inc. purchased the copyright to a book for $15,000 and agreed to pay royalties equal to 10 percent of book sales, with a guaranteed minimum royalty of $60,000. VIP had book sales of $800,000 in 1992. In its 1992 income statement, what amount should VIP report as royalty expense?
    A. $60,000
    B. $75,000
    C. $80,000
    D. $95,000

3. Dunne Co. sells equipment service contracts that cover a two-year period. The sales price of each contract is $600. Dunne's past experience is that, of the total dollars spent for repairs on service

contracts, 40 percent is incurred evenly during the first contract year and 60 percent evenly during the second contract year. Dunne sold 1,000 contracts evenly throughout 1992. In its December 31, 1992, balance sheet, what amount should Dunne report as deferred service contract revenue?

A. $540,000
B. $480,000
C. $360,000
D. $300,000

4. On July 1, 1992, York Co. purchased as a long-term investment $1,000,000 of Park, Inc.'s 8 percent bonds for $946,000, including accrued interest of $40,000. The bonds were purchased to yield 10 percent interest. The bonds mature on January 1, 1999, and pay interest annually on January 1. York uses the effective interest method of amortization. In its December 31, 1992, balance sheet, what amount should York report as investment in bonds?

A. $911,300
B. $916,600
C. $953,300
D. $960,600

5. Lance Corp.'s statement of cash flows for the year ended September 30, 1992, was prepared using the indirect method and included the following:

Net income	$60,000
Noncash adjustments:	
Depreciation expense	9,000
Increase in accounts receivable	(5,000)
Decrease in inventory	40,000
Decrease in accounts payable	(12,000)
Net cash flows from operating activities	$92,000

Lance reported revenues from customers of $75,000 in its 1992 income statement. What amount of cash did Lance receive from its customers during the year ended September 30, 1992?

A. $80,000
B. $70,000
C. $65,000
D. $55,000

6. On September 1, 1992, Canary Co. sold used equipment for a cash amount equaling its carrying amount for both book and tax purposes. On September 15, 1992, Canary replaced the equipment by paying cash and signing a note payable for new equipment. The cash paid for the new equipment exceeded the cash received for the old equipment. How should these equipment transactions be reported in Canary's 1992 statement of cash flows?

A. Cash outflow equal to the cash paid less the cash received.
B. Cash outflow equal to the cash paid and note payable less the cash received.
C. Cash inflow equal to the cash received and a cash outflow equal to the cash paid and note payable.
D. Cash inflow equal to the cash received and a cash outflow equal to the cash paid.

7. Parker Corp. owns 80 percent of Smith Inc.'s common stock. During 1991, Parker sold Smith $250,000 of inventory on the same terms as sales made to third parties. Smith sold all of the inventory purchased from Parker in 1991. The following information pertains to Smith and Parker's sales for 1991:

	Parker	Smith
Sales	$1,000,000	$700,000
Cost of sales	400,000	350,000
	$ 600,000	$350,000

What amount should Parker report as cost of sales in its 1991 consolidated income statement?

A. $750,000
B. $680,000
C. $500,000
D. $430,000

8. Penn, Inc., a manufacturing company, owns 75 percent of the common stock of Sell, Inc., an investment company. Sell owns 60 percent of the common stock of Vane, Inc., an insurance company. In Penn's consolidated financial statements, should consolidation accounting or equity method accounting be used for Sell and Vane?

A. Consolidation used for Sell and equity method used for Vane.
B. Consolidation used for both Sell and Vane.
C. Equity method used for Sell and consolidation used for Vane.
D. Equity method used for both Sell and Vane.

9. Tod Corp. wrote off $100,000 of obsolete inventory at December 31, 1990. The effect of this write-off was to decrease

A. Both the current and acid-test ratios.
B. Only the current ratio.
C. Only the acid-test ratio.
D. Neither the current nor the acid-test ratios.

10. On January 2, 1991, Air, Inc. agreed to pay its former president $300,000 under a deferred compensation arrangement. Air should have recorded this expense in 1990 but did not do so. Air's reported income tax expense would have been $70,000 lower in 1990 had it properly accrued this deferred compensation. In its December 31, 1991, financial statements, Air should adjust the beginning balance of its retained earnings by a
   A. $230,000 credit.
   B. $230,000 debit.
   C. $300,000 credit.
   D. $370,000 debit.

11. South Co. purchased a machine that was installed and placed in service on January 1, 1990, at a cost of $240,000. Salvage value was estimated at $40,000. The machine is being depreciated over 10 years by the double-declining-balance method. For the year ended December 31, 1991, what amount should South report as depreciation expense?
   A. $48,000
   B. $38,400
   C. $32,000
   D. $21,600

12. Bensol Co. and Sable Co. exchanged similar trucks with fair values in excess of carrying amounts. In addition, Bensol paid Sable to compensate for the difference in truck values. As a consequence of the exchange, Sable recognizes
   A. A gain equal to the difference between the fair value and carrying amount of the truck given up.
   B. A gain determined by the proportion of cash received to the total consideration.
   C. A loss determined by the proportion of cash received to the total consideration.
   D. Neither a gain **nor** a loss.

13. On September 1, 1990, Cano & Co., a U.S. corporation, sold merchandise to a foreign firm for 250,000 francs. Terms of the sale require payment in francs on February 1, 1991. On September 1, 1990, the spot exchange rate was $.20 per franc. At December 31, 1990, Cano's year end, the spot rate was $.19, but the rate increased to $.22 by February 1, 1991, when payment was received. How much should Cano report as foreign exchange gain or loss in its 1991 income statement?
   A. $0
   B. $2,500 loss.

C. $5,000 gain.
D. $7,500 gain.

14. West Corp. leased a building and received the $36,000 annual rental payment on June 15, 1992. The beginning of the lease was July 1, 1992. Rental income is taxable when received. West's tax rates are 30 percent for 1992 and 40 percent thereafter. West has elected early adoption of FASB Statement No. 109, "Accounting for Income Taxes." West had no other permanent or temporary differences. West determined that no valuation allowance was needed. What amount of deferred tax asset should West report in its December 31, 1992, balance sheet?
   A. $ 5,400
   B. $ 7,200
   C. $10,800
   D. $14,400

15. Dolce Co., which began operations on January 1, 1990, appropriately uses the installment method of accounting to record revenues. The following information is available for the years ended December 31, 1990 and 1991:

	1990	1991
Sales	$1,000,000	$2,000,000
Gross profit realized on sales made in:		
1990	150,000	90,000
1991	—	200,000
Gross profit percentages	30%	40%

   What amount of installment accounts receivable should Dolce report in its December 31, 1991, balance sheet?
   A. $ 1,225,000
   B. $ 1,300,000
   C. $ 1,700,000
   D. $ 1,775,000

16. Malden, Inc., has two patents that have allegedly been infringed by competitors. After investigation, legal counsel informed Malden that it had a weak case on patent A34 and a strong case in regard to patent B19. Malden incurred additional legal fees to stop infringement on B19. Both patents have a remaining legal life of 8 years. How should Malden account for these legal costs incurred relating to the two patents?
   A. Expense costs for A34 and capitalize costs for B19.
   B. Expense costs for both A34 and B19.

C. Capitalize costs for both A34 and B19.

D. Capitalize costs for A34 and expense costs for B19.

17. Jel Co., a consignee, paid the freight costs for goods shipped from Dale Co., a consignor. These freight costs are to be deducted from Jel's payment to Dale when the consignment goods are sold. Until Jel sells the goods, the freight costs should be included in Jel's

A. Cost of goods sold.

B. Freight-out costs.

C. Selling expenses.

D. Accounts receivable.

18. The following information pertains to Lark Corp.'s available-for-sale securities portfolio:

	December	
	1991	1990
Cost	$200,000	$200,000
Market value	240,000	180,000

Differences between cost and market values are considered to be temporary. The decline in market value was properly accounted for at December 31, 1990 under the provisions of FASB Statement #115, "Accounting for Certain Investments in Debt and Equity Securities." By what amount should the unrealized holding gain or loss account on available-for-sale securities be credited from December 31, 1990, to December 31, 1991?

A. $60,000

B. $40,000

C. $20,000

D. $0

19. Pal Corp.'s 1991 dividend income included only part of the dividend received from its Ima Corp. investment. Ima Corp.'s common stock is not publicly traded. The balance of the dividend reduced Pal's carrying amount for its Ima investment. This reflects that Pal accounts for its Ima investment by the

A. Cost method, and only a portion of Ima's 1991 dividends represent earnings after Pal's acquisition.

B. Cost method, and its carrying amount exceeded the proportionate share of Ima's market value.

C. Equity method, and Ima incurred a loss in 1991.

D. Equity method, and its carrying amount exceeded the proportionate share of Ima's market value.

20. On December 31, 1990, Day Co. leased a new machine from Parr with the following pertinent information:

Lease term	6 years
Annual rental payable at beginning of each year	$50,000
Useful life of machine	8 years
Day's incremental borrowing rate	15%
Implicit interest rate in lease (known by Day)	12%
Present value of an annuity of 1 in advance for 6 periods at	
12%	4.61
15%	4.35

The lease is not renewable, and the machine reverts to Parr at the termination of the lease. The cost of the machine on Parr's accounting records is $375,500. At the beginning of the lease term, Day should record a lease liability of

A. $375,500.

B. $230,500.

C. $217,500.

D. $0.

21. Jay's lease payments are made at the end of each period. Jay's liability for a capital lease would be reduced periodically by the

A. Minimum lease payment less the portion of the minimum lease payment allocable to interest.

B. Minimum lease payment plus the amortization of the related asset.

C. Minimum lease payment less the amortization of the related asset.

D. Minimum lease payment.

22. Case Cereal Co. frequently distributes coupons to promote new products. On October 1, 1991, Case mailed 1,000,000 coupons for $.45 off each box of cereal purchased. Case expects 120,000 of these coupons to be redeemed before the December 31, 1991, expiration date. It takes 30 days from the redemption date for Case to receive the coupons from the retailers. Case reimburses the retailers an additional $.05 for each coupon redeemed. As of December 31, 1991, Case had paid retailers $25,000 related to these coupons and had 50,000 coupons on hand that had not been processed for payments. What amount should Case report as a liability for coupons in its December 31, 1991, balance sheet?

A. $35,000
B. $29,000
C. $25,000
D. $22,500

23. In 1991, a contract dispute between Dollis Co. and Brooks Co. was submitted to binding arbitration. In 1991, each party's attorney indicated privately that the probable award in Dollis' favor could be reasonably estimated. In 1992, the arbitrator decided in favor of Dollis. When should Dollis and Brooks recognize their respective gain and loss?

	Dollis' gain	Brooks' loss
A.	1991	1991
B.	1991	1992
C.	1992	1991
D.	1992	1992

24. A company uses the completed-contract method to account for a long-term construction contract. Revenue is recognized when recorded progress billings

	Are collected	Exceed recorded costs
A.	Yes	Yes
B.	No	No
C.	Yes	No
D.	No	Yes

25. Roberts and Smith drafted a partnership agreement that lists the following assets contributed at the partnership's formation:

	Contributed by	
	Roberts	Smith
Cash	$20,000	$30,000
Inventory	—	15,000
Building	—	40,000
Furniture & Equipment	15,000	—

The building is subject to a mortgage of $10,000, which the partnership has assumed. The partnership agreement also specifies that profits and losses are to be distributed evenly. What amounts should be recorded as capital for Roberts and Smith at the formation of the partnership?

	Roberts	Smith
A.	$35,000	$85,000
B.	$35,000	$75,000
C.	$55,000	$55,000
D.	$60,000	$60,000

26. Nome Co. sponsors a defined benefit plan covering all employees. Benefits are based on years of service and compensation levels at the time of retirement. Nome determined that, as of September 30, 1992, its accumulated benefit obligation was $380,000, and its plan assets had a $290,000 fair value. Nome's September 30, 1992, trial balance showed prepaid pension cost of $20,000. In its September 30, 1992, balance sheet, what amount should Nome report as additional pension liability?
A. $110,000
B. $360,000
C. $380,000
D. $400,000

27. The following information pertains to Tara Co.'s accounts receivable at December 31, 1992:

Days outstanding	Amount	Estimated % uncollectible
0 - 60	$120,000	1%
61 - 120	90,000	2%
Over 120	100,000	6%
	$310,000	

During 1992, Tara wrote off $7,000 in receivables and recovered $4,000 that had been written off in prior years. Tara's December 31, 1991, allowance for uncollectible accounts was $22,000. Under the aging method, what amount of allowance for uncollectible accounts should Tara report at December 31, 1992?
A. $ 9,000
B. $10,000
C. $13,000
D. $19,000

28. On Merf's April 30, 1993, balance sheet a note receivable was reported as a noncurrent asset and its accrued interest for eight months was reported as a current asset. Which of the following terms would fit Merf's note receivable?
A. Both principal and interest amounts are payable on August 31, 1993, and August 31, 1994.
B. Principal and interest are due December 31, 1993.
C. Both principal and interest amounts are payable on December 31, 1993, and December 31, 1994.
D. Principal is due August 31, 1994, and interest is due August 31, 1993, and August 31, 1994.

29. Rudd Corp. had 700,000 shares of common stock authorized and 300,000 shares outstanding at December 31, 1991. The following events occurred during 1992:

January 31	Declared 10% stock dividend
June 30	Purchased 100,000 shares
August 1	Reissued 50,000 shares
November 30	Declared 2-for-1 stock split

At December 31, 1992, how many shares of common stock did Rudd have outstanding?

A. 560,000
B. 600,000
C. 630,000
D. 660,000

30. Quoit, Inc. issued preferred stock with detachable common stock warrants. The issue price exceeded the sum of the warrants' fair value and the preferred stocks' par value. The preferred stocks' fair value was not determinable. What amount should be assigned to the warrants outstanding?

A. Total proceeds.
B. Excess of proceeds preferred stock over the par value of the preferred stock.
C. The proportion of the proceeds that the warrants' fair value bears to the preferred stocks' par value.
D. The fair value of the warrants.

Question #	Answer	Topical Area
4	B	Bankruptcy
5	C	Bankruptcy
6	A	Commercial Paper
7	A	Commercial Paper
8	A	Contracts
9	B	Contracts
10	B	Corporations
11	A	Corporations
12	D	Documents of Title
13	A	Employment Regulations
14	D	Estates and Trusts
15	C	Estates and Trusts
16	C	Federal Securities Regulations
17	C	Federal Securities Regulations
18	D	Insurance
19	D	Investment Securities
20	C	Partnerships
21	B	Partnerships
22	B	Professional Responsibilities
23	D	Property
24	B	Property
25	A	Sales
26	D	Sales
27	A	Secured Transactions
28	A	Secured Transactions
29	B	Suretyship and Creditor's Rights
30	C	Suretyship and Creditor's Rights

ANSWER KEY— FOUR-OPTION MULTIPLE-CHOICE QUESTIONS

Be sure to read "Chapter 6—Chart Your Progress and Plan Your Course of Action." It will help you analyze your test and plan your study program.

Business Law & Professional Responsibilities (LPR)

Question #	Answer	Topical Area
1	C	Accountants' Legal Responsibility
2	D	Accountants' Legal Responsibility
3	C	Agency

Auditing (AUDIT)

Question #	Answer	Topical Area
1	A	Audit Evidence
2	C	Audit Evidence
3	D	Audit Evidence
4	A	Audit Evidence
5	B	Audit Evidence
6	B	Audit Evidence
7	B	Audit Planning
8	D	Audit Planning
9	B	Audit Planning
10	C	Audit Planning
11	A	Audit Reporting Standards
12	D	Audit Reporting Standards
13	A	Audit Reporting Standards
14	C	Audit Reporting Standards
15	D	Audit Reporting Standards

QUESTION #	ANSWER	TOPICAL AREA
16	A	Auditing Concepts and Standards
17	D	Auditing Concepts and Standards
18	C	Auditing Concepts and Standards
19	D	Electronic Data Processing
20	C	Electronic Data Processing
21	D	Internal Control
22	A	Internal Control
23	C	Internal Control
24	B	Internal Control
25	D	Internal Control
26	B	Other Reporting Areas
27	D	Other Reporting Areas
28	C	Other Reporting Areas
29	B	Statistical Sampling
30	A	Statistical Sampling

Accounting & Reporting— Taxation, Managerial, and Governmental and Not-for-Profit Organizations (ARE)

QUESTION #	ANSWER	TOPICAL AREA
1	B	Cost Accounting
2	A	Cost Accounting
3	D	Cost Accounting
4	C	Cost Accounting
5	B	Cost Accounting
6	B	Federal Income Taxes— Capital Gains and Losses
7	D	Federal Income Taxes— Corporations
8	A	Federal Income Taxes— Corporations
9	D	Federal Income Taxes— Corporations
10	A	Federal Income Taxes— Estates and Trusts
11	B	Federal Income Taxes— Exempt Organizations
12	A	Federal Income Taxes— Individuals
13	D	Federal Income Taxes— Individuals
14	C	Federal Income Taxes— Individuals

QUESTION #	ANSWER	TOPICAL AREA
15	C	Federal Income Taxes— Partnerships
16	D	Managerial Accounting & Quantitative Methods
17	C	Managerial Accounting & Quantitative Methods
18	C	Managerial Accounting & Quantitative Methods
19	C	Managerial Accounting & Quantitative Methods
20	D	Managerial Accounting & Quantitative Methods
21	D	Not-for-Profit Accounting— Governmental Units
22	D	Not-for-Profit Accounting— Governmental Units
23	D	Not-for-Profit Accounting— Governmental Units
24	A	Not-for-Profit Accounting— Governmental Units
25	B	Not-for-Profit Accounting— Governmental Units
26	C	Not-for-Profit Accounting— Other Than Governmental Units
27	C	Not-for-Profit Accounting— Other Than Governmental Units
28	A	Not-for-Profit Accounting— Other Than Governmental Units
29	D	Not-for-Profit Accounting— Other Than Governmental Units
30	B	Not-for-Profit Accounting— Other Than Governmental Units

Financial Accounting & Reporting—Business Enterprises (FARE)

QUESTION #	ANSWER	TOPICAL AREA
1	A	Accounting Concepts
2	C	Accounting Fundamentals
3	B	Accounting Fundamentals
4	A	Bonds, Accounting for
5	B	Cash Flows
6	D	Cash Flows

Question #	Answer	Topical Area	Question #	Answer	Topical Area
7	C	Consolidation and Business Combination	18	A	Investments
			19	A	Investments
8	B	Consolidation and Business Combination	20	B	Leases
			21	A	Leases
9	B	Financial Statement Analysis	22	A	Liabilities
10	B	Financial Statements	23	C	Liabilities
11	B	Fixed Assets	24	B	Long-Term Contracts
12	B	Fixed Assets	25	B	Partnerships
13	D	Foreign Currency Translation	26	A	Pension Costs
14	B	Income Taxes, Accounting for	27	A	Receivables
			28	D	Receivables
15	C	Installment Sales	29	A	Stockholders' Equity
16	A	Intangibles	30	D	Stockholders' Equity
17	D	Inventories			

Answer Sheet

Simulated CPA Examination

LPR   **AUDIT**

1. Ⓐ Ⓑ Ⓒ Ⓓ	31. Ⓐ Ⓑ Ⓒ Ⓓ	1. Ⓐ Ⓑ Ⓒ Ⓓ	31. Ⓐ Ⓑ Ⓒ Ⓓ	61. Ⓐ Ⓑ Ⓒ Ⓓ
2. Ⓐ Ⓑ Ⓒ Ⓓ	32. Ⓐ Ⓑ Ⓒ Ⓓ	2. Ⓐ Ⓑ Ⓒ Ⓓ	32. Ⓐ Ⓑ Ⓒ Ⓓ	62. Ⓐ Ⓑ Ⓒ Ⓓ
3. Ⓐ Ⓑ Ⓒ Ⓓ	33. Ⓐ Ⓑ Ⓒ Ⓓ	3. Ⓐ Ⓑ Ⓒ Ⓓ	33. Ⓐ Ⓑ Ⓒ Ⓓ	63. Ⓐ Ⓑ Ⓒ Ⓓ
4. Ⓐ Ⓑ Ⓒ Ⓓ	34. Ⓐ Ⓑ Ⓒ Ⓓ	4. Ⓐ Ⓑ Ⓒ Ⓓ	34. Ⓐ Ⓑ Ⓒ Ⓓ	64. Ⓐ Ⓑ Ⓒ Ⓓ
5. Ⓐ Ⓑ Ⓒ Ⓓ	35. Ⓐ Ⓑ Ⓒ Ⓓ	5. Ⓐ Ⓑ Ⓒ Ⓓ	35. Ⓐ Ⓑ Ⓒ Ⓓ	65. Ⓐ Ⓑ Ⓒ Ⓓ
6. Ⓐ Ⓑ Ⓒ Ⓓ	36. Ⓐ Ⓑ Ⓒ Ⓓ	6. Ⓐ Ⓑ Ⓒ Ⓓ	36. Ⓐ Ⓑ Ⓒ Ⓓ	66. Ⓐ Ⓑ Ⓒ Ⓓ
7. Ⓐ Ⓑ Ⓒ Ⓓ	37. Ⓐ Ⓑ Ⓒ Ⓓ	7. Ⓐ Ⓑ Ⓒ Ⓓ	37. Ⓐ Ⓑ Ⓒ Ⓓ	67. Ⓐ Ⓑ Ⓒ Ⓓ
8. Ⓐ Ⓑ Ⓒ Ⓓ	38. Ⓐ Ⓑ Ⓒ Ⓓ	8. Ⓐ Ⓑ Ⓒ Ⓓ	38. Ⓐ Ⓑ Ⓒ Ⓓ	68. Ⓐ Ⓑ Ⓒ Ⓓ
9. Ⓐ Ⓑ Ⓒ Ⓓ	39. Ⓐ Ⓑ Ⓒ Ⓓ	9. Ⓐ Ⓑ Ⓒ Ⓓ	39. Ⓐ Ⓑ Ⓒ Ⓓ	69. Ⓐ Ⓑ Ⓒ Ⓓ
10. Ⓐ Ⓑ Ⓒ Ⓓ	40. Ⓐ Ⓑ Ⓒ Ⓓ	10. Ⓐ Ⓑ Ⓒ Ⓓ	40. Ⓐ Ⓑ Ⓒ Ⓓ	70. Ⓐ Ⓑ Ⓒ Ⓓ
11. Ⓐ Ⓑ Ⓒ Ⓓ	41. Ⓐ Ⓑ Ⓒ Ⓓ	11. Ⓐ Ⓑ Ⓒ Ⓓ	41. Ⓐ Ⓑ Ⓒ Ⓓ	71. Ⓐ Ⓑ Ⓒ Ⓓ
12. Ⓐ Ⓑ Ⓒ Ⓓ	42. Ⓐ Ⓑ Ⓒ Ⓓ	12. Ⓐ Ⓑ Ⓒ Ⓓ	42. Ⓐ Ⓑ Ⓒ Ⓓ	72. Ⓐ Ⓑ Ⓒ Ⓓ
13. Ⓐ Ⓑ Ⓒ Ⓓ	43. Ⓐ Ⓑ Ⓒ Ⓓ	13. Ⓐ Ⓑ Ⓒ Ⓓ	43. Ⓐ Ⓑ Ⓒ Ⓓ	73. Ⓐ Ⓑ Ⓒ Ⓓ
14. Ⓐ Ⓑ Ⓒ Ⓓ	44. Ⓐ Ⓑ Ⓒ Ⓓ	14. Ⓐ Ⓑ Ⓒ Ⓓ	44. Ⓐ Ⓑ Ⓒ Ⓓ	74. Ⓐ Ⓑ Ⓒ Ⓓ
15. Ⓐ Ⓑ Ⓒ Ⓓ	45. Ⓐ Ⓑ Ⓒ Ⓓ	15. Ⓐ Ⓑ Ⓒ Ⓓ	45. Ⓐ Ⓑ Ⓒ Ⓓ	75. Ⓐ Ⓑ Ⓒ Ⓓ
16. Ⓐ Ⓑ Ⓒ Ⓓ	46. Ⓐ Ⓑ Ⓒ Ⓓ	16. Ⓐ Ⓑ Ⓒ Ⓓ	46. Ⓐ Ⓑ Ⓒ Ⓓ	76. Ⓐ Ⓑ Ⓒ Ⓓ
17. Ⓐ Ⓑ Ⓒ Ⓓ	47. Ⓐ Ⓑ Ⓒ Ⓓ	17. Ⓐ Ⓑ Ⓒ Ⓓ	47. Ⓐ Ⓑ Ⓒ Ⓓ	77. Ⓐ Ⓑ Ⓒ Ⓓ
18. Ⓐ Ⓑ Ⓒ Ⓓ	48. Ⓐ Ⓑ Ⓒ Ⓓ	18. Ⓐ Ⓑ Ⓒ Ⓓ	48. Ⓐ Ⓑ Ⓒ Ⓓ	78. Ⓐ Ⓑ Ⓒ Ⓓ
19. Ⓐ Ⓑ Ⓒ Ⓓ	49. Ⓐ Ⓑ Ⓒ Ⓓ	19. Ⓐ Ⓑ Ⓒ Ⓓ	49. Ⓐ Ⓑ Ⓒ Ⓓ	79. Ⓐ Ⓑ Ⓒ Ⓓ
20. Ⓐ Ⓑ Ⓒ Ⓓ	50. Ⓐ Ⓑ Ⓒ Ⓓ	20. Ⓐ Ⓑ Ⓒ Ⓓ	50. Ⓐ Ⓑ Ⓒ Ⓓ	80. Ⓐ Ⓑ Ⓒ Ⓓ
21. Ⓐ Ⓑ Ⓒ Ⓓ	51. Ⓐ Ⓑ Ⓒ Ⓓ	21. Ⓐ Ⓑ Ⓒ Ⓓ	51. Ⓐ Ⓑ Ⓒ Ⓓ	81. Ⓐ Ⓑ Ⓒ Ⓓ
22. Ⓐ Ⓑ Ⓒ Ⓓ	52. Ⓐ Ⓑ Ⓒ Ⓓ	22. Ⓐ Ⓑ Ⓒ Ⓓ	52. Ⓐ Ⓑ Ⓒ Ⓓ	82. Ⓐ Ⓑ Ⓒ Ⓓ
23. Ⓐ Ⓑ Ⓒ Ⓓ	53. Ⓐ Ⓑ Ⓒ Ⓓ	23. Ⓐ Ⓑ Ⓒ Ⓓ	53. Ⓐ Ⓑ Ⓒ Ⓓ	83. Ⓐ Ⓑ Ⓒ Ⓓ
24. Ⓐ Ⓑ Ⓒ Ⓓ	54. Ⓐ Ⓑ Ⓒ Ⓓ	24. Ⓐ Ⓑ Ⓒ Ⓓ	54. Ⓐ Ⓑ Ⓒ Ⓓ	84. Ⓐ Ⓑ Ⓒ Ⓓ
25. Ⓐ Ⓑ Ⓒ Ⓓ	55. Ⓐ Ⓑ Ⓒ Ⓓ	25. Ⓐ Ⓑ Ⓒ Ⓓ	55. Ⓐ Ⓑ Ⓒ Ⓓ	85. Ⓐ Ⓑ Ⓒ Ⓓ
26. Ⓐ Ⓑ Ⓒ Ⓓ	56. Ⓐ Ⓑ Ⓒ Ⓓ	26. Ⓐ Ⓑ Ⓒ Ⓓ	56. Ⓐ Ⓑ Ⓒ Ⓓ	86. Ⓐ Ⓑ Ⓒ Ⓓ
27. Ⓐ Ⓑ Ⓒ Ⓓ	57. Ⓐ Ⓑ Ⓒ Ⓓ	27. Ⓐ Ⓑ Ⓒ Ⓓ	57. Ⓐ Ⓑ Ⓒ Ⓓ	87. Ⓐ Ⓑ Ⓒ Ⓓ
28. Ⓐ Ⓑ Ⓒ Ⓓ	58. Ⓐ Ⓑ Ⓒ Ⓓ	28. Ⓐ Ⓑ Ⓒ Ⓓ	58. Ⓐ Ⓑ Ⓒ Ⓓ	88. Ⓐ Ⓑ Ⓒ Ⓓ
29. Ⓐ Ⓑ Ⓒ Ⓓ	59. Ⓐ Ⓑ Ⓒ Ⓓ	29. Ⓐ Ⓑ Ⓒ Ⓓ	59. Ⓐ Ⓑ Ⓒ Ⓓ	89. Ⓐ Ⓑ Ⓒ Ⓓ
30. Ⓐ Ⓑ Ⓒ Ⓓ	60. Ⓐ Ⓑ Ⓒ Ⓓ	30. Ⓐ Ⓑ Ⓒ Ⓓ	60. Ⓐ Ⓑ Ⓒ Ⓓ	90. Ⓐ Ⓑ Ⓒ Ⓓ

Answer Sheet

ARE

1. Ⓐ Ⓑ Ⓒ Ⓓ	31. Ⓐ Ⓑ Ⓒ Ⓓ
2. Ⓐ Ⓑ Ⓒ Ⓓ	32. Ⓐ Ⓑ Ⓒ Ⓓ
3. Ⓐ Ⓑ Ⓒ Ⓓ	33. Ⓐ Ⓑ Ⓒ Ⓓ
4. Ⓐ Ⓑ Ⓒ Ⓓ	34. Ⓐ Ⓑ Ⓒ Ⓓ
5. Ⓐ Ⓑ Ⓒ Ⓓ	35. Ⓐ Ⓑ Ⓒ Ⓓ
6. Ⓐ Ⓑ Ⓒ Ⓓ	36. Ⓐ Ⓑ Ⓒ Ⓓ
7. Ⓐ Ⓑ Ⓒ Ⓓ	37. Ⓐ Ⓑ Ⓒ Ⓓ
8. Ⓐ Ⓑ Ⓒ Ⓓ	38. Ⓐ Ⓑ Ⓒ Ⓓ
9. Ⓐ Ⓑ Ⓒ Ⓓ	39. Ⓐ Ⓑ Ⓒ Ⓓ
10. Ⓐ Ⓑ Ⓒ Ⓓ	40. Ⓐ Ⓑ Ⓒ Ⓓ
11. Ⓐ Ⓑ Ⓒ Ⓓ	41. Ⓐ Ⓑ Ⓒ Ⓓ
12. Ⓐ Ⓑ Ⓒ Ⓓ	42. Ⓐ Ⓑ Ⓒ Ⓓ
13. Ⓐ Ⓑ Ⓒ Ⓓ	43. Ⓐ Ⓑ Ⓒ Ⓓ
14. Ⓐ Ⓑ Ⓒ Ⓓ	44. Ⓐ Ⓑ Ⓒ Ⓓ
15. Ⓐ Ⓑ Ⓒ Ⓓ	45. Ⓐ Ⓑ Ⓒ Ⓓ
16. Ⓐ Ⓑ Ⓒ Ⓓ	46. Ⓐ Ⓑ Ⓒ Ⓓ
17. Ⓐ Ⓑ Ⓒ Ⓓ	47. Ⓐ Ⓑ Ⓒ Ⓓ
18. Ⓐ Ⓑ Ⓒ Ⓓ	48. Ⓐ Ⓑ Ⓒ Ⓓ
19. Ⓐ Ⓑ Ⓒ Ⓓ	49. Ⓐ Ⓑ Ⓒ Ⓓ
20. Ⓐ Ⓑ Ⓒ Ⓓ	50. Ⓐ Ⓑ Ⓒ Ⓓ
21. Ⓐ Ⓑ Ⓒ Ⓓ	51. Ⓐ Ⓑ Ⓒ Ⓓ
22. Ⓐ Ⓑ Ⓒ Ⓓ	52. Ⓐ Ⓑ Ⓒ Ⓓ
23. Ⓐ Ⓑ Ⓒ Ⓓ	53. Ⓐ Ⓑ Ⓒ Ⓓ
24. Ⓐ Ⓑ Ⓒ Ⓓ	54. Ⓐ Ⓑ Ⓒ Ⓓ
25. Ⓐ Ⓑ Ⓒ Ⓓ	55. Ⓐ Ⓑ Ⓒ Ⓓ
26. Ⓐ Ⓑ Ⓒ Ⓓ	56. Ⓐ Ⓑ Ⓒ Ⓓ
27. Ⓐ Ⓑ Ⓒ Ⓓ	57. Ⓐ Ⓑ Ⓒ Ⓓ
28. Ⓐ Ⓑ Ⓒ Ⓓ	58. Ⓐ Ⓑ Ⓒ Ⓓ
29. Ⓐ Ⓑ Ⓒ Ⓓ	59. Ⓐ Ⓑ Ⓒ Ⓓ
30. Ⓐ Ⓑ Ⓒ Ⓓ	60. Ⓐ Ⓑ Ⓒ Ⓓ

FARE

1. Ⓐ Ⓑ Ⓒ Ⓓ	31. Ⓐ Ⓑ Ⓒ Ⓓ
2. Ⓐ Ⓑ Ⓒ Ⓓ	32. Ⓐ Ⓑ Ⓒ Ⓓ
3. Ⓐ Ⓑ Ⓒ Ⓓ	33. Ⓐ Ⓑ Ⓒ Ⓓ
4. Ⓐ Ⓑ Ⓒ Ⓓ	34. Ⓐ Ⓑ Ⓒ Ⓓ
5. Ⓐ Ⓑ Ⓒ Ⓓ	35. Ⓐ Ⓑ Ⓒ Ⓓ
6. Ⓐ Ⓑ Ⓒ Ⓓ	36. Ⓐ Ⓑ Ⓒ Ⓓ
7. Ⓐ Ⓑ Ⓒ Ⓓ	37. Ⓐ Ⓑ Ⓒ Ⓓ
8. Ⓐ Ⓑ Ⓒ Ⓓ	38. Ⓐ Ⓑ Ⓒ Ⓓ
9. Ⓐ Ⓑ Ⓒ Ⓓ	39. Ⓐ Ⓑ Ⓒ Ⓓ
10. Ⓐ Ⓑ Ⓒ Ⓓ	40. Ⓐ Ⓑ Ⓒ Ⓓ
11. Ⓐ Ⓑ Ⓒ Ⓓ	41. Ⓐ Ⓑ Ⓒ Ⓓ
12. Ⓐ Ⓑ Ⓒ Ⓓ	42. Ⓐ Ⓑ Ⓒ Ⓓ
13. Ⓐ Ⓑ Ⓒ Ⓓ	43. Ⓐ Ⓑ Ⓒ Ⓓ
14. Ⓐ Ⓑ Ⓒ Ⓓ	44. Ⓐ Ⓑ Ⓒ Ⓓ
15. Ⓐ Ⓑ Ⓒ Ⓓ	45. Ⓐ Ⓑ Ⓒ Ⓓ
16. Ⓐ Ⓑ Ⓒ Ⓓ	46. Ⓐ Ⓑ Ⓒ Ⓓ
17. Ⓐ Ⓑ Ⓒ Ⓓ	47. Ⓐ Ⓑ Ⓒ Ⓓ
18. Ⓐ Ⓑ Ⓒ Ⓓ	48. Ⓐ Ⓑ Ⓒ Ⓓ
19. Ⓐ Ⓑ Ⓒ Ⓓ	49. Ⓐ Ⓑ Ⓒ Ⓓ
20. Ⓐ Ⓑ Ⓒ Ⓓ	50. Ⓐ Ⓑ Ⓒ Ⓓ
21. Ⓐ Ⓑ Ⓒ Ⓓ	51. Ⓐ Ⓑ Ⓒ Ⓓ
22. Ⓐ Ⓑ Ⓒ Ⓓ	52. Ⓐ Ⓑ Ⓒ Ⓓ
23. Ⓐ Ⓑ Ⓒ Ⓓ	53. Ⓐ Ⓑ Ⓒ Ⓓ
24. Ⓐ Ⓑ Ⓒ Ⓓ	54. Ⓐ Ⓑ Ⓒ Ⓓ
25. Ⓐ Ⓑ Ⓒ Ⓓ	55. Ⓐ Ⓑ Ⓒ Ⓓ
26. Ⓐ Ⓑ Ⓒ Ⓓ	56. Ⓐ Ⓑ Ⓒ Ⓓ
27. Ⓐ Ⓑ Ⓒ Ⓓ	57. Ⓐ Ⓑ Ⓒ Ⓓ
28. Ⓐ Ⓑ Ⓒ Ⓓ	58. Ⓐ Ⓑ Ⓒ Ⓓ
29. Ⓐ Ⓑ Ⓒ Ⓓ	59. Ⓐ Ⓑ Ⓒ Ⓓ
30. Ⓐ Ⓑ Ⓒ Ⓓ	60. Ⓐ Ⓑ Ⓒ Ⓓ

Step 4: Two Sample Examinations— Practice Your Strategy

with • *Solutions to Essay and Computational Questions*
• *Explanatory Answers for Objective Questions*

8. Simulated CPA Examination

This chapter includes the first of two practice examinations that you will be taking. This examination consists of questions from actual CPA examinations given prior to May 1994. Accordingly, the ARE and FARE sections of this Simulated CPA Examination include questions from the former "Accounting Practice" and "Accounting Theory" examinations, which form the basis for the ARE and FARE sections. The LPR section includes questions pertaining to professional responsibilities, which were previously included on the Auditing Examination.*

Be sure to take each of the four sections of this examination just as you would the actual test. *Allow no more time than each examination section indicates. Take each test in one sitting, and do no more than two sections in a day.* You will then become accustomed to concentrating for the duration of a test period and to working efficiently during this time.

Before beginning this practice examination, be sure to review the test tactics outlined in "Chapter 5—How to Approach CPA Examination Questions." After completing this examination, turn to "Chapter 6—Chart Your Progress and Plan Your Course of Action" for guidance in analyzing your score and planning your review program.

Remember: Read directions carefully!

---

*Note: All answer explanations are the authors'.

(Note: These instructions have been adapted from the May 1994 CPA Examination Booklet.)

 *Uniform Certified Public Accountant Examination*

EXAMINATION QUESTION BOOKLET

LPR — 9:00 A.M. to 12:00 noon

The point values for each question, and estimated time allotments based primarily on point value, are as follows:

	Point Value	Estimated Minutes Minimum	Maximum
No. 1	60	90	100
No. 2	10	10	15
No. 3	10	10	15
No. 4	10	15	25
No. 5	10	15	25
Totals	100	140	180

INSTRUCTIONS TO CANDIDATES

Failure to follow these instructions may have an adverse effect on your Examination grade.

1. Record your 7-digit candidate number in the boxes provided at the upper right-hand corner of this page.

2. Question numbers 1, 2, and 3 should be answered on the *Objective Answer Sheet,* which is pages 11 and 12 of your *Examination Answer Booklet.* You should attempt to answer all objective items. There is no penalty for incorrect responses. Since the objective items are computer-graded, your comments and calculations associated with them are not considered. Be certain that you have entered your answers on the *Objective Answer Sheet* before the examination time is up. The objective portion of your examination will not be graded if you fail to record your answers on the *Objective Answer Sheet.* You will not be given additional time to record your answers.

3. Question numbers 4 and 5 should be answered beginning on page 3 of the *Examination Answer Booklet.* If you have not completed answering a question on a page, fill in the appropriate spaces in the wording on the bottom of the page **"QUESTION NUMBER _____ CONTINUES ON PAGE _____."** If you have completed answering a question, fill in the appropriate space in the wording on the bottom of the page **"QUESTION NUMBER _____ ENDS ON THIS PAGE."** Always begin the start of an answer to a question on the top of a new page (which may be the back side of a sheet of paper).

4. Record your 7-digit candidate number, state, and question number where indicated on pages 3 through 10 of the *Examination Answer Booklet.*

5. Although the primary purpose of the examination is to test your knowledge and application of the subject matter, selected essay responses will be graded for writing skills.

6. You are required to turn in by the end of each session:
   a. Attendance Record Form, front page of *Examination Answer Booklet;*
   b. *Objective Answer Sheet,* pages 11 and 12 of *Examination Answer Booklet;*
   c. Remaining Portion of *Examination Answer Booklet;*
   d. *Examination Question Booklet;* and
   e. All unused examination materials.

   Your examination will not be graded unless the above listed items are handed in before leaving the examination room.

7. Unless otherwise instructed, if you want your *Examination Question Booklet* mailed to you, write your name and address in both places indicated on the back cover and place 52 cents postage in the space provided. *Examination Question Booklets* will be distributed no sooner than the day following the administration of this examination.

SIMULATED CPA EXAMINATION

Business Law & Professional Responsibilities (LPR)

Number 1 (Estimated time—90 to 100 minutes)

Instructions

Select the **best** answer for each of the following items. Use a No. 2 pencil to blacken the appropriate ovals on the Objective Answer Sheet to indicate your answers. **Mark only one answer for each item. Answer all items.** Your grade will be based on the total number of correct answers.

1. Beckler & Associates, CPAs, audited and gave an unqualified opinion on the financial statements of Queen Co. The financial statements contained misstatements that resulted in a material overstatement of Queen's net worth. Queen provided the audited financial statements to Mac Bank in connection with a loan made by Mac to Queen. Beckler knew that the financial statements would be provided to Mac. Queen defaulted on the loan. Mac sued Beckler to recover for its losses associated with Queen's default. Which of the following must Mac prove in order to recover?

  I. Beckler was negligent in conducting the audit.
  II. Mac relied on the financial statements.

    A. I only.
    B. II only.
    C. Both I and II.
    D. Neither I nor II.

2. Which of the following statements best describes whether a CPA has met the required standard of care in conducting an audit of a client's financial statements?
    A. The client's expectations with regard to the accuracy of audited financial statements.
    B. The accuracy of the financial statements and whether the statements conform to generally accepted accounting principles.
    C. Whether the CPA conducted the audit with the same skill and care expected of an ordinarily prudent CPA under the circumstances.
    D. Whether the audit was conducted to investigate and discover all acts of fraud.

Items 3 through 5 are based on the following:

While conducting an audit, Larson Associates, CPAs, failed to detect material misstatements included in its client's financial statements. Larson's unqualified opinion was included with the financial statements in a registration statement and prospectus for a public offering of securities made by the client. Larson knew that its opinion and the financial statements would be used for this purpose.

3. Which of the following statements is correct with regard to a suit against Larson and the client by a purchaser of the securities under Section 11 of the Securities Act of 1933?
    A. The purchaser must prove that Larson was negligent in conducting the audit.
    B. The purchaser must prove that Larson knew of the material misstatements.
    C. Larson will **not** be liable if it had reasonable grounds to believe the financial statements were accurate.
    D. Larson will be liable unless the purchaser did **not** rely on the financial statements.

4. In a suit by a purchaser against Larson for common law negligence, Larson's best defense would be that the
    A. Audit was conducted in accordance with generally accepted auditing standards.
    B. Client was aware of the misstatements.
    C. Purchaser was **not** in privity of contract with Larson.
    D. Identity of the purchaser was **not** known to Larson at the time of the audit.

5. In a suit by a purchaser against Larson for common law fraud, Larson's best defense would be that
    A. Larson did **not** have actual or constructive knowledge of the misstatements.
    B. Larson's client knew or should have known of the misstatements.
    C. Larson did **not** have actual knowledge that the purchaser was an intended beneficiary of the audit.
    D. Larson was **not** in privity of contract with its client.

6. Jay and Co., CPAs, audited the financial statements of Maco Corp. Jay intentionally gave an unqualified opinion on the financial statements even though material misstatements were discovered. The financial statements and Jay's unqualified opinion were included in a registration statement and prospectus for an original public offering of Maco stock. Which of the following statements is correct regarding Jay's liability to a purchaser of the offering under Section 10(b) and Rule 10b-5 of the Securities Exchange Act of 1934?

A. Jay will be liable if the purchaser relied on Jay's unqualified opinion on the financial statements.

B. Jay will be liable if Jay was negligent in conducting the audit.

C. Jay will **not** be liable if the purchaser's loss was under $500.

D. Jay will **not** be liable if the misstatement resulted from an omission of a material fact by Jay.

7. Which of the following is the best defense a CPA firm can assert in defense to a suit for common law fraud based on their unqualified opinion on materially false financial statements?

A. Lack of privity.

B. Lack of scienter.

C. Contributory negligence on the part of the client.

D. A disclaimer contained in the engagement letter.

8. Ivor and Associates, CPAs, audited the financial statements of Jaymo Corporation. As a result of Ivor's negligence in conducting the audit, the financial statements included material misstatements. Ivor was unaware of this fact. The financial statements and Ivor's unqualified opinion were included in a registration statement and prospectus for an original public offering of stock by Jaymo. Thorp purchased shares in the offering. Thorp received a copy of the prospectus prior to the purchase but did not read it. The shares declined in value as a result of the misstatements in Jaymo's financial statements becoming known. Under which of the following Acts is Thorp most likely to prevail in a lawsuit against Ivor?

	Securities Act of 1933, Section 11	Securities Exchange Act of 1934, Section 10(b), Rule 10b-5
A.	Yes	Yes
B.	Yes	No
C.	No	Yes
D.	No	No

9. Clark, a professional tax return preparer, prepared and signed a client's 1992 federal income tax return that resulted in a $600 refund. Which one of the following statements is correct with regard to an Internal Revenue Code penalty Clark may be subject to for endorsing and cashing the client's refund check?

A. Clark will be subject to the penalty if Clark endorses and cashes the check.

B. Clark may endorse and cash the check, without penalty, if Clark is enrolled to practice before the Internal Revenue Service.

C. Clark may **not** endorse and cash the check, without penalty, because the check is for more than $500.

D. Clark may endorse and cash the check, without penalty, if the amount does **not** exceed Clark's fee for preparation of the return.

10. According to the profession's ethical standards, a CPA would be considered independent in which of the following instances?

A. A client leases part of an office building from the CPA, resulting in a material indirect financial interest to the CPA.

B. The CPA has a material direct financial interest in a client, but transfers the interest into a blind trust.

C. The CPA owns an office building and the mortgage on the building is guaranteed by a client.

D. The CPA belongs to a country club client in which membership requires the acquisition of a pro rata share of equity.

11. Noll gives Carr a written power of attorney. Which of the following statements is correct regarding this power of attorney?

A. It must be signed by both Noll and Carr.

B. It must be for a definite period of time.

C. It may continue in existence after Noll's death.

D. It may limit Carr's authority to specific transactions.

12. The apparent authority of a partner to bind the partnership in dealing with third parties

A. Will be effectively limited by a formal resolution of the partners of which third parties are aware.

B. Will be effectively limited by a formal resolution of the partners of which third parties are unaware.

C. Would permit a partner to submit a claim against the partnership to arbitration.

D. Must be derived from the express powers and purposes contained in the partnership agreement.

13. Generally, a disclosed principal will be liable to third parties for its agent's unauthorized misrepresentations if the agent is an

	Employee	Independent Contractor
A.	Yes	Yes
B.	Yes	No
C.	No	Yes
D.	No	No

14. Which of the following rights will a third party be entitled to after validly contracting with an agent representing an undisclosed principal?
   A. Disclosure of the principal by the agent.
   B. Ratification of the contract by the principal.
   C. Performance of the contract by the agent.
   D. Election to void the contract after disclosure of the principal.

15. North, Inc., hired Sutter as a purchasing agent. North gave Sutter written authorization to purchase, without limit, electronic appliances. Later, Sutter was told not to purchase more than 300 of each appliance. Sutter contracted with Orr Corp. to purchase 500 tape recorders. Orr had been shown Sutter's written authorization. Which of the following statements is correct?
   A. Sutter will be liable to Orr because Sutter's actual authority was exceeded.
   B. Sutter will **not** be liable to reimburse North if North is liable to Orr.
   C. North will be liable to Orr because of Sutter's actual and apparent authority.
   D. North will **not** be liable to Orr because Sutter's actual authority was exceeded.

16. Which of the following requirements must be met to have a valid partnership exist?
   I. Co-ownership of all property used in a business.
   II. Co-ownership of a business for profit.

   A. I only.
   B. II only.
   C. Both I and II.
   D. Neither I nor II.

17. Which of the following securities are corporate debt securities?

	Convertible bonds	Debenture bonds	Warrants
A.	Yes	Yes	Yes
B.	Yes	No	Yes
C.	Yes	Yes	No
D.	No	Yes	Yes

18. Unless the partnership agreement prohibits it, a partner in a general partnership may validly assign rights to

	Partnership property	Partnership distributions
A.	Yes	Yes
B.	Yes	No
C.	No	Yes
D.	No	No

19. Which of the following provisions must a for-profit-corporation include in its Articles of Incorporation to obtain a corporate charter?

   I. Provision for the issuance of voting stock.
   II. Name of the corporation.

   A. I only.
   B. II only.
   C. Both I and II.
   D. Neither I nor II.

20. The corporate veil is most likely to be pierced and the shareholders held personally liable if
   A. The corporation has elected S corporation status under the Internal Revenue Code.
   B. The shareholders have commingled their personal funds with those of the corporation.
   C. An ultra vires act has been committed.
   D. A partnership incorporates its business solely to limit the liability of its partners.

21. Egan, a minor, contracted with Baker to purchase Baker's used computer for $400. The computer was purchased for Egan's personal use. The agreement provided that Egan would pay $200 down on delivery and $200 thirty days later. Egan took delivery and paid the $200 down payment. Twenty days later, the computer was damaged seriously as a result of Egan's negligence. Five days after the damage occurred and one day after Egan reached the age of majority, Egan attempted to disaffirm the contract with Baker. Egan will
   A. Be able to disaffirm despite the fact that Egan was **not** a minor at the time of disaffirmance.
   B. Be able to disaffirm only if Egan does so in writing.
   C. Not be able to disaffirm because Egan had failed to pay the balance of the purchase price.
   D. Not be able to disaffirm because the computer was damaged as a result of Egan's negligence.

22. Teller brought a lawsuit against Kerr ten years after an oral contract was made and eight years after it was breached. Kerr raised the statute of limitations as a defense. Which of the following allegations would be most important to Kerr's defense?
    A. The contract was oral.
    B. The contract could **not** be performed within one year from the date made.
    C. The action was **not** timely brought because the contract was entered into ten years prior to the commencement of the lawsuit.
    D. The action was **not** timely brought because the contract was allegedly breached eight years prior to the commencement of the lawsuit.

23. To prevail in a common law action for fraud in the inducement, a plaintiff must prove that the
    A. Defendant was an expert with regard to the misrepresentations.
    B. Defendant made the misrepresentations with knowledge of their falsity and with an intention to deceive.
    C. Misrepresentations were in writing.
    D. Plaintiff was in a fiduciary relationship with the defendant.

24. Which of the following offers of proof are inadmissible under the parol evidence rule when a written contract is intended as the complete agreement of the parties?
    I. Proof of the existence of a subsequent oral modification of the contract.
    II. Proof of the existence of a prior oral agreement that contradicts the written contract.

    A. I only.
    B. II only.
    C. Both I and II.
    D. Neither I nor II.

25. Nash, Owen, and Polk are co-sureties with maximum liabilities of $40,000, $60,000 and $80,000, respectively. The amount of the loan on which they have agreed to act as co-sureties is $180,000. The debtor defaulted at a time when the loan balance was $180,000. Nash paid the lender $36,000 in full settlement of all claims against Nash, Owen, and Polk. The total amount that Nash may recover from Owen and Polk is
    A. $0
    B. $ 24,000
    C. $ 28,000
    D. $140,000

26. Ames Construction Co. contracted to build a warehouse for White Corp. The construction specifications required Ames to use Ace lighting fixtures. Inadvertently, Ames installed Perfection lighting fixtures, which are of slightly lesser quality than Ace fixtures, but in all other respects meet White's needs. Which of the following statements is correct?
    A. White's recovery will be limited to monetary damages because Ames' breach of the construction contract was **not** material.
    B. White will **not** be able to recover any damages from Ames because the breach was inadvertent.
    C. Ames did **not** breach the construction contract because the Perfection fixtures were substantially as good as the Ace fixtures.
    D. Ames must install Ace fixtures or White will **not** be obligated to accept the warehouse.

27. The filing of an involuntary bankruptcy petition under the Federal Bankruptcy Code
    A. Terminates liens on exempt property.
    B. Terminates all security interests in property in the bankruptcy estate.
    C. Stops the debtor from incurring new debts.
    D. Stops the enforcement of judgment liens against property in the bankruptcy estate.

28. Which of the following requirements must be met for creditors to file an involuntary bankruptcy petition under Chapter 7 of the Federal Bankruptcy Code?
    A. The debtor must owe one creditor more than $5,000.
    B. The debtor has **not** been paying its *bona fide* debts as they become due.
    C. There must **not** be more than 12 creditors.
    D. At least one fully secured creditor must join in the petition.

29. Which of the following conditions, if any, must a debtor meet to file a voluntary bankruptcy petition under Chapter 7 of the Federal Bankruptcy Code?

	Insolvency	Three or more creditors
A.	Yes	Yes
B.	Yes	No
C.	No	Yes
D.	No	No

30. Which of the following transfers by a debtor, within ninety days of filing for bankruptcy, could be set aside as a preferential payment?
    A. Making a gift to charity.
    B. Paying a business utility bill.
    C. Borrowing money from a bank secured by giving a mortgage on business property.
    D. Prepaying an installment loan on inventory.

31. Which of the following acts by a debtor could result in a bankruptcy court revoking the debtor's discharge?
    I. Failure to list one creditor.
    II. Failure to answer correctly material questions on the bankruptcy petition.

    A. I only.
    B. II only.
    C. Both I and II.
    D. Neither I nor II.

32. Robin Corp. incurred substantial operating losses for the past three years. Unable to meet its current obligations, Robin filed a petition for reorganization under Chapter 11 of the Federal Bankruptcy Code. Which of the following statements is correct?
    A. The creditors' committee must select a trustee to manage Robin's affairs.
    B. The reorganization plan may only be filed by Robin.
    C. A creditors' committee, if appointed, will consist of unsecured creditors.
    D. Robin may continue in business only with the approval of a trustee.

33. A reorganization under Chapter 11 of the Federal Bankruptcy Code requires all of the following **except** the
    A. Liquidation of the debtor.
    B. Filing of a reorganization plan.
    C. Confirmation of the reorganization plan by the court.
    D. Opportunity for each class of claims to accept the reorganization plan.

34. May a CPA hire for the CPA's public accounting firm a non-CPA systems analyst who specializes in developing computer systems?
    A. Yes, provided the CPA is qualified to perform each of the specialist's tasks.
    B. Yes, provided the CPA is able to supervise the specialist and evaluate the specialist's end product.
    C. No, because non-CPA professionals are **not** permitted to be associated with CPA firms in public practice.

    D. No, because developing computer systems is **not** recognized as a service performed by public accountants.

35. After serving as an active director of Lee Corp. for 20 years, Ryan was appointed an honorary director with the obligation to attend directors' meetings with no voting power. In 1992, Ryan received an honorary director's fee of $5,000. This fee is
    A. Reportable by Lee as employee compensation subject to social security tax.
    B. Reportable by Ryan as self-employment income subject to social security self-employment tax.
    C. Taxable as "Other income" by Ryan, **not** subject to any social security tax.
    D. Considered to be a gift **not** subject to social security self-employment or income tax.

36. Which of the following statements concerning workers' compensation laws is generally correct?
    A. Employers are strictly liable without regard to whether or **not** they are at fault.
    B. Workers' compensation benefits are **not** available if the employee is negligent.
    C. Workers' compensation awards are **not** reviewable by the courts.
    D. The amount of damages recoverable is based on comparative negligence.

37. One of the elements necessary to recover damages if there has been a material misstatement in a registration statement filed under the Securities Act of 1933 is that the
    A. Issuer and plaintiff were in privity of contract with each other.
    B. Issuer failed to exercise due care in connection with the sale of the securities.
    C. Plaintiff gave value for the security.
    D. Plaintiff suffered a loss.

38. Lux Limited Partnership intends to offer $300,000 of its limited partnership interests under Rule 504 of Regulation D of the Securities Act of 1933. Which of the following statements is correct?
    A. The resale of the limited partnership interests by a purchaser generally will be restricted.
    B. The limited partnership interests may be sold only to accredited investors.
    C. The exemption under Rule 504 is **not** available to an issuer of limited partnership interests.
    D. The limited partnership interests may **not** be sold to more than 35 investors.

39. Which of the following types of claims would be paid first in the distribution of a bankruptcy estate under the liquidation provisions of Chapter 7 of the Federal Bankruptcy Code if the petition was filed July 15, 1993?
   A. A secured debt properly perfected on March 20, 1993.
   B. Inventory purchased and delivered August 1, 1993.
   C. Employee wages due April 30, 1993.
   D. Federal tax lien filed June 30, 1993.

40. An offering made under the provisions of Regulation A of the Securities Act of 1933 requires that the issuer
   A. File an offering circular with the SEC.
   B. Sell only to accredited investors.
   C. Provide investors with the prior four years' audited financial statements.
   D. Provide investors with a proxy registration statement.

41. Adler, Inc., is a reporting company under the Securities Exchange Act of 1934. The only security it has issued is voting common stock. Which of the following statements is correct?
   A. Because Adler is a reporting company, it is **not** required to file a registration statement under the Securities Act of 1933 for any future offerings of its common stock.
   B. Adler need **not** file its proxy statements with the SEC because it has only one class of stock outstanding.
   C. Any person who owns more than 10 percent of Adler's common stock must file a report with the SEC.
   D. It is unnecessary for the required annual report (Form 10K) to include audited financial statements.

42. Which of the following persons is **not** an insider of a corporation subject to the Securities Exchange Act of 1934 registration and reporting requirements?
   A. An attorney for the corporation.
   B. An owner of 5 percent of the corporation's outstanding debentures.
   C. A member of the board of directors.
   D. A stockholder who owns 10 percent of the outstanding common stock.

43. Pix Corp. is making a $6,000,000 stock offering. Pix wants the offering exempt from registration under the Securities Act of 1933.

Which of the following provisions of the Act would Pix have to comply with for the offering to be exempt?
   A. Regulation A.
   B. Regulation D, Rule 504.
   C. Regulation D, Rule 505.
   D. Regulation D, Rule 506.

44. When a CPA prepares a client's federal income tax return, the CPA has the responsibility to
   A. Be an advocate for the entity's realistically sustainable position.
   B. Verify the data to be used in preparing the return.
   C. Take a position of independent neutrality.
   D. Argue the position of the Internal Revenue Service.

45. Frey, Inc., intends to make a $2,000,000 common stock offering under Rule 505 of Regulation D of the Securities Act of 1933. Frey
   A. May sell the stock to an unlimited number of investors.
   B. May make the offering through a general advertising.
   C. Must notify the SEC within 15 days after the first sale of the offering.
   D. Must provide all investors with a prospectus.

46. Field Corp. issued a negotiable warehouse receipt to Hall for goods stored in Field's warehouse. Hall's goods were lost due to Field's failure to exercise such care as a reasonably careful person would under like circumstances. The state in which this transaction occurred follows the UCC rule with respect to a warehouseman's liability for lost goods. The warehouse receipt is silent on this point. Under the circumstances, Field is
   A. Liable because it is strictly liable for any loss.
   B. Liable because it was negligent.
   C. Not liable because the warehouse receipt was negotiable.
   D. Not liable unless Hall can establish that Field was grossly negligent.

47. Which of the following statements is correct concerning a bill of lading in the possession of Major Corp. that was issued by a common carrier and provides that the goods are to be delivered "to bearer"?
   A. The carrier's lien for any unpaid shipping charges does **not** entitle it to sell the goods to enforce the lien.
   B. The carrier will **not** be liable for delivering the goods to a person other than Major.
   C. The carrier may require Major to endorse the bill of lading prior to delivering the goods.
   D. The bill of lading can be negotiated by Major by delivery alone and without endorsement.

48. A person who loses a stock certificate is entitled to a new certificate to replace the lost one, provided certain requirements are satisfied. Which of the following is **not** such a requirement?
   A. The request for a new certificate is made before the issuer has notice that the lost certificate has been acquired by a bona fide purchaser.
   B. The owner files a sufficient indemnity bond with the issuer.
   C. The owner satisfies any reasonable requirements of the issuer.
   D. The fair market value of the security is placed in escrow with the issuer for six months.

49. Which of the following statements applies to a sale on approval under the UCC Sales Article?
   A. Both the buyer and seller must be merchants.
   B. The buyer must be purchasing the goods for resale.
   C. Risk of loss for the goods passes to the buyer when the goods are accepted after the trial period.
   D. Title to the goods passes to the buyer on delivery of the goods to the buyer.

50. Which of the following statements would **not** apply to a written contract governed by the provisions of the UCC Sales Article?
   A. The contract may involve the sale of personal property.
   B. The obligations of a nonmerchant may be different from those of a merchant.
   C. The obligations of the parties must be performed in good faith.
   D. The contract must involve the sale of goods for a price of $500 or more.

Items 51 and 52 are based on the following:

On May 2, Handy Hardware sent Ram Industries a signed purchase order that stated, in part, as follows:

"Ship for May 8 delivery 300 Model A-X socket sets at current dealer price. Terms 2/10/net 30."

Ram received Handy's purchase order on May 4. On May 5, Ram discovered that it had only 200 Model A-X socket sets and 100 Model W-Z socket sets in stock. Ram shipped the Model A-X and Model W-Z sets to Handy without any explanation concerning the shipment. The socket sets were received by Handy on May 8.

51. Which of the following statements concerning the shipment is correct?
   A. Ram's shipment is an acceptance of Handy's offer.
   B. Ram's shipment is a counteroffer.
   C. Handy's order must be accepted by Ram in writing before Ram ships the socket sets.
   D. Handy's order can only be accepted by Ram shipping conforming goods.

52. Assuming a contract exists between Handy and Ram, which of the following implied warranties would result?

   I. Implied warranty of merchantability.
   II. Implied warranty of fitness for a particular purpose.
   III. Implied warranty of title.

   A. I only.
   B. III only.
   C. I and III only.
   D. I, II and III.

53. In what order are the following obligations paid after a secured creditor rightfully sells the debtor's collateral after repossession?

   I. Debt owed to any junior security holder.
   II. Secured party's reasonable sale expenses.
   III. Debt owed to the secured party.

   A. I, II, III.
   B. II, I, III.
   C. II, III, I.
   D. III, II, I.

54. A CPA firm evaluates its personnel advancement experience to ascertain whether individuals meeting stated criteria are assigned increased degrees of responsibility. This is evidence of the firm's adherence to which of the following prescribed standards?

    A. Professional ethics.

    B. Supervision and review.

    C. Accounting and review services.

    D. Quality control.

55. Which of the following statements applies to consultation services engagements?

    A. A practitioner should obtain an understanding of the internal control structure to assess control risk.

    B. A practitioner is **not** permitted to compile a financial forecast.

    C. A practitioner should obtain sufficient relevant data to complete the engagement.

    D. A practitioner is to maintain an appearance of independence.

56. Smith contracted in writing to sell Peters a used personal computer for $600. The contract did not specifically address the time for payment, place of delivery, or Peters' right to inspect the computer. Which of the following statements is correct?

    A. Smith is obligated to deliver the computer to Peters' home.

    B. Peters is entitled to inspect the computer before paying for it.

    C. Peters may **not** pay for the computer using a personal check unless Smith agrees.

    D. Smith is **not** entitled to payment until 30 days after Peters receives the computer.

57. Cara Fabricating Co. and Taso Corp. agreed orally that Taso would custom manufacture a compressor for Cara at a price of $120,000. After Taso completed the work at a cost of $90,000, Cara notified Taso that the compressor was no longer needed. Taso is holding the compressor and has requested payment from Cara. Taso has been unable to resell the compressor for any price. Taso incurred storage fees of $2,000. If Cara refuses to pay Taso and Taso sues Cara, the most Taso will be entitled to recover is

    A. $ 92,000

    B. $105,000

    C. $120,000

    D. $122,000

58. Winslow Co., which is in the business of selling furniture, borrowed $60,000 from Pine Bank. Winslow executed a promissory note for that amount and used all of its accounts receivable as collateral for the loan. Winslow executed a security agreement that described the collateral. Winslow did not file a financing statement. Which of the following statements best describes this transaction?

    A. Perfection of the security interest occurred even though Winslow did **not** file a financing statement.

    B. Perfection of the security interest occurred by Pine having an interest in accounts receivable.

    C. Attachment of the security interest did **not** occur because Winslow failed to file a financing statement.

    D. Attachment of the security interest occurred when the loan was made and Winslow executed the security agreement.

59. Grey Corp. sells computers to the public. Grey sold and delivered a computer to West on credit. West executed and delivered to Grey a promissory note for the purchase price and a security agreement covering the computer. West purchased the computer for personal use. Grey did not file a financing statement. Is Grey's security interest perfected?

    A. Yes, because Grey retained ownership of the computer.

    B. Yes, because it was perfected at the time of attachment.

    C. No, because the computer was a consumer good.

    D. No, because Grey failed to file a financing statement

60. Noninventory goods were purchased and delivered on June 15, 1993. Several security interests exist in these goods. Which of the following security interests has priority over the others?

    A. Security interest in future goods attached June 10, 1993.

    B. Security interest attached June 15, 1993.

    C. Security interest perfected June 20, 1993.

    D. Purchase money security interest perfected June 24, 1993.

Number 2 (Estimated time—15 to 25 minutes)

Instructions

Question Number 2 consists of 12 items. Select the **best** answer for each item. Use a No. 2 pencil to blacken the appropriate ovals on the Objective Answer Sheet to indicate your answers. **Answer all items.** Your grade will be based on the total number of correct answers.

On June 1, 1990, Anderson bought a one family house from Beach for $240,000. At the time of the purchase, the house had a market value of $200,000 and the land was valued at $40,000. Anderson assumed the recorded $150,000 mortgage Beach owed Long Bank, gave a $70,000 mortgage to Rogers Loan Co., and paid $20,000 cash. Rogers did not record its mortgage. Rogers did not know about the Long mortgage.

Beach gave Anderson a quitclaim deed that failed to mention a recorded easement on the property held by Dalton, the owner of the adjacent piece of property. Anderson purchased a title insurance policy from Edge Title Insurance Co. Edge's policy neither disclosed nor excepted Dalton's easement.

On August 1, 1992, Anderson borrowed $30,000 from Forrest Finance to have a swimming pool dug. Anderson gave Forrest a $30,000 mortgage on the property. Forrest, knowing about the Long mortgage but not the Rogers mortgage, recorded its mortgage on August 10, 1992. After the digging began, Dalton sued to stop the work claiming violation of the easement. The court decided in Dalton's favor.

At the time of the purchase, Anderson had taken out two fire insurance policies; a $120,000 face value policy with Harvest Fire Insurance Co., and a $60,000 face value policy with Grant Fire Insurance Corp. Both policies contained a standard 80 percent coinsurance clause.

On December 1, 1992, a fire caused $180,000 damage to the house. At that time, the house had a market value of $250,000. Harvest and Grant refused to honor the policies claiming that the house was under insured.

Anderson made no mortgage payments after the fire and on June 1, 1993, after the house had been rebuilt, the mortgages were foreclosed. The balances due for principal and accrued interest were as follows: Long, $140,000; Rogers, $65,000; and Forrest, $28,000. At a foreclosure sale, the house and land were sold. After payment of all expenses, $200,000 of the proceeds remained for distribution. As a result of the above events, the following actions took place:

- Anderson sued Harvest and Grant for the face values of the fire insurance policies.
- Anderson sued Beach for failing to mention Dalton's easement in the quitclaim deed.
- Anderson sued Edge for failing to disclose Dalton's easement.
- Long, Rogers, and Forrest all demanded full payment of their mortgages from the proceeds of the foreclosure sale.

The preceding took place in a "Notice-Race" jurisdiction.

Required:

a. Items 61 through 63 relate to Anderson's suit against Harvest and Grant. For each item, select from *List I* the dollar amount Anderson will receive.

		List I
61.	What will be the dollar amount of Anderson's total fire insurance recovery?	A. $ 0
		B. $ 20,000
		C. $ 48,000
62.	What dollar amount will be payable by Harvest?	D. $ 54,000
		E. $ 60,000
63.	What dollar amount will be payable by Grant?	F. $ 80,000
		G. $ 96,000
		H. $108,000
		I. $120,000
		J. $144,000
		K. $162,000
		L. $180,000

b. Items 64 through 66 relate to Anderson's suit against Beach. For each item, determine whether that statement is True or False.

64. Anderson will win the suit against Beach.
65. A quitclaim deed conveys only the grantor's interest in the property.
66. A warranty deed protects the purchaser against any adverse title claim against the property.

c. Items 67 through 69 relate to Anderson's suit against Edge. For each item, determine whether the statement is True or False.

67. Anderson will win the suit against Edge.
68. Edge's policy should insure against all title defects of record.
69. Edge's failure to disclose Dalton's easement voids Anderson's contract with Beach.

d. Items 70 through 72 relate to the demands Long, Rogers, and Forrest have made to have their mortgages satisfied out of the foreclosure proceeds. For each item, select from *List II* the dollar amount to be paid.

		List II
70.	What dollar amount of the foreclosure proceeds will Long receive?	A. $ 0
		B. $ 28,000
		C. $ 32,000
71.	What dollar amount of the foreclosure proceeds will Rogers receive?	D. $ 65,000
		E. $107,000
		F. $135,000
72.	What dollar amount of the foreclosure proceeds will Forrest receive?	G. $140,000

Number 3 (Estimated time—15 to 25 minutes)

Instructions

Question Number 3 consists of 15 items. Select the **best** answer for each item. Use a No. 2 pencil to blacken the appropriate ovals on the Objective Answer Sheet to indicate your answers. **Answer all items.** Your grade will be based on the total number of correct answers.

On April 15, 1992, Wren Corp., an appliance wholesaler, was petitioned involuntarily into bankruptcy under the liquidation provisions of Chapter 7 of the Federal Bankruptcy Code.

When the petition was filed, Wren's creditors included:

Secured creditors	*Amount owed*
Fifth Bank - 1st mortgage on warehouse owned by Wren	$50,000
Hart Manufacturing Corp. - perfected purchase money security interest in inventory	30,000
TVN Computers, Inc. - perfected security interest in office computers	15,000

Unsecured creditors	*Amount owed*
IRS - 1990 federal income taxes	$20,000
Acme Office Cleaners - services for January, February, and March 1992	750
Ted Smith (employee) - February and March 1992 wages	2,400
Joan Sims (employee) - March 1992 commissions	1,500
Power Electric Co. - electricity charges for January, February, and March 1992	600
Soft Office Supplies - supplies purchased in 1991	2,000

The following transactions occurred before the bankruptcy petition was filed:

- On December 31, 1991, Wren paid off a $5,000 loan from Mary Lake, the sister of one of Wren's directors.
- On January 30, 1992, Wren donated $2,000 to Universal Charities.
- On February 1, 1992, Wren gave Young Finance Co. a security agreement covering Wren's office fixtures to secure a loan previously made by Young.
- On March 1, 1992, Wren made the final $1,000 monthly payment to Integral Appliance Corp. on a two-year note.
- On April 1, 1992, Wren purchased from Safety Co., a new burglar alarm system for its factory, for $5,000 cash.

All of Wren's assets were liquidated. The warehouse was sold for $75,000, the computers were sold for $12,000, and the inventory was sold for $25,000. After paying the bankruptcy administration expenses of $8,000, secured creditors, and priority general creditors, there was enough cash to pay each nonpriority general creditor 50 cents on the dollar.

Required:
a. Items 73 through 77 represent the transactions that occurred before the filing of the bankruptcy petition. For each transaction, determine if the transaction would be set aside as a preferential transfer by the bankruptcy court. On the Objective Answer Sheet, blacken (Y) if the transaction would be set aside or (N) if the transaction would **not** be set aside.

    73. Payment to Mary Lake
    74 Donation to Universal Charities
    75. Security agreement to Young Finance Co.
    76. Payment to Integral Appliance Corp.
    77. Purchase from Safety Co.

b. Items 78 through 82 represent creditor claims against the bankruptcy estate. Select from List I each creditor's order of payment in relation to the other creditors named in items 78 through 82 and blacken the corresponding oval on the Objective Answer Sheet.

		List I
78.	Bankruptcy administration expense	A. First
79.	Acme Office Cleaners	B. Second
80.	Fifth Bank	C. Third
81.	IRS	D. Fourth
82.	Joan Sims	E. Fifth

c. Items 83 through 87 also represent creditor claims against the bankruptcy estate. For each of the creditors listed in Items 83 through 87, select from List II the amount that creditor will receive and blacken the corresponding oval on the Objective Answer Sheet.

		List II
83.	TVN Computers Inc.	A. $0
84.	Hart Manufacturing Corp.	B. $ 300
85.	Ted Smith	C. $ 600
86.	Power Electric Co.	D. $ 1,000
87.	Soft Office Supplies	E. $ 1,200
		F. $ 2,000
		G. $ 2,200
		H. $ 2,400
		I. $12,000
		J. $13,500
		K. $15,000
		L. $25,000
		M. $27,500
		N. $30,000

Number 4 (Estimated time—15 to 25 minutes)

In 1990, Park, after consulting a CPA and an attorney, decided to have an *inter vivos* trust and will prepared. Park wanted to provide for the welfare of three close relatives: Archer, Book, and Cable, during Park's lifetime and after Park's death.

The trust was funded by cash and real estate transfers. The trust contained spendthrift provisions directing the trustees to pay the income to only the trust beneficiaries, Archer, Book, and Cable. Park also provided for $10,000 "sprinkling" provisions allowing for the annual distribution of up to $10,000 of principal to each beneficiary at the trustees' discretion.

Park's will provided for a "pour-over" transfer of any residuary estate to the trust.

Young, a CPA, and Zack, a stockbroker, were named trustees of the trust and executors of the will. Young and Zack were directed to perform their duties as "prudent business people" in investing and protecting the assets of the trust and estate.

During 1991, Young and Zack properly allocated income and principal and paid the trust income to Park's relatives as directed. They also made $5,000 principal payments to two of the beneficiaries for a medical emergency and to pay college tuition.

During 1992, Zack, with Young's consent, borrowed $10,000 from the trust. Zack agreed to repay the loan at a higher interest rate than the trust normally received on its investments. Archer, one of the trust beneficiaries, asked for and received a $15,000 principal payment. The money was used to enable Archer to invest in a joint venture with Zack.

In January 1993, Park died and the will was probated. After payment of all taxes, debts, and bequests, the residuary estate was transferred to the trust. Archer, Book, and Cable sued:

- To have the court allow distribution of the residuary estate instead of the residuary being transferred to the trust.
- To have the spendthrift trust terminated.
- To remove Young and Zack as trustees for making the $5,000 principal payments.
- To remove Young and Zack as trustees for allowing Zack to borrow money from the trust.
- To remove Young and Zack as trustees for making the $15,000 principal payment to Archer.

Required:

Determine whether Archer, Book, and Cable will be successful in the lawsuits and give the reasons for your conclusions.

Number 5 (Estimated time—15 to 25 minutes)

Williams Co. provides financial consulting services to the business community. On occasion, Williams will purchase promissory notes from its clients. The following transactions involving promissory notes purchased by Williams have resulted in disputes:

- Williams purchased the following promissory note from Jason Computers, Inc.:

> January 3, 1992
>
> For value received, Helco Distributors Corp. promises to pay $3,000 to the order of Jason Computers, Inc. with such payment to be made out of the proceeds of the resale of the computer components purchased this day from Jason Computers, Inc. and to be used as part of the customized computer systems sold to our customers. Payment shall be made two weeks after such proceeds become available.
>
> *J. Helco*
> ———————————
> J. Helco, President

Helco executed and delivered the note to Jason in payment for the computer components referred to in the note. Jason represented to Helco that all the components were new when, in fact, a large number of them were used and had been reconditioned. Williams was unaware of this fact at the time it acquired the note from Jason for $2,000. Jason endorsed and delivered the note to Williams in exchange for the $2,000 payment. Williams presented the promissory note to Helco for payment. Helco refused to pay, alleging that Jason misrepresented the condition of the components. Helco also advised Williams that the components had been returned to Jason within a few days after Helco had taken delivery.

Williams commenced an action against Helco, claiming that:

- the note is negotiable;
- Williams is a holder in due course; and
- Helco cannot raise Jason's misrepresentation as a defense to payment of the note.
- Williams Co. purchased a negotiable promissory note from Oliver International, Inc. that Oliver had received from Abco Products Corp., as partial payment on the sale of goods by Oliver to Abco. The maker of the note was Grover Corp., which had executed and delivered the note to Abco as payment for services rendered by Abco. When Oliver received the note from Abco, Oliver was unaware of the fact that

Grover disputed its obligation under the note because Grover was dissatisfied with the quality of the services Abco rendered. Williams was aware of Grover's claims at the time Williams purchased the note from Oliver. The reverse side of the note was endorsed as follows:

Pay to the order of Oliver

F. Smith
_____
F. Smith, President of Abco Products Corp.

Pay to the order of Williams Co. without recourse

N. Oliver
_____
N. Oliver, President of Oliver International Inc.

When the promissory note became due Williams demanded that Grover pay the note. Grover refused, claiming that Abco breached its contractual obligations to Grover and that Williams was aware of this fact at the time Williams acquired the note. Williams immediately advised both Abco and Oliver of Grover's refusal to pay and demanded payment from Oliver in the event Grover fails to pay the note.

Required:

Answer the following questions and give the reasons for your conclusions.

a. Are Williams' claims correct regarding the Helco promissory note?

b. Is Grover correct in refusing to pay its note?

c. What are the rights of Williams against Oliver in the event Grover is not required to pay its note?

(Note: These instructions have been adapted from the May 1994 CPA Examination Booklet.)

Uniform Certified Public Accountant Examination

EXAMINATION QUESTION BOOKLET

AUDITING – 1:30 P.M. to 6:00 P.M.

The point values for each question, and estimated time allotments based primarily on point value, are as follows:

	Point Value	Estimated Minutes	
		Minimum	*Maximum*
No. 1	60	140	150
No. 2	10	15	25
No. 3	10	15	25
No. 4	10	25	35
No. 5	10	25	35
Totals	100	220	270

INSTRUCTIONS TO CANDIDATES

Failure to follow these instructions may have an adverse effect on your Examination grade.

1. Record your 7-digit candidate number in the boxes provided at the upper right-hand corner of this page.

2. Question numbers 1, 2, and 3 should be answered on the *Objective Answer Sheet*, which is pages 11 and 12 of your *Examination Answer Booklet*. You should attempt to answer all objective items. There is no penalty for incorrect responses. Since the objective items are computer-graded, your comments and calculations associated with them are not considered. Be certain that you have entered your answers on the *Objective Answer Sheet* before the examination time is up. The objective portion of your examination will not be graded if you fail to record your answers on the *Objective Answer Sheet*. You will not be given additional time to record your answers.

3. Question numbers 4 and 5 should be answered beginning on page 3 of the *Examination Answer Booklet*. If you have not completed answering a question on a page, fill in the appropriate spaces in the wording on the bottom of the page **"QUESTION NUMBER _____ CONTINUES ON PAGE _____ ."** If you have completed answering a question, fill in the appropriate space in the wording on the bottom of the page **"QUESTION NUMBER _____ ENDS ON THIS PAGE."** Always begin the start of an answer to a question on the top of a new page (which may be the back side of a sheet of paper).

4. Record your 7-digit candidate number, state, and question number where indicated on pages 3 through 10 of the *Examination Answer Booklet*.

5. Although the primary purpose of the examination is to test your knowledge and application of the subject matter, selected essay responses will be graded for writing skills.

6. You are required to turn in by the end of each session:
   a. Attendance Record Form, front page of *Examination Answer Booklet*;
   b. *Objective Answer Sheet*, pages 11 and 12 of *Examination Answer Booklet*;
   c. Remaining Portion of *Examination Answer Booklet*;
   d. *Examination Question Booklet*; and
   e. All unused examination materials.

   Your examination will not be graded unless the above listed items are handed in before leaving the examination room.

7. Unless otherwise instructed, if you want your *Examination Question Booklet* mailed to you, write your name and address in both places indicated on the back cover and place 52 cents postage in the space provided. *Examination Question Booklets* will be distributed no sooner than the day following the administration of this examination.

Auditing (AUDIT)

Number 1 (Estimated time—140 to 150 minutes)

Instructions

Select the **best** answer for each of the following items. Use a No. 2 pencil to blacken the appropriate ovals on the Objective Answer Sheet to indicate your answers. **Mark only one answer for each item. Answer all items.** Your grade will be based on the total number of correct answers.

1. An auditor would **least** likely use computer software to
   A. Construct parallel simulations.
   B. Access client data files.
   C. Prepare spreadsheets.
   D. Assess EDP control risk.

2. Which of the following best describes what is meant by the term generally accepted auditing standards?
   A. Pronouncements issued by the Auditing Standards Board.
   B. Rules acknowledged by the accounting profession because of their universal application.
   C. Procedures to be used to gather evidence to support financial statements.
   D. Measures of the quality of the auditor's performance.

3. To obtain evidence that online access controls are properly functioning, an auditor most likely would
   A. Create checkpoints at periodic intervals after live data processing to test for unauthorized use of the system.
   B. Examine the transaction log to discover whether any transactions were lost or entered twice due to a system malfunction.
   C. Enter invalid identification numbers or passwords to ascertain whether the system rejects them.
   D. Vouch a random sample of processed transactions to assure proper authorization.

4. The auditor with final responsibility for an engagement and one of the assistants have a difference of opinion about the results of an auditing procedure. If the assistant believes it is necessary to be disassociated from the matter's resolution, the CPA firm's procedures should enable the assistant to
   A. Refer the disagreement to the AICPA's Quality Review Committee.
   B. Document the details of the disagreement with the conclusion reached.
   C. Discuss the disagreement with the entity's management or its audit committee.
   D. Report the disagreement to an impartial peer review monitoring team.

5. Before accepting an engagement to audit a new client, an auditor is required to
   A. Make inquiries of the predecessor auditor after obtaining the consent of the prospective client.
   B. Obtain the prospective client's signature to the engagement letter.
   C. Prepare a memorandum setting forth the staffing requirements and documenting the preliminary audit plan.
   D. Discuss the management representation letter with the prospective client's audit committee.

6. In considering materiality for planning purposes, an auditor believes that misstatements aggregating $10,000 would have a material effect on an entity's income statement, but that misstatements would have to aggregate $20,000 to materially affect the balance sheet. Ordinarily, it would be appropriate to design auditing procedures that would be expected to detect misstatements that aggregate
   A. $10,000
   B. $15,000
   C. $20,000
   D. $30,000

7. On the basis of audit evidence gathered and evaluated, an auditor decides to increase the assessed level of control risk from that originally planned. To achieve an overall audit risk level that is substantially the same as the planned audit risk level, the auditor would
   A. Increase inherent risk.
   B. Increase materiality levels.
   C. Decrease substantive testing.
   D. Decrease detection risk.

8. Analytical procedures used in planning an audit should focus on
    A. Evaluating the adequacy of evidence gathered concerning unusual balances.
    B. Testing individual account balances that depend on accounting estimates.
    C. Enhancing the auditor's understanding of the client's business.
    D. Identifying material weaknesses in the internal control structure.

9. In performing an attestation engagement, a CPA typically
    A. Supplies litigation support services.
    B. Assesses control risk at a low level.
    C. Expresses a conclusion about an assertion.
    D. Provides management consulting advice.

10. An advantage of statistical sampling over nonstatistical sampling is that statistical sampling helps an auditor to
    A. Minimize the failure to detect errors and irregularities.
    B. Eliminate the risk of nonsampling errors.
    C. Reduce the level of audit risk and materiality to a relatively low amount.
    D. Measure the sufficiency of the evidential matter obtained.

11. An auditor who discovers that client employees have committed an illegal act that has a material effect on the client's financial statements most likely would withdraw from the engagement if
    A. The illegal act is a violation of generally accepted accounting principles.
    B. The client does **not** take the remedial action that the auditor considers necessary.
    C. The illegal act was committed during a prior year that was **not** audited.
    D. The auditor has already assessed control risk at the maximum level.

12. A CPA is required to comply with the provisions of "Statements on Standards for Accounting and Review Services" when

	Processing financial data for clients of other CPA firms	Consulting on accounting matters
A.	Yes	Yes
B.	Yes	No
C.	No	Yes
D.	No	No

13. Which of the following most likely would be an advantage in using classical variables sampling rather than probability-proportional-to-size (PPS) sampling?
    A. An estimate of the standard deviation of the population's recorded amounts is **not** required.
    B. The auditor rarely needs the assistance of a computer program to design an efficient sample.
    C. Inclusion of zero and negative balances generally does **not** require special design considerations.
    D. Any amount that is individually significant is automatically identified and selected.

14. An auditor most likely would modify an unqualified opinion if the entity's financial statements include a footnote on related party transactions
    A. Disclosing loans to related parties at interest rates significantly below prevailing market rates.
    B. Describing an exchange of real estate for similar property in a nonmonetary related party transaction.
    C. Stating that a particular related party transaction occurred on terms equivalent to those that would have prevailed in an arm's-length transaction.
    D. Presenting the dollar volume of related party transactions and the effects of any change in the method of establishing terms from prior periods.

15. Which of the following circumstances most likely would cause an auditor to believe that material misstatements may exist in an entity's financial statements?
    A. Accounts receivable confirmation requests yield significantly fewer responses than expected.
    B. Audit trails of computer-generated transactions exist only for a short time.
    C. The chief financial officer does **not** sign the management representation letter until the last day of the auditor's field work.
    D. Management consults with other accountants about significant accounting matters.

16. An advantage of using systems flowcharts to document information about internal control instead of using internal control questionnaires is that systems flowcharts
    A. Identify internal control weaknesses more prominently.
    B. Provide a visual depiction of clients' activities.
    C. Indicate whether control procedures are operating effectively.
    D. Reduce the need to observe clients' employees performing routine tasks.

17. For which of the following judgments may an independent auditor share responsibility with an entity's internal auditor who is assessed to be both competent and objective?

	Materiality of misstatements	Evaluation of accounting estimates
A.	Yes	No
B.	No	Yes
C.	No	No
D.	Yes	Yes

18. Which of the following statements is **not** true of the test data approach to testing an accounting system?
   A. Test data are processed by the client's computer programs under the auditor's control.
   B. The test data need consist of only those valid and invalid conditions that interest the auditor.
   C. Only one transaction of each type need be tested.
   D. The test data must consist of all possible valid and invalid conditions.

19. In obtaining an understanding of an entity's internal control structure in a financial statement audit, an auditor is **not** obligated to
   A. Determine whether the control procedures have been placed in operation.
   B. Perform procedures to understand the design of the internal control structure policies.
   C. Document the understanding of the entity's internal control structure elements.
   D. Search for significant deficiencies in the operation of the internal control structure.

20. As a result of sampling procedures applied as tests of controls, an auditor incorrectly assesses control risk lower than appropriate. The most likely explanation for this situation is that
   A. The deviation rates of both the auditor's sample and the population exceed the tolerable rate.
   B. The deviation rates of both the auditor's sample and the population is less than the tolerable rate.
   C. The deviation rate in the auditor's sample is less than the tolerable rate, but the deviation rate in the population exceeds the tolerable rate.
   D. The deviation rate in the auditor's sample exceeds the tolerable rate, but the deviation rate in the population is less than the tolerable rate.

21. An auditor may decide to assess control risk at the maximum level for certain assertions because the auditor believes
   A. Control policies and procedures are unlikely to pertain to the assertions.
   B. The entity's control environment, accounting system, and control procedures are interrelated.
   C. Sufficient evidential matter to support the assertions is likely to be available.
   D. More emphasis on tests of controls than substantive tests is warranted.

22. Which of the following statements concerning control risk is correct?
   A. Assessing control risk and obtaining an understanding of an entity's internal control structure may be performed concurrently.
   B. When control risk is at the maximum level, an auditor is required to document the basis for that assessment.
   C. Control risk may be assessed sufficiently low to eliminate substantive testing for significant transaction classes.
   D. When assessing control risk an auditor should **not** consider evidence obtained in prior audits about the operation of control procedures.

23. Regardless of the assessed level of control risk, an auditor would perform some
   A. Tests of controls to determine the effectiveness of internal control policies.
   B. Analytical procedures to verify the design of internal control procedures.
   C. Substantive tests to restrict detection risk for significant transaction classes.
   D. Dual-purpose tests to evaluate both the risk of monetary misstatement and preliminary control risk.

24. Which of the following audit techniques most likely would provide an auditor with the most assurance about the effectiveness of the operation on an internal control procedure?
   A. Confirmation with outside parties.
   B. Inquiry of client personnel.
   C. Recomputation of account balance amounts.
   D. Observation of client personnel.

25. When communicating internal control structure related matters noted in an audit, an auditor's report issued on reportable conditions should indicate that

A. Errors or irregularities may occur and **not** be detected because there are inherent limitations in any internal control structure.

B. The issuance of an unqualified opinion on the financial statements may be dependent on corrective follow-up action.

C. The deficiencies noted were **not** detected within a timely period by employees in the normal course of performing their assigned functions.

D. The purpose of the audit was to report on the financial statements and **not** to provide assurance on the internal control structure.

26. To determine whether accounts payable are complete, an auditor performs a test to verify that all merchandise received is recorded. The population of documents for this test consists of all

A. Payment vouchers.

B. Receiving reports.

C. Purchase requisitions.

D. Vendor's invoices.

27. Which of the following internal control procedures is **not** usually performed in the treasurer's department?

A. Verifying the accuracy of checks and vouchers.

B. Controlling the mailing of checks to vendors.

C. Approving vendors' invoices for payment.

D. Canceling payment vouchers when paid.

28. The objectives of the internal control structure for a production cycle are to provide assurance that transactions are properly executed and recorded, and that

A. Production orders are prenumbered and signed by a supervisor.

B. Custody of work in process and of finished goods is properly maintained.

C. Independent internal verification of activity reports is established.

D. Transfers to finished goods are documented by a completed production report and a quality control report.

29. In a well designed internal control structure, employees in the same department most likely would approve purchase orders, and also

A. Reconcile the open invoice file.

B. Inspect goods upon receipt.

C. Authorize requisitions of goods.

D. Negotiate terms with vendors.

30. The purpose of segregating the duties of hiring personnel and distributing payroll checks is to separate the

A. Human resources function from the controllership function.

B. Administrative controls from the internal accounting controls.

C. Authorization of transactions from the custody of related assets.

D. Operational responsibility from the record keeping responsibility.

31. Which of the following departments most likely would approve changes in pay rates and deductions from employee salaries?

A. Personnel.

B. Treasurer.

C. Controller.

D. Payroll.

32. Which of the following questions would an auditor most likely include on an internal control questionnaire for notes payable?

A. Are assets that collateralize notes payable critically needed for the entity's continued existence?

B. Are two or more authorized signatures required on checks that repay notes payable?

C. Are the proceeds from notes payable used for the purchase of noncurrent assets?

D. Are direct borrowings on notes payable authorized by the board of directors?

33. Which of the following internal control procedures would an entity most likely use to assist in satisfying the completeness assertion related to long-term investments?

A. Senior management verifies that securities in the bank safe deposit box are registered in the entity's name.

B. The internal auditor compares the securities in the bank safe deposit box with recorded investments.

C. The treasurer vouches the acquisition of securities by comparing brokers' advices with canceled checks.

D. The controller compares the current market prices of recorded investments with the brokers' advices on file.

34. Equipment acquisitions that are misclassified as maintenance expense most likely would be detected by an internal control procedure that provides for
    A. Segregation of duties of employees in the accounts payable department.
    B. Independent verification of invoices for disbursements recorded as equipment acquisitions.
    C. Investigation of variances within a formal budgeting system.
    D. Authorization by the board of directors of significant equipment acquisitions.

35. When performing an engagement to review a non-public entity's financial statements, an accountant most likely would
    A. Confirm a sample of significant accounts receivable balances.
    B. Ask about actions taken at board of directors' meetings.
    C. Obtain an understanding of the internal control structure.
    D. Limit the distribution of the accountant's report.

36. Which of the following statements concerning audit evidence is correct?
    A. To be competent, audit evidence should be either persuasive or relevant, but need **not** be both.
    B. The measure of the validity of audit evidence lies in the auditor's judgment.
    C. The difficulty and expense of obtaining audit evidence concerning an account balance is a valid basis for omitting the test.
    D. A client's accounting data can be sufficient audit evidence to support the financial statements.

37. In auditing accounts payable, an auditor's procedures most likely would focus primarily on management's assertion of
    A. Existence or occurrence.
    B. Presentation and disclosure.
    C. Completeness.
    D. Valuation or allocation.

38. For audits of financial statements made in accordance with generally accepted auditing standards, the use of analytical procedures is required to some extent

	As a substantive test	In the final review stage
A.	Yes	Yes
B.	Yes	No
C.	No	Yes
D.	No	No

39. The primary source of information to be reported about litigation, claims, and assessments is the
    A. Client's lawyer.
    B. Court records.
    C. Client's management.
    D. Independent auditor.

40. In which of the following circumstances would the use of the negative form of accounts receivable confirmation most likely be justified?
    A. A substantial number of accounts may be in dispute and the accounts receivable balance arises from sales to a few major customers.
    B. A substantial number of accounts may be in dispute and the accounts receivable balance arises from sales to many customers with small balances.
    C. A small number of accounts may be in dispute and the accounts receivable balance arises from sales to a few major customers.
    D. A small number of accounts may be in dispute and the accounts receivable balance arises from sales to many customers with small balances.

41. Which of the following procedures would an auditor most likely perform in searching for unrecorded payables?
    A. Reconcile receiving reports with related cash payments made just prior to year-end.
    B. Contrast the ratio of accounts payable to purchases with the prior year's ratio.
    C. Vouch a sample of creditor balances to supporting invoices, receiving reports, and purchase orders.
    D. Compare cash payments occurring after the balance sheet date with the accounts payable trial balance.

42. The permanent (continuing) file of an auditor's working papers most likely would include copies of the
    A. Bank statements.
    B. Debt agreements.
    C. Lead schedules.
    D. Attorney's letters.

43. A primary advantage of using generalized audit software packages to audit the financial statements of a client that uses an EDP system is that the auditor may

A. Substantiate the accuracy of data through self-checking digits and hash totals.
B. Reduce the level of required tests of controls to a relatively small amount.
C. Access information stored on computer files while having a limited understanding of the client's hardware and software features.
D. Consider increasing the use of substantive tests of transactions in place of analytical procedures.

44. Which of the following is a documentation requirement that an auditor should follow when auditing in accordance with "Government Auditing Standards"?

A. The auditor should obtain written representations from management acknowledging responsibility for correcting instances of fraud, abuse, and waste.
B. The auditor's working papers should contain sufficient information so that supplementary oral explanations are **not** required.
C. The auditor should document the procedures that assure discovery of all illegal acts and contingent liabilities resulting from noncompliance.
D. The auditor's working papers should contain a caveat that all instances of material errors and irregularities may **not** be identified.

45. When auditing an entity's financial statements in accordance with "Government Auditing Standards," an auditor should prepare a written report on the auditor's

A. Identification of the causes of performance problems and recommendations for actions to improve operations.
B. Understanding of the internal control structure and assessment of control risk.
C. Field work and procedures that substantiated the auditor's specific findings and conclusions.
D. Opinion on the entity's attainment of the goals and objectives specified by applicable laws and regulations.

46. When disclaiming an opinion due to a client-imposed scope limitation, an auditor should indicate in a separate paragraph why the audit did not comply with generally accepted auditing standards. The auditor should also omit the

	Scope paragraph	Opinion paragraph
A.	No	Yes
B.	Yes	Yes
C.	No	No
D.	Yes	No

47. Management believes and the auditor is satisfied that the chance of a material loss resulting from the resolution of a lawsuit is more than remote but less than probable. Which of the following matters should the auditor consider in deciding whether to add an explanatory paragraph?

	Likelihood that the loss is closer to probable than remote	Magnitude by which the loss exceeds the auditor's materiality
A.	Yes	Yes
B.	Yes	No
C.	No	Yes
D.	No	No

48. Comparative financial statements include the financial statements of the prior year that were audited by a predecessor auditor whose report is not presented. If the predecessor's report was qualified, the successor should

A. Indicate the substantive reasons for the qualification in the predecessor auditor's opinion.
B. Request the client to reissue the predecessor's report on the prior year's statements.
C. Issue an updated comparative audit report indicating the division of responsibility.
D. Express an opinion only on the current year's statements and make **no** reference to the prior year's statements.

49. An auditor decides to issue a qualified opinion on an entity's financial statements because a major inadequacy in its computerized accounting records prevents the auditor from applying necessary procedures. The opinion paragraph of the auditor's report should state that the qualification pertains to

A. A client-imposed scope limitation.
B. A departure from generally accepted auditing standards.
C. The possible effects on the financial statements.
D. Inadequate disclosure of necessary information.

50. When unaudited financial statements are presented in comparative form with audited financial statements in a document filed with the Securities and Exchange Commission, such statements should be

	Marked as "unaudited"	Withheld until audited	Referred to in the auditor's report
A.	Yes	No	No
B.	Yes	No	Yes
C.	No	Yes	Yes
D.	No	Yes	No

51. When an auditor qualifies an opinion because of inadequate disclosure, the auditor should describe the nature of the omission in a separate explanatory paragraph and modify the

	Introductory paragraph	Scope paragraph
A.	Yes	Yes
B.	Yes	No
C.	No	Yes
D.	No	No

52. Several sources of GAAP consulted by an auditor are in conflict as to the application of an accounting principle. Which of the following should the auditor consider the most authoritative?
   A. FASB Technical Bulletins.
   B. AICPA Accounting Interpretations.
   C. FASB Statements of Financial Accounting Concepts.
   D. AICPA Technical Practice Aids.

53. During an engagement to review the financial statements of a nonpublic entity, an accountant becomes aware of a material departure from GAAP. If the accountant decides to modify the standard review report because management will **not** revise the financial statements, the accountant should
   A. Express negative assurance on the accounting principles that do **not** conform with GAAP.
   B. Disclose the departure from GAAP in a separate paragraph of the report.
   C. Issue an adverse or an "except for" qualified opinion, depending on materiality.
   D. Express positive assurance on the accounting principles that conform with GAAP.

54. Which of the following representations does an accountant make implicitly when issuing the standard report for the compilation of a nonpublic entity's financial statements?
   A. The accountant is independent with respect to the entity.
   B. The financial statements have **not** been audited.
   C. A compilation consists principally of inquiries and analytical procedures.
   D. The accountant does **not** express any assurance on the financial statements.

55. An entity changed from the straight-line method to the declining balance method of depreciation for all newly acquired assets. This change has no material effect on the current year's financial statements, but is reasonably certain to have a substantial effect in later years. If the change is disclosed in the notes to the financial statements, the auditor should issue a report with a(an)
   A. "Except for" qualified opinion.
   B. Explanatory paragraph.
   C. Unqualified opinion.
   D. Consistency modification.

56. A CPA is permitted to accept a separate engagement (**not** in conjunction with an audit of financial statements) to audit an entity's

	Schedule of accounts receivable	Schedule of royalties
A.	Yes	Yes
B.	Yes	No
C.	No	Yes
D.	No	No

57. An accountant's standard report on a compilation of a projection should **not** include a
   A. Statement that a compilation of a projection is limited in scope.
   B. Disclaimer of responsibility to update the report for events occurring after the report's date.
   C. Statement that the accountant expresses only limited assurance that the results may be achieved.
   D. Separate paragraph that describes the limitations on the presentation's usefulness.

58. In performing a financial statement audit in accordance with "Government Auditing Standards," an auditor is required to report on the entity's compliance with laws and regulations. This report should
    A. State that compliance with laws and regulations is the responsibility of the entity's management.
    B. Describe the laws and regulations that the entity must comply with.
    C. Provide an opinion on overall compliance with laws and regulations.
    D. Indicate that the auditor does **not** possess legal skills and **cannot** make legal judgments.

59. Which of the following events occurring after the issuance of an auditor's report most likely would cause the auditor to make further inquiries about the previously issued financial statements?
    A. A technological development that could affect the entity's future ability to continue as a going concern.
    B. The discovery of information regarding a contingency that existed before the financial statements were issued.
    C. The entity's sale of a subsidiary that accounts for 30 percent of the entity's consolidated sales.
    D. The final resolution of a lawsuit explained in a separate paragraph of the auditor's report.

60. An auditor is obligated to communicate a proposed audit adjustment to an entity's audit committee only if the adjustment
    A. Has **not** been recorded before the end of the auditor's field work.
    B. Has a significant effect on the entity's financial reporting process.
    C. Is a recurring matter that was proposed to management the prior year.
    D. Results from the correction of a prior period's departure from GAAP.

61. Which of the following procedures should an auditor generally perform regarding subsequent events?
    A. Compare the latest available interim financial statements with the financial statements being audited.
    B. Send second requests to the client's customers who failed to respond to initial accounts receivable confirmation requests.
    C. Communicate material weaknesses in the internal control structure to the client's audit committee.
    D. Review the cut-off bank statements for several months after the year end.

62. In the auditor's report, the principal auditor decides not to make reference to another CPA who audited a client's subsidiary. The principal auditor could justify this decision if, among other requirements, the principal auditor
    A. Issues an unqualified opinion on the consolidated financial statements.
    B. Learns that the other CPA issued an unqualified opinion on the subsidiary's financial statements.
    C. Is unable to review the audit programs and working papers of the other CPA.
    D. Is satisfied as to the independence and professional reputation of the other CPA.

63. Which of the following matters is covered in a typical comfort letter?
    A. Negative assurance concerning whether the entity's internal control procedures operated as designed during the period being audited.
    B. An opinion regarding whether the entity complied with laws and regulations under "Government Auditing Standards" and the Single Audit Act of 1984.
    C. Positive assurance concerning whether unaudited condensed financial information complied with generally accepted accounting principles.
    D. An opinion as to whether the audited financial statements comply in form with the accounting requirements of the SEC.

64. An auditor most likely would be responsible for assuring that management communicates significant deficiencies in the design of the internal control structure
    A. To a court-appointed creditors' committee when the client is operating under Chapter 11 of the Federal Bankruptcy Code.
    B. To shareholders with significant influence (more than 20 percent equity ownership) when the reportable conditions are deemed to be material weaknesses.
    C. To the Securities and Exchange Commission when the client is a publicly held entity.
    D. To specific legislative and regulatory bodies when reporting under "Government Auditing Standards."

65. The objective of a review of interim financial information of a public entity is to provide an accountant with a basis for reporting whether
    A. A reasonable basis exists for expressing an updated opinion regarding the financial statements that were previously audited.
    B. Material modifications should be made to conform with generally accepted accounting principles.
    C. The financial statements are presented fairly in accordance with standards of interim reporting.
    D. The financial statements are presented fairly in accordance with generally accepted accounting principles.

66. The ultimate purpose of assessing control risk is to contribute to the auditor's evaluation of the
    A. Factors that raise doubts about the auditability of the financial statements.
    B. Operating effectiveness of internal control policies and procedures.
    C. Risk that material misstatements exist in the financial statements.
    D. Possibility that the nature and extent of substantive tests may be reduced.

67. When an auditor assesses control risk below the maximum level, the auditor is required to document the auditor's

	Basis for concluding that control risk is below the maximum level	Understanding of the entity's internal control structure elements
A.	No	No
B.	Yes	Yes
C.	Yes	No
D.	No	Yes

68. Audit evidence concerning segregation of duties ordinarily is best obtained by
    A. Performing tests of transactions that corroborate management's financial statement assertions.
    B. Observing the employees as they apply control procedures.
    C. Obtaining a flowchart of activities performed by available personnel.
    D. Developing audit objectives that reduce control risk.

69. In obtaining an understanding of an entity's internal control structure, an auditor is required to obtain knowledge about the

	Operating effectiveness of policies and procedures	Design of policies and procedures
A.	Yes	Yes
B.	No	Yes
C.	Yes	No
D.	No	No

70. Assessing control risk at below the maximum most likely would involve
    A. Changing the timing of substantive tests by omitting interim-date testing and performing the tests at year end.
    B. Identifying specific internal control structure policies and procedures relevant to specific assertions.
    C. Performing more extensive substantive tests with larger sample sizes than originally planned.
    D. Reducing inherent risk for most of the assertions relevant to significant account balances.

71. Which of the following internal control procedures most likely would deter lapping of collections from customers?
    A. Independent internal verification of dates of entry in the cash receipts journal with dates of daily cash summaries.
    B. Authorization of write-offs of uncollectible accounts by a supervisor independent of credit approval.
    C. Segregation of duties between receiving cash and posting the accounts receivable ledger.
    D. Supervisory comparison of the daily cash summary with the sum of the cash receipts journal entries.

72. Which of the following most likely would be the result of ineffective internal control policies and procedures in the revenue cycle?
    A. Final authorization of credit memos by personnel in the sales department could permit an employee defalcation scheme.
    B. Fictitious transactions could be recorded, causing an understatement of revenues and an overstatement of receivables.
    C. Irregularities in recording transactions in the subsidiary accounts could result in a delay in goods shipped.
    D. Omission of shipping documents could go undetected, causing an understatement of inventory.

73. The authority to accept incoming goods in receiving should be based on a(an)
    A. Vendor's invoice.
    B. Materials requisition.
    C. Bill of lading.
    D. Approved purchase order.

74. Mailing disbursement checks and remittance advices should be controlled by the employee who
    A. Matches the receiving reports, purchase orders, and vendors' invoices.
    B. Signs the checks last.
    C. Prepares the daily voucher summary.
    D. Agrees the check register to the daily check summary.

75. Which of the following procedures would an auditor **least** likely perform in planning a financial statement audit?
    A. Coordinating the assistance of entity personnel in data preparation.
    B. Discussing matters that may affect the audit with firm personnel responsible for non-audit services to the entity.
    C. Selecting a sample of vendors' invoices for comparison to receiving reports.
    D. Reading the current year's interim financial statements.

76. Which of the following audit risk components may be assessed in nonquantitative terms?

	Control risk	Detection risk	Inherent risk
A.	Yes	Yes	Yes
B.	No	Yes	Yes
C.	Yes	Yes	No
D.	Yes	No	Yes

77. When assessing an internal auditor's competence, a CPA ordinarily obtains information about all of the following **except**
    A. Quality of working paper documentation.
    B. Educational level and professional experience.
    C. Audit programs and procedures.
    D. Access to information about related parties.

78. In testing long-term investments, an auditor ordinarily would use analytical procedures to ascertain the reasonableness of the
    A. Completeness of recorded investment income.
    B. Classification between current and noncurrent portfolios.
    C. Valuation of marketable equity securities.
    D. Existence of unrealized gains or losses in the portfolio.

79. Which of the following statements is correct concerning analytical procedures?
    A. Analytical procedures usually involve comparisons of ratios developed from recorded amounts to assertions developed by management.
    B. Analytical procedures used in planning an audit generally use data aggregated at a high level.
    C. Analytical procedures can replace tests of controls in gathering evidence to support the assessed level of control risk.
    D. Analytical procedures are more efficient, but **not** more effective, than tests of details and transactions.

80. Although the quantity and content of audit working papers vary with each particular engagement, an auditor's permanent files most likely include
    A. Schedules that support the current year's adjusting entries.
    B. Prior years' accounts receivable confirmations that were classified as exceptions.
    C. Documentation indicating that the audit work was adequately planned and supervised.
    D. Analyses of capital stock and other owners' equity accounts.

81. Sound internal control procedures dictate that defective merchandise returned by customers should be presented initially to the
    A. Accounts receivable supervisor.
    B. Receiving clerk.
    C. Shipping department supervisor.
    D. Sales clerk.

82. Davis, CPA, believes there is substantial doubt about the ability of Hill Co. to continue as a going concern for a reasonable period of time. In evaluating Hill's plans for dealing with the adverse effects of future conditions and events, Davis most likely would consider, as a mitigating factor, Hill's plans to
    A. Accelerate research and development projects related to future products.
    B. Accumulate treasury stock at prices favorable to Hill's historic price range.
    C. Purchase equipment and production facilities currently being leased.
    D. Negotiate reductions in required dividends being paid on preferred stock.

83. Which of the following procedures would provide the most reliable audit evidence?
    A. Inquiries of the client's internal audit staff held in private.
    B. Inspection of prenumbered client purchase orders filed in the vouchers payable department.
    C. Analytical procedures performed by the auditor on the entity's trial balance.
    D. Inspection of bank statements obtained directly from the client's financial institution.

84. An auditor most likely would review an entity's periodic accounting for the numerical sequence of shipping documents and invoices to support management's financial statement assertion of
    A. Existence or occurrence.
    B. Rights and obligations.
    C. Valuation or allocation.
    D. Completeness.

85. When auditing inventories, an auditor would **least** likely verify that
    A. The financial statement presentation of inventories is appropriate.
    B. Damaged goods and obsolete items have been properly accounted for.
    C. All inventory owned by the client is on hand at the time of the count.
    D. The client has used proper inventory pricing.

86. In evaluating the adequacy of the allowance for doubtful accounts, an auditor most likely reviews the entity's aging of receivables to support management's financial statement assertion of
    A. Existence or occurrence.
    B. Valuation or allocation.
    C. Completeness.
    D. Rights and obligations.

87. An auditor who uses the work of a specialist may refer to the specialist in the auditor's report if the
    A. Specialist's findings provide the auditor greater assurance of reliability about management's representations.
    B. Auditor adds an explanatory paragraph to an unqualified opinion describing an uncertainty resulting from the specialist's findings.
    C. Auditor's use of the specialist's findings is different from that of prior years.
    D. Specialist is a related party whose findings fully corroborate management's financial statement assertions.

88. The primary purpose of sending a standard confirmation request to financial institutions with which the client has done business during the year is to
    A. Detect kiting activities that may otherwise **not** be discovered.
    B. Corroborate information regarding deposit and loan balances.
    C. Provide the data necessary to prepare a proof of cash.
    D. Request information about contingent liabilities and secured transactions.

89. Which of the following procedures would an auditor most likely perform for year-end accounts receivable confirmations when the auditor did **not** receive replies to second requests?
    A. Review the cash receipts journal for the month prior to the year end.
    B. Intensify the study of the internal control structure concerning the revenue cycle.
    C. Increase the assessed level of detection risk for the existence assertion.
    D. Inspect the shipping records documenting the merchandise sold to the debtors.

90. An auditor most likely would perform substantive tests of details on payroll transactions and balances when
    A. Cutoff tests indicate a substantial amount of accrued payroll expense.
    B. The assessed level of control risk relative to payroll transactions is low.
    C. Analytical procedures indicate unusual fluctuations in recurring payroll entries.
    D. Accrued payroll expense consists primarily of unpaid commissions.

Number 2 (Estimated time—15 to 25 minutes)

Instructions

Question Number 2 consists of 13 items pertaining to possible deficiencies in an accountant's review report. Select the **best** answer for each item. Use a No. 2 pencil to blacken the appropriate ovals on the Objective Answer Sheet to indicate your answers. **Answer all items.** Your grade will be based on the total number of correct answers.

Jordan & Stone, CPAs, audited the financial statements of Tech Co., a nonpublic entity, for the year ended December 31, 1991, and expressed an unqualified opinion. For the year ended December 31, 1992, Tech issued comparative financial statements. Jordan & Stone reviewed Tech's 1992 financial statements and Kent, an assistant on the engagement, drafted the accountants' review report below. Land, the engagement supervisor, decided not to reissue the prior year's auditors' report, but instructed Kent to include a separate paragraph in the current year's review report describing the responsibility assumed for the prior year's audited financial statements. This is an appropriate reporting procedure.

Land reviewed Kent's draft and indicated in the *Supervisor's Review Notes* below that there were several deficiencies in Kent's draft.

Accountant's Review Report

We have reviewed and audited the accompanying balance sheets of Tech Co. as of December 31, 1992 and 1991, and the related statements of income, retained earnings, and cash flows for the years then ended, in accordance with Statements on Standards for Accounting and Review Services issued by the American Institute of Certified Public Accountants and generally accepted auditing standards. All information included in these financial statements is the representation of the management of Tech Co.

A review consists principally of inquiries of company personnel and analytical procedures applied to financial data. It is substantially less in scope than an audit in accordance with generally accepted auditing standards, the objective of which is the expression of an opinion regarding the financial statements taken as a whole.

Based on our review, we are not aware of any material modifications that should be made to the accompanying financial statements. Because of the inherent limitations of a review engagement, this report is intended for the information of management and should not be used for any other purpose.

The financial statements for the year ended December 31, 1991, were audited by us and our report was dated March 2, 1992. We have no responsibility for updating that report for events and circumstances occurring after that date.

Jordan and Stone, CPAs
March 1, 1993

Required:

Items 61 through 73 represent deficiencies noted by Land. For each deficiency, indicate whether Land is correct (C) or incorrect (I) in the criticism of Kent's draft and blacken the corresponding oval on the Objective Answer Sheet.

Items to be Answered:

Supervisor's Review Notes

61. There should be **no** reference to the prior year's audited financial statements in the first (introductory) paragraph.
62. All the current-year basic financial statements are **not** properly identified in the first (introductory) paragraph.
63. There should be **no** reference to the American Institute of Certified Public Accountants in the first (introductory) paragraph.
64. The accountant's review and audit responsibilities should follow management's responsibilities in the first (introductory) paragraph.
65. There should be **no** comparison of the scope of a review to an audit in the second (scope) paragraph.
66. Negative assurance should be expressed on the current year's reviewed financial statements in the second (scope) paragraph.
67. There should be a statement that **no** opinion is expressed on the current year's financial statements in the second (scope) paragraph.
68. There should be a reference to "conformity with generally accepted accounting principles" in the third paragraph.
69. There should be **no** restriction on the distribution of the accountant's review report in the third paragraph.
70. There should be **no** reference to "material modifications" in the third paragraph.
71. There should be an indication of the type of opinion expressed on the prior year's audited financial statements in the fourth (separate) paragraph.
72. There should be an indication that **no** auditing procedures were performed after the date of the report on the prior year's financial statements in the fourth (separate) paragraph.
73. There should be **no** reference to "updating the prior year's auditor's report for events and circumstances occurring after that date" in the fourth (separate) paragraph.

Number 3 (Estimated time—15 to 25 minutes)

Instructions

Question Number 3 consists of 10 items. Select the **best** answer for each item. Use a No. 2 pencil to blacken the appropriate ovals on the Objective Answer Sheet to indicate your answers. **Answer all items.** Your grade will be based on the total number of correct answers.

To support financial statement assertions, an auditor develops specific audit objectives. The auditor then designs substantive tests to satisfy or accomplish each objective.

Required:

Items 74 through 83 represent audit objectives for the investments, accounts receivable, and property and equipment accounts. To the right of each set of audit objectives is a listing of possible audit procedures for that account. For each audit objective, select the audit procedure that would primarily respond to the objective and blacken the corresponding oval on the Objective Answer Sheet. Select only one procedure for each audit objective. A procedure may be selected only once, or not at all.

Items to be Answered:

Audit Objectives for Investments

74. Investments are properly described and classified in the financial statements.
75. Recorded investments represent investments actually owned at the balance sheet date.
76. Investments are properly valued at the lower of cost or market at the balance sheet date.

Audit Procedures for Investments

A. Trace opening balances in the subsidiary ledger to prior year's audit working papers.
B. Determine that employees who are authorized to sell investments do not have access to cash.
C. Examine supporting documents for a sample of investment transactions to verify that prenumbered documents are used.
D. Determine that any impairments in the price of investments have been properly recorded.
E. Verify that transfers from the current to the noncurrent investment portfolio have been properly recorded.
F. Obtain positive confirmations as of the balance sheet date of investments held by independent custodians.
G. Trace investment transactions to minutes of the Board of Directors meetings to determine that transactions were properly authorized.

Audit Objectives for Accounts Receivable

77. Accounts receivable represent all amounts owed to the entity at the balance sheet date.
78. The entity has legal right to all accounts receivable at the balance sheet date.
79. Accounts receivable are stated at net realizable value.
80. Accounts receivable are properly described and presented in the financial statements.

Audit Procedures for Accounts Receivable

A. Analyze the relationship of accounts receivable and sales and compare it with relationships for preceding periods.
B. Perform sales cut-off tests to obtain assurance that sales transactions and corresponding entries for inventories and cost of goods sold are recorded in the same and proper period.
C. Review the aged trial balance for significant past due accounts.
D. Obtain an understanding of the business purpose of transactions that resulted in accounts receivable balances.
E. Review loan agreements for indications of whether accounts receivable have been factored or pledged.
F. Review the accounts receivable trial balance for amounts due from officers and employees.
G. Analyze unusual relationships between monthly accounts receivable balances and monthly accounts payable balances.

Audit Objectives for Property & Equipment

81. The entity has legal right to property and equipment acquired during the year.
82. Recorded property and equipment represent assets that actually exist at the balance sheet date.
83. Net property and equipment are properly valued at the balance sheet date.

Audit Procedures for Property & Equipment

A. Trace opening balances in the summary schedules to the prior year's audit working papers.
B. Review the provision for depreciation expense and determine that depreciable lives and methods used in the current year are consistent with those used in the prior year.
C. Determine that the responsibility for maintaining the property and equipment records is segregated from the responsibility for custody of property and equipment.
D. Examine deeds and title insurance certificates.
E. Perform cut-off tests to verify that property and equipment additions are recorded in the proper period.
F. Determine that property and equipment is adequately insured.
G. Physically examine all major property and equipment additions.

Number 4 (Estimated time—15 to 25 minutes)

Post, CPA, accepted an engagement to audit the financial statements of General Co., a new client. General is a publicly held retailing entity that recently replaced its operating management. In the course of applying auditing procedures, Post discovered that General's financial statements may be materially misstated due to the existence of irregularities.

Required:

a. Describe Post's responsibilities on the circumstances described above.

b. Describe Post's responsibilities for reporting on General's financial statements and other communications if Post is precluded from applying necessary procedures in searching for irregularities.

c. Describe Post's responsibilities for reporting on General's financial statements and other communications if Post concludes that General's financial statements are materially affected by irregularities.

d. Describe the circumstances in which Post may have a duty to disclose irregularities to third parties outside General's management and its audit committee.

Number 5 (Estimated time—15 to 25 minutes)

Butler, CPA, has been engaged to audit the financial statements of Young Computer Outlets, Inc., a new client. Young is a privately owned chain of retail stores that sells a variety of computer software and video products. Young uses an in-house payroll department at its corporate headquarters to compute payroll data, and to prepare and distribute payroll checks to its 300 salaried employees.

Butler is preparing an internal control questionnaire to assist in obtaining an understanding of Young's internal control structure and in assessing control risk.

Required:

Prepare a "Payroll" segment of Butler's internal control questionnaire that would assist in obtaining an understanding of Young's internal control structure and in assessing control risk.

Do **not** prepare questions relating to cash payrolls, EDP applications, payments based on hourly rates, piecework, commissions, employee benefits (pensions, health care, vacations, etc.), or payroll tax accruals other than withholdings.

Use the format in the following example:

Question	*Yes*	*No*
Are paychecks prenumbered and accounted for?		

Uniform Certified Public Accountant Examination

EXAMINATION QUESTION BOOKLET

ACCOUNTING AND REPORTING—TAXATION, MANAGERIAL, AND
GOVERNMENTAL AND NOT-FOR-PROFIT ORGANIZATIONS — 8:30 A.M. to 12:00 noon

The point values for each question, and estimated time allotments based primarily on point value, are as follows:

	Point Value	Estimated Minutes Minimum	Estimated Minutes Maximum
No. 1	60	120	130
No. 2	20	25	40
No. 3	20	25	40
Totals	100	170	210

INSTRUCTIONS TO CANDIDATES

Failure to follow these instructions may have an adverse effect on your Examination grade.

1. Record your 7-digit candidate number in the boxes provided at the upper right-hand corner of this page.

2. Question numbers 1, 2, and 3 should be answered on the *Objective Answer Sheet,* which is pages 23 and 24 of your *Examination Question and Answer Booklet.* You should attempt to answer all objective items. There is no penalty for incorrect responses. Work space to solve the objective questions is provided in this *Examination Question and Answer Booklet* on pages 5 through 20. Since the objective items are computer-graded, your comments and calculations associated with them are not considered. Be certain that you have entered your answers on the *Objective Answer Sheet* before the examination time is up. Your examination will not be graded if you fail to record your answers on the *Objective Answer Sheet.* You will not be given additional time to record your answers.

3. Record your 7-digit candidate number, state, and question number where indicated on pages 1 and 24 of the *Examination Question and Answer Booklet.*

4. You are required to turn in by the end of each session:
   a. Attendance Record and Calculator Sign-off Record Form, front page of *Examination Question and Answer Booklet;*
   b. *Objective Answer Sheet,* pages 23 and 24 of *Examination Question and Answer Booklet;*
   c. *Examination Question Booklet,* pages 5 through 22; of *Examination Question and Answer Booklet;*
   d. Calculator; and
   e. All unused examination materials.

   Your examination will not be graded unless the above listed items are handed in before leaving the examination room.

5. Unless otherwise instructed, if you want your *Examination Question Booklet* mailed to you, write your name and address in both places indicated on the back cover (page 22) and place 52 cents postage in the space provided. *Examination Question Booklets* will be distributed no sooner than the day following the administration of this examination.

Accounting and Reporting (ARE)

Number 1 (Estimated time—120 to 130 minutes)

Instructions

Select the **best** answer for each of the following items. Use a No. 2 pencil to blacken the appropriate ovals on the Objective Answer Sheet to indicate your answers. **Mark only one answer for each item. Answer all items.** Your grade will be based on the total number of correct answers.

1. The rule limiting the allowability of passive activity losses and credits applies to
    A. Partnerships.
    B. S corporations.
    C. Personal service corporations.
    D. Widely held C corporations.

2. Corporate dividends-received deduction
    A. Must exceed the applicable percentage of the recipient shareholder's taxable income.
    B. Is affected by a requirement that the investor corporation must own the investee's stock for a specified minimum holding period.
    C. Is unaffected by the percentage of the investee's stock owned by the investor corporation.
    D. May be claimed by S corporations.

3. During 1993, Nale Corp. received dividends of $1,000 from a 10 percent-owned taxable domestic corporation. When Nale computes the maximum allowable deduction for contributions in its 1993 return, the amount of dividends to be included in the computation of taxable income is
    A. $0
    B. $ 200
    C. $ 300
    D. $1,000

4. Foreign income taxes paid by a corporation
    A. May be claimed either as a deduction or as a credit, at the option of the corporation.
    B. May be claimed only as a deduction.
    C. May be claimed only as a credit.
    D. Do **not** qualify either as a deduction or as a credit.

5. In 1993, Acorn Inc. had the following items of income and expense:

Sales	$500,000
Cost of sales	250,000
Dividends received	25,000

The dividends were received from a corporation of which Acorn owns 30 percent. In Acorn's 1993 corporate income tax return, what amount should be reported as income before special deductions?
    A. $525,000
    B. $505,000
    C. $275,000
    D. $250,000

6. Ace Rentals Inc., an accrual-basis taxpayer, reported rent receivable of $35,000 and $25,000 in its 1993 and 1992 balance sheets, respectively. During 1993, Ace received $50,000 in rent payments and $5,000 in nonrefundable rent deposits. In Ace's 1993 corporate income tax return, what amount should Ace include as rent revenue?
    A. $50,000
    B. $55,000
    C. $60,000
    D. $65,000

7. In 1993, Portal Corp. received $100,000 in dividends from Sal Corp., its 80 percent-owned subsidiary. What net amount of dividend income should Portal include in its 1993 consolidated tax return?
    A. $100,000
    B. $ 80,000
    C. $ 70,000
    D. $0

8. Brown Corp., a calendar-year taxpayer, was organized and actively began operations on July 1, 1993, and incurred the following costs:

Legal fees to obtain corporate charter	$40,000
Commission paid to underwriter	25,000
Other stock issue costs	10,000

Brown wishes to amortize its organizational costs over the shortest period allowed for tax purposes. In 1993, what amount should Brown deduct for the amortization of organizational expenses?
    A. $8,000
    B. $7,500
    C. $5,000
    D. $4,000

9.   In 1993, Garland Corp. contributed $40,000 to a qualified charitable organization. Garland's 1993 taxable income before the deduction for charitable contributions was $410,000. Included in that amount is a $20,000 dividends-received deduction. Garland also had carryover contributions of $5,000 from the prior year. In 1993, what amount can Garland deduct as charitable contributions?

A. $40,000
B. $41,000
C. $43,000
D. $45,000

10.   In 1993, Cero Corp.'s second year of operation, Cero's book income before federal income taxes was $400,000. Included in that amount were the following items:

State income tax refunds	$10,000
Amortization of goodwill (acquired in 1987)	5,000

On its 1992 federal tax return, Cero deducted the payments it made for state income taxes. Cero's policy is to maximize its deductible expenses. What is Cero's 1993 taxable income?

A. $405,000
B. $400,000
C. $395,000
D. $390,000

11.   When a corporation has an unused net capital loss that is carried back or carried forward to another tax year,

A. It retains its original identity as short-term or long-term.
B. It is treated as a short-term capital loss whether or not it was short-term when sustained.
C. It is treated as a long-term capital loss whether or not it was long-term when sustained.
D. It can be used to offset ordinary income up to the amount of the carryback or carryover.

12.   Soma Corp. had $600,000 in compensation expense for book purposes in 1993. Included in this amount was a $50,000 accrual for 1993 nonshareholder bonuses. Soma paid the actual 1993 bonus of $60,000 on March 1, 1994. In its 1993 tax return, what amount should Soma deduct as compensation expense?

A. $600,000
B. $610,000
C. $550,000
D. $540,000

13.   Potter Corp. and Sly Corp. file consolidated tax returns. In January 1992, Potter sold land, with a basis of $60,000 and a fair value of $75,000, to Sly for $100,000. Sly sold the land in December 1993 for $125,000. In its 1993 and 1992 tax returns, what amount of gain should be reported for these transactions in the consolidated return?

	1993	1992
A.	$25,000	$40,000
B.	$50,000	$0
C.	$50,000	$25,000
D.	$65,000	$0

14.   Which of the following tax credits **cannot** be claimed by a corporation?

A. Foreign tax credit.
B. Earned income credit.
C. Alternative fuel production credit.
D. General business credit.

15.   Which of the following conditions will prevent a corporation from qualifying as an S Corporation?

A. The corporation has both common and preferred stock.
B. The corporation has one class of stock with different voting rights.
C. One shareholder is an estate.
D. One shareholder is a grantor trust.

16.   Acme Corp. has two common stockholders. Acme derives all of its income from investments in stocks and securities, and it regularly distributes 51 percent of its taxable income as dividends to its stockholders. Acme is a

A. Corporation subject to tax only on income **not** distributed to stockholders.
B. Corporation subject to the accumulated earnings tax.
C. Regulated investment company.
D. Personal holding company.

17. In 1993, Stone, a cash basis taxpayer, incorporated her CPA practice. No liabilities were transferred. The following assets were transferred to the corporation:

Cash (checking account)	$ 500
Computer equipment	
Adjusted basis	30,000
Fair market value	34,000
Cost	40,000

Immediately after the transfer, Stone owned 100 percent of the corporation's stock. The corporation's total basis for the transferred assets is
A. $30,000
B. $30,500
C. $34,500
D. $40,500

18. What is the usual result to the shareholders of a distribution in complete liquidation of a corporation?
A. No taxable effect.
B. Ordinary gain to the extent of cash received.
C. Ordinary gain or loss.
D. Capital gain or loss.

19. Kari Corp., a manufacturing company, was organized on January 2, 1993. Its 1993 federal taxable income was $400,000 and its federal income tax was $100,000. What is the maximum amount of accumulated taxable income that may be subject to the accumulated earnings tax for 1993 if Kari takes only the minimum accumulated earnings credit?
A. $300,000
B. $150,000
C. $ 50,000
D. $0

20. Corporations A and B combine in a qualifying reorganization, and form Corporation C, the only surviving corporation. This reorganization is tax-free to the

	Shareholders	Corporation
A.	Yes	Yes
B.	Yes	No
C.	No	No
D.	No	Yes

21. If a corporation's tentative minimum tax exceeds the regular tax, the excess amount is
A. Carried back to the first preceding taxable year.
B. Carried back to the third preceding taxable year.
C. Payable in addition to the regular tax.
D. Subtracted from the regular tax.

22. In 1993, Cape Co. reported book income of $140,000. Included in that amount was $50,000 for meals and entertainment expense and $40,000 for federal income tax expense. In Cape's Schedule M-1 of Form 1120, which reconciles book income and taxable income, what amount should be reported as taxable income?
A. $190,000
B. $180,000
C. $150,000
D. $140,000

23. If an S corporation has **no** accumulated earnings or profits, the amount distributed to a shareholder
A. Must be returned to the S corporation.
B. Increases the shareholder's basis for the stock.
C. Decreases the shareholder's basis for the stock.
D. Has **no** effect on the shareholder's basis for the stock.

24. Jones incorporated a sole proprietorship by exchanging all the proprietorship's assets for the stock of Nu Co., a new corporation. To qualify for tax-free incorporation, Jones must be in control of Nu immediately after the exchange. What percentage of Nu's stock must Jones own to qualify as "control" for this purpose?
A. 50.00 percent
B. 51.00 percent
C. 66.67 percent
D. 80.00 percent

25. A corporation was completely liquidated and dissolved during 1993. The filing fees, professional fees, and other expenditures incurred in connection with the liquidation and dissolution are
A. Deductible in full by the dissolved corporation.
B. Deductible by the shareholders and **not** by the corporation.
C. Treated as capital losses by the corporation.
D. Not deductible either by the corporation or shareholders.

26. Pert contributed land with a fair market value of $20,000 to a new partnership in exchange for a 50 percent partnership interest. The land had an adjusted basis to Pert of $12,000 and was subject to a $4,000 mortgage, which the partnership assumed. What is the adjusted basis of Pert's partnership interest?
A. $10,000
B. $12,000
C. $18,000
D. $20,000

27. On June 1, 1993, Kelly received a 10 percent interest in Rock Co., a partnership, for services contributed to the partnership. Rock's net assets at that date had a basis of $70,000 and fair market value of $100,000. In Kelly's 1993 income tax return, what amount must Kelly include as income from transfer of partnership interest?

A. $ 7,000 ordinary income.
B. $ 7,000 capital gain.
C. $10,000 ordinary income.
D. $10,000 capital gain.

28. Under Section 444 of the Internal Revenue Code, certain partnerships can elect to use a tax year different from their required tax year. One of the conditions for eligibility to make a Section 444 election is that the partnership must

A. Be a limited partnership.
B. Be a member of a tiered structure.
C. Choose a tax year where the deferral period is **not** longer than three months.
D. Have less than 35 partners.

29. In computing the ordinary income of a partnership, a deduction is allowed for

A. Contributions to recognized charities.
B. The first $100 of dividends received from qualifying domestic corporations.
C. Short-term capital losses.
D. Guaranteed payments to partners.

30. When a partner's share of partnership liabilities increases, that partner's basis in the partnership

A. Increases by the partner's share of the increase.
B. Decreases by the partner's share of the increase.
C. Decreases, but **not** to less than zero.
D. Is **not** affected.

Items 31 and 32 are based on the following:

The adjusted basis of Jody's partnership interest was $50,000 immediately before Jody received a current distribution of $20,000 cash and property with an adjusted basis to the partnership of $40,000 and a fair market value of $35,000.

31. What amount of taxable gain must Jody report as a result of this distribution?

A. $0
B. $ 5,000
C. $10,000
D. $20,000

32. What is Jody's basis in the distributed property?
A. $0
B. $30,000
C. $35,000
D. $40,000

33. What amount of a decedent's taxable estate is effectively tax-free if the maximum unified estate and gift credit is taken?

A. $0
B. $ 10,000
C. $192,800
D. $600,000

34. Which of the following is(are) deductible from a decedent's gross estate?

I. Expenses of administering and settling the estate.
II. State inheritance or estate tax.

A. I only.
B. II only.
C. Both I and II.
D. Neither I nor II.

35. Which of the following statements is correct regarding the unrelated business income of exempt organizations?

A. If an exempt organization has any unrelated business income, it may result in the loss of the organization's exempt status.
B. Unrelated business income relates to the performance of services, but **not** to the sale of goods.
C. An unrelated business does **not** include any activity where all the work is performed for the organization by unpaid volunteers.
D. Unrelated business income tax will **not** be imposed if profits from the unrelated business are used to support the exempt organization's charitable activities.

36. In an activity-based costing system, cost reduction is accomplished by identifying and eliminating

	All cost drivers	Nonvalue-adding activities
A.	No	No
B.	Yes	Yes
C.	No	Yes
D.	Yes	No

37. When production levels are expected to increase within a relevant range, and a flexible budget is used, what effect would be anticipated with respect to each of the following costs?

	Fixed costs per unit	Variable costs per unit
A.	Decrease	Decrease
B.	No change	No change
C.	No change	Decrease
D.	Decrease	No change

38. At the break-even point, the contribution margin equals total
A. Variable costs.
B. Sales revenues.
C. Selling and administrative costs.
D. Fixed costs.

39. Controllable revenue would be included in a performance report for a

	Profit center	Cost center
A.	No	No
B.	No	Yes
C.	Yes	No
D.	Yes	Yes

40. Vince Inc. has developed and patented a new laser disc reading device that will be marketed internationally. Which of the following factors should Vince consider in pricing the device?

I. Quality of the new device.
II. Life of the new device.
III. Customers' relative preference for quality compared to price.

A. I and II only.
B. I and III only.
C. II and III only.
D. I, II, and III.

41. Cook Co.'s total costs of operating five sales offices last year were $500,000, of which $70,000 represented fixed costs. Cook has determined that total costs are significantly influenced by the number of sales offices operated. Last year's costs and number of sales offices can be used as the bases for predicting annual costs. What would be the budgeted costs for the coming year if Cook were to operate seven sales offices?
A. $700,000
B. $672,000
C. $614,000
D. $586,000

42. Lon Co.'s budget committee is preparing its master budget on the basis of the following projections:

Sales	$2,800,000
Decrease in inventories	70,000
Decrease in accounts payable	150,000
Gross margin	40%

What are Lon's estimated cash disbursements for inventories?

A. $1,040,000
B. $1,200,000
C. $1,600,000
D. $1,760,000

43. The following information pertains to Syl Co.:

Sales	$800,000
Variable costs	160,000
Fixed costs	40,000

What is Syl's breakeven point in sales dollars?
A. $200,000
B. $160,000
C. $ 50,000
D. $ 40,000

44. Neu Co. is considering the purchase of an investment that has a positive net present value based on Neu's 12 percent hurdle rate. The internal rate of return would be
A. 0.
B. 12 percent.
C. > 12 percent.
D. < 12 percent.

45. Major Corp. is considering the purchase of a new machine for $5,000 that will have an estimated useful life of five years and no salvage value. The machine will increase Major's after-tax cash flow by $2,000 annually for five years. Major uses the straight-line method of depreciation and has an incremental borrowing rate of 10 percent. The present value factors for 10 percent are as follows:

Ordinary annuity with five payments	3.79
Annuity due for five payments	4.17

Using the payback method, how many years will it take to pay back Major's initial investment in the machine?
A. 2.50
B. 5.00
C. 7.58
D. 8.34

46. Lin Co. is buying machinery it expects will increase average annual operating income by $40,000. The initial increase in the required investment is $60,000, and the average increase in required investment is $30,000. To compute the accrual accounting rate of return, what amount should be used as the numerator in the ratio?

    A. $20,000
    B. $30,000
    C. $40,000
    D. $60,000

47. The following information pertains to Krel Co.'s computation of net present value relating to a contemplated project:

Discounted expected cash inflows	$1,000,000
Discounted expected cash outflows	700,000

Net present value is
    A. $ 300,000
    B. $ 700,000
    C. $ 850,000
    D. $1,000,000

48. In a traditional job order cost system, the issue of indirect materials to a production department increases
    A. Stores control.
    B. Work in process control.
    C. Factory overhead control.
    D. Factory overhead applied.

49. For purposes of allocating joint costs to joint products, the sales price at point of sale, reduced by cost to complete after split-off, is assumed to be equal to the
    A. Total costs.
    B. Joint costs.
    C. Sales price less a normal profit margin at point of sale.
    D. Relative sales value at split-off.

50. Which of the following standard costing variances would be **least** controllable by a production supervisor?
    A. Overhead volume.
    B. Overhead efficiency.
    C. Labor efficiency.
    D. Material usage.

51. The modified accrual basis of accounting should be used for which of the following funds?
    A. Capital projects fund.
    B. Enterprise fund.
    C. Pension trust fund.
    D. Proprietary fund.

52. The town of Hill operates municipal electric and water utilities. In which of the following funds should the operations of the utilities be accounted for?
    A. Enterprise fund.
    B. Internal service fund.
    C. Agency fund.
    D. Special revenue fund.

53. Bay Creek's municipal motor pool maintains all city-owned vehicles and charges the various departments for the cost of rendering those services. In which of the following funds should Bay account for the cost of such maintenance?
    A. General fund.
    B. Internal service fund.
    C. Special revenue fund.
    D. Special assessment fund.

54. Central County received proceeds from various towns and cities for capital projects financed by Central's long-term debt. A special tax was assessed by each local government, and a portion of the tax was restricted to repay the long-term debt of Central's capital projects. Central should account for the restricted portion of the special tax in which of the following funds?
    A. Internal service fund.
    B. Enterprise fund.
    C. Capital projects fund.
    D. Debt service fund.

55. Stone Corp. donated investments to Pine City and stipulated that the income from the investments be used to acquire art for the city's museum. Which of the following funds should be used to account for the investments?
    A. Endowment fund.
    B. Special revenue fund.
    C. Expendable trust fund.
    D. Nonexpendable trust fund.

56. Which of the following accounts would appear in the plant fund of a not-for-profit private college?

	Fuel inventory for power plant	Equipment
A.	Yes	Yes
B.	No	Yes
C.	No	No
D.	Yes	No

57. When a nonprofit organization combines fund-raising efforts with educational materials or program services, the total combined costs incurred are
    A. Reported as program services expenses.
    B. Allocated between fund-raising and program services expenses using an appropriate allocation basis.
    C. Reported as fund-raising costs.
    D. Reported as management and general expenses.

58. A hospital should report earnings from endowment funds that are restricted to a specific operating purpose as
    A. An increase in temporarily restricted net assets.
    B. An increase in permanently restricted net assets.
    C. An increase in unrestricted net assets.
    D. An increase in current fund revenues.

59. In the loan fund of a college, each of the following types of loans would be found **except**
    A. Faculty.
    B. Computer.
    C. Staff.
    D. Student.

60. Is the recognition of depreciation expense required for public colleges and private not-for-profit colleges?

	Public	Private
A.	No	Yes
B.	No	No
C.	Yes	Yes
D.	Yes	No

Number 2 (Estimated time—40 to 50 minutes)

Instructions

Question Number 2 consists of 25 items. Select the **best** answer for each item. Use a No. 2 pencil to blacken the appropriate ovals on the Objective Answer Sheet to indicate your answers. **Answer all items.** Your grade will be based on the total number of correct answers.

Green is self-employed as a human resources consultant and reports on the cash basis for income tax purposes. Listed below are Green's 1993 business and nonbusiness transactions, as well as possible tax treatments.

Required:

For each of Green's transactions (Items 61 through 85), select the appropriate tax treatment and blacken the corresponding oval on the Objective Answer Sheet. A tax treatment may be selected once, more than once, or not at all.

Items to be Answered:

Transactions

61. Retainer fees received from clients.
62. Oil royalties received.
63. Interest income on general obligation state and local government bonds.
64. Interest on refund of federal taxes.
65. Death benefits from term life insurance policy on parent.
66. Interest income on U.S. Treasury bonds.
67. Share of ordinary income from an investment in a limited partnership reported in Form 1065, Schedule K-1.
68. Taxable income from rental of a townhouse owned by Green.
69. Prize won as a contestant on a TV quiz show.
70. Payment received for jury service.
71. Dividends received from mutual funds that invest in tax-free government obligations.
72. Qualifying medical expenses not reimbursed by insurance.
73. Personal life insurance premiums paid by Green.
74. Expenses for business-related meals where clients were present.
75. Depreciation on personal computer purchased in 1992 used for business.
76. Business lodging expenses, while out of town.
77. Subscriptions to professional journals used for business.
78. Self-employment taxes paid.
79. Qualifying contributions to a simplified employee pension plan.
80. Election to expense business equipment purchased in 1992.
81. Qualifying alimony payments made by Green.
82. Subscriptions for investment-related publications.
83. Interest expense on a home-equity line of credit for an amount borrowed to finance Green's business.
84. Interest expense on a loan for an auto used 75 percent for business.
85. Loss on sale of residence.

Tax Treatments

A. Taxable as other income on Form 1040.
B. Reported in Schedule B - Interest and Dividend Income.
C. Reported in Schedule C as trade or business income.
D. Reported in Schedule E - Supplemental Income and Loss.
E. Not taxable.
F. Fully deductible on Form 1040 to arrive at adjusted gross income.
G. Fifty percent deductible on Form 1040 to arrive at adjusted gross income.
H. Reported in Schedule A - Itemized Deductions (deductibility subject to threshold of 7.5 percent of adjusted gross income).
I. Reported in Schedule A - Itemized Deductions (deductibility subject to threshold of 2 percent of adjusted gross income).
J. Reported in Form 4562 - Depreciation and Amortization and deductible in Schedule A - Itemized Deductions (deductibility subject to threshold of 2 percent of adjusted gross income).
K. Reported in Form 4562 - Depreciation and Amortization, and deductible in Schedule C - Profit or Loss from Business.
L. Fully deductible in Schedule C - Profit or Loss from Business.
M. Partially deductible in Schedule C - Profit or Loss from Business.
N. Reported in Form 2119 - Sale of Your Home, and deductible in Schedule D - Capital Gains and Losses.
O. Not deductible.

Number 3 (Estimated time—45 to 55 minutes)

Instructions

Question Number 3 consists of 20 items relating to a municipal government. Select the **best** answer for each item. Use a No. 2 pencil to blacken the appropriate ovals on the Objective Answer Sheet to indicate your answers. **Answer all items.** Your grade will be based on the total number of correct answers.

Items 86 through 95, in the left-hand column, represent various transactions pertaining to a municipality that uses encumbrance accounting. To the right of these items is a listing of possible ways to record the transactions. Items 96 through 105, also listed in the left-hand column, represent the funds, accounts, and account groups used by the municipality. To the right of these items is a list of possible accounting and reporting methods.

Required:

a. For each of the municipality's transactions (Items 86 through 95), select the appropriate recording of the transaction and blacken the corresponding oval on the Objective Answer Sheet. A method of recording the transactions may be selected once, more than once, or not at all.

b. For each of the municipality's funds, accounts, and account groups (Items 96 through 105), select the appropriate method of accounting and reporting and blacken the corresponding oval on the Objective Answer Sheet. An accounting and reporting method may be selected once, more than once, or not at all.

Items to be Answered:

3(a)   Transactions

86. General obligation bonds were issued at par.
87. Approved purchase orders were issued for supplies.
88. The above-mentioned supplies were received and the related invoices were approved.
89. General fund salaries and wages were incurred.
90. The internal service fund had interfund billings.
91. Revenues were earned from a previously awarded grant.
92. Property taxes were collected in advance.
93. Appropriations were recorded on adoption of the budget.
94. Short-term financing was received from a bank, secured by the city's taxing power.
95. There was an excess of estimated inflows over estimated outflows.

Recording of Transactions

A. Credit appropriations control.
B. Credit budgetary fund balance - unreserved.
C. Credit expenditures control.
D. Credit deferred revenues.
E. Credit interfund revenues.
F. Credit tax anticipation notes payable.
G. Credit other financing sources.
H. Credit other financing uses.
I. Debit appropriations control.
J. Debit deferred revenues.
K. Debit encumbrances control.
L. Debit expenditures control.

3(b)   Funds, Accounts and Account Groups

96. Enterprise fund fixed assets.
97. Capital projects fund.
98. General fixed assets.
99. Infrastructure fixed assets.
100. Enterprise fund cash.
101. General fund.
102. Agency fund cash.
103. General long-term debt.
104. Special revenue fund.
105. Debt services fund.

Accounting and Reporting by Funds and Account Groups

A. Accounted for in a fiduciary fund.
B. Accounted for in a proprietary fund.
C. Accounted for in a quasi-endowment fund.
D. Accounted for in a self-balancing account group.
E. Accounted for in a special assessment fund.
F. Accounts for major construction activities.
G. Accounts for property tax revenues.
H. Accounts for payment of interest and principal on tax supported debt.
I. Accounts for revenues from earmarked sources to finance designated activities.
J. Reporting is optional.

(Note: These instructions have been adapted from the May 1994 CPA Examination Booklet.)

 *Uniform Certified Public Accountant Examination*

EXAMINATION QUESTION BOOKLET

FINANCIAL ACCOUNTING & REPORTING— BUSINESS ENTERPRISES — 1:30 P.M. to 6:00 P.M.

The point values for each question, and estimated time allotments based primarily on point value, are as follows:

	Point Value	Estimated Minutes	
		Minimum	Maximum
No. 1	60	130	140
No. 2	10	15	25
No. 3	10	15	25
No. 4	10	30	40
No. 5	10	30	40
Totals	100	220	270

INSTRUCTIONS TO CANDIDATES

Failure to follow these instructions may have an adverse effect on your Examination grade.

1. Record your 7-digit candidate number in the boxes provided at the upper right-hand corner of this page.

2. Question numbers 1, 2, and 3 should be answered on the *Objective Answer Sheet,* which is pages 11 and 12 of your *Examination Answer Booklet.* You should attempt to answer all objective items. There is no penalty for incorrect responses. Work space to solve the objective questions is provided in this *Examination Question Booklet* on pages 3 through 14. Since the objective items are computer-graded, your comments and calculations associated with them are not considered. Be certain that you have entered your answers on the *Objective Answer Sheet* before the examination time is up. The objective portion of your examination will not be graded if you fail to record your answers on the *Objective Answer Sheet.* You will not be given additional time to record your answers.

3. Question numbers 4 and 5 should be answered beginning on page 3 of the *Examination Answer Booklet.* Support **all** answers with properly labeled and legible calculations that can be identified as sources of amounts used to derive your final answer. If you have not completed answering a question on a page, fill in the appropriate spaces in the wording on the bottom of the page **"QUES-TION NUMBER ____ CONTINUES ON PAGE ____ ."** If you have completed answering a question, fill in the appropriate space in the wording on the bottom of the page **"QUESTION**

NUMBER ____ ENDS ON THIS PAGE." Always begin the start of an answer to a question on the top of a new page (which may be the back side of a sheet of paper). Use the entire width of the page to answer requirements of a noncomputational nature. To answer requirements of a computational nature, you may wish to use the three vertical columns provided on the right side of each page.

4. Record your 7-digit candidate number, state, and question number where indicated on pages 3 through 10 of the *Examination Answer Booklet.*

5. Although the primary purpose of the examination is to test your knowledge and application of the subject matter, selected essay responses will be graded for writing skills.

6. You are required to turn in by the end of each session:
   a. Attendance Record and Calculator Sign-off Record Form, front page of *Examination Answer Booklet;*
   b. *Objective Answer Sheet,* pages 11 and 12 of *Examination Answer Booklet;*
   c. Remaining Portion of *Examination Answer Booklet;*
   d. *Examination Question Booklet;*
   e. Calculator; and
   f. All unused examination materials.

Your examination will not be graded unless the above listed items are handed in before leaving the examination room.

Financial Accounting & Reporting (FARE)

Number 1 (Estimated time—130 to 140 minutes)

Instructions

Select the **best** answer for each of the following items. Use a No. 2 pencil to blacken the appropriate ovals on the Objective Answer Sheet to indicate your answers. **Mark only one answer for each item. Answer all items.** Your grade will be based on the total number of correct answers.

1. On January 10, 1992, Box, Inc. purchased marketable securities of Knox, Inc. and Scot, Inc. Box classified both securities as available-for-sale investments over which it could not exercise significant influence. At December 31, 1992, the cost of each investment was greater than its fair market value. The loss on the Knox investment was considered permanent and that on Scot was considered temporary. How should Box report the effects of these investing activities in its 1992 income statement, assuming the application of FASB Statement #115, "Accounting for Certain Investments in Debt and Equity Securities"?

   I. Excess of cost of Knox stock over its market value.
  II. Excess of cost of Scot stock over its market value.

    A. An unrealized loss equal to I plus II.
    B. An unrealized loss equal to I only.
    C. A realized loss equal to I only.
    D. No income statement effect.

2. Based on a physical inventory taken on December 31, 1992, Chewy Co. determined its chocolate inventory on a FIFO basis at $26,000 with a replacement cost of $20,000. Chewy estimated that, after further processing costs of $12,000, the chocolate could be sold as finished candy bars for $40,000. Chewy's normal profit margin is 10 percent of sales. Under the lower of cost or market rule, what amount should Chewy report as chocolate inventory in its December 31, 1992, balance sheet?
    A. $28,000
    B. $26,000
    C. $24,000
    D. $20,000

3. Merry Co. purchased a machine costing $125,000 for its manufacturing operations and paid shipping costs of $20,000. Merry spent an additional $10,000 testing and preparing the machine for use. What amount should Merry record as the cost of the machine?
    A. $155,000
    B. $145,000
    C. $135,000
    D. $125,000

4. Weir Co. uses straight-line depreciation for its property, plant, and equipment, which, stated at cost, consisted of the following:

	12/31/92	12/31/91
Land	$ 25,000	$ 25,000
Buildings	195,000	195,000
Machinery and equipment	695,000	650,000
	915,000	870,000
Less accumulated depreciation	400,000	370,000
	$515,000	$500,000

Weir's depreciation expense for 1992 and 1991 was $55,000 and $50,000, respectively. What amount was debited to accumulated depreciation during 1992 because of property, plant, and equipment retirements?
    A. $40,000
    B. $25,000
    C. $20,000
    D. $10,000

5. Gei Co. determined that, due to obsolescence, equipment with an original cost of $900,000 and accumulated depreciation at January 1, 1992, of $420,000 had suffered permanent impairment, and as a result should have a carrying value of only $300,000 as of the beginning of the year. In addition, the remaining useful life of the equipment was reduced from 8 years to 3. In its December 31, 1992, balance sheet, what amount should Gei report as accumulated depreciation?
    A. $100,000
    B. $520,000
    C. $600,000
    D. $700,000

6. On January 2, 1992, Judd Co. bought a trademark from Krug Co. for $500,000. Judd retained an independent consultant, who estimated the trademark's remaining life to be 50 years. Its unamortized cost on Krug's accounting records was $380,000. Judd decided to amortize the trademark over the maximum period allowed. In Judd's December 31, 1992, balance sheet, what amount should be reported as accumulated amortization?

    A. $ 7,600
    B. $ 9,500
    C. $10,000
    D. $12,500

Items 7 and 8 are based on the following:

On January 2, 1992, Emme Co. sold equipment with a carrying amount of $480,000 in exchange for a $600,000 noninterest bearing note due January 2, 1995. There was no established exchange price for the equipment. The prevailing rate of interest for a note of this type at January 2, 1992, was 10 percent. The present value of 1 at 10 percent for three periods is 0.75.

7. In Emme's 1992 income statement, what amount should be reported as interest income?

    A. $ 9,000
    B. $45,000
    C. $50,000
    D. $60,000

8. In Emme's 1992 income statement, what amount should be reported as gain (loss) on sale of machinery?

    A. ($ 30,000) loss.
    B. $ 30,000 gain.
    C. $120,000 gain.
    D. $270,000 gain.

9. After being held for 40 days, a 120-day 12 percent interest-bearing note receivable was discounted at a bank at 15 percent. The proceeds received from the bank equal

    A. Maturity value less the discount at 12 percent.
    B. Maturity value less the discount at 15 percent.
    C. Face value less the discount at 12 percent.
    D. Face value less the discount at 15 percent.

10. At December 31, 1992, Date Co. awaits judgment on a lawsuit for a competitor's infringement of Date's patent. Legal counsel believes it is probable that Date will win the suit and indicated the most likely award together with a range of possible awards. How should the lawsuit be reported in Date's 1992 financial statements?

    A. In note disclosure only.
    B. By accrual for the most likely award.
    C. By accrual for the lowest amount of the range of possible awards.
    D. Neither in note disclosure **nor** by accrual.

11. Compared to its 1992 cash basis net income, Potoma Co.'s 1992 accrual basis net income increased when it

    A. Declared a cash dividend in 1991 that it paid in 1992.
    B. Wrote off more accounts receivable balances than it reported as uncollectible accounts expense in 1992.
    C. Had lower accrued expenses on December 31, 1992, than on January 1, 1992.
    D. Sold used equipment for cash at a gain in 1992.

12. On December 31, 1992, Brooks Co. decided to end operations and dispose of its assets within three months. At December 31, 1992, the net realizable value of the equipment was below historical cost. What is the appropriate measurement basis for equipment included in Brooks' December 31, 1992, balance sheet?

    A. Historical cost.
    B. Current reproduction cost.
    C. Net realizable value.
    D. Current replacement cost.

13. Delect Co. provides repair services for the AZ195 TV set. Customers prepay the fee on the standard one-year service contract. The 1991 and 1992 contracts were identical, and the number of contracts outstanding was substantially the same at end of each year. However, Delect's December 31, 1992, deferred revenues' balance on unperformed service contracts was significantly less than the balance at December 31, 1991. Which of the following situations might account for this reduction in the deferred revenue balance?

    A. Most 1992 contracts were signed later in the calendar year than were the 1991 contracts.
    B. Most 1992 contracts were signed earlier in the calendar year than were the 1991 contracts.
    C. The 1992 contract contribution margin was greater than the 1991 contract contribution margin.
    D. The 1992 contribution margin was less than the 1991 contract contribution margin.

14. Luge Co., which began operations on January 2, 1992, appropriately uses the installment sales method of accounting. The following information is available for 1992:

Installment accounts receivable,
December 31, 1992 $800,000
Deferred gross profit, December 31,
1992 (before recognition of realized
gross profit for 1992)   560,000
Gross profit on sales   40 percent

For the year ended December 31, 1992, cash collections and realized gross profit on sales should be

	Cash collections	Realized gross profit
A.	$400,000	$320,000
B.	$400,000	$240,000
C.	$600,000	$320,000
D.	$600,000	$240,000

15. Dunne Co. sells equipment service contracts that cover a two-year period. The sales price of each contract is $600. Dunne's past experience is that, of the total dollars spent for repairs on service contracts, 40 percent is incurred evenly during the first contract year and 60 percent evenly during the second contract year. Dunne sold 1,000 contracts evenly throughout 1992. In its December 31, 1992, balance sheet, what amount should Dunne report as deferred service contract revenue?
   A. $540,000
   B. $480,000
   C. $360,000
   D. $300,000

16. On September 1, 1992, Brady Corp. entered into a foreign exchange contract for speculative purposes by purchasing 50,000 deutsche marks for delivery in 60 days. The rates to exchange $1 for 1 deutsche mark follow:

	9/1/92	9/30/92
Spot rate	.75	.70
30-day forward rate	.73	.72
60-day forward rate	.74	.73

In its September 30, 1992, income statement, what amount should Brady report as foreign exchange loss?
   A. $2,500
   B. $1,500
   C. $1,000
   D. $ 500

17. On April 1, 1993, Ivy began operating a service proprietorship with an initial cash investment of $1,000. The proprietorship provided $3,200 of services in April and received full payment in May. The proprietorship incurred expenses of $1,500 in April which were paid in June. During May, Ivy drew $500 against her capital account.

What was the proprietorship's income for the two months ended May 31, 1993, under the following methods of accounting?

	Cash-basis	Accrual-basis
A.	$1,200	$1,200
B.	$1,700	$1,700
C.	$2,700	$1,200
D.	$3,200	$1,700

18. On January 2, 1991, Blake Co. sold a used machine to Cooper, Inc., for $900,000, resulting in a gain of $270,000. On that date, Cooper paid $150,000 cash and signed a $750,000 note bearing interest at 10 percent. The note was payable in three annual installments of $250,000 beginning January 2, 1992. Blake appropriately accounted for the sale under the installment method. Cooper made a timely payment of the first installment on January 2, 1992, of $325,000, which included accrued interest of $75,000. What amount of deferred gross profit should Blake report at December 31, 1992?
   A. $150,000
   B. $172,500
   C. $180,000
   D. $225,000

19. Mill Co.'s trial balance included the following account balances at December 31, 1992:

Accounts payable	$15,000
Bonds payable, due 1993	25,000
Discount on bonds payable, due 1993	3,000
Dividends payable 1/31/93	8,000
Notes payable, due 1994	20,000

What amount should be included in the current liability section of Mill's December 31, 1992, balance sheet?
   A. $45,000
   B. $51,000
   C. $65,000
   D. $78,000

20. On December 31, 1992, Roth Co. issued a $10,000 face value note payable to Wake Co. in exchange for services rendered to Roth. The note, made at usual trade terms, is due in nine months and bears interest, payable at maturity, at the annual rate of 3 percent. The market interest rate is 8 percent. The compound interest factor of $1 due in nine months at 8 percent is .944. At what amount should the note payable be reported in Roth's December 31, 1992, balance sheet?

    A. $10,300
    B. $10,000
    C. $ 9,652
    D. $ 9,440

21. Ross Co. pays all salaried employees on a Monday for the five-day workweek ended the previous Friday. The last payroll recorded for the year ended December 31, 1992, was for the week ended December 25, 1992. The payroll for the week ended January 1, 1993, included regular weekly salaries of $80,000 and vacation pay of $25,000 for vacation time earned in 1992 not taken by December 31, 1992. Ross had accrued a liability of $20,000 for vacation pay at December 31, 1991. In its December 31, 1992, balance sheet, what amount should Ross report as accrued salary and vacation pay?

    A. $64,000
    B. $68,000
    C. $69,000
    D. $89,000

22. On January 31, 1992, Beau Corp. issued $300,000 maturity value, 12 percent bonds for $300,000 cash. The bonds are dated December 31, 1991, and mature on December 31, 2001. Interest will be paid semiannually on June 30 and December 31. What amount of accrued interest payable should Beau report in its September 30, 1992, balance sheet?

    A. $27,000
    B. $24,000
    C. $18,000
    D. $ 9,000

23. Lyle, Inc., is preparing its financial statements for the year ended December 31, 1992. Accounts payable amounted to $360,000 before any necessary year-end adjustment related to the following:

• At December 31, 1992, Lyle has a $50,000 debit balance in its accounts payable to Ross, a supplier, resulting from a $50,000 advance payment for goods to be manufactured to Lyle's specifications.

• Checks in the amount of $100,000 were written to vendors and recorded on December 29, 1992. The checks were mailed on January 5, 1993.

What amount should Lyle report as accounts payable in its December 31, 1992, balance sheet?

    A. $510,000
    B. $410,000
    C. $310,000
    D. $210,000

24. On September 1, 1991, Brak Co. borrowed on a $1,350,000 note payable from Federal Bank. The note bears interest at 12 percent and is payable in three equal annual principal payments of $450,000. On this date, the bank's prime rate was 11 percent. The first annual payment for interest and principal was made on September 1, 1992. At December 31, 1992, what amount should Brak report as accrued interest payable?

    A. $54,000
    B. $49,500
    C. $36,000
    D. $33,000

25. Kent Co., a division of National Realty, Inc., maintains escrow accounts and pays real estate taxes for National's mortgage customers. Escrow funds are kept in interest-bearing accounts. Interest, less a 10 percent service fee, is credited to the mortgagee's account and used to reduce future escrow payments. Additional information follows:

Escrow accounts liability, 1/1/92	$ 700,000
Escrow payments received during 1992	1,580,000
Real estate taxes paid during 1992	1,720,000
Interest on escrow funds during 1992	50,000

What amount should Kent report as escrow accounts liability in its December 31, 1992, balance sheet?

    A. $510,000
    B. $515,000
    C. $605,000
    D. $610,000

Items 26 and 27 are based on the following:

The following information pertains to the transfer of real estate pursuant to a troubled debt restructuring by Knob Co. to Mene Corp. in full liquidation of Knob's liability to Mene:

Carrying amount of liability liquidated	$150,000
Carrying amount of real estate transferred	100,000
Fair value of real estate transferred	90,000

26. What amount should Knob report as a pretax extraordinary gain (loss) on restructuring of payables?
   A. ($10,000)
   B. $0
   C. $50,000
   D. $60,000

27. What amount should Knob report as ordinary gain (loss) on transfer of real estate?
   A. ($10,000)
   B. $0
   C. $50,000
   D. $60,000

28. Lease M does not contain a bargain purchase option, but the lease term is equal to 90 percent of the estimated economic life of the leased property. Lease P does not transfer ownership of the property to the lessee at the end of the lease term, but the lease term is equal to 75 percent of the estimated economic life of the leased property. How should the lessee classify these leases?

	Lease M	Lease P
A.	Capital lease	Operating lease
B.	Capital lease	Capital lease
C.	Operating lease	Capital lease
D.	Operating lease	Operating lease

29. On May 18, 1992, Sol Corp.'s board of directors declared a 10 percent stock dividend. The market price of Sol's 3,000 outstanding shares of $2 par value common stock was $9 per share on that date. The stock dividend was distributed on July 21, 1992, when the stock's market price was $10 per share. What amount should Sol credit to additional paid-in capital for this stock dividend?
   A. $2,100
   B. $2,400
   C. $2,700
   D. $3,000

30. Cross Corp. had outstanding 2,000 shares of 11 percent preferred stock, $50 par. On August 8, 1992, Cross redeemed and retired 25 percent of these shares for $22,500. On that date, Cross' additional paid-in capital from preferred stock totaled $30,000. To record this transaction, Cross should debit (credit) its capital accounts as follows:

	Preferred stock	Additional paid-in capital	Retained earnings
A.	$25,000	$7,500	($10,000)
B.	$25,000	—	($ 2,500)
C.	$25,000	($2,500)	—
D.	$22,500	—	—

31. Boe Corp.'s stockholders' equity at December 31, 1991, was as follows:

6 percent noncumulative preferred stock, $100 par (liquidation value $105 per share)	$100,000
Common stock, $10 par	300,000
Retained earnings	95,000

At December 31, 1991, Boe's book value per common share was
   A. $13.17
   B. $13.00
   C. $12.97
   D. $12.80

32. Which of the following should be reported as a stockholders' equity contra account?
   A. Discount on convertible bonds that are common stock equivalents.
   B. Premium on convertible bonds that are common stock equivalents.
   C. Cumulative foreign exchange translation loss.
   D. Organization costs.

33. On November 2, 1992, Finsbury, Inc. issued warrants to its stockholders giving them the right to purchase additional $20 par value common shares at a price of $30. The stockholders exercised all warrants on March 1, 1993. The shares had market prices of $33, $35, and $40 on November 2, 1992, December 31, 1992, and March 1, 1993, respectively. What were the effects of the warrants on Finsbury's additional paid-in capital and net income?

	Additional paid-in capital	Net income
A.	Increased in 1993	No effect
B.	Increased in 1992	No effect
C.	Increased in 1993	Decreased in 1992 and 1993
D.	Increased in 1992	Decreased in 1992 and 1993

34. When computing primary earnings per share, convertible securities that are common stock equivalents are
   A. Ignored.
   B. Recognized whether they are dilutive or anti-dilutive.
   C. Recognized only if they are anti-dilutive.
   D. Recognized only if they are dilutive.

35. In a comparison of 1992 to 1991, Neir Co.'s inventory turnover ratio increased substantially although sales and inventory amounts were essentially unchanged. Which of the following statements explains the increased inventory turnover ratio?
   A. Cost of goods sold decreased.
   B. Accounts receivable turnover increased.
   C. Total asset turnover increased.
   D. Gross profit percentage decreased.

36. Lino Co.'s worksheet for the preparation of its 1992 statement of cash flows included the following:

	December 31	January 1
Accounts receivable	$29,000	$23,000
Allowance for uncollectible accounts	1,000	800
Prepaid rent expense	8,200	12,400
Accounts payable	22,400	19,400

Lino's 1992 net income is $150,000. What amount should Lino include as net cash provided by operating activities in the statement of cash flows?
   A. $151,400
   B. $151,000
   C. $148,600
   D. $145,400

Items 37 and 38 are based on the following:

Karr, Inc., reported net income of $300,000 for 1992. Changes occurred in several balance sheet accounts as follows:

Equipment	$25,000 increase
Accumulated depreciation	40,000 increase
Note payable	30,000 increase

Additional information:
• During 1992, Karr sold equipment costing $25,000, with accumulated depreciation of $12,000, for a gain of $5,000.

• In December 1992, Karr purchased equipment costing $50,000 with $20,000 cash and a 12 percent note payable of $30,000.
• Depreciation expense for the year was $52,000.

37. In Karr's 1992 statement of cash flows, net cash provided by operating activities should be
   A. $340,000
   B. $347,000
   C. $352,000
   D. $357,000

38. In Karr's 1992 statement of cash flows, net cash used in investing activities should be
   A. $ 2,000
   B. $12,000
   C. $22,000
   D. $35,000

39. Bounty Co. provides postretirement health care benefits to employees who have completed at least 10 years service and are aged 55 years or older when retiring. Employees retiring from Bounty have a median age of 62, and no one has worked beyond age 65. Fletcher is hired at 48 years old. The attribution period for accruing Bounty's expected postretirement health care benefit obligation to Fletcher is during the period when Fletcher is aged
   A. 48 to 65.
   B. 48 to 58.
   C. 55 to 65.
   D. 55 to 62.

40. A company that maintains a defined benefit pension plan for its employees reports an unfunded accrued pension cost. This cost represents the amount that the
   A. Cumulative net pension cost accrued exceeds contributions to the plan
   B. Cumulative net pension cost accrued exceeds the vested benefit obligation.
   C. Vested benefit obligation exceeds plan assets.
   D. Vested benefit obligation exceeds contributions to the plan.

41. Visor Co. maintains a defined benefit pension plan for its employees. The service cost component of Visor's net periodic pension cost is measured using the
   A. Unfunded accumulated benefit obligation.
   B. Unfunded vested benefit obligation.
   C. Projected benefit obligation.
   D. Expected return on plan assets.

42. The following information pertains to each unit of merchandise purchased for resale by Vend Co.:

March 1, 1991

Purchase price	$ 8
Selling price	$12
Price level index	110

December 31, 1991

Replacement cost	$10
Selling price	$15
Price level index	121

Under current cost accounting, what is the amount of Vend's holding gain on each unit of this merchandise?
   A. $0
   B. $0.80
   C. $1.20
   D. $2.00

43. On January 2, 1992, to better reflect the variable use of its only machine, Holly, Inc., elected to change its method of depreciation from the straight-line method to the units of production method. The original cost of the machine on January 2, 1990, was $50,000, and its estimated life was 10 years. Holly estimates that the machine's total life is 50,000 machine hours.

Machine hours usage was 8,500 during 1991 and 3,500 during 1990.

Holly's income tax rate is 30 percent. Holly should report the accounting change in its 1992 financial statements as a(an)
   A. Cumulative effect of a change in accounting principle of $2,000 in its income statement.
   B. Adjustment to beginning retained earnings of $2,000.
   C. Cumulative effect of a change in accounting principle of $1,400 in its income statement.
   D. Adjustment to beginning retained earnings of $1,400.

44. Conn Co. reported a retained earnings balance of $400,000 at December 31, 1991. In August 1992, Conn determined that insurance premiums of $60,000 for the three-year period beginning January 1, 1991, had been paid and fully expensed in 1991. Conn has a 30 percent income tax rate. What amount should Conn report as adjusted beginning retained earnings in its 1992 statement of retained earnings?
   A. $420,000
   B. $428,000
   C. $440,000
   D. $442,000

45. The following costs were incurred by Griff Co., a manufacturer, during 1992:

Accounting and legal fees	$ 2,500
Freight-in	175,000
Freight-out	160,000
Officers salaries	150,000
Insurance	85,000
Sales representatives salaries	215,000

What amount of these costs should be reported as general and administrative expenses for 1992?
   A. $260,000
   B. $550,000
   C. $635,000
   D. $810,000

46. In Yew Co.'s 1992 annual report, Yew described its social awareness expenditures during the year as follows:
   "The Company contributed $250,000 in cash to youth and educational programs. The Company also gave $140,000 to health and human-service organizations, of which $80,000 was contributed by employees through payroll deductions. In addition, consistent with the Company's commitment to the environment, the Company spent $100,000 to redesign product packaging."

What amount of the above should be included in Yew's income statement as charitable contributions expense?
   A. $310,000
   B. $390,000
   C. $410,000
   D. $490,000

Items 47 and 48 are based on the following:

The following data pertains to Tyne Co.'s investments in marketable equity securities:

		Market value	
	Cost	12/31/92	12/31/91
Trading	$150,000	$155,000	$100,000
Available-for-sale	150,000	130,000	120,000

47. Assuming the application of FASB Statement #115, "Accounting for Certain Investments in Debt and Equity Securities," what amount should Tyne report as an unrealized holding gain in its 1992 income statement?
   A. $50,000
   B. $55,000
   C. $60,000
   D. $65,000

48.   Assuming the application of FASB Statement #115, "Accounting for Certain Investments in Debt and Equity Securities," what amount should Tyne report as net unrealized loss on available-for-sale marketable securities at December 31, 1992, in it statement of stockholders' equity?

    A. $0
    B. $10,000
    C. $15,000
    D. $20,000

49.   On January 1, 1990, JCK Co. signed a contract for an eight-year lease of its equipment with a 10-year life. The present value of the 16 equal semiannual payments in advance equaled 85 percent of the equipment's fair value. The contract had no provision for JCK, the lessor, to give up legal ownership of the equipment. Should JCK recognize rent or interest revenue in 1992, and should the revenue recognized in 1992 be the same or smaller than the revenue recognized in 1991?

	1992 revenues recognized	1992 amount recognized compared to 1991
A.	Rent	The same
B.	Rent	Smaller
C.	Interest	The same
D.	Interest	Smaller

50.   For a capital lease, the amount recorded initially by the lessee as a liability should normally

    A. Exceed the total of the minimum lease payments.
    B. Exceed the present value of the minimum lease payments at the beginning of the lease.
    C. Equal the total of the minimum lease payments.
    D. Equal the present value of the minimum lease payments at the beginning of the lease.

51.   On March 1, 1987, Somar Co. issued 20-year bonds at a discount. By September 1, 1992, the bonds were quoted at 106 when Somar exercised its right to retire the bonds at 105. How should Somar report the bond retirement on its 1992 income statement?

    A. A gain in continuing operations.
    B. A loss in continuing operations.
    C. An extraordinary gain.
    D. An extraordinary loss.

52.   On June 2, 1988, Tory, Inc., issued $500,000 of 10 percent, 15-year bonds at par. Interest is payable semi-annually on June 1 and December 1. Bond issue costs were $6,000. On June 2, 1993, Tory retired half of the bonds at 98. What is the net amount that Tory should use in computing the gain or loss on retirement of debt?

    A. $249,000
    B. $248,500
    C. $248,000
    D. $247,000

Items 53 and 54 are based on the following:

On January 1, 1991, Dallas, Inc. purchased 80 percent of Style, Inc.'s outstanding common stock for $120,000. On that date, the carrying amounts of Style's assets and liabilities approximated their fair values. During 1991, Style paid $5,000 cash dividends to its stockholders. Summarized balance sheet information for the two companies follows:

	Dallas	Style	
	12/31/91	12/31/91	1/1/91
Investment in Style (equity method)	$132,000		
Other assets	138,000	$115,000	$100,000
	$270,000	$115,000	$100,000
Common stock	$ 50,000	$ 20,000	$ 20,000
Additional paid-in capital	80,250	4,000	44,000
Retained earnings	139,750	51,000	36,000
	$270,000	$115,000	$100,000

53.   What amount should Dallas report as earnings from subsidiary, before amortization of goodwill, in its 1991 income statement?

    A. $12,000
    B. $15,000
    C. $16,000
    D. $20,000

54.   What amount of total stockholders' equity should be reported in Dallas' December 31, 1991, consolidated balance sheet?

    A. $270,000
    B. $286,000
    C. $362,000
    D. $385,000

Items 55 and 56 are based on the following:

Scroll, Inc., a wholly owned subsidiary of Pirn, Inc., began operations on January 1, 1991. The following information is from the condensed 1991 income statements of Pirn and Scroll:

	Pirn	Scroll
Sales to Scroll	$100,000	$ —
Sales to others	400,000	300,000
	500,000	300,000
Cost of goods sold:		
Acquired from Pirn	—	80,000
Acquired from others	350,000	190,000
Gross profit	150,000	30,000
Depreciation	40,000	10,000
Other expenses	60,000	15,000
Income from operations	50,000	5,000
Gain on sale of equipment to Scroll	12,000	—
Income before income taxes	$ 38,000	$ 5,000

Additional information:

• Sales by Pirn to Scroll are made on the same terms as those made to third parties.
• Equipment purchased by Scroll from Pirn for $36,000 on January 1, 1991, is depreciated using the straight-line method over four years.

55. In Pirn's December 31, 1991, consolidating worksheet, how much intercompany profit should be eliminated from Scroll's inventory?
   A. $30,000
   B. $20,000
   C. $10,000
   D. $ 6,000

56. What amount should be reported as depreciation expense in Pirn's 1991 consolidated income statement?
   A. $50,000
   B. $47,000
   C. $44,000
   D. $41,000

57. Heath Co.'s current ratio is 4:1. Which of the following transactions would normally increase its current ratio?
   A. Purchasing inventory on account.
   B. Selling inventory on account.
   C. Collecting an account receivable.
   D. Purchasing machinery for cash.

58. Seco Corp. was forced into bankruptcy and is in the process of liquidating assets and paying claims. Unsecured claims will be paid at the rate of forty cents on the dollar. Hale holds a $30,000 noninterest-bearing note receivable from Seco collateralized by an asset with a book value of $35,000 and a liquidation value of $5,000. The amount to be realized by Hale on this note is
   A. $ 5,000
   B. $12,000
   C. $15,000
   D. $17,000

59. On April 30, 1993, Algee, Belger, and Ceda formed a partnership by combining their separate business proprietorships. Algee contributed cash of $50,000. Belger contributed property with a $36,000 carrying amount, a $40,000 original cost, and $80,000 fair value. The partnership accepted responsibility for the $35,000 mortgage attached to the property. Ceda contributed equipment with a $30,000 carrying amount, a $75,000 original cost, and $55,000 fair value. The partnership agreement specifies that profits and losses are to be shared equally but is silent regarding capital contributions. Which partner has the largest April 30, 1993, capital account balance?
   A. Algee.
   B. Belger.
   C. Ceda.
   D. All capital account balances are equal

60. In its first four years of operations ending December 31, 1992, Alder, Inc.'s depreciation for income tax purposes exceeded its depreciation for financial statement purposes. This temporary difference was expected to reverse in 1992, 1994, and 1995. Alder had no other temporary difference and elected early adoption of FASB 109. Alder's 1992 balance sheet should include
   A. A noncurrent contra asset for the effects of the difference between asset bases for financial statement and income tax purposes.
   B. Both current and noncurrent deferred tax assets.
   C. A current deferred tax liability only.
   D. A noncurrent deferred tax liability only.

Number 2 (Estimated time for total question—15 to 25 minutes)

Instructions

Question 2 consists of two unrelated parts. Select the best answer for each item. Use a No. 2 pencil to blacken the appropriate ovals on the Objective Answer Sheet to indicate your answers. **Answer all items.** Your grade will be based on the total number of correct answers.

Part 2(a)

Items 61 through 65 are based on the following:

Hamnoff, Inc.'s $50 par value common stock has always traded above par. During 1992, Hamnoff had several transactions that affected the following balance sheet accounts:

   I. Bond discount
  II. Bond premium
 III. Bonds payable
  IV. Common stock
   V. Additional paid-in capital
  VI. Retained earnings

Required:
  For items 61 through 65, determine whether the transaction increased (I), decreased (D), or had no effect (N) on each of the balances in the above accounts.

61. Hamnoff issued bonds payable with a nominal rate of interest that was less than the market rate of interest.
62. Hamnoff issued convertible bonds, which are common stock equivalents, for an amount in excess of the bonds' face amount.
63. Hamnoff issued common stock when the convertible bonds described in item 62 were submitted for conversion. Each $1,000 bond was converted into 20 common shares. The book value method was used for the early conversion.
64. Hamnoff issued bonds, with detachable stock warrants, for an amount equal to the face amount of the bonds. The stock warrants have a determinable value.
65. Hamnoff declared and issued a 2 percent stock dividend.

Part 2(b)

Items 66 through 71 are based on the following:

Daley, Inc. is consistently profitable. Daley's normal financial statement relationships are as follows:

I.	Current ratio	3 to 1
II.	Inventory turnover	4 times
III.	Total debt/total assets ratio	0.5 to 1

Required:
  For items 66 through 71, determine whether each 1992 transaction or event increased (I), decreased (D), or had no effect (N) on each of the 1992 ratios.

66. Daley issued a stock dividend.
67. Daley declared, but did not pay, a cash dividend.
68. Customers returned invoiced goods for which they had not paid.
69. Accounts payable were paid on December 31, 1992.
70. Daley recorded both a receivable from an insurance company and a loss from fire damage to a factory building.
71. Early in 1992, Daley increased the selling price of one of its products that had a demand in excess of capacity. The number of units sold in 1991 and 1992 was the same.

Number 3 (Estimated time—15 to 25 minutes)

Instructions

Question 3 consists of two unrelated parts. Select the best answer for each item. Use a No. 2 pencil to blacken the appropriate ovals on the Objective Answer Sheet to indicate your answers. **Answer all items.** Your grade will be based on the total number of correct answers.

Part 3(a)

Items 72 through 79 are based on the following:

During 1992, Sloan, Inc. began a project to construct new corporate headquarters. Sloan purchased land with an existing building for $750,000. The land was valued at $700,000 and the building at $50,000. Sloan planned to demolish the building and construct a new office building on the site. Items 61 through 68 represent various expenditures by Sloan for this project.

Required:
For each expenditure in Items 72 through 79, select from the list below the appropriate accounting treatment and blacken the corresponding oval on the Objective Answer Sheet.

L. Classify as land and do not depreciate.
B. Classify as building and depreciate.
E. Expense.

72. Purchase of land for $700,000.
73. Interest of $147,000 on construction financing incurred after completion of construction.
74. Interest of $186,000 on construction financing paid during construction.
75. Purchase of building for $50,000.
76. $18,500 payment of delinquent real estate taxes assumed by Sloan on purchase.
77. $12,000 liability insurance premium during the construction period.
78. $65,000 cost of razing existing building.
79. Moving costs of $136,000.

Part 3(b)

Items 80 through 89 are based on the following:

The following information pertains to Sparta Co.'s defined benefit pension plan.

Discount rate	8 percent
Expected rate of return	10 percent
Average service life	12 years

At January 1, 1992:

Projected benefit obligation	$600,000
Fair value of pension plan assets	720,000
Unrecognized prior service cost	240,000
Unamortized prior pension gain	96,000

At December 31, 1992:

Projected benefit obligation	910,000
Fair value of pension plan assets	825,000

Service cost for 1992 was $90,000. There were no contributions made or benefits paid during the year. Sparta's unfunded accrued pension liability was $8,000 at January 1, 1992. Sparta uses the straight-line method of amortization over the maximum period permitted.

Required:
1. For items 80 through 84, calculate the amounts to be recognized as components of Sparta's unfunded accrued pension liability at December 31, 1992.

Amounts to be calculated:

80. Interest cost.
81. Expected return on plan assets.
82. Actual return on plan assets.
83. Amortization of prior service costs.
84. Minimum amortization of unrecognized pension gain.

2. For items 85 through 89, determine whether the component increases (I) or decreases (D) Sparta's unfunded accrued pension liability.

Items to be answered:

85. Service cost.
86. Deferral of gain on pension plan assets.
87. Actual return on plan assets.
88. Amortization of prior service costs.
89. Amortization of unrecognized pension gain.

Number 4 (Estimated time—35 to 40 minutes)

Question 4 consists of two unrelated parts.

Part 4(a)

Mono Tech Co. began operations in 1989 and confined its activities to one project. It purchased equipment to be used exclusively for research and development on the project, and other equipment that is to be used initially for research and development and subsequently for production. In 1990, Mono constructed and paid for a pilot plant that was used until December 1991 to determine the best manufacturing process for the project's product. In December 1991, Mono obtained a patent and received cash from the sale of the pilot plant. In 1992, a factory was constructed and commercial manufacture of the product began.

Required:

1. According to the FASB conceptual framework, what are the three essential characteristics of an asset?

2. How do Mono's project expenditures through 1991 meet the FASB conceptual framework's three essential characteristics of an asset? Do **not** discuss why the expenditures may **not** meet the characteristics of an asset.

3. Why is it difficult to justify the classification of research and development expenditures as assets?

Part 4(b)

London, Inc. began operation of its construction division on October 1, 1991, and entered into contracts for two separate projects. The Beta project contract price was $600,000 and provided for penalties of $10,000 per week for late completion. Although during 1992 the Beta project had been on schedule for timely completion, it was completed four weeks late in August 1993. The Gamma project's original contract price was $800,000. Change orders during 1993 added $40,000 to the original contract price.

The following data pertains to the separate long-term construction projects in progress:

	Beta	Gamma
As of September 30, 1992:		
Costs incurred to date	$360,000	$410,000
Estimated costs to complete	40,000	410,000
Billings	315,000	440,000
Cash collections	275,000	365,000
As of September 30, 1993:		
Costs incurred to date	450,000	720,000
Estimated costs to complete	—	180,000
Billings	560,000	710,000
Cash collections	560,000	625,000

Additional information:

• London accounts for its long-term construction contracts using the percentage-of-completion method for financial reporting purposes and the completed-contract method for income tax purposes.

• London elected early application of FASB 109, *Accounting for Income Taxes,* for the year ended September 30, 1992. Enacted rates are 25 percent for 1992 and 30 percent for future years.

• London's income before income taxes from all divisions, before considering revenues from long-term construction projects, was $300,000 for the year ended September 30, 1992. There was no other temporary or permanent differences.

Required:

Prepare a schedule showing London's gross profit (loss) recognized for the years ended September 30, 1992, and 1993, under the percentage-of-completion method.

Number 5 (Estimated time—35 to 40 minutes)

Question 5 consists of two unrelated parts.

Part 5(a)

Gregor Wholesalers Co. sells industrial equipment for a standard three-year note receivable. Revenue is recognized at time of sale. Each note is secured by a lien on the equipment and has a face amount equal to the equipment's list price. Each note's stated interest rate is below the customer's market rate at date of sale. All notes are to be collected in three equal annual installments beginning one year after sale. Some of the notes are subsequently discounted at a bank with recourse, some are subsequently discounted without recourse, and some are retained by Gregor. At year end, Gregor evaluates all outstanding notes receivable and provides for estimated losses arising from defaults.

Required:

What is the appropriate valuation basis for Gregor's notes receivable at the date it sells equipment?

Part 5(b)

Trask Corp., a public company whose shares are traded in the over-the-counter market, had the following stockholders' equity account balances at December 31, 1991:

Common stock	$ 7,875,000
Additional paid-in capital	15,750,000
Retained earnings	16,445,000
Treasury common stock	750,000

Transactions during 1992, and other information relating to the stockholders' equity accounts, were as follows:

- Trask had 4,000,000 authorized shares of $5 par value common stock; 1,575,000 shares were issued, of which 75,000 were held in treasury.
- On January 21, 1992, Trask issued 50,000 shares of $100 par value, 6 percent cumulative preferred stock in exchange for all of Rover Co.'s assets and liabilities. On that date, the net carrying amount of Rover's assets and liabilities was $5,000,000. The carrying amounts of Rover's assets and liabilities equalled their fair values. On January 22, 1992, Rover distributed the Trask shares to its stockholders in complete liquidation and dissolution of Rover. Trask had 150,000 authorized shares of preferred stock.

- On February 17, 1992, Trask formally retired 25,000 of its 75,000 treasury common stock shares. The shares were originally issued at $15 per share and had been acquired on September 25, 1991, for $10 per share. Trask uses the cost method to account for treasury stock.
- Trask owned 15,000 shares of Harbor, Inc. common stock purchased in 1989 for $600,000. The Harbor stock was included in Trask's short-term marketable securities portfolio. On March 5, 1992, Trask declared a property dividend of one share of Harbor common stock for every 100 shares of Trask common stock held by a stockholder of record on April 16, 1992. The market price of Harbor stock on March 5, 1992, was $60 per share. The property dividend was distributed on April 29, 1992.
- On January 2, 1990, Trask granted stock options to employees to purchase 200,000 shares of the company's common stock at $12 per share, which was also the market price on that date. The options are exercisable within a three-year period beginning January 2, 1992. The measurement date is the same as the grant date. On June 1, 1992, employees exercised 150,000 options when the market value of the stock was $25 per share. Trask issued new shares to settle the transaction.
- On October 27, 1992, Trask declared a 2-for-1 stock split on its common stock and reduced the per share par value accordingly. Trask stockholders of record on August 2, 1992, received one additional share of Trask common stock for each share of Trask common stock held. The laws in Trask's state of incorporation protect treasury stock from dilution.
- On December 12, 1992, Trask declared the yearly cash dividend on preferred stock, payable on January 11, 1993, to stockholders of record on December 31, 1992.
- On January 16, 1993, before the accounting records were closed for 1992, Trask became aware that depreciation expense was understated by $350,000 for the year ended December 31, 1991. The after-tax effect on 1991 net income was $245,000. The appropriate correcting entry was recorded on the same day.
- Net income for 1992 was $2,400,000.

Required:

Prepare Trask's statement of retained earnings for the year ended December 31, 1992. Assume that Trask prepares only single-period financial statements for 1992.

ANSWER KEY FOUR-OPTION MULTIPLE-CHOICE QUESTIONS

Be sure to read "Chapter 6—Chart Your Progress and Plan Your Course of Action." It will help you analyze your test and plan your study program.

Business Law & Professional Responsibilities (LPR)

QUESTION #	ANSWER	TOPICAL AREA
1	C	Accountants' Legal Responsibility
2	C	Accountants' Legal Responsibility
3	C	Accountants' Legal Responsibility
4	A	Accountants' Legal Responsibility
5	A	Accountants' Legal Responsibility
6	A	Accountants' Legal Responsibility
7	B	Accountants' Legal Responsibility
8	B	Accountants' Legal Responsibility
9	A	Accountants' Legal Responsibility
10	D	Professional Responsibilities
11	D	Agency
12	A	Partnerships
13	B	Agency
14	C	Agency
15	C	Agency
16	B	Partnerships
17	C	Corporations
18	C	Partnerships
19	C	Corporations
20	B	Corporations
21	A	Contracts
22	D	Contracts
23	B	Contracts
24	B	Contracts
25	C	Suretyship and Creditor's Rights
26	A	Contracts
27	D	Bankruptcy
28	B	Bankruptcy

QUESTION #	ANSWER	TOPICAL AREA
29	D	Bankruptcy
30	D	Bankruptcy
31	B	Bankruptcy
32	C	Bankruptcy
33	A	Bankruptcy
34	B	Professional Responsibilities
35	B	Employment Regulations
36	A	Employment Regulations
37	D	Federal Securities Regulations
38	A	Federal Securities Regulations
39	A	Bankruptcy
40	A	Federal Securities Regulations
41	C	Federal Securities Regulations
42	B	Federal Securities Regulations
43	D	Federal Securities Regulations
44	A	Professional Responsibilities
45	C	Federal Securities Regulations
46	B	Documents of Title
47	D	Documents of Title
48	D	Investment Securities
49	C	Sales
50	D	Sales
51	A	Sales
52	C	Sales
53	C	Secured Transactions
54	D	Professional Responsibilities
55	C	Professional Responsibilities
56	B	Sales
57	D	Sales
58	D	Secured Transactions
59	B	Secured Transactions
60	D	Secured Transactions

Auditing (AUDIT)

QUESTION #	ANSWER	TOPICAL AREA
1	D	Electronic Data Procession (EDP)
2	D	Auditing Concepts and Standards
3	C	Electronic Data Procession (EDP)

Question #	Answer	Topical Area
4	B	Audit Planning
5	A	Audit Planning
6	A	Audit Planning
7	D	Audit Planning
8	C	Audit Planning
9	C	Other Reporting Areas
10	D	Statistical Sampling
11	B	Audit Evidence
12	D	Other Reporting Areas
13	C	Statistical Sampling
14	C	Audit Reporting Standards
15	A	Audit Evidence
16	B	Internal Control
17	C	Audit Planning
18	D	Electronic Data Processing (EDP)
19	D	Internal Control
20	C	Statistical Sampling
21	A	Internal Control
22	A	Internal Control
23	C	Internal Control
24	D	Internal Control
25	D	Internal Control
26	B	Audit Evidence
27	C	Internal Control
28	B	Internal Control
29	D	Internal Control
30	C	Internal Control
31	A	Internal Control
32	D	Internal Control
33	B	Internal Control
34	C	Internal Control
35	B	Other Reporting Areas
36	B	Audit Evidence
37	C	Audit Evidence
38	C	Audit Planning
39	C	Audit Evidence
40	D	Audit Evidence
41	D	Audit Evidence
42	B	Audit Planning
43	C	Electronic Data Processing (EDP)
44	B	Other Reporting Areas
45	B	Other Reporting Areas
46	D	Audit Reporting Standards
47	A	Audit Reporting Standards
48	A	Audit Reporting Standards
49	C	Audit Reporting Standards
50	A	Other Reporting Areas
51	D	Audit Reporting Standards
52	A	Auditing Concepts and Standards

Question #	Answer	Topical Area
53	B	Other Reporting Areas
54	A	Other Reporting Areas
55	C	Audit Reporting Standards
56	A	Other Reporting Areas
57	C	Other Reporting Areas
58	A	Other Reporting Areas
59	B	Audit Reporting Standards
60	B	Internal Control
61	A	Audit Reporting Standards
62	D	Audit Reporting Standards
63	D	Other Reporting Areas
64	D	Other Reporting Areas
65	B	Other Reporting Areas
66	C	Internal Control
67	B	Internal Control
68	B	Internal Control
69	B	Internal Control
70	B	Internal Control
71	C	Internal Control
72	A	Internal Control
73	D	Internal Control
74	B	Internal Control
75	C	Audit Planning
76	A	Audit Planning
77	D	Audit Planning
78	A	Audit Planning
79	B	Audit Planning
80	D	Audit Planning
81	B	Internal Control
82	D	Audit Evidence
83	D	Audit Evidence
84	D	Audit Evidence
85	C	Audit Evidence
86	B	Audit Evidence
87	B	Audit Planning
88	B	Audit Evidence
89	D	Audit Evidence
90	C	Audit Evidence

Accounting & Reporting— Taxation, Managerial, and Governmental and Not-For-Profit Organizations (ARE)

Question #	Answer	Topical Area
1	C	Federal Income Taxes— Corporations
2	B	Federal Income Taxes— Corporations

Question #	Answer	Topical Area
3	D	Federal Income Taxes—Corporations
4	A	Federal Income Taxes—Corporations
5	C	Federal Income Taxes—Corporations
6	D	Federal Income Taxes—Corporations
7	D	Federal Income Taxes—Corporations
8	D	Federal Income Taxes—Corporations
9	C	Federal Income Taxes—Corporations
10	A	Federal Income Taxes—Corporations
11	B	Federal Income Taxes—Corporations
12	B	Federal Income Taxes—Corporations
13	D	Federal Income Taxes—Corporations
14	B	Federal Income Taxes—Corporations
15	A	Federal Income Taxes—Corporations
16	D	Federal Income Taxes—Corporations
17	B	Federal Income Taxes—Corporations
18	D	Federal Income Taxes—Corporations
19	C	Federal Income Taxes—Corporations
20	A	Federal Income Taxes—Corporations
21	C	Federal Income Taxes—Corporations
22	A	Federal Income Taxes—Corporations
23	C	Federal Income Taxes—Corporations
24	D	Federal Income Taxes—Corporations
25	A	Federal Income Taxes—Corporations
26	A	Federal Income Taxes—Partnerships
27	C	Federal Income Taxes—Partnerships
28	C	Federal Income Taxes—Partnerships

Question #	Answer	Topical Area
29	D	Federal Income Taxes—Partnerships
30	A	Federal Income Taxes—Partnerships
31	A	Federal Income Taxes—Partnerships
32	B	Federal Income Taxes—Partnerships
33	D	Federal Income Taxes—Estates & Trusts
34	A	Federal Income Taxes—Estates & Trusts
35	C	Federal Income Taxes—Exempt Organizations
36	C	Managerial Accounting and Quantitative Methods
37	D	Managerial Accounting and Quantitative Methods
38	D	Managerial Accounting and Quantitative Methods
39	C	Managerial Accounting and Quantitative Methods
40	D	Managerial Accounting and Quantitative Methods
41	B	Managerial Accounting and Quantitative Methods
42	D	Managerial Accounting and Quantitative Methods
43	C	Managerial Accounting and Quantitative Methods
44	C	Managerial Accounting and Quantitative Methods
45	A	Managerial Accounting and Quantitative Methods
46	C	Managerial Accounting and Quantitative Methods
47	A	Managerial Accounting and QuantitativeMethods
48	C	Cost Accounting
49	D	Cost Accounting
50	A	Cost Accounting
51	A	Not-for-Profit Accounting—Governmental Units
52	A	Not-for-Profit Accounting—Governmental Units
53	B	Not-for-Profit Accounting—Governmental Units
54	D	Not-for-Profit Accounting—Governmental Units
55	D	Not-for-Profit Accounting—Governmental Units

Question #	Answer	Topical Area
56	B	Not-for-Profit Accounting—Other Than Governmental Units
57	B	Not-for-Profit Accounting—Other Than Governmental Units
58	A	Not-for-Profit Accounting—Other Than Governmental Units
59	B	Not-for-Profit Accounting—Other Than Governmental Units
60	A	Not-for-Profit Accounting—Other Than Governmental Units

Financial Accounting & Reporting—Business Enterprises (FARE)

Question #	Answer	Topical Area
1	C	Investments
2	C	Inventories
3	A	Fixed Assets
4	B	Fixed Assets
5	D	Fixed Assets
6	D	Intangibles
7	B	Receivables
8	A	Receivables
9	B	Receivables
10	A	Accounting Concepts
11	C	Accounting Concepts
12	C	Accounting Concepts
13	B	Accounting Concepts
14	D	Installment Sales
15	B	Accounting Fundamentals
16	C	Foreign Currency Translation
17	D	Accounting Fundamentals
18	A	Installment Sales
19	A	Liabilities
20	B	Liabilities

Question #	Answer	Topical Area
21	D	Liabilities
22	D	Liabilities
23	A	Liabilities
24	C	Liabilities
25	C	Liabilities
26	D	Liabilities
27	A	Liabilities
28	B	Leases
29	A	Stockholders' Equity
30	C	Stockholders' Equity
31	B	Stockholders' Equity
32	C	Stockholders' Equity
33	A	Stockholders' Equity
34	D	Stockholders' Equity
35	D	Financial Statement Analysis
36	A	Cash Flows
37	B	Cash Flows
38	A	Cash Flows
39	B	Pension Costs
40	A	Pension Costs
41	C	Pension Costs
42	D	Inflation Accounting
43	C	Financial Statements
44	B	Financial Statements
45	A	Financial Statements
46	A	Financial Statements
47	B	Investments
48	D	Investments
49	D	Leases
50	D	Leases
51	D	Bonds, Accounting for
52	C	Bonds, Accounting for
53	C	Consolidation and Business Combination
54	A	Consolidation and Business Combination
55	D	Consolidation and Business Combination
56	B	Consolidation and Business Combination
57	B	Financial Statement Analysis
58	C	Bankruptcy
59	C	Partnerships
60	D	Income Taxes, Accounting for

SOLUTIONS AND EXPLAINED ANSWERS

Business Law and Professional Responsibilities (LPR)

FOUR-OPTION MULTIPLE-CHOICE QUESTIONS

Answer 1

1.   C   An accountant's common-law liability to a client may be based upon negligence or upon fraud.

The elements of negligence include:
1. A duty of due professional care and competence.
2. Failure to act in accordance with that duty.
3. Proximate cause.
4. Loss or damage resulting from failure to act.

The elements of fraud include:
1. A material, false statement or omission.
2. <u>Scienter</u> - knowledge of the falsity or omission.
3. Intention that plaintiff rely.
4. Justifiable reliance by plaintiff.
5. Damages caused by reliance.

Therefore, in order for Mac to recover from Beckler for its losses associated with Queen's default, Mac must prove that <u>Beckler</u> <u>was</u> <u>negligent</u> <u>in</u> <u>conducting</u> <u>the</u> <u>audit</u>, <u>and</u> <u>that</u> <u>Mac</u> <u>relied</u> <u>on</u> <u>the</u> <u>financial</u> <u>statements</u>.

Answer choices other than "C" are based on incorrect assumptions and/or interpretations of the law.

2.   C   An accountant does not guarantee that he/she will not make mistakes but only that the accountant will perform the engagement in accordance with industry standards. <u>Whether</u> <u>the</u> <u>CPA</u> <u>conducted</u> <u>the</u> <u>audit</u> <u>with</u> <u>the</u> <u>same</u> <u>skill</u> <u>and</u> <u>care</u> <u>expected</u> <u>of</u> <u>an</u> <u>ordinarily</u> <u>prudent</u> <u>CPA</u> <u>under</u> <u>the</u> <u>circumstances</u> best describes whether a CPA has met the required standard of care in conducting an audit of a client's financial statements.

Answer choice "A" is incorrect because the standard of care required for a CPA in conducting an audit of a client's financial statements is not determined by the client's expectations with regard to the accuracy of audited financial statements. Industry standards, rather than client expectations, determine the required standard of care.

Answer choice "B" is incorrect because the accuracy of the financial statements and whether the statements conform to generally accepted accounting principles are not determinative of whether a CPA has met the required standard of care in conducting an audit of a client's financial statements. An accountant is not liable for mistakes as long as the accountant exercised reasonable care and followed generally accepted auditing standards in performing the audit.

Answer choice "D" is incorrect because a CPA has no special duty to discover all acts of fraud. A CPA will be liable for failing to discover fraud only where such fraud would have been discovered by an ordinarily prudent CPA performing the audit in a nonnegligent manner.

3.   C   An accountant may avoid civil liability for material misstatements or omissions in a registration statement for publicly offered securities by establishing the affirmative defense of "due diligence." The due diligence defense places the burden on the CPA to prove that the CPA followed proper accounting standards and had reasonable grounds to believe, and did believe, in the truth, accuracy, and completeness of the accountant's work. Thus, if Larson is sued by a securities purchaser under Section 11 of the Securities Act of 1933, Larson will not be liable if it had reasonable grounds to believe the financial statements were accurate.

Answer choice "A" is incorrect because the purchaser of the securities does not need to prove that Larson was negligent in conducting the audit. Under Section 11 of the Securities Act of 1933, the purchaser need only prove (1) the securities were purchased, (2) the registration statement or prospectus contained omitted material information or materially false information, and (3) a loss was incurred.

Answer choice "B" is incorrect because the purchaser is not required to prove that Larson knew of the material misstatements. Under Section 11 of the Securities Act of 1933, the purchaser need only prove (1) the securities were purchased, (2) the registration statement or prospectus contained omitted material information or materially false information, and (3) a loss was incurred.

Answer choice "D" is incorrect because the purchaser's reliance on the financial statements is not a condition precedent to Larson's liability under Section 11 of the Securities Act of 1933.

4.   A   An accountant is liable to clients and known third-party beneficiaries for damages resulting from the accountant's common law negligence. A successful suit for negligence requires proof of:
1.   A duty of due professional care and competence that is owed by the accountant.
2.   The accountant's failure to act in accordance with that duty.
3.   Proximate cause.
4.   Loss or damage resulting from failure to act.

Thus, in a suit by a purchaser against Larson for common law negligence, Larson's best defense would be that the audit was conducted in accordance with generally accepted auditing standards.

Answer choice "B" is incorrect because the fact that the client was aware of the misstatements will not shield Larson from liability for negligence in a suit by the purchaser of the securities. If the purchaser was aware of the misstatement, then Larson could defend with a contributory negligence defense.

Answer choice "C" is incorrect because most states do not recognize lack of privity between the accountant and the plaintiff as a valid defense to a negligence action against the accountant by the client. Most states hold that an accountant is liable for damages resulting from negligence to the client and all known third-party users of the accountant's work product.

Answer choice "D" is incorrect because most states hold that an accountant is liable for damages resulting from negligence to the client and all known third-party users of the accountant's work product. The fact that the identity of that third-party user was not known to the accountant at the time the service was rendered is not a valid defense for the accountant.

5.   A   Clients, known third parties, and reasonably foreseeable third parties may sue an accountant for common law fraud. A suit for fraud requires proof of the following.
1.   A material, false statement or omission.
2.   Scienter - knowledge of the falsity or omission.
3.   Intention that plaintiff rely.
4.   Justifiable reliance by plaintiff.
5.   Damages caused by reliance.

Thus, Larson's best defense to a suit by a purchaser for common law fraud would be that Larson did not have actual or constructive knowledge of the misstatements (i.e., lacked scienter).

Answer choice "B" is incorrect because the fact that Larson's client knew or should have known of the misstatements will not shield Larson from liability for fraud in a suit by a purchaser of the securities.

Answer choice "C" is incorrect because an accountant is liable for damages resulting from fraud to reasonably foreseeable third parties, as well as to clients and known third parties. Thus, Larson's lack of actual knowledge that the purchaser of the securities was an intended beneficiary of the audit is not a valid defense to a suit by that purchaser based on common law fraud.

Answer choice "D" is incorrect because lack of privity of contract with an accountant's client will not provide an accountant with a valid defense to a securities purchaser's suit for damages resulting from fraud.

6.   A   A CPA is civilly liable under Section 10(b) and Rule 10b-5 of the Securities Exchange Act of 1934 for damages resulting from fraud. Fraud requires proof of the following.

1. A material, false statement or omission.
2. <u>Scienter</u> - knowledge of the falsity or omission.
3. Intention that plaintiff rely.
4. Justifiable reliance by plaintiff.
5. Damages caused by reliance.

Thus, under Section 10(b) and Rule 10b-5 of the Securities Exchange Act of 1934, <u>Jay will be liable if the purchaser relied on Jay's unqualified opinion on the financial statements</u>.

Answer choice "B" is incorrect because a CPA is not liable for mere negligence where the CPA is sued under Section 10(b) and Rule 10b-5 of the Securities Exchange Act of 1934. The plaintiff must prove to be successful in a lawsuit under the Securities Exchange Act of 1934.

Answer choice "C" is incorrect because Section 10(b) and Rule 10b-5 of the Securities Exchange Act of 1934 do not preclude suits for losses of less than $500.

Answer choice "D" is incorrect because an accountant is not shielded from liability for the accountant's own fraudulent omission under Section 10(b) and Rule 10b-5 of the Securities Exchange Act of 1934. Thus, the fact that Jay is the party responsible for the material omission will not preclude Jay from liability.

7. B A suit based on common law fraud requires the plaintiff to prove the following.
1. A material, false statement or omission.
2. <u>Scienter</u> - knowledge of the falsity or omission.
3. Intention that plaintiff rely.
4. Justifiable reliance by plaintiff.
5. Damages caused by reliance.

Thus, a CPA firm's best defense to a suit for common law fraud based on their unqualified opinion on materially false financial statements would be <u>lack of scienter</u>.

Answer choice "A" is incorrect because lack of privity is not a valid defense to a suit for common law fraud.

Answer choice "C" is incorrect because contributory negligence on the part of the client is not a valid defense to a suit for common law fraud.

Answer choice "D" is incorrect because a disclaimer contained in an engagement letter will not be a valid defense to a suit for common law fraud. Such a disclaimer is generally against public policy.

8. B An accountant is civilly liable for damages resulting from violations of Section 11 of the Securities Act of 1933 and Section 10(b) and Rule 10b-5 of the Securities Exchange Act of 1934. A suit based on Section 11 of the Securities Act of 1933 requires proof of the following.

1. The security was purchased.
2. The registration statement or prospectus omitted material information or contained materially false information.
3. A loss was incurred.

A suit based on Section 10(b) and Rule 10b-5 of the Securities Exchange Act of 1934 requires proof of:
1. A material, false statement or omission.
2. <u>Scienter</u> - knowledge of the falsity or omission.
3. Intention that plaintiff rely.
4. Justifiable reliance by plaintiff.
5. Damages caused by reliance.

Thus, Thorp is most likely to prevail in a suit against Ivor based upon the <u>Section 11 of the Securities Act of 1933</u>. Thorp will not prevail under Section 10(b) and Rule 10b-5 of the Securities Exchange Act of 1934 because of the lack of scienter and the lack of reliance by Thorp.

Answer choices other than "B" are based on incorrect assumptions and/or interpretations of the law.

9.   A   In preparing a tax return, a tax practitioner must adhere to the IRC and the regulations thereunder. Failure to do so may result in the imposition of criminal and/or civil penalties. One of the common civil penalties is a $500 civil fine for negotiating a taxpayer's income tax refund check. Thus, <u>Clark will be subject to the penalty if Clark endorses and cashes the check</u>.

Answer choice "B" is incorrect because Clark will be subject to the penalty, despite the fact that Clark is enrolled to practice before the Internal Revenue Service.

Answer choice "C" is incorrect because Clark will be liable for a civil penalty for cashing a client's income tax refund check, without regard to the amount of the check.

Answer choice "D" is incorrect because Clark will be liable for a civil penalty for cashing a client's income tax refund check, without regard to the amount of the check or the relationship of the amount of the check to the accountant's fee for preparing the return.

10.   D   It is essential that CPAs maintain an independent attitude in fulfilling their responsibilities. It is also important that the users of financial statements have confidence in the existence of that independence. These two objectives are identified, respectively, as independence in fact and independence in appearance.

Independence in fact exists when the auditor is able to maintain an unbiased attitude throughout the audit. Independence in appearance is dependent on how others perceive this independence. Independence in appearance enhances public confidence in the profession.

Generally, independence will be considered to be impaired if the auditor, during the period of his or her engagement, or at the time of expressing his or her opinion:

1. Had any direct or material indirect financial interest in the client.
2. Was a trustee, executor, or administrator committed to acquiring a direct or material indirect interest in the client.
3. Had any joint closely held business investment with the client.
4. Had any loan to or from the client, with the exception of "grandfathered loans" and "other permitted loans." "Grandfathered loans" include home mortgages, other secured loans, or loans that are not considered material to the CPA's net worth, that existed prior to January 1, 1992. "Other permitted loans" include automobile loans, loans on the cash surrender value under terms of an insurance policy, borrowings fully collateralized by cash deposits (e.g., "passbook loans"), or credit cards and cash advances on checking accounts not exceeding $5,000.
5. Acted in any capacity equivalent to that of a member of management.
6. Was a trustee for any pension or profit-sharing trust of the client.

A CPA may belong to a social club (for example, country club or tennis club) in which membership requirements involve the acquisition of a pro rata share of equity.

As long as membership in a club is essentially a social matter, independence of the CPA would not be considered to be impaired, because such equity ownership is not considered to be a direct financial interest. However, the member should not serve on the club's governing board or take part in its management.

Answer choice "A" is incorrect because the leasing of property to a client results in an indirect financial interest in that client. Independence would be considered to be impaired if the indirect financial interest in that client is material to the CPA's net worth.

Answer choice "B" is incorrect because the independence of the CPA would be considered impaired if the CPA has any direct financial interest in an audit client, whether or not the financial interest is placed in a blind trust.

Answer choice "C" is incorrect because the CPA's independence would be impaired because the mortgage on the building guaranteed by a client is considered to be a loan from the client.

11. D Generally, no formalities are required to create an agency relationship. A power of attorney is a formal appointment of an agent who is called an attorney in fact (as distinguished from an attorney at law). Thus, if Noll gives Carr a written power of attorney, it may limit Carr's authority to specific transactions.

Answer choice "A" is incorrect because a document creating a power of attorney need not be signed by both the principal and the agent, but only by the principal (i.e., Noll).

Answer choice "B" is incorrect because a written power of attorney need not be for a definite period of time.

Answer choice "C" is incorrect because a written power of attorney is terminated automatically by operation of law upon the death of the principal (i.e., Noll).

12.   A   Each partner is an agent of the partnership and the other partners for partnership business. The firm and its partners are contractually bound by a partner's action for which apparent authority exists in carrying on the partnership business in the normal way, unless the third party has notice or actual knowledge that the partner lacks authority for the action. Thus, the apparent authority of a partner to bind the partnership in dealing with third parties <u>will be effectively limited by a formal resolution of the partners of which third parties are aware</u>.

Answer choice "B" is incorrect because third parties who are unaware of a formal resolution of the partners that limits a partner's apparent authority are not limited by the resolution and may deal with the partner within the partner's apparent authority.

Answer choice "C" is incorrect because the authority of a partner to submit a claim against the partnership to arbitration requires the unanimous consent of all partners and thus is not within the scope of a partner's apparent authority.

Answer choice "D" is incorrect because apparent authority is not derived from the express powers and purposes contained in the partnership agreement. Apparent authority is derived from the customs in the industry, the partner's position in the firm, and/or other circumstances apparent to the third party.

13.   B   Generally, an employer of an employee who is an agent is liable for the torts of the employee committed within the scope of the employee's job, but is not liable for the torts of an employee who is an independent contractor. Thus, generally a disclosed principal will be liable to a third parties for its agent's unauthorized misrepresentations <u>if the agent is an employee</u>, but <u>not if the agent is an independent contractor</u>.

Answer choices other than "B" are based on incorrect assumptions and/or interpretations of the law.

14.   C   An agent who contracts on behalf of an undisclosed principal is personally liable to the third party for breach of the contract. The third party, upon learning of the existence and identity of the principal, may elect to sue the agent, or the principal. Thus, a third party who validly contracts with an agent representing an

undisclosed principal will be entitled to <u>performance</u> <u>of</u> <u>the</u> <u>contract</u> <u>by</u> <u>the</u> <u>agent</u>.

Answer choice "A" is incorrect because an agent for an undisclosed principal may not disclose the identity of the principal to the third party without the consent of the principal.

Answer choice "B" is incorrect because the concept of ratification is not applicable to contracts made by an agent for an undisclosed principal. Ratification can only apply to acts of the agent purportedly on behalf of the principal. An agent for an undisclosed principal does not purport to act for a principal but only for the agent.

Answer choice "D" is incorrect because a third party who contracts with an agent for an undisclosed principal may not void the contract after discovery of the existence of the principal. The third party may elect, instead, to enforce the contract against either the agent or the principal.

15. C   An agent's apparent authority is actual authority from the third party's perspective, and the third party can enforce a contract made with an agent acting within the agent's apparent authority. A limitation upon an agent's actual authority, of which the third party has neither notice nor knowledge, does not limit the agent's apparent authority. Thus, <u>North</u> <u>will</u> <u>be</u> <u>liable</u> <u>to</u> <u>Orr</u> <u>because</u> <u>of</u> <u>Sutter's</u> <u>actual</u> <u>and</u> <u>apparent</u> <u>authority</u>.

Answer choice "A" is incorrect because Sutter will not be liable to Orr. Sutter will be liable to North for breach of the fiduciary duty to obey the reasonable instructions of the principal and therefore to honor the limitation on his/her actual authority.

Answer choice "B" is incorrect because Sutter will be liable to reimburse North if North is liable to Orr, since Sutter breached his fiduciary duty to obey the reasonable instructions of the principal. The limitation on Sutter's actual authority was a reasonable instruction.

Answer choice "D" is incorrect because North will be liable to Orr since the contract Orr made with North's agent, Sutter, was within Sutter's apparent authority.

16. B   A partnership is an association of two or more persons to carry on a business as co-owners for profit. In order to have a valid partnership, the parties must have <u>co-ownership</u> <u>of</u> <u>a</u> <u>business</u> <u>for</u> <u>profit</u>. However, the parties need not have co-ownership of all property used in business.

Answer choices other than "B" are based on incorrect assumptions and/or interpretations of the law.

17.   C   Debt securities normally involve a corporation's promise to repay a stated sum of money (i.e., the principal) plus a stated rate of interest on a fixed date. Debt securities create a debtor-creditor relationship between the holder of the security and the corporation. <u>Convertible</u> <u>bonds</u> <u>and</u> <u>debenture</u> <u>bonds</u> are debt securities, but warrants are equity securities. Equity securities create ownership rights in the corporation for the holder of the security.

Answer choices other than "C" are based on incorrect assumptions and/or interpretations of the law.

18.   C   Partnership property includes all property originally brought into the partnership and/or subsequently acquired with partnership funds. <u>Partnership</u> <u>property</u> is co-owned and therefore <u>is</u> <u>not</u> <u>assignable</u> or inheritable by the heirs of an individual partner. However, a partnership distribution is a transfer of partnership property to a partner. Examples include distributions of profit shares and returns of capital contributions. A <u>partnership</u> <u>distribution</u> <u>is</u> <u>assignable</u> because the right to distribution belongs to the partners individually, rather than the partners as a group.

Answer choices other than "C" are based on incorrect assumptions and/or interpretations of the law.

19.   C   A corporation is a statutory creation and derives its powers from the state corporation statutes and the express provisions of the Articles of Incorporation. A for-profit-corporation must include the <u>name</u> <u>of</u> <u>the</u> <u>corporation</u> <u>and</u> <u>a</u> <u>provision</u> <u>for</u> <u>the</u> <u>issuance</u> <u>of</u> <u>voting</u> <u>stock</u> in its Articles of Incorporation to obtain a corporate charter.

Answer choices other than "C" are based on incorrect assumptions and/or interpretations of the law.

20.   B   One of the features of a corporation is the limited liability afforded its owners, the shareholders. The liability of corporate shareholders is normally limited to their investment. However, courts will pierce the corporate veil (i.e., disregard the separate corporate entity) to prevent the corporation from being used to perpetrate a fraud or otherwise circumvent the law. Thus, the corporate veil is most likely to be pierced and the shareholders held personally liable if <u>the</u> <u>shareholders</u> <u>have</u> <u>commingled</u> <u>their</u> <u>personal</u> <u>funds</u> <u>with</u> <u>those</u> <u>of</u> <u>the</u> <u>corporation</u>.

Answer choice "A" is incorrect because electing S corporation status under the IRC is not fraudulent and will not cause the corporate veil to be pierced.

Answer choice "C" is incorrect because the commission of an ultra vires act will not cause the corporate veil to be pierced. An ultra vires act is one outside of the corporation's authority as set forth in its Articles of Incorporation and/or in the applicable state corporation statutes.

Answer choice "D" is incorrect because incorporation of a partnership solely to limit the liability of its partners is not fraudulent and will not cause the corporate veil to be pierced. In fact, this is often the primary reason for the formation of a corporation.

21. A   Minors' contracts are voidable at the option of the minor. A minor can disaffirm a contract on the grounds of age at any time while he/she is a minor, and for a reasonable time after reaching the age of majority. Since Egan attempted to disaffirm the contract for the used computer one day after reaching the age of majority, Egan will <u>be able to disaffirm despite the fact that Egan was not a minor at the time of disaffirmance</u>.

Answer choice "B" is incorrect because a minor can disaffirm a contract verbally, as well as in writing.

Answer choice "C" is incorrect because a minor retains the right to disaffirm a contract, even where the balance of the purchase price for the item contracted for is unpaid.

Answer choice "D" is incorrect because damage to the item purchased does not eliminate the minor's right to disaffirm, even where the damage was the fault of the minor.

22. D   The statute of limitations fixes the time within which a lawsuit to enforce legal rights must be initiated. The statute of limitations for contracts normally begins to run at the time of the breach of contract. Thus the most important allegation for Kerr's defense would be that <u>the action was not timely brought because the contract was allegedly breached eight years prior to the commencement of the lawsuit</u>.

Answer choice "A" is incorrect because the fact that the contract was oral would not be very important to Kerr's defense of the statute of limitations. Normally the statute of limitations for an oral contract is shorter than the statute of limitations for a written contract.

Answer choice "B" is incorrect because the fact that the contract could not be performed within one year from the date made would not be very important to Kerr's defense of the statute of limitations. It would be important to a defense of the statute of frauds.

Answer choice "C" is incorrect because the statute of limitations normally begins to run as of the date the contract was breached, rather than the date the contract was entered into.

23. B   Fraud in the inducement occurs where the defendant's fraud induces the plaintiff to act. Fraud in the inducement requires proof of the following.

1. A material, false statement or omission.
2. <u>Scienter</u> - knowledge of the falsity or omission.
3. Intention that plaintiff rely.
4. Justifiable reliance by plaintiff.
5. Damages caused by reliance.

Thus, to prevail in a common law action for fraud in the inducement, the plaintiff must prove that the <u>defendant</u> <u>made</u> <u>the</u> <u>misrepresentations</u> <u>with</u> <u>knowledge</u> <u>of</u> <u>their</u> <u>falsity</u> <u>and</u> <u>with</u> <u>an</u> <u>intention</u> <u>to</u> <u>deceive</u>.

Answer choice "A" is incorrect because fraud in the inducement does not require the plaintiff to prove that the defendant was an expert with regard to the misrepresentations.

Answer choice "C" is incorrect because fraud in the inducement does not require the plaintiff to prove that the misrepresentations were in writing.

Answer choice "D" is incorrect because fraud in the inducement does not require the plaintiff to prove that the plaintiff was in a fiduciary relationship with the defendant. However, proof of undue influence requires the plaintiff to prove a fiduciary relationship existed with the defendant.

24. B The parol evidence rule applies when there exists a contract in which the parties have assented to a certain writing or writings as the full statement of the agreement between them. The rule states that no parol evidence of any prior or contemporaneous agreement will be permitted to vary, change, alter, or modify any of the terms or provisions of the written agreement.

The rule does not apply:
1. If contract is partly written and partly oral.
2. To a clerical or typographical error that is obvious.
3. In order to prove a condition precedent.
4. To a later oral agreement to modify or rescind.
5. To prove fraud, innocent misrepresentation, duress, undue influence, mistake, illegality, or unconscionability.
6. To prove lack of contractual capacity by one party to the contract.
7. To explain ambiguous terms in the contract.

Thus, <u>proof</u> <u>of</u> <u>the</u> <u>existence</u> <u>of</u> <u>a</u> <u>prior</u> <u>oral</u> <u>agreement</u> <u>that</u> <u>contradicts</u> <u>the</u> <u>written</u> <u>contract</u> would be inadmissible under the parol evidence rule when a written contract is intended as the complete agreement of the parties.

Answer choices other than "B" are based on incorrect assumptions and/or interpretations of the law.

25. C Co-suretyship exists where two or more sureties are bound to answer for the same debt. Where one co-surety pays the entire debt of the

principal debtor to the creditor, then that co-surety may seek to compel the other co-sureties to contribute their proportionate shares of the debt.

Since Nash paid $36,000 in full settlement of all claims against the co-sureties, Nash may recover $12,000 from Owen ($60,000/$180,000 x $36,000) and $16,000 from Polk ($80,000/$180,000 x $36,000), for a total of $28,000.

Answer choices other than "C" are based on incorrect assumptions and/or interpretations of the law.

26.   A   Most contractual obligations are discharged by the parties rendering full performance according to the terms of the contract. Normally, a breach of contract occurs if less than full performance is rendered. However, substantial performance is allowed in construction contracts where:
1.   The breach was immaterial.
2.   The breach was not willful.
3.   A good-faith effort was made to comply with the contract's terms.

Where substantial performance has been rendered in a construction contract, the other party must fulfill the contract and sue for damages for the unperformed portion of the contract. Thus, White's recovery will be limited to monetary damages because Ames' breach of the construction contract was not material.

Answer choice "B" is incorrect because White will be permitted to recover damages from Ames.

Answer choice "C" is incorrect because Ames did breach the construction contract. However its substantial performance of the contract permits it to recover fully from White, less the monetary damages for the unperformed portion of the contract.

Answer choice "D" is incorrect because White must accept the warehouse whether or not Ames installs the correct brand of fixtures. If Ames fails to install the correct brand of fixtures, White may sue Ames for damages equal to the cost of installing the correct brand of lighting fixtures.

27.   D   The filing of a petition, voluntary or involuntary, under the Federal Bankruptcy Code operates as an automatic "stay" (i.e., restraint) on the following.
1.   Commencement or continuation of a judicial, administrative, or other proceeding against the debtor regarding bankruptcy matters.
2.   Enforcement of judgments.
3.   Any act to obtain possession of property of the estate.
4.   Any acts to create, perfect, or enforce any lien against the property of the estate.

Thus, the filing of an involuntary bankruptcy petition under the Federal Bankruptcy Code stops the enforcement of judgment liens against property in the bankruptcy estate.

Answer choice "A" is incorrect because the filing of an involuntary bankruptcy petition does not terminate liens on exempt property. Instead, filing the petition stops the enforcement of liens against most of the debtor's property. Further, while the debtor may choose to avoid judicial liens on exempt property, filing an involuntary bankruptcy petition does not automatically terminate or provide the debtor with the option of terminating other types of liens on exempt property.

Answer choice "B" is incorrect because filing an involuntary bankruptcy petition does not terminate "all" security interests in property in the bankruptcy estate. Instead filing the petition provides the debtor the option to avoid only consensual liens that (1) are nonpossessory, (2) are nonpurchase money, and (3) encumber household goods, tools of a trade, and professionally prescribed health aids.

Answer choice "C" is incorrect because filing an involuntary petition in bankruptcy does not stop the debtor from incurring new debts. The debtor may continue to incur new debts as long as willing creditors can be found.

28.   B   The primary basis for judging a petition for bankruptcy under the involuntary provisions of the Federal Bankruptcy Code is the debtor's inability to pay debts as they become due. Thus, in order for creditors to file an involuntary bankruptcy petition under Chapter 7 of the Federal Bankruptcy Code, the creditors must prove that the debtor has not been paying its "bona fide" debts as they become due.

Answer choice "A" is incorrect because for creditors to file an involuntary bankruptcy petition, the debtor must owe $5,000 or more to unsecured creditors. Thus a debtor who owed exactly $5,000 to only one creditor might be eligible for involuntary bankruptcy but only if the creditor was unsecured.

Answer choice "C" is incorrect because creditors may file an involuntary bankruptcy petition when more than 12 creditors exist. Thus there is no limit on the number of creditors a debtor may have in order to be eligible to be petitioned involuntarily into bankruptcy.

Answer choice "D" is incorrect because creditors may file an involuntary bankruptcy petition without having at least one fully secured creditor sign the petition. If the debtor has less than 12 creditors, only one unsecured creditor must sign the involuntary petition. If the debtor has 12 or more creditors, then at least 3 unsecured creditors must sign the involuntary bankruptcy petition. In addition, the petition must also, in good faith, allege that the debtor has unsecured debts of $5,000 or more and is unable to pay his/her debts as they mature.

29.   D   All debtors except railroads, insurance companies, banks, savings and loans, homestead associations, and credit unions are eligible to file a voluntary petition for bankruptcy under Chapter 7 of the Federal Bankruptcy Code. The debtor need not be insolvent and need not have three or more creditors. The debtor needs only to be eligible to file for voluntary bankruptcy.

Answer choices other than "D" are based on incorrect assumptions and/or interpretations of the law.

30.   D   A bankruptcy trustee is a representative of the debtor's estate and is concurrently responsible for the equitable treatment of the debtor's creditors. The bankruptcy trustee may invalidate certain prebankruptcy transfers by the debtor, including preferential transfers (i.e., asset transfers that enable a creditor to obtain a greater percentage of that creditor's claims than the creditor would have received had the debtor's assets been liquidated in bankruptcy).

A preferential transfer has five elements.
1.   Made to or for the benefit of a creditor.
2.   Enables a creditor to obtain a preference over other creditors.
3.   Made in connection with an antecedent debt.
4.   Made within 90 days of petition filing. (One year if transferee is an insider; i.e., one with whom the debtor has close ties.)
5.   Made while the debtor is insolvent.

Thus, prepaying an installment loan on inventory within ninety days of filing for bankruptcy could be set aside as a preferential payment.

Answer choice "A" is incorrect because making a gift to charity within ninety days of filing for bankruptcy does not qualify as a preferential transfer, since the transfer is not for the benefit of a creditor.

Answer choice "B" is incorrect because not all asset transfers by a debtor that are made within ninety days of filing a bankruptcy petition are considered preferential. For example, a trustee may not avoid a transfer in payment of a debt incurred in the ordinary course of business of the debtor and the transferee. Thus, payment of a utility bill within ninety days of filing for bankruptcy is not voidable as a preferential payment.

Answer choice "C" is incorrect because borrowing money from a bank secured by giving a mortgage on business property is not a preferential payment, since the transfer is not made in connection with an antecedent debt.

31. B A creditor, trustee, or other interested party can have a discharge revoked by a bankruptcy court if:
1. The discharge was obtained through fraud.
2. The debtor fraudulently failed to tell the trustee that the debtor had other properties.
3. The debtor failed to answer correctly material questions on the bankruptcy petition or within one year thereafter.

However, the failure to list one creditor will not result in revocation of the debtor's discharge, but will make the discharge ineffective against that creditor.

Answer choices other than "B" are based on incorrect assumptions and/or interpretations of the law.

32. C Chapter 11 of the Federal Bankruptcy Code provides for reorganization by business debtors. An attractive feature of Chapter 11 from the debtor's perspective is that the debtor may continue to operate the financially troubled business during the bankruptcy proceedings. Chapter 11 is available to any debtor who is eligible for Chapter 7 relief, and to railroads.

If the Chapter 11 petition has been filed by an eligible debtor, no formal adjudication is necessary and the petition operates as an order for relief. The petition may be voluntary or involuntary, and the requirements for such mirror the requirements of Chapter 7. The debtor often has such a large number of creditors that it would be impractical for the debtor to negotiate the reorganization plan with each creditor individually. Thus, a creditor's committee, if appointed, will consist of unsecured creditors and will be appointed as soon as practicable after the order for relief.

Answer choice "A" is incorrect because the creditor's committee may not select a trustee. A trustee is appointed by the bankruptcy court, rather than the creditor's committee. Further, a trustee often is not appointed. Chapter 11 requires the appointment of a trustee only for cause (such as fraud or dishonesty) or if the appointment is in the best interests of the creditors or equity security holders.

Answer choice "B" is incorrect because parties other than the debtor may file a reorganization plan once 180 days have passed following the order for relief if (1) the debtor has not filed a plan within 120 days after the order for relief, or (2) the plan has not been accepted within 180 days after the order for relief.

Answer choice "D" is incorrect because Chapter 11 permits the debtor to continue the business where the approval of a trustee has not been obtained. In fact, it may be impossible to obtain the trustee's approval for the debtor to continue the business, since a trustee often is not appointed in a Chapter 11 case.

33. A A reorganization under Chapter 11 of the Federal Bankruptcy Code requires:

1. The filing of a reorganization plan.
2. Creditor acceptance of the plan.
3. Confirmation of the plan by the court.

Acceptance of the plan by the creditors must include an opportunity for each class of claims to accept or reject the plan. A class of claims accepts a plan where the plan is approved by creditors holding at least two-thirds of the amount of debts the creditor owes, and more than one-half of the total number of claims allowed for that class.

Thus, Chapter 11 of the Federal Bankruptcy Code does not require <u>liquidation</u> <u>of</u> <u>the</u> <u>debtor</u>.

Answer choices other than "A" are based on incorrect assumptions and/or interpretations of the law.

34.   B   A CPA's agreement to perform professional services implies that the CPA has the necessary competence to complete those professional services according to professional standards, applying the CPA's knowledge and skill with reasonable care and diligence. The member does not assume a responsibility for infallibility of knowledge or judgment. Competence to perform professional services involves both the technical qualifications of the CPA and the CPA's staff and the ability to supervise and evaluate the quality of the work performed.

Competence relates both to knowledge of the profession's standards, techniques, and the technical subject matter involved, and to the capability to exercise sound judgment in applying such knowledge in the performance of professional services.

Therefore, <u>if a CPA hires a non-CPA systems analyst who specializes in developing computer systems, the CPA must be qualified to supervise the specialist and evaluate the specialist's end product</u>. Although supervision does not require that the CPA be qualified to perform each of the specialist's tasks, the CPA should be able to define the tasks and evaluate the end product.

Answer choice "A" is incorrect because supervision does not require that the CPA be qualified to perform each of the specialist's tasks.

Answer choice "C" is incorrect because non-CPA professionals are permitted to be associated with CPA firms in public practice; e.g., computer specialists, actuaries, and attorneys.

Answer choice "D" is incorrect because developing computer systems is recognized as a service performed by public accountants; this type of service is considered a consulting service.

35.   B   Persons who are self-employed must report all taxable income to the IRS and pay social security tax on that income. Director's fees are reportable as income. Thus, the $5,000 honorary director's fee is <u>reportable by Ryan as self-employment income subject to social security self-employment tax</u>.

Answer choice "A" is incorrect because Ryan was not an employee of Lee Corp. In an employment relationship, the employer has the right to exert control over the employee. Lee Corp. had no right to control Ryan. Thus Ryan was a self-employed, independent contractor and should report the honorary director's fee as self-employment income.

Answer choice "C" is incorrect because the honorary director's fee was self-employment income and therefore is not taxable as "Other income" by Ryan.

Answer choice "D" is incorrect because the honorary director's fee is considered self-employment income subject to social security tax. The fee would not be considered a gift.

36. A Workers' compensation laws require employers to provide medical treatment, income maintenance, and death and disability benefits to employees for job-related injuries and illnesses. Employers are strictly liable without regard to whether or not they are at fault. In return for this no-fault liability, employers are shielded from employee lawsuits for work-related injuries or illnesses.

Answer choice "B" is incorrect because negligence by an employee does not preclude recovery under workers' compensation laws.

Answer choice "C" is incorrect because workers' compensation awards are reviewable by the courts, but only to confirm that the awards comply with the workers' compensation laws.

Answer choice "D" is incorrect because recoveries under workers' compensation laws are not based upon comparative negligence. The injured employee's negligence does not preclude or reduce the employee's recovery for a work-related injury or illness.

37. D In order to recover damages for a material misstatement in a registration statement filed under the Securities Act of 1933, the plaintiff must prove the following.
1. The securities were purchased.
2. The registration statement or prospectus contained either a material omission or a material misstatement.
3. Plaintiff suffered a loss.

Answer choice "A" is incorrect because it is not necessary for a plaintiff filing a suit for damages under the Securities Act of 1933 to establish privity of contract between the issuer and the plaintiff.

Answer choice "B" is incorrect because it is not necessary for a plaintiff filing a suit for damages under the Securities Act of 1933 to prove that the issuer failed to exercise due care in connection with the sale of the securities.

Answer choice "C" is incorrect because it is not necessary for a plaintiff filing a suit for damages under the Securities Act of 1933 to prove that the plaintiff gave value for the security. The plaintiff need only prove that the securities were purchased. Section 11 gives a cause of action to any person acquiring the security.

38. A   All purchases under Regulation D result in ownership of restricted securities. Such securities must be held for two years or registered with the SEC before resale. Thus, <u>the</u> <u>resale</u> <u>of</u> <u>the</u> <u>limited</u> <u>partnership</u> <u>interests</u> <u>by</u> <u>a</u> <u>purchaser</u> <u>generally</u> <u>will</u> <u>be</u> <u>restricted</u>.

Answer choice "B" is incorrect because Rule 504 of Regulation D permits offerings of up to $500,000 to an unlimited number of investors, accredited or unaccredited.

Answer choice "C" is incorrect because the exemption under Rule 504 of Regulation D is available to all types of securities, including limited partnership interests.

Answer choice "D" is incorrect because under Rule 504 of Regulation D the exempt securities may be sold to an unlimited number of investors.

39. A   Under the liquidation provisions of Chapter 7 of the Federal Bankruptcy Code, creditors with secured claims have priority over creditors with unsecured claims. The unsecured claims are then given priority over other unsecured claims, as follows:
1. Administrative expenses.
2. Debts incurred after the commencement of an involuntary bankruptcy case, but before the order for relief or appointment of a trustee (the so-called "involuntary gap").
3. Unsecured claims for wages earned within 90 days before filing of petition or cessation of business, whichever is first, limited to $2,000 for each employee.
4. Claims for contributions to employee benefit plans arising from services rendered within 180 days before petition filing.
5. Monies, to the extent of $900 per individual, deposited with debtor for purchase, rental, or lease of real property or personal services, for family or household use.
6. Taxes.

Thus, a <u>secured</u> <u>debt</u> <u>properly</u> <u>perfected</u> <u>on</u> <u>March</u> <u>20,</u> <u>1993</u>, would be paid first in the distribution of a bankruptcy estate under the liquidation provisions of Chapter 7 of the Federal Bankruptcy Code.

Answer choices other than "A" are based on incorrect assumptions and/or interpretations of the law.

40. A   Regulation A provides issuers of securities with an abbreviated registration option. An offering of up to $1.5 million of securities in any 12-month period qualifies under Regulation A. There are no restrictions on the number or types of investors. An offering

circular is substituted for a full prospectus, and the financial statements that accompany the circular do not need to be audited.

Thus, an offering made under the provisions of Regulation A of the Securities Act of 1933 requires that the issuer file an offering circular with the SEC.

Answer choice "B" is incorrect because Regulation A does not place limits on the types of investors who can participate in the offering. Thus, both accredited and nonaccredited investors may participate in a Regulation A offering.

Answer choice "C" is incorrect because Regulation A does not require that audited financial statements be submitted with the abbreviated registration.

Answer choice "D" is incorrect because Regulation A does not require a proxy registration statement, but only an offering circular that contains less detailed information than a full registration statement.

41. C The Securities Exchange Act of 1934 contains both registration and reporting requirements. The Act requires each director, officer, and investor owning 10 percent or more of a registered equity security to file a report with the SEC in any month in which there have been ownership changes for those equity securities. Thus, if Adler is a reporting company under the Securities Exchange Act of 1934, any person who owns more than 10 percent of Adler's common stock must file a report with the SEC.

Answer choice "A" is incorrect because the requirements of the Securities Act of 1933 and the Securities Exchange Act of 1934 apply independently. A reporting company under the Securities Exchange Act of 1934 must file a registration statement with the SEC for any future offerings of common stock that do not qualify for a registration exemption.

Answer choice "B" is incorrect because all proxy solicitations of reporting companies must be filed with the SEC.

Answer choice "D" is incorrect because the required annual report for reporting companies (Form 10K) must include audited financial statements.

42. B Section 10(b) and Rule 10b-5 prohibit fraud in connection with the purchase or sale of securities (registered or unregistered) in interstate commerce. The prohibition applies to a broad range of fraudulent practices, including insider trading. Insiders, for the purpose of Rule 10b-5, include attorneys, accountants, and consultants, as well as directors, officers, and employees of the security issuer. Thus, an owner of 5 percent of the corporation's outstanding debentures would not be considered an insider under the Securities Exchange Act of 1934.

Answer choices other than "B" are based on incorrect assumptions and/or interpretations of the law.

43. D   Rule 506 of Regulation D permits an unlimited dollar amount of securities to be sold without registration. The exempt securities are restricted for two years and may not be sold to more than 35 nonaccredited investors. Thus, if Pix is making a $6 million stock offering and wishes to be exempt from the registration provisions of the Securities Act of 1933, it must comply with <u>Regulation D, Rule 506</u>.

Answer choices other than "D" are based on incorrect assumptions and/or interpretations of the law.

44. A   A CPA should apply the same standards of professional conduct in performing tax work for a client as the CPA does in audit and other services. The CPA should not knowingly prepare any return or related document that the CPA has reason to believe is false or misleading.

When preparing an entity's tax return, <u>the CPA should be an advocate for the entity's realistically sustainable position</u>. That is, the CPA should not recommend to a client that a position be taken with respect to a particular tax treatment unless the CPA believes that the position has a realistic possibility of being sustained if it is challenged.

Answer choice "B" is incorrect because the CPA may rely on information provided by the client, without verification, unless the data appear to be incorrect or incomplete.

Answer choice "C" is incorrect because in providing tax services, the CPA's position is one of objectivity, not independent neutrality.

Answer choice "D" is incorrect because the CPA, when preparing a tax return, should be an advocate of the client, not of the Internal Revenue Service.

45. C   Rule 505 of Regulation D of the Securities Exchange Act of 1934 provides a registration exemption for securities offerings of up to $5 million to an unlimited number of accredited investors and up to 35 nonaccredited investors.

All Regulation D offerings require that:
1. The offer be made in a nonpublic manner.
2. The sale be completed within a 12-month period.
3. The sale be reported to the SEC within 15 days after the first sale of exempted securities.

Thus, Frey <u>must notify the SEC within 15 days after the first sale of the offering</u>.

Answer choice "A" is incorrect because Rule 505 of Regulation D limits the number of permissible nonaccredited investors to 35.

Answer choice "B" is incorrect because Rule 505 of Regulation D requires the offering to be made in a nonpublic manner.

Answer choice "D" is incorrect because Rule 505 of Regulation D requires only that audited financial statements be provided if any nonaccredited investors are in the group.

46. B A warehouse receipt is a document of title issued by a party called a warehouser who is engaged in the business of storing goods for a fee. A warehouse receipt is negotiable if it states that the stored goods are to be delivered to "bearer" or to the "order of" a named person. The warehouser is liable for losses or damage to the stored goods caused by the failure to exercise ordinary care. Thus, Field is <u>liable because it was negligent</u>.

Answer choice "A" is incorrect because a warehouser is not strictly liable for "any" loss to the stored goods. The warehouser is only liable where the warehouser failed to exercise ordinary care to protect the goods.

Answer choice "C" is incorrect because whether or not the warehouse receipt is negotiable is not determinative of the warehouser's liability for lost goods.

Answer choice "D" is incorrect because Field will be liable for the loss if Hall can establish ordinary negligence by Field. Thus, Hall need not establish that Field was grossly negligent.

47. D A bill of lading is a document of title issued by a common carrier that evidences the receipt of goods for shipment. If the goods are to be delivered to a specified person, then the document is nonnegotiable. If the goods are to be delivered to "bearer" or to the "order of" a named person, then the document is negotiable.

Thus, when a bill of lading that is in the possession of Major Corp. was issued by a common carrier and provides that the goods are to be delivered "to bearer," <u>the bill of lading can be negotiated by Major by delivery alone and without endorsement</u>.

Answer choice "A" is incorrect because the carrier's lien for any unpaid shipping charges does permit the carrier to sell the goods by public or private sale to enforce the lien.

Answer choice "B" is incorrect because the carrier is liable for delivering the goods to a party other than the one in possession of the bill of lading. Major Corp. is in possession of the bill of lading, and thus the carrier is liable for delivering the goods to a party other than Major.

Answer choice "C" is incorrect because the carrier is obligated to deliver possession of the goods to anyone in possession of the negotiable bearer document of title, and may not require Major to endorse the bill of lading prior to delivering the goods.

48.   D   If a negotiable investment security has been lost, the owner is entitled to a replacement certificate provided that the owner:
1.   Initiates the request before the issuer has notice that the lost certificate has been acquired by a bona fide purchaser.
2.   Files a sufficient indemnity bond with the issuer.
3.   Satisfies other reasonable requirements of the issuer.

Thus, for a person who loses a stock certificate, the fair market value of the security need not be placed in escrow with the issuer for six months.

Answer choices other than "D" are based on incorrect assumptions and/or interpretations of the law.

49.   C   A sale on approval is a type of trial sale where the goods are delivered primarily for the buyer's use. In a sale on approval, both title and risk of loss remain with the seller until the buyer approves the purchase of the goods, or until the buyer commits an act inconsistent with the title of the seller. Thus, with a sale on approval, risk of loss for the goods passes to the buyer when the goods are accepted after the trial period.

Answer choice "A" is incorrect because a sale on approval does not require that both the buyer and seller be merchants.

Answer choice "B" is incorrect because in a sale on approval the goods are delivered primarily for the buyer's use. If the goods are primarily for resale, then the transaction is a sale or return.

Answer choice "D" is incorrect because in a sale on approval title passes to the buyer after delivery of the goods to the buyer, and then only after the buyer has accepted the goods.

50.   D   The statement that the contract must involve the sale of goods for a price of $500 or more does not apply to a written contract governed by the provisions of the UCC Sales Article. It is possible to have a written contract to sell goods for a price of less than $500.

Answer choice "A" is incorrect because the UCC Sales Article applies to contracts for the sale of goods. Goods are tangible, personal property. Thus, the contract may involve the sale of personal property.

Answer choice "B" is incorrect because under the UCC Sales Article the obligations of a nonmerchant may be different from those of a merchant.

Answer choice "C" is incorrect because under the UCC Sales Article the obligations of the parties must be performed in good faith.

51.   A   According to Article 2 of the UCC, an order or other offer to buy
          goods for prompt or current shipment may be interpreted as inviting
          acceptance, either by a prompt promise to ship or by the shipment of
          either conforming or nonconforming goods. Thus, Ram's shipment is an
          acceptance of Handy's offer and a concurrent breach of their
          contract.

          Answer choice "B" is incorrect because Ram's shipment was without
          any explanation and would therefore be considered an effort to
          accept the purchase order, rather than a counteroffer.

          Answer choice "C" is incorrect because Handy's order need not be
          accepted by Ram in writing. It may be accepted either by a prompt
          promise to ship or by a prompt shipment of goods.

          Answer choice "D" is incorrect because Handy's order can be accepted
          by shipping either conforming goods or nonconforming goods, or by a
          prompt promise to ship.

52.   C   Implied warranties occur automatically, by operation of law in a
          contract for the sale of goods. The following implied warranties
          arise under Article 2 of the UCC.
          1. Warranty of title - seller warrants good title and rightful
              transfer; may include warranty against encumbrances (i.e.,
              liens).
          2. Warranty of merchantability (applies only to merchant seller) -
              warranty guarantees item is fit for ordinary purposes and
              extends to the packaging of the item.
          3. Warranty of fitness for a particular purpose - will apply where
              buyer has made known the intended use to seller and where buyer
              has relied upon the judgment of the seller in making purchase.
              Seller need not be a merchant to create this warranty.

          Thus, the contract between Handy and Ram contains the implied
          warranty of merchantability and the implied warranty of title.

          Answer choices other than "C" are based on incorrect assumptions
          and/or interpretations of the law.

53.   C   Article 9 of the UCC provides that the proceeds from a secured
          party's sale of collateral following repossession thereof shall be
          applied first to the secured party's reasonable sale expenses;
          second to the debt owed to the secured party; and third to the debt
          owed any junior security holder.

          Answer choices other than "C" are based on incorrect assumptions
          and/or interpretations of the law.

54.   D   Reasonable assurance of achieving the basic objective of providing
          professional services that conform to professional standards can be
          accomplished through adherence to prescribed standards of quality
          control.

There are four basic elements of quality control for a CPA firm: (1) personnel, (2) independence, (3) acceptance and continuance of clients, and (4) inspection. Further, the personnel-related element concerns hiring, supervision, assigning personnel to engagements, advancement, professional development, and consultation.

Answer choice "A" is incorrect because professional ethics do not include personnel advancement considerations.

Answer choice "B" is incorrect because "supervision and review" is a specific area relating to the "personnel" quality control element.

Answer choice "C" is incorrect because standards for accounting and review services relate specifically to compilations and reviews and not to the firm's personnel advancement policies.

55. C When performing consultation services engagements, the CPA should adhere to professional standards. Pursuant to the following compliance standards that address the distinctive nature of consulting services, the CPA shall:
1. Serve the client's interests, to meet stated objectives, while maintaining integrity and objectivity.
2. Obtain a written or oral understanding with the client concerning the responsibilities of the parties and the nature, scope, and limitations of services to be performed.
3. Inform the client of conflicts of interests, significant reservations of the engagement, and/or significant findings or events.

The following general standards apply to all services performed in the practice of public accounting, inclusive of consulting services. The CPA shall:
1. Perform with professional competence.
2. Exercise due professional care.
3. Adequately plan and supervise an engagement.
4. Obtain sufficient relevant data to afford a reasonable basis for conclusions or recommendations.

Answer choice "A" is incorrect because obtaining an understanding of the internal control structure to assess control risk is part of an audit and is not part of a consulting service.

Answer choice "B" is incorrect because a practitioner is permitted to compile a financial forecast as part of an engagement concerning prospective financial information.

Answer choice "D" is incorrect because, although independence is encouraged, regardless of the services rendered by the CPA, it is not required in the case of consulting services.

56. B In a contract for the sale of goods, if the parties do not specify terms such as the time of payment, the place of delivery, or the buyer's right to inspect goods before payment, then the provisions

of Article 2 of the UCC supply those missing terms. Unless otherwise agreed, the buyer has the right to inspect the goods before payment for or acceptance of the goods. Thus, <u>Peters is entitled to inspect the computer before paying for it</u>.

Answer choice "A" is incorrect because if the contract does not specify the place of delivery, it is the seller's place of business.

Answer choice "C" is incorrect because unless otherwise agreed, payment for goods may be by any means. Thus, Peters may pay Smith by check.

Answer choice "D" is incorrect because, unless otherwise agreed, payment is due at the time and place at which the buyer is to receive the goods.

57.   D   Article 2 of the UCC permits the seller to recover the contract price plus appropriate incidental damages where:
1. The goods have been accepted by the buyer.
2. Conforming goods were destroyed after the risk of loss passed to the buyer.
3. The goods have been identified to the contract and the seller cannot, after reasonable effort, resell them.

Thus, if Cara refuses to pay Taso and Taso sues Cara, the most Taso will be entitled to recover is <u>$122,000</u>, as Taso has been unable to resell the compressor for any price.

Answer choices other than "D" are based on incorrect assumptions and/or interpretations of the law.

58.   D   A security interest must attach before the rights of the creditor or secured party are enforceable. Attachment of a security interest occurs when all three of the following happen.
1. Secured party has possession of the collateral pursuant to an agreement with the debtor, or debtor has signed a security agreement describing collateral (Winslow executed a security agreement describing the collateral).
2. Creditor gives value (Pine Bank made loan to Winslow).
3. Debtor has property rights in collateral (Winslow owned the accounts receivable).

Thus, <u>attachment of the security interest occurred when the loan was made and Winslow executed the security agreement</u>.

Answer choice "A" is incorrect because the security interest was not perfected. Perfection normally occurs after the security interest has attached and may be accomplished by (1) filing a financing statement, (2) creditor taking possession of the collateral, or (3) attachment of the security agreement where the creditor has a purchase money security interest in consumer goods. Since the financing statement has not been filed, perfection of Pine's security interest was not achieved.

Answer choice "B" is incorrect because the financing statement was not filed and thus perfection of Pine's security interest was not achieved.

Answer choice "C" is incorrect because attachment of Pine's security interest did occur despite the fact that Winslow failed to file a financing statement. Filing a financing statement is a method of perfecting a security interest but is not a method for attachment of a security interest.

59. B   Perfection makes a security interest effective against most third parties. Perfection may be achieved in three ways.
1. Filing a financing statement.
2. The creditor taking possession of the collateral.
3. Attachment of the security interest where the creditor has a purchase money security interest in consumer goods.

Grey's security interest had attached (West executed a security agreement; Grey extended credit to West; and West had rights in the computer). In addition, Grey had a purchase money security interest (extended the funds to West that West used to purchase the computer) in consumer goods (West bought the computer for a personal use). Grey's security interest was perfected (i.e., Yes) because it was perfected at the time of attachment.

Answer choice "A" is incorrect because Grey's retention of ownership of the computer is not the reason that Grey's security interest was perfected. Grey's security interest was perfected because Grey had a purchase money security interest in consumer goods, and because Grey's security interest had attached. Perfection and attachment occurred simultaneously without Grey filing a financing statement.

Answer choice "C" is incorrect because Grey's security interest is perfected. Since the computer was a consumer good, and Grey had a purchase money security interest in the consumer goods, perfection of Grey's interest occurred simultaneously with attachment of its security interest.

Answer choice "D" is incorrect because Grey's security interest is perfected since the computer was a consumer good and Grey had a purchase money security interest in the consumer goods; perfection of Grey's interest occurred simultaneously with attachment of the interest. Grey's failure to file a financing statement does not preclude perfection of its security interest.

60. D   Perfected security interests prevail over unperfected security interests. If two or more security interests are perfected, they have priority according to the time of perfection.

A purchase money security interest in noninventory collateral takes priority over a conflicting security interest if the purchase money security interest is perfected either at the time the debtor receives possession of the collateral or within ten days of such receipt. Thus, the purchase money security interest perfected June 24, 1993, and has priority over the other security interests.

Answer choices "A" and "B" are incorrect because perfected security interests have priority over unperfected security interests.

Answer choice "C" is incorrect because perfection of a purchase money security interest in noninventory collateral relates back to the date the interest was created, as long as the purchase money security interest is perfected within ten days from the date the purchase money security interest was created. Thus, the interest perfected on June 24, 1993, is treated as perfected on June 15, 1993, and has priority over the security interest perfected on June 20, 1993.

OTHER OBJECTIVE FORMATS/ESSAY QUESTIONS

Answer 2

61. K   If an insured insures his/her property for less than the percent required by a co-insurance clause, then the insurer is liable only for its appropriate share of a loss per the following formula:

$$\text{Recovery} = \frac{\text{Face Amount of Policy}}{\text{Co-Insurance \% } \times \text{ Value at time of loss}} \times \text{Loss}$$

Thus, Anderson's total fire insurance recovery will be $162,000; i.e., ($180,000/[.8 × $250,000]) × $180,000.

62. H   Recovery under property insurance contracts is normally limited by "other insurance" clauses that require pro-rata distribution of the loss among the various insurers based on their respective policy amounts. Thus, the amount of the fire loss payable by Harvest is $108,000 (i.e., $120,000/$180,000 × $162,000).

63. D   The amount of the fire loss payable by Grant is $54,000 (i.e., $60,000/$180,000 × $162,000).

64. F   Beach gave Anderson a quitclaim deed to the property. In a quitclaim deed, the grantor gives to the grantee whatever rights he/she possesses, if any. Thus, Anderson will not win the suit against Beach, because Beach satisfied the terms of the quitclaim deed.

65. T   A quitclaim deed contains no warranties concerning the seller's title. Thus, a quitclaim deed conveys only the grantor's interest in the property.

66. T   In a warranty deed, the grantor warrants the following to the grantee.
         a. Ownership and right to transfer.
         b. Grantee's right to possession.
         c. No encumbrances other than those specified.
         d. Procurement of any additional assurances necessary to perfect the title.
         e. Grantor's defense of grantee's title against adverse claimants.

67. T   Title insurance protects the insured from any loss due to a failure of or defect in title up to the date of title transfer from the seller to the buyer. Since Dalton's easement was recorded, and Edge's policy neither disclosed nor excepted Dalton's easement, Anderson will win the suit against Edge.

68. T   One function of title insurance is to ensure the accuracy of the recording system. Thus, Edge's policy should insure against all title defects of record.

69. F   Edge's failure to disclose Dalton's easement has no impact upon the enforceability of the contract between Anderson and Beach. Thus,

<u>Edge's</u> <u>failure</u> <u>to</u> <u>disclose</u> <u>Dalton's</u> <u>easement</u> <u>does</u> <u>not</u> <u>void</u> <u>Anderson's</u> <u>contract</u> <u>with</u> <u>Beach</u>.

70.   G   In a "Notice-Race" jurisdiction, an unrecorded mortgage is invalid against any subsequent mortgagee without notice of such who records first. Long Bank's mortgage was the first mortgage recorded and was recorded without notice of a prior mortgage because there was none. Thus, Long will recover <u>$140,000</u> of the foreclosure proceeds.

71.   C   Rogers' mortgage was never recorded and has the lowest claim priority of the three mortgages. Thus, Rogers will receive <u>$32,000</u> of the foreclosure proceeds.

72.   B   Forrest Finance was the second mortgagee to record and Forrest recorded its mortgage without knowing about the Rogers' mortgage. Thus, Forrest Finance's mortgage has the second highest priority of the three mortgages and Forrest will receive <u>$28,000</u> of the foreclosure proceeds.

Answer 3

73.   Yes   A preferential transfer is voidable by a bankruptcy trustee because it enables a creditor to obtain a greater percentage of the creditor's claim than the creditor would have received had the debtor's assets been liquidated in bankruptcy. Preferential transfers have five elements.
1. Made to or for the benefit of a creditor.
2. Enables a creditor to obtain a preference over other creditors.
3. Made in connection with an antecedent debt.
4. Made within 90 days of the filing of a bankruptcy petition (one year if the transferee is an insider).
5. Made while the debtor is insolvent.

The payment to Mary Lake would be set aside as preferential. Lake is considered an insider because she is the sister of a director. Thus, a transfer to her in connection with an antecedent debt made within one year of filing the bankruptcy petition is considered preferential.

74.   No   The donation to Universal Charities was not made in connection with an antecedent debt and thus was not voidable as a preferential transfer.

75.   Yes   The transfer of a security agreement to Young Finance on February 1 (1) was for the benefit of a creditor (Young Finance); (2) enabled a creditor to obtain a preference over other creditors (as a secured creditor, Young Finance has priority over unsecured creditors); (3) was made in connection with an antecedent debt (a loan previously made by Young to Wren for office furniture); (4) was made within ninety days of filing the petition (February 1 is within 90 days of April 15); and (5) was made while the debtor was insolvent (it is assumed as a matter of law that a debtor was insolvent) for the ninety days preceding the filing of a bankruptcy petition.

76. No Wren's $1,000 payment to Integral Appliance Corp. was not a preferential transfer because it did not enable Integral to gain a benefit over other creditors. Wren was merely paying a debt in the ordinary course of business pursuant to a prearranged payment schedule.

77. No Wren's payment of $5,000 cash to Safety Co. was not a preferential transfer because it was not made for an antecedent debt. This transaction constituted a contemporaneous exchange of assets of equivalent value.

78. B After secured creditors' claims are satisfied, the remaining assets are utilized to satisfy the claims of unsecured creditors. Bankruptcy administration expenses have first priority in the class of unsecured claims. This claim must be paid in full before any party possessing an unsecured claim with a lower priority is paid. Thus, the bankruptcy administration expense will be the <u>second</u> claim paid.

79. E The claim of Acme Office Cleaners is in the group of unsecured creditors with no priority of claim. This group of creditors shares proportionately in the proceeds of any remaining assets. Acme will be the <u>fifth</u> creditor paid.

80. A The claim of a secured creditor has first priority of claim to the proceeds from the sale of the property securing its claim. Fifth Bank will be the <u>first</u> creditor paid.

81. D The IRS claim for 1990 income taxes is among the class of unsecured claims given priority. However, it has the lowest priority in its class. The IRS claim will be the <u>fourth</u> claim paid.

82. C The Sims' claim for commissions earned in March of 1992 is also in the group of unsecured claims granted payment priority. Sims' claim has a lower priority than the bankruptcy administration expense claim but a higher priority than the tax claim. Sims' claim will be the <u>third</u> claim paid.

83. J TVN Computers is a secured creditor with highest priority claim against the proceeds from the sale of the office computers. It will receive the $12,000 proceeds from the sale of the computers. TVN is also a general unsecured creditor for the $3,000 deficiency. Since general creditors received 50 cents per dollar of claim, TVN will receive an additional $1,500 as a general creditor. Thus, TVN will receive a total of <u>$13,500</u>.

84. M Hart Manufacturing is a secured creditor and has highest priority claim to the proceeds from the sale of Wren's inventory (i.e., $25,000), and is a general creditor receiving 50 cents per dollar for the $5,000 deficiency (i.e., $2,500). Thus, Hart will receive a total of <u>$27,500</u>.

85.   G   Ted Smith's claim for wages earned in February and March of 1992 is an unsecured claim in the class of claims given priority over other unsecured claims. Smith's claim for unpaid wages earned within 40 days of filing the petition has priority for up to $2,000. Thereafter, Smith is a general unsecured creditor who will receive an additional $200 (50 cents per dollar of claim) for a total of $2,200.

86.   B   Power Electric is a general unsecured creditor and will receive 50 cents per dollar of claim for a total of $300.

87.   D   Soft Office Supplies is a general unsecured creditor and will receive 50 cents per dollar of claim for a total of $1,000.

Answer 4

Suit #1 - Unsuccessful
Archer, Book, and Cable will be unsuccessful in the suit to have the court allow distribution of the residuary estate instead of transferring the residuary estate to the trust. A will is a formally executed, written document whereby a person known as the testator directs the distribution of his/her estate. The terms of the will do not take effect until the testator's death. The executor of an estate must comply with the directions of the testator as specified in the will. Since Park directed that any residuary from the estate be transferred to the trust, via the "pour-over" clause, the court will enforce the provisions of the will. Thus the effort to gain court authorization to distribute the residuary estate to the beneficiaries will fail.

Suit #2 - Unsuccessful
Archer, Book, and Cable will be unsuccessful in their suit to have the spendthrift trust terminated. The majority rule is that a trust will not be terminated until all the trust's purposes have been accomplished. This rule is followed even where all the trust beneficiaries request termination of the trust. Since Park created the trust for the dual purposes of providing for the welfare of the beneficiaries "during Park's lifetime and after Park's death," and protecting them from their own financial shortcomings, the purposes of the trust have not been fully accomplished. Thus, the court will deny the beneficiaries' suit to terminate the spendthrift trust.

Suit #3 - Unsuccessful
Archer, Book, and Cable will be unsuccessful in their suit to remove Young and Zack as trustees for making the $5,000 principal payments. Removal of a trustee is considered an extraordinary action and is done only in extreme situations where continuation of the trustee poses a serious danger to the interests of the beneficiaries. A disagreement or conflict between the trustee and the beneficiaries of the trust does not pose a sufficiently seriously threat to the welfare of the beneficiaries to justify removal of a trustee. While trustees may not normally distribute the trust principal to income beneficiaries, Young and Zack were authorized by the terms of the trust (i.e., the "sprinkling" provisions) to make annual discretionary distributions of up to $10,000 from the trust principal, the two $5,000 distributions of principal will not justify their removal. Thus, the court will deny the suit by the beneficiaries.

Suit #4 - Successful
Archer, Book, and Cable will be successful in their suit to remove Young and Zack as trustees for allowing Zack to borrow money from the trust. Courts are reluctant to remove a trustee and do so only where continuation of the trustee poses a serious danger to the interests of the beneficiaries. The duty of loyalty is considered the most important of the trustee's fiduciary duties. Breach of the duty of loyalty by the trustee is considered a sufficiently serious threat to the interests of the trust beneficiaries to justify removal of the trustee. A trustee may not borrow money from the trust unless authorized by the trust instrument. Therefore, Zack's loan of trust funds to himself constitutes a breach of the duty of loyalty because a trustee may not borrow money from a trust unless authorized by the trust instrument. The loan also created the appearance of a conflict of interest between Zack and the beneficiaries.

This is true despite Zack's agreement to pay an interest rate higher than that normally received by the trust on its investments and despite Young's consent to the loan. Thus, the court will order the removal of Zack and Young as trustees.

Suit #5 - Successful
Archer, Book, and Cable will be successful in their suit to remove Young and Zack as trustees for making the $15,000 principal payment to Archer. While courts are reluctant to remove a trustee and normally do so only where continuation of the trustee poses a danger to the interests of the beneficiaries, a trustee's breach of the terms of the trust is sufficiently serious to justify removal. This loan also constitutes a breach of the fiduciary duties of loyalty and to safeguard the trust res. Since Young and Zack breached the terms of the trust, as well as their duties as fiduciaries, by making a larger-than-authorized principal distribution to Archer, the beneficiaries' suit to remove Young and Zack will be successful.

Answer 5

Part 5(a)

William's first claim - Incorrect
Williams' claim that the note is negotiable is incorrect. In order to be negotiable the note must:
1.   Be payable at fixed or determinable time or on demand.
2.   Be in writing.
3.   Be payable to order or bearer.
4.   Be signed by the maker or drawer.
5.   Contain an unconditional promise or order.
6.   Be payable in money only.
7.   Be a sum certain.

This instrument is nonnegotiable for two reasons. First, an instrument that is payable only upon an act or event uncertain as to time of occurrence is not payable at a definite time and thus not negotiable. Since Helco's note is payable two weeks after the proceeds from the resale of the computer components become available, the note is not negotiable because it is not payable at a definite time. Second, an instrument payable only out of the proceeds from the sale of a specific item constitutes a conditional promise to pay. Since Helco's obligation to pay the note was limited to the proceeds from the sale of the computer components, the note was also not negotiable because it contained a conditional promise to pay.

Williams' second claim - Incorrect
Williams' claim that it is a holder in due course of the note is incorrect. To be a holder in due course one must be a holder of a negotiable instrument. Since Helco's note is not negotiable, Williams is not a holder in due course of the note.

Williams' third claim - Incorrect
Williams' claim that Helco cannot raise Jason's misrepresentation as a defense to payment of the note is incorrect. The only method for transferring rights in a nonnegotiable instrument is by the process of assignment. Helco's note was not negotiable. Thus, when Jason transferred its rights under the note to Williams, it did so by assigning the note to Williams. As an assignee of the note from Jason, Williams "steps into the shoes" of Jason, the assignor of the note. Since Helco could raise the defense of Jason's misrepresentation against Jason, Helco can also raise Jason's misrepresentation against Williams and use the misrepresentation as a defense to payment of the note.

Part 5(b)

Grover is not correct in refusing to pay its note. The "shelter rule" permits a transferee of negotiable commercial paper to acquire the "status" of a holder in due course through a holder in due course. Oliver was a holder in due course of Grover's note since Oliver took the properly endorsed, negotiable note from Abco in good faith, for value, and without notice of Grover's defense to payment of the note.

Since Williams was the transferee of the note from Oliver, Williams gains the status of a holder in due course from Oliver via the "shelter rule."

A party with the status of a holder in due course is shielded from personal defenses such as failure of consideration. Grover's dissatisfaction with the quality of Abco's services rendered constitutes the defense of failure of consideration. Since failure of consideration is an invalid defense against a party with the status of a holder in due course, Grover was incorrect in refusing to pay the note because Williams has the status of a holder in due course.

Part 5(c)

If Grover is not required to pay the note, then Williams has no rights against Oliver. Generally an endorser has secondary (i.e., conditional) liability on a note based upon his/her signature on the note. If the holder makes timely presentment of the note for payment, and the note is dishonored by the maker, and the holder promptly notifies the endorser of both the dishonor and the holder's intent to proceed against the endorser for payment, then the endorser is liable to pay the note to the holder. However, where a party endorses "without recourse," liability based upon the endorser's signature is disclaimed.

Similarly, all parties who transfer a note for value make the following implied warranties to all subsequent holders.
1.   All signatures are genuine.
2.   Transferor has good title.
3.   Instrument has not been materially altered.
4.   Transferor has no knowledge of insolvency proceedings against any part to the instrument.
5.   No defense of any party is good against the transferor.

A qualified endorser makes essentially the same warranties but impliedly warrants only that the qualified endorser has no knowledge of a defense of any party that is good against him/her. Since Oliver endorsed the note to Williams "without recourse" and was unaware of Grover's dissatisfaction with Abco's services rendered at the time the note was purchased, Oliver has no liability to Williams.

Auditing (AUDIT)

FOUR-OPTION MULTIPLE-CHOICE QUESTIONS

Answer 1

1.   D   Generalized audit software (i.e., computer software) commonly consists of individual computer programs, or routines, designed to perform a variety of functions. Typically, the software can perform all of the normal data handling and processing functions provided by the client's own software. Information can be sorted, stratified, sampled, evaluated, included or excluded, and summarized as desired. The software also has the capability of processing transactions, updating master files for current transactions, generating printed reports, and performing data search and retrieval. Data files may be reviewed for completeness, reasonableness, and mathematical accuracy.

The use of a generalized audit software program, in and of itself, would not necessarily <u>assess</u> <u>EDP</u> <u>control</u> <u>risk</u>. Such risks are generally ascertained through the tests of controls of the client's internal control structure by such means as inquiry, observation, and inspection.

Answer choice "A" is incorrect because generalized audit software can verify the reliability of the client's computer programs through a process known as "parallel simulation." As such, the generalized audit software includes programs that can perform processing functions essentially equivalent to those of the client's programs. These programs use the same files (transaction and master files) as do the client's programs and should ideally produce the same results as were produced by the client. Thus, generalized audit programs simulate the client's processing of live data. Any discrepancies between the results generated through application of the auditor's program and the results produced by the application of the client's system should be identified.

Answer choice "B" is incorrect because accessing client data files would be a primary use of generalized audit software. Once computer files are accessed, all other useful functions can be performed.

Answer choice "C" is incorrect because the preparation of spreadsheets, along with a variety of other reports, represents a major use of computer software.

2.   D   Generally accepted auditing standards relate both to the professional qualities of the auditor and the judgment that must be exercised while performing an audit report. Standards deal with <u>measures</u> <u>of</u> <u>the</u> <u>quality</u> <u>of</u> <u>the</u> <u>auditor's</u> <u>performance</u> and the objectives to be attained by the use of the procedures undertaken.

Answer choice "A" is incorrect because pronouncements issued by the Auditing Standards Board (i.e., Statements on Auditing Standards) are intended to define the nature and extent of auditors' responsibilities and provide guidance to auditors in carrying out their duties. In essence, they are interpretations of the generally accepted auditing standards.

Answer choice "B" is based on an incorrect assumption.

Answer choice "C" is incorrect because procedures relate to specific auditing actions; i.e., how the auditor accomplishes the task of performing the audit under generally accepted auditing standards.

3.   C   To obtain evidence that online access controls are properly functioning, an auditor most likely would <u>enter invalid identification numbers or passwords to ascertain whether the system rejects them</u>. This is referred to as a test-data approach. The auditor's test data must include both valid and invalid transactions in order to determine whether the client's computer programs will react properly to the different kinds of data, such as IDs and passwords. By using test data, which the auditor controls and which has a known output, the auditor is able to gain certain assurances relating to the procedures contained within the program.

Answer choices other than "C" would not provide evidence that online access controls are properly functioning.

4.   B   The first standard of field work requires that the work is to be adequately planned and assistants, if any, are to be properly supervised. Supervision involves directing the efforts of assistants who are involved in accomplishing the objectives of the audit and determining whether those objectives were accomplished. Elements of supervision include instructing assistants, keeping informed of significant problems encountered, reviewing the work performed, and dealing with differences of opinion among firm personnel.

Assistants should be informed of their responsibilities and the objectives of the procedures that they are to perform. They should be informed of matters that may affect the nature, extent, and timing of procedures they are to perform.

The auditor with final responsibility for the audit and assistants should be aware of the procedures to be followed when differences of opinion concerning accounting and auditing issues exist among firm personnel involved in the audit; such procedures should enable an assistant to <u>document the details of the disagreement with the conclusions reached</u>.

Answer choices other than "B" are based on incorrect assumptions.

5.   A   Before accepting an engagement with a client that has been previously audited, <u>the successor auditor should take the initiative to communicate with the predecessor auditor</u>. Permission must be obtained from the client before communication can be made, because of the confidentiality requirement of the AICPA Code of Conduct.

If a client will not permit such communication, the successor should carefully consider the desirability of accepting the engagement.

The successor's inquiries should focus on the predecessor's understanding of the reasons for the change in auditors, and should include specific questions concerning facts that might bear on the integrity of management and disagreements the predecessor had with the client concerning auditing procedures, accounting principles, or other similarly significant matters.

Answer choices other than "A" are incorrect because they occur after acceptance of the engagement by the successor auditor.

6. A The auditor plans the audit to obtain reasonable assurance of detecting misstatements that the auditor believes could be large enough, individually or in the aggregate, to be quantitatively material to the financial statements. The concept of materiality recognizes that some matters, either individually or in the aggregate, are important for fair presentation of financial statements in conformity with generally accepted accounting principles, while other matters are not important. The phrase "present fairly, in all material respects, in conformity with generally accepted accounting principles" indicates the auditor's belief that the financial statements taken as a whole are not materially misstated.

In planning the audit, the auditor should use his or her preliminary judgment about materiality levels in a manner that can be expected to provide the auditor, within the inherent limitations of the auditing process, with sufficient evidential matter to obtain reasonable assurance about whether the financial statements are free of material misstatement.

Materiality levels include an overall level for each statement; however, because the statements are interrelated, and for reasons of efficiency, the auditor ordinarily considers materiality for planning purposes in terms of the smallest aggregate level of misstatements that could be considered material to any one of the financial statements. For example, suppose the auditor believes that misstatements aggregating approximately $10,000 would have a material effect on income, but that such misstatements would have to aggregate approximately $20,000 to materially affect financial position. It would not be appropriate to design auditing procedures that would be expected to detect misstatements only if they aggregate approximately $20,000; accordingly, the $10,000 amount would be appropriate for materiality.

Answer choices other than "A" are incorrect because they are above the smallest aggregate level of misstatements that would be considered material to any one of the financial statements.

7. D The second standard of fieldwork indicates that a sufficient understanding of the internal control structure is to be obtained to

plan the audit and to determine the nature, timing, and extent of the substantive tests to be performed.

An auditor uses the knowledge provided by the understanding of the internal control structure and the assessed level of control risk primarily to determine the nature, timing, and extent of substantive tests for financial statement assertions. The substantive tests that the auditor performs consist of tests of transactions, tests of details of account balances, and analytical procedures. As the assessed level of control risk increases on the basis of audit evidence gathered and evaluated concerning the internal control structure, the acceptable level of detection risk should decrease.

Answer choice "A" is incorrect because the level of inherent risk would remain unchanged.

Answer choice "B" is incorrect because materiality levels would either remain unchanged or decrease, but not increase.

Answer choice "C" is incorrect because the level of substantive testing would increase.

8. C The purpose of applying analytical procedures in planning the audit is to assist in planning the nature, timing, and extent of auditing procedures that will be used to obtain evidential matter for specific account balances or classes of transactions.

In order to achieve this, the analytical procedures used in planning the audit should focus on:
1. Enhancing the auditor's understanding of the client's business and the transactions and events that have occurred since the last audit date.
2. Identifying areas that represent specific risks relevant to the audit.

As such, the objective of the procedures is to identify such things as the existence of unusual transactions and events, and the amounts, ratios, and trends that might indicate matters having financial statement and audit-planning ramifications.

Answer choices "A" and "B" are incorrect because they represent actions the auditor would take in connection with substantive testing.

Answer choice "D" is incorrect because analytical procedures are not designed to identify material weaknesses in the internal control structure.

9. C An attestation engagement is an engagement wherein a CPA is requested to issue, or does issue, a written communication containing the expression of a conclusion as to the reliability of a written assertion that is the responsibility of another party. Standards for attestation engagements are:

1. General
   a. Training in the attest function.
   b. Knowledge in the subject matter.
   c. Acceptance of engagement only if:
      (1) Reasonable criteria against which assertion can be evaluated.
      (2) Reasonable consistent estimation or measurement.
   d. Mental independence.
   e. Due care.
2. Standards of fieldwork
   a. Planning work adequately.
   b. Evidence sufficient to support conclusion expressed.
3. Standards of reporting
   a. Identification of assertion and character of engagement.
   b. Conclusion as to conformity with established or stated criteria.
   c. Significant reservations as to the engagement and presentation of assertion.
   d. Limit the report's use, when prepared in conformity with agreed-upon criteria or when the engagement is based upon agreed-upon procedures, to the parties who have agreed upon such criteria or procedures.

In view of points "3.a." and "3.b.," the CPA typically _expresses a conclusion about an assertion_ in an attestation engagement.

Answer choice "A" is incorrect because litigation support services do not represent a typical attestation engagement.

Answer choice "B" is incorrect because a CPA does not typically assess control risk as part of an attestation engagement. A CPA may, however, examine and report on management's assertion about the effectiveness of an entity's internal control structure.

Answer choice "D" is incorrect because providing management consulting advice is considered to be a consulting service, not an attestation engagement.

10. D In performing audit tests in accordance with GAAS, the auditor may use either nonstatistical or statistical sampling, or both. Both types of sampling require the exercise of judgment in planning and executing the sampling plan and evaluating the results. Additionally, both types can provide sufficient evidential matter as required by the third standard of field work, and both are subject to risk.

In nonstatistical sampling, the auditor determines sample size and evaluates sample results entirely on the basis of the subjective criteria growing out of his or her own experience. Thus, the auditor may unknowingly use too large a sample in one area and too small a sample in another. However, statistical sampling should benefit the auditor in designing an efficient sample and _measuring the sufficiency of the evidential matter obtained_.

Answer choice "A" is incorrect because both statistical and nonstatistical sampling are subject to the risk of failure to detect errors and irregularities.

Answer choice "B" is incorrect because neither statistical nor nonstatistical sampling eliminates the risk of nonsampling errors.

Answer choice "C" is incorrect because the use of statistical versus nonstatistical sampling does not imply that the level of audit risk and materiality is reduced to a relatively low amount.

11.   B   Illegal acts refer to violations of laws or governmental regulations by the audited entity, its management, or employees acting on behalf of the entity.

When the auditor becomes aware of information concerning a possible illegal act, the auditor should inquire of management at a level above those involved.

If the auditor concludes that an illegal act has or is likely to have occurred, the auditor should:
1.   Consider the effects on the financial statement.
2.   Consider the implications for other aspects of the audit, particularly the reliability of management representations.
3.   Inform the audit committee, or others with equivalent authority, about all but clearly inconsequential illegal acts. Oral communication is permissible but should be documented in the workpapers.

The auditor should:
1.   Express a qualified or adverse opinion if an illegal act has a material effect on the financial statements and has not been properly accounted for or disclosed.
2.   Disclaim an opinion if the auditor is precluded by the client from obtaining sufficient competent evidential matter needed to evaluate whether an illegal act that could be material has, or is likely to have, occurred.
3.   Withdraw from the engagement if the client:
     a.   Refuses to accept the auditor's report.
     b.   Does not take the remedial action the auditor considers necessary in the circumstances, even when the illegal act is not material to the financial statements.

Answer choice "A" is incorrect because the auditor should modify the audit report if the illegal act had a material effect on the financial statements and was not properly accounted for or disclosed.

Answer choice "C" is incorrect because the auditor would inform management at a level above those involved, but would not withdraw based on when the act occurred.

Answer choice "D" is incorrect because assessing control risk at the maximum level is not related to circumstances that would cause the auditor to withdraw from the engagement.

12.　D　Accountants may perform the following accounting services either in connection with a compilation or review of financial statements, <u>or as a separate service</u>.

1.　Preparing a working trial balance.
2.　Assisting in adjusting the books (i.e., preparing monthly standard journal entries).
3.　<u>Consulting on accounting</u>, tax, and similar <u>matters</u>.
4.　Preparing tax returns.
5.　Providing bookkeeping services (but not the preparation of financial statements).
6.　<u>Processing financial data for clients of other accounting firms</u>.

In view of points "3" and "6," a CPA <u>is not required to comply with Statements on Standards for Accounting and Review Services for these services</u>, as they do not establish standards or procedures for such services.

Answer choices other than "D" represent illogical combinations and/or are based on incorrect assumptions.

13.　C　Classical variables sampling is the method most often used for substantive testing. It estimates the total dollar amount of a population, or the dollar amount of error in a population. Because it provides an answer in dollars, it is also referred to as dollar-value estimation. The computation of the sample size for variables sampling involves the following formula.

$$\frac{(\underline{\text{Factor for Complement of Risk}} \times \underline{\text{Standard Deviation}} \times \underline{\text{Population}})^2}{\text{Tolerable Misstatement in Dollars (Materiality)}}$$

Probability-proportional-to-size (PPS) sampling, sometimes referred to as "dollar-unit" sampling, is a plan or approach that utilizes the attribute sampling theory to express a conclusion in dollar amounts. Accordingly, this method may be used in lieu of classical variables sampling approaches. PPS sampling is most useful in testing transactions and account balances for overstatement.

PPS calculates a projected error (i.e., misstatement in dollars) from the sample of "dollars" by calculating the difference between the recorded amount (i.e., book value) and the audited value. A "tainting percentage" is determined, which is the amount of misstatement in the sampled unit divided by the recorded book value of the unit, expressed as a percentage. This "tainting percentage" is applied to the sampling interval to determine the projected error associated with the sampled unit. When the recorded amount is greater than the sampling interval, the projected error is equal to the actual error.

Based on the foregoing, the PPS approach relies on recorded dollar amounts of account balances. Consequently, existence of zero and negative dollar amounts would require special design considerations to utilize PPS. Since the variables sampling approach relies on accounts rather than the dollar amounts recorded in the accounts, <u>no special design considerations are required for inclusion of zero and negative balances</u>.

Answer choice "A" is incorrect because the variables sampling approach requires an estimate of the population standard deviation, while PPS does not.

Answer choice "B" is incorrect because a computer program may be needed to assist in either approach to sampling.

Answer choice "D" is incorrect because neither method will automatically identify and select a large (i.e., significant) dollar amount. Under the PPS approach, however, an account with a large dollar amount is more likely to be selected than an account with a small dollar balance.

14.   C   During the course of an audit, the auditor should be alert to the possibility of the existence of material related party transactions that could have an effect on the financial statements. Related parties exist when any one party with which the reporting entity may deal has the ability to significantly influence the management or operating policies of the other, to the extent that one of the transacting parties might be prevented from fully pursuing its own separate interests.

It is difficult to substantiate <u>representations that a particular related party transaction occurred on terms equivalent to those that would have prevailed in an arm's-length transaction</u>. If such a representation is included in the financial statements, and the auditor believes that the representation is unsubstantiated by the client, the auditor should express a qualified or adverse opinion because of a departure from GAAP.

Answer choices other than "C" are incorrect because they all involve appropriate disclosures concerning related party transactions.

15.   A   In performing procedures and gathering evidential matter, the auditor continually maintains an attitude of professional skepticism. The performance of auditing procedures during the audit may result in the detection of conditions or circumstances that should cause the auditor to consider whether material misstatements exist.

Circumstances likely to cause an auditor to consider whether a material misstatement exists include:
1.   Analytical procedures that disclose unexpected differences.
2.   Unreconciled differences that are not appropriately investigated and corrected on a timely basis.

3. <u>Confirmation</u> <u>requests</u> <u>that</u> disclose significant differences or <u>yield</u> <u>significantly</u> <u>fewer</u> <u>responses</u> <u>than</u> <u>expected</u>.
4. Transactions selected for testing that are not supported by proper documentation or are not appropriately authorized.
5. Supporting records or files which are not readily available.
6. Audit tests that indicate errors that apparently were known to client personnel but were not voluntarily disclosed to the auditor.

When such conditions or circumstances exist, the planned scope of audit procedures should be reconsidered.

Answer choice "B" is incorrect because short-lived audit trails are characteristic of many computer-generated transactions and therefore are not necessarily indicative of material misstatements.

Answer choice "C" is incorrect because the management representation letter should be signed as of the date of the audit report; i.e., the completion of the fieldwork.

Answer choice "D" is incorrect because management's consultation with other accountants about significant accounting matters is not necessarily indicative of the existence of material misstatements in an entity's financial statements.

16.   B   A flowchart of internal control is a symbolic, diagrammatic representation of the client's documents and their sequential flow in the organization. An adequate flowchart shows the origin of each document and record in the system, the subsequent processing, and the final disposition of any document or record included in the chart. In addition, it is possible for the flowchart to show the separation of duties, authorization, approvals, and internal verifications that take place within the system.

<u>Flowcharting</u> <u>is</u> <u>advantageous</u> <u>primarily</u> <u>because</u> <u>it</u> <u>can</u> <u>provide</u> <u>a</u> concise picture (i.e., a <u>visual</u> <u>depiction</u>) <u>of</u> <u>clients'</u> <u>activities</u>, which is useful as an analytical tool. A well-prepared flowchart aids in identifying inadequacies by facilitating a clear understanding of how the system operates.

Answer choice "A" is incorrect because a flowchart, by itself, will not identify internal control weaknesses; the analysis of the flowchart, however, will facilitate the identification of internal control weaknesses.

Answer choice "C" is incorrect because a flowchart does not indicate how effectively the internal control procedures are operating.

Answer choice "D" is incorrect because the auditor would still need to observe task performance to determine how the system actually operates.

17. C If the independent auditor decides that it would be efficient to consider how the internal auditors' work might affect the nature, timing, and extent of audit procedures, the auditor should assess the competence and objectivity of the internal audit function.

If the auditor decides to utilize the work of internal auditors, the auditor should test some of that work related to significant financial statement assertions by examining some of the controls, transactions, or account balances that the internal auditors examined, as well as those not actually examined by the internal auditors.

In reaching conclusions about the internal auditors' work, the independent auditor should compare the results of his or her tests with the results of the internal auditors' work.

However, the responsibility to report on the financial statements rests solely with the independent auditor; this responsibility cannot be shared with the internal auditors. Because the auditor has the ultimate responsibility to express an opinion on the financial statements, <u>judgments</u> <u>about</u> assessments of inherent and control risks, <u>the materiality of misstatements</u>, the sufficiency of tests performed, <u>the evaluation of significant accounting estimates</u>, and other matters affecting the auditor's report <u>should always be those of the auditor</u>.

Answer choices other than "C" are incorrect because they are based on incorrect assumptions.

18. D The objective of using the test data (sometimes referred to as test deck) approach is to determine whether the client's computer programs can correctly handle valid and invalid transactions as they arise. To fulfill this objective, the auditor develops input for different types of transactions, which are then processed under the auditor's control, using the client's computer programs and equipment.

However, preparing <u>test data consisting of all possible valid and invalid transactions would not be warranted and probably would be impossible</u> to do from a cost/benefit point of view.

Answer choices other than "D" are incorrect because they all represent true statements concerning the test data approach.

19. D To properly plan an audit, the auditor should obtain a sufficient knowledge of the internal control structure in order to understand:
1. The design of the policies, procedures, and records pertaining to each internal control structure element (i.e., control environment, accounting system, and control procedures).
2. Whether they have been placed in operation.

<u>The auditor, however, need not search for significant deficiencies in the</u> design or <u>operation of the internal control structure</u>.

This knowledge is obtained through previous experience with the entity, inquiry, observation, inspection, client descriptions, etc.

The understanding obtained must be documented in the working papers through means such as flowcharts, questionnaires, narrative memos, and decision tables.

Answer choices other than "D" are incorrect because they all represent procedures the auditor performs when obtaining an understanding of the internal control structure.

20. C Sampling risk arises from the possibility that, when a test of controls or a substantive test is limited to a sample, the auditor's conclusions may be different from the conclusions that would have been drawn had the test been applied to all of the items in the population.

The auditor is concerned with two aspects of sampling risk in conducting tests of controls. They are:
1. The risk of assessing control risk too low - In performing tests of controls, the risk that the assessed level of control risk based on the sample is less than the true operating effectiveness of the control structure policy or procedure.
2. The risk of assessing control risk too high - In performing tests of controls, the risk that the assessed level of control risk based on the sample is greater than the true operating effectiveness of the control structure policy or procedure.

The risk of assessing control risk too low relates to the effectiveness of the audit; the risk of assessing control risk too high relates to the efficiency of the audit.

When the deviation rate in the auditor's sample (plus the allowance for sample risk) is less than the tolerable rate, but the deviation rate in the population exceeds the tolerable rate, the auditor will assess control risk too low. As a result, the auditor will reach the wrong conclusion regarding the effectiveness of the control.

Answer choices other than "C" are based on incorrect assumptions.

21. A Assessing control risk is the process of evaluating the effectiveness of an entity's internal control structure policies and procedures in preventing or detecting material misstatements in the financial statements.

Control risk is the risk that a material misstatement that could occur in an assertion will not be prevented or detected on a timely basis by an entity's internal control structure. The auditor may assess control risk at the maximum level (i.e., 100 percent), which is the greatest probability that a material misstatement in a financial statement assertion will not be prevented or detected by an entity's internal control structure, for some or all assertions, because the auditor believes that:

1. <u>Internal control policies and procedures are unlikely to pertain to the assertions</u>.
2. Policies and procedures are unlikely to be effective.
3. Evaluating their effectiveness would be inefficient.

Answer choices other than "A" are based on incorrect assumptions.

22. A To properly plan an audit, the auditor should obtain a sufficient knowledge of the internal control structure in order to understand:
1. The design of the policies, procedures, and records pertaining to each internal control structure element (i.e., control environment, accounting system, and control procedures).
2. Whether they have been placed in operation.

This knowledge is obtained through previous experience with the entity, inquiry, observation, inspection, client descriptions, etc.

Assessing control risk is the process of evaluating the effectiveness of an entity's internal control structure policies and procedures in preventing or detecting material misstatements in the financial statements.

Control risk is the risk that a material misstatement that could occur in an assertion will not be prevented or detected on a timely basis by an entity's internal control structure.

The auditor may assess control risk at the maximum level (i.e., 100 percent, which is the greatest probability that a material misstatement in a financial statement assertion will not be prevented or detected by an entity's internal control structure) for some or all assertions because the auditor believes that:
1. Policies and procedures are unlikely to pertain to an assertion.
2. Policies and procedures are unlikely to be effective.
3. Evaluating their effectiveness would be inefficient.

When control risk is assessed at the maximum level for some or all assertions, no reliance on controls is planned. Accordingly, the auditor would concentrate on substantive testing. Although <u>obtaining an understanding of the internal control structure and assessing control risk</u> are separate steps, they <u>may be performed concurrently</u> in an audit.

Answer choice "B" is incorrect because when control risk is assessed at the maximum level, the auditor is not required to document the basis for that assessment.

Answer choice "C" is incorrect because reliance on tests of controls that results from assessing control risk at a low level may reduce substantive testing, but does not eliminate it.

Answer choice "D" is incorrect because evidence from prior audits may be useful in obtaining an understanding of the current internal control structure and assessing control risk.

23. C The auditor should use the assessed levels of control risk and inherent risk (i.e., the susceptibility of an assertion to material misstatement regardless of the internal control structure) to determine the acceptable level of detection risk. The acceptable level of detection risk, in turn should be used to determine the nature, extent, and timing of substantive tests. Substantive tests usually comprise tests of transactions and balances, and analytical procedures.

There should be a direct relationship between the assessed level of control risk and the required amount of substantive tests. Substantive testing should be sufficient to restrict detection risk to an acceptable level.

When the assessment of control risk is at the maximum level, there is no planned reliance on the related control; therefore, the auditor will normally plan for maximum substantive tests. Conversely, when the assessment of control risk is at the minimum level, there is considerable planned reliance on the related control; therefore, minimum substantive testing is anticipated.

Therefore, after considering the level to which he or she seeks to restrict the risk of a material misstatement in the financial statements and the assessed levels of inherent risk and control risk, the auditor performs substantive tests to restrict detection risk to an acceptable level.

Answer choice "A" is incorrect because if the auditor initially assesses control risk at the maximum level, the auditor may choose not to perform any tests of controls.

Answer choice "B" is incorrect because analytical procedures are not used to verify the design of internal control procedures.

Answer choice "D" is incorrect because dual-purpose tests may be used to meet the objectives of both substantive and control tests. However, if control risk is assessed at the maximum level, no control-test objective would be established.

24. D Generally, evidential matter about the effectiveness of the design and operation of internal control structure policies and procedures obtained directly by the auditor, such as through observation of client personnel, provides more assurance than evidential matter obtained indirectly or by inference, such as through inquiry of client personnel.

Answer choices "A" and "C" are incorrect because they relate to substantive testing.

Answer choice "B" is incorrect because inquiry provides less assurance than observation.

25. D Reportable conditions are those matters coming to the auditor's attention that, in the auditor's judgment, should be communicated to the audit committee (or its equivalent) because they represent significant deficiencies in the design or operation of the internal control structure, which could adversely affect the organization's ability to record, process, summarize, and report financial data consistent with the assertions of management in the financial statements.

Such deficiencies may involve aspects of the internal control structure procedures; e.g., the lack of segregation of duties, and the absence of approvals of transactions.

While the communication is usually made after the audit is concluded, interim communication may be warranted and is acceptable. The auditor should not issue a report indicating that no reportable conditions were noted during the audit.

The communication may be oral or written. If the auditor chooses to communicate orally, the auditor should document the communication in the working papers.

A written report issued on reportable conditions should:
1. Indicate that the purpose of the audit was to report on the financial statements and not to provide assurance on the internal control structure.
2. Include the definition of reportable conditions.
3. Include a restriction on the distribution; i.e., the distribution is intended for the audit committee, management, others within the organization, or, under certain circumstances, specific regulatory agencies.
4. Describe the reportable conditions noted.

Answer choice "A" is incorrect because such a statement is not part of the report communicating reportable conditions to the audit committee.

Answer choice "B" is incorrect because the audit opinion is not based on reportable conditions.

Answer choice "C" is based on incorrect assumptions.

26. B The auditor undertakes audit procedures to verify management's assertion of completeness for account balances in the financial statements.

In order to determine whether all merchandise received by the client is recorded, the auditor begins with the population of all receiving reports for the period under audit. In turn, the auditor would then select a sample of these receiving reports and trace them to the applicable invoices. The invoices would then be traced to the entries in the accounts payable subsidiary ledger.

Answer choice "A" is incorrect because payment vouchers provide evidence that invoices for merchandise have been received and receiving reports exist. However, payment vouchers would not be the population used to determine that all merchandise received has been recorded. These vouchers would aid in establishing the existence of, but not the completeness of, recorded accounts payable.

Answer choice "C" is incorrect because purchase requisitions do not even provide evidence that the merchandise has been received, which is a prerequisite for recording related accounts payable.

Answer choice "D" is incorrect because some of the merchandise may have been billed but not yet received.

27. C A voucher system helps gain control over cash disbursements by providing a routine that (1) permits only designated departments and individuals to incur obligations that will result in cash disbursements, (2) establishes procedures for incurring such obligations, and for their verification, approval, and recording, and (3) permits checks to be issued by the treasurer's department only in payment of properly verified, approved, and recorded obligations.

Typically, upon receipt of a vendor's invoice, the invoice is checked for mathematical accuracy by the vouchers (accounts) payable department, and then matched against copies of the receiving report, inspection report, purchase order, and purchase requisition. This procedure provides the most assurance that recorded purchases are free of material misstatements.

The vouchers (accounts) payable department is then in a position to approve the invoice, and a voucher (i.e., a request for payment) is prepared. The entire voucher package is then checked and approved by a responsible individual in the vouchers (accounts) payable department, and the amount is posted to the expense ledger.

After being approved for payment and recorded, a voucher is filed until its due date, at which time it is sent to the company's cashier (i.e., treasurer's department) for payment. A check is then prepared and signed in the treasurer's department, and the accuracy of the check and related voucher is verified. In turn, the check signer should control the mailing of the check and the related remittance advice. The voucher package is then canceled in the treasurer's department and sent back to the vouchers (accounts) payable department for filing.

In light of the above, approving vendors' invoices is not usually performed in the treasurer's department.

Answer choices other than "C" are incorrect because they represent functions that are usually performed in the treasurer's department.

28. B The production cycle relates to the conversion of raw materials into finished goods. Included in this cycle are production planning and

control of the types and quantities of goods to be manufactured, the inventory levels to be maintained, and the transactions and events pertaining to the manufacturing process. Transactions in this cycle begin at the point where raw materials are requisitioned for production and end with the transfer of the manufactured product to finished goods.

The production cycle interrelates with both the expenditure and revenue cycles. The former involves the acquisition of goods and services needed in production; the latter involves the custody and subsequent sale of finished goods.

The objectives of the internal control structure for a production cycle are to assure that transactions are properly executed and recorded, and that <u>custody of</u> assets (including <u>work in process and finished goods</u>) <u>is properly maintained</u>.

Answer choices other than "B" are incorrect because they are all concerned with the proper execution and recording of transactions, rather than the safeguarding of assets.

29.   D   Segregation of functions, which is a necessary characteristic of an effective internal control structure, is present when the authorization, recording, and custodial functions are segregated from one another.

The documentation normally associated with the purchase cycle consists of a two-part purchase requisition and a multi-part purchase order. The purchase requisition initiates the procurement cycle, with one copy sent to accounting (accounts payable) and the other sent to the originating organizational element (i.e., the user department). The purchasing department prepares the multi-part purchase order and sends the original and one copy to the vendor, a copy to the originator, a copy to receiving (with the quantities omitted), and a copy to accounting. Thus, the purchasing department would approve the purchase order based on the authorization from the purchase requisition and the terms negotiated with vendors. The copy of the purchase order used by the receiving department aids in confirming that what was ordered was in fact received.

In light of the above, <u>employees in the same department</u>, i.e., purchasing, <u>would both approve purchase orders and negotiate terms with vendors</u>.

Answer choice "A" is incorrect because the open invoice file would be reconciled in the accounting department.

Answer choice "B" is incorrect because the receiving department would inspect goods upon receipt.

Answer choice "C" is incorrect because the authorization of requisitions of goods takes place in the user department.

30. C Proper internal control over the payroll function involves segregating the duties involved with hiring employees, determining payroll amounts due, and distributing payroll payments. This is consistent with <u>segregating the authorization of transactions</u> (i.e., hiring personnel) <u>from the custody of related assets</u> (i.e., distributing payroll checks).

Answer choices other than "C" are incorrect because they do not properly indicate the purpose of segregating the duties specified.

31. A Segregation of duties is important in payroll-related transactions. The personnel department is an independent source of records for the internal verification of wage information.

The most important internal controls in the <u>personnel department</u> involve <u>authorization for</u> hiring new employees, initial and periodic <u>changes in pay rates</u>, <u>deductions from employee salaries</u>, and the termination dates of employees. No individual with access to time cards, payroll records, or checks should also be permitted access to personnel records.

Answer choices other than "A" are incorrect because they represent departments that are not responsibile for approving changes in pay rates and deductions from employee salaries.

32. D In obtaining information about notes payable, the auditor's internal control questionnaire would include questions that relate to specific control policies and procedures considered by the auditor to be necessary for effective control. In general, an internal control questionnaire asks a series of questions about the controls, including the control environment, as a means of indicating to the auditor aspects of the internal control structure that may be inadequate. In most instances, it is designed to require a "yes" or "no" response, with "no" responses indicating potential internal control deficiencies.

Questions concerning notes payable would be concerned with whether:
1. <u>Borrowings on notes payable are properly authorized by the board of directors</u>. Whenever notes are renewed, it is important that they are subjected to the same authorization procedures as those for the issuance of new notes.
2. Adequate controls exist for the repayment of principal and interest. The periodic payments of interest and principal should be controlled as a part of the acquisition and payment cycle.
3. Proper documents and records exist; this includes the maintenance of subsidiary records and control over blank and paid notes by a responsible person. Paid notes should be canceled and retained by an authorized official.
4. Periodic independent verification is made of notes payable. Accordingly, the detailed note records should be reconciled with the general ledger by an employee who is not responsible for maintaining the detailed records.

Answer choice "A" is incorrect because it relates to a questionnaire pertaining to assets owned by the organization.

Answer choice "B" is incorrect because it would most likely be found on the questionnaire relating to cash disbursements.

Answer choice "C" is incorrect because it does not relate to the authorization, custody, or recording of the notes payable.

33. B Assertions are representations by management that are embodied in financial statement components. They can be classified as to:
   1. <u>Existence or occurrence</u> - Deals with whether assets or liabilities of the entity exist at a given date, or whether recorded transactions have occurred during a given period.
   2. <u>Completeness</u> - Deals with whether all transactions and accounts that should be presented in the financial statements are so included.
   3. <u>Rights and obligations</u> - Deals with whether assets are the rights of the entity (i.e., owned) at a given time.
   4. <u>Valuation and allocation</u> - Deals with whether asset, liability, revenue, or expense components have been included in the financial statements at the appropriate amounts.
   5. <u>Presentation and disclosure</u> - Deals with whether particular components of the financial statements are properly classified, described, and disclosed.

With respect to long-term investments, the auditor's <u>comparison of the securities in the bank safe deposit box with recorded investments</u> would assist in satisfying the completeness assertion.

Answer choice "A" is incorrect because it would assist in satisfying the rights and obligations assertion.

Answer choice "C" is incorrect because it would assist in satisfying the existence or occurrence assertion, as well as the rights and obligations assertion and the valuation and allocation assertion.

Answer choice "D" is incorrect because it would assist in satisfying the valuation and allocation assertion.

34. C Control procedures are those policies and procedures in addition to the control environment and accounting system that management has established to provide reasonable assurance that an entity's established objectives will be achieved.

Control procedures include:
   1. <u>Segregation of functions</u> - to avoid a position that can both perpetrate and conceal an error, etc.
   2. <u>Proper authorization of transactions and activities</u> - need for independent evidence that authorizations are issued by personnel acting within the scope of their authority, and that transactions conform to such authorization.
   3. Adequate safeguards over access to and use of assets and records.

4. Recording of transactions - design and use of adequate documents and records to help ensure proper recording of transactions and events; e.g., use of prenumbered invoices.
5. Checks on performance and proper valuation of recorded amounts; e.g., clerical checks, reconciliations, comparison of assets with recorded amounts.

In view of item "2" above, equipment acquisitions that are misclassified as maintenance expense would be reflected as a variance in a formal budgeting system because the acquisition would likely cause the budgeted maintenance to exceed authorized amounts.

Answer choice "A" is incorrect because segregation of duties would not highlight a misclassification.

Answer choice "B" is incorrect because independent verification of invoices for disbursements recorded as equipment would not identify acquisitions recorded as expenses.

Answer choice "D" is incorrect because the authorization of acquisitions would not in and of itself identify improper classification.

35.   B   The purpose of a review is to provide the accountant with a basis for expressing limited assurance that the financial statements conform to GAAP, or to a comprehensive basis of accounting other than GAAP.

In performing a review, the accountant makes inquiries of the entity's personnel and employs analytical procedures. Specific review procedures include the following.
1. Inquiries concerning the entity's accounting principles and practices, and the methods followed in applying them.
2. Inquiries concerning the entity's procedures for recording, classifying, and summarizing transactions.
3. Analytical procedures designed to identify relationships and individual items that appear to be unusual.
4. Inquiries concerning actions taken at meetings of stockholders and the board of directors that may affect the financial statements.
5. Reading the financial statements to consider whether they appear to be in conformity with GAAP.

In view of item "4" above, the accountant most likely would ask about actions taken at board of directors' meetings.

Answer choices "A" and "C" are incorrect because such procedures are performed as part of an audit engagement.

Answer choice "D" is incorrect because distribution of the review report may not be limited.

36.   B   The gathering of sufficient, competent evidential matter, from which the auditor can form an opinion as to the fairness of financial statements, is mandated under GAAS and is covered by the third standard of fieldwork.

Most of the independent auditor's work in forming an opinion on financial statements consists of obtaining and evaluating evidential matter concerning the assertions in such financial statements. The measure of the validity of such evidence for audit purposes lies in the judgment of the auditor.

The following presumptions about the validity of evidential matter should be considered.
1. Evidential matter obtained from independent sources outside an entity provides greater assurance of reliability than evidence obtained solely from within the organization.
2. When accounting data and financial statements are developed under strong internal control, reliability is enhanced.
3. The auditor's direct personal knowledge, obtained through physical examination, observation, computation and inspection, is more persuasive than information obtained indirectly from independent outside sources.

Underlying accounting data, which includes the books of original entry, the general and subsidiary ledgers, related accounting manuals, worksheets, reconciliations, etc., constitute evidence in support of the financial statements. However, by itself, underlying accounting data cannot be considered sufficient audit evidence to support the opinion on the financial statements.

Answer choice "A" is incorrect because to be competent, audit evidence should be both persuasive and relevant.

Answer choice "C" is incorrect because, although the auditor should consider the cost of obtaining evidence relative to the usefulness of the information obtained, the difficulty and expense of a test is not, by itself, a valid basis for omitting the test.

Answer choice "D" is incorrect because, as noted, underlying accounting data by itself cannot be considered sufficient audit evidence to support the financial statements.

37.   C   Assertions are management representations embodied in financial statement components. They can be classified as to:
1. Existence or occurrence - Deals with whether assets or liabilities of the entity exist at a given date, or whether recorded transactions have occurred during a given period.
2. Completeness - Deals with whether all transactions and accounts that should be presented in the financial statements are included.
3. Rights and obligations - Deals with whether assets are the rights of the entity (i.e., owned) at a given time.
4. Valuation and allocation - Deals with whether asset, liability,

revenue, or expense components have been included in the
financial statements at the appropriate amounts.

5. <u>Presentation and disclosure</u> - Deals with whether particular
   components of the financial statements are properly classified,
   described, and disclosed.

<u>In</u> <u>the</u> <u>audit</u> <u>of</u> <u>accounts</u> <u>payable</u>, <u>the</u> <u>primary</u> <u>focus</u> <u>is</u> <u>on</u> <u>the</u>
<u>discovery</u> <u>of</u> understated or omitted liabilities; that is, the
<u>completeness</u> assertion.

Answer choices other than "C" are incorrect because, although these
assertions are relevant concerns for the auditor, they are all
secondary considerations.

38.   C   Analytical procedures consist of evaluations of financial
          information made by a study of plausible relationships among both
          financial and nonfinancial data. A basic premise underlying the
          application of analytical procedures is that plausible relationships
          among data may reasonably be expected to exist and continue to exist
          in the absence of known conditions to the contrary.

          Analytical procedures:
          1. Should be used to assist the auditor in planning the nature,
             timing, and extent of other auditing procedures.
          2. May be used as a substantive test to obtain evidential matter
             about particular assertions related to account balances or
             classes of transactions.
          3. Should be used to perform an overall review of the financial
             information in the final review stage of the audit.

          In view of items "2" and "3" above, the use of analytical procedures
          <u>is</u> <u>not</u> <u>required</u> <u>as</u> <u>a</u> <u>substantive</u> <u>test</u> but <u>is</u> <u>required</u> to some extent
          <u>in</u> <u>the</u> <u>final</u> <u>review</u> <u>stage</u> of an audit.

          Answer choices other than "C" are based on incorrect assumptions and
          illogical combinations of responses.

39.   C   Since the events or conditions that should be considered in the
          financial accounting for and reporting of litigation, claims, and
          assessments are matters within the direct knowledge and, often,
          control of management of an entity, <u>management</u> <u>is</u> <u>the</u> <u>primary</u> <u>source</u>
          <u>of</u> <u>information</u> <u>about</u> <u>litigation</u>, <u>claims</u>, <u>and</u> <u>assessments</u>.

          A letter of audit inquiry sent to the client's lawyer is the
          auditor's primary means of obtaining corroboration of the
          information furnished by management concerning litigation, claims,
          and assessments. Evidential matter obtained from the client's legal
          department may provide the auditor with some corroboration, but it
          is not a substitute for information that should be obtained from the
          outside counsel, which represents an independent source.

          Answer choice "A" is incorrect because the client's lawyer is the
          primary source of evidence corroborating or supporting information
          furnished by management.

Answer choices "B" and "D" are clearly based on incorrect assumptions.

40. D Confirmations represent written evidence received directly by the auditor from an independent third party verifying the accuracy of requested information. Since confirmations come from sources independent of the client, they are the most highly regarded type of evidential matter.

One type of confirmation deals with accounts receivable. Accounts receivable may be confirmed by using the positive form, the negative form, or a combination of both. With the positive form, the debtor is asked to reply directly to the auditor, stating whether the balance as indicated on the request is correct or, if it is incorrect, to indicate the correct balance and any possible explanation for the difference.

The positive form is usually used (1) for individual account balances that are material in amount, (2) when the internal control structure relating to receivables is weak, (3) when there is reason to believe that the possibility of disputes or irregularities in the accounts is greater than usual, and (4) when there is reason to believe that a negative form will not receive adequate consideration.

With the negative form, the debtor is asked to reply only if the balance, as stated on the request, is not in agreement with its records. This type of request is useful when (1) the assessed level of control risk relating to receivables is low, (2) <u>a small number of accounts may be in dispute</u>, (3) <u>there are many customers with small balances</u>, and (4) there are indications that the requests will receive proper consideration.

Answer choices other than "D" are incorrect because they describe conditions for which the auditor would be better served by the positive form of accounts receivable confirmation.

41. D The overall objective in the audit of accounts payable is to determine whether accounts payable is fairly stated and properly disclosed. The auditor should focus on the detection of unrecorded liabilities.

In searching for unrecorded liabilities, the auditor might perform the following procedures.
1. Examine documentation for cash payments occurring after the balance sheet date. <u>Cash payments occurring after the balance sheet date should be compared with the accounts payable trial balance</u>.
2. Trace receiving reports issued before year-end to related vendors' invoices.
3. Examine vendors' statements and compare any stated balances due to the accounts payable trial balance.

4. Mail confirmations to active vendors for which a balance has not been included in the accounts payable trial balance.

Answer choice "A" is incorrect because it involves cash payments made prior to year-end.

Answer choice "B" is incorrect because this analytical procedure would not enable detection of actual unrecorded payables; it might, however, reveal the possible existence of unrecorded payables.

Answer choice "C" is incorrect because vouching creditor balances would not identify unrecorded payables; rather, it would only verify that documentation exists to support payables already recorded.

42.   B   Working papers are generally filed under two categories: (1) a current file and (2) a permanent (continuing) file. The current file contains corroborating information pertaining to the execution of the current year's audit program; the permanent file contains data that are expected to be useful to the auditor during current and future engagements.

Items contained in the current file include:
1. Schedules and analyses of accounts.
2. The current year's audit program.
3. Correspondence with third parties confirming balances, transactions, and other data.
4. Schedule of time spent on the engagement by each individual auditor.
5. A copy of the current year's financial statements.
6. Review notes pertaining to questions and comments regarding the audit work performed.

Items contained in the permanent file include:
1. Copies of articles of incorporation and bylaws.
2. Organization charts.
3. Plant layouts and descriptions of manufacturing processes.
4. Details of capital stock and bond issues.
5. Charts of accounts.
6. Narrative descriptions and flowcharts of the client's internal control structure.
7. Copies of pension plans, lease agreements, bond and note indentures, etc.
8. Summaries of accounting principles used by the client.

In light of items "4" and "7" above, the permanent (continuing) file of working papers most likely would include copies of the debt agreements.

Answer choices other than "B" are incorrect because they represent items that should be included in the current file and not in the permanent file of the auditor's working papers.

43. C Generalized audit software commonly consists of individual computer programs, or routines, designed to perform a variety of functions. Typically, the software can perform all of the normal data handling and processing functions provided by the client's own software. Information can be sorted, stratified, sampled, evaluated, included or excluded, and summarized as desired. The software also has the capability of processing transactions, updating master files for current transactions, generating printed reports, and performing data search and retrieval. In addition, data files may be reviewed for completeness, reasonableness, and mathematical accuracy.

A primary advantage of using generalized audit software is that the auditor may <u>access information stored on computer files while having a limited understanding of the client's hardware and software features</u>.

Answer choice "A" is incorrect because it is secondary and not primary in nature. Once computer files are accessed, all other functions, such as verifying data accuracy, can be performed.

Answer choice "B" is incorrect because the use of a generalized audit software program, in and of itself, would not necessarily reduce the level of required tests of controls to a relatively small amount.

Answer choice "D" is incorrect because generalized audit software may assist in performing analytical procedures as a substantive test, as well as aiding substantive tests of transactions.

44. B Both Generally Accepted Auditing Standards (GAAS) and Generally Accepted Government Auditing Standards (GAGAS) require that a record of the auditor's work be retained in the form of working papers.

Under GAGAS, supplemental working paper requirements for financial audits are that <u>working papers should</u>:
1. Contain a written audit program cross-referenced to the working papers.
2. Contain the objective, scope, methodology, and results of the audit.
3. <u>Contain sufficient information so that supplementary oral explanations are not required</u>.
4. Be legible with adequate indexing and cross-referencing, and include summaries and lead schedules, as appropriate.
5. Restrict information included to matters that are materially important and relevant to the objectives of the audit.
6. Contain evidence of supervisory reviews of the work conducted.

Answer choice "A" is incorrect because such a written representation is not a requirement of GAGAS.

Answer choice "C" is incorrect because the auditor should document the procedures used to test compliance with certain provisions of laws, regulations, contracts, and grants, rather than all illegal acts.

Answer choice "D" is incorrect because it does not represent a documentation requirement of GAGAS.

45. B Generally Accepted Government Auditing Standards (GAGAS) incorporate the Generally Accepted Auditing Standards (GAAS) of reporting for financial audits, and the following supplemental standards of reporting needed to satisfy the unique needs of government financial audits.
   1. A statement that the audit was made in accordance with generally accepted government auditing standards.
   2. Report on compliance - A written report that contains a statement of positive assurance on items tested for compliance, and negative assurance on those items not tested. It should include all material instances of noncompliance and all instances or indications of illegal acts that could result in criminal prosecution.
   3. Report on internal controls - A written report on the understanding of the entity's internal control structure and assessment of control risk made. Include, as a minimum, a description of the scope of the work performed, significant controls, and any reportable conditions noted (including those considered to be material weaknesses).
   4. Written audit reports on the results of each financial-related audit.
   5. Privileged and confidential information - If certain information is prohibited from general disclosure, report the nature of the information omitted and the requirement that makes the omission necessary.
   6. Report distribution - Submit written audit reports to the appropriate officials, both within and outside the organization audited. Unless restricted by law or regulation, copies should be made available for public inspection.

In light of item "3" above, when auditing an entity's financial statements in accordance with GAGAS, the auditor should prepare a written report on the auditor's understanding of the entity's internal control structure and the assessment of control risk made.

Answer choice "A" is incorrect because this type of report may be made as part of a performance audit conducted under GAGAS.

Answer choice "C" is incorrect because this documentation is part of the auditor's working papers.

Answer choice "D" is incorrect because this type of opinion is not rendered under GAGAS for a financial statement audit.

46. D A disclaimer of opinion is issued whenever the auditor has been unable to satisfy himself or herself that the overall financial statements are fairly presented. The necessity for disclaiming an opinion may arise because of a severe limitation on the scope of the audit.

When a disclaimer of opinion is warranted, the auditor should indicate in a separate paragraph why the audit did not comply with generally accepted auditing standards. Further, <u>the scope paragraph is deleted and the opinion paragraph is changed to a disclaimer</u>.

Answer choices other than "D" are incorrect because of illogical combinations of responses or incorrect assumptions.

47.   A   Certain circumstances, while not affecting the auditor's unqualified opinion, may require that the auditor add an explanatory paragraph to the standard report. These circumstances include the financial statements being affected by uncertainties concerning future events, the outcome of which are not susceptible to reasonable estimation at the date of the auditor's report.

In deciding whether to add an explanatory paragraph to the report because of a matter involving an uncertainty, the auditor should consider the likelihood of a material loss resulting from the resolution of the uncertainty.

If management believes, and the auditor is satisfied, that there is only a remote likelihood of a material loss resulting from the resolution of a matter involving an uncertainty, the auditor should not add an explanatory paragraph to the audit report.

If management believes, and the auditor is satisfied, that it is probable that a material loss will occur, but management is unable to make a reasonable estimate of the amount or range of potential loss, and thus has not made an accrual in the financial statements, the auditor should add an explanatory paragraph to the audit report.

If management believes, and the auditor is satisfied, that the chance of a material loss resulting from the resolution of a matter involving an uncertainty is more than remote but less than probable, the auditor should consider the following matters in deciding whether to add an explanatory paragraph to the audit report.
1. The magnitude by which the amount of reasonably possible loss exceeds the auditor's judgment about materiality.
2. The likelihood of occurrence of a material loss (i.e., whether that likelihood is closer to remote or to probable).

<u>The auditor is more likely to add an explanatory paragraph to the auditor's report as the amount of reasonably possible loss becomes larger, or the likelihood of occurrence of a material loss increases</u>.

Answer choices other than "A" are based on incorrect assumptions or illogical combinations of responses.

48.   A   When comparative financial statements are presented, and there has been a change in auditors between years, the predecessor's audit report may or may not be presented. <u>When the predecessor's audit report is not presented</u>, regardless of the type of opinion

expressed, the successor auditor should specify in the introductory paragraph that the prior year's financial statements were audited by another auditor. The introductory paragraph should also indicate the date of the predecessor's report, the type of opinion expressed and, if other than an unqualified opinion was issued, the reasons for such an opinion.

Answer choices other than "A" are improper forms of reporting and/or incorrect procedures.

49. C An auditor's qualified opinion states that "except for" the effects of the matter(s) to which the qualification relates, the financial statements present fairly, in all material respects, the financial position, results of operations, and cash flows of the entity in conformity with GAAP.

A qualified opinion may result from a scope limitation that prevents the auditor from applying necessary procedures. Scope limitations occur when there is a lack of sufficient competent evidential matter, or there are restrictions on the scope of the audit and a disclaimer of opinion is not warranted.

The wording of the opinion paragraph in a scope limitation situation should include the word "except" or "exception" in a phrase such as "except for" or "with the exception of." The wording of the opinion paragraph should indicate that the qualification pertains to the possible effects on the financial statements and not to the scope limitation itself.

Answer choice "A" is incorrect because the explanatory paragraph preceding the opinion paragraph should explain the limitation on the scope of the audit.

Answer choice "B" is incorrect because the explanatory paragraph preceding the opinion paragraph should explain a departure from generally accepted auditing standards.

Answer choice "D" is incorrect because inadequate disclosure of necessary information would lead to a qualified or adverse opinion; inadequate disclosure of necessary information does not represent a scope limitation.

50. A The independent accountant's responsibility with respect to filings under federal securities statutes is generally, in substance, no different from the independent accountant's responsibility with respect to other forms of reporting.

In general, a report based on a review of interim financial information of a public entity is not considered to be a report governed by federal securities statutes.

When audited financial statements are presented in comparative form with financial statements in a document filed with the Securities and Exchange Commission, such statements <u>should</u> <u>be</u> <u>marked</u> <u>as</u> "<u>unaudited</u>." The unaudited financial statements, however, <u>should</u> <u>not</u> <u>be</u> <u>referred</u> <u>to</u> <u>in</u> <u>the</u> <u>auditor's</u> <u>report</u>. Finally, it should be obvious that the unaudited financial statements <u>do</u> <u>not</u> <u>have</u> <u>to</u> <u>be</u> <u>withheld</u> <u>until</u> <u>audited</u>.

Answer choices other than "A" are based on incorrect assumptions or illogical combinations of responses.

51. D An auditor's qualified opinion states that "except for" the effects of the matter(s) to which the qualification relates, the financial statements present fairly, in all material respects, the financial position, results of operations, and cash flows of the entity in conformity with GAAP.

When financial statements fail to disclose information required by generally accepted accounting principles, the auditor should express a qualified opinion if the effects do not warrant an adverse opinion.

When an auditor qualifies an opinion because of inadequate disclosure, <u>the</u> <u>introductory</u> <u>and</u> <u>scope</u> <u>paragraphs</u> <u>should</u> <u>not</u> <u>be</u> <u>modified</u>. A separate explanatory paragraph, added before the opinion paragraph, should describe the nature of the omitted disclosure. The opinion paragraph should be modified to reflect the "except for" qualified opinion, as well as the reference to the explanatory paragraph.

Answer choices other than "D" are based on incorrect assumptions or illogical combinations of responses.

52. A Accounting principles selected and applied by management have general acceptance according to the following ranking of the sources of established accounting principles. (The degree of authority is highest at level one, etc.)
1. <u>Level one</u>
    a. <u>Nongovernmental entities</u> - FASB Statements and Interpretations, APB Opinions, and AICPA Accounting Research Bulletins.
    b. <u>State and local governments</u> - GASB Statements and Interpretations, plus AICPA and FASB pronouncements if made applicable to state and local governments by a GASB Statement or Interpretation.
2. <u>Level two</u>
    a. <u>Nongovernmental entities</u> - FASB Technical Bulletins, AICPA Industry Audit and Accounting Guides, and AICPA Statements of Position.
    b. <u>State and local governments</u> - GASB Technical Bulletins, and the following pronouncements if specifically made applicable to state and local governments by the AICPA: AICPA Industry Audit and Accounting Guides, and AICPA Statements of Position.

3. <u>Level three</u>
   a. <u>Nongovernmental entities</u> - Consensus positions of the FASB Emerging Issues Task Force and AICPA Practice Bulletins.
   b. <u>State and local governments</u> - Consensus positions of the GASB Emerging Issues Task Force and AICPA Practice Bulletins if specifically made applicable to state and local governments by the AICPA.

4. <u>Level four</u>
   a. <u>Nongovernmental entities</u> - AICPA Accounting Interpretations, "Qs and As" published by the FASB staff, as well as industry practices widely recognized and prevalent.
   b. <u>State and local governments</u> - "Qs and As" published by the GASB staff, as well as industry practices widely recognized and prevalent.

5. <u>Level five</u> (i.e., "other accounting literature")

   These sources should be considered only in the absence of sources identified in Levels one through four.
   a. <u>Nongovernmental entities</u> - Other accounting literature, including FASB Concepts Statements, etc.
   b. <u>State and local governments</u> - Other accounting literature, including GASB Concepts Statements and pronouncements in Levels one through four which were not made specifically applicable to state and local governments.

Of the choices provided, <u>FASB Technical Bulletins are the most authoritative</u>.

Answer choices other than "A" are incorrect because they are not as authoritative as FASB Technical Bulletins.

53.　B　During a review of financial statements, the accountant may become aware of a material departure from GAAP. The accountant should recommend that the financial statements be appropriately revised to conform with GAAP. If the client does not agree to revise the financial statements, the accountant must consider whether to modify his or her review report or withdraw from the engagement.

If the accountant concludes that modifying the report is sufficient, the <u>departure from GAAP should be disclosed in a separate paragraph of the report</u>.

Answer choice "A" is incorrect because a review report would not provide negative assurance on accounting principles that do not conform with GAAP.

Answer choice "C" is incorrect because adverse opinions and "except for" qualified opinions are only associated with audited financial statements.

Answer choice "D" is incorrect because positive assurance is not provided in a review report.

54.   A   A compilation of financial statements is a service, provided to a nonpublic entity, in which an accountant prepares or assists in preparing financial statements without expressing any assurance that the statements are in conformity with GAAP.

The accountant's compilation report, which should accompany the financial statements, states that:
1.   The accountant has compiled the financial statements in accordance with Statements on Standards for Accounting and Review Services issued by the American Institute of Certified Public Accountants.
2.   A compilation is limited to presenting in the form of financial statements information that is the representation of management.
3.   No audit or review of the financial statements has taken place and the accountant does not express an opinion or any other form of assurance on the statements.
4.   The report date is the date on which the compilation was completed.

Furthermore, each page of the financial statements should be marked, "See Accountant's Compilation Report."

An additional paragraph is added when the accountant is not independent.

It should be noted that the accountant may lack independence and still issue a compilation report. However, an additional (final) paragraph, in which the lack of independence is disclosed, must be added to the compilation report.

In view of the above, the "independence" representation is made implicitly. Accordingly, the accountant only explicitly indicates the lack of independence.

Answer choices "B" and "D" are incorrect because such representations are made explicitly.

Answer choice "C" is incorrect because this representation is not made implicitly or explicitly in a compilation report.

55.   C   The auditor's standard report implies that the auditor is satisfied that there have been no material changes in GAAP affecting comparability. The second reporting standard under GAAS requires the auditor to identify circumstances in which accounting principles have not been consistently observed in the current period in relation to the preceding period.

If a change in GAAP has no material effect on the current year's financial statements, but is reasonably certain to have a substantial effect in later years, the auditor should issue a standard unqualified opinion if the change is disclosed in the notes to the financial statements.

Answer choices other than "C" are based on incorrect assumptions.

56.   A   Auditor's reports issued in connection with the following criteria constitute special reports.

1.   Financial statements prepared in accordance with a comprehensive basis of accounting other than GAAP. A comprehensive basis of accounting other than GAAP may be a basis prescribed by a regulatory body, a basis used for income-tax purposes, the cash or modified-cash basis, or a basis having substantial support, such as the constant-dollar or replacement-cost basis.

2.   Specified elements, accounts, or items of a financial statement. Examples include rentals, royalties, accounts receivable profit participation, or a provision for income taxes.

3.   Compliance with contractual agreements or regulatory requirements related to audited financial statements.

4.   Financial presentations to comply with contractual agreements or regulatory provisions that are incomplete or are not in conformity with GAAP or another comprehensive basis of accounting.

5.   Financial information and/or auditor's report required in a prescribed form.

In view of point "2" above, a CPA may accept a separate engagement to <u>audit</u> <u>an</u> <u>entity's</u> <u>schedule</u> <u>of</u> <u>accounts</u> <u>receivable</u> <u>or</u> <u>an</u> <u>entity's</u> <u>schedule</u> <u>of</u> <u>royalties</u>.

Answer choices other than "A" are based on incorrect assumptions or illogical combinations of responses.

57.   C   A financial projection presents to the best of the responsible party's knowledge and belief, given one or more hypothetical assumptions (i.e., assumptions used to present a condition or course of action that is not necessarily expected to occur), an entity's expected financial position, results of operations, and cash flows. A financial projection is, therefore, based on "what if" assumptions.

The accountant's standard report on a compilation of prospective financial statements should include:

1.   An identification of the prospective financial statements.

2.   A statement that the prospective financial statements have been compiled in accordance with standards established by the AICPA.

3.   A statement that the compilation is limited in scope, and does not enable the accountant to express an opinion or any other form of assurance that the results may be achieved.

4.   A disclaimer of responsibility to update the report for events occurring after the report date.

5.   A separate paragraph that describes the limitations on the presentation's usefulness.

Thus, an accountant's standard compilation report on a projection should not include a <u>statement</u> <u>expressing</u> <u>any</u> <u>assurance</u>, limited or otherwise.

Answer choices other than "C" are incorrect because each of the items indicated should be included in the report.

58. A   In performing a financial audit in accordance with Government Auditing Standards, an auditor is required to prepare a written report on the entity's compliance with applicable laws and regulations. The report may be included with the report on the audited financial statements or presented separately.

The written report on compliance with laws and regulations should include, in addition to the manual (or printed) signature of the auditor and the date of the auditor's report:
1. References to the audit of the financial statements and the auditor's report thereon.
2. References to GAAS and Government Auditing Standards issued by the Comptroller General of the U.S.
3. A statement indicating that those standards require the auditor to obtain reasonable assurance about whether the financial statements are free of material misstatement.
4. A statement that management is responsible for compliance with laws, regulations, contracts, and grants.
5. A statement that the auditor performed tests of compliance with certain provisions of laws, regulations, contracts, and grants.
6. A statement that the auditor's objective was not to provide an opinion on overall compliance with such provisions, and a disclaimer of opinion on compliance with laws, regulations, contracts, and grants.
7. Positive assurance with respect to items tested.
8. Negative assurance with respect to items not tested.
9. The intended distribution of the report (e.g., audit committee, management, regulatory bodies, and if a matter of public record, that limited distribution is not intended).

In view of point "4" above, the auditor's report should <u>state that compliance with laws and regulations is the responsibility of management</u>.

Answer choices other than "A" are incorrect because they are not elements of the written report on compliance with laws and regulations.

59. B   After the financial statements and the auditor's report are released, the auditor continues to have a responsibility with respect to the subsequent discovery of facts; i.e., the discovery of material facts existing at the audit report date that were not known to the auditor when the report was issued.

Upon such discovery, the auditor should determine whether the information is reliable and whether the facts actually existed at the date of the auditor's report. If so, the auditor should discuss the matter with the client's management, including the board of directors.

When the subsequently discovered information is found to be both reliable and to have existed at the date of the auditor's report, the auditor should determine if:

1. The audit report would have been affected if the information had been known to the auditor at the date of the report.
2. The auditor believes there are persons who currently rely, or are likely to rely, on the financial statements and who would attach importance to the information.

When the auditor has concluded that action should be taken, the auditor should advise the client to make appropriate disclosure of the newly discovered facts. In addition, the client should issue revised financial statements and the auditor should issue a revised report.

Thus, an auditor has no obligation to make continuing inquiries or perform other procedures concerning the audited financial statements, unless information that existed at the report date, that may affect the report, comes to the auditor's attention.

In view of the above, the discovery of information regarding a contingency that existed before the financial statements were issued would require the auditor to make inquiries or perform other procedures.

Answer choices other than "B" are incorrect because they involve subsequent events, and not subsequent discovery of facts. The auditor has no additional obligation as to inquiries and/or procedures relative to subsequent events after the auditor's report and the financial statements are issued.

60.   B   The auditor must determine whether certain matters related to the audit should be communicated (orally or in writing) to the audit committee (or, in the absence of an audit committee, to other financial oversight groups, such as finance or budget committees). Such communication need not be made before the issuance of the auditor's report.

Matters to be communicated include the following:

1. The level of responsibility an auditor assumes for the internal control structure and the financial statements under GAAS.
2. The initial selection of, and changes in, significant policies, methods used to account for significant unusual transactions, and the effect of continuing accounting policies in controversial areas.
3. The processes used by management in formulating accounting estimates, and the basis for the auditor's conclusions about the reasonableness of those estimates.
4. Any adjustments arising from the audit that could have a significant effect on the entity's reporting process.
5. The auditor's responsibility for information, other than the audited financial statements, in documents such as corporate annual reports.

6. Any disagreements between the auditor and management, whether or not satisfactorily resolved.

7. Significant matters that were the subject of consultations with other accountants.

8. Any major issues discussed by management and the auditor before the auditor was hired.

9. Any serious difficulties the auditor encountered that were detrimental to the effective completion of the audit.

As noted in point "4" above, significant audit adjustments that could have a significant effect on the entity's financial reporting process are required to be communicated to the audit committee by the auditor.

Answer choices other than "B" are based on incorrect assumptions and/or combinations.

61. A The auditor should perform auditing procedures with respect to the period after the balance sheet date for the purpose of ascertaining the occurrence of subsequent events that may require either adjustments to, or disclosures in, the financial statements in order for them to be in conformity with GAAP.

The auditor should perform procedures to identify subsequent events at or near the completion of fieldwork. These procedures include:

1. Reading the latest available interim statements.

2. Inquiries and discussions with officers and other executives having responsibility for such financial and accounting matters as:
    a. Substantial contingent liabilities.
    b. Significant changes in capital stock, long-term debt, or working capital.
    c. Unusual adjustments.

3. Reading the available minutes of meetings of stockholders and the board of directors.

4. Inquiries of client's attorneys concerning any pending litigation, unasserted claims, or assessments.

5. Obtaining a letter of representation.

6. Any other additional inquiries or procedures considered necessary.

As noted in point #1 above, during the review of subsequent events, the auditor would ordinarily read and compare the latest available interim financial statements with the financial statements being audited.

Answer choice "B" is incorrect because, while it is an appropriate audit procedure, it is not relevant to subsequent events.

Answer choice "C" is incorrect because the communication of material weaknesses (and other reportable conditions) in the internal control structure to the client's audit committee is a required communication; it is not related to subsequent events.

Answer choice "D" is incorrect because, when considering subsequent events, the auditor would not review the cut-off bank statements for several months after the year end; rather, the auditor would review bank statements cut off only in the month following year end.

62. D   When part of the audit is performed by another auditor, the principal auditor must be able to gain satisfaction as to the independence and professional reputation of the other CPA, as well as to the quality of the audit. Having done so, the principal auditor must then decide whether he or she is willing to express an opinion on the financial statements taken as a whole without referring to the audit of the other auditor. If the auditor decides to do so, it should not be stated that part of the audit was performed by another auditor, because to do so may cause a reader to misinterpret the degree of responsibility being assumed. As such, a standard audit report is issued when the principal auditor decides not to make reference to the other auditor.

Generally, no reference to the other auditor is necessary when:
1. The other auditor is associated with the principal auditor.
2. The principal auditor retained, supervised, or guided and controlled the other auditor.
3. The principal auditor becomes satisfied as to the work of the other auditor.
4. The work of the other auditor is not material in relation to the financial statements.

Based on the above, the principal auditor would be justified in his or her decision not to make reference to another CPA if the principal auditor is satisfied as to the independence and professional reputation of the other CPA.

Answer choice "A" is incorrect because reference to the other auditor does not depend on the type of opinion expressed.

Answer choice "B" is incorrect because the type of opinion issued by the other auditor does not provide the auditor with evidence of the work of the other auditor and, therefore, has no impact on the decision of whether or not to make reference to the other auditor.

Answer choice "C" is incorrect because the auditor may decide to refer to the other auditor if he or she is unable to become satisfied as to the work of the other auditor.

63. D   A "comfort letter" is a letter written by the accountant and sent to an underwriter of securities during client registration procedures with the SEC. The letter is so named because it is designed to give comfort (i.e., assurance) to underwriters that the financial and accounting data not covered by the auditor's opinion on the financial statements, but included in the prospectus, are in (a) compliance with the Securities Act of 1933, and (b) conformity with GAAP.

The contents of a typical comfort letter include:
1. A statement regarding the independence of the accountants.
2. An opinion as to whether the audited financial statements and financial schedules included in the registration statement comply as to form in all material respects with the applicable accounting requirements and related published rules and regulations of the SEC.
3. Negative assurance on whether:
   a. The unaudited condensed interim financial information included in the registration statement complies as to form in all material respects with the applicable accounting requirements of the Act and related published rules and regulations.
   b. Any material modifications should be made to the unaudited condensed financial statements included in the registration statement in order for them to be in conformity with generally accepted accounting principles.
   c. There has been any change in capital stock, increase in long-term debt, or decrease in other specified financial statement items during a specified period following the date of the latest financial statements included in the registration statement and prospectus.

The comfort letter should conclude with a statement indicating that the letter is solely for the use of the underwriter in connection with the specific security issue. Furthermore, the letter should be dated at the time, or shortly before, the securities are delivered to the underwriter in exchange for the proceeds of the offering.

Answer choice "A" is incorrect because the negative assurance provided does not relate to the entity's internal control structure.

Answer choice "B" is incorrect because "Government Auditing Standards" and the Single Audit Act of 1984 do not apply to matters discussed in comfort letters.

Answer choice "C" is incorrect because negative assurance, and not positive assurance, is provided concerning whether the unaudited condensed financial information is in compliance with generally accepted accounting principles.

64.   D   "Government Auditing Standards" requires a written report on the internal control structure, and a written report on compliance with laws and regulations. Therefore, the auditor would be responsible for assuring that management reported significant deficiencies in the design of the internal control structure to specific legislative and regulatory bodies when reporting under "Government Auditing Standards."

Answer choice "A" is incorrect because there are no reporting requirements with respect to internal control structure deficiencies under Chapter 11 of the Federal Bankruptcy Code.

Answer choice "B" is incorrect because reportable conditions, including those considered material weaknesses, are communicated by the auditor to the audit committee (or its equivalent) and not to the shareholders.

Answer choice "C" is incorrect because internal control structure deficiencies are not reported to the Securities and Exchange Commission.

65. B A review of interim financial information is substantially less in scope than an audit. It does not provide the basis for expressing an opinion, since it omits many standard audit procedures. Its objective is to provide the accountant with a basis for reporting to the board of directors or stockholders whether <u>material modifications</u> <u>should</u> <u>be</u> <u>made</u> for such information <u>to</u> <u>conform</u> <u>with</u> <u>GAAP</u>.

Answer choice "A" is incorrect because a review does not provide a basis for the expression of an updated opinion.

Answer choice "C" is incorrect because standards of interim reporting do not exist.

Answer choice "D" is incorrect because only an audit would provide a basis for reporting whether the financial statements are presented fairly in accordance with generally accepted accounting principles.

66. C Assessing control risk is the process of evaluating the effectiveness of an entity's internal control structure policies and procedures to prevent or detect material misstatements in the financial statements.

Thus, the ultimate purpose of assessing control risk is to contribute to the auditor's evaluation of the <u>risk</u> <u>that</u> <u>material</u> <u>misstatements</u> may <u>exist</u> <u>in</u> <u>the</u> <u>financial</u> <u>statements</u>.

Answer choice "A" is incorrect because the auditor's evaluation of factors that raise doubts about the auditability of the financial statements may contribute to the evaluation that material misstatements may exist in the financial statements; as such, these factors are part of the process of assessing control risk, rather than the ultimate purpose.

Answer choice "B" is incorrect because the auditor's evaluation of the operating effectiveness of internal control policies and procedures may affect the final assessed level of control risk, rather than being the purpose of assessing control risk.

Answer choice "D" is incorrect because the assessed level of control risk will affect the nature and extent of substantive testing. This testing will depend on the risk that material misstatements exist, and will only be reduced if the assessed level of control risk is low.

67. B When an auditor assess control risk below the maximum level, the auditor is required to document his or her understanding of the entity's internal control structure elements. Such documentation may include flowcharts, questionnaires, narrative memoranda, and/or decision tables.

In addition, the auditor is required to document his or her basis for concluding that control risk is below the maximum level.

Answer choices other than "B" are based on incorrect assumptions and/or illogical combinations.

68. B If an auditor wishes to assess control risk at below the maximum level, the auditor must perform tests of controls. Four types of procedures that are used in tests of controls are:
1. Inquiries of appropriate entity personnel. Although an inquiry is not generally a strong source of evidence about the effective operation of controls, it is an appropriate source of evidence (e.g., inquiries of the computer librarian).
2. Inspection of documents, records, and reports; i.e., the auditor examines a customer order and the related approved sales order to ensure that they are complete and properly matched, and that the required signatures or initials are present.
3. Observation - segregation of duties relies on specific persons performing specific tasks. As such, the auditor generally observes them being applied.
4. Reperformance involves control-related activities for which there are related documents and records, but that contain insufficient data for the auditor's purpose of assessing whether the controls are operating effectively; i.e., client personnel fail to indicate if they have verified prices on a sales invoice to a standard price list. As such, the auditor would reperform the control activity to ascertain that proper results were obtained.

Audit evidence concerning segregation of duties ordinarily is best obtained by observing the employees as they apply control procedures.

Answer choice "A" is incorrect because tests of transactions to corroborate management's financial statement assertions are substantive tests, and not tests of controls.

Answer choice "C" is incorrect because obtaining flowcharts involves inspection. As such, it would indicate whether segregation of duties should exist, but would not provide evidence as to whether segregation of duties actually exists.

Answer choice "D" is incorrect because audit objectives relate to management's assertions and not to reducing control risk.

69. B The auditor should obtain a sufficient understanding of each of the three elements of the entity's internal control structure (i.e.,

control environment, accounting system, and control procedures) to plan the audit of the entity's financial statements. The understanding <u>should</u> <u>include</u> <u>knowledge</u> <u>about</u> <u>the</u> <u>design</u> <u>of</u> relevant <u>policies</u>, <u>procedures</u>, and records, and whether they have been placed in operation by the client.

The fact that an internal control structure policy or procedure has been placed in operation has no bearing on its operating effectiveness. In obtaining knowledge about whether policies, procedures, or records have been placed in operation, the auditor must determine if the client is using them. On the other hand, operating effectiveness is concerned with the consistency with which they were applied, and by whom. As such, when obtaining an understanding of the internal control structure, <u>the</u> <u>auditor</u> <u>is</u> <u>not</u> <u>required</u> <u>to</u> <u>obtain</u> <u>knowledge</u> <u>about</u> <u>the</u> <u>operating</u> <u>effectiveness</u> <u>of</u> <u>policies</u> <u>and</u> <u>procedures</u>.

Answer choices other than "B" are incorrect because they are based on illogical combinations and/or incorrect assumptions.

70. B Assessing control risk is the process of evaluating the effectiveness of an entity's internal control structure policies and procedures in preventing or detecting material misstatements in the financial statements.

Control risk is the risk that a material misstatement that could occur in an assertion will not be prevented or detected on a timely basis by an entity's internal control structure.

After obtaining an understanding of the internal control structure, the auditor may assess control risk at the maximum level.

The auditor may assess control risk at the maximum level (i.e., 100 percent, which is the greatest probability that a material misstatement in a financial statement assertion will not be prevented or detected by an entity's internal control structure) for some or all assertions because the auditor believes that:
1. Policies and procedures are unlikely to pertain to an assertion.
2. Policies and procedures are unlikely to be effective.
3. Evaluating the effectiveness of the policies and procedures would be inefficient.

Assessing control risk at below the maximum level involves:
1. <u>Identifying</u> <u>specific</u> <u>internal</u> <u>control</u> <u>structure</u> <u>policies</u> <u>and</u> <u>procedures</u> <u>relevant</u> <u>to</u> <u>specific</u> <u>assertions</u> that are likely to prevent or detect material misstatements in those assertions.
2. Performing tests of controls to evaluate the effectiveness of such policies and procedures.

Answer choices "A" and "C" are incorrect because they involve substantive testing, which would be based on the assessed level of control risk, rather than the process of assessing control risk.

Answer choice "D" is incorrect because assessing control risk follows the assessment of inherent risk, rather than involving inherent risk.

71. C For proper functioning of internal controls, there must be a segregation of:
1. The custody of, or access to, assets from the accounting or record keeping responsibility for the assets.
2. The proper authorization of transactions from the custody of, or access to, the related assets.
3. Duties within the accounting function.
4. Operational responsibility from record keeping responsibility.

Lapping is the postponement of entries for the collection of receivables to conceal cash shortages. Cash receipts from one customer that are unrecorded are covered by the receipts from another customer; these receipts in turn are covered by other receipts. This type of irregularity can be perpetrated by a person who records receipts of cash in both the cash receipts journal and the accounts receivable ledger. Therefore, segregation of duties between receiving cash and posting the accounts receivable ledger would deter lapping of collections from customers.

Answer choice "A" is incorrect because the independent internal verification of dates of entry in the cash receipts journal with dates of daily cash summaries does not involve the accounts receivable subsidiary ledger.

Answer choice "B" is incorrect because the authorization of write-offs of uncollectible accounts by a supervisor independent of credit approval does not involve the cash receipts function.

Answer choice "D" is incorrect because supervisory comparison of daily cash summaries with the sum of the cash receipts journal entries does not consider the accounts receivable subsidiary ledger.

72. A An entity's revenue cycle consists of the activities relating to the exchange of goods and services with customers, and the collection of cash. For a merchandising company, the classes of transactions in the revenue cycle include (a) sales, (b) sales adjustments (i.e., discounts, returns, allowances, and write-offs), and (c) cash receipts. Each of the functions involved in executing sales transactions should be assigned to different departments and/or individuals.

In the question situation, the most likely result of ineffective internal controls in the revenue cycle is that final authorization of credit memos by sales personnel could permit an employee defalcation scheme. Accordingly, erroneous credit memos may be issued, and, upon collection of receipts, the legitimate higher amount may be skimmed off the top. In order to prevent such a situation, customer requests for adjustments for returned goods should be reviewed by personnel independent of sales department employees.

Answer choice "B" is incorrect because fictitious transactions would likely lead to overstatement of both revenues and receivables.

Answer choice "C" is incorrect because irregularities in recording transactions would not likely lead to a delay in goods shipped.

Answer choice "D" is incorrect because the omission of shipping documents would cause an overstatement of inventory, rather than an understatement.

73. D   Documentation is necessary for each of the major steps in the purchasing and cash disbursement functions. The documents in ordering goods and services begin with a two-part purchase requisition and a multi-part (usually 5 parts) purchase order.

One copy of the purchase requisition is sent to the accounts payable department and the other copy to the purchasing department.

Upon receipt of the purchase requisition, the purchasing department prepares a purchase order, with the original and a copy going to the vendor, and copies distributed internally to receiving, vouchers payable, and the department that made the request. On the receiving department copy, the quantity ordered is generally blacked out so that receiving clerks will take a blind count of the goods received.

Upon receipt of the merchandise by the receiving department, the receiving clerk should match the goods with the vendor's shipping document and the copy of the approved purchase order on file.

In turn, an independent count of the merchandise is made and a three-part receiving report is prepared, indicating the quantity, description of goods, and vendor name and address. Copies of the receiving report are distributed to the initiating department, purchasing department, and accounts payable.

Answer choice "A" is incorrect because the vendor's invoice is received directly by the accounts payable department.

Answer choice "B" is incorrect because the materials requisition is generally used for inventory control to request that materials be issued from the storeroom to production.

Answer choice "C" is incorrect because the bill of lading is used to document the shipment of goods.

74. B   A voucher system is often used to handle cash disbursements. A voucher system helps gain control over cash disbursements by providing a routine that (1) permits only designated departments and individuals to incur obligations that will result in cash disbursements, (2) establishes procedures for incurring such obligations, and for their verification, approval, and recording, and (3) permits checks to be issued only in payment of properly verified, approved, and recorded obligations.

Typically, upon receipt of a vendor's invoice (which includes an attached remittance advice), the invoice is checked for mathematical accuracy by the vouchers (accounts) payable department, and then matched against copies of the receiving report, inspection report, purchase order, and purchase requisition. This procedure provides the most effective assurance that recorded purchases are free of material misstatements.

The accounting department is then in a position to approve the invoice, and a voucher (i.e., a request for payment) is prepared. The entire voucher package is then checked and approved by a responsible individual in the vouchers (accounts) payable department, and the amount is posted to the expense ledger.

After being approved for payment and recorded, a voucher is filed until its due date, at which time it is sent to the company's cashier (i.e., treasurer's department) for payment. A check is then prepared and signed by the treasurer's department. In turn, the check signer should control the mailing of the check and the related remittance advice. The voucher package is then canceled by the treasurer's department and sent back to the vouchers (accounts) payable department for filing.

Thus, mailing disbursement checks and remittance advices should be controlled by the employee who <u>signs</u> <u>the</u> <u>checks</u> <u>last</u>.

Answer choices "A" and "C" are incorrect because they are functions of the vouchers (accounts) payable department, which has no responsibility to sign checks, mail checks, or mail remittance advices.

Answer choice "D" is incorrect because this function would not be performed by the individual who mailed the checks.

75. C The first standard of field work indicates that the audit is to be adequately planned and assistants, if any, are to be properly supervised.

Planning of the audit involves developing an overall strategy for the expected conduct and scope of the audit. Adequate planning includes the auditor's acquiring an understanding of the client's business, its organization, the location of its facilities, the products sold or services rendered, its financial structure, etc. To acquire the requisite level of knowledge, the auditor makes use of any prior experience with the client or the industry, including the review of prior years' audit work papers, financial statements, and auditor's reports. Discussions on matters that potentially could influence the audit should be held with audit and nonaudit personnel. Discussions with management personnel will prove to be an important source of information, as will a review of interim financial statements. The auditor should coordinate the assistance of client personnel, including the internal auditor and any anticipated use of consultants. All planning should be well documented and should include an audit program.

The client's internal control structure has a major impact on the design of the audit program. The auditor should plan to perform audit steps on a timely basis. However, selecting a sample of vendors' invoices for comparison to receiving reports would be a substantive test in gathering evidence; it is least likely to be done in the planning for the audit.

Answer choices other than "C" are incorrect because they are procedures the auditor would likely perform in planning a financial statement audit.

76.   A   The basis for the answer to this question is SAS #47, "Audit Risk and Materiality in Conducting an Audit." The definitions of the various types of risks described in SAS #47 are as follows:
Audit risk - the risk that the auditor may unknowingly fail to appropriately modify his or her opinion on financial statements that are materially misstated. Audit risk consists of inherent risk, control risk, and detection risk.
Inherent risk - the susceptibility of an assertion to a material misstatement, assuming there are no related internal control structure policies or procedures.
Control risk - the risk that a material misstatement that could occur in an assertion will not be prevented or detected on a timely basis by an entity's internal control structure policies or procedures.
Detection risk - the risk that the auditor will not detect a material misstatement that exists in an assertion.

Detection risk should bear an inverse relationship to inherent and control risks. That is, the lesser the inherent and control risk the auditor believes exists, the greater the detection risk he or she can accept, and vice versa.

Control risk, detection risk, and inherent risk may be assessed in nonquantitative terms that range, for example, from a minimum to a maximum, or in quantitative terms, such as percentages.

Answer choices other than "A" are incorrect because each answer precludes one of the risk components being assessed in nonquantitative terms.

77.   D   The competence of an internal auditor may be judged utilizing the following procedures.
1. Inquire about qualifications of the internal audit staff, including education, professional experience, and/or certification.
2. Consider audit policies, programs, and procedures.
3. Inquire about assignments, supervision, and review.

Based on the foregoing, the competence of the internal auditor would not be based on access to information about related parties.

Answer choices other than "D" are incorrect because they all represent matters for which the CPA would normally obtain information as a basis for assessing the competence of the internal auditor.

78. A Analytical procedures can be used as substantive tests designed to evaluate the reasonableness of financial information. They are performed by studying and comparing relationships among data. Analytical procedures involve comparisons of recorded amounts, or ratios developed from recorded amounts, to expectations developed by the auditor, including the following.
    1. Comparison of the current-year financial information with the financial information of a comparable prior period or periods.
    2. Comparison of the financial information with anticipated results (e.g., budgets and forecasts).
    3. Study of the relationships among elements of financial information that would be expected to conform to a predictable pattern based on the entity's experience.
    4. Comparison of financial information with similar information regarding the industry in which the entity operates.
    5. Study of the relationships of the financial information with relevant nonfinancial information.

    Analytical procedures applied to long-term investments to ascertain the reasonableness of the <u>completeness of recorded investment income</u> would be accomplished by comparing the ratio of investment income (i.e., dividends and interest) to balances in investment accounts for current and prior years.

    Answer choices other than "A" are incorrect because audit procedures other than analytical procedures would be used to ascertain the audit objectives listed.

79. B Analytical procedures consist of evaluations of financial information made by a study of plausible relationships among both financial and nonfinancial data. A basic premise underlying the application of analytical procedures is that these plausible relationships among data may reasonably be expected to exist and continue in the absence of known conditions to the contrary.

    Analytical procedures should be used to assist the auditor in planning the nature, timing, and extent of other auditing procedures. They may be used in substantive testing to obtain evidential matter, and should be used as an overall review of the financial information in the final review stage of the audit.

    Analytical procedures involve comparisons of recorded amounts, or ratios developed from recorded amounts, to expectations developed by the auditor, including the following.
    1. Comparison of the current-year financial information with the financial information of a comparable prior period or periods.
    2. Comparison of financial information with anticipated results (e.g., budgets and forecasts).

3. Study of the relationships among elements of financial information that would be expected to conform to a predictable pattern based on the entity's experience.
4. Comparison of financial information with similar information regarding the industry in which the entity operates.
5. Study of the relationships of the financial information with relevant nonfinancial information (e.g., number of units produced).

Based on the foregoing, analytical procedures used in planning an audit generally use data aggregated at a high level.

Answer choice "A" is incorrect because analytical procedures involve comparisons of recorded amounts, or ratios developed from recorded amounts, to expectations developed by the auditor.

Answer choice "C" is incorrect because analytical procedures may not be used in lieu of tests of controls.

Answer choice "D" is incorrect because, for some assertions, analytical procedures may be more effective than tests of details and transactions.

80. D Working papers are generally filed under two categories: (1) current files and (2) permanent files. The current files contain corroborating information pertaining only to the execution of the current year's audit. The permanent files contain data that are expected to be useful to the auditor during current and future engagements.

Items contained in the permanent files include:
1. Copies of articles of incorporation and bylaws.
2. Organization charts.
3. Plant layouts and descriptions of manufacturing processes.
4. Details (analyses) of capital stock (and other owners' equity accounts) and bond issues.
5. Charts of accounts.
6. Narrative descriptions and flowcharts of the client's internal control structure.
7. Copies of pension plans, lease agreements, bond and note indentures, etc.
8. Summaries of accounting principles used by the client.

Items contained in the current files include:
1. Schedules and analyses of accounts.
2. An audit program.
3. Correspondence with third parties confirming balances, transactions, and other data.
4. Schedule of time spent on the engagement by each individual auditor.
5. A copy of the current year's financial statements.
6. Review notes pertaining to questions and comments regarding the audit work performed.

As noted above, the permanent files generally should include <u>analyses</u> <u>of</u> <u>capital</u> <u>stock</u> <u>and</u> <u>other</u> <u>owners'</u> <u>equity</u> <u>accounts</u>.

Answer choices other than "D" are incorrect because they represent items that should be included in the current files and not the permanent files.

81. B Segregation of functions is a necessary characteristic of an effective internal control structure. Such control is present when the authorization, recording, and custodial functions are segregated from one another.

The primary functions of the receiving clerk are counting, inspecting, and noting quantities and conditions as a basis for later determining the credit to be given to the customer, and whether the goods need repair or can be placed back in stock. Receipt of goods returned for credit should be handled by the receiving clerk. Therefore, defective merchandise returned by customers should be presented initially to the <u>receiving</u> <u>clerk</u>.

Answer choices other than "B" are incorrect because they refer to personnel engaged in activities that are all separate and apart from the receiving function. None of the persons indicated should receive merchandise.

82. D A special type of significant uncertainty concerns the ability of a client company to continue as a going concern. When a question arises about an entity's continued existence, the auditor should consider mitigating factors. These factors relate primarily to an entity's alternative means for maintaining adequate cash flows. The following factors might be considered.
  1. <u>Assets</u>
      a. Marketability of assets that management plans to sell.
      b. Leasing, rather than purchasing, certain assets.
      c. Using assets for factoring or sale-leaseback arrangements.
  2. <u>Debts</u>
      a. Availability of unused credit lines or similar borrowing capacity.
      b. Capacity of extending the due dates of existing loans.
      c. Entering into debt-restricting agreements.
  3. <u>Equity</u>
      a. Reducing dividends.
      b. Obtaining additional equity capital.

As indicated by point "3-a," <u>negotiating</u> <u>reductions</u> <u>in</u> <u>required</u> <u>dividends</u> <u>being</u> <u>paid</u> <u>on</u> <u>preferred</u> <u>stock</u> would improve cash flows and, as such, would represent a mitigating factor that Davis would most likely consider.

Answer choices other than "D" are incorrect because they represent actions that would worsen cash flows and, accordingly, would not represent mitigating factors.

83.   D   Audit evidence must be both competent (valid and relevant) and sufficient. With respect to the validity of evidential matter:

1.   Evidence obtained from independent external sources is more reliable than that secured from within the entity.
2.   The presence of good internal control adds to the validity of the evidential matter.
3.   Computations made by the auditor are more persuasive than those made by the client.

Therefore, <u>inspection of bank statements obtained directly from the client's financial institution</u> represents an externally generated source of evidence that is more reliable than evidence generated from within the entity.

Answer choices "A" and "B" are incorrect because the evidence is secured from within the entity.

Answer choice "C" is incorrect because analytical procedures are applied to evidence secured from within the entity.

84.   D   Assertions are management representations embodied in financial statement components. They can be classified as to:

1.   <u>Existence or occurrence</u> - deals with whether assets or liabilities of the entity exist at a given date, or whether recorded transactions have occurred during a given period.
2.   <u>Completeness</u> - deals with whether all transactions and accounts that should be presented in the financial statements are included.
3.   <u>Rights and obligations</u> - deals with whether assets are the rights of the entity (i.e., owned) at a given time.
4.   <u>Valuation or allocation</u> - deals with whether asset, liability, revenue, or expense components have been included in the financial statements at the appropriate amounts.
5.   <u>Presentation and disclosure</u> - deals with whether particular components of the financial statements are properly classified, described, and disclosed.

In the question situation, by reviewing the periodic accounting for the numerical sequence of shipping documents and invoices, the auditor could determine whether each shipment was supported by a sales invoice; this would provide the auditor with support for management's assertion of <u>completeness</u>.

Answer choices other than "D" are incorrect because the periodic accounting for the numerical sequence of documents does not provide support for the assertions provided.

85.   C   Observing the count of the physical inventory is not likely to reveal either the existence of inventory held on consignment by others or the existence of goods in transit. Verifying that <u>all inventory owned by the client is on hand at the time of the count</u> is usually unlikely, and, therefore, is not one of the independent auditor's objectives regarding the audit of inventories. Alternative

procedures must be used by the auditor to gain satisfaction as to the existence of goods in transit and goods held by others on consignment.

Answer choice "A" is incorrect because the auditor's overall objective in auditing inventories is to determine whether inventories are presented fairly (appropriately) in the financial statements.

Answer choice "B" is incorrect because obsolete and damaged items will affect the valuation of inventories.

Answer choice "D" is incorrect because the auditor must ascertain that inventories are priced correctly.

86. B   Management's assertion about valuation or allocation deals with whether asset, liability, revenue, or expense components have been included in the financial statements at the appropriate amounts. For the allowance for doubtful accounts, management asserts that the allowance has been properly established, and accounts receivable are stated at net realizable value. The auditor's analysis would provide evidence concerning the reasonableness of the allowance based on an aging of receivables, credit and collection files, previous years' experience, review of write-offs, and other factors. The auditor's objective is to obtain evidence for management's assertion concerning proper <u>valuation</u> <u>or</u> <u>allocation</u> of the allowance and its impact on the related bad-debt expense and accounts receivable accounts.

Answer choice "A" is incorrect because management's assertion of existence or occurrence relates to the validity of recorded accounts receivable and allowance for doubtful account balances, or whether transactions have actually occurred. To obtain evidence pertaining to the assertion of existence or occurrence, the auditor would use the confirmation process.

Answer choice "C" is incorrect because management's assertion of completeness relates to whether all accounts receivable have been recorded as a basis to determine the aging for valuation purposes.

Answer choice "D" is incorrect because management's assertion of rights and obligations pertaining to accounts receivable would principally relate to whether the accounts receivable are owned by the client, and whether any commitments or other restrictions concerning receivables exist.

87. B   In accordance with SAS #11, "Using the Work of a Specialist," a specialist is one who possesses special skill or knowledge in a field other than accounting or auditing; i.e., an actuary, appraiser, engineer, etc.

When expressing an unqualified opinion, the auditor should generally not refer to the work or findings of a specialist. Such reference might be construed as a qualification of the auditor's opinion or a division of responsibility, neither of which is intended. A matter that has not been resolved between the auditor and the specialist may lead to a qualified, adverse, or disclaimer of opinion. It should be understood that a modification of the auditor's opinion may arise because of the inability to obtain sufficient competent evidential matter (i.e., a scope limitation) or, because after obtaining the findings of a specialist, the auditor may conclude that the representations in the financial statements are not in conformity with GAAP.

If the <u>auditor</u>, <u>as</u> <u>a</u> <u>result</u> <u>of</u> <u>the</u> report or <u>findings</u> <u>of</u> <u>the</u> <u>specialist</u>, <u>decides</u> <u>to</u> (1) <u>add</u> <u>an</u> <u>explanatory</u> <u>paragraph</u> <u>describing</u> <u>an</u> <u>uncertainty</u>, (2) add an explanatory paragraph describing his or her substantial doubt about the entity's ability to continue as a going concern, (3) add an explanatory paragraph to emphasize a matter regarding the financial statements, or (4) depart from an unqualified opinion, reference to and identification of the specialist may be made in the auditor's report if the auditor believes such reference will facilitate an understanding of the reason for the explanatory paragraph or the departure from the unqualified opinion.

Answer choice "A" is incorrect because the auditor should not refer to the specialist merely because the specialist's work provides the auditor greater assurance of reliability.

Answer choice "C" is incorrect because the auditor's use of the specialist's findings is based on the current-year understanding between the auditor, the specialist, and the client, and not on the use made in prior years.

Answer choice "D" is incorrect because a specialist does not have to be independent of the client. This is permissible and should be documented in the working papers, but should not be referred to in the auditor's report.

88. B A standard confirmation request should be sent to all banks in which the client has an account, including those accounts that may have a zero balance at the end of the year. Such communications may disclose the existence of a balance in the account. The standard confirmation request extends beyond the verification of the actual cash balances. The confirmation requests not only the cash balances on deposit as of the balance sheet date, and any applicable interest rate(s), but also information pertaining to direct indebtedness to the bank. Accordingly, the primary purpose is to <u>corroborate information</u> <u>regarding</u> <u>deposit</u> <u>and</u> <u>loan</u> <u>balances</u>.

Answer choice "A" is incorrect because the detection of kiting is in no way assured by the use of confirmations. Kiting is a method used to cover a cash shortage. It involves writing a check on one bank account and depositing it in another just before the end of the accounting period.

Answer choice "C" is incorrect because the data necessary to prepare a proof of cash is usually derived from the bank statement, cash receipts and cash disbursements journals, and the general ledger.

Answer choice "D" is incorrect because information about contingent liabilities and secured transactions cannot be confirmed by using the "Standard Form to Confirm Account Balance Information with Financial Institutions"; rather, the auditor must request this information in a separate communication.

89. D   Confirmations represent written evidence received directly by the auditor from an independent third party verifying the accuracy of information. Confirmation of accounts receivable balances provides primary evidence as to the rights and obligations and existence assertions.

Since confirmations come from sources independent of the client, they are the most highly regarded type of evidential matter. Therefore, when the auditor does not receive replies to second requests for accounts receivable confirmations, the existence of the accounts receivable balances is uncertain. Consequently, the auditor would most likely <u>inspect</u> <u>the</u> <u>shipping</u> <u>records</u> <u>documenting</u> <u>the</u> <u>merchandise</u> <u>sold</u> <u>to</u> <u>the</u> <u>debtors</u>.

Answer choice "A" is incorrect because the auditor should review the cash receipts journal for payments received from customers after year-end.

Answer choice "B" is incorrect because the study of the internal control structure would not provide evidence concerning accounts receivable.

Answer choice "C" is incorrect because the auditor might decrease, and not increase, the level of detection risk for the existence assertion.

90. C   An auditor performs substantive tests of details on payroll transactions and balances based on the assessed level of control risk for payroll. Substantive tests may be performed when payroll has a significant effect on manufactured inventory, or when the internal control structure for payroll is weak. To aid this determination, analytical procedures are useful.

Analytical procedures consist of evaluations of financial information made by a study of plausible relationships among both financial and nonfinancial data. A basic premise underlying the application of analytical procedures is that these plausible relationships among data may reasonably be expected to exist and continue in the absence of known conditions to the contrary.

Analytical procedures should be used to assist the auditor in planning the nature, timing, and extent of other auditing procedures. Relationships in a stable environment are usually more predictable than relationships in a dynamic or unstable environment. Relationships involving income statement accounts that are not subject to management discretion, such as payroll expense, tend to be more predictable than relationships involving only balance sheet accounts, since income statement accounts represent transactions over a period of time, whereas balance sheet accounts represent amounts as of a particular point in time. In performing analytical procedures, the auditor should evaluate significant unexpected fluctuations.

In light of the foregoing, the auditor most likely would perform substantive tests of details on payroll transactions and balances when <u>analytical procedures indicate unusual fluctuations in recurring payroll entries</u>.

Answer choices "A" and "D" are incorrect because accrued payroll expense is a typical liability at the end of the accounting period.

Answer choice "B" is incorrect because if the assessed level of control risk is low, the auditor is less likely to perform substantive tests.

OTHER OBJECTIVE FORMATS/ESSAY QUESTIONS

Answer 2

61. C   The current period report should include a fourth (separate) paragraph describing the responsibility assumed for the audit of the prior period.

62. I   The balance sheet and related statements of income, retained earnings, and cash flows are all properly identified.

63. I   The American Institute of Certified Public Accountants should be identified as the source of the review standards.

64. I   A review report does not explicitly state the accountant's responsibility; further, the auditor's responsibilities are discussed in the fourth (separate) paragraph.

65. I   The scope of the review is properly described in the second (scope) paragraph.

66. I   The term "limited," rather than "negative," assurance applies to a review; further, such assurance should be expressed in the third paragraph. (As an aside "negative" assurance is used in connection with audit engagements; otherwise, the two terms are synonymous.)

67. C   The second (scope) paragraph should also contain the sentence: "Accordingly, we do not express such an opinion."

68. C The phrase "in order for them to be in conformity with generally accepted accounting principles" should be added to the first sentence in the third paragraph.

69. C Distribution of a review report may not be limited.

70. I The report as drafted, correctly refers to the phrase "material modifications."

71. C The fourth (separate) paragraph should indicate the date of the previous report and the type of opinion expressed.

72. C The fourth (separate) paragraph should state that no additional auditing procedures were performed after the date of the report on the prior years' financial statements.

73. C The fourth (separate) paragraph should describe the responsibility assumed for the prior period, inclusive of the date and type of opinion expressed in the previous report, and state that no additional auditing procedures were performed.

Answer 3

74. E To determine that investments are properly described and classified in the financial statements, the auditor should verify that transfers from the current to the noncurrent investment portfolio have been properly recorded.

75. F To ascertain that recorded investments represent investments actually owned at the balance sheet date, the auditor should obtain positive confirmations as of the balance sheet date of investments held by independent custodians.

76. D To gain audit satisfaction that investments are properly valued at the lower of cost or market at the balance sheet date, the auditor should determine that any impairments in the price of investments have been properly recorded.

77. B To verify that accounts receivable represent all amounts owed to the entity at the balance sheet date, the auditor should perform sales cut-off tests to obtain assurance that sales transactions and corresponding entries for inventories and cost of goods sold are recorded in the same and proper period.

78. E To determine that the entity has legal right to all accounts receivable at the balance sheet date, the auditor should review loan agreements for indications of whether accounts receivable have been factored or pledged.

79. C To determine that accounts receivable are stated at net realizable value, the auditor should review the aged trial balance for significant past due accounts.

80.   F   To ascertain that accounts receivable are properly described and presented in the financial statements, the auditor should review the accounts receivable trial balance for amounts due from officers and employees.

81.   D   To verify that the entity has legal right to property and equipment acquired during the year, the auditor should examine deeds and title insurance certificates.

82.   G   To determine that recorded property and equipment represent assets that actually exist at the balance sheet date, the auditor should physically examine all major property and equipment additions.

83.   B   To gain audit satisfaction that net property and equipment are properly valued at the balance sheet date, the auditor should review the provision for depreciation expense and determine that depreciable lives and methods used in the current year are consistent with those used in the prior year.

Answer 4

Part 4(a)
In general, if the financial statements are materially affected by an irregularity, or the effects of the irregularity cannot be ascertained, the auditor should:
1.   Consider the implications for other aspects of the audit.
2.   Discuss the matter and the approach to further investigation with an appropriate level of management at least one level above those involved.
3.   Attempt to obtain sufficient evidential matter to determine whether, in fact, material irregularities exist and, if so, their effect.
4.   If appropriate, suggest that the client consult with legal counsel on matters concerning questions of law.

Part 4(b)
If the auditor is precluded from applying necessary procedures in searching for irregularities, or is unable to conclude whether possible irregularities may materially affect the financial statements, then the auditor's responsibility for reporting on the client's financial statements and other communications is to disclaim or qualify an opinion.

The auditor should also communicate findings to the audit committee or board of directors.

The auditor should consider withdrawing from the engagement if the client refuses to accept the auditor's report, as modified, in these circumstances.

The auditor should communicate the reasons for withdrawal to the audit committee or board of directors.

Part 4(c)
If the auditor concludes that the client's financial statements are materially affected by irregularities, then the auditor's responsibility for reporting on the client's financial statements and other communications is to insist that the financial statements be revised.

If they are not revised, the auditor should express a qualified or adverse opinion.

Part 4(d)
All irregularities, except those that are clearly inconsequential, should be communicated to the audit committee or board of directors.

The auditor may have a duty to disclose irregularities to third parties outside the client's management and its audit committee in the following circumstances.
1.   When a successor auditor makes inquiries of a predecessor auditor.
2.   When the auditor responds to a subpoena.
3.   When the entity reports an auditor change under the appropriate securities law.

Answer 5

<u>Young Computer Outlets, Inc.</u>
<u>PAYROLL</u>
<u>Internal Control Questionnaire</u>

<u>Question</u>   <u>YES</u>   <u>NO</u>

1.   Are the following duties appropriately segregated?
     a.   Personnel-hiring authorization.
     b.   Payroll preparation.
     c.   Payroll approval.
     d.   Payroll check distribution.
     e.   Payroll records.
     f.   Payroll bank reconciliation.
2.   Are the following appropriately authorized?
     a.   Hires.
     b.   Terminations.
     c.   Wage rates.
3.   Do policies exist for vacations, holidays, leave, etc.?
4.   Are time changes in employment status recorded and
     maintained by someone outside the payroll
     processing function?
5.   Are time and attendance records approved by
     nonaccounting personnel?
6.   Does the payroll register accompany checks
     for signature?
7.   Are payroll registers reviewed and initialed by
     the check signer?
8.   Are all disbursements made by prenumbered checks
     and accounted for? (<u>given</u> <u>as</u> <u>example</u> <u>in</u> <u>question</u>)
9.   Must two persons sign each payroll check, or all
     checks over a certain amount?
10. Is the number of authorized signatures on each
     payroll check limited to the minimum practical number?
11. Are signed checks distributed promptly under the
     control of the check signer?
12. Is the payroll register, initialed by the check
     signer, compared with the payroll summary prepared
     by the payroll processing function for use in
     posting the general ledger?
13. Is the summary of the payroll register posted to
     the general ledger by a person independent of the
     payroll processing, check signing, and
     authorization functions?
14. Are unclaimed payroll checks controlled by an
     individual not involved in payroll processing,
     check signing, or distribution functions?
15. Is payroll classified in proper accounts
     (e.g., by function) and is classification
     periodically reviewed?

Accounting & Reporting—Taxation, Managerial, and Governmental and Not-for-Profit Organizations (ARE)

FOUR-OPTION MULTIPLE-CHOICE QUESTIONS

Answer 1

1. C   In general, losses from passive activities may only be used to offset income from such activities. Accordingly, passive losses may not be offset against earned income (such as wage income) or portfolio income (which includes interest and dividends). Passive losses that are not deductible in the current year by virtue of this rule may be carried forward indefinitely, but may only offset passive income in future years.

    If a taxpayer disposes of the interest in the passive activity, all loss carryforwards may be used to offset the taxpayer's entire income. This benefit is only available if the disposition of the interest resulted in a taxable transaction.

    Passive activities are those activities that involve the conduct of any trade or business and in which the taxpayer does not materially participate. Additionally, passive activities include any rental activity (even those in which the taxpayer materially participates), and any activity conducted by a limited partnership.

    A taxpayer is considered to be materially participating in an activity if the taxpayer is involved in the operations of the activity on a regular, continuous, and substantial basis.

    The rule limiting the allowability of passive activity losses as well as credits applies to individuals, closely-held C corporations, and to <u>personal</u> <u>service</u> <u>corporations</u>.

    Answer choice "A" is incorrect since partnerships generally are not subject to the passive activity rules. Partners, however, are subject to the passive activity rules on items passed through to them by partnerships.

    Answer choice "B" is incorrect since S corporations, like partnerships, are not subject to the passive activity rules; S corporation shareholders, on the other hand, are subject to such rules.

    Answer choice "D" is incorrect since closely-held C corporations, and not widely-held C corporations, are subject to the passive activity rules.

2. B   The dividends-received deduction is generally 70 percent (80 percent as to dividends received from a 20 percent-or-more-owned corporation) of dividends received from taxable domestic corporations limited to 70 percent (80 percent as noted) of the

corporation's taxable income computed without regard to the dividends-received deduction and net operating loss deduction.

If a corporation sustains a net operating loss for the year, the limitation of 70 percent (80 percent as noted) of taxable income does not apply.

The 70 percent (80 percent as noted) of taxable income limitation will not apply if the full dividends-received deduction results in a net operating loss.

Dividends-received deductions for "affiliated corporations" are subject to different rules. Under certain circumstances, 100 percent of such dividends may be excluded.

It should be noted that the corporate dividends-received deduction is allowed only <u>if the investor corporation owns the investee's stock for a specified minimum holding period</u>, which in general is at least 46 days.

Answer choice "A" is incorrect since a corporation's dividends-received deduction may generally not exceed the applicable percentage of the recipient shareholder's taxable income.

Answer choice "C" is incorrect because the percentage of the investee's stock owned by the investor corporation governs the percentage applicable to the dividends-received deduction.

Answer choice "D" is incorrect since the dividends-received deduction is available only to C corporations. S corporations may not claim the dividends-received deduction.

3.   D   A corporation may claim a deduction for charitable contributions made in cash or property. The deduction is limited to 10 percent of taxable income without taking into account:
1. The deduction for contributions.
2. The dividends-received deduction.
3. Any net operating loss carryback to the tax year.
4. Any capital loss carryback to the tax year.

Any charitable contributions made during the year in excess of the limitation may be carried over five (5) succeeding years. However, contributions actually made during the later year plus the carryover must fall within the limitation. Any excess not used up within the five-year period is lost forever. Also, a contributions carryover is not allowed to the extent that it increases a net operating loss carryover.

An accrual basis taxpayer may elect to deduct contributions authorized by the Board of Directors but not paid during the tax year if payment is made within 2-1/2 months after close of the tax year.

In view of the above, when Nale computes the maximum allowable deduction for contributions in its 1993 return, <u>Nale</u> <u>must</u> <u>include</u> <u>the</u> <u>full</u> <u>amount</u> <u>of</u> <u>the</u> <u>dividends</u> <u>received</u>, <u>or</u> <u>$1,000</u>.

Answer choices other than "D" are based on assumptions that are not valid under current tax law.

4. A   In general, foreign income taxes paid by a corporation <u>may</u> <u>be</u> <u>claimed</u> <u>either</u> <u>as</u> <u>a</u> <u>deduction</u> <u>or</u> <u>as</u> <u>a</u> <u>credit</u>, <u>at</u> <u>the</u> <u>option</u> <u>of</u> <u>the</u> <u>corporation</u>.

If the foreign tax credit is elected, the credit may not reduce the U.S. tax liability on income from U.S. sources. The computation to determine the allowable credit is:

$$\frac{\text{Foreign source income}}{\text{Worldwide income}} \times \text{Tentative U.S. liability} = \text{Foreign Tax Credit}$$

It should be understood that the election to claim the foreign tax credit is usually more advantageous, since a tax credit reduces a taxpayer's liability on a dollar-for-dollar basis.

Answer choices other than "A" are based on assumptions that are not valid under current tax law.

5. C   In general, the special deductions available to a C Corporation are the net operating loss deduction and the dividends-received deduction.

The dividends-received deduction is generally 70 percent (80 percent as to dividends received from a 20 percent-or-more-owned corporation) of dividends received from taxable domestic corporations limited to 70 percent (80 percent as noted) of the corporation's taxable income computed without regard to the dividends-received deduction and net operating loss deduction.

If a corporation sustains a net operating loss for the year, the limitation of 70 percent (80 percent as noted) of taxable income does not apply.

The 70 percent (80 percent as noted) of taxable income limitation will not apply if the full dividends-received deduction results in a net operating loss.

Dividends-received deductions for "affiliated corporations" are subject to different rules. Under certain circumstances, 100 percent of such dividends may be excluded.

It should be noted that the corporate dividends-received deduction is allowed only if the investor corporation owns the investee's stock for a minimum holding period, which in general is at least 46 days.

In general, a corporation's net operating loss is determined by making the following adjustments to the net loss on a tax return.
1. No deduction is allowed for any net operating loss carryover or carryback from another year.
2. The deduction for dividends received is permitted without regard to the provision that otherwise limits it.

In view of the above, Acorn should report $275,000 as income before special deductions, which is equal to gross profit of $250,000 (i.e., $500,000 - $250,000) plus the $25,000 of dividends received.

Answer choice "A" is incorrect because the cost of sales is not claimed as a deduction, and should be.

Answer choice "B" is incorrect because it erroneously includes 20 percent of the dividends received (i.e., 20 percent of $25,000, or $5,000) and it fails to claim cost of sales as a deduction.

Answer choice "D" is incorrect because it does not include the dividends received as income before special deductions.

6.   D   Amounts received as rent must be included in gross income. Advance rental receipts must also be included in gross income regardless of the period covered or the method of accounting used (i.e., cash basis or accrual basis). An accrual-basis taxpayer must reflect income on the accrual basis, without regard to the fact that advance rentals must also be included as revenue. Thus, an increase in rent receivable represents revenue to an accrual-basis taxpayer.

Receipt of a security deposit is not included in gross income if the lessor plans to return it to the tenant at the end of the lease. If, during the course of the lease, the lessor keeps part or all of the security deposit because the tenant breaks a term of the lease, then the amount retained is treated as rental income.

Finally, if an amount called a security deposit is to be used as a final payment of the rent, it is considered to be advance rent and therefore includible in income in the year received.

Ace's 1993 rent revenue would therefore be $65,000, which includes the $50,000 in rent payments, the $5,000 nonrefundable rent deposits, and the $10,000 increase in rents receivable (i.e., $35,000 - $25,000), which represents revenue to an accrual basis taxpayer).

Answer choice "A" is incorrect because it does not include the $5,000 nonrefundable rent deposits or the $10,000 increase in rents receivable, and both should be included.

Answer choice "B" is incorrect because it does not include the $10,000 increase in rents receivable.

Answer choice "C" is incorrect because it fails to include the $5,000 nonrefundable rent deposits.

7.   D   A group of affiliated corporations may file consolidated tax returns for the period that they are affiliated, but only if all the corporations that were members of the affiliated group at any time during the tax year consent before the last day for filing the return.

An affiliated group may be defined as one or more chains of includible corporations connected through stock ownership with a common parent corporation which is an includible corporation, but only if (1) the common parent owns stock possessing at least 80 percent of the total voting power and at least 80 percent of the total value of the stock of at least one includible corporation, and (2) stock meeting the 80 percent requirement in each of the includible corporations (except the common parent) is owned directly by one or more of the other includible corporations.

An "includible corporation" means all corporations except: (1) exempt corporations, (2) life insurance or mutual insurance companies, (3) foreign corporations, (4) corporations with 80 percent income from U.S. possessions, (5) regulated investment companies, (6) real estate investment trusts, and (7) certain domestic international sales corporations (DISCS).

Logically, affiliated corporations that file a consolidated tax return will not be taxed on dividends paid from one includible corporation to another. (Practically, this is as a result of the intercompany eliminations necessary to prevent double taxation.)

(Affiliated corporations that do not file a consolidated tax return similarly are entitled to a 100-percent-dividends-received deduction for qualifying dividends received from members of the affiliated group.)

Answer choices other than "D" are clearly based on incorrect assumptions.

8.   D   A corporation's organization costs may be amortized over a period of not less than 60 months (i.e., the "shortest period allowed") by a newly organized corporation that elects to do so. Failing the election, the amount is deductible only upon liquidation.

Organization costs do not include expenses for the sale or issuance of stock or securities.

Brown's only amortizable organizational costs are the $40,000 of legal fees to obtain the corporate charter.

Since Brown began operations on July 1, 1993, it is entitled to deduct amortization for six months. Brown should deduct $4,000 (i.e., 6/60 × $40,000) for the amortization of organizational expenses in 1993.

Answer choice "A" is incorrect because it reflects amortization of the legal fees for a full year (i.e., $40,000 × 12/60 equals $8,000).

Answer choices "B" and "C" are incorrect because they include amortization of the commission paid to the underwriter and/or the other stock issue costs, and should not.

9.   C   A corporation may claim a deduction for charitable contributions made in cash or property. The deduction is limited to 10 percent of taxable income without taking into account:
1. The deduction for contributions.
2. The dividends-received deduction.
3. Any net operating loss carryback to the tax year.
4. Any capital loss carryback to the tax year.

Any charitable contributions made during the year in excess of the 10 percent limitation may be carried over five succeeding years. However, contributions actually made during the later years plus the carryover must fall within the 10 percent limit. Any excess not used up within the five-year period is lost forever. Also, a contributions carryover is not allowed to the extent that it increases a net operating loss carryover.

An accrual basis taxpayer may elect to deduct contributions authorized by the Board of Directors but not paid during the tax year if payment is made within 2-1/2 months after close of the tax year.

The $410,000 taxable income before deducting charitable contributions includes a $20,000 dividends-received deduction, which must be added back in order to calculate the maximum contributions deduction. As such, the maximum amount Garland can deduct would be 10 percent of $430,000 (i.e., taxable income of $410,000 plus the dividends-received deduction of $20,000), or $43,000, as charitable contributions.

(It should be noted that $43,000 is inclusive of 1993 contributions and the $5,000 carryover, and that the contributions not deductible would be carried over as discussed above.)

Answer choice "A" is incorrect because it fails to apply the 10 percent limitation to the applicable base amount, and because the carryover contributions are not considered.

Answer choice "B" is incorrect because it does not reflect the addback of the dividends-received deduction in the applicable base amount.

Answer choice "D" is incorrect because it fails to consider the 10 percent limitation of the applicable base amount.

10.   A   State and local income taxes are deductible by a corporation; refunds of state and local income taxes represent taxable income.

Amortization of the goodwill acquired in 1987, while allowable for financial statement (book) purposes, is not deductible for tax purposes. It should be noted that goodwill (like other acquired intangibles) acquired after August 10, 1993 (or July 25, 1991, if an election is made), must be amortized over a 15-year period (beginning with the month of acquisition) utilizing the straight-line method.

Cero's 1993 taxable income would therefore be $405,000 (i.e., $400,000 + $5,000).

Answer choice "B" is incorrect because the amortization of the goodwill acquired in 1987 is treated as a deductible expense for income tax purposes, and should not be.

Answer choice "C" is not logical in view of the explanation provided for answer choice "A."

Answer choice "D" is incorrect because the state income tax refunds are treated as nontaxable, and the amortization of goodwill is treated as deductible; neither is appropriate.

11. B   Corporations may deduct capital losses only to the extent of capital gains. Capital losses may never offset ordinary income.

Any capital loss that exceeds capital gains is carried back to the three years preceding the year of the loss, and if not completely absorbed, is then carried forward for up to five years succeeding the loss year. A corporation's capital loss carryback or carryforward is always treated as a short-term capital loss whether or not it was short-term when sustained.

Answer choice "A" is incorrect because long-term capital losses do not retain their character when carried back or carried forward; rather, they are treated as short-term capital losses.

Answer choice "C" is incorrect because a corporation's capital loss carryback or carryforward is never treated as a long-term capital loss.

Answer choice "D" is incorrect because a corporation's capital losses may never offset ordinary income.

12. B   An accrual-basis corporation may generally deduct compensation to nonshareholder employees authorized by the Board of Directors but not paid during the tax year if payment is made within 2-1/2 months after the close of the tax year (i.e., the due date of the tax return).

With respect to compensation to shareholder-employees, an accrual-basis corporation may claim a deduction only when payment is made and the amount involved is includible in the gross income of the recipient.

Since Soma paid actual 1993 nonshareholder bonuses in the amount of $60,000 before the March 15, 1994, due date of its corporate income tax return, it may properly deduct the $60,000 bonus, rather than the $50,000 bonus it accrued on its books.

As such, <u>Soma</u> <u>should</u> <u>deduct</u> <u>$610,000</u> <u>as</u> <u>compensation</u> <u>expense</u> (i.e., $600,000 + $60,000 - $50,000).

Answer choice "A" is incorrect because it fails to consider the actual $60,000 bonus paid; rather, it reflects the $50,000 bonus accrued for book purposes.

Answer choice "C" is incorrect because it presumes that an accrual-basis corporation may not accrue and deduct nonshareholder bonuses.

Answer choice "D" is incorrect in view of the explanation provided for choice "B."

13. D Generally, the gain or loss on intercompany transactions is attributed to the member of the affiliated group that actually earns or incurs the gain or loss. In this connection, the transaction is finalized when it passes through the affiliated group and involves an outsider.

Thus, when one member of the group sells an asset to another member at a profit in a consolidated return year, the selling member defers the gain on its books and the buying member's basis for the asset is its cost. When the buying member later sells the asset to an outsider, the selling member then reports its gain.

The character of the gain is the same as it would have been had the transaction taken place between the selling member and the outsider.

In the consolidated return <u>for</u> <u>1993</u>, <u>a</u> <u>$65,000</u> (i.e., $125,000 - $60,000) <u>gain</u> <u>should</u> <u>be</u> <u>reported</u> for the transactions involving the sale of the land. In the consolidated return <u>for</u> <u>1992</u>, <u>$0</u> <u>gain</u> <u>should</u> <u>be</u> <u>reported</u> because of the intercompany elimination of gain between the members of the affiliated group.

It is interesting to note that in 1993, Potter would report a $40,000 gain on the sale of the land (i.e., $100,000 - $60,000), and Sly would report the balance of the gain, or $25,000.

Answer choices other than "D" are based on incorrect assumptions and/or combinations.

14. B A corporation may claim a credit for income taxes paid to a foreign country. However, the foreign tax credit cannot be used to reduce the U.S. liability on income from U.S. sources.

A credit is also available for the production of fuels from nonconventional (alternative) sources, including oil from shale, certain synthetic fuels, and certain types of natural gas.

Finally, a corporation is entitled to claim the general business credit. The general business credit consists of the following components: the investment tax credit, the targeted jobs credit, the alcohol fuel credit, the incremental research credit, the low-income housing credit, the enhanced oil recovery credit, and the disabled access credit.

The computation of the alternative fuel production and general business credits can be quite complex and therefore has never been tested on the CPA exam per se.

The earned income credit is a tax credit that is available only to individual taxpayers; accordingly, a corporation cannot claim the earned income credit.

Answer choices other than "B" are incorrect because they represent credits which can be claimed by corporations.

15. A   To be eligible for the S Corporation election, a corporation must:
1. Be a domestic corporation.
2. Not be an active member of an affiliated group.
3. Have one class of stock. Differences in voting power attached to shares of stock will not be deemed to create more than one class of stock.
4. Have no more than 35 shareholders who are individuals, estates, and certain trusts (including, but not limited to, grantor and voting trusts). All stockholdings, whether jointly or individually held, of a husband, wife, or their estates, are counted as one shareholder. (In the case of a grantor trust, the grantor is treated as the shareholder; with respect to voting trusts, each beneficiary is counted as a shareholder.)

Given proper election, there will be no federal tax except for the tax on "built-in" gains (which is beyond the scope of the CPA examination), and the tax on excessive passive investment income.

The election may be made at any time during the previous taxable year and at any time on or before the 15th day of the third month of the current taxable year.

In view of item "3" above, preferred stock represents a second class of stock; accordingly, if the corporation has both common and preferred stock, it will be prevented from qualifying as an S Corporation.

Answer choice "B" is incorrect because the common stock is one class of stock, despite the fact that there are both voting and nonvoting shares.

Answer choice "C" is incorrect because estates may be shareholders in an S Corporation.

Answer choice "D" is incorrect because a grantor trust may be a shareholder in an S Corporation.

16. D   Determination of whether a corporation is to be treated as a personal holding company, and therefore subject to a 39.6 percent tax on undistributed income in addition to other corporate taxes, is based on two tests—as to income and stock ownership.

The income test provides that a corporation is a personal holding company when 60 percent of adjusted gross income consists of dividends, interest, certain royalties, annuities, certain rents, personal service contract income, and certain income from estates and trusts.

As to stock ownership, if during the period of the last half of the taxable year more than 50 percent of the value of the outstanding stock is owned by or for not more than five individuals, the corporation is deemed to be a personal holding company. (For purposes of determining the five individuals, the rules of constructive stock ownership apply.)

Should the corporation be liable for the tax on undistributed income, it should be self-assessed by filing a separate schedule (Form 1120-PH) along with the regular tax return.

Since the tax is imposed on undistributed personal holding company income, sufficient distribution of dividends can mitigate the tax.

In view of the above, Acme is a personal holding company.

Answer choice "A" is incorrect because a corporation is subject to tax on income regardless of the distributions it makes to its stockholders.

Answer choice "B" is incorrect since Acme cannot be treated as a corporation subject to the accumulated earnings tax since it is a personal holding company. Otherwise, two "penalty" taxes could be levied against the same corporation.

Answer choice "C" is incorrect because a regulated investment company is one that distributes 90 percent or more of its taxable income (with adjustments).

17. B   No gain or loss will be recognized by a corporation upon the contribution of capital to the corporation.

As to the corporation, the basis of the property is the fair market value of the stock at the time the property is acquired, unless the transferors of the property "control" the property after the transfer, as discussed following.

No gain or loss is recognized if property of any kind is transferred by one or more persons (individuals, trusts or estates, partnerships, or corporations) solely in exchange for stock of the same corporation, and if immediately after the exchange the same person or persons are in "control" of the transferee corporation; that is, own 80 percent of the voting stock and 80 percent of all other stock of the corporation. If, in addition to stock, the transferor/stockholder receives other property or cash, the gain (but not a loss) is recognized, but only in an amount not in excess of the cash or fair market value of the other property received.

In a "controlled" transaction, the basis of the property is the same as it would be in the hands of the transferor, increased by any gain which is recognized on the exchange.

(A controlled corporation for this purpose is one in which more than 80 percent in value of all outstanding common stock is beneficially owned by an individual, his or her spouse, minor children, and minor grandchildren.)

Since Stone is clearly in control of the corporation, the corporation's total basis is the same as Stone's basis, which is $500 + $30,000, or $30,500.

Answer choice "A" is incorrect because it fails to include the cash transferred by Stone.

Answer choice "C" is incorrect because the fair market value, rather than the adjusted basis, of the computer equipment is included in the corporation's basis for the transferred assets (i.e., $500 + $34,000 equals $34,500).

Answer choice "D" is incorrect because the cost, rather than the adjusted basis, of the equipment is included in the corporation's basis for the transferred assets (i.e., $500 + $40,000 equals $40,500).

18.   D   The general rule is that a shareholder will recognize gain or loss (usually capital in character) on the receipt of cash or other property distributed in complete liquidation.

The gain or loss will be measured by the difference between the fair market value of the assets distributed and the adjusted basis of the stock. The basis of the assets distributed to the shareholders will be their fair market value on the date of distribution, and the asset's holding period shall start with the date of distribution.

The corporation will generally recognize income or loss on business transactions, including sales and distributions of its assets, during the period of liquidation. The rules relating to depreciation recapture are also applicable.

Liquidating distributions result in gain (capital gain or ordinary income, depending on the asset) at the corporate level to the extent that the fair market value of the distributed property exceeds the adjusted basis of such property. In the event an asset is subject to a liability, for purposes of determining the gain, the asset's fair market value cannot be less than the amount of the liability.

Answer choice "A" is incorrect because there is a taxable effect, as explained in answer choice "D."

Answer choice "B" is incorrect because the receipt of money as a liquidating distribution, by itself, does not create ordinary income.

Answer choice "C" is incorrect because shares of stock usually represent capital assets; accordingly, upon disposition (including liquidation), capital gain or loss, not ordinary gain or loss, will usually result.

19. C   In addition to liability for regular income taxes, every corporation (other than a domestic or foreign personal holding company, a domestic international sales corporation, or an exempt organization) is liable for an extra tax (in the nature of a penalty) if it is formed or availed of for the purpose of preventing the imposition of income tax upon its shareholders, or the shareholders of any other corporation, by permitting earnings and profits to accumulate instead of being divided or distributed.

The rate of tax is 39.6 percent.

The tax is imposed on "accumulated taxable income" of the taxable year, which is taxable income with the following adjustments, minus the sum of the dividends-paid deduction and the accumulated earnings credit.
1. Deduction is allowed for federal income taxes and income and profit taxes of foreign countries and U.S. possessions (but not including the accumulated earnings tax or personal holding company tax).
2. The deduction for charitable contributions is unlimited.
3. No deduction is allowed for dividends received.
4. The net operating loss deduction is not allowed.
5. Deduction is allowed for net capital losses.
6. Deduction is allowed for the net capital gain for the year, minus the taxes attributed thereto.
7. No capital loss carryback or carryover is allowed.

The accumulated earnings credit is measured by the reasonable retained earnings (undistributed earnings and profits) of the business. There is a minimum credit of $250,000, limited to $150,000 for personal service corporations.

The dividends-paid deduction includes dividends paid during the taxable year plus those paid on or before the 15th day of the third month following the close of the taxable year.

The accumulated earnings tax can be imposed regardless of the number of stockholders of a corporation.

In view of the above, Kari's <u>accumulated</u> <u>taxable</u> <u>income</u> <u>is</u> <u>$50,000</u>, which is taxable income of $400,000, less the sum of the $100,000 federal income tax paid, and the minimum accumulated earnings credit of $250,000.

Answer choice "A" is incorrect because the $250,000 minimum accumulated earnings credit is not deducted, and should be.

Answer choice "B" is incorrect because the $100,000 federal income tax paid is not deducted, and should be.

Answer choice "D" is incorrect in view of the explanation provided for choice "C."

20. A   The Internal Revenue Code specifically defines seven types of corporate reorganizations.
1. A statutory merger or consolidation. (A type "A" reorganization.)
2. The acquisition by one corporation, in exchange solely for all or a part of its voting stock, of stock of another corporation, if, immediately after the acquisition, the acquiring corporation has control of such other corporation. (A type "B" reorganization.)
3. The acquisition by one corporation, in exchange solely for all or a part of its voting stock, of substantially all of the properties of another corporation. (A type "C" reorganization.)
4. A transfer by a corporation of all or a part of its assets to another corporation if immediately after the transfer the transferor, or one or more of its shareholders, or any combination thereof, is in control of the corporation to which the assets are transferred. (A type "D" reorganization.)
5. A recapitalization. (A type "E" reorganization.)
6. A mere change in identity, form, or place of organization. (A type "F" reorganization.)
7. A reorganization pursuant to Title 11 of the Bankruptcy Code. (A type "G" reorganization.)

It should be noted that a stock redemption (which occurs when a corporation cancels or redeems its own stock) is not a corporate reorganization.

The requirements for each type of reorganization are beyond the scope of the CPA examination.

An examination question that contains the phrase "pursuant to a corporate reorganization" should be answered utilizing the following general rules.
1. No gain will be recognized by the shareholders unless "boot" is received in addition to the receipt of stock. In addition, no gain will be recognized by the corporation(s) involved.
2. Three types of "boot" may trigger recognition of gain.
    a. Cash.
    b. Bonds - gain will be recognized if the principal amount of

the bonds received exceeds the principal amount of the bonds surrendered, or, if bonds are received and none are surrendered.

The fair market value of the bonds will be utilized in measuring the gain.

    c. Payments equivalent to a dividend when one of the parties to the reorganization has accumulated earnings and profits.

In the question situation, Corporations A and B combine and form Corporation C, the only surviving corporation. It should be readily apparent that this is a consolidation, which is a type "A" reorganization. Accordingly, the reorganization is tax-free to the shareholders and the corporation.

Answer choices other than "A" are based on incorrect assumptions and/or combinations.

21. C   In effect, if a corporation's tentative minimum tax exceeds the regular tax, the excess amount is payable in addition to the regular tax.

Technically referred to as the "alternative minimum tax," the minimum tax is equal to 20 percent of alternative minimum taxable income (in excess of the exemption amount) reduced by the corporation's regular tax liability. The exemption amount is $40,000, but must be reduced by 25 percent of the excess of AMTI over $150,000.

Alternative minimum taxable income is equal to taxable income, after certain adjustments, plus tax preference items. The adjustments to taxable income are complex and are beyond the scope of the CPA examination.

In computing the alternative minimum tax, the following are some of the more general types of tax preference items to be considered.
1. Excess accelerated depreciation on real property.
2. Excess percentage depletion for coal and iron ore.
3. Excess amortization of pollution control facilities.
4. With respect to personal property placed into service after 1986, the excess of accelerated depreciation over the amount calculated using the 150 percent declining balance method with a switch to straight-line.
5. Seventy-five percent of the excess of book income (before deduction of federal income tax) over AMTI.

Answer choices "A" and "B" are incorrect and should have been easily eliminated since the purpose of a "minimum" tax is to impose a tax in the current year.

Answer choice "D" is incorrect because the excess is not subtracted.

22. A   Schedule M-1 of the corporation income tax return (Form 1120) is used to show the reconciliation of income per books with income per the tax return.

In preparing Schedule M-1, the starting point is net income per books. Items to be added are (1) federal income tax, (2) the excess of capital losses over capital gains, (3) income subject to tax but not recorded on the books in the tax year, and (4) expenses recorded on the books but not deducted on the tax return in the tax year. Items to be subtracted are (1) income recorded on the books but not includible on the return in the tax year and (2) deductions on the return not charged against book income in the tax year.

It should be noted that only 80 percent (50 percent, beginning in 1994) of meals and entertainment is deductible in arriving at a corporation's taxable income.

Accordingly, in Cape's Schedule M-1 of Form 1120, the amount reported as 1993 taxable income is $190,000:

Book income		$140,000
Add: Federal income tax expense	$40,000	
Meals and entertainment (20% × $50,000)	10,000	50,000
1993 taxable income		$190,000

Answer choice "B" is incorrect because it fails to consider the required addback for 20 percent of the meals and entertainment (i.e., 20% × $50,000, or $10,000).

Answer choice "C" is incorrect because it fails to consider the required addback for the nondeductible $40,000 federal income tax expense.

Answer choice "D" is incorrect because it fails to consider the required addbacks for 20 percent of the meals and entertainment (i.e., $10,000), and the $40,000 federal income tax expense.

23. C An S Corporation will not have earnings and profits for tax years beginning after 1982.

A distribution made by an S Corporation with no earnings and profits at all will be treated first as a nontaxable return of capital (resulting in a decrease of the shareholder's basis for the stock) to the extent of the shareholder's basis, and second, as a capital gain.

A distribution made by an S Corporation with earnings and profits (as in the case of a corporation that is making the election after operating as a C Corporation) is subject to a four-tier system.
1. Nontaxable return of capital - The distribution, to the extent of the corporation's accumulated adjustments account ("AAA"), will be deemed to be a nontaxable return of capital. The accumulated adjustments account is basically the taxable income of the corporation for all years beginning after 1982 (which is reported as income by the stockholders), reduced by nondeductible expenses which do not relate to tax-exempt income.

2. <u>Dividend</u> - Taxation as a dividend will result to the extent of the corporation's accumulated earnings and profits earned while not under Subchapter S.

3. <u>Additional nontaxable return of capital</u> - If the shareholder has any basis in his or her stock after taking into account the reductions from the first two tiers, then the remaining basis may be recovered tax free.

4. <u>Capital gain</u> - Any additional distribution will be treated as capital gain.

Answer choices other than "C" are clearly based on incorrect assumptions.

24.   D   If property is transferred to a corporation by one or more persons (individuals, trusts, estates, partnerships, or corporations) solely in exchange for stock in that corporation, and immediately after the exchange such person or persons are in control of the corporation to which the property was transferred, ordinarily no gain or loss will be recognized.

To be in control of the corporation, the person or persons making the transfer must own, immediately after the exchange, at least <u>80 percent</u> <u>of</u> <u>the</u> <u>total</u> <u>combined</u> <u>voting</u> <u>power</u> <u>of</u> <u>all</u> <u>classes</u> <u>of</u> <u>stock</u> entitled to vote and at least 80 percent of the total number of shares in each class of nonvoting stock outstanding.

The term "property" does not include services rendered, or to be rendered, to the issuing corporation. Stock received for services is taxable income to the recipient to the extent of the stock's fair market value.

If, in addition to stock, the persons transferring property to the corporation receive other property or cash, gain is recognized, but only to the extent of the cash and fair market value of the other property received. No loss, however, will be recognized.

The assumption of liabilities by a corporation is not regarded as the receipt of cash or other property in determining the gain or loss recognized. However, when the liabilities exceed the adjusted basis of the property transferred, gain is recognized to the extent of this excess.

The shareholder's basis in the stock received is equal to the cash plus the adjusted basis of the property transferred to the corporation, increased by any gain recognized. The basis is decreased to the extent of the cash and the fair market value of the other property, if any, received by the shareholder.

The corporation's basis in the property is generally the same as the shareholder's basis immediately before the transfer, increased by any gain recognized by the shareholder as a result of the transfer.

Answer choices other than "D" are based on incorrect assumptions.

25. A The general rule is that a shareholder will recognize gain or loss (usually capital in character) on the receipt of cash or other property distributed in complete liquidation. The gain or loss will be measured by the difference between the fair market value of the assets distributed and the adjusted basis of the stock. The basis of the assets distributed to the shareholders will be their fair market value on the date of distribution, and the asset's holding period shall start with the date of distribution.

The corporation will generally recognize income or loss on business transactions, including sales and distributions of its assets, during the period of liquidation. The rules relating to depreciation recapture are also applicable.

If a corporation is completely liquidated and dissolved, filing fees, professional (e.g., legal and accounting) fees, and other expenditures incurred in connection with the liquidation are deductible in full by the dissolved corporation.

Liquidating distributions result in gain (capital gain or ordinary income, depending on the asset) at the corporate level to the extent that the fair market value of the distributed property exceeds the adjusted basis of such property. In the event an asset is subject to a liability, for purposes of determining the gain, the asset's fair market value cannot be less than the amount of the liability.

Answer choices other than "A" are based on assumptions that are not valid under current tax laws.

26. A The original basis of a partner's interest includes the amount of money paid, plus the adjusted basis of any contributed property, reduced by the portion of any indebtedness on such property assumed by the other partners.

The adjusted basis of Pert's partnership interest is $10,000:

Adjusted basis of property contributed	$12,000
Less: Portion of mortgage assumed by other partners:	
50% × $4,000	2,000
Adjusted basis of Pert's 50 percent interest	$10,000

Answer choice "B" is incorrect because it fails to reduce the basis of Pert's partnership interest by the portion of the mortgage assumed by the other partners (i.e., 50 percent × $4,000, or $2,000).

Answer choice "C" is incorrect because it reduces the fair market value of the contributed property (i.e., $20,000), rather than reducing Pert's adjusted basis of the contributed property (i.e., $12,000) by the portion of the mortgage assumed by the other partners (i.e., 50% × $4,000, or $2,000). This results in the incorrect answer choice of $18,000.

Answer choice "D" is clearly incorrect because (1) the fair market value of the property is irrelevant in determining the adjusted basis of Pert's partnership interest, and (2) no adjustment is made for the portion of the mortgage assumed by the other partners.

27.   C   When a person receives property other than cash (including an interest in a partnership) in exchange for services, the fair market value of the property is ordinary income and becomes the basis of the property to the recipient. Accordingly, in Kelly's 1993 income tax return, Kelly must include 10 percent of $100,000, or $10,000, as ordinary income from the transfer of the partnership interest.

Answer choice "A" is incorrect because instead of treating 10 percent of the fair market value of the partnership's net assets as ordinary income, it treats 10 percent of the basis of the partnership's net assets (i.e., 10 percent of $70,000, or $7,000) as ordinary income.

Answer choice "B" is incorrect because (1) instead of treating 10 percent of the fair market value of the partnership's net assets as income to Kelly, it treats 10 percent of the basis of the partnership's net assets (i.e., 10 percent of $70,000, or $7,000) as income to Kelly, and (2) it treats the income on the transfer of the partnership interest as capital gain, when in fact it is ordinary income.

Answer choice "D" is incorrect because, while the amount of income to be recognized by Kelly is $10,000, it is not recognized as capital gain; rather, it is recognized as ordinary income.

28.   C   A partnership must use a "required tax year," which is generally the calendar year. Under Section 444 of the Internal Revenue Code, the "required tax year" may be other than the calendar year if (1) there is a valid business purpose for such use, or (2) the deferral period for the tax year elected does not exceed three months.

If a "required tax year" other than the calendar year is elected, the partnership may be liable for an annual "required payment," which essentially represents the prepayment of the partners' tax on the income of the deferral period. (The calculation of the annual "required payment" is beyond the scope of the CPA examination.)

Answer choice "A" is incorrect because all partnerships, and not just limited partnerships, may elect to use a "required tax year" other than the calendar year.

Answer choice "B" is incorrect because the Section 444 election is generally not available to a partnership that is a member of a tiered structure. (A tiered structure exists, for example, when one partnership owns any part of another partnership).

Answer choice "D" is incorrect because the Section 444 election is not dependent on the number of partners in the partnership.

29. D Certain partnership items, which are not deductible by a partnership, retain their identity and flow through to the returns of the individual partners. The distributive items to be considered separately by each partner are those that are subject to special handling or limitation on the individual returns of the partner, and include contributions to recognized charities and capital gains and losses.

In computing the ordinary income of a partnership, a deduction is allowed for fixed salaries, determined without regard to the income of the partnership, paid to partners for services. Similarly, a partnership may deduct fixed payments, determined without regard to the income of the partnership, paid to partners for the use of their capital. Such payments, frequently called "guaranteed payments," merely alter the manner in which respective partners share profits.

Answer choices "A" and "C" are incorrect because they represent items that are not deductible by a partnership since they retain their identity and flow through to the returns of the individual partners.

Answer choice "B" is incorrect because there is no such provision under current tax law.

30. A The basis of a partner's interest in a partnership is the original basis and subsequent adjustments thereto.

When one receives a partnership interest in exchange for services, the value of the interest is ordinary income and the basis is its fair market value.

The original basis equals the amount of money paid plus the adjusted basis of any contributed property reduced by the portion of indebtedness on such property, if any, assumed by the other partners. (In general, no gain or loss is recognized either to the partnership or any partner upon a contribution of property in exchange for a partnership interest.)

Subsequent increases to a partner's basis in a partnership result from further contributions, the sum of the partner's distributive shares of partnership income, and increases in partnership liabilities that increase each partner's share of the liabilities.

Subsequent decreases in basis result from the amount of money and the adjusted basis of property distributed, the sum of distributive shares of partnership losses, and nondeductible, noncapital expenditures. The adjusted basis for an interest in a partnership can never be less than zero.

Answer choices "B" and "C" are incorrect because when a partner's share of partnership liabilities increases, that partner's basis in the partnership is increased, and not decreased, by the partner's share of the increase.

Answer choice "D" is incorrect because the basis of a partner's interest is affected by partnership liabilities.

31.   A   When property is distributed as a current nonliquidating distribution (as in the question situation), no gain is recognized by the partner until he or she sells or otherwise disposes of the property.

The receipt of unrealized receivables and inventory items will result in ordinary income when sold, except when inventory items representing a capital asset are held by the partner in excess of five years. In that instance, any gain or loss will be treated as a capital asset transaction.

Accordingly, <u>the amount of taxable gain that Jody must report as a result of the distribution is $0</u>.

Answer choices other than "A" are clearly based on incorrect assumptions.

32.   B   When property is distributed as a current nonliquidating distribution, its basis is equal to the lower of (1) the adjusted basis of the property in the hands of the partnership immediately prior to the distribution, or (2) the adjusted basis of the partner's partnership interest immediately prior to the distribution, reduced by any money distributed simultaneously.

<u>Jody's basis in the distributed property is $30,000</u>, which is the lower of (1) $40,000, the adjusted basis of the property to the partnership, or (2) $30,000, the adjusted basis of Jody's partnership interest ($50,000) reduced by the cash ($20,000) distributed in the same transaction.

Answer choices other than "B" are based on assumptions that are not valid under current tax law.

33.   D   The unified transfer tax system is designed to eliminate most of the tax advantages of making lifetime gifts as opposed to making transfers at death (i.e., testamentary transfers).

Pursuant to the unified transfer tax system, a unified rate schedule is used to calculate the tax on both lifetime gifts and transfers at death. Under the unified rate schedule, lifetime taxable gifts and transfers at death are taxed on a cumulative basis.

Accordingly, the estate tax base consists of the taxable estate plus the taxable gifts made during the lifetime of the decedent. The taxable estate is generally determined by subtracting the allowable deductions from the gross estate, which includes all assets owned and/or controlled by the decedent. Allowable deductions include all administrative expenses, debts and, most important, the marital deduction (i.e., the total of all transfers by an estate from one spouse to another).

Once the taxable estate is determined, the unified rate schedule is applied and then a special unified credit (i.e., $192,800) comes into play that, if available to the decedent, can reduce the tax liability. In essence, if the maximum unified estate and gift credit is taken, then the amount of a decedent's taxable estate that is effectively tax-free is $600,000.

Answer choice "A" is incorrect because it fails to consider the unified estate and gift credit.

Answer choice "B" is incorrect because it merely refers to the annual gift tax exclusion of $10,000.

Answer choice "C" is incorrect because it refers to the unified estate and gift credit; it fails to consider the amount of the taxable estate against which the unified credit may be claimed.

34.   A   Valid deductions from a decedent's gross estate, to arrive at the taxable estate, include expenses of administering and settling the estate, debts, and the marital deduction.

Once the taxable estate is determined, the applicable tax rate is applied in order to determine the gross estate tax liability. The gross estate tax liability is then reduced by the unified credit (if available to the decedent), and allowable credits for such items as state inheritance (estate) taxes, gift taxes on pre-1977 gifts, and foreign death taxes.

Answer choices other than "A" are based on incorrect assumptions and/or combinations.

35.   C   Exempt organizations are liable for income tax on unrelated business income in excess of a $1,000 exemption and allowable deductions for ordinary and necessary expenses. If the entity is a corporation, the regular corporate income tax rates will prevail. An exempt organization, subject to tax on unrelated business taxable income, must comply with the code provisions regarding installment payments of estimated income tax by corporations, even if it is operating as a trust. Accordingly, quarterly payments of estimated tax may be necessary.

Unrelated business income is any income derived from a trade or business regularly carried on by the exempt organization that is not substantially related to the purpose giving rise to the exempt status. Specifically excluded from the category of an unrelated trade or business are (1) any activities where substantially all work is performed for the organization without compensation (i.e., by <u>volunteers</u>), (2) any activities carried on for the convenience of its members, students, patients, or employees, (3) any activities involving the selling of merchandise, substantially all of which has been received by the organization as gifts or contributions, or (4) any activity involving games of chance (e.g., bingo) if such games are (a) conducted in accordance with local laws and (b) confined to nonprofit organizations (i.e., do not compete with profit-motivated businesses).

Answer choice "A" is incorrect because if an exempt organization has unrelated business income, it would not lose its exempt status; rather, it could only be liable for a tax on the unrelated business taxable income.

Answer choice "B" is incorrect because unrelated business income may relate to the sale of goods, unless substantially all of the goods have been received by the organization as gifts or contributions.

Answer choice "D" is incorrect because the tax on unrelated business income will be imposed even if profits from the unrelated business are used to support the exempt organization's charitable activities.

36. C Activity-based costing assigns costs to products on the basis of the types and quantities of activities that must be performed to produce those products.

The following relevant background should be understood.
1. Costs are assigned on the basis of activities performed to produce, distribute, or support products (i.e., purchasing, administrative, and engineering functions). In this sense, costs are not accumulated by department or function, as they are in traditional systems such as job order costing or process costing, etc.
2. Cost drivers are actions or conditions that directly influence and create costs; they are used as a basis for cost allocation. (For example, cost drivers for the purchasing activity would include the number of purchase orders, the number of supplier contracts, and the number of shipments received.)
3. Activity-based costing allows management to identify value-adding and nonvalue-adding activities. Clearly, a value-adding activity increases the worth (i.e., "value") of a product, while a nonvalue-adding activity increases the time spent on a product or service, but does not increase its worth. The objective is therefore to ensure that activities that do not add value to the product are identified and reduced to the extent possible.

Based on the facts above, <u>nonvalue-adding</u> <u>activities</u> <u>are</u> <u>identified</u> <u>and</u> <u>eliminated</u> <u>to</u> <u>the</u> <u>extent</u> <u>possible</u>, whereas, <u>cost</u> <u>drivers</u> <u>do</u> <u>not</u> <u>reduce</u> <u>costs</u>; rather they are actions or conditions that directly influence and create costs.

Answer choices other than "C" are based on incorrect assumptions and/or combinations.

37. D Flexible budgets, as contrasted with fixed, static, or master budgets, require the separation of fixed and variable costs. Once this is accomplished under flexible budgeting, it becomes possible to compare actual and budgeted results at virtually any level of activity. This, of course, is bounded by the relevant range. The usefulness of a flexible budget is founded on adequate knowledge of both fixed and variable cost behavior patterns.

"Relevant range" refers to the level of production assumed in constructing a breakeven model. Within the assumed range of production activity, certain sales and expense relationships are considered to remain valid. Outside of the assumed range the relationships are not valid and the particular model is irrelevant.

(While flexible budgets are generally associated with the control of overhead factors, they may also be used to control direct materials and direct labor, as well as nonmanufacturing costs.)

Within a relevant range, an increase in production levels would decrease fixed costs per unit since the same total fixed costs would be allocated over a greater number of units. However, variable costs per unit are constant and do not change.

Answer choices other than "D" are based on incorrect assumptions and/or combinations.

38. D In general, break-even is the point at which there is neither profit nor loss. It represents the amount of fixed cost and expense that must be covered by contribution margin, which equals sales less variable costs.

As such, at the break-even point, the contribution margin equals total fixed costs.

Answer choices "A" and "B" are incorrect because the difference between variable costs and sales revenues equals the contribution margin.

Answer choice "C" is incorrect because selling and administrative costs are generally semivariable costs, having both a variable and fixed cost element. By definition, these costs would not equal the contribution margin.

39. C Responsibility accounting relates income, costs, and expenses to positions and people in the organizational structure who control and are directly responsible for creating them; it fixes responsibility for performance.

Controllable revenue would be included in a performance report for a profit center, but not cost a center, since the latter does not have revenue by definition.

Answer choices other than "C" are based on incorrect assumptions and/or combinations.

40. D   Pricing decisions, including product profitability decisions, are among the most challenging decisions facing managers. Three major factors that influence pricing decisions include customers, competitors, and costs.

Managers must always examine pricing problems through the eyes of customers. A price increase may cause a customer to reject the company's product and chose one from a competitor; or a price increase may drive a customer to choose a substitute product that fits desired quality specifications in a more cost-effective way.

A business with knowledge of its rival's technology, plant size, and operating policies is better able to estimate its rival's costs, which is valuable information in setting competitive prices.

Cost information is an important input into many pricing decisions. Costs are incurred at all stages of the life of a product. These stages are research and development, product design, manufacturing, marketing, distribution, and customer service. The systematic budgeting and tracking of costs at all stages provides important information to managers making decisions about product introduction, product pricing, and determining relative product profitability.

Thus, the quality of a new product, the expected life of a new product, and customers' relative preference for quality compared to price are all factors that should be considered by management in pricing the product.

Answer choices other than "D" are based on incorrect assumptions and/or combinations.

41. B   Since the fact situation presented is not clear-cut, a general awareness of cost patterns should be applied. While it is rather clear that variable costs would increase in direct proportion to volume (i.e., the number of sales offices), there is no reason to believe that fixed costs would.

Thus, it should be concluded that the budgeted costs to operate seven sales offices would be $672,000:

Variable costs; ($500,000 - $70,000) × 7/5	$602,000
Fixed costs	70,000
Budgeted costs to operate seven sales offices	$672,000

Answer choice "A" is incorrect because the fixed costs of $70,000 that are included in the total of $500,000 are assumed to increase in direct proportion to the number of sales offices (i.e., $500,000 × 7/5 equals $700,000); there is no logical basis to assume such an increase.

Answer choices "C" and "D" are not logical in view of the explanation provided.

42. D The following should be noted.
1. Estimated cash disbursements for inventories would include amounts needed for projected sales, and an increase in inventory, if any.
2. A decrease in inventories would reduce disbursements necessary for projected sales.
3. A decrease in accounts payable represents payments for prior purchases; as such, cash disbursements would increase.
4. Since the gross margin is 40 percent, the cost of goods sold is 60 percent.

The estimated cash disbursements are $1,760,000:

Required for projected sales; $2,800,000 × 60%	$1,680,000
Decrease in inventories	(70,000)
Decrease in accounts payable	150,000
Estimated cash disbursements for inventories	$1,760,000

Answer choice "A" is incorrect for several reasons. First, the projected sales are based on the 40 percent gross margin rather than the 60 percent cost of goods sold (i.e., $2,800,000 × 40% equals $1,120,000). In addition, the decrease in inventories is added, and should be subtracted, and the decrease in accounts payable is subtracted and should be added. (Thus, $1,120,000 plus $70,000, and minus $150,000, equals $1,040,000.)

Answer choice "B" is incorrect because the projected sales are based on the 40 percent gross margin, and should be based on the 60 percent cost of goods sold (i.e., [$2,800,000 × 40%] minus $70,000, and plus $150,000, equals $1,200,000).

Answer choice "C" is incorrect because the decrease in inventories is added, and should be subtracted, and the decrease in accounts payable is subtracted, and should be added (i.e., $1,680,000 plus $70,000, and minus $150,000, equals $1,600,000).

43. C Generally, the computations to determine the breakeven point are as follows:
1. Units to breakeven - Fixed costs and expenses are divided by the contribution margin (or "marginal income") per unit, which is sales revenue less variable costs.
2. Dollars to breakeven - Fixed costs and expenses are divided by the contribution margin percentage, which is contribution margin divided by sales.

Thus, the $40,000 of fixed costs should be divided by 80 percent (i.e., [$800,000 - $160,000]/$800,000) to yield Syl's breakeven point in sales dollars, which is $50,000 (i.e., $40,000/80%).

Answer choices "A" and "B" are not logical in view of the explanation provided.

Answer choice "D" is incorrect because it represents fixed costs, and the breakeven point must be in excess of fixed costs in order to recover both fixed and variable costs.

44. C Both the net present value method and the internal rate of return method of capital budgeting adjust for the time value of money. The difference between the two methods is that the net present value method is based on a rate known in advance (i.e., the "desired" or "hurdle" rate), while the internal rate of return method infers an interest rate, which must therefore be approximated.

The following should be observed.
1. Net present value method - At a desired (i.e., "hurdle") rate of return, the discounted cash flow generated is equal to the original investment. Any excess of the discounted cash flow over the original investment is positive net present value, which indicates a rate of return higher than the desired rate; any excess of the original investment over the discounted cash flow indicates negative net present value and a lesser return. (The desired rate of return is built into the tables which are used.) Discounted cash flow is determined by applying the desired rate of return to cash inflow for each period. When the inflows are uniform for each period, an annuity table is issued. When the cash inflows are not uniform, they must be discounted separately by using the present value of $1.
2. Internal rate of return method - The "internal rate of return," which, again, is not known and must be approximated, is defined as the discount rate which makes the net present value of a project equal to zero; it is the point at which the initial outlay is equal to the discounted cash flows.

Based on this awareness, a positive net present value indicates a rate of return greater than (i.e., ">") the desired (hurdle) rate of return of 12 percent. Hence, the internal rate of return would be greater than 12 percent.

Answer choice "A" is incorrect because a positive net present value indicates a return in excess of 12 percent, which is greater than 0.

Answer choice "B" is incorrect because an internal rate of return of exactly 12 percent would indicate that the net present value was equal to zero, and not positive.

Answer choice "D" is incorrect because an internal rate of return less than 12 percent would indicate negative net present value, and not positive net present value.

45. A The payback period is the amount of time a project requires to recover the initial cash outlay. It is an elementary method of capital budgeting; other methods include return on capital and cash flow techniques. It is determined by dividing the initial cash outlay by the net cash benefit per year.

Generally, in arriving at an answer, it must be considered that there are two sources of cash benefit. First is the after-tax cash inflow generated by additional revenue and/or decreased costs. Also, the cash savings generated by depreciation must be considered since depreciation provides cash by lowering taxes.

However, in this question, the effect of depreciation is already considered in the language "after-tax cash flow." Accordingly, this amount of cash inflow is the net cash benefit.

The payback period is <u>2.50</u> <u>years</u>:

Initial cash outlay	<u>$5,000</u>
After-tax cash flow per year	<u>$2,000</u>
<u>Payback</u> <u>period</u>: $5,000/$2,000	<u>2.50 years</u>

(The present value information given was not relevant.)

Answer choices other than "A" are not logical based on the explanation provided.

46. C   The accounting rate of return (i.e., "accrual" accounting rate of return) is a capital budgeting concept based on book values, which represents historical costs, and does not consider the time value of money (present value). In effect, it is income statement oriented.

In essence, under this method, the numerator is the increase in expected future average annual income (on an accrual accounting basis). The denominator is the increase in required investment, utilizing either the initial increase, or an average increase.

The only matter specifically addressed in the question is <u>the amount</u> <u>to be used as the numerator in the ratio</u>, which <u>would be</u> the <u>$40,000</u> expected average increase in annual operating income.

Answer choice "A" is incorrect because it merely represents the $60,000 initial increase in the required investment reduced by the $40,000 expected average increase in annual operating income; this amount has no basis in fact.

Answer choice "B" is incorrect because it represents the average increase in required investment, which could appear in the denominator, but not the numerator.

Answer choice "D" is incorrect because it represents the initial increase in required investment, which could appear in the denominator, but not the numerator.

47. A   The net present value method of capital budgeting holds that at a desired rate of return, the discounted cash flow generated is equal to the original investment. Any excess of the discounted cash flow over the original investment is positive net present value, which indicates a rate of return higher than the desired rate; any excess

of the original investment over the discounted cash flow indicates negative net present value and a lesser return. (The desired rate of return is built into the tables which are used.)

Discounted cash flow is determined by applying the desired rate of return to cash inflow for each period. When the inflows are uniform for each period, an annuity table is issued. When the cash inflows are not uniform, they must be discounted separately by using the present value of $1.

Given discounted expected cash inflows of $1,000,000, and discounted expected cash outflows of $700,000, net present value is $300,000.

Answer choice "B" is incorrect because it represents the discounted expected cash outflows, and ignores the discounted expected cash inflows.

Answer choice "C" is incorrect because it is an average of the two numbers provided, which has no basis in fact.

Answer choice "D" is incorrect because the $700,000 of discounted expected cash outflows has not been deducted, and should be.

48. C   Indirect materials are those that cannot be traced to the finished goods in an economically practical manner; they are therefore included as an element of factory overhead when used.

When indirect materials are purchased, there is an increase in stores control. Consequently, the issue of indirect materials previously purchased would result in an increase in factory overhead control and a decrease in stores control.

Answer choice "A" is incorrect because stores control would decrease, not increase, from the issuance of indirect materials.

Answer choices "B" and "D" are incorrect because an increase (i.e., debit) to work in process control with an increase (i.e., credit) to factory overhead applied occurs when overhead is applied to production, and not from the actual use of indirect materials.

49. D   Joint costs are those that arise from a common process yielding two or more goods or services having differing and significant economic unit values.

Under the relative sales value at split-off method, the established sales value at split-off is used as the basis for allocation of the joint costs. In establishing relative sales value at split-off, it is usually necessary to ascertain sales value at completion and to deduct therefrom any after-split-off costs to arrive at the relative sales value at split-off.

(An underlying assumption is that the incremental revenue from further processing is equal to the incremental cost of further processing and selling.)

Answer choices other than "D" are incorrect conclusions. As indicated, the sales price at point of sale, reduced by cost to complete after split-off, is assumed to equal the relative sales value at split-off.

50.　A　The variances indicated in the answer choices and their related definitions are described as follows:

1. <u>Overhead volume variance</u> - the difference between the budget allowance based on standard hours allowed and overhead applied for standard hours allowed.
(It should be noted that the terms "volume," "noncontrollable," "capacity," and "fixed volume" are synonymous as used in connection with this definition.)

2. <u>Overhead efficiency variance</u> - standard unit variable rate multiplied by the difference between actual hours and standard hours allowed.

3. <u>Labor efficiency variance</u> - standard unit rate multiplied by the difference between actual and standard hours allowed.

4. <u>Material usage variance</u> - standard unit price multiplied by the difference between actual and standard quantity allowed.

In essence, an overhead volume variance addresses the over- or under-application of fixed costs, which are constant within the relevant range. As such, the factors in the variance are related to capacity, as the name might imply, and the overhead volume variance would not be useful in calling attention to a possible short-term problem in the control of overhead costs. Logically, therefore, an <u>overhead volume variance would be least controllable by a production supervisor</u>.

Answer choices other than "A" are incorrect because the factors relating to these variances all give rise to variable costs, which are considered controllable by management.

51.　A　The answer to this question is based on an awareness of accounting bases for governmental units. In general, governmental units will use either the accrual basis or the modified accrual basis; use of the cash basis is generally not appropriate.

Under the accrual basis, revenue is recognized when it is earned and becomes measurable, and expenses are recognized in the period incurred. The accrual basis is recommended for use by proprietary funds (enterprise and internal service funds), and certain types of trust funds (including nonexpendable trust funds and pension trust funds).

Under the modified accrual basis, revenues are recognized in the accounting period in which they become available and measurable. Expenditures are generally recognized in the period in which the liability is incurred.

The modified accrual basis is recommended for use by governmental funds. The <u>capital projects fund</u> is classified as a governmental fund.

Answer choice "B" is incorrect because an enterprise fund is classified as a proprietary fund, which uses the accrual basis of accounting.

Answer choice "C" is incorrect because a pension trust fund uses the accrual basis of accounting.

Answer choice "D" is incorrect because a proprietary fund uses the accrual basis of accounting.

52.   A   In governmental accounting, there are three broad types of funds and two "account groups." The three broad types are governmental funds, proprietary funds, and fiduciary funds. The two account groups, which are self-balancing sets of accounts and not funds in the strict sense, are the general fixed assets account group and the general long-term debt account group.

Governmental-type funds include general funds, special revenue funds, capital projects funds, and debt service funds. Proprietary funds include enterprise funds and internal service funds. Fiduciary funds include trust funds and agency funds.

Long-term debt, inclusive of bonds and/or liabilities under a lease-purchase agreement, is accounted for in the general long-term debt account group, except debt payable by a proprietary fund, or a trust fund; the latter two fund types account for their own debt.

The two types of proprietary funds share the common characteristic of providing goods and/or services for which user fees are charged. They emulate the activities of for-profit organizations, inclusive of the recognition of depreciation, and differ in that enterprise funds provide goods and/or services to the general public as well as other government departments. On the other hand, internal service funds provide goods and/or services exclusively for other government departments on a cost-reimbursement basis.

Examples of activities for which user fees are charged and therefore may be conducted through enterprise funds are electricity generation systems, sewer systems, water supply systems, hospitals and nursing homes, parking facilities, airports, amusement parks, swimming pools, golf courses, public transportation systems, etc.

To the extent that municipal electric and water services would logically be provided to the general population, the operations of the utilities should be accounted for in an enterprise fund.

Answer choice "B" is incorrect because electric and water utility services would logically be provided to the general public; hence, operations should be accounted for by an enterprise fund, not an internal service fund.

Answer choices "C" and "D" are incorrect because neither an agency fund nor a special revenue fund would be used to account for the operations of a utility.

53. B   A municipal motor pool would provide services only for other departments within the governmental unit; hence, the cost of maintenance <u>should</u> <u>be</u> <u>accounted</u> <u>for</u> <u>in</u> <u>an</u> <u>internal</u> <u>service</u> <u>fund</u>.

Answer choice "A" is incorrect because the general fund would be billed for its share of vehicle usage, but would not account for the maintenance costs <u>per</u> <u>se</u>, which would be accounted for in the internal service fund.

Answer choice "C" is incorrect because a special revenue fund is used to account for the proceeds of specific revenue sources (other than expendable trusts or for major capital projects); it would not be used to account for goods and/or services of the type indicated.

Answer choice "D" is incorrect because the "special assessment fund" is no longer used in governmental accounting. Rather, transactions formerly accounted for in a special assessment fund are now accounted for in other funds, generally a capital projects fund.

54. D   A debt service fund, which is a governmental-type fund, is used to account for the accumulation of resources for, and the payment of, general long-term debt principal and interest. Repayment of internal service fund and enterprise fund long-term debt is accounted for in these individual funds.

The money for repaying general long-term debt usually comes from property taxes. Typically, such resources are transferred to the debt service fund from the general fund.

The facts indicate that a special tax was assessed with an allocated portion earmarked for repayment of long-term debt. The proceeds of the special tax would be accounted for in a special revenue fund. The amount of this special tax dedicated to debt service would be transferred to the <u>debt</u> <u>service</u> <u>fund</u>.

Answer choices other than "D" are not logical in view of the explanation provided.

55. D   A governmental unit would account for donated investments that stipulate a specific purpose for investment income in a trust fund. The funds used to account for this fiduciary responsibility are the nonexpendable trust fund and the expendable trust fund.

In general, a nonexpendable trust fund requires that principal be maintained while income may be available to support a specific activity. In the case of an expendable trust fund, principal need not be maintained.

Since the donor stipulated that the earnings from the investment be used for acquiring art, the donor intended the principal (investments) to be held intact and only the income expended. Therefore, the investments should be accounted for in a <u>nonexpendable</u> <u>trust</u> <u>fund</u>.

Answer choice "A" is incorrect because the term "endowment fund" is not usually used by governments. A governmental unit classifies trust funds as either nonexpendable or expendable.

Answer choice "B" is incorrect because the special revenue fund is not used when the governmental unit is acting in a fiduciary capacity (managing assets that belong to others). The special revenue fund is used to account for financial resources of the government that are dedicated to specific purposes.

Answer choice "C" is incorrect because the donor intended the investments to be preserved intact. An expendable trust fund is appropriate when both the investments and earnings can be spent.

56. B "Plant funds" of a hospital is a generic term for the plant assets and related long-term debt, along with assets to be used for future acquisitions and/or replacements.

Based on the background provided, <u>equipment</u> <u>would</u> <u>appear</u> <u>in</u> <u>the</u> <u>plant</u> <u>fund</u>. However, <u>fuel</u> <u>inventory</u> does not represent a plant asset and would be included in current funds; it <u>would</u> <u>not</u> <u>appear</u> <u>in</u> <u>the</u> <u>plant</u> <u>fund</u>.

Answer choices other than "B" are based on incorrect assumptions and/or combinations.

57. B In accounting for certain types of not-for-profit organizations, most notably voluntary health and welfare organizations, there is a distinction between program services and supporting services.

Program services include the costs and expenses incurred in connection with the organization's programs; i.e., research, community services, etc. ("Programs" may be viewed as broad activities that constitute the organization's not-for-profit reason to exist.)

Supporting services, as the name logically implies, include fund-raising, general and administrative activities, membership development, etc.

Logically, therefore, the total combined costs incurred are <u>allocated</u> <u>between</u> <u>fund-raising</u> <u>and</u> <u>program</u> <u>services</u> <u>expenses</u> <u>using</u> <u>an</u> <u>appropriate</u> <u>allocation</u> <u>basis</u>.

Answer choice "A" is incorrect because fund-raising costs should not be included as program services expenses.

Answer choice "C" is incorrect because program services expenses should not be combined with fund-raising costs.

Answer choice "D" is incorrect because program services expenses should not be reported as management and general expenses, which represent supporting services.

58.   A   Endowment funds that are restricted to a specific operating purpose are classified as temporarily restricted funds. Earnings from such funds should generally be considered <u>an increase in temporarily restricted net assets</u>.

            Answer choice "B" is incorrect because specific purpose funds are temporarily restricted, not permanently restricted.

            Answer choice "C" is incorrect because specific purpose funds are not unrestricted.

            Answer choice "D" is incorrect because earnings restricted to specific endowment purposes would appropriately be an increase in temporarily restricted net assets.

59.   B   Loan funds of a college or university are available for use by students, faculty, and/or staff. "<u>Computer</u>" <u>loans would not be found in the loan fund</u>; it is essentially a nonexistent term.

            Answer choices other than "B" are incorrect because they represent types of loans that <u>would</u> be found in the loan fund of a college.

60.   A   Generally speaking, depreciation is recognized as an expense by all not-for-profit organizations other than governmental units. Thus, the recognition of depreciation expense <u>is not required by public</u> (i.e., "government") <u>colleges, but is required by private colleges</u>.

            Answer choices other than "A" are based on incorrect assumptions and/or combinations.

OTHER OBJECTIVE FORMATS/ESSAY QUESTIONS

Answer 2

61.   C   Retainer fees received from clients are <u>reported in Schedule C as trade or business income</u>.

62.   D   Oil royalties received are <u>reported in Schedule E - Supplemental Income and Loss</u>.

            (It should be noted that Schedule E is also used to report rental income, as well as ordinary income from partnerships, S Corporations, estates, and trusts, etc.)

63.   E   Interest income on general obligation state and local government bonds is <u>not taxable</u>.

            In general, to be tax exempt, interest income must be interest on obligations of a state or one of its political subdivisions (i.e., local governments), the District of Columbia, a possession of the U.S., or one of its political subdivisions.

64.   B   Interest on refund of federal taxes is <u>reported in Schedule B</u> - <u>Interest and Dividend Income</u>.

65.   E   Death benefits from a term life insurance policy on a parent are <u>not taxable</u>.

In addition, a deceased employee's beneficiary may receive and exclude from income a one-time death benefit of up to $5,000. If the decedent had more than one beneficiary, the $5,000 exclusion must be apportioned among the beneficiaries.

66.   B   Interest income on U.S. Treasury bonds is <u>reported in Schedule B</u> - <u>Interest and Dividend Income</u>.

It should be noted that an exclusion may be available for interest income on Series EE U.S. Savings bonds.

67.   D   A share of ordinary income from an investment in a limited partnership reported in Form 1065, Schedule K-1 is <u>reported in Schedule E - Supplemental Income and Loss</u>.

A partner's share of items separately stated on Form 1065, Schedule K-1 will not necessarily be reported in Schedule E. The character of the separately stated items will determine in which form(s) they must be reported. For example, a partner's share of a partnership's capital gains must be reported in Schedule D - Capital Gains and Losses.

68.   D   Taxable income from rental of a townhouse owned by Green is <u>reported in Schedule E - Supplemental Income and Loss</u>.

It should be noted that rental activity is subject to the passive activity rules that limit the amount of losses that may be deducted.

69.   A   A prize won as a contestant on a TV quiz show is <u>taxable as other income on Form 1040</u>.

It should be obvious that the fair market value of the prize must be used when reporting the income on Form 1040.

70.   A   Payment received for jury service is <u>taxable as other income on Form 1040</u>.

(If an employer requires an employee to remit jury duty fees in exchange for his or her regular compensation during the period of jury service, then the jury duty pay remitted may be deducted from gross income on page 1 of Form 1040 in arriving at adjusted gross income.)

71.   E   Dividends received from mutual funds that invest in tax-free government obligations are <u>not taxable</u>.

It should be noted that these nontaxable dividends in essence represent the pass-through from the mutual fund of nontaxable interest income.

72. H   Qualifying medical expenses not reimbursed by insurance are <u>reported in Schedule A - Itemized Deductions</u> (deductibility <u>subject to threshold of 7.5 percent of adjusted gross income</u>).

Qualifying medical expenses include, among other items, health and dental insurance premiums, fees paid to doctors, dentists and laboratories, as well as prescription drugs.

73. O   Personal life insurance premiums paid by Green are <u>not deductible</u>.

The only personal insurance premiums deductible are for medical and dental insurance. These premiums represent qualifying medical expenses that may be claimed in Schedule A - Itemized Deductions (deductibility subject to threshold of 7.5 percent of adjusted gross income).

74. M   Expenses for business-related meals where clients were present are <u>partially deductible in Schedule C - Profit or Loss from Business</u>.

It should be noted that only 80 percent (50 percent beginning in 1994) of a self-employed individual's business-related meals and entertainment expenses qualifies for the deduction.

If an individual is not self-employed, 80 percent (50 percent beginning in 1994) of any employment-related meals and entertainment expenses is deductible as a miscellaneous itemized deduction, subject to a threshold of 2 percent of adjusted gross income.

75. K   Depreciation on a personal computer purchased in 1992 used for business is <u>reported in Form 4562 - Depreciation and Amortization, and deductible in Schedule C - Profit or Loss from Business</u>.

A taxpayer who is not self-employed may deduct depreciation on a personal computer to the extent that it is used to produce income. To be deducted as an employee business expense, the computer must be used for the convenience of the employer and required as a condition of employment. Depreciation claimed as an employee business expense is reported on Form 4562 and deductible in Schedule A - Itemized Deductions (deductibility subject to threshold of 2 percent of adjusted gross income).

76. L   Business lodging expenses, while out of town, are <u>fully deductible in Schedule C - Profit or Loss from Business</u>.

If an individual is not self-employed, the business lodging expenses would be reportable as a miscellaneous itemized deduction in Schedule A - Itemized Deductions (deductibility subject to threshold of 2 percent of adjusted gross income).

77.   L   Subscriptions to professional journals used for business are <u>fully deductible</u> in <u>Schedule</u> <u>C</u> - <u>Profit</u> <u>or</u> <u>Loss</u> <u>from</u> <u>Business</u>.

If an individual is not self-employed, the subscriptions to professional journals would be reportable as a miscellaneous itemized deduction in Schedule A - Itemized Deductions (deductibility subject to threshold of 2 percent of adjusted gross income).

78.   G   Self-employment taxes paid are <u>fifty</u> <u>percent</u> <u>deductible</u> <u>on</u> <u>Form</u> <u>1040</u> <u>to</u> <u>arrive</u> <u>at</u> <u>adjusted</u> <u>gross</u> <u>income</u>.

It should be understood that the computation of self-employment tax is based on net earnings from self-employment. When calculating the amount of self-employment tax owed, a deduction is allowed for the self-employment tax, based on a formula that changes each year.

79.   F   Qualifying contributions to a simplified employee pension plan are <u>fully</u> <u>deductible</u> <u>on</u> <u>Form</u> <u>1040</u> <u>to</u> <u>arrive</u> <u>at</u> <u>adjusted</u> <u>gross</u> <u>income</u>.

80.   K   The election (under Section 179) to expense business equipment purchased in 1992 is <u>reported</u> <u>in</u> <u>Form</u> <u>4562</u> - <u>Depreciation</u> <u>and</u> <u>Amortization</u>, <u>and</u> <u>deductible</u> <u>in</u> <u>Schedule</u> <u>C</u> - <u>Profit</u> <u>or</u> <u>Loss</u> <u>from</u> <u>Business</u>.

81.   F   Qualifying alimony payments made by Green are <u>fully</u> <u>deductible</u> <u>on</u> <u>Form</u> <u>1040</u> <u>to</u> <u>arrive</u> <u>at</u> <u>adjusted</u> <u>gross</u> <u>income</u>.

82.   I   Subscriptions for investment-related publications are <u>reported</u> <u>in</u> <u>Schedule</u> <u>A</u> - <u>Itemized</u> <u>Deductions</u> (<u>deductibility</u> <u>subject</u> <u>to</u> <u>threshold</u> <u>of</u> <u>2</u> <u>percent</u> <u>of</u> <u>adjusted</u> <u>gross</u> <u>income</u>).

If Green were a self-employed investment adviser, the subscriptions for investment-related publications would be fully deductible in Schedule C - Profit or Loss from Business.

83.   L   Interest expense on a home-equity line of credit for an amount borrowed to finance Green's business is <u>fully</u> <u>deductible</u> <u>in</u> <u>Schedule</u> <u>C</u> - <u>Profit</u> <u>or</u> <u>Loss</u> <u>from</u> <u>Business</u>.

The amount of home-equity indebtedness, however, is limited to $100,000.

If the loan proceeds are used for personal purposes, the deduction is reported in Schedule A - Itemized Deductions.

84.   M   Interest expense on a loan for an auto used 75 percent for business is <u>partially</u> <u>deductible</u> <u>in</u> <u>Schedule</u> <u>C</u> - <u>Profit</u> <u>or</u> <u>Loss</u> <u>from</u> <u>Business</u>.

It should be obvious that the interest expense is only deductible to the extent of the business use of the automobile (i.e., 75 percent).

Interest expense on a loan for an automobile used only for personal purposes is treated as personal interest and, accordingly, is not deductible.

85. O Loss on a sale of residence is generally <u>not</u> <u>deductible</u>.

If a residence is used both for personal and business use, and the residence is disposed of at a loss, a loss will be deductible, but only to the extent of the loss attributable to the portion of the residence used for business.

Answer 3

Part 3(a)

86. G General obligation bonds of a municipality (as opposed to bonds specifically issued by proprietary or trust funds, which account for their own bonds) are usually recorded in connection with a capital project. In general, the following entries are made in connection with such bonds.

1. <u>Capital projects fund</u>
    Dr. Cash
        Cr. Other financing sources (bond issue proceeds)

2. <u>General long-term debt account group</u>
    Dr. Amount to be provided for the retirement
        of general long-term debt
        Cr. General obligation bonds payable

By reference to the answer choices provided, the <u>credit</u> had to be <u>other</u> <u>financing</u> <u>sources</u>.

87. K Questions #87, #88, and #89 relate to encumbrance accounting.

Encumbrance accounting is peculiar to governmental accounting, particularly with respect to governmental-type funds. It is an integral part of budgetary accountability.

Encumbrances represent commitments related to unfilled contracts for goods and services; they are in the nature of estimated liabilities, and are evidenced by purchase orders, etc. (It should also be noted that unpaid wages and salaries, a significant expenditure by governmental units, represent a known, incurred liability and, hence, are not encumbered.)

The purpose of encumbrance accounting is to prevent further expenditure of funds in light of commitments already made.

At year-end, encumbrances still open are not accounted for as expenditures and liabilities but, rather, as reservations of fund balance.

There are several points involved in encumbrance accounting. These are summarized following:

1. <u>Recording of an encumbrance</u>
   When an estimated or contractual liability is entered into, and/or a purchase order is recorded, the entry made is as follows:

   Dr. Encumbrances control   XXX
       Cr. Reserve for encumbrances   XXX

   Again, this is an estimated amount. It will be reversed when an actual invoice, etc., is received.

2. <u>Actual expenditure for item previously encumbered</u>
   When the actual expenditure for an amount previously encumbered is made, there are two entries; one reverses the original encumbrance, the second records the expenditure:

   a. Dr. Reserve for encumbrances   XXX
           Cr. Encumbrances control   XXX
   b. Dr. Expenditures control   XXX
           Cr. Vouchers payable   XXX

Based on the answer choices provided, the issuance of an approved purchase order requires a <u>debit</u> <u>to</u> <u>encumbrances</u> <u>control</u>.

88.   L   As noted in the background to question #87, receipt of supplies previously ordered requires a <u>debit</u> <u>to</u> <u>expenditures</u> <u>control</u>.

89.   L   As noted in the background to question #87, salaries and wages need not be encumbered. Rather, they result in a <u>debit</u> to <u>expenditures</u> <u>control</u> when incurred.

90.   E   An internal service fund is one of the two proprietary fund types (the other being an enterprise fund). Both fund types are used to account for operations in much the same manner as a for-profit entity.

                The difference between them is that an enterprise fund will deal with users of services within and/or without the governmental entity, while an internal service fund will deal within the governmental entity only. As such, interfund billings will result in a <u>credit</u> to revenue; i.e., <u>interfund</u> <u>revenues</u>.

91.   J   It is a general axiom of accounting for municipalities that grant revenues are recorded as deferred revenues until earned.

                Since the grant was "previously awarded," the only appropriate treatment is to <u>debit</u> <u>deferred</u> <u>revenues</u>.

92.   D   In accounting for municipalities, it is appropriate for revenue (i.e., property taxes) collected in advance to result in a <u>credit</u> to <u>deferred</u> <u>revenues</u>.

93.   A   Questions #93 and #95 relate to the adoption of a budget.

In general, budgets are recorded in connection with general funds and special revenue funds.

In the broad sense, the journal entry to record the adoption of a budget would appear as follows:

Dr. Estimated revenues control
Dr. Estimated other financing sources control
    Cr. Appropriations control
    Cr. Estimated other financing uses control
Dr. or Cr. Budgetary fund balance

The accounts indicated above for estimated revenues, appropriations, and estimated other financing sources and uses are budgetary (nominal) accounts that will be closed out at year-end along with actual transactions.

It should be noted that while "transfers in" and "transfers out" have the same impact as revenues and expenditures, they are classified separately in the financial statements under the captions "other financing sources" and "other financing uses," and not as revenues and/or expenditures per se.

As noted above, the recording of appropriations results in a <u>credit</u> to <u>appropriations control</u>.

94.   F   Short-term financing is usually in anticipation of tax revenues, and is recorded as a <u>credit</u> <u>to</u> <u>tax</u> <u>anticipation</u> <u>notes</u> <u>payable</u>.

95.   B   An excess of estimated inflows over estimated outflows is a budgetary concept; as such, there should be <u>credit</u> to <u>budgetary</u> <u>fund</u> <u>balance</u> — <u>unreserved</u>.

Part 3(b)

96.   B   An enterprise fund is a proprietary fund; fixed assets of a proprietary fund are <u>accounted</u> <u>for</u> <u>in</u> <u>a</u> <u>proprietary</u> <u>fund</u>.

97.   F   A capital projects fund is used to <u>account</u> <u>for</u> financial resources to be expended for the acquisition or <u>construction</u> <u>of</u> <u>major</u> <u>capital</u> facilities or <u>activities</u> (other than those financed by proprietary funds and trust funds).

98.   D   Fixed assets other than those accounted for in proprietary funds or trust funds are general fixed assets, which are <u>accounted</u> <u>for</u> <u>in</u> <u>a</u> <u>self-balancing</u> <u>account</u> <u>group</u> (i.e., the general fixed assets account group).

99.   J   On extremely rare occasions, the term "infrastructure fixed assets" has appeared on the examination.

It refers to general fixed assets that are immovable and that are of value only to the governmental entity. Common examples are highways, bridges, and sidewalks, etc.

The <u>reporting</u> of infrastructure fixed assets <u>is</u> <u>optional</u>.

100. B   An enterprise fund is a proprietary fund; its cash would be <u>accounted</u> <u>for</u> <u>in</u> <u>a</u> <u>proprietary</u> <u>fund</u>.

101. G   The general fund is used to account for all financial resources, except those required to be accounted for in another fund.

The general fund <u>accounts</u> <u>for</u> <u>property</u> <u>tax</u> <u>revenues</u> since these are not levied by another fund in the regular course of operations.

(Note that taxes collected by a fund other than the general fund would likely have a more descriptive title than "property tax revenues.")

102. A   Fiduciary funds include trust and agency funds. As such, agency fund cash would be <u>accounted</u> <u>for</u> <u>in</u> <u>a</u> <u>fiduciary</u> <u>fund</u>.

103. D   Long-term debt other than debt of a proprietary fund or trust fund is general long-term debt, which is <u>accounted</u> <u>for</u> <u>in</u> <u>a</u> <u>self-balancing</u> <u>group</u> (i.e., the general long-term debt account group).

104. I   A special revenue fund is <u>used</u> <u>to</u> <u>account</u> <u>for</u> the proceeds of specific (i.e., <u>earmarked</u>) <u>revenue</u> <u>sources</u> (other than expendable trusts or for major capital projects) that are legally restricted (i.e., <u>designated</u>) <u>to</u> <u>finance</u> <u>specified</u> purposes (i.e., <u>activities</u>).

105. H   A debt services fund is <u>used</u> <u>to</u> <u>account</u> <u>for</u> the accumulation of resources for, and the <u>payment</u> <u>of</u>, <u>interest</u> <u>and</u> <u>principal</u> <u>on</u> general long-term debt (i.e., <u>tax-supported</u> <u>debt</u>).

Financial Accounting & Reporting—Business Enterprises (FARE)

FOUR-OPTION MULTIPLE-CHOICE QUESTIONS

Answer 1

1.　C　This question is based on FASB Statement #115, "Accounting for Certain Investments in Debt and Equity Securities." According to that Statement, investments in available-for-sale securities should be valued at their market value on the balance sheet date.

Unrealized holding gains and losses are accumulated in a separate component of stockholders' equity. When a decline is considered as other than temporary (i.e., permanent), the security is written down to market value, and a loss is recognized as a realized loss.

Accordingly, the excess of the cost of the Knox stock over its market value should be treated as a realized loss on the income statement because the decline in value is considered permanent. The excess of cost of the Scot stock over its market value is considered an unrealized loss because it is not permanent, and included in a separate component of stockholders' equity.

Answer choices "A" and "B" are incorrect because the permanent decline in value of the Knox stock is considered a realized loss.

Answer choice "D" is incorrect because the decline in value of the Knox stock is treated as a realized loss and, thus, does affect income.

2.　C　The lower of cost or market method of inventory valuation follows the concept of conservatism: losses are recognized upon downward changes in value; gains are not recognized until realized.

As used in the term "lower of cost or market," market generally means replacement cost by purchase or reproduction, except that market should never be more than net realizable value (selling price reduced by the estimated costs of completion and disposal) nor less than net realizable value reduced by an allowance for a normal profit margin. (These limits are generally referred to as the "ceiling" and "floor," respectively.)

In applying the rule, the decision process is to:
1. Compute cost.
2. Compute market by taking into account the ceiling and floor limitations.
3. Compare cost and market, and value the inventory at the lower of the two.

In accordance with the preceding discussion, at December 31, 1992, Chewy should report its chocolate inventory at $24,000.

FIFO cost	$26,000

Ceiling - Net realizable value (estimated sales price
   less estimated cost of disposal); $40,000 - $12,000 $28,000
Floor - Net realizable value less normal profit margin;
   $28,000 - $4,000 $24,000
Current replacement cost $20,000

Market is $24,000, which is the "floor" amount (i.e., the lowest amount at which inventory should be valued in the circumstances).

Answer choices other than "C" are inconsistent with the information provided.

3. A In general, the cost of a fixed asset should include all costs incurred to bring that asset to the state of intended use.

Clearly, all the costs incurred, or $155,000, should be the amount recorded by Merry as the cost of the machine.

Answer choice "B" is incorrect because the $10,000 of testing costs are not included, and should be.

Answer choice "C" is incorrect because the $20,000 of shipping costs are not included, and should be.

Answer choice "D" is incorrect because neither the $20,000 of shipping costs nor the $10,000 of testing costs are included, and should be.

4. B The increase in the accumulated depreciation account must be deducted from the depreciation charged to operations during 1992. This provides the amount that was debited to accumulated depreciation during 1992 as a result of property, plant, and equipment retirements.

Depreciation charged to operations in 1992 $55,000
Less: Gross increase in accumulated depreciation;
   $400,000 - $370,000   30,000
Accumulated depreciation debited during 1992 $25,000

Answer choices other than "B" are incorrect in view of the facts presented.

5. D Permanent impairment in the value of a plant asset is recorded by recognizing a loss and reducing the book value of the asset through a credit to accumulated depreciation. If the asset is to continue in use, estimates of the remaining useful life and the salvage value may be revised as well.

The loss of $180,000 is presented separately as a component of income from continuing operations; it is not an extraordinary item because such items are a normal consequence of business operations.

Future depreciation will be based on the new carrying value of $300,000 over its remaining life of three years, or $100,000 per year.

In the circumstances, accumulated depreciation would be increased by $180,000 (i.e., [$900,000 - $420,000] - $300,000), which represents the loss.

Consequently, Gei should report accumulated depreciation as of December 31, 1992, of $700,000:

Accumulated depreciation balance at January 1, 1992	$420,000
Amount of loss on permanent impairment	180,000
1992 depreciation: $300,000/3	100,000
Accumulated depreciation, December 31, 1992	$700,000

Answer choice "A" is incorrect because it does not include the $420,000 balance at January 1, 1992, and the $180,000 due to the loss on permanent impairment, and both should be included.

Answer choice "B" is incorrect because it does not include the $180,000 due to permanent impairment, and should.

Answer choice "C" is incorrect because it does not include the current year's depreciation of $100,000, and should.

6. D   Intangibles are divided into two groups.
1. Those with limited lives generally growing out of statutes or contracts; i.e., patents, copyrights, franchises, and the like.
2. Those without limited lives, having no clear limitation as to existence; i.e., trade names and/or marks, goodwill, organization costs, etc.

In general, the amortization period should not exceed the lesser of useful life or forty (40) years.

Limited life intangibles should be amortized over their economic or legal life, whichever is shorter.

Unlimited life intangibles may be amortized over a period not to exceed forty years.

The straight-line method of amortization should be used unless another systematic method is demonstrated to be more appropriate. Note also that if estimates of useful lives change, the remaining unamortized cost should be allocated to the revised life, but not to exceed forty years.

Since the trademark had a fifty-year estimated life, Judd's cost of $500,000 should be amortized over forty years, which is the maximum period. Consequently, accumulated amortization at December 31, 1992, should be $500,000/40, or $12,500.

Answer choice "A" is incorrect for two reasons. First, the amortization period represented is fifty years, and forty is appropriate. In addition, the cost is Krug's unamortized cost of $380,000 (i.e., $380,000/50 is $7,600), and not the $500,000 cost to Judd; the latter is appropriate.

Answer choice "B" is incorrect because it represents Krug's unamortized cost of $380,000 amortized over forty years (i.e., $380,000/40 is $9,500); Krug's cost is not relevant.

Answer choice "C" is incorrect because it represents cost of $500,000 amortized over fifty years, which is not appropriate.

7.   B   As per APB Opinion #21, "Interest on Receivables and Payables," when notes are exchanged for property, goods, or services, there is a general presumption that the stipulated rate of interest is fair and adequate compensation. If this presumption is not valid, substance must prevail over form and the notes should be recorded at the fair value of the goods or services or at an amount which approximates fair value, whichever is more clearly determinable.

Further, in the absence of established measures of value, an imputed rate of interest should be used to determine present value, which would then be the basis upon which the exchange (sale) would be recorded.

In this question, given a noninterest-bearing note, no other measure of fair value, and a prevailing rate of interest of 10 percent, it is clear that the sale must be recorded at the present value of future payments, using a 10 percent discount rate.

The difference between the face value of the note and its present value represents unearned interest income, which is amortized under the "interest method" by applying the discount rate to the net amount outstanding for the period.

Here, only one note payment is involved. Therefore, the factor to determine present value is the present value of $1. Given that the note is to be paid in three years, the present value is $600,000 × .75, or $450,000, and Emme's 1992 interest income is $450,000 × 10%, or $45,000.

Answer choices "A" and "C" are based on incorrect assumptions in light of the explanation provided.

Answer choice "D" is incorrect because it uses the face value of the noninterest-bearing note (i.e., $600,000) in calculating the interest income, instead of the discounted amount (i.e., $450,000).

8.   A   See the answer to question #7 for background information on APB Opinion #21, "Interest on Receivables and Payables."

In general, when a noninterest-bearing note is exchanged for property, plant, or equipment, a gain or loss is recognized at the date of exchange, measured by the difference between the present value of the noninterest-bearing note and the carrying amount of the property, plant, or equipment given up.

Consequently, the amount reported in Emme's 1992 income statement is a ($30,000) loss, equal to the difference between the $480,000 carrying value of the equipment, and the $450,000 present value of the note (i.e., $600,000 × .75).

Answer choice "B" is incorrect because a loss of $30,000, rather than a gain of $30,000, should be reported.

Answer choice "C" is incorrect because it uses the face value of the noninterest-bearing note, rather than the present value of the note in determining the gain or loss (i.e., $600,000 - $480,000 is $120,000).

Answer choice "D" is not logical based upon the explanation provided.

9.   B   When a note receivable is discounted, the proceeds (cash) received are equal to the maturity value of the note (i.e., face value plus interest to maturity) less the interest (i.e., "discount") on the maturity value determined by use of the discount rate.

Accordingly, the proceeds received from the bank equal maturity value less the discount at 15 percent.

Answer choice "A" is incorrect because the discount rate should be 15 percent, not 12 percent.

Answer choice "C" is incorrect because the maturity value, not the face value, should be used and because the rate should be 15 percent, not 12 percent.

Answer choice "D" is incorrect because the maturity value, not the face value, should be used.

10.   A   A contingency is an existing condition involving uncertainty as to possible gain or loss that will be resolved when future events occur or fail to occur.

A loss contingency is accrued by a charge to income if the loss is both probable and can be reasonably estimated. However, based on conservatism, a gain contingency should be included in note disclosure only, but should not be recognized in the financial statements prior to realization.

Answer choices "B" and "C" are incorrect because no amount of gain should be recognized prior to realization.

Answer choice "D" is incorrect because gain contingencies should be disclosed in order to keep the financial statements from being misleading.

11.   C   Under the cash basis of accounting, which is not appropriate under generally accepted accounting principles, net income is affected by inflows and outflows of cash rather than appropriate accrual basis considerations.

Under accrual basis accounting, revenues are recognized when earned and expenses are recognized when incurred, without regard to the inflows and outflows of cash.

Consequently, 1992 accrual basis net income will exceed 1992 cash basis net income (i.e., increased compared to the cash basis) when Potoma had lower accrued expenses on December 31, 1992, than on January 1, 1992, because cash paid for expenses will exceed expenses recognized according to the accrual basis.

Answer choice "A" is incorrect because the payment of cash dividends will not affect income under either the cash basis or accrual basis.

Answer choice "B" is incorrect because the accounting for uncollectible accounts receivable will not influence cash basis net income; accounts receivable are not recognized under the cash basis, and uncollectible accounts expense will not appear in a cash basis income statement.

Answer choice "D" is incorrect because the sale of used equipment for cash at a gain will result in higher cash basis net income than accrual basis net income. Under the cash basis, the entire proceeds of the sale will be included in net income, and under the accrual basis, only the excess of the cash proceeds over the carrying value of the asset will be included in net income.

12.   C   When an entity has decided to end operations, the balance sheet is prepared on the basis of an assumption of liquidation, rather than on the going-concern assumption. The appropriate emphasis is no longer one of reporting historical costs or future service potential of assets, but one of reporting assets at their expected net realizable value. As such, the appropriate measurement basis for equipment included in Brooks' December 31, 1992, balance sheet is net realizable value.

Answer choice "A" is incorrect because in a liquidation situation, the historical cost of an asset is not relevant. Further, even under a going-concern assumption, historical cost is an appropriate measurement basis only at the time the equipment was acquired. Subsequent to acquisition, the equipment should be measured at book value (cost less accumulated depreciation).

Answer choice "B" is incorrect because current reproduction cost is an input measure (a measure of the cost of acquiring an asset), rather than an output measure, and is irrelevant in a liquidation assumption.

Answer choice "D" is incorrect because current replacement cost is an input measure (a measure of the cost of acquiring an asset), rather than an output measure, and is irrelevant in a liquidation assumption.

13. B Clearly, the proper matching of revenue with the period of benefit requires that revenue that is collected in advance should be reported as deferred revenues at the amount of cash received.

It should be noted that revenues would be earned ratably over each twelve-month contract year. As such, if, at December 31, 1992, the deferred revenues' balance on unperformed service contracts was significantly less than the balance at December 31, 1991, then most 1992 contracts were signed earlier in the calendar year (and hence more was earned) than were the 1991 contracts.

Answer choice "A" is incorrect because the December 31, 1992, deferred revenues would have been more, and not less, than the December 31, 1991, deferred revenues if most 1992 contracts were signed later in the calendar year than were the 1991 contracts.

Answer choices "C" and "D" are incorrect because contribution margin (i.e., revenue less variable costs) has no bearing on changes in deferred revenue balances.

14. D This question indicates that use of the installment sales method is appropriate. The installment sales method should be used for financial accounting purposes only when there is a significant risk of not collecting the sales price, and where the degree of collectibility cannot be estimated. Under the installment sales method, gross profit is realized only as cash is collected.

Revenue realized under the installment method is equal to the cash collected multiplied by the applicable gross profit percentage for the period in which the sale was made. Any gross profit not collected is "deferred" on the balance sheet pending collection. When collections are subsequently made, realized gross profit is increased via debit to the deferred gross profit account.

Note the following with respect to this question.
1. The gross profit percentage is 40 percent.
2. The deferred gross profit at December 31, 1992, before recognition of realized gross profit would help establish the total installment sales for 1992, which are otherwise unknown.

The answer is determined as follows:

Installment sales, 1992; $560,000/40%	$1,400,000
Installment accounts receivable, December 31, 1992	800,000
Cash collections, 1992	$ 600,000
Realized gross profit, 1992; $600,000 × 40%	$ 240,000

Answer choices other than "D" are based on incorrect assumptions and/or combinations.

15. B Under the accrual basis for financial statement purposes, revenue is recognized when the service is performed; any collections received prior to completion of the service constitute deferred revenue.

The basis for recognition of revenue should consider that 40 percent of the total dollars spent for repairs are "incurred evenly during the first contract year." Given the sale of 1,000 two-year contracts "evenly throughout the year," revenue should be recognized as 40 percent of one-half (i.e., the first year) of the contracts. Consequently, at December 31, 1992, Dunne should report as deferred service contract revenue the amount of the equipment service contracts due to expire after 1992, or $480,000:

1992 equipment service contracts revenue received in advance; 1,000 × $600	$600,000
Less: 1992 equipment service contract revenue earned ($600,000 × .40)/2	(120,000)
Deferred service contract revenue, December 31, 1992	$480,000

Answer choice "A" is incorrect because it considers only $60,000 as being earned in 1992, rather than $120,000.

Answer choice "C" is incorrect because it assumes $240,000 as being earned in 1992, rather than one-half of the $240,000, or $120,000.

Answer choice "D" is incorrect because it assumes one-half of $600,000, or $300,000, as being earned in 1992, and $120,000 is the appropriate amount earned.

16. C This question is based on FASB Statement #52, "Foreign Currency Translation."

Gains and losses on foreign currency transactions are generally included in determining net income for the period in which the exchange rate changes. Likewise, a transaction gain or loss realized upon settlement of a foreign currency transaction generally should be included in determining net income for the period in which the transaction is settled.

When the balance sheet date falls between the date of a transaction and the date of settlement, any receivable or payable must be adjusted to its dollar equivalent as of the balance sheet date. The difference between the current balance and the new balance is an exchange gain or loss. Obviously, upon settlement of the transaction, the gain or loss will be finalized.

While this question does not deal with translation adjustments, it should be noted that the latter are reported separately as a component of stockholders' equity; they are not included in income unless there is a sale or liquidation of the investment in the foreign entity.

This question essentially deals with a forward exchange contract, which is an agreement to exchange different currencies at a specified future date and at a specified rate; such contracts result in transaction gain or loss.

The following should be noted with respect to forward exchange contracts.
1. Computation of transaction gain or loss
   a. Speculative forward exchange contracts
      Gain or loss on such a contract (one that does not hedge an exposure) is computed by multiplying the foreign currency amount by the difference between the forward rate available for the remaining maturity of the contract and the contracted forward rate (or the last rate used to measure gain or loss).
   b. Contracts other than speculative contracts (hedges, etc.)
      Gain or loss is computed by multiplying the foreign currency amount by the difference between the spot rate at the balance sheet date and the spot rate at the inception of the forward contract (or the spot rate last used to measure gain or loss on that contract for an earlier period).

2. Nonrecognition of gains and losses
   A gain or loss on a forward contract that is intended to hedge an identifiable foreign currency commitment (such as an agreement to purchase or sell equipment) shall be deferred and included in the measurement of the related foreign currency transaction (i.e., the purchase or sale).
   (Losses should not be deferred, however, if it is estimated that deferral would lead to recognizing losses in later periods.)

The transaction in this question involves a contract for speculation. As such, the transaction gain or loss is equal to the foreign currency amount multiplied by the difference between the forward rate for the remaining maturity of the contract (i.e., the 30-day rate as of 9/30/92 since the contract was for 60 days beginning 9/1/92) and the contracted forward rate.

Accordingly, Brady should report 50,000 × (.$74 - $.72), or $1,000, as foreign exchange loss at September 30, 1992.

Answer choice "A" is incorrect because it is based on the spot rate (i.e., 50,000 × [$.75 - $.70] equals $2,500), and should be based on the appropriate forward rate.

Answer choices "B" and "D" are not logical in view of the explanation provided in the answer to "C."

17. D   Under the accrual basis of accounting, in contrast to the cash basis of accounting, revenue is recognized when earned rather than when cash is received. Likewise, under the accrual basis of accounting, in contrast to the cash basis, expenses are recognized when the cost is incurred rather than when cash is paid.

Cash-basis income:

Revenue, collected in May	$3,200
Expenses	0
Cash-basis net income	$3,200

Accrual-basis income:

Revenue, earned in April	$3,200
Expenses incurred in April	1,500
Accrual-basis income	$1,700

It should be noted that the $1,000 cash investment and the $500 cash withdrawals impact capital, and have no effect on income on either the accrual basis or cash basis of accounting.

Answer choices other than "D" are based upon incorrect assumptions and/or combinations.

18.   A   Revenue realized under the installment method is equal to the cash collected multiplied by the applicable gross profit percentage for the period in which the sale was made. Any gross profit not collected is "deferred" on the balance sheet pending collection. When collections are subsequently made, realized gross profit is increased via a debit to the deferred gross profit account.

The following should also be noted.
1.   Interest should not be included in installment cash collections. Thus, the cash collections equal the $150,000 down payment on January 2, 1991, plus $325,000 - $75,000, or $250,000, on January 2, 1992; obviously, the total is $400,000.
2.   The installment sales method should not be used for financial accounting purposes unless there is a significant risk as to the collection of the sales price, and when the degree of collectibility cannot be estimated. Since it was stated that the method was appropriately used, no decision in this connection was necessary.

The deferred gross profit should be $150,000:

Installment sales	$900,000
Cost of installment sales; $900,000 - $270,000	630,000
Gross profit	$270,000
Gross profit percentage; $270,000/$900,000	30%
Installment receivables; $900,000 - $400,000	$500,000
Deferred gross profit, December 31, 1992; $500,000 × 30%	$150,000

Answer choices other than "A" are based on incorrect assumptions.

19.   A   A current liability is one that will require liquidation within one year, or the operating cycle, whichever is longer. Accordingly, each of the items listed are elements of current liabilities at December 31, 1992, except the notes payable, due 1994.

Total current liabilities should be <u>$45,000</u>:

Accounts payable		$15,000
Bonds payable, due 1993	$25,000	
Less: Bond discount	(3,000)	22,000
Dividends payable 1/31/93		8,000
Total current liabilities		$45,000

Answer choice "B" is incorrect because the $3,000 discount on bonds payable is added, and should be subtracted.

Answer choice "C" is incorrect because $65,000 incorrectly includes the notes payable due in 1994; such notes are noncurrent liabilities.

Answer choice "D" is not logical in view of the explanation provided.

20. B   According to APB Opinion #21, "Interest on Receivables and Payables," when a receivable or payable is noninterest bearing, or bears interest at an unrealistic rate, interest at a reasonable rate must be imputed. As such, receivables and payables are stated at their present values.

However, APB Opinion #21 is only applicable to receivables or payables with terms in excess of one year. For this reason, on Roth's December 31, 1992, balance sheet, the <u>note payable</u> due in nine months <u>should be reported at $10,000</u>, the face amount of the note.

Answer choice "A" is incorrect because $10,300 would be the maturity value of the note if its term were 1 year rather than 9 months (i.e., $10,000 + [$10,000 × 3 percent] is $10,300).

Answer choice "C" is incorrect because $9,652 is the present value of the note's maturity value discounted at 8 percent; the note should be presented at its face amount because the term is less than one year.

Answer choice "D" is incorrect because $9,440 is the present value of the face amount of the note discounted at 8 percent; the note should be reported at its face amount because its term is less than one year.

21. D   This question requires a determination of the amount of liability for services to be recognized on the balance sheet.

At December 31, 1992, Ross had an accrued liability for four of the five days worked in 1992, and paid in 1993 for the week ended January 1, 1993, or 80 percent (i.e., 4/5) of $80,000, which is $64,000. In addition, there was a $25,000 liability for vacation pay earned, but not taken. Therefore, <u>Ross should report</u> a total <u>accrued salary and vacation pay of $89,000</u> in its December 31, 1992, balance sheet.

Answer choice "A" is incorrect because $64,000 (i.e., 80% ×
$80,000) is the amount of the accrued salaries; the accrued vacation
pay of $25,000 should also be included.

Answer choice "B" is incorrect because $68,000 represents the
accrued salaries of $64,000 (i.e., 80% × $80,000), plus 80 percent
of the $5,000 increase in the accrued vacation pay from the
beginning to the end of the year. The correct liability for accrued
vacation pay is $25,000, not $4,000.

Answer choice "C" is incorrect because $69,000 is accrued salaries
of $64,000 (i.e., 80% × $80,000), plus the $5,000 increase in the
accrued vacation pay from the beginning to the end of the year. The
correct liability for accrued vacation pay is $25,000, not $5,000.

22. D Accrued interest payable is the amount of interest that has been
incurred from the last interest payment date to the balance sheet
date. Beau last paid interest on June 30, 1992; therefore, at
September 30, 1992, interest has accrued for 3 months. Accrued
interest payable at September 30, 1992, is $9,000 (i.e., 300,000 ×
12% × 3/12).

Answer choice "A" is incorrect because $27,000 is the amount of
interest expense that would have been incurred had no interest been
paid for 9 months (i.e., $300,000 × 12% × 9/12); only 3 months had
elapsed since the last payment date.

Answer choice "B" is incorrect because $24,000 is the amount of
interest expense incurred for the period January 31, 1992, to
September 30, 1992 (i.e., $300,000 × 12% × 8/12), not the amount
of accrued interest payable. Interest was paid on June 30, 1992.

Answer choice "C" is incorrect because $18,000 is the amount of
interest payable at each semiannual interest date (i.e., $300,000 ×
12% × 6/12); it is not the amount payable at September 30, 1992.

23. A The customer's account with a debit balance is not an element of
accounts payable at December 31, 1992; rather, it should be included
as a current asset at that date. Therefore, the amount of the debit
balance, $50,000, should be added back to accounts payable.

Since the checks were not mailed until January 5, 1993, the funds
were not legally disbursed, and the liability extinguished at
December 31, 1992. Therefore, the amount of the checks; i.e.,
$100,000, should be added back to accounts payable and to cash.

Lyle should report accounts payable of $510,000 in it December 31,
1992, balance sheet.

Unadjusted balance	$360,000
Customer with debit balance	50,000
Unmailed checks	100,000
Adjusted accounts payable	$510,000

Answer choice "B" is incorrect because the $100,000 adjustment for the checks not mailed is excluded; it should be included.

Answer choice "C" is incorrect because the $100,000 adjustment for checks not mailed is excluded, and should be included, and because the $50,000 debit balance is subtracted, and should be added (i.e., $360,000 - $50,000 is $310,000).

Answer choice "D" is incorrect because both the $100,000 and $50,000 adjustments are subtracted, and should be added (i.e., $360,000 - $150,000 equals $210,000).

24.   C   Accrued <u>interest payable would be</u> equal to the $900,000 note balance at December 31, 1992 (i.e., $1,350,000 less the $450,000 payment on September 1, 1992), at 12 percent for four months, or <u>$36,000</u>.

It should be noted that the 11 percent prime rate is irrelevant because 12 percent is a reasonable rate of interest for a note of this term.

Answer choices other than "C" are incorrect in view of the explanation provided.

25.   C   Kent's escrow liability at December 31, 1992, is <u>$605,000</u>:

Balance in escrow account, January 1, 1992	$ 700,000
Escrow payments received during 1992	1,580,000
Real estate taxes paid during 1992	(1,720,000)
Interest on escrow funds during 1992,	
net of 10% service fee; $50,000 × 90%	45,000
Escrow liability at December 31, 1992	$ 605,000

Answer choices other than "C" are incorrect in view of the explanation provided.

26.   D   The background for this question is FASB Statement #15, "Accounting by Debtors and Creditors for Troubled Debt Restructuring."

In accordance with Statement #15, there can be a transfer in full settlement of the debt, or a modification of the terms of the indebtedness. Background for the debtor's accounting for each is as follows:

1.   Transfer in full settlement
     The debtor has two elements of the gain and/or loss.
     a.   The debtor's extraordinary gain on the debt restructuring is equal to the difference between the fair value of the assets exchanged and the carrying amount of the debt, inclusive of accrued interest. As an extraordinary item, it is presented net of income taxes.
     b.   In addition, there is a gain or loss on disposal of any assets exchanged in the transaction, equal to the difference between the fair value and the carrying amount of the

assets. This element of gain or loss is not a gain or loss on the restructuring but is treated as any other asset disposal; usually, as an ordinary item.

2. Modification of terms
   a. Carrying value of debt (including accrued interest) does not exceed future cash payments - The effects are accounted for prospectively, and the carrying amount of the debt is not changed. No gain or loss is recognized. Interest expense is determined based upon the implicit interest rate using the "interest method," which equates the present value of the future cash payments with the carrying amount of the debt. (This, however, can be a complex situation to measure and is not likely to be encountered on the exam.)
   b. Carrying value of debt (including accrued interest) exceeds future cash payments - The carrying amount of the debt is reduced to an amount equal to future cash payments, and an extraordinary gain is recognized by the debtor. Further, no interest expense is recognized from reduction until maturity; all future payments are a reduction of the adjusted carrying value of the debt.

This question concerns a transfer in full settlement.

Knob should report a pretax extraordinary gain on the restructuring of $60,000, which is equal to the difference between the carrying amount of the liability liquidated (i.e., $150,000) and the fair value of the real estate transferred (i.e., $90,000).

Answer choice "A" is incorrect because ($10,000) is the loss on the disposal of the real estate (i.e., $100,000 - $90,000).

Answer choice "B" is incorrect because a gain must be recognized in this case. A gain would not be recognized only if the carrying value of the debt did not exceed the future cash payments in a modification of terms.

Answer choice "C" is incorrect because $50,000 is the net gain on both the restructuring and the disposal of the real estate (i.e., $150,000 - $100,000).

27. A Refer to the explanation of question #26, above, for a full discussion of FASB #15.

The loss on the transfer of the real estate that Knob should report as an ordinary loss on its income statement is ($10,000), which is the excess of the carrying amount of the real estate transferred (i.e., $100,000) over its fair value (i.e., $90,000).

Answer choice "B" is incorrect because an ordinary gain or loss on disposal of an asset must be recognized for the difference between the carrying value of the asset transferred and its fair value.

Answer choice "C" is incorrect because $50,000 is the net gain on both the transfer of the real estate and the restructuring of the payable (i.e., $150,000 - $100,000).

Answer choice "D" is incorrect because $60,000 is the amount of pretax extraordinary gain to be recognized on the restructuring (i.e., the difference between the $150,000 liability liquidated, and the $90,000 fair value of the real estate transferred).

28. B   As to a lessee, a lease is a capital lease if it meets one or more of the following criteria; any other lease is an operating lease.
1. Property ownership transfers to the lessee by the end of the lease term.
2. The lease contains a bargain purchase option.
3. The lease term is at least 75 percent of the estimated life of the property.
4. The present value of minimum lease payments at the inception of the lease (excluding such executory costs as property taxes, maintenance, insurance, etc.) equals or exceeds 90 percent of the fair value of the property.

Examination of the facts indicates that both lease M and lease P are capital leases since the third criterion above has been met.

Answer choices other than "B" are based on incorrect assumptions and/or combinations.

29. A   A stock dividend that is less than 20 percent to 25 percent of the shares issued and outstanding at the date of declaration decreases retained earnings and increases capital stock and additional paid-in capital in an amount equal to the fair market value of the shares to be issued. A stock dividend in excess of this range decreases retained earnings in an amount equal to the par value of the shares issued.

The fair market value used is the value as of the date of declaration.

Therefore, the stock dividend of 10 percent would result in a decrease in retained earnings equal to the fair market value of $2,700 (i.e., 3,000 shares × 10% × $9), an increase in common stock for the par value of $600 (i.e., 3,000 × 10% × $2), and a credit to additional paid-in capital for the difference, or $2,100.

Answer choice "B" is incorrect because it is based on the fair market value at the distribution date, and should be based on the value at the declaration date.

Answer choice "C" is incorrect because it represents the entire amount of the dividend, and not the credit to additional paid-in capital.

Answer choice "D" is incorrect for two reasons. First, it is based on the fair market value at the date of distribution (i.e., 10% × 3,000 shares × $10 equals $3,000), and should be based on the value at the declaration date. In addition, it represents the entire amount of the dividend, and not the credit to additional paid-in capital.

30.   C   If capital stock is retired at its par or stated value, the capital stock account is debited and cash is credited.

If stock is retired for less than the par or stated value, the difference is credited to additional paid-in capital.

If the stock is retired at a price that is in excess of the par or stated value, there are two alternate treatments that are acceptable.

Under the first treatment, which is preferable, the capital stock account is debited for the par or stated value and additional paid-in capital is debited for a pro-rata amount associated with the same issue of stock. Any excess of the acquisition price over the total paid-in capital (capital stock plus additional paid-in capital) is charged to retained earnings.

Under the second treatment, the entire excess of the acquisition price over the total paid-in capital is charged to retained earnings.

Here, the stock was retired at a price which was less than its par value. Clearly, the $22,500 paid was less than the $25,000 attributable to 25 percent of the shares (i.e., 2,000 × 25% × $50).

Accordingly, $50 per share, or $25,000, is debited to preferred stock, and the difference, or $2,500, is credited to additional paid-in capital.

Answer choices other than "C" are based on incorrect assumptions and/or combinations.

31.   B   Book value per share of common stock equals common stockholders' equity divided by the shares of common stock outstanding.

When there is preferred stock outstanding and there is a liquidation or redemption value in excess of the par value thereof, and/or preferred dividends in arrears on cumulative preferred stock, the equity available to common stockholders is reduced by such amounts.

In this situation, there is a liquidation value in excess of par of 5 percent (i.e., $105 − $100 equals $5, or 5 percent per share). The book value per common share is $13.00:

Total stockholders' equity;
($100,000 + $300,000 + $95,000) $495,000
Less: Preferred stock at liquidation value;
$100,000 × 105%   (105,000)
Equity available for common stockholders $390,000
Book value per common share; $390,000/(300,000/$10) $13.00

Answer choice "A" is incorrect because the equity available for common stockholders is not reduced by the $5,000 liquidation premium (i.e., $395,000/30,000 shares equals $13.17).

Answer choices "C" and "D" are not logical in view of the explanation provided.

32.   C   In general, in accordance with FASB Statement #52, "Foreign Currency Translation," translation adjustments should be distinguished from transaction gains and losses.

Translation adjustments result from the process of translating financial statements from an entity's functional currency into the reporting currency. Translation adjustment gains and losses should not be included in determining net income but should be accumulated and reported separately as a component of stockholders' equity.

Transaction gains and losses result from exchange rate differentials that occur when there is a time lapse between a transaction date in a foreign currency and a settlement date in that currency; e.g., a sale on account with payment 30 days later. Such gains and losses should be included as components of income from continuing operations. (It should also be noted that when the balance sheet falls between the date of a transaction and final settlement, receivables/payables must be adjusted to the dollar equivalent as of the balance sheet date; the difference is an exchange gain or loss. Upon settlement of the transaction, there will be a further gain or loss based on the recorded balance at that time.)

Therefore, a cumulative foreign exchange translation loss should be reported as a stockholders' equity contra account.

Answer choices "A" and "B" are incorrect because both discounts and premiums on convertible bonds are reported in the liability section of the balance sheet as deductions from or additions to the related bonds, regardless of the fact that the bonds are common stock equivalents.

Answer choice "D" is incorrect because organization costs are assets, and would not be reported as a stockholders' equity contra account.

33.   A   Stock rights (i.e., "warrants") represent the rights of existing stockholders to buy additional shares within a specified future time at a specified price.

No entry in connection with stock rights is made until the rights are exercised. It should also be considered that net income is not affected by reason of the exercise of stock rights. Rather, any difference between the issue price and par or stated value is recorded as an element of additional paid-in capital.

Since the exercise price is greater than par value, when the rights are exercised, additional paid-in capital would increase. However, as noted, net income would not be affected.

Answer choices other than "A" are based on incorrect assumptions and/or combinations.

34. D Common stock equivalents consist of stock options, warrants and the like, plus convertible securities that, at the time of issuance, have an effective yield of less than 66-2/3 percent of the average Aa corporate bond yield. Common stock equivalents are a consideration in computing primary earnings per share.

In computing fully diluted earnings per share, the denominator of the fraction broadens. It includes not only common stock outstanding and common stock equivalents, but convertible securities that were not a factor in computing primary earnings per share.

Securities that produce antidilutive effects (increase earnings per share or decrease a loss per share) are excluded from earnings per share computations, either for primary earnings per share, or for fully diluted earnings per share.

Hence, when computing primary earnings per share, convertible securities that are common stock equivalents are recognized only if they are dilutive.

Answer choice "A" is incorrect because convertible securities that are common stock equivalents are recognized when computing primary earnings per share, unless they are antidilutive.

Answer choices "B" and "C" are incorrect because securities that produce antidilutive effects are excluded from earnings per share computations, either for primary or for fully diluted earnings per share, and hence are not recognized.

35. D The inventory turnover ratio provides information about the length of time a company holds its inventory prior to sale. It is computed by dividing the cost of goods sold by average inventory.

The turnover ratio would increase if either cost of goods sold increased, or average inventory decreased.

The information presented indicates that sales and inventory remained essentially unchanged; therefore, an increase in cost of goods sold is the only feasible explanation for an increase in the turnover ratio. It must logically follow that with sales constant, cost of goods sold and the inventory turnover would increase only if the gross profit percentage decreased.

Answer choice "A" is incorrect because a decrease in the cost of goods sold would result in a decrease in the inventory turnover ratio.

Answer choices "B" and "C" are incorrect because neither the accounts receivable turnover ratio nor the total asset turnover ratio would impact the inventory turnover ratio.

36.   A   Questions #36 through #38 are based on the provisions of FASB Statement #95, "Statement of Cash Flows."

The Statement classifies cash receipts and cash payments as cash inflows and cash outflows from investing activities, financing activities, and operating activities.

The following should be noted for background.
1.   Cash flows from investing activities
   a.   Making and collecting loans (but not related interest).
   b.   Acquiring and disposing of debt or equity instruments of other entities, except for investments in "trading securities," as per FASB Statement #115, which are treated as operating cash flows (but not related interest or dividends).
   c.   Acquiring and disposing of property, plant, and equipment and other productive assets.

2.   Cash flows from financing activities
   a.   Obtaining resources from owners and providing them with a return on, and a return of, their investment (but not related interest).
   b.   Borrowing money and repaying amounts involved, or otherwise settling the obligation (but not related interest).
   c.   Obtaining and paying for other resources obtained from creditors on long-term credit (but not related interest).

3.   Cash flows from operating activities
   Operating activities include the cash effects of all transactions and other events that are neither investing activities nor financing activities; essentially, operating activities relate to income statement items. They generally involve producing and delivering goods and providing services.

   It should be noted that receipts of interest and dividends from all sources, and interest paid to creditors, represent operating activities.

4.   Noncash activities
   Information about investing and financing activities not resulting in cash receipts or cash payments, such as issuing a mortgage note in exchange for a building, converting debt to

equity, or exchanging common stock for plant and equipment, should be reported separately (as supplementary information) and not be included in the body of the statement.

5. Direct and indirect methods
Statement #95 encourages use of the direct method of presenting cash flow information, but also permits use of the indirect method.

Under the direct method, individual income statement items are presented as gross cash receipts and gross cash payments. In addition, a reconciliation of net income and net cash flows from operating activities is presented as a separate schedule; this schedule has the same net result as gross cash receipts and cash payments from operating activities.

Under the indirect method, the reconciliation of net income and net cash flows from operating activities is the key element in the statement. It is presented either in the body of the statement, or in a separate schedule. If presented in a separate schedule, the net cash flow from operating activities is presented as a single line item. There is no presentation of gross cash receipts and gross cash payments from operating activities.

In effect, this question requires a reconciliation of net income and net cash (flows) provided by operations. Each element of information provided must be examined and reacted to.

Net cash provided by operating activities was $151,400:

Net income	$150,000
Add (subtract):	
Increase in accounts receivable; $29,000 - $23,000	(6,000)
Increase in allowance for uncollectible accounts; $1,000 - $800	200
Decrease in prepaid rent expense; $12,400 - $8,200	4,200
Increase in accounts payable; $22,400 - $19,400	3,000
Net cash provided by operating activities, 1992	$151,400

Parenthetically, the following should be noted.
1. An increase in accounts receivable has the effect of increasing net income (i.e., sales). Since the increase of $6,000 did not provide cash per se, it is subtracted.
2. An increase in allowance for uncollectibles has the effect of decreasing net income (i.e., bad debt expense). Since the increase of $200 did not use cash per se, it is added back.
3. A decrease in prepaid rent expense has the effect of decreasing net income (i.e., rent expense). Since the decrease of $4,200 did not use cash per se, it is added back.
4. An increase in accounts payable has the effect of decreasing net income (i.e., purchases). Since the increase of $3,000 did not use cash per se, it is added back.

Answer choices other than "A" are incorrect in view of the explanation provided.

37. B   Refer to question #36 for background on the provisions of FASB #95, "Statement of Cash Flows," and in particular on cash flows from operating activities.

Net cash provided by operating activities was <u>$347,000</u>:

Net income	$300,000
Add (subtract):	
Depreciation expense	52,000
Gain on sale of equipment	(5,000)
<u>Net cash provided by operating activities, 1992</u>	<u>$347,000</u>

The following should be noted.
1. Depreciation expense is added because it decreases net income and does not require cash.
2. The $5,000 gain on the sale of equipment increased net income and did not provide cash per se (the proceeds of the sale did, which is an investing activity); thus, the gain is subtracted.

Answer choices other than "B" are not logical in view of the explanation provided.

38. A   In accordance with FASB Statement #95, cash flows from investing activities includes:
1. Making and collecting loans (but not related interest).
2. Acquiring and disposing of debt or equity instruments of other entities, except for investments in "trading securities," as per FASB #115, which are treated as operating cash flows (but not related interest or dividends).
3. Acquiring and disposing of property, plant, and equipment and other productive assets.

The net cash used in investing activities amounts to <u>$2,000</u>:

Sale of equipment (cash inflow):	
$25,000 - $12,000 + $5,000	($18,000)
Acquisition of equipment (cash outflow)	20,000
<u>Net cash used in investing activities, 1992</u>	<u>$ 2,000</u>

The following should be noted.
1. Cash inflows and outflows, and not carrying amounts, are the items to report. Thus, the sale of equipment would have resulted in a cash inflow equal to the carrying value of $13,000 (i.e., $25,000 - $12,000), plus the $5,000 gain, or $18,000.
2. Since the requirement was "net cash used," which implies a net cash outflow, cash inflows appear above in brackets.
3. Information about investing activities not resulting in cash receipts or cash payments, such as the acquisition of $30,000 (i.e., $50,000 - $20,000) of equipment through the issuance of long-term debt, is reported as supplementary information only.

Answer choices other than "A" are not logical in view of the explanation provided.

39. B In accordance with FASB Statement #109, "Employers' Accounting for Postretirement Benefits Other than Pensions," the attribution period is the period during which an employee earns the right to receive postretirement benefits; that is, the period from the time that credits begin to accumulate to the time the employee reaches full eligibility for benefits.

In order to receive benefits, an employee of Bounty must work at least 10 years and be aged 55 or older when retiring. Since Fletcher was hired at age 48, he will earn credits over the next ten years, until he is age 58. Accordingly, the attribution period is when Fletcher is aged 48 to 58.

Answer choices other than "B" are inconsistent with the information presented.

40. A According to FASB Statement #87, "Employers' Accounting for Pensions," the difference between the amount of pension cost recognized and the amount funded with the pension trustee represents an adjustment to the accrued or prepaid pension cost.

An expense in excess of funding results in an accrued pension cost (a liability), while funding in excess of pension expense results in a prepaid pension cost (an asset).

Under Statement #87, net periodic pension cost is the sum of the following components.
1. Service cost - The increase in the projected benefit obligation resulting from services rendered by employees in the current period. (Will increase the periodic cost.)

2. Amortization of prior service cost - The amount allocated to the current period resulting from retroactive amendments to the pension plan. (Will increase the periodic cost.)

    Prior service costs are generally the result of a plan adoption or amendment; while they relate to the past, they benefit the future. Further, these costs are recognized only as they are amortized over current and future years; they are not booked as liabilities.

3. Return on plan assets - Generally, a decrease in the net periodic pension cost based on either expected or actual return. (While generally a decrease in the cost, can increase it as well.)
    a. Expected return - The fair value of plan assets as of the beginning of the year multiplied by the expected rate.
    b. Actual return - The change in the fair value of plan assets during the period.

4. <u>Interest cost</u> - The interest cost component recognized in a period shall be determined as the increase in the projected benefit obligation due to the passage of time. It is measured by applying the discount rate to the projected benefit obligation as of the beginning of the year. (Will increase the periodic cost.)

5. <u>Amortization of unrecognized gains or losses</u> - The amount added to or subtracted from the net periodic pension cost when the actual return on plan assets is materially different than the expected return. The difference is deferred and amortized when the cumulative unrecognized gain or loss exceeds 10 percent of the greater of the beginning of year balances of either the fair value of plan assets or projected benefit obligation; this excess is referred to as the "corridor" amount.

The amount of amortization is the excess of the unrecognized gain or loss over the corridor amount divided by the average remaining service period of active employees.

Based on the background provided, the company reports a liability for unfunded accrued pension cost equal to the amount that <u>cumulative net pension cost accrued exceeds contributions to the plan</u>.

Answer choices other than "A" are incorrect because each inappropriately considers the vested benefit obligation as influencing the accrued pension cost.

41. C See the answer to question #40 for background information on FASB #87, "Employers' Accounting for Pensions."

In the absence of prior service costs, the change in the projected benefit obligation of a defined benefit pension plan will be equal to the sum of the interest cost and service cost components of net periodic pension cost. Accordingly, the service cost component is measured using the <u>projected benefit obligation</u>.

The projected benefit obligation is the actuarial present value of benefits attributed by the pension benefit formula to employee service earned to date using projected salary levels.

Answer choice "A" is incorrect because the unfunded accumulated benefit obligation is used only to determine the amount of the additional pension obligation that must be recognized on the balance sheet. It does not relate to the measurement of net periodic pension cost.

Answer choice "B" is incorrect because the unfunded vested benefit obligation is not a determining factor in the service cost component.

Answer choice "D" is incorrect because the expected return on plan assets is a separate component of net pension cost, and not part of the service cost component.

42.   D   Under current cost accounting, assets and related expenses resulting
          from use are measured in terms of current costs or lower recoverable
          amounts (net realizable value). Current cost may be determined in a
          variety of ways; e.g., LIFO cost flow, specific price indexes,
          supplier invoices, present value, appraisal, etc.

          Current cost accounting also requires recognition of holding gains
          or losses prior to realization through a sale or exchange.

          Obviously, a holding gain could arise with respect to inventory
          (i.e., inventory is "held" prior to realization [sale]).

          In summary, the holding gain is the change in value between current
          cost (i.e., "replacement cost") of $10 per unit at December 31,
          1991, and the historical cost of $8 on March 31, 1991. Hence, Vend's
          holding gain on each unit is $10 - $8, or $2.00.

          Parenthetically, it should be noted that the price index information
          was not relevant.

          Answer choices other than "D" are not logical in view of the
          explanation provided.

43.   C   The "cumulative effect of an accounting change" is a separate income
          statement item provided for in APB Opinion #20, "Accounting
          Changes." "Cumulative effect" type items appear on the income
          statement (net of tax effect) after extraordinary items.

          In accordance with Opinion #20, "cumulative effect" items arise from
          changes in accounting principles (including changes in accounting
          methods). Not only is the new principle to be used in current and
          future periods, there is additional income statement disclosure of
          the "cumulative effect," the measure of which is the difference
          between beginning retained earnings and the retained earnings
          balance had the method been retroactively applied.

          Changes in accounting estimate, as opposed to changes in principle,
          require presentation only in current and future years. There is no
          "cumulative effect" involved.

          The cumulative effect of the change to the units of production
          method from the straight-line method is the after-tax difference in
          retained earnings that would have existed if the units of production
          method had been used since acquisition.

          The cumulative effect should be $1,400:

          Accumulated depreciation:
             Units of production method;
                 ($50,000/50,000) × 12,000 hours $12,000
             Straight line; ($50,000/10) × 2   10,000
          Cumulative effect before taxes $ 2,000
          Cumulative effect, net of taxes, 1992; $2,000 × 70% $ 1,400

Answer choice "A" is incorrect because the cumulative effect is presented before taxes, and should be net of taxes.

Answer choice "B" is incorrect because the cumulative effect should be presented net of tax effect, and it is not. Also the cumulative effect should be presented on the income statement, and not as an adjustment to beginning retained earnings.

Answer choice "D" is incorrect because the cumulative effect should be presented on the income statement, and not as an adjustment to beginning retained earnings.

44.   B   This question is based on APB Opinion #20, "Accounting Changes," and FASB Statement #16, "Prior Period Adjustments."

The following selected background information should be noted.
1.   "Cumulative effect" type items
     The "cumulative effect of an accounting change" is a separate income statement item provided for in Opinion #20. Such items appear on the income statement (net of tax effect) after extraordinary items.

     In accordance with Opinion #20, "cumulative effect" items arise from changes in accounting principles (including changes in accounting methods). Not only is the new principle to be used in current and future periods, there is additional disclosure of the "cumulative effect," the measure of which is the difference between beginning retained earnings and the retained earnings balance had the method been retroactively applied.

2.   Changes in accounting estimate
     Such changes require presentation within income from continuing operations on a before-tax basis. They are accounted for in the current and future years, if the change affects both; there is no "cumulative effect" involved.

3.   Prior period adjustments
     For all practical exam purposes, the only prior period adjustments of which a candidate should be aware are corrections of errors. The correction of an error is appropriately reported on the retained earnings statement as an adjustment of the beginning balance, net of tax effect. This, of course, represents a retroactive adjustment.

     (While there are other items which are treated as prior period adjustments, they are beyond the scope of the CPA exam.)

     Errors may be broadly classified into two categories.

     a.   Those resulting from mathematical mistakes, mistakes in the application of accounting principles, or oversight or misuse of facts that existed at the time the financial statements were prepared. (The last type of error should not be confused with an appropriate change in estimate, which is not a prior period adjustment.)

b. A change from an accounting principle that is not generally accepted to one that is generally accepted is a correction of an error.

Clearly, the $60,000 of insurance premiums paid in 1991 should not have been expensed in total. Since the premiums were for three years, 2/3, or $40,000, should have been prepaid in 1991.

The error made in 1991 understated (i.e., decreased) income and retained earnings in the net of tax amount of $28,000 (i.e., $40,000 less the $12,000 income tax expense). Consequently, Conn should report $428,000 as adjusted beginning retained earnings in its 1992 statement of retained earnings (i.e., $400,000 plus the $28,000 net of tax adjustment).

Answer choice "A" has no logical basis in view of the explanation provided in "B."

Answer choice "C" is incorrect because the correction of an error should be presented net of the tax effect, and not on a gross basis.

Answer choice "D" is incorrect because it implies an adjustment amount of $60,000, net of its tax effect, (i.e., $400,000 + [70% × $60,000] equals $442,000), and the adjustment should be $40,000, net of tax effect, since 1/3 was an appropriate expense in 1991.

45. A   General and administrative expenses include all items connected with the administrative functions of the organization and/or such items that are not included in the cost of goods sold, selling expenses, or other revenue and expense.

Inclusions in the cost of goods sold are obvious; these are costs directly associated with the product. Selling expenses include items connected with the sales function. Other revenue and expense typically includes interest revenue, interest expense, gains and losses on the disposal of assets, etc.

Based on the facts provided, general and administrative expenses would include $25,000 of accounting and legal fees, $150,000 of officers' salaries, and $85,000 of insurance; the total is $260,000.

Answer choice "B" is incorrect because it includes "cost of goods sold" (i.e., freight-in) and "selling expenses" (i.e., freight-out and sales representatives salaries); none of the general and administrative expenses were included.

Answer choice "C" is incorrect because it includes the freight-out of $160,000 and the sales representatives salaries of $215,000; such items should be included in "selling expenses."

Answer choice "D" is incorrect because it includes the freight-out and the sales representatives salaries; such items are appropriately included in "selling expenses." In addition, it includes the freight-in, which should be included in "cost of goods sold."

46.   A   A charitable contribution is cash or other corporate assets given to a charity without consideration. The $250,000 in cash contributed by Yew to youth and educational programs is a charitable contribution. Of the $140,000 contributed to health and human-service organizations, $80,000 was given by employees, not by Yew; therefore, Yew only contributed $60,000 (i.e., $140,000 - $80,000). The $100,000 paid to redesign product packaging is not a charitable contribution, but rather a cost of operations.

Yew should report charitable contributions on its income statement in the amount of $310,000 (i.e., $250,000 + $60,000).

Answer choice "B" is incorrect because $390,000 incorrectly includes the $80,000 of employees' contributions through payroll deductions.

Answer choice "C" is incorrect because $410,000 incorrectly includes the $100,000 cost of redesigning product packaging, which is not a charitable contribution.

Answer choice "D" is incorrect because $490,000 incorrectly includes both the employee contributions of $80,000, and the $100,000 cost of redesigning product packaging.

47.   B   This question is based upon FASB Statement #115, "Accounting for Certain Investments in Debt and Equity Securities." Under that Statement, investments are presented on the balance sheet and unrealized gains and losses are accounted for as follows:

Trading securities are measured in the statement of financial position at market value on the statement date, with unrealized holding gains and losses included in earnings.

Held-to-maturity securities are measured at amortized cost in the statement of financial position; unrealized holding gains and losses are not recognized.

Available-for-sale securities are measured in the statement of financial position at market value at the statement date, with unrealized holding gains and losses reported as a separate component of shareholders' equity.

Accordingly, Tyne should report an unrealized holding gain of $55,000 in its 1992 income statement. This amount is the increase in the market value of the trading securities during the year.

Answer choice "A" is incorrect because $50,000 (i.e., $150,000 - $100,000) is the recovery of the previously recognized unrealized holding loss at December 31, 1991. It does not include the unrealized holding gain; this would be the correct answer for investments in current marketable equity securities under FASB #12, which has been superseded by FASB #115.

Answer choice "C" is not logical in view of the explanation provided for the answer to "B."

Answer choice "D" is incorrect because $65,000 is the increase in the market value of all investments from 12/31/91 to 12/31/92; only the change in value of the trading securities should be reflected in income.

48. D   See the answer to question #47 for background on FASB Statement #115, Accounting for Certain Investments in Debt and Equity Securities."

The amount of the <u>net</u> <u>unrealized</u> <u>holding</u> <u>loss</u> on available-for-sale securities at December 31, 1992, in Tyne's statement of stockholders' equity <u>is</u> $20,000, the difference between the cost and market value of the portfolio at December 31, 1992 (i.e., $150,000 - $130,000 = $20,000).

Answer choice "A" is not logical in view of the facts presented.

Answer choice "B" is incorrect because $10,000 is the recovery of the 1991 unrealized holding loss in 1992, (i.e., $130,000 - $120,000), and not the unrealized loss.

Answer choice "C" is incorrect because $15,000 is the difference between the aggregate cost of both the trading and available-for-sale securities (i.e., $150,000 + $150,000 = $300,000), and the aggregate market value of both investment categories at December 31, 1992 (i.e., $155,000 + $130,000 = $285,000). Only the unrealized losses for available-for-sale securities are included in a separate component of stockholders' equity.

49. D   As to a lessee, a lease is a capital lease if it meets one or more of the following criteria; any other lease is an operating lease.
1. Property ownership transfers to the lessee by the end of the lease term.
2. The lease contains a bargain purchase option.
3. The lease term is at least 75 percent of the estimated life of the property.
4. The present value of minimum lease payments at the inception of the lease (excluding such executory costs as property taxes, maintenance, insurance, etc.) equals or exceeds 90 percent of the fair value of the property.

Examination of the facts indicates that the lease is a capital lease, since the third criterion above has been met.

The following should be noted with respect to capital leases.
1. The amount capitalized is the present value of minimum lease payments (plus the present value of any bargain purchase option); this is the "net lease liability." (It should be noted, however, that the leased asset cannot be reported at an amount exceeding its fair value.)
2. The difference between the gross lease payments and the net lease liability is unamortized discount. It is amortized over the life of the lease under the interest method; i.e., the implicit rate is applied to the net lease liability outstanding for the period.
3. Each minimum (gross) lease payment is allocated between a reduction of the net lease liability and interest expense.
4. With the passing of time, the net lease liability obviously decreases; therefore, the portion of the minimum lease payment applicable to interest expense decreases, and the portion applicable to a reduction of the liability increases.

Any lease that is classified as a capital lease to the lessee is either classified as a direct-financing or sales-type lease to the lessor. The following should be noted.
1. In a direct-financing lease, the lessor purchases the property for the purpose of leasing it, and there is interest income only. The cost (or carrying amount, if different) and the fair value of the leased property are the same at the inception of the lease.
2. In a sales-type lease, there is a profit or loss resulting from the sale, as well as interest income. The cost and fair value of the leased property are not the same at the inception of the lease.
3. Under either type of lease, there is unearned interest income that is amortized over the lease period.

Unearned interest income at the inception of the lease is the difference between minimum (i.e., gross) lease payments and the present value thereof, which is amortized and recognized as income over the period of the lease using the interest method.

When utilizing the interest method, the implicit rate is applied to the present value of the lease payments outstanding at the beginning of the period to determine interest revenue. As time passes, the present value of the minimum lease payment decreases. Thus, <u>JCK should recognize interest revenue in 1992, which would be smaller than the revenue recognized in 1991</u>.

Answer choices other than "D" are based on incorrect assumptions and/or combinations.

50.   D   The following should be noted with respect to capital leases.
1. The amount capitalized is the present value of minimum lease payments (plus the present value of any bargain purchase option); this is the "net lease liability." (It should be noted,

however, that the leased asset cannot be reported at an amount exceeding its fair value.)

2. The difference between the gross lease payments and the net lease liability is unamortized discount. It is amortized over the life of the lease under the interest method; i.e., the implicit rate is applied to the net lease liability outstanding for the period.

3. Each minimum (gross) lease payment is allocated between a reduction of the net lease liability and interest expense.

4. With the passing of time, the net lease liability obviously decreases; therefore, the portion of the minimum lease payment applicable to interest expense decreases, and the portion applicable to a reduction of the liability increases.

Essentially, as noted in point "1" above, for a capital lease, the amount recorded initially by the lessee as a liability should normally equal the present value of the minimum lease payments at the beginning of the lease.

Answer choices "A" and "B" are not logical in view of the explanation provided in answer choice "D."

Answer choice "C" is incorrect because the amount recorded initially as a liability should normally equal the present value of the minimum lease payments, and not the total of the minimum lease payments.

51.   D   FASB Statement #4 provides that gains or losses on extinguishment of debt shall be aggregated and, if material, classified as an extraordinary item, net of applicable income tax effect.

The appropriate period to recognize the extraordinary item is in the period of extinguishment.

An extraordinary loss results when the retirement price paid exceeds the carrying amount of the bonds, and an extraordinary gain results when the opposite is true; i.e., when the carrying amount of the bonds exceeds the retirement price.

In this situation, the bonds were sold at a discount, which means that the carrying amount had to be less than the retirement price, which was in excess of par. Thus, Somar should report the bond retirement on its 1992 income statement as an extraordinary loss.

Answer choice "A" is incorrect because there is an extraordinary loss, not a gain (i.e., the retirement price exceeded the carrying value). In addition, the transaction would be extraordinary in any event; as such, it would not be included in continuing operations.

Answer choice "B" is incorrect because the loss is extraordinary, and would not be included in continuing operations.

Answer choice "C" is incorrect because the bonds were retired at an amount greater than their carrying value, resulting in an extraordinary loss, and not an extraordinary gain.

52.   C   Gain or loss on the retirement of bonds is equal to the difference between the price paid on retirement and the carrying, or book value (face plus unamortized premium or minus unamortized discount), of the bonds.

Unamortized bond issue costs, if any, are a reduction of the carrying value of the bonds for the purpose of determining gain or loss on retirement. (On the balance sheet they are presented as deferred charges and are not included in the carrying value of the bonds.)

FASB Statement #4 provides that gains or losses on extinguishment of debt shall be aggregated and, if material, classified as an extraordinary item (net of tax).

In the circumstances, Tory should use a net amount of <u>$248,000</u> in computing the gain or loss on retirement of debt:

Face value of bonds; $500,000 × 1/2	$250,000
Less: Unamortized issue costs; $6,000 × 2/3 × 1/2	2,000
<u>Net amount of bonds used in computing gain or loss on retirement of debt</u>	<u>$248,000</u>

As of June 2, 1993, the bonds would have been outstanding for five years, or one-third of the 15-year life; as such, two-thirds of the bond issue costs would have been unamortized on that date.

Answer choice "A" is incorrect because 1/6 of the unamortized bond issue costs, or $1,000, is subtracted, rather than $2,000 (i.e., 2/3 × $3,000).

Answer choice "B" is incorrect because 1/4 of the unamortized bond issue costs, or $1,500, is subtracted, rather than $2,000 (i.e., 2/3 × $3,000).

Answer choice "D" is incorrect because 1/2 of the unamortized bond issue costs, or $3,000, is subtracted, rather than $2,000 (i.e., 2/3 × $3,000).

53.   C   In a purchase, consolidated net income will include the parent's share of subsidiary net income (i.e., "earnings") for the period subsequent to acquisition, which in this case occurred on January 1, 1991.

The parent's share of subsidiary earnings is modified by reason of any adjustments made for purposes of consolidation, inclusive of the amortization of goodwill and/or fair value adjustments, as well as intercompany profit eliminations.

In this situation there are no intercompany profit eliminations or fair value adjustments (i.e., "the carrying amount of Style's assets and liabilities approximated their fair values"). Likewise, the question requires an answer "before amortization of goodwill."

It should also be noted that Dallas, Inc., recorded its investment in Style under the equity method; this means that Dallas' share of earnings has already been included in the investment account, and its share of Style's dividends has already been reflected as a reduction of the investment account.

Accordingly, Dallas should report $16,000 as earnings from subsidiary for 1991, based on "grossing up" the change in Style's retained earnings:

Net increase in Style, Inc., retained earnings during 1991;	
$51,000 - $36,000	$15,000
Add: Cash dividends paid	5,000
Earnings, 1991	$20,000
Earnings from subsidiary, 1991; $20,000 × 80%	$16,000

Clearly, the $12,000 net increase in Dallas' investment account (i.e., $132,000 - $120,000) during 1991 is equal to its 80 percent share of $15,000.

Answer choice "A" is incorrect because $12,000 represents the net increase in the investment account, which has appropriately been reduced by dividends (i.e., Dallas' share of Style's dividends is 80 percent of $5,000, or $4,000).

Answer choice "B" is incorrect because it merely represents the increase in Style's retained earnings during 1991 (i.e., $51,000 - $36,000 is $15,000). The impact of the 20 percent minority interest, as well as the dividends paid, has been ignored.

Answer choice "D" is incorrect because the 20 percent minority interest is ignored. While $20,000 represents earnings, as noted in the explanation to answer choice "C," Style's share is only 80 percent thereof.

54.   A   In a purchase, the consolidated stockholders' equity is equal to the parent's stockholders' equity plus its share of the net increase in the subsidiary's retained earnings since acquisition.

Since Dallas, Inc., records its investment in Style, Inc., under the equity method, it has already reflected its increase for 1991 (the first year of acquisition) in the investment account.

This is clear since the investment account has increased by 80 percent of the net $15,000 increase in Style's retained earnings for 1991 (i.e., $51,000 - $36,000), or $12,000.

Accordingly, total stockholders' equity in the consolidated balance sheet at December 31, 1991, is Dallas' total of $270,000.

Parenthetically, it should be noted that since the net increase in Style's retained earnings was $15,000, and dividends of $5,000 were paid, net income (i.e., "earnings") for 1991 would have been $20,000.

Answer choice "B" is incorrect because it includes Dallas' $16,000 share of Style's earnings (i.e., $20,000 × 80%) for 1991; under the equity method, this amount has already been included, as noted in the explanation to answer choice "A."

Answer choice "C" is not logical in light of the facts presented.

Answer choice "D" is incorrect because it represents the total of Dallas' stockholders' equity and Style's stockholders' equity (i.e., $270,000 plus $115,000 is $385,000). As noted in the explanation to answer choice "A," since the equity method was used, and the parent's increase in subsidiary retained earnings has been appropriately handled, the subsidiary's stockholders' equity is not relevant.

55. D In preparing consolidated or combined financial statements, 100 percent of unrealized profits on intercompany items still on hand are eliminated, and the balance sheet amount for inventory represents cost to the consolidated or combined group.

Since "sales by Pirn to Scroll are made on the same terms as those made to third parties," the applicable gross profit percentage is $150,000 divided by $500,000, or 30%.

Accordingly, $6,000 of intercompany profit should be eliminated:

Intercompany purchases still on hand; $100,000 - $80,000 $20,000
Intercompany profit to be eliminated; $20,000 × 30% $ 6,000

Answer choice "A" is incorrect because it represents the 30 percent gross profit percentage applied to the $100,000 total purchases by Scroll from Pirn (i.e., "Pirn's sales to Scroll"). As noted in the explanation to answer choice "D," the profit to be eliminated is with respect to items still on hand, and not total purchases.

Answer choice "B" is incorrect because $20,000 represents the total intercompany purchases still on hand (i.e., the $100,000 of Pirn's sales to Scroll less Scroll's $80,000 cost of goods sold acquired from Pirn), and not the intercompany profit.

Answer choice "C" is incorrect because it represents the entire $30,000 gross profit on intercompany sales (i.e., $100,000 × 30%) less the $20,000 intercompany purchases still on hand (i.e., $100,000 - $80,000), and not the intercompany profit.

56.   B   This question involves an intercompany transaction in fixed assets.

In essence, the carrying value of fixed assets is appropriately based on cost to the consolidated group. Any intercompany gain or loss on the transaction is eliminated in the preparation of a consolidated balance sheet.

Likewise, depreciation expense on such fixed assets is based on cost to the consolidated group, without regard to intercompany gains or losses.

Since equipment was purchased by Scroll from Pirn for $36,000, and there was a gain of $12,000, consolidated cost is $24,000. Depreciation expense is therefore $47,000:

Total depreciation expense; $40,000 + $10,000	$50,000
Less depreciation on increment above cost (gain);	
$12,000 × 1/4	3,000
Depreciation expense in Pirn's 1991 consolidated income statement	$47,000

Answer choice "A" is incorrect because $50,000 of depreciation expense is inclusive of the $3,000 of depreciation on the intercompany gain, which is inappropriate.

Answer choices "C" and "D" are not logical in view of the explanation provided.

57.   B   The current ratio is defined as current assets divided by current liabilities.

In order for a transaction to increase the current ratio, one of the following would have to occur.
1.   Current assets could increase with no change in current liabilities.
2.   Current liabilities could decrease with no change in current assets.
3.   If both current assets and current liabilities were to change, the increase or decrease in current assets would need to be proportionately greater or smaller than the increase or decrease in current liabilities.

Selling inventory on account will result in an increase in accounts receivable and a decrease in inventory. As long as the sale was made at a profit, the net current assets would increase, thereby resulting in an increase in the current ratio.

Answer choice "A" is incorrect because purchasing inventory on account will increase both inventory and accounts payable by the same amount. Thus, the current ratio would decrease.

Answer choice "C" is incorrect because collecting an account receivable will increase cash and decrease accounts receivable by the same amount; therefore, total current assets would not change, nor would the current ratio.

Answer choice "D" is incorrect because purchasing machinery for cash would decrease cash and increase a noncurrent asset, thereby decreasing the current ratio.

58. C If Hale holds a noninterest-bearing note in the amount of $30,000 that is collateralized by an asset with a liquidation value of $5,000, Hale is a partially secured creditor.

As such, the total amount to be received by Hale includes the $5,000 of equipment plus 40 percent (i.e., forty cents on the dollar) on the $25,000 balance of the note (as reduced by the equipment), which of course is $10,000. Accordingly, Hale will realize $15,000 in total.

Answer choice "A" is incorrect because the $10,000 balance of the note (i.e., 40 percent of $25,000) is not included, and should be.

Answer choice "B" is incorrect because $12,000 represents 40 percent of the $30,000 face of the note; Hale will receive only 40 percent of $25,000, or $10,000, with respect to the note. In addition, the $5,000 liquidation value of the equipment is not included, and should be.

Answer choice "D" is incorrect because it represents both the $5,000 with respect to the liquidation value of the equipment, and 40 percent of the $30,000 face amount of the note. Hale will only receive 40 percent of $25,000, or $10,000, with respect to the note.

59. C The transfer of property other than cash to a partnership should be recorded at the fair value of the property at the date of the transfer, less any mortgage thereon assumed by the partnership.

The formation of a partnership results in the creation of a new entity; from a financial accounting standpoint, this requires a new basis of accountability. Proprietors' book values are not relevant.

Accordingly, Ceda would have the largest initial capital account balance (i.e., $55,000), which is equal to the fair value of the contributed equipment.

Answer choice "A" is incorrect because Algee would have an initial capital account balance equal to the $50,000 of cash contributed.

Answer choice "B" is incorrect because Belger would have an initial capital account balance of $45,000 (i.e., $80,000 - $35,000), which is equal to the fair value of the contributed equipment less the mortgage assumed by the partnership.

Answer choice "D" is incorrect because initial capital account balances are based upon fair value of property contributed to the partnership, and not according to the partnership's profit and loss ratio.

60.   D   In accordance with FASB Statement #109, "Accounting for Income Taxes," a temporary difference arises when the tax basis of an asset or liability differs from its financial accounting basis. If the financial accounting basis of an asset exceeds its tax basis, or if the tax basis of a liability exceeds its financial accounting basis, a deferred tax liability will arise. In a classified balance sheet, a deferred tax liability (or asset) is classified based upon the classification of the related asset or liability for financial accounting purposes.

When accumulated depreciation for tax purposes exceeds that for financial statement purposes, a noncurrent deferred tax liability will arise because the related asset is noncurrent.

Answer choice "A" is incorrect because the application of FASB #109 does not result in a contra asset for this temporary difference. A contra asset (i.e., valuation allowance) may be needed for a deferred tax asset if it is more likely than not that some or all of the deferred tax asset will not be realized.

Answer choice "B" is incorrect because the deferred tax item is classified based upon the classification of the item to which it relates; clearly, depreciation relates to plant and equipment, which is noncurrent.

Answer choice "C" is incorrect because a deferred tax liability related to a noncurrent asset will be classified as noncurrent, not current.

OTHER OBJECTIVE FORMATS/ESSAY QUESTIONS

Answer 2

Part 2(a)

61.   I, N, I, N, N, N

The issuance of bonds with a nominal rate of interest that is less than the market rate will result in the bonds being issued at a discount. Therefore, the only accounts that were affected were the bond discount and the bonds payable, both of which increased; none of the other accounts presented were affected.

62.   N, I, I, N, N, N

When convertible bonds are issued, no portion of the proceeds is allocated to equity; rather, at issuance, convertible bonds are accounted for in the same fashion as nonconvertible bonds. Because the bonds were issued at more than their face amount, they were issued at a premium. The only accounts that were affected were the bond premium and the bonds payable, both of which increased; none of the other accounts presented were affected.

63. N, D, D, I, I, N

When convertible bonds are converted, the carrying value of the bonds must be eliminated; under the book value method the issuance of the stock should be recorded at the carrying amount of the bonds with no gain or loss being recognized. Therefore, both the bond premium and the bonds payable decreased, and common stock and additional paid-in capital increased; neither of the other accounts presented were affected.

64. I, N, I, N, I, N

When bonds are issued with detachable stock warrants, the proceeds must be allocated between the bonds and the warrants based upon the relative fair values of the two securities issued. Since the bonds and warrants were issued at the face value of the bonds, and the warrants have a determinable value, the amount allocated to the bonds must be less than their face value (i.e., a discount). Therefore, this issuance resulted in an increase in the bond discount, bonds payable and additional paid-in capital; none of the other accounts presented were affected.

65. N, N, N, I, I, D

When a stock dividend of less than 20 to 25 percent is declared and issued, retained earnings is decreased based on the market value of the common stock on the declaration date. Therefore, the declaration and issuance of a 2 percent stock dividend resulted in an increase in both common stock and additional paid-in capital and a decrease in retained earnings; none of the other accounts presented were affected.

Part 2(b)

GENERAL BACKGROUND
1. A brief description of each ratio follows.
   a. Current ratio - Current assets/current liabilities
      This ratio measures the liquidity of an entity; that is, the ability to repay current liabilities out of current assets.
   b. Inventory turnover - Cost of sales/average inventory
      This ratio measures the ability of the entity to sell its inventory.
   c. Total debt/total assets ratio
      This ratio measures financial leverage; that is, the extent to which the entity has relied upon liabilities to finance the acquisition of assets.

2. Illustration
    Since many of the situations described will impact both the
    numerator and the denominator of the ratio, it is useful to
    approach a question of this type by inserting some actual
    numbers into the ratios, and then adjust them for the given
    event to determine how the ratio has changed as a result of the
    event.

    Assume that prior to the events described, the ratios were
    derived as follows:
    a. Current ratio - Current assets/current liabilities =
        $300/$100 = 3 to 1
    b. Inventory turnover - Cost of sales/average inventory =
        $200/$50 = 4 times
    c. Total debt/total assets ratio - $500/$1,000 = 0.5 to 1

66.   N, N, N

    The issuance of a stock dividend is accounted for solely within
    stockholders' equity. Retained earnings is reduced and paid-in
    capital is increased; however, total stockholders' equity does not
    change. The issuance of a stock dividend will not impact any of the
    components of the ratios presented; therefore, this event had no
    effect on any of the ratios.

67.   D, N, I

    The declaration of a cash dividend will decrease retained earnings
    and increase current liabilities.

    The current ratio has decreased because current liabilities have
    increased while current assets have not changed.

    This event has no effect on the inventory turnover.

    The total debt/total assets ratio has increased as a result of the
    declaration of the cash dividend because total liabilities have
    increased by the amount of the dividend payable.

68.   D, D, I

    The return by customers of invoiced goods that had not been paid
    will result in a reduction in sales, accounts receivable, and cost
    of sales, and an increase in inventory. In addition, income and
    equity will be reduced by the gross profit on the sale.

    Assume the recorded amount of the sale was $50, the cost of the
    inventory was $30, and, therefore, the gross profit was $20.

    Current ratio: $280/$100 = 2.8 to 1 - The current ratio has
    decreased because current assets have been reduced (i.e., $50
    decrease in accounts receivable less $30 increase in inventory) by
    the gross profit on the sale.

Inventory turnover: $170/$65 = 2.6 times - The inventory turnover ratio has _decreased_ because cost of sales has decreased and average inventory has increased because of the returned goods.

Total debt/total assets ratio: $500/$980 = 0.51 to 1 - The total debt to total assets ratio has _increased_ because total assets have decreased by the gross profit on the return (i.e., $20).

69. I, N, D

The payment of accounts payable on December 31, 1992, will reduce both current assets and current liabilities by the amount of the payment, assumed to be $50 for this example.

Current ratio: $250/$50 = 5 to 1 - The current ratio has _increased_ because the proportional change in current assets is less than the proportional change in current liabilities.

There is _no effect_ on inventory turnover as the result of the payment of accounts payable.

Total debt/total assets ratio: $450/$950 = 0.47 to 1 - The total debt/total assets ratio has _decreased_ because both liabilities and assets have decreased, but the proportional decrease in liabilities is greater than the proportional change in assets.

70. I, N, I

The recording of a receivable from an insurance company and a loss from fire damage will have the following effect on the accounts: current assets will increase by the amount of the receivable, total assets will decrease by the amount of the loss, and total equity will decrease by the amount of the loss.

The current ratio will _increase_ because current assets increased by the amount of the receivable with no change in current liabilities.

There will be _no effect_ on inventory turnover as a result of this event, because neither cost of sales nor inventory was affected.

The total debt/total assets ratio will be _increased_ because total assets will be reduced by the amount of the loss and total liabilities will not change.

71. I, N, D

When Daley increased the selling price of one of its products, with no change in volume of sales, the following financial statement elements will be changed: current assets will increase because of both higher cash collection from sales and higher accounts receivable resulting from higher sales prices, and total equity will increase as a result of the higher profits earned because of the higher sales price.

The current ratio will <u>increase</u> because current assets have increased.

There is <u>no effect</u> on inventory turnover because the only impact of this event is on sales; the number of units sold and their cost is unaffected.

The total debt/total assets ratio will <u>decrease</u> because total assets have increased by reason of the higher sales price, and liabilities have not changed.

Answer 3

Part 3(a)

72.   L   When land and an existing building thereon have been acquired in a lump-sum transaction and the existing building is immediately razed (demolished) prior to the construction of a new building, the acquisition cost of the land and original building (net of any salvage realized on the demolition) <u>should</u> <u>be</u> <u>charged</u> <u>to</u> the <u>land</u> account, which is <u>not subject to depreciation</u>.

73.   E   Questions #73 and #74 are based on FASB Statement #34, "Capitalization of Interest Cost."

Interest capitalization is appropriate when a period of time is required to make assets ready for their intended use. Interest capitalization is required for those assets if its effect, compared with the effect of expensing interest, is material.

1.   <u>Interest should be capitalized for</u>
   a.   Assets constructed or produced for company's own use.
   b.   Assets intended for sale or lease that are constructed or produced as discrete projects (e.g., ships or real estate developments).
2.   <u>Interest should not be capitalized for</u>
   a.   Inventory items routinely manufactured in large quantities on a repetitive basis.
   b.   Assets already in use or ready for use.
   c.   Assets not used in the earning activities of the enterprise.

Based on point "2.b." above, the interest of $147,000 on construction financing incurred after completion of construction <u>should</u> <u>be</u> classified as <u>an expense</u>.

74.   B   See question #73 for background information.

Based on the facts provided, it is clear that, in general, interest on construction financing paid during construction should be capitalized.

Since the construction relates to the building, which is a depreciable asset, the interest paid during construction <u>should be classified as</u> an addition to <u>building and depreciated</u>.

75. L As indicated in the answer to question #72, when land and building are acquired in a lump-sum transaction, and the existing building is demolished prior to construction of a new building, the acquisition cost of the land and old building are charged to land.

The facts indicate a total purchase price for the land and existing building of $750,000, with $50,000 being assigned to the building. While the $50,000 is nominally the value of the building, the intent was to acquire the land. Therefore, the $50,000 is <u>classified as land, and not depreciated</u>.

76. L Since the basic intent was to acquire the land, and not the building, the payment of delinquent real estate taxes assumed by the buyer (Sloan) is <u>classified as land, and not depreciated</u>.

77. B In general, the costs of an asset include the acquisition price and any other costs associated with making the asset ready for its intended use.

Thus, once construction had begun, insurance premiums paid during the construction period <u>should be classified as</u> part of the <u>building, and</u> would, of course, be <u>depreciated</u>.

78. L As noted in question #72, costs of razing an existing building to prepare for construction of a new building <u>should be classified as land, and not depreciated</u>.

79. E "Moving costs" implies that construction is complete and the building is in the process of being occupied. As such, moving costs would generally not benefit future periods, and <u>should be classified as an expense</u>.

Part 3(b)
Part (b)1.

80. $48,000

Projected benefit obligation, January 1, 1992	$600,000
Discount rate	.08
<u>Interest cost</u>	<u>$ 48,000</u>

81. $72,000

Fair value of pension plan assets, January 1, 1992	$720,000
Expected rate of return	.10
<u>Expected return on plan assets</u>	<u>$ 72,000</u>

82. $105,000

Fair value of pension plan assets, December 31, 1992	$825,000
Fair value of pension plan assets, January 1, 1992	720,000
<u>Actual return on plan assets</u>	<u>$105,000</u>

83. $20,000

<u>Amortization of prior service costs</u>; $240,000/12   <u>$ 20,000</u>

84. $2,000

Unamortized prior pension gain, January 1, 1992 $96,000
Fair value of pension plan assets, January 1, 1992;
    $720,000 at 10%   <u>72,000</u>
Unrecognized pension gain   <u>$ 24,000</u>
<u>Minimum amortization of unrecognized</u>
    <u>pension gain</u>; $24,000/12 years   <u>$ 2,000</u>

Part (b)2

85.   I   Service cost is the increase in the projected benefit obligation resulting from services rendered by employees in the current period.

In general, the various elements of the net periodic pension cost will either increase or decrease the unfunded accrued pension liability. (It should be noted that this is the case without regard to contributions to the plan, which in and of themselves would decrease the unfunded accrued pension liability.)

Without regard to contributions to the plan, the service cost component <u>increases</u> the unfunded accrued pension liability.

86.   I   A gain on pension plan assets would have the effect of decreasing the net pension cost, which would decrease the unfunded accrued pension liability. Therefore, if the gain, or any portion thereof, is deferred, the net periodic pension cost would be higher than it would otherwise be. As a general rule, the higher the cost, the higher the liability.

Thus, deferral of gain on pension plan assets <u>increases</u> the unfunded accrued pension liability.

87.   D   Actual return on plan assets is the change in the fair value of pension plan assets during the period. Since Sparta's actual return on plan assets increased, both net periodic pension cost and unfunded accrued pension liability for the period <u>decrease</u>.

88.   I   Amortization of prior service costs is the amount allocated to the current period resulting from retroactive amendments to the pension plan. This cost element will increase the net periodic pension cost. As such, the unfunded accrued pension liability <u>increases</u> for the period, in and of itself, and without regard to whether or not contributions were made to the plan.

89.   D   The amortization of unrecognized pension gain <u>decreases</u> both Sparta's net periodic pension cost and unfunded accrued pension liability.

Answer 4

Part 4(a)

1. According to the FASB conceptual framework, assets are probable future economic benefits obtained or controlled by a particular entity as a result of a past transaction or event. This definition embodies the three essential characteristics of an asset. First, an asset must have probable future economic benefit. Second, the benefit must be obtained or controlled by the entity. Third, the resource must have arisen as the result of a past transaction or event.

2. The expenditures made through 1991 meet the above three characteristics of an asset if they:
    a. Have probable future economic benefit; that is, the service potential of the expenditure must be reasonably expected or believed. Mono's expenditure for the equipment that has alternative use gives rise to an asset because the equipment can be used in the future to obtain revenue.
    b. Have been obtained or controlled by the entity; that is, the expenditure must result in a right or privilege that accrues to the benefit of the entity. The expenditures for equipment give rise to assets because Mono has the legal right to the exclusive use of the equipment.
    c. Have arisen as the result of a past transaction or event; that is, the resource must have been secured by the entity. All of the expenditures have been made and are the result of a past transaction.

3. It is difficult to justify the classification of research and development expenditures as assets because the future economic benefit of such expenditures is uncertain. Further, the realization of the future benefit may not be known until some future date, and the amount of the future benefit will not be known with sufficient certainty until the project reaches maturity.

Part 4(b)

<u>London, Inc.</u>
<u>Schedule of Gross Profit (Loss)</u>
<u>For the Years September 30, 1992</u>
<u>and September 30, 1993</u>
<u>Under the Percentage-of-Completion Method</u>

<u>1992</u>

<u>Beta</u>

Revenue; ($360,000/$400,000) × $600,000		$540,000
Less costs incurred to date		360,000
Gross profit, 1992		180,000

<u>Gamma</u> (Note)

Total costs incurred and estimated	$820,000	
Contract price	800,000	
Loss, 1992		(20,000)
<u>Total gross profit, year ended September 30, 1992</u>		$160,000

<u>1993</u>

<u>Beta</u>

Revenue; $600,000 - $40,000		$560,000
Less costs incurred to date		450,000
Cumulative gross profit		110,000
Less gross profit recognized in 1992		180,000
Loss, 1993		(70,000)

<u>Gamma</u> (Note)

Total costs incurred and estimated	$900,000	
Contract price; $800,000 + $40,000	840,000	
Cumulative loss	(60,000)	
Less loss recognized, 1992	20,000	
Loss, 1993		(40,000)
<u>Total loss, year ended September 30, 1993</u>		$(110,000)

<u>NOTE</u> - As to Gamma, there is a recognized loss in both years because total
costs, inclusive of estimated costs, will exceed contract revenue.

Answer 5

Part 5(a)

When goods are exchanged for a note receivable, there is a general presumption that the stipulated interest rate is fair and adequate compensation. However, where this presumption is not valid, substance over form must prevail. In this circumstance, the notes receivable should be valued at either the fair value of the goods transferred or the fair value of the notes, whichever is more clearly determinable. The fair value of the notes can be estimated by discounting the amount of the three annual installments at the market rate of interest at the date of sale.

Part 5(b)

WORKSHEET FOR SOLUTION (NOT REQUIRED)

	Common Stock	Add'l P-I-C Common	Ret'd Earnings	Treasury Stock Common
Beginning balances (1)	7,875,000	15,750,000	16,445,000	(750,000)
2/17/92; retirement of treasury stock (3)	(125,000)	(125,000)		250,000
3/5/92; declaration of property dividend (4) $60 × ([1,550,000 − 50,000]/100)			(900,000)	
6/1/92; exercise of options (5)	750,000	1,050,000		
12/12/92; declaration of cash dividend on preferred (6) $100 × 6% × 50,000			(300,000)	
12/31/92; correction of 1991 error (7)			(245,000)	
12/31/92; 1992 net income (8)			2,400,000	
Ending balances	8,500,000	16,675,000	17,400,000	(500,000)

	Pf'd Stock
1/21/92; issuance of preferred (2)	5,000,000
Ending balances	5,000,000

NOTE: SEE THE ABOVE WORKSHEET FOR SUPPORTING COMPUTATIONS

<u>Trask Corp.</u>
<u>Statement of Retained Earnings</u>
<u>Year Ended December 31, 1992</u>

Balance, January 1, 1992		$16,445,000
Less: Prior period adjustment (correction of error), net of $105,000 tax effect		245,000
Adjusted balance, January 1, 1992		16,200,000
Add: Net income, 1992		2,400,000
		18,600,000
Less: Preferred stock dividends (cash)	$300,000	
Common stock dividends (property)	900,000	1,200,000
Balance, December 31, 1992		$17,400,000

Objective Answer Sheet

May 1994 CPA Examination

LPR   **AUDIT**

1. Ⓐ Ⓑ Ⓒ Ⓓ	31. Ⓐ Ⓑ Ⓒ Ⓓ	1. Ⓐ Ⓑ Ⓒ Ⓓ	31. Ⓐ Ⓑ Ⓒ Ⓓ	61. Ⓐ Ⓑ Ⓒ Ⓓ
2. Ⓐ Ⓑ Ⓒ Ⓓ	32. Ⓐ Ⓑ Ⓒ Ⓓ	2. Ⓐ Ⓑ Ⓒ Ⓓ	32. Ⓐ Ⓑ Ⓒ Ⓓ	62. Ⓐ Ⓑ Ⓒ Ⓓ
3. Ⓐ Ⓑ Ⓒ Ⓓ	33. Ⓐ Ⓑ Ⓒ Ⓓ	3. Ⓐ Ⓑ Ⓒ Ⓓ	33. Ⓐ Ⓑ Ⓒ Ⓓ	63. Ⓐ Ⓑ Ⓒ Ⓓ
4. Ⓐ Ⓑ Ⓒ Ⓓ	34. Ⓐ Ⓑ Ⓒ Ⓓ	4. Ⓐ Ⓑ Ⓒ Ⓓ	34. Ⓐ Ⓑ Ⓒ Ⓓ	64. Ⓐ Ⓑ Ⓒ Ⓓ
5. Ⓐ Ⓑ Ⓒ Ⓓ	35. Ⓐ Ⓑ Ⓒ Ⓓ	5. Ⓐ Ⓑ Ⓒ Ⓓ	35. Ⓐ Ⓑ Ⓒ Ⓓ	65. Ⓐ Ⓑ Ⓒ Ⓓ
6. Ⓐ Ⓑ Ⓒ Ⓓ	36. Ⓐ Ⓑ Ⓒ Ⓓ	6. Ⓐ Ⓑ Ⓒ Ⓓ	36. Ⓐ Ⓑ Ⓒ Ⓓ	66. Ⓐ Ⓑ Ⓒ Ⓓ
7. Ⓐ Ⓑ Ⓒ Ⓓ	37. Ⓐ Ⓑ Ⓒ Ⓓ	7. Ⓐ Ⓑ Ⓒ Ⓓ	37. Ⓐ Ⓑ Ⓒ Ⓓ	67. Ⓐ Ⓑ Ⓒ Ⓓ
8. Ⓐ Ⓑ Ⓒ Ⓓ	38. Ⓐ Ⓑ Ⓒ Ⓓ	8. Ⓐ Ⓑ Ⓒ Ⓓ	38. Ⓐ Ⓑ Ⓒ Ⓓ	68. Ⓐ Ⓑ Ⓒ Ⓓ
9. Ⓐ Ⓑ Ⓒ Ⓓ	39. Ⓐ Ⓑ Ⓒ Ⓓ	9. Ⓐ Ⓑ Ⓒ Ⓓ	39. Ⓐ Ⓑ Ⓒ Ⓓ	69. Ⓐ Ⓑ Ⓒ Ⓓ
10. Ⓐ Ⓑ Ⓒ Ⓓ	40. Ⓐ Ⓑ Ⓒ Ⓓ	10. Ⓐ Ⓑ Ⓒ Ⓓ	40. Ⓐ Ⓑ Ⓒ Ⓓ	70. Ⓐ Ⓑ Ⓒ Ⓓ
11. Ⓐ Ⓑ Ⓒ Ⓓ	41. Ⓐ Ⓑ Ⓒ Ⓓ	11. Ⓐ Ⓑ Ⓒ Ⓓ	41. Ⓐ Ⓑ Ⓒ Ⓓ	71. Ⓐ Ⓑ Ⓒ Ⓓ
12. Ⓐ Ⓑ Ⓒ Ⓓ	42. Ⓐ Ⓑ Ⓒ Ⓓ	12. Ⓐ Ⓑ Ⓒ Ⓓ	42. Ⓐ Ⓑ Ⓒ Ⓓ	72. Ⓐ Ⓑ Ⓒ Ⓓ
13. Ⓐ Ⓑ Ⓒ Ⓓ	43. Ⓐ Ⓑ Ⓒ Ⓓ	13. Ⓐ Ⓑ Ⓒ Ⓓ	43. Ⓐ Ⓑ Ⓒ Ⓓ	73. Ⓐ Ⓑ Ⓒ Ⓓ
14. Ⓐ Ⓑ Ⓒ Ⓓ	44. Ⓐ Ⓑ Ⓒ Ⓓ	14. Ⓐ Ⓑ Ⓒ Ⓓ	44. Ⓐ Ⓑ Ⓒ Ⓓ	74. Ⓐ Ⓑ Ⓒ Ⓓ
15. Ⓐ Ⓑ Ⓒ Ⓓ	45. Ⓐ Ⓑ Ⓒ Ⓓ	15. Ⓐ Ⓑ Ⓒ Ⓓ	45. Ⓐ Ⓑ Ⓒ Ⓓ	75. Ⓐ Ⓑ Ⓒ Ⓓ
16. Ⓐ Ⓑ Ⓒ Ⓓ	46. Ⓐ Ⓑ Ⓒ Ⓓ	16. Ⓐ Ⓑ Ⓒ Ⓓ	46. Ⓐ Ⓑ Ⓒ Ⓓ	76. Ⓐ Ⓑ Ⓒ Ⓓ
17. Ⓐ Ⓑ Ⓒ Ⓓ	47. Ⓐ Ⓑ Ⓒ Ⓓ	17. Ⓐ Ⓑ Ⓒ Ⓓ	47. Ⓐ Ⓑ Ⓒ Ⓓ	77. Ⓐ Ⓑ Ⓒ Ⓓ
18. Ⓐ Ⓑ Ⓒ Ⓓ	48. Ⓐ Ⓑ Ⓒ Ⓓ	18. Ⓐ Ⓑ Ⓒ Ⓓ	48. Ⓐ Ⓑ Ⓒ Ⓓ	78. Ⓐ Ⓑ Ⓒ Ⓓ
19. Ⓐ Ⓑ Ⓒ Ⓓ	49. Ⓐ Ⓑ Ⓒ Ⓓ	19. Ⓐ Ⓑ Ⓒ Ⓓ	49. Ⓐ Ⓑ Ⓒ Ⓓ	79. Ⓐ Ⓑ Ⓒ Ⓓ
20. Ⓐ Ⓑ Ⓒ Ⓓ	50. Ⓐ Ⓑ Ⓒ Ⓓ	20. Ⓐ Ⓑ Ⓒ Ⓓ	50. Ⓐ Ⓑ Ⓒ Ⓓ	80. Ⓐ Ⓑ Ⓒ Ⓓ
21. Ⓐ Ⓑ Ⓒ Ⓓ	51. Ⓐ Ⓑ Ⓒ Ⓓ	21. Ⓐ Ⓑ Ⓒ Ⓓ	51. Ⓐ Ⓑ Ⓒ Ⓓ	81. Ⓐ Ⓑ Ⓒ Ⓓ
22. Ⓐ Ⓑ Ⓒ Ⓓ	52. Ⓐ Ⓑ Ⓒ Ⓓ	22. Ⓐ Ⓑ Ⓒ Ⓓ	52. Ⓐ Ⓑ Ⓒ Ⓓ	82. Ⓐ Ⓑ Ⓒ Ⓓ
23. Ⓐ Ⓑ Ⓒ Ⓓ	53. Ⓐ Ⓑ Ⓒ Ⓓ	23. Ⓐ Ⓑ Ⓒ Ⓓ	53. Ⓐ Ⓑ Ⓒ Ⓓ	83. Ⓐ Ⓑ Ⓒ Ⓓ
24. Ⓐ Ⓑ Ⓒ Ⓓ	54. Ⓐ Ⓑ Ⓒ Ⓓ	24. Ⓐ Ⓑ Ⓒ Ⓓ	54. Ⓐ Ⓑ Ⓒ Ⓓ	84. Ⓐ Ⓑ Ⓒ Ⓓ
25. Ⓐ Ⓑ Ⓒ Ⓓ	55. Ⓐ Ⓑ Ⓒ Ⓓ	25. Ⓐ Ⓑ Ⓒ Ⓓ	55. Ⓐ Ⓑ Ⓒ Ⓓ	85. Ⓐ Ⓑ Ⓒ Ⓓ
26. Ⓐ Ⓑ Ⓒ Ⓓ	56. Ⓐ Ⓑ Ⓒ Ⓓ	26. Ⓐ Ⓑ Ⓒ Ⓓ	56. Ⓐ Ⓑ Ⓒ Ⓓ	86. Ⓐ Ⓑ Ⓒ Ⓓ
27. Ⓐ Ⓑ Ⓒ Ⓓ	57. Ⓐ Ⓑ Ⓒ Ⓓ	27. Ⓐ Ⓑ Ⓒ Ⓓ	57. Ⓐ Ⓑ Ⓒ Ⓓ	87. Ⓐ Ⓑ Ⓒ Ⓓ
28. Ⓐ Ⓑ Ⓒ Ⓓ	58. Ⓐ Ⓑ Ⓒ Ⓓ	28. Ⓐ Ⓑ Ⓒ Ⓓ	58. Ⓐ Ⓑ Ⓒ Ⓓ	88. Ⓐ Ⓑ Ⓒ Ⓓ
29. Ⓐ Ⓑ Ⓒ Ⓓ	59. Ⓐ Ⓑ Ⓒ Ⓓ	29. Ⓐ Ⓑ Ⓒ Ⓓ	59. Ⓐ Ⓑ Ⓒ Ⓓ	89. Ⓐ Ⓑ Ⓒ Ⓓ
30. Ⓐ Ⓑ Ⓒ Ⓓ	60. Ⓐ Ⓑ Ⓒ Ⓓ	30. Ⓐ Ⓑ Ⓒ Ⓓ	60. Ⓐ Ⓑ Ⓒ Ⓓ	90. Ⓐ Ⓑ Ⓒ Ⓓ

Objective Answer Sheet

ARE

1. Ⓐ Ⓑ Ⓒ Ⓓ
2. Ⓐ Ⓑ Ⓒ Ⓓ
3. Ⓐ Ⓑ Ⓒ Ⓓ
4. Ⓐ Ⓑ Ⓒ Ⓓ
5. Ⓐ Ⓑ Ⓒ Ⓓ
6. Ⓐ Ⓑ Ⓒ Ⓓ
7. Ⓐ Ⓑ Ⓒ Ⓓ
8. Ⓐ Ⓑ Ⓒ Ⓓ
9. Ⓐ Ⓑ Ⓒ Ⓓ
10. Ⓐ Ⓑ Ⓒ Ⓓ
11. Ⓐ Ⓑ Ⓒ Ⓓ
12. Ⓐ Ⓑ Ⓒ Ⓓ
13. Ⓐ Ⓑ Ⓒ Ⓓ
14. Ⓐ Ⓑ Ⓒ Ⓓ
15. Ⓐ Ⓑ Ⓒ Ⓓ
16. Ⓐ Ⓑ Ⓒ Ⓓ
17. Ⓐ Ⓑ Ⓒ Ⓓ
18. Ⓐ Ⓑ Ⓒ Ⓓ
19. Ⓐ Ⓑ Ⓒ Ⓓ
20. Ⓐ Ⓑ Ⓒ Ⓓ
21. Ⓐ Ⓑ Ⓒ Ⓓ
22. Ⓐ Ⓑ Ⓒ Ⓓ
23. Ⓐ Ⓑ Ⓒ Ⓓ
24. Ⓐ Ⓑ Ⓒ Ⓓ
25. Ⓐ Ⓑ Ⓒ Ⓓ
26. Ⓐ Ⓑ Ⓒ Ⓓ
27. Ⓐ Ⓑ Ⓒ Ⓓ
28. Ⓐ Ⓑ Ⓒ Ⓓ
29. Ⓐ Ⓑ Ⓒ Ⓓ
30. Ⓐ Ⓑ Ⓒ Ⓓ

31. Ⓐ Ⓑ Ⓒ Ⓓ
32. Ⓐ Ⓑ Ⓒ Ⓓ
33. Ⓐ Ⓑ Ⓒ Ⓓ
34. Ⓐ Ⓑ Ⓒ Ⓓ
35. Ⓐ Ⓑ Ⓒ Ⓓ
36. Ⓐ Ⓑ Ⓒ Ⓓ
37. Ⓐ Ⓑ Ⓒ Ⓓ
38. Ⓐ Ⓑ Ⓒ Ⓓ
39. Ⓐ Ⓑ Ⓒ Ⓓ
40. Ⓐ Ⓑ Ⓒ Ⓓ
41. Ⓐ Ⓑ Ⓒ Ⓓ
42. Ⓐ Ⓑ Ⓒ Ⓓ
43. Ⓐ Ⓑ Ⓒ Ⓓ
44. Ⓐ Ⓑ Ⓒ Ⓓ
45. Ⓐ Ⓑ Ⓒ Ⓓ
46. Ⓐ Ⓑ Ⓒ Ⓓ
47. Ⓐ Ⓑ Ⓒ Ⓓ
48. Ⓐ Ⓑ Ⓒ Ⓓ
49. Ⓐ Ⓑ Ⓒ Ⓓ
50. Ⓐ Ⓑ Ⓒ Ⓓ
51. Ⓐ Ⓑ Ⓒ Ⓓ
52. Ⓐ Ⓑ Ⓒ Ⓓ
53. Ⓐ Ⓑ Ⓒ Ⓓ
54. Ⓐ Ⓑ Ⓒ Ⓓ
55. Ⓐ Ⓑ Ⓒ Ⓓ
56. Ⓐ Ⓑ Ⓒ Ⓓ
57. Ⓐ Ⓑ Ⓒ Ⓓ
58. Ⓐ Ⓑ Ⓒ Ⓓ
59. Ⓐ Ⓑ Ⓒ Ⓓ
60. Ⓐ Ⓑ Ⓒ Ⓓ

FARE

1. Ⓐ Ⓑ Ⓒ Ⓓ
2. Ⓐ Ⓑ Ⓒ Ⓓ
3. Ⓐ Ⓑ Ⓒ Ⓓ
4. Ⓐ Ⓑ Ⓒ Ⓓ
5. Ⓐ Ⓑ Ⓒ Ⓓ
6. Ⓐ Ⓑ Ⓒ Ⓓ
7. Ⓐ Ⓑ Ⓒ Ⓓ
8. Ⓐ Ⓑ Ⓒ Ⓓ
9. Ⓐ Ⓑ Ⓒ Ⓓ
10. Ⓐ Ⓑ Ⓒ Ⓓ
11. Ⓐ Ⓑ Ⓒ Ⓓ
12. Ⓐ Ⓑ Ⓒ Ⓓ
13. Ⓐ Ⓑ Ⓒ Ⓓ
14. Ⓐ Ⓑ Ⓒ Ⓓ
15. Ⓐ Ⓑ Ⓒ Ⓓ
16. Ⓐ Ⓑ Ⓒ Ⓓ
17. Ⓐ Ⓑ Ⓒ Ⓓ
18. Ⓐ Ⓑ Ⓒ Ⓓ
19. Ⓐ Ⓑ Ⓒ Ⓓ
20. Ⓐ Ⓑ Ⓒ Ⓓ
21. Ⓐ Ⓑ Ⓒ Ⓓ
22. Ⓐ Ⓑ Ⓒ Ⓓ
23. Ⓐ Ⓑ Ⓒ Ⓓ
24. Ⓐ Ⓑ Ⓒ Ⓓ
25. Ⓐ Ⓑ Ⓒ Ⓓ
26. Ⓐ Ⓑ Ⓒ Ⓓ
27. Ⓐ Ⓑ Ⓒ Ⓓ
28. Ⓐ Ⓑ Ⓒ Ⓓ
29. Ⓐ Ⓑ Ⓒ Ⓓ
30. Ⓐ Ⓑ Ⓒ Ⓓ

31. Ⓐ Ⓑ Ⓒ Ⓓ
32. Ⓐ Ⓑ Ⓒ Ⓓ
33. Ⓐ Ⓑ Ⓒ Ⓓ
34. Ⓐ Ⓑ Ⓒ Ⓓ
35. Ⓐ Ⓑ Ⓒ Ⓓ
36. Ⓐ Ⓑ Ⓒ Ⓓ
37. Ⓐ Ⓑ Ⓒ Ⓓ
38. Ⓐ Ⓑ Ⓒ Ⓓ
39. Ⓐ Ⓑ Ⓒ Ⓓ
40. Ⓐ Ⓑ Ⓒ Ⓓ
41. Ⓐ Ⓑ Ⓒ Ⓓ
42. Ⓐ Ⓑ Ⓒ Ⓓ
43. Ⓐ Ⓑ Ⓒ Ⓓ
44. Ⓐ Ⓑ Ⓒ Ⓓ
45. Ⓐ Ⓑ Ⓒ Ⓓ
46. Ⓐ Ⓑ Ⓒ Ⓓ
47. Ⓐ Ⓑ Ⓒ Ⓓ
48. Ⓐ Ⓑ Ⓒ Ⓓ
49. Ⓐ Ⓑ Ⓒ Ⓓ
50. Ⓐ Ⓑ Ⓒ Ⓓ
51. Ⓐ Ⓑ Ⓒ Ⓓ
52. Ⓐ Ⓑ Ⓒ Ⓓ
53. Ⓐ Ⓑ Ⓒ Ⓓ
54. Ⓐ Ⓑ Ⓒ Ⓓ
55. Ⓐ Ⓑ Ⓒ Ⓓ
56. Ⓐ Ⓑ Ⓒ Ⓓ
57. Ⓐ Ⓑ Ⓒ Ⓓ
58. Ⓐ Ⓑ Ⓒ Ⓓ
59. Ⓐ Ⓑ Ⓒ Ⓓ
60. Ⓐ Ⓑ Ⓒ Ⓓ

9. May 1994 CPA Examination

This chapter includes the second of two practice examinations that you were to take. This examination is the actual AICPA examination given in May 1994.*

By this time, you should have taken the Preliminary Readiness Tests in Chapter 7 and the Simulated CPA Examination in Chapter 8, and you should have seen steady improvement. If not, you should spend more time reviewing those topical areas in which you have performed poorly. In order to do this, analyze your weak areas in "Chapter 6—Chart Your Progress and Plan Your Course of Action." Then review using one of the recommended methods described in Chapter 3.

Be sure to take each of the four sections of this examination just as you would the actual test. *Allow no more time than each examination section indicates. Take each section in one sitting, and do no more than two sections in a day.* You will then become accustomed to concentrating for the duration of a test period and to working efficiently during this time.

Before beginning this practice examination, be sure to review the test tactics outlined in "Chapter 5—How to Approach CPA Examination Questions." After completing this examination, turn to "Chapter 6—Chart Your Progress and Plan Your Course of Action" for guidance in analyzing your score and in planning your review program.

Remember: Read directions carefully!

---

*Note: All answer explanations are the authors'.

(Note: These instructions have been adapted from the May 1994 CPA Examination Booklet.)

Uniform Certified Public Accountant Examination

EXAMINATION QUESTION BOOKLET

CANDIDATE NUMBER

Record your 7-digit candidate number in the boxes.

Q - LPR

The point values for each question, and estimated time allotments based primarily on point value, are as follows:

	Point Value	Estimated Minutes Minimum	Maximum
No. 1	60	90	100
No. 2	10	10	15
No. 3	10	10	15
No. 4	10	15	25
No. 5	10	15	25
Totals	100	140	180

BUSINESS LAW & PROFESSIONAL RESPONSIBILITIES

May 4, 1994; 9:00 A.M. to 12:00 NOON

INSTRUCTIONS TO CANDIDATES *Failure to follow these instructions may have an adverse effect on your Examination grade.*

1. Record your 7-digit candidate number in the boxes provided at the upper right-hand corner of this page.

2. Question numbers 1, 2, and 3 should be answered on the *Objective Answer Sheet,* which is pages 11 and 12 of your *Examination Answer Booklet.* You should attempt to answer all objective items. There is no penalty for incorrect responses. Since the objective items are computer-graded, your comments and calculations associated with them are not considered. Be certain that you have entered your answers on the *Objective Answer Sheet* before the examination time is up. The objective portion of your examination will not be graded if you fail to record your answers on the *Objective Answer Sheet.* You will not be given additional time to record your answers.

3. Question numbers 4 and 5 should be answered beginning on page 3 of the *Examination Answer Booklet.* If you have not completed answering a question on a page, fill in the appropriate spaces in the wording on the bottom of the page "QUESTION NUMBER ____ CONTINUES ON PAGE ____ ." If you have completed answering a question, fill in the appropriate space in the wording on the bottom of the page "QUESTION NUMBER ____ ENDS ON THIS PAGE." Always begin the start of an answer to a question on the top of a new page (which may be the back side of a sheet of paper).

4. Record your 7-digit candidate number, state, an question number where indicated on pages through 10 of the *Examination Answer Booklet.*

5. Although the primary purpose of the examinatio is to test your knowledge and application of th subject matter, selected essay responses will b graded for writing skills.

6. You are required to turn in by the end of eac session:
   a. Attendance Record Form, front page o *Examination Answer Booklet;*
   b. *Objective Answer Sheet,* pages 11 and 12 o *Examination Answer Booklet;*
   c. Remaining Portion of *Examination Answe Booklet;*
   d. *Examination Question Booklet;* and
   e. All unused examination materials.

Your examination will not be graded unless th above listed items are handed in before leaving the examination room.

7. Unless otherwise instructed, if you want your *Examination Question Booklet* mailed to you write your name and address in both places indicated on the back cover and place 52 cents postage in the space provided. *Examination Question Booklets* will be distributed no sooner than the day following the administration of this examination.

Prepared by the Board of Examiners of the American Institute of Certified Public Accountants and adopted by the examining boards of all states, the District of Columbia, Guam, Puerto Rico, and the Virgin Islands of the United States.

Copyright © 1994 by the American Institute of Certified Public Accountants, Inc.

Number 1 (Estimated time—90 to 100 minutes)

Instructions

Select the **best** answer for each of the following items. Use a No. 2 pencil to blacken the appropriate ovals on the Objective Answer Sheet to indicate your answers. **Mark only one answer for each item. Answer all items.** Your grade will be based on the total number of correct answers.

1. Which of the following actions by a CPA most likely violates the profession's ethical standards?
   A. Arranging with a financial institution to collect notes issued by a client in payment of fees due.
   B. Compiling the financial statements of a client that employed the CPA's spouse as a bookkeeper.
   C. Retaining client records after the client has demanded their return.
   D. Purchasing a segment of an insurance company's business that performs actuarial services for employee benefit plans.

2. Which of the following statements best explains why the CPA profession has found it essential to promulgate ethical standards and to establish means for ensuring their observance?
   A. A distinguishing mark of a profession is its acceptance of responsibility to the public.
   B. A requirement for a profession is to establish ethical standards that stress primary responsibility to clients and colleagues.
   C. Ethical standards that emphasize excellence in performance over material rewards establish a reputation for competence and character.
   D. Vigorous enforcement of an established code of ethics is the best way to prevent unscrupulous acts.

3. Which of the following reports may be issued only by an accountant who is independent of a client?
   A. Standard report on an examination of a financial forecast.
   B. Report on consulting services.
   C. Compilation report on historical financial statements.
   D. Compilation report on a financial projection.

4. According to the profession's ethical standards, an auditor would be considered independent in which of the following instances?
   A. The auditor is the officially appointed stock transfer agent of a client.
   B. The auditor's checking account that is fully insured by a federal agency, is held at a client financial institution.
   C. The client owes the auditor fees for more than two years prior to the issuance of the audit report.
   D. The client is the only tenant in a commercial building owned by the auditor.

5. Which of the following services may a CPA perform in carrying out a consulting service for a client?

   I. Analysis of the client's accounting system.

   II. Review of the client's prepared business plan.

   III. Preparation of information for obtaining financing.

   A. I and II only.
   B. I and III only.
   C. II and III only.
   D. I, II, and III.

6. Nile, CPA, on completing an audit, was asked by the client to provide technical assistance in implementing a new EDP system. The set of pronouncements designed to guide Nile in this engagement is the Statement(s) on
   A. Quality Control Standards.
   B. Auditing Standards.
   C. Standards for Accountants' EDP Services.
   D. Standards for Consulting Services.

7. According to the profession's ethical standards, a CPA preparing a client's tax return may rely on unsupported information furnished by the client, without examining underlying information, unless the information
   A. Is derived from a pass-through entity.
   B. Appears to be incomplete on its face.
   C. Concerns dividends received.
   D. Lists charitable contributions.

8. Which of the following acts by a CPA will **not** result in a CPA incurring an IRS penalty?
   A. Failing, without reasonable cause, to provide the client with a copy of an income tax return.
   B. Failing, without reasonable cause, to sign a client's tax return as preparer.
   C. Understating a client's tax liability as a result of an error in calculation.
   D. Negotiating a client's tax refund check when the CPA prepared the tax return.

9. If a CPA recklessly departs from the standards of due care when conducting an audit, the CPA will be liable to third parties who are unknown to the CPA based on
   A. Negligence.
   B. Gross negligence.
   C. Strict liability.
   D. Criminal deceit.

10. Which of the following statements is correct with respect to ownership, possession, or access to a CPA firm's audit working papers?
   A. Working papers may **never** be obtained by third parties unless the client consents.
   B. Working papers are **not** transferable to a purchaser of a CPA practice unless the client consents.
   C. Working papers are subject to the privileged communication rule which, in most jurisdictions, prevents any third-party access to the working papers.
   D. Working papers are the client's exclusive property.

11. Under the Revised Model Business Corporation Act, which of the following must be contained in a corporation's articles of incorporation?
   A. Quorum voting requirements.
   B. Names of stockholders.
   C. Provisions for issuance of par and non-par shares.
   D. The number of shares the corporation is authorized to issue.

12. Under the Revised Model Business Corporation Act, which of the following statements is correct regarding corporate officers of a public corporation?
   A. An officer may **not** simultaneously serve as a director.
   B. A corporation may be authorized to indemnify its officers for liability incurred in a suit by stockholders.
   C. Stockholders always have the right to elect a corporation's officers.
   D. An officer of a corporation is required to own at least one share of the corporation's stock.

13. Which of the following rights is a holder of a public corporation's cumulative preferred stock always entitled to?
   A. Conversion of the preferred stock into common stock.
   B. Voting rights.
   C. Dividend carryovers from years in which dividends were **not** paid, to future years.
   D. Guaranteed dividends.

14. Under the Revised Model Business Corporation Act, a merger of two public corporations usually requires all of the following **except**
   A. A formal plan of merger.
   B. An affirmative vote by the holders of a majority of each corporation's voting shares.
   C. Receipt of voting stock by all stockholders of the original corporations.
   D. Approval by the board of directors of each corporation.

15. Which of the following is **not** necessary to create an express trust?
   A. A successor trustee.
   B. A trust corpus.
   C. A beneficiary.
   D. A valid trust purpose.

16. Which of the following expenditures resulting from a trust's ownership of commercial real estate should be allocated to the trust's principal?
   A. Building management fees.
   B. Insurance premiums.
   C. Sidewalk assessments.
   D. Depreciation.

17. In a written trust containing **no** specific powers, the trustee will have all of the following implied powers **except**
   A. Sell trust property.
   B. Pay management expenses.
   C. Accumulate income.
   D. Employ a CPA to prepare trust tax returns.

18. Which of the following fiduciary duties will a trustee violate by borrowing money from the trust?
   A. Duty of loyalty.
   B. Duty to properly account.
   C. Duty to safeguard the trust res.
   D. Duty to properly manage the trust.

19. An irrevocable testamentary trust was created by Park, with Gordon named as trustee. The trust provided that the income will be paid to Hardy for life with the principal then reverting to Park's estate to be paid to King. The trust will automatically end on the death of
   A. Park.
   B. Gordon.
   C. Hardy.
   D. King.

20. Which of the following events will terminate an irrevocable spendthrift trust established for a period of five years?
   A. Grantor dies.
   B. Income beneficiaries die.
   C. Grantor decides to terminate the trust.
   D. Income beneficiaries agree to the trust's termination.

21. A debtor may attempt to conceal or transfer property to prevent a creditor from satisfying a judgment. Which of the following actions will be considered an indication of fraudulent conveyance?

	Debtor remaining in possession after conveyance	Secret conveyance	Debtor retains an equitable benefit in the property conveyed
A.	Yes	Yes	Yes
B.	No	Yes	Yes
C.	Yes	Yes	No
D.	Yes	No	Yes

22. A homestead exemption ordinarily could exempt a debtor's equity in certain property from post-judgment collection by a creditor. To which of the following creditors will this exemption apply?

	Valid home mortgage lien	Valid IRS Tax lien
A.	Yes	Yes
B.	Yes	No
C.	No	Yes
D.	No	No

23. Which of the following methods will allow a creditor to collect money from a debtor's wages?
   A. Arrest.
   B. Mechanic's lien.
   C. Order of receivership.
   D. Writ of garnishment.

24. A party contracts to guaranty the collection of the debts of another. As a result of the guaranty, which of the following statements is correct?
   A. The creditor may proceed against the guarantor without attempting to collect from the debtor.
   B. The guaranty must be in writing.
   C. The guarantor may use any defenses available to the debtor.
   D. The creditor must be notified of the debtor's default by the guarantor.

25. Which of the following events will release a noncompensated surety from liability?
   A. Release of the principal debtor's obligation by the creditor but with the reservation of the creditor's rights against the surety.
   B. Modification by the principal debtor and creditor of their contract that materially increases the surety's risk of loss.
   C. Filing of an involuntary petition in bankruptcy against the principal debtor.
   D. Insanity of the principal debtor at the time the contract was entered into with the creditor.

26. Syl Corp. does not withhold FICA taxes from its employees' compensation. Syl voluntarily pays the entire FICA tax for its share and the amounts that it could have withheld from the employees. The employees' share of FICA taxes paid by Syl to the IRS is
   A. Deductible by Syl as additional compensation that is includible in the employees' taxable income.
   B. Not deductible by Syl because it does **not** meet the deductibility requirement as an ordinary and necessary business expense.
   C. A nontaxable gift to each employee, provided that the amount is less than $1,000 annually to each employee.
   D. Subject to prescribed penalties imposed on Syl for its failure to withhold required payroll taxes.

27. Which of the following statements is correct regarding the scope and provisions of the Occupational Safety and Health Act (OSHA)?
   A. OSHA requires employers to provide employees a workplace free from risk.
   B. OSHA prohibits an employer from discharging an employee for revealing OSHA violations.
   C. OSHA may inspect a workplace at any time regardless of employer objection.
   D. OSHA preempts state regulation of workplace safety.

28. Under Title VII of the 1964 Civil Rights Act, which of the following forms of discrimination is **not** prohibited?
   A. Sex.
   B. Age.
   C. Race.
   D. Religion.

29. Which of the following statements is correct under the Federal Fair Labor Standards Act?
   A. Some workers may be included within the minimum wage provisions but exempt from the overtime provisions.
   B. Some workers may be included within the overtime provisions but exempt from the minimum wage provisions.
   C. All workers are required to be included within both the minimum wage provisions and the overtime provisions.
   D. Possible exemptions from the minimum wage provisions and the overtime provisions must be determined by the union contract in effect at the time.

30. Under the Federal Consolidated Budget Reconciliation Act of 1985 (COBRA), when an employee voluntarily resigns from a job, the former employee's group health insurance coverage that was in effect during the period of employment with the company
   A. Automatically ceases for the former employee and spouse, if the resignation occurred before normal retirement age.
   B. Automatically ceases for the former employee's spouse, but continues for the former employee for an 18-month period at the former employer's expense.
   C. May be retained by the former employee at the former employee's expense for at least 18 months after leaving the company, but must be terminated for the former employee's spouse.
   D. May be retained for the former employee and spouse at the former employee's expense for at least 18 months after leaving the company.

31. Which of the following statements concerning the prospectus required by the Securities Act of 1933 is correct?
   A. The prospectus is a part of the registration statement.
   B. The prospectus should enable the SEC to pass on the merits of the securities.
   C. The prospectus must be filed after an offer to sell.
   D. The prospectus is prohibited from being distributed to the public until the SEC approves the accuracy of the facts embodied therein.

32. A preliminary prospectus, permitted under SEC Regulations, is known as the
   A. Unaudited prospectus.
   B. Qualified prospectus.
   C. "Blue-sky" prospectus.
   D. "Red-herring" prospectus.

33. A tombstone advertisement
   A. May be substituted for the prospectus under certain circumstances.
   B. May contain an offer to sell securities.
   C. Notifies prospective investors that a previously offered security has been withdrawn from the market and is therefore effectively "dead."
   D. Makes known the availability of a prospectus.

34. Which of the following factors, by itself, requires a corporation to comply with the reporting requirements of the Securities Exchange Act of 1934?
   A. Six hundred employees.
   B. Shares listed on a national securities exchange.
   C. Total assets of $2 million.
   D. Four hundred holders of equity securities.

35. Which of the following events must be reported to the SEC under the reporting provisions of the Securities Exchange Act of 1934?

	Tender offers	Insider trading	Soliciting proxies
A.	Yes	Yes	Yes
B.	Yes	Yes	No
C.	Yes	No	Yes
D.	No	Yes	Yes

36. Under the Securities Act of 1933, which of the following statements is correct concerning a public issuer of securities who has made a registered offering?
   A. The issuer is required to distribute an annual report to its stockholders.
   B. The issuer is subject to the proxy rules of the SEC.
   C. The issuer must file an annual report (Form 10-K) with the SEC.
   D. The issuer is **not** required to file a quarterly report (Form 10-Q) with the SEC, unless a material event occurs.

37. Which of the following transactions will be exempt from the full registration requirements of the Securities Act of 1933?
   A. All intrastate offerings.
   B. All offerings made under Regulation A.
   C. Any resale of a security purchased under a Regulation D offering.
   D. Any stockbroker transaction.

38. Under the Securities Exchange Act of 1934, which of the following types of instruments is excluded from the definition of "securities"?
   A. Investment contracts.
   B. Convertible debentures.
   C. Nonconvertible debentures.
   D. Certificates of deposit.

39. If securities are exempt from the registration provisions of the Securities Act of 1933, any fraud committed in the course of selling such securities can be challenged by

	SEC	Person defrauded
A.	Yes	Yes
B.	Yes	No
C.	No	Yes
D.	No	No

40. Under Regulation D of the Securities Act of 1933, which of the following conditions apply to private placement offerings? The securities
   A. Cannot be sold for longer than a six month period.
   B. Cannot be the subject of an immediate unregistered reoffering to the public.
   C. Must be sold to accredited institutional investors.
   D. Must be sold to fewer than 20 non-accredited investors.

41. Under the UCC Sales Article, which of the following conditions will prevent the formation of an enforceable sale of goods contract?
   A. Open price.
   B. Open delivery.
   C. Open quantity.
   D. Open acceptance.

42. Under the UCC Sales Article, which of the following statements is correct concerning a contract involving a merchant seller and a non-merchant buyer?
   A. Whether the UCC Sales Article is applicable does **not** depend on the price of the goods involved.
   B. Only the seller is obligated to perform the contract in good faith.
   C. The contract will be either a sale or return or sale on approval contract.
   D. The contract may **not** involve the sale of personal property with a price of more than $500.

43. Vick bought a used boat from Ocean Marina that disclaimed "any and all warranties" in connection with the sale. Ocean was unaware the boat had been stolen from Kidd. Vick surrendered it to Kidd when confronted with proof of the theft. Vick sued Ocean. Who is likely to prevail and why?
   A. Vick, because the implied warranty of title has been breached.
   B. Vick, because a merchant **cannot** disclaim implied warranties.
   C. Ocean, because of the disclaimer of warranties.
   D. Ocean, because Vick surrendered the boat to Kidd.

44. Larch Corp. manufactured and sold Oak a stove. The sale documents included a disclaimer of warranty for personal injury. The stove was defective. It exploded causing serious injuries to Oak's spouse. Larch was notified one week after the explosion. Under the UCC Sales Article, which of the following statements concerning Larch's liability for personal injury to Oak's spouse would be correct?
   A. Larch **cannot** be liable because of a lack of privity with Oak's spouse.
   B. Larch will **not** be liable because of a failure to give proper notice.
   C. Larch will be liable because the disclaimer was **not** a disclaimer of all liability.
   D. Larch will be liable because liability for personal injury **cannot** be disclaimed.

45. Quick Corp. agreed to purchase 200 typewriters from Union Suppliers, Inc. Union is a wholesaler of appliances and Quick is an appliance retailer. The contract required Union to ship the typewriters to Quick by common carrier, "F.O.B. Union Suppliers, Inc. Loading Dock." Which of the parties bears the risk of loss during shipment?
   A. Union, because the risk of loss passes only when Quick receives the typewriters.
   B. Union, because both parties are merchants.
   C. Quick, because title to the typewriters passed to Quick at the time of shipment.
   D. Quick, because the risk of loss passes when the typewriters are delivered to the carrier.

46. Webstar Corp. orally agreed to sell Northco, Inc. a computer for $20,000. Northco sent a signed purchase order to Webstar confirming the agreement. Webstar received the purchase order and did not respond. Webstar refused to deliver the computer to Northco, claiming that the purchase order did not satisfy the UCC Statute of Frauds because it was not signed by Webstar. Northco sells computers to the general public and Webstar is a computer wholesaler. Under the UCC Sales Article, Webstar's position is
   A. Incorrect because it failed to object to Northco's purchase order.
   B. Incorrect because only the buyer in a sale-of-goods transaction must sign the contract.
   C. Correct because it was the party against whom enforcement of the contract is being sought.
   D. Correct because the purchase price of the computer exceeded $500.

47. Under the UCC Sales Article, which of the following legal remedies would a buyer **not** have when a seller fails to transfer and deliver goods identified to the contract?
   A. Suit for specific performance.
   B. Suit for punitive damages.
   C. Purchase substitute goods (cover).
   D. Recover the identified goods (capture).

48. Under the UCC Secured Transactions Article, which of the following events will always prevent a security interest from attaching?
   A. Failure to have a written security agreement.
   B. Failure of the creditor to have possession of the collateral.
   C. Failure of the debtor to have rights in the collateral.
   D. Failure of the creditor to give present consideration for the security interest.

49. Under the UCC Secured Transactions Article, which of the following after-acquired property may be attached to a security agreement given to a secured lender?

	Inventory	Equipment
A.	Yes	Yes
B.	Yes	No
C.	No	Yes
D.	No	No

50. Under the UCC Secured Transactions Article, which of the following actions will best perfect a security interest in a negotiable instrument against any other party?
  A. Filing a security agreement.
  B. Taking possession of the instrument.
  C. Perfecting by attachment.
  D. Obtaining a duly executed financing statement.

51. Under the UCC Secured Transactions Article, perfection of a security interest by a creditor provides added protection against other parties in the event the debtor does not pay its debts. Which of the following parties is **not** affected by perfection of a security interest?
  A. Other prospective creditors of the debtor.
  B. The trustee in a bankruptcy case.
  C. A buyer in the ordinary course of business.
  D. A subsequent personal injury judgment creditor.

52. Under the UCC Secured Transactions Article, what is the order of priority for the following security interests in store equipment?

  I. Security interest perfected by filing on April 15, 1994.

  II. Security interest attached on April 1, 1994.

  III. Purchase money security interest attached April 11, 1994 and perfected by filing on April 20, 1994.

  A. I, III, II.
  B. II, I, III.
  C. III, I, II.
  D. III, II, I.

53. Larkin is a wholesaler of computers. Larkin sold 40 computers to Elk Appliance for $80,000. Elk paid $20,000 down and signed a promissory note for the balance. Elk also executed a security agreement giving Larkin a security interest in Elk's inventory, including the computers. Larkin perfected its security interest by properly filing a financing statement in the state of Whiteacre. Six months later, Elk moved its business to the state of Blackacre, taking the computers. On arriving in Blackacre, Elk secured a loan from Quarry Bank and signed a security agreement putting up all inventory (including the computers) as collateral. Quarry perfected its security interest by properly filing a financing statement in the state of Blackacre. Two months after arriving in Blackacre, Elk went into default on both debts. Which of the following statements is correct?
  A. Quarry's security interest is superior because Larkin's time to file a financing statement in Blackacre had expired prior to Quarry's filing.
  B. Quarry's security interest is superior because Quarry had **no** actual notice of Larkin's security interest.
  C. Larkin's security interest is superior even though at the time of Elk's default Larkin had **not** perfected its security interest in the state of Blackacre.
  D. Larkin's security interest is superior provided it repossesses the computers before Quarry does.

Items 54 and 55 are based on the following:

Drew bought a computer for personal use from Hale Corp. for $3,000. Drew paid $2,000 in cash and signed a security agreement for the balance. Hale properly filed the security agreement. Drew defaulted in paying the balance of the purchase price. Hale asked Drew to pay the balance. When Drew refused, Hale peacefully repossessed the computer.

54. Under the UCC Secured Transactions Article, which of the following remedies will Hale have?
   A. Obtain a deficiency judgment against Drew for the amount owed.
   B. Sell the computer and retain any surplus over the amount owed.
   C. Retain the computer over Drew's objection.
   D. Sell the computer without notifying Drew.

55. Under the UCC Secured Transactions Article, which of the following rights will Drew have?
   A. Redeem the computer after Hale sells it.
   B. Recover the sale price from Hale after Hale sells the computer.
   C. Force Hale to sell the computer.
   D. Prevent Hale from selling the computer.

56. Court, Fell, and Miles own a parcel of land as joint tenants with right of survivorship. Court's interest was sold to Plank. As a result of the sale from Court to Plank,
   A. Fell, Miles, and Plank each own one-third of the land as joint tenants.
   B. Fell and Miles each own one-third of the land as tenants in common.
   C. Plank owns one-third of the land as a tenant in common.
   D. Plank owns one-third of the land as a joint tenant.

57. Which of the following is a defect in marketable title to real property?
   A. Recorded zoning restrictions.
   B. Recorded easements referred to in the contract of sale
   C. Unrecorded lawsuit for negligence against the seller.
   D. Unrecorded easement.

58. Which of the following conditions must be met to have an enforceable mortgage?
   A. An accurate description of the property must be included in the mortgage.
   B. A negotiable promissory note must accompany the mortgage.
   C. Present consideration must be given in exchange for the mortgage.
   D. The amount of the debt and the interest rate must be stated in the mortgage.

59. Which of the following remedies is available against a real property owner to enforce the provisions of federal acts regulating air and water pollution?

	Citizen suits against the Environmental Protection Agency to enforce compliance with the laws	*State suits against violators*	*Citizen suits against violators*
A.	Yes	Yes	Yes
B.	Yes	Yes	No
C.	No	Yes	Yes
D.	Yes	No	Yes

60. Which of the following requirements must be met to create a bailment?

   I. Delivery of personal property to the intended bailee.

   II. Possession by the intended bailee.

   III. An absolute duty on the intended bailee to return or dispose of the property according to the bailor's directions.

   A. I and II only.
   B. I and III only.
   C. II and III only.
   D. I, II, and III.

Number 2 (Estimated time—10 to 15 minutes)

Question Number 2 consists of 2 parts. Each part consists of 6 items. Select the **best** answer for each item. Use a No. 2 pencil to blacken the appropriate ovals on the Objective Answer Sheet to indicate your answers. **Answer all items.** Your grade will be based on the total number of correct answers.

A.   Items 61 through 66 are based on the following:

Under Section 11 of the Securities Act of 1933 and Section 10(b), Rule 10b-5 of the Securities Exchange Act of 1934, a CPA may be sued by a purchaser of registered securities.

Required:

Items 61 through 66 relate to what a plaintiff who purchased securities must prove in a civil liability suit against a CPA. For each item determine whether the statement must be proven under Section 11 of the Securities Act of 1933, under Section 10(b), Rule 10b-5, of the Securities Exchange Act of 1934, both Acts, or neither Act, and blacken the corresponding oval on the Objective Answer Sheet.

- If the item must be proven **only** under Section 11 of the Securities Act of 1933, blacken Ⓐ on the Objective Answer Sheet.

- If the item must be proven **only** under Section 10(b), Rule 10b-5, of the Securities Exchange Act of 1934, blacken Ⓑ on the Objective Answer Sheet.

- If the item must be proven under **both** Acts, blacken Ⓒ on the Objective Answer Sheet.

- If the item must be proven under **neither** of the Acts, blacken Ⓓ on the Objective Answer Sheet.

Only Section 11	*Only Section 10(b)*	*Both*	*Neither*
Ⓐ	Ⓑ	Ⓒ	Ⓓ

The plaintiff security purchaser must
   allege or prove:

61. Material misstatements were included
     in a filed document.
62. A monetary loss occurred.
63. Lack of due diligence by the CPA.
64. Privity with the CPA.
65. Reliance on the document.
66. The CPA had scienter.

Number 2 (continued)

B. Items 67 through 72 are based on the following:

On May 1, 1994, Able Corp. was petitioned involuntarily into bankruptcy under the provisions of Chapter 7 of the Federal Bankruptcy Code.

When the petition was filed, Able had the following unsecured creditors:

Creditor	Amount owed
Cole	$5,000
Lake	2,000
Young	1,500
Thorn	1,000

The following transactions occurred before the bankruptcy petition was filed:

- On January 15, 1994, Able paid Vista Bank the $1,000 balance due on an unsecured business loan.

- On February 28, 1994, Able paid $1,000 to Owen, an officer of Able, who had lent Able money.

- On March 1, 1994, Able bought a computer for use in its business from Core Computer Co. for $2,000 cash.

Required:

Items 67 through 69 refer to the bankruptcy filing. For each item, determine whether the statement is True Ⓣ or False Ⓕ and blacken the corresponding oval on the Objective Answer Sheet.

67. Able can file a voluntary petition for bankruptcy if it is solvent.
68. Lake, Young, and Thorn can file a valid involuntary petition.
69. Cole alone can file a valid involuntary petition.

Items 70 through 72 refer to the transactions that occurred before the filing of the involuntary bankruptcy petition. Assuming the bankruptcy petition was validly filed, for each item determine whether the statement is True Ⓣ or False Ⓕ and blacken the corresponding oval on the Objective Answer Sheet.

70. The payment to Vista Bank would be set aside as a preferential transfer.
71. The payment to Owen would be set aside as a preferential transfer.
72. The purchase from Core Computer Co. would be set aside as a preferential transfer.

Number 3 (Estimated time—10 to 15 minutes)

Question Number 3 consists of 2 parts. Each part consists of 6 items. Select the **best** answer for each item. Use a No. 2 pencil to blacken the appropriate oval on the Objective Answer Sheet to indicate your answers. **Answer all items.** Your grade will be based on the total number of correct answers.

A. Items 73 through 78 are based on the following documents:

Document I (face)

> April 1, 1994
>
> On demand, the undersigned promises to pay to the order of
>
> MARK EDEN
>
> Three Thousand Two Hundred and ᴺᴼ/100 ($3,300.00)...dollars
>
> *Alice Long*
> Alice Long

Document I (back)

> *Mark Eden*
>
> Pay Joyce Noon
> *Harold Storm*

Document II (face)

> April 15, 1994
>
> On May 1, 1994, or sooner, pay to the order of
>
> EDWARD THARP
>
> Two Thousand and ᴺᴼ/100 ($2,000.00) .... dollars
>
> To: Henry Gage   *Patricia Rite*
> 100 East Way   Patricia Rite
> Capital City, ND

Document II (back)

> *Edward Tharp*
>
> *Nancy Ferry*
> without recourse
>
> *Ann Archer*

Required:

Items 73 through 78 relate to the nature and negotiability of the above documents and the nature of several of the endorsements. For each item select from List A the response that best completes that statement and blacken the corresponding oval on the Objective Answer Sheet. A response may be selected more than once.

List A

73. Document I is a (type of instrument)	A. Blank
74. Document II is a (type of instrument)	B. Check
75. Document I is (negotiability)	C. Draft
76. Document II is (negotiability)	D. Negotiable
77. The endorsement by Mark Eden is (type of endorsement)	E. Nonnegotiable
78. The endorsement by Nancy Ferry is (type of endorsement)	F. Promissory Note
	G. Qualified
	H. Special

Number 3 (continued)

B. **Items 79 through 84** are based on the following:

On January 12, 1994, Frank, Inc. contracted in writing to purchase a factory building from Henderson for $250,000 cash. Closing took place on March 15, 1994. Henderson had purchased the building in 1990 for $225,000 and had, at that time, taken out a $180,000 fire insurance policy with Summit Insurance Co.

On January 15, 1994, Frank took out a $140,000 fire insurance policy with Unity Insurance Co. and a $70,000 fire insurance policy with Imperial Insurance, Inc.

On March 16, 1994, a fire caused $150,000 damage to the building. At that time the building had a market value of $250,000. All fire insurance policies contain a standard 80 percent coinsurance clause. The insurance carriers have refused any payment to Frank or Henderson alleging lack of insurable interest and insufficient coverage. Frank and Henderson have sued to collect on the policies.

Required:
Items 79 through 84 relate to the suits by Frank and Henderson. For each item, determine whether the statement is True **T** or False **F** and blacken the corresponding oval on the Objective Answer Sheet.

79. Frank had an insurable interest at the time the Unity and Imperial policies were taken out.
80. Henderson had an insurable interest at the time of the fire.
81. Assuming Frank had an insurable interest, Frank's coverage would be insufficient under the Unity and Imperial coinsurance clauses.
82. Assuming Henderson had an insurable interest, Henderson's coverage would be insufficient under the Summit coinsurance clause.
83. Assuming only Frank had an insurable interest, Frank will recover $100,000 from Unity and $50,000 from Imperial.
84. Assuming only Henderson had an insurable interest, Henderson will recover $135,000 from Summit.

Number 4 (Estimated time—15 to 25 minutes)

Best Aviation Associates is a general partnership engaged in the business of buying, selling and servicing used airplanes. Best's original partners were Martin and Kent. They formed the partnership on January 1, 1992, under an oral partnership agreement which provided that the partners would share profits equally. There was no agreement as to how the partners would share losses. At the time the partnership was formed, Martin contributed $320,000 and Kent contributed $80,000.

On December 1, 1993, Best hired Baker to be a salesperson and to assist in purchasing used aircraft for Best's inventory. On December 15, 1993, Martin instructed Baker to negotiate the purchase of a used airplane from Jackson without disclosing that Baker was acting on Best's behalf. Martin thought that a better price could be negotiated by Baker if Jackson was not aware that the aircraft was being acquired for Best. Baker contracted with Jackson without disclosing that the airplane was being purchased for Best. The agreement provided that Jackson would deliver the airplane to Baker on January 2, 1994, at which time the purchase price was to be paid. On January 2, 1994, Jackson attempted to deliver the used airplane purchased for Best by Baker. Baker, acting on Martin's instructions, refused to accept delivery or pay the purchase price.

On December 20, 1993, Kent assigned Kent's partnership interest in Best to Green. On December 31, 1993, Kent advised Martin of the assignment to Green. On January 11, 1994, Green contacted Martin and demanded to inspect the partnership books and to participate in the management of partnership affairs, including voting on partnership decisions.

On January 13, 1994, it was determined that Best had incurred an operating loss of $160,000 in 1993. Martin demanded that Kent contribute $80,000 to the partnership to account for Kent's share of the loss. Kent refused to contribute.

On January 28, 1993, Laco Supplies, Inc., a creditor of Best, sued Best and Martin for unpaid bills totalling $92,000. Best had not paid the bills because of a cash shortfall caused by the 1993 operating loss.

Jackson has taken the following position:

- Baker is responsible for any damages incurred by Jackson as a result of Best's refusal to accept delivery or pay the purchase price.

Martin has taken the following positions:

- Green is not entitled to inspect the partnership books or participate in the management of the partnership.

- Only the partnership is liable for the amounts owed to Laco, or, in the alternative, Martin's personal liability is limited to 50 percent of the total of the unpaid bills.

Kent has taken the following positions:

- Only Martin is liable for the 1993 operating loss because of the assignment to Green of Kent's partnership interest.

- Any personal liability of the partners for the 1993 operating loss should be allocated between them on the basis of their original capital contributions.

Required:

a. Determine whether Jackson's position is correct and state the reasons for your conclusions.

b. Determine whether Martin's positions are correct and state the reasons for your conclusions.

c. Determine whether Kent's positions are correct and state the reasons for your conclusions.

Number 5 (Estimated time—15 to 25 minutes)

Suburban Properties, Inc. owns and manages several shopping centers.

On May 4, 1993, Suburban received from Bridge Hardware, Inc., one of its tenants, a signed letter proposing that the existing lease between Suburban and Bridge be modified to provide that certain utility costs be equally shared by Bridge and Suburban, effective June 1, 1993. Under the terms of the original lease, Bridge was obligated to pay all utility costs. On May 5, 1993, Suburban sent Bridge a signed letter agreeing to share the utility costs as proposed. Suburban later changed its opinion and refused to share in the utility costs.

On June 4, 1993, Suburban received from Dart Associates, Inc. a signed offer to purchase one of the shopping centers owned by Suburban. The offer provided as follows: a price of $9,250,000; it would not be withdrawn before July 1, 1993; and an acceptance must be received by Dart to be effective. On June 9, 1993, Suburban mailed Dart a signed acceptance. On June 10, before Dart had received Suburban's acceptance, Dart telephoned Suburban and withdrew its offer. Suburban's acceptance was received by Dart on June 12, 1993.

On June 22, 1993, one of Suburban's shopping centers was damaged by a fire, which started when the center was struck by lightning. As a result of the fire, one of the tenants in the shopping center, World Popcorn Corp., was forced to close its business and will be unable to reopen until the damage is repaired. World sued Suburban claiming that Suburban is liable for World's losses resulting from the fire. The lease between Suburban and World is silent in this regard.

Suburban has taken the following positions:

- Suburban's May 5, 1994, agreement to share equally the utility costs with Bridge is not binding on Suburban.

- Dart could not properly revoke its June 4 offer and must purchase the shopping center.

- Suburban is not liable to World for World's losses resulting from the fire.

Required:

In separate paragraphs, determine whether Suburban's positions are correct and state the reasons for your conclusions.

EXAMINATION QUESTION BOOKLET

CANDIDATE NUMBER

Record your 7-digit candidate number in the boxes.

Q-AUD

AUDITING

May 4, 1994; 1:30 P.M. to 6:00 P.M.

The point values for each question, and estimated time allotments based primarily on point value, are as follows:

	Point Value	Estimated Minutes Minimum	Estimated Minutes Maximum
No. 1	60	140	150
No. 2	10	15	25
No. 3	10	15	25
No. 4	10	25	35
No. 5	10	25	35
Totals	100	220	270

INSTRUCTIONS TO CANDIDATES *Failure to follow these instructions may have an adverse effect on your Examination grade.*

1. Record your 7-digit candidate number in the boxes provided at the upper right-hand corner of this page.

2. Question numbers 1, 2, and 3 should be answered on the *Objective Answer Sheet*, which is pages 11 and 12 of your *Examination Answer Booklet*. You should attempt to answer all objective items. There is no penalty for incorrect responses. Since the objective items are computer-graded, your comments and calculations associated with them are not considered. Be certain that you have entered your answers on the *Objective Answer Sheet* before the examination time is up. The objective portion of your examination will not be graded if you fail to record your answers on the *Objective Answer Sheet*. You will not be given additional time to record your answers.

3. Question numbers 4 and 5 should be answered beginning on page 3 of the *Examination Answer Booklet*. If you have not completed answering a question on a page, fill in the appropriate spaces in the wording on the bottom of the page **"QUESTION NUMBER ___ CONTINUES ON PAGE ___"** If you have completed answering a question, fill in the appropriate space in the wording on the bottom of the page **"QUESTION NUMBER ___ ENDS ON THIS PAGE."** Always begin the start of an answer to a question on the top of a new page (which may be the back side of a sheet of paper).

4. Record your 7-digit candidate number, state, and question number where indicated on pages 3 through 10 of the *Examination Answer Booklet*.

5. Although the primary purpose of the examination is to test your knowledge and application of the subject matter, selected essay responses will be graded for writing skills.

6. You are required to turn in by the end of each session:

   a. Attendance Record Form, front page of *Examination Answer Booklet*;
   b. *Objective Answer Sheet*, pages 11 and 12 of *Examination Answer Booklet*;
   c. Remaining Portion of *Examination Answer Booklet*;
   d. *Examination Question Booklet*; and
   e. All unused examination materials.

   Your examination will not be graded unless the above listed items are handed in before leaving the examination room.

7. Unless otherwise instructed, if you want your *Examination Question Booklet* mailed to you, write your name and address in both places indicated on the back cover and place 52 cents postage in the space provided. Examination Question Booklets will be distributed no sooner than the day following the administration of this examination.

Prepared by the Board of Examiners of the American Institute of Certified Public Accountants and adopted by the examining boards of all states, the District of Columbia, Guam, Puerto Rico, and the Virgin Islands of the United States.

Number 1 (Estimated time — 140 to 150 minutes)

Instructions

Select the **best** answer for each of the following items. Use a No. 2 pencil to blacken the appropriate ovals on the Objective Answer Sheet to indicate your answers. **Mark only one answer for each item. Answer all items.** Your grade will be based on the total number of correct answers.

1. Before accepting an audit engagement, a successor auditor should make specific inquiries of the predecessor auditor regarding the predecessor's
   A. Opinion of any subsequent events occurring since the predecessor's audit report was issued.
   B. Understanding as to the reasons for the change of auditors.
   C. Awareness of the consistency in the application of GAAP between periods.
   D. Evaluation of all matters of continuing accounting significance.

2. Which of the following factors most likely would cause an auditor **not** to accept a new audit engagement?
   A. An inadequate understanding of the entity's internal control structure.
   B. The close proximity to the end of the entity's fiscal year.
   C. Concluding that the entity's management probably lacks integrity.
   D. An inability to perform preliminary analytical procedures before assessing control risk.

3. The audit work performed by each assistant should be reviewed to determine whether it was adequately performed and to evaluate whether the
   A. Auditor's system of quality control has been maintained at a high level.
   B. Results are consistent with the conclusions to be presented in the auditor's report.
   C. Audit procedures performed are approved in the professional standards.
   D. Audit has been performed by persons having adequate technical training and proficiency as auditors.

4. An auditor obtains knowledge about a new client's business and its industry to
   A. Make constructive suggestions concerning improvements to the client's internal control structure.
   B. Develop an attitude of professional skepticism concerning management's financial statement assertions.
   C. Evaluate whether the aggregation of known misstatements causes the financial statements taken as a whole to be materially misstated.
   D. Understand the events and transactions that may have an effect on the client's financial statements.

5. The objective of performing analytical procedures in planning an audit is to identify the existence of
   A. Unusual transactions and events.
   B. Illegal acts that went undetected because of internal control weaknesses.
   C. Related party transactions.
   D. Recorded transactions that were **not** properly authorized.

6. Jones, CPA, is auditing the financial statements of XYZ Retailing, Inc. What assurance does Jones provide that direct effect illegal acts that are material to XYZ's financial statements, and illegal acts that have a material, but indirect effect on the financial statements will be detected?

	Direct effect illegal acts	*Indirect effect illegal acts*
A.	Reasonable	None
B.	Reasonable	Reasonable
C.	Limited	None
D.	Limited	Reasonable

7. An auditor concludes that a client has committed an illegal act that has not been properly accounted for or disclosed. The auditor should withdraw from the engagement if the
   A. Auditor is precluded from obtaining sufficient competent evidence about the illegal act.
   B. Illegal act has an effect on the financial statements that is both material and direct.
   C. Auditor **cannot** reasonably estimate the effect of the illegal act on the financial statements.
   D. Client refuses to accept the auditor's report as modified for the illegal act.

8. In designing written audit programs, an auditor should establish specific audit objectives that relate primarily to the
    A. Timing of audit procedures.
    B. Cost-benefit of gathering evidence.
    C. Selected audit techniques.
    D. Financial statement assertions.

9. North Co., a privately-held entity, asked its tax accountant, King, a CPA in public practice, to generate North's interim financial statements on King's microcomputer when King prepared North's quarterly tax return. King should **not** submit these financial statements to North unless, as a minimum, King complies with the provisions of
    A. Statements on Standards for Accounting and Review Services.
    B. Statements on Standards for Unaudited Financial Services.
    C. Statements on Standards for Consulting Services.
    D. Statements on Standards for Attestation Engagements.

10. Which of the following is a conceptual difference between the attestation standards and generally accepted auditing standards?
    A. The attestation standards provide a framework for the attest function beyond historical financial statements.
    B. The requirement that the practitioner be independent in mental attitude is omitted from the attestation standards.
    C. The attestation standards do **not** permit an attest engagement to be part of a business acquisition study or a feasibility study.
    D. **None** of the standards of fieldwork in generally accepted auditing standards are included in the attestation standards.

11. Because of the risk of material misstatement, an audit of financial statements in accordance with generally accepted auditing standards should be planned and performed with an attitude of
    A. Objective judgment.
    B. Independent integrity.
    C. Professional skepticism.
    D. Impartial conservatism.

12. Davis, CPA, accepted an engagement to audit the financial statements of Tech Resources, a nonpublic entity. Before the completion of the audit, Tech requested Davis to change the engagement to a compilation of financial statements. Before Davis agrees to change the engagement, Davis is required to consider the

	Additional audit effort necessary to complete the audit	Reason given for Tech's request
A.	No	No
B.	Yes	Yes
C.	Yes	No
D.	No	Yes

13. Smith, CPA, has been asked to issue a review report on the balance sheet of Cone Company, a nonpublic entity, and not on the other related financial statements. Smith may do so only if
    A. Smith compiles and reports on the related statements of income, retained earnings, and cash flows.
    B. Smith is **not** aware of any material modifications needed for the balance sheet to conform with GAAP.
    C. The scope of Smith's inquiry and analytical procedures is **not** restricted.
    D. Cone is a new client and Smith accepts the engagement after the end of Cone's fiscal year.

14. Accepting an engagement to examine an entity's financial projection most likely would be appropriate if the projection were to be distributed to
    A. All employees who work for the entity.
    B. Potential stockholders who request a prospectus or a registration statement.
    C. A bank with which the entity is negotiating for a loan.
    D. All stockholders of record as of the report date.

15. Which of the following is an element of a CPA firm's quality control system that should be considered in establishing its quality control policies and procedures?
    A. Complying with laws and regulations.
    B. Using statistical sampling techniques.
    C. Assigning personnel to engagements.
    D. Considering audit risk and materiality.

16. Which of the following statements most likely represents a disadvantage for an entity that keeps microcomputer-prepared data files rather than manually prepared files?
   A. Attention is focused on the accuracy of the programming process rather than errors in individual transactions.
   B. It is usually easier for unauthorized persons to access and alter the files.
   C. Random error associated with processing similar transactions in different ways is usually greater.
   D. It is usually more difficult to compare recorded accountability with physical count of assets.

17. For which of the following audit tests would an auditor most likely use attribute sampling?
   A. Making an independent estimate of the amount of a LIFO inventory.
   B. Examining invoices in support of the valuation of fixed asset additions.
   C. Selecting accounts receivable for confirmation of account balances.
   D. Inspecting employee time cards for proper approval by supervisors.

18. An auditor's flowchart of a client's accounting system is a diagrammatic representation that depicts the auditor's
   A. Assessment of control risk.
   B. Identification of weaknesses in the system.
   C. Assessment of the control environment's effectiveness.
   D. Understanding of the system.

19. Management's attitude toward aggressive financial reporting and its emphasis on meeting projected profit goals most likely would significantly influence an entity's control environment when
   A. The audit committee is active in overseeing the entity's financial reporting policies.
   B. External policies established by parties outside the entity affect its accounting practices.
   C. Management is dominated by one individual who is also a shareholder.
   D. Internal auditors have direct access to the board of directors and entity management.

20. An auditor should obtain sufficient knowledge of an entity's accounting system to understand the
   A. Safeguards used to limit access to computer facilities.
   B. Process used to prepare significant accounting estimates.
   C. Procedures used to assure proper authorization of transactions.
   D. Policies used to detect the concealment of irregularities.

21. When obtaining an understanding of an entity's internal control procedures, an auditor should concentrate on the substance of the procedures rather than their form because
   A. The procedures may be operating effectively but may **not** be documented.
   B. Management may establish appropriate procedures but **not** enforce compliance with them.
   C. The procedures may be so inappropriate that **no** reliance is contemplated by the auditor.
   D. Management may implement procedures whose costs exceed their benefits.

22. Which of the following most likely would **not** be considered an inherent limitation of the potential effectiveness of an entity's internal control structure?
   A. Incompatible duties.
   B. Management override.
   C. Mistakes in judgment.
   D. Collusion among employees.

23. When an auditor increases the assessed level of control risk because certain control procedures were determined to be ineffective, the auditor would most likely increase the
   A. Extent of tests of controls.
   B. Level of detection risk.
   C. Extent of tests of details.
   D. Level of inherent risk.

24. An auditor uses the assessed level of control risk to
   A. Evaluate the effectiveness of the entity's internal control policies and procedures.
   B. Identify transactions and account balances where inherent risk is at the maximum.
   C. Indicate whether materiality thresholds for planning and evaluation purposes are sufficiently high.
   D. Determine the acceptable level of detection risk for financial statement assertions.

25. After obtaining an understanding of the internal control structure and assessing control risk, an auditor decided not to perform additional tests of controls. The auditor most likely concluded that the
  A. Additional evidence to support a further reduction in control risk was **not** cost-beneficial to obtain.
  B. Assessed level of inherent risk exceeded the assessed level of control risk.
  C. Internal control structure was properly designed and justifiably may be relied on.
  D. Evidence obtainable through tests of controls would **not** support an increased level of control risk.

26. An auditor wishes to perform tests of controls on a client's cash disbursements procedures. If the control procedures leave **no** audit trail of documentary evidence, the auditor most likely will test the procedures by
  A. Confirmation and observation.
  B. Observation and inquiry.
  C. Analytical procedures and confirmation.
  D. Inquiry and analytical procedures.

27. Which of the following audit procedures would an auditor most likely perform to test controls relating to management's assertion concerning the completeness of sales transactions?
  A. Verify that extensions and footings on the entity's sales invoices and monthly customer statements have been recomputed.
  B. Inspect the entity's reports of prenumbered shipping documents that have **not** been recorded in the sales journal.
  C. Compare the invoiced prices on prenumbered sales invoices to the entity's authorized price list.
  D. Inquire about the entity's credit granting policies and the consistent application of credit checks.

28. Which of the following internal control procedures most likely would assure that all billed sales are correctly posted to the accounts receivable ledger?
  A. Daily sales summaries are compared to daily postings to the accounts receivable ledger.
  B. Each sales invoice is supported by a prenumbered shipping document.
  C. The accounts receivable ledger is reconciled daily to the control account in the general ledger.
  D. Each shipment on credit is supported by a prenumbered sales invoice.

29. An auditor most likely would assess control risk at the maximum if the payroll department supervisor is responsible for
  A. Examining authorization forms for new employees.
  B. Comparing payroll registers with original batch transmittal data.
  C. Authorizing payroll rate changes for all employees.
  D. Hiring all subordinate payroll department employees.

30. In a properly designed internal control structure, the same employee most likely would match vendors' invoices with receiving reports and also
  A. Post the detailed accounts payable records.
  B. Recompute the calculations on vendors' invoices.
  C. Reconcile the accounts payable ledger.
  D. Cancel vendors' invoices after payment.

31. An auditor most likely would introduce test data into a computerized payroll system to test internal controls related to the
  A. Existence of unclaimed payroll checks held by supervisors.
  B. Early cashing of payroll checks by employees.
  C. Discovery of invalid employee I.D. numbers.
  D. Proper approval of overtime by supervisors.

32. Which of the following internal control procedures most likely would prevent direct labor hours from being charged to manufacturing overhead?
  A. Periodic independent counts of work in process for comparison to recorded amounts.
  B. Comparison of daily journal entries with approved production orders.
  C. Use of time tickets to record actual labor worked on production orders.
  D. Reconciliation of work-in-process inventory with periodic cost budgets.

33. Which of the following internal control procedures most likely would be used to maintain accurate inventory records?
  A. Perpetual inventory records are periodically compared with the current cost of individual inventory items.
  B. A just-in-time inventory ordering system keeps inventory levels to a desired minimum.
  C. Requisitions, receiving reports, and purchase orders are independently matched before payment is approved.
  D. Periodic inventory counts are used to adjust the perpetual inventory records.

34. When an entity uses a trust company as custodian of its marketable securities, the possibility of concealing fraud most likely would be reduced if the
  A. Trust company has **no** direct contact with the entity employees responsible for maintaining investment accounting records.
  B. Securities are registered in the name of the trust company, rather than the entity itself.
  C. Interest and dividend checks are mailed directly to an entity employee who is authorized to sell securities.
  D. Trust company places the securities in a bank safe-deposit vault under the custodian's exclusive control.

35. An auditor tests an entity's policy of obtaining credit approval before shipping goods to customers in support of management's financial statement assertion of
  A. Valuation or allocation.
  B. Completeness.
  C. Existence or occurrence.
  D. Rights and obligations.

36. Lake, CPA, is auditing the financial statements of Gill Co. Gill uses the EDP Service Center, Inc. to process its payroll transactions. EDP's financial statements are audited by Cope, CPA, who recently issued a report on EDP's internal control structure. Lake is considering Cope's report on EDP's internal control structure in assessing control risk on the Gill engagement. What is Lake's responsibility concerning making reference to Cope as a basis, in part, for Lake's own opinion?
  A. Lake may refer to Cope only if Lake is satisfied as to Cope's professional reputation and independence.
  B. Lake may refer to Cope only if Lake relies on Cope's report in restricting the extent of substantive tests.
  C. Lake may refer to Cope only if Lake's report indicates the division of responsibility.
  D. Lake may **not** refer to Cope under the circumstances above.

37. Which of the following best describes a CPA's engagement to report on an entity's internal control structure over financial reporting?
  A. An attestation engagement to examine and report on management's written assertions about the effectiveness of its internal control structure.
  B. An audit engagement to render an opinion on the entity's internal control structure.
  C. A prospective engagement to project, for a period of time **not** to exceed one year, and report on the expected benefits of the entity's internal control structure.
  D. A consulting engagement to provide constructive advice to the entity on its internal control structure.

38. Which of the following presumptions does **not** relate to the competence of audit evidence?
   A. The more effective the internal control structure, the more assurance it provides about the accounting data and financial statements.
   B. An auditor's opinion, to be economically useful, is formed within reasonable time and based on evidence obtained at a reasonable cost.
   C. Evidence obtained from independent sources outside the entity is more reliable than evidence secured solely within the entity.
   D. The independent auditor's direct personal knowledge, obtained through observation and inspection, is more persuasive than information obtained indirectly.

39. An auditor concluded that no excessive costs for idle plant were charged to inventory. This conclusion most likely related to the auditor's objective to obtain evidence about the financial statement assertions regarding inventory, including presentation and disclosure and
   A. Valuation and allocation.
   B. Completeness.
   C. Existence or occurrence.
   D. Rights and obligations.

40. Auditors try to identify predictable relationships when using analytical procedures. Relationships involving transactions from which of the following accounts most likely would yield the highest level of evidence?
   A. Accounts receivable.
   B. Interest expense.
   C. Accounts payable.
   D. Travel and entertainment expense.

41. An auditor selected items for test counts while observing a client's physical inventory. The auditor then traced the test counts to the client's inventory listing. This procedure most likely obtained evidence concerning management's assertion of
   A. Rights and obligations.
   B. Completeness.
   C. Existence or occurrence.
   D. Valuation.

42. In testing plant and equipment balances, an auditor examines new additions listed on an analysis of plant and equipment. This procedure most likely obtains evidence concerning management's assertion of
   A. Completeness.
   B. Existence or occurrence.
   C. Presentation and disclosure.
   D. Valuation or allocation.

43. While performing a test of details during an audit, an auditor determined that the sample results supported the conclusion that the recorded account balance was materially misstated. It was, in fact, not materially misstated. This situation illustrates the risk of
   A. Assessing control risk too high.
   B. Assessing control risk too low.
   C. Incorrect rejection.
   D. Incorrect acceptance.

44. The sample size of a test of controls varies inversely with

	Expected population deviation rate	Tolerable rate
A.	Yes	Yes
B.	No	No
C.	Yes	No
D.	No	Yes

45. In evaluating an entity's accounting estimates, one of an auditor's objectives is to determine whether the estimates are
   A. Not subject to bias.
   B. Consistent with industry guidelines.
   C. Based on objective assumptions.
   D. Reasonable in the circumstances.

46. May an accountant accept an engagement to compile or review the financial statements of a not-for-profit entity if the accountant is unfamiliar with the specialized industry accounting principles, but plans to obtain the required level of knowledge before compiling or reviewing the financial statements?

	Compilation	Review
A.	No	No
B.	Yes	No
C.	No	Yes
D.	Yes	Yes

47. Which of the following audit procedures is best for identifying unrecorded trade accounts payable?
- A. Reviewing cash disbursements recorded subsequent to the balance sheet date to determine whether the related payables apply to the prior period.
- B. Investigating payables recorded just prior to and just subsequent to the balance sheet date to determine whether they are supported by receiving reports.
- C. Examining unusual relationships between monthly accounts payable balances and recorded cash payments.
- D. Reconciling vendors' statements to the file of receiving reports to identify items received just prior to the balance sheet date.

48. In testing for unrecorded retirements of equipment, an auditor most likely would
- A. Select items of equipment from the accounting records and then locate them during the plant tour.
- B. Compare depreciation journal entries with similar prior-year entries in search of fully depreciated equipment.
- C. Inspect items of equipment observed during the plant tour and then trace them to the equipment subsidiary ledger.
- D. Scan the general journal for unusual equipment additions and excessive debits to repairs and maintenance expense.

49. An auditor most likely would extend substantive tests of payroll when
- A. Payroll is extensively audited by the state government.
- B. Payroll expense is substantially higher than in the prior year.
- C. Overpayments are discovered in performing tests of details.
- D. Employees complain to management about too much overtime.

50. A client has a large and active investment portfolio that is kept in a bank safe deposit box. If the auditor is unable to count the securities at the balance sheet date, the auditor most likely will
- A. Request the bank to confirm to the auditor the contents of the safe deposit box at the balance sheet date.
- B. Examine supporting evidence for transactions occurring during the year.
- C. Count the securities at a subsequent date and confirm with the bank whether securities were added or removed since the balance sheet date.
- D. Request the client to have the bank seal the safe deposit box until the auditor can count the securities at a subsequent date.

51. Which of the following is required documentation in an audit in accordance with generally accepted auditing standards?
- A. A flowchart or narrative of the accounting system describing the recording and classification of transactions for financial reporting.
- B. An audit program setting forth in detail the procedures necessary to accomplish the engagement's objectives.
- C. A planning memorandum establishing the timing of the audit procedures and coordinating the assistance of entity personnel.
- D. An internal control questionnaire identifying policies and procedures that assure specific objectives will be achieved.

52. In using the work of a specialist, an auditor referred to the specialist's findings in the auditor's report. This would be an appropriate reporting practice if the
- A. Client is **not** familiar with the professional certification, personal reputation, or particular competence of the specialist.
- B. Auditor, as a result of the specialist's findings, adds an explanatory paragraph emphasizing a matter regarding the financial statements.
- C. Client understands the auditor's corroborative use of the specialist's findings in relation to the representations in the financial statements.
- D. Auditor, as a result of the specialist's findings, decides to indicate a division of responsibility with the specialist.

53. Zero Corp. suffered a loss that would have a material effect on its financial statements on an uncollectible trade account receivable due to a customer's bankruptcy. This occurred suddenly due to a natural disaster ten days after Zero's balance sheet date, but one month before the issuance of the financial statements and the auditor's report. Under these circumstances,

	The financial statements should be adjusted	The event requires financial statement disclosure, but no adjustment	The auditor's report should be modified for a lack of consistency
A.	Yes	No	No
B.	Yes	No	Yes
C.	No	Yes	Yes
D.	No	Yes	No

54. Which of the following statements ordinarily is included among the written client representations obtained by the auditor?
   A. Compensating balances and other arrangements involving restrictions on cash balances have been disclosed.
   B. Management acknowledges responsibility for illegal actions committed by employees.
   C. Sufficient evidential matter has been made available to permit the issuance of an unqualified opinion.
   D. Management acknowledges that there are no material weaknesses in the internal control.

55. Which of the following auditing procedures most likely would assist an auditor in identifying conditions and events that may indicate substantial doubt about an entity's ability to continue as a going concern?
   A. Inspecting title documents to verify whether any assets are pledged as collateral.
   B. Confirming with third parties the details of arrangements to maintain financial support.
   C. Reconciling the cash balance per books with the cut-off bank statement and the bank confirmation.
   D. Comparing the entity's depreciation and asset capitalization policies to other entities in the industry.

56. Using microcomputers in auditing may affect the methods used to review the work of staff assistants because
   A. The audit field work standards for supervision may differ.
   B. Documenting the supervisory review may require assistance of consulting services personnel.
   C. Supervisory personnel may not have an understanding of the capabilities and limitations of microcomputers.
   D. Working paper documentation may not contain readily observable details of calculations.

57. Which of the following auditing procedures most likely would assist an auditor in identifying related party transactions?
   A. Retesting ineffective internal control procedures previously reported to the audit committee.
   B. Sending second requests for unanswered positive confirmations of accounts receivable.
   C. Reviewing accounting records for nonrecurring transactions recognized near the balance sheet date.
   D. Inspecting communications with law firms for evidence of unreported contingent liabilities.

58. Before applying principal substantive tests to the details of accounts at an interim date prior to the balance sheet date, an auditor should
   A. Assess control risk at below the maximum for the assertions embodied in the accounts selected for interim testing.
   B. Determine that the accounts selected for interim testing are not material to the financial statements taken as a whole.
   C. Consider whether the amounts of the year-end balances selected for interim testing are reasonably predictable.
   D. Obtain written representations from management that all financial records and related data will be made available.

59. An accountant should perform analytical procedures during an engagement to

	Compile a nonpublic entity's financial statements	Review a nonpublic entity's financial statements
A.	No	No
B.	Yes	Yes
C.	Yes	No
D.	No	Yes

60. Which of the following procedures most likely would **not** be included in a review engagement of a nonpublic entity?
  A. Obtaining a management representation letter.
  B. Considering whether the financial statements conform with GAAP.
  C. Assessing control risk.
  D. Inquiring about subsequent events.

61. When an independent CPA assists in preparing the financial statements of a publicly held entity, but has **not** audited or reviewed them, the CPA should issue a disclaimer of opinion. In such situations, the CPA has **no** responsibility to apply any procedures beyond
  A. Documenting that the internal control structure is **not** being relied on.
  B. Reading the financial statements for obvious material misstatements.
  C. Ascertaining whether the financial statements are in conformity with GAAP.
  D. Determining whether management has elected to omit substantially all required disclosures.

62. When an auditor concludes there is substantial doubt about a continuing audit client's ability to continue as a going concern for a reasonable period of time, the auditor's responsibility is to
  A. Issue a qualified or adverse opinion, depending upon materiality, due to the possible effects on the financial statements.
  B. Consider the adequacy of disclosure about the client's possible inability to continue as a going concern.
  C. Report to the client's audit committee that management's accounting estimates may need to be adjusted.
  D. Reissue the prior year's auditor's report and add an explanatory paragraph that specifically refers to "substantial doubt" and "going concern."

63. Investment and property schedules are presented for purposes of additional analysis in an auditor-submitted document. The schedules are not required parts of the basic financial statements, but accompany the basic financial statements. When reporting on such additional information, the measurement of materiality is the
  A. Same as that used in forming an opinion on the basic financial statements taken as a whole.
  B. Lesser of the individual schedule of investments or schedule of property taken by itself.
  C. Greater of the individual schedule of investments or schedule of property taken by itself.
  D. Combined total of both the individual schedules of investments and property taken as a whole.

64. An independent accountant's report is based on a review of interim financial information. If this report is presented in a registration statement, a prospectus should include a statement clarifying that the
  A. Accountant's review report is **not** a part of the registration statement within the meaning of the Securities Act of 1933.
  B. Accountant assumes **no** responsibility to update the report for events and circumstances occurring after the date of the report.
  C. Accountant's review was performed in accordance with standards established by the Securities and Exchange Commission.
  D. Accountant obtained corroborating evidence to determine whether material modifications are needed for such information to conform with GAAP.

65. Reference in a principal auditor's report to the fact that part of the audit was performed by another auditor most likely would be an indication of the
  A. Divided responsibility between the auditors who conducted the audits of the components of the overall financial statements.
  B. Lack of materiality of the portion of the financial statements audited by the other auditor.
  C. Principal auditor's recognition of the other auditor's competence, reputation, and professional certification.
  D. Different opinions the auditors are expressing on the components of the financial statements that each audited.

66. In May 1994, an auditor reissues the auditor's report on the 1992 financial statements at a continuing client's request. The 1992 financial statements are not restated and the auditor does not revise the wording of the report. The auditor should
  A. Dual date the reissued report.
  B. Use the release date of the reissued report.
  C. Use the original report date on the reissued report.
  D. Use the current-period auditor's report date on the reissued report.

67. In connection with a proposal to obtain a new client, an accountant in public practice is asked to prepare a written report on the application of accounting principles to a specific transaction. The accountant's report should include a statement that
  A. Any difference in the facts, circumstances, or assumptions presented may change the report.
  B. The engagement was performed in accordance with Statements on Standards for Consulting Services.
  C. The guidance provided is for management use only and may **not** be communicated to the prior or continuing auditors.
  D. Nothing came to the accountant's attention that caused the accountant to believe that the accounting principles violated GAAP.

68. An accountant's report on a review of pro forma financial information should include a
  A. Statement that the entity's internal control structure was **not** relied on in the review.
  B. Disclaimer of opinion on the financial statements from which the pro forma financial information is derived.
  C. Caveat that it is uncertain whether the transaction or event reflected in the pro forma financial information will ever occur.
  D. Reference to the financial statements from which the historical financial information is derived.

69. An auditor includes a separate paragraph in an otherwise unmodified report to emphasize that the entity being reported on had significant transactions with related parties. The inclusion of this separate paragraph
  A. Is considered an "except for" qualification of the opinion.
  B. Violates generally accepted auditing standards if this information is already disclosed in footnotes to the financial statements.
  C. Necessitates a revision of the opinion paragraph to include the phrase "with the foregoing explanation."
  D. Is appropriate and would **not** negate the unqualified opinion.

70. On March 15, 1994, Kent, CPA, issued an unqualified opinion on a client's audited financial statements for the year ended December 31, 1993. On May 4, 1994, Kent's internal inspection program disclosed that engagement personnel failed to observe the client's physical inventory. Omission of this procedure impairs Kent's present ability to support the unqualified opinion. If the stockholders are currently relying on the opinion, Kent should first
  A. Advise management to disclose to the stockholders that Kent's unqualified opinion should **not** be relied on.
  B. Undertake to apply alternative procedures that would provide a satisfactory basis for the unqualified opinion.
  C. Reissue the auditor's report and add an explanatory paragraph describing the departure from generally accepted auditing standards.
  D. Compensate for the omitted procedure by performing tests of controls to reduce audit risk to a sufficiently low level.

71. For an entity that does **not** receive governmental financial assistance, an auditor's standard report on financial statements generally would **not** refer to
  A. Significant estimates made by management.
  B. An assessment of the entity's accounting principles.
  C. Management's responsibility for the financial statements.
  D. The entity's internal control structure.

72. Due to a scope limitation, an auditor disclaimed an opinion on the financial statements taken as a whole, but the auditor's report included a statement that the current asset portion of the entity's balance sheet was fairly stated. The inclusion of this statement is
   A. Not appropriate because it may tend to overshadow the auditor's disclaimer of opinion.
   B. Not appropriate because the auditor is prohibited from reporting on only one basic financial statement.
   C. Appropriate provided the auditor's scope paragraph adequately describes the scope limitation.
   D. Appropriate provided the statement is in a separate paragraph preceding the disclaimer of opinion paragraph.

73. When there has been a change in accounting principles, but the effect of the change on the comparability of the financial statements is **not** material, the auditor should
   A. Refer to the change in an explanatory paragraph.
   B. Explicitly concur that the change is preferred.
   C. Not refer to consistency in the auditor's report.
   D. Refer to the change in the opinion paragraph.

74. When single-year financial statements are presented, an auditor ordinarily would express an unqualified opinion in an unmodified report if the
   A. Auditor is unable to obtain audited financial statements supporting the entity's investment in a foreign affiliate.
   B. Entity declines to present a statement of cash flows with its balance sheet and related statements of income and retained earnings.
   C. Auditor wishes to emphasize an accounting matter affecting the comparability of the financial statements with those of the prior year.
   D. Prior year's financial statements were audited by another CPA whose report, which expressed an unqualified opinion, is **not** presented.

75. When financial statements contain a departure from GAAP because, due to unusual circumstances, the statements would otherwise be misleading, the auditor should explain the unusual circumstances in a separate paragraph and express an opinion that is
   A. Unqualified.
   B. Qualified.
   C. Adverse.
   D. Qualified or adverse, depending on materiality.

76. Park, CPA, was engaged to audit the financial statements of Tech Co., a new client, for the year ended December 31, 1993. Park obtained sufficient audit evidence for all of Tech's financial statement items except Tech's opening inventory. Due to inadequate financial records, Park could not verify Tech's January 1, 1993, inventory balances. Park's opinion on Tech's 1993 financial statements most likely will be

	Balance sheet	Income statement
A.	Disclaimer	Disclaimer
B.	Unqualified	Disclaimer
C.	Disclaimer	Adverse
D.	Unqualified	Adverse

77. Which paragraphs of an auditor's standard report on financial statements should refer to generally accepted auditing standards (GAAS) and generally accepted accounting principles (GAAP) in which paragraphs?

	GAAS	GAAP
A.	Opening	Scope
B.	Scope	Scope
C.	Scope	Opinion
D.	Opening	Opinion

78. Compiled financial statements should be accompanied by a report stating that
   A. A compilation is substantially less in scope than a review or an audit in accordance with generally accepted auditing standards.
   B. The accountant does **not** express an opinion but expresses only limited assurance on the compiled financial statements.
   C. A compilation is limited to presenting in the form of financial statements information that is the representation of management.
   D. The accountant has compiled the financial statements in accordance with standards established by the Auditing Standards Board.

79. An accountant may compile a nonpublic entity's financial statements that omit all of the disclosures required by GAAP only if the omission is

I. Clearly indicated in the accountant's report.

II. Not undertaken with the intention of misleading the financial statement users.

   A. I only.
   B. II only.
   C. Both I and II.
   D. Either I or II.

80. An accountant's standard report on a review of the financial statements of a nonpublic entity should state that the accountant
   A. Does **not** express an opinion or any form of limited assurance on the financial statements.
   B. Is **not** aware of any material modifications that should be made to the financial statements for them to conform with GAAP.
   C. Obtained reasonable assurance about whether the financial statements are free of material misstatement.
   D. Examined evidence, on a test basis, supporting the amounts and disclosures in the financial statements.

81. An accountant has been asked to issue a review report on the balance sheet of a nonpublic company but not to report on the other basic financial statements. The accountant may **not** do so
   A. Because compliance with this request would result in a violation of the ethical standards of the profession.
   B. Because compliance with this request would result in an incomplete review.
   C. If the review of the balance sheet discloses material departures from GAAP.
   D. If the scope of the inquiry and analytical procedures has been restricted.

82. What is an auditor's responsibility for supplementary information, such as segment information, which is outside the basic financial statements, but required by the FASB?
   A. The auditor has **no** responsibility for required supplementary information as long as it is outside the basic financial statements.
   B. The auditor's only responsibility for required supplementary information is to determine that such information has **not** been omitted.
   C. The auditor should apply certain limited procedures to the required supplementary information, and report deficiencies in, or omissions of, such information.
   D. The auditor should apply tests of details of transactions and balances to the required supplementary information, and report any material misstatements in such information.

83. When an auditor reports on financial statements prepared on an entity's income tax basis, the auditor's report should
   A. Disclaim an opinion on whether the statements were examined in accordance with generally accepted auditing standards.
   B. Not express an opinion on whether the statements are presented in conformity with the comprehensive basis of accounting used.
   C. Include an explanation of how the results of operations differ from the cash receipts and disbursements basis of accounting.
   D. State that the basis of presentation is a comprehensive basis of accounting other than GAAP.

84. Because of the pervasive effects of laws and regulations on the financial statements of governmental units, an auditor should obtain written management representations acknowledging that management has
   A. Identified and disclosed all laws and regulations that have a direct and material effect on its financial statements.
   B. Implemented internal control policies and procedures designed to detect all illegal acts.
   C. Expressed both positive and negative assurance to the auditor that the entity complied with all laws and regulations.
   D. Employed internal auditors who can report their findings, opinions, and conclusions objectively without fear of political repercussion.

85. An auditor notes reportable conditions in a financial statement audit conducted in accordance with *Government Auditing Standards*. In reporting on the internal control structure, the auditor should state that
   A. Expressing an opinion on the entity's financial statements provides **no** assurance on the internal control structure.
   B. The auditor obtained an understanding of the design of relevant policies and procedures, and determined whether they have been placed in operation.
   C. The specified government funding or legislative body is responsible for reviewing the internal control structure as a condition of continued funding.
   D. The auditor has **not** determined whether any of the reportable conditions described in the report are so severe as to be material weaknesses.

86. Management believes and the auditor is satisfied that a material loss probably will occur when pending litigation is resolved. Management is unable to make a reasonable estimate of the amount or range of the potential loss, but fully discloses the situation in the notes to the financial statements. If management does **not** make an accrual in the financial statements, the auditor should express a(an)
   A. Qualified opinion due to a scope limitation.
   B. Qualified opinion due to a departure from GAAP.
   C. Unqualified opinion with an explanatory paragraph.
   D. Unqualified opinion in a standard auditor's report.

87. In which of the following circumstances would an auditor be most likely to express an adverse opinion?
   A. The chief executive officer refuses the auditor access to minutes of board of directors' meetings.
   B. Tests of controls show that the entity's internal control structure is so poor that it **cannot** be relied upon.
   C. The financial statements are **not** in conformity with the FASB Statements regarding the capitalization of leases.
   D. Information comes to the auditor's attention that raises substantial doubt about the entity's ability to continue as a going concern.

88. When qualifying an opinion because of an insufficiency of audit evidence, an auditor should refer to the situation in the

	Opening (introductory) paragraph	*Scope paragraph*
A.	No	No
B.	Yes	No
C.	Yes	Yes
D.	No	Yes

89. When unaudited financial statements of a nonpublic entity are presented in comparative form with audited financial statements in the subsequent year, the unaudited financial statements should be clearly marked to indicate their status and

I. The report on the unaudited financial statements should be reissued.

II. The report on the audited financial statements should include a separate paragraph describing the responsibility assumed for the unaudited financial statements.

   A. I only.
   B. II only.
   C. Both I and II.
   D. Either I or II.

90. An auditor expressed a qualified opinion on the prior year's financial statements because of a lack of adequate disclosure. These financial statements are properly restated in the current year and presented in comparative form with the current year's financial statements. The auditor's updated report on the prior year's financial statements should
   A. Be accompanied by the auditor's original report on the prior year's financial statements.
   B. Continue to express a qualified opinion on the prior year's financial statements.
   C. Make **no** reference to the type of opinion expressed on the prior year's financial statements.
   D. Express an unqualified opinion on the restated financial statements of the prior year.

Question Number 2 Begins on Page 382

Number 2 (Estimated time—15 to 25 minutes)

Instructions

Question Number 2 consists of 15 items pertaining to possible deficiencies in an auditor's communication of internal control structure related matters noted in an audit. Select the **best** answer for each item. Use a No. 2 pencil to blacken the appropriate ovals on the Objective Answer Sheet to indicate your answers. **Answer all items.** Your grade will be based on the total number of correct answers.

Land & Hale, CPAs, are auditing the financial statements of Stone Co., a nonpublic entity, for the year ended December 31, 1993. Land, the engagement supervisor, anticipates expressing an unqualified opinion on May 20, 1994.

Wood, an assistant on the engagement, drafted the auditor's communication of internal control structure related matters that Land plans to send to Stone's board of directors with the May 20th auditor's report.

Land reviewed Wood's draft and indicated in the *Supervisor's Review Notes* that there were deficiencies in Wood's draft.

Independent Auditor's Report

To the Board of Directors of Stone Company:

In planning and performing our audit of the financial statements of Stone, Co. for the year ended December 31, 1993, we considered its internal control structure in order to determine our auditing procedures for the purpose of expressing our opinion on the financial statements and to provide assurance on the internal control structure. However, we noted certain matters involving the internal control structure and its operations that we consider to be reportable conditions under standards established by the American Institute of Certified Public Accountants. Reportable conditions involve matters coming to our attention relating to significant deficiencies in the design or operation of the internal control structure that, in our judgment, could adversely affect the organization's ability to record, process, summarize, and report financial data consistent with our assessment of control risk.

We noted that deficiencies in the internal control structure design included inadequate provisions for the safeguarding of assets, especially concerning cash receipts and inventory stored at remote locations. Additionally, we noted failures in the operation of the internal control structure. Reconciliations of subsidiary ledgers to control accounts were not timely prepared and senior employees in authority intentionally overrode the internal control structure concerning cash payments to the detriment of the overall objectives of the structure.

A material weakness is not necessarily a reportable condition, but is a design defect in which the internal control structure elements do not reduce to a relatively low level the risk that errors or irregularities in amounts that would be material in relation to the financial statements being audited may occur and not be detected by the auditor during the audit.

Our consideration of the internal control structure would not necessarily disclose all matters in the internal control structure that might be reportable conditions and, accordingly, would not necessarily disclose all reportable conditions that are also considered to be material weaknesses as defined above. However, none of the reportable conditions described above is believed to be a material weakness.

This report is intended solely for the information and use of the Board of Directors of Stone Co. Accordingly, it is not intended to be distributed to stockholders, management, or those who are not responsible for these matters.

Land & Hale, CPAs
May 4, 1994

Required:

Items 91 through 105 represent the deficiencies noted by Land. For each deficiency, indicate whether Land is correct ⓒ or incorrect ⓘ in the criticism of Wood's draft and blacken the corresponding oval on the Objective Answer Sheet.

Number 2 (continued)

Items to be Answered:

Supervisor's Review Notes

In the 1st paragraph

91. There should be **no** reference to "our audit of the financial statements."

92. The report should indicate that providing assurance is **not** the purpose of our consideration of the internal control structure.

93. The reference to "our assessment of control risk" at the end of the paragraph should have been a reference to "the assertions of management in the financial statements."

94. There should be a reference to "conformity with generally accepted accounting principles."

In the 2nd paragraph

95. There should be **no** reference to deficiencies because such reference is inconsistent with the expression of an unqualified opinion on the financial statements.

96. When deficiencies (reportable conditions) are noted, the report should include a description of the assessed level of control risk.

In the 3rd paragraph

97. The definition of "material weakness" is incorrect. A material weakness is a reportable condition.

98. The report should indicate that the auditor assumes **no** responsibility for errors or irregularities resulting from the deficiencies (reportable conditions) identified in the report.

99. The report should refer to detection by the entity's employees at the end of the paragraph, **not** detection by the auditor.

In the 4th paragraph

100. The report should indicate that our consideration of the internal control structure is expected to disclose all reportable conditions.

101. It is inappropriate to state that "none of the reportable conditions... is believed to be a material weakness."

In the final paragraph

102. The restriction on the report's distribution is inappropriate because management ordinarily would receive the report.

103. The report should indicate that the financial statement audit resulted in an unqualified opinion.

104. The report should indicate that the auditor is **not** responsible to update the report for events or circumstances occurring after the date of the report.

Dating the Report

105. The report may **not** be dated before the auditor's report on the financial statements.

Number 3 (Estimated time—15 to 25 minutes)

Instructions

Question Number 3 consists of 15 items pertaining to an auditor's risk analysis of an entity. Select the **best** answer for each item. Use a No. 2 pencil to blacken the appropriate ovals on the Objective Answer Sheet to indicate your answers. **Answer all items.** Your grade will be based on the total number of correct answers.

Bond, CPA, is considering audit risk at the financial statement level in planning the audit of Toxic Waste Disposal (TWD) Company's financial statements for the year ended December 31, 1993. TWD is a privately-owned entity that contracts with municipal governments to remove environmental wastes. Audit risk at the financial statement level is influenced by the risk of material misstatements, which may be indicated by a combination of factors related to management, the industry, and the entity.

Required:
Based only on the information below, indicate whether each of the following factors **(Items 106 through 120)** would most likely increase audit risk ①, decrease audit risk ⑩, or have **no** effect on audit risk ⑭, and blacken the corresponding oval on the Objective Answer Sheet.

Items to be Answered:

Company Profile

106. This was the first year TWD operated at a profit since 1989 because the municipalities received increased federal and state funding for environmental purposes.

107. TWD's Board of Directors is controlled by Mead, the majority stockholder, who also acts as the chief executive officer.

108. The internal auditor reports to the controller and the controller reports to Mead.

109. The accounting department has experienced a high rate of turnover of key personnel.

110. TWD's bank has a loan officer who meets regularly with TWD's CEO and controller to monitor TWD's financial performance.

111. TWD's employees are paid biweekly.

112. Bond has audited TWD for five years.

Recent developments

113. During 1993, TWD changed its method of preparing its financial statements from the cash basis to generally accepted accounting principles.

114. During 1993, TWD sold one half of its controlling interest in United Equipment Leasing (UEL) Co. TWD retained significant interest in UEL.

115. During 1993, litigation filed against TWD in 1988 alleging that TWD discharged pollutants into state waterways was dropped by the state. Loss contingency disclosures that TWD included in prior years' financial statements are being removed for the 1993 financial statements.

116. During December 1993, TWD signed a contract to lease disposal equipment from an entity owned by Mead's parents. This related party transaction is not disclosed in TWD's notes to its 1993 financial statements.

117. During December 1993, TWD completed a barter transaction with a municipality. TWD removed waste from a municipally-owned site and acquired title to another contaminated site at below market price. TWD intends to service this new site in 1994.

118. During December 1993, TWD increased its casualty insurance coverage on several pieces of sophisticated machinery from historical cost to replacement cost.

119. Inquiries about the substantial increase in revenue TWD recorded in the fourth quarter of 1993 disclosed a new policy. TWD guaranteed to several municipalities that it would refund the federal and state funding paid to TWD if any municipality fails federal or state site clean-up inspection in 1994.

120. An initial public offering of TWD's stock is planned for late 1994.

Number 4 (Estimated time—25 to 35 minutes)

North, CPA, is planning an audit of the financial statements of General Co. In determining the nature, timing, and extent of the auditing procedures, North is considering General's internal audit function, which is staffed by Tyler.

Required:

    a. In what ways may Tyler's work be relevant to North, the independent auditor?

    b. What factors should North consider and what inquiries should North make in deciding whether to use Tyler's work?

Number 5 (Estimated time— 25 to 35 minutes)

King, CPA, is auditing the financial statements of Cycle Co., an entity that has receivables from customers, which have arisen from the sale of goods in the normal course of business. King is aware that the confirmation of accounts receivable is a generally accepted auditing procedure.

Required:

    a. Under what circumstances could King justify omitting the confirmation of Cycle's accounts receivable?

    b. In designing confirmation requests, what factors are likely to affect King's assessment of the reliability of confirmations that King sends?

    c. What alternative procedures would King consider performing when replies to positive confirmation requests are **not** received?

EXAMINATION QUESTION BOOKLET

CANDIDATE NUMBER

Record your 7-digit candidate number in the boxes.

Q - ARE

ACCOUNTING AND REPORTING—TAXATION, MANAGERIAL, AND GOVERNMENTAL AND NOT-FOR-PROFIT ORGANIZATIONS

May 5, 1994; 8:30 A.M. to 12:00 NOON

The point values for each question, and estimated time allotments based primarily on point value, are as follows:

	Point Value	Estimated Minutes Minimum	Estimated Minutes Maximum
No. 1	60	120	130
No. 2	20	25	40
No. 3	20	25	40
Totals	100	170	210

INSTRUCTIONS TO CANDIDATES *Failure to follow these instructions may have an adverse effect on your Examination grade.*

1. Record your 7-digit candidate number in the boxes provided at the upper right-hand corner of this page.

2. Question numbers 1, 2, and 3 should be answered on the *Objective Answer Sheet*, which is pages 23 and 24 of your *Examination Question and Answer Booklet.* You should attempt to answer all objective items. There is no penalty for incorrect responses. Work space to solve the objective questions is provided in this *Examination Question and Answer Booklet* on pages 5 through 20. Since the objective items are computer-graded, your comments and calculations associated with them are not considered. Be certain that you have entered your answers on the *Objective Answer Sheet* before the examination time is up. Your examination will not be graded if you fail to record your answers on the *Objective Answer Sheet.* You will not be given additional time to record your answers.

3. Record your 7-digit candidate number, state, and question number where indicated on pages 1 and 24 of the *Examination Question and Answer Booklet.*

4. You are required to turn in by the end of each session:

   a. Attendance Record and Calculator Sign-off Record Form, front page of *Examination Question and Answer Booklet;*
   b. *Objective Answer Sheet,* pages 23 and 24 of *Examination Question and Answer Booklet;*
   c. *Examination Question Booklet,* pages 5 through 22; of *Examination Question and Answer Booklet;*
   d. Calculator; and
   e. All unused examination materials.

   Your examination will not be graded unless the above listed items are handed in before leaving the examination room.

5. Unless otherwise instructed, if you want your *Examination Question Booklet* mailed to you, write your name and address in both places indicated on the back cover (page **22**) and place 52 cents postage in the space provided. *Examination Question Booklets* will be distributed no sooner than the day following the administration of this examination.

Prepared by the Board of Examiners of the American Institute of Certified Public Accountants and adopted by the examining boards of all states, the District of Columbia, Guam, Puerto Rico, and the Virgin Islands of the United States.

Copyright © 1994 by the American Institute of Certified Public Accountants, Inc.

6. To turn the calculator on press (CA). Display will read "0". The calculator automatically turns itself off approximately 8 minutes after the last entry. All data in the calculator will be lost once the calculator is off. We recommend that when you press (=), you press (CA) before beginning a new calculation. The basic key descriptions are as follows:

(CA) **On and Clear** — Clears the calculator of all entries, including entries in memory, once calculator is on.

(C.CE) **Clear Calculation** — Clears the Display.

(0) ... (9) **Numericals** — Inputs that number.

(.) **Decimal** — Indicates that all numbers to follow are decimals.

(+/−) **Change sign** — Changes plus (minus) to minus (plus).

(+) & (−) **Add & Subtract** — Adds the next number entered to, or subtracts the next number entered from, the displayed number.

(x) & (÷) **Multiply & Divide** — Multiplies or divides the displayed number by the next number entered.

(=) **Equal** — Displays the results of all previously entered operations.

(√) **Square Root** — Calculates the square root of the displayed number. It is unlikely that you will need to use this key during the exam.

(%) **Percentage** — Converts the displayed number to a percentage (i.e., divides it by 100) and completes all previously entered operations. It is unlikely that you will need to use this key during the exam.

(M+) **Memory Add** — Adds the displayed number to the balance in memory.

(M−) **Memory Subtract** — Subtracts the displayed number from the balance in memory.

(R.CM) **Recall Memory** — Pressed once, displays the balance in memory. Pressed twice in a row, eliminates the balance in memory but not the displayed number.

If your calculator does not work or malfunctions, a replacement calculator will be available from the proctor.

Number 1 (Estimated time—120 to 130 minutes)

Instructions

Select the **best** answer for each of the following items. Use a No. 2 pencil to blacken the appropriate ovals on the Objective Answer Sheet to indicate your answers. **Mark only one answer for each item. Answer all items.** Your grade will be based on the total number of correct answers.

Items 1 through 35 are in the areas of federal taxation. The answers should be based on the Internal Revenue Code and Tax Regulations in effect for the tax period specified in the item. If *no* tax period is specified, use the *current* Internal Revenue Code and Tax Regulations.

1. In December 1993, Davis purchased a new residence for $200,000. During that same month he sold his former residence for $80,000 and paid the realtor a $5,000 commission. The former residence, his first home, had cost $65,000 in 1990. Davis added a bathroom for $5,000 in 1991. What amount of gain is recognized from the sale of the former residence on Davis' 1993 tax return?
   A. $15,000
   B. $10,000
   C. $ 5,000
   D. $0

2. In a tax year where the taxpayer pays qualified education expenses, interest income on the redemption of qualified U.S. Series EE Bonds may be excluded from gross income. The exclusion is subject to a modified gross income limitation and a limit of aggregate bond proceeds in excess of qualified higher education expenses. Which of the following is (are) true?

I. The exclusion applies for education expenses incurred by the taxpayer, the taxpayer's spouse, or any person whom the taxpayer may claim as a dependent for the year.

II. "Otherwise qualified higher education expenses" must be reduced by qualified scholarships not includible in gross income.

   A. I only.
   B. II only.
   C. Both I and II.
   D. Neither I nor II.

3. During 1993 Kay received interest income as follows:

On U.S. Treasury certificates	$4,000
On refund of 1991 federal income tax	500

The total amount of interest subject to tax in Kay's 1993 tax return is
   A. $4,500
   B. $4,000
   C. $ 500.
   D. $0

MULTIPLE-CHOICE WORK SPACE—This information will **not** be graded. Only answers recorded on the Objective Answer Sheet will be graded.

4. With regard to the inclusion of social security benefits in gross income, for the 1993 tax year, which of the following statements is correct?

A. The social security benefits in excess of modified adjusted gross income are included in gross income.

B. The social security benefits in excess of one half the modified adjusted gross income are included in gross income.

C. One half of the social security benefits is the maximum amount of benefits to be included in gross income.

D. The social security benefits in excess of the modified adjusted gross income over $32,000 are included in gross income.

5. Rich is a cash basis self-employed air-conditioning repairman with 1993 gross business receipts of $20,000. Rich's cash disbursements were as follows:

Air conditioning parts	$2,500
Yellow Pages listing	2,000
Estimated federal income taxes on self-employment income	1,000
Business long-distance telephone calls	400
Charitable contributions	200

What amount should Rich report as net self-employment income?

A. $15,100
B. $14,900
C. $14,100
D. $13,900

6. The self-employment tax is

A. Fully deductible as an itemized deduction.

B. Fully deductible in determining net income from self-employment.

C. One-half deductible from gross income in arriving at adjusted gross income.

D. Not deductible.

7. For 1993, Val and Pat White filed a joint return. Val earned $35,000 in wages and was covered by his employer's qualified pension plan. Pat was unemployed and received $5,000 in alimony payments for the first 4 months of the year before remarrying. The couple had no other income. Each contributed $2,000 to an IRA account. The allowable IRA deduction on their 1993 joint tax return is

A. $4,000
B. $2,250
C. $2,000
D. $0

8. The 1993 deduction by an individual taxpayer for interest on investment indebtedness is

A. Limited to the investment interest paid in 1993.

B. Limited to the taxpayer's 1993 interest income.

C. Limited to the taxpayer's 1993 net investment income.

D. Not limited.

9. Which of the following is **not** a miscellaneous itemized deduction?

A. An individual's tax return preparation fee.

B. Education expense to meet minimum entry level education requirements at an individual's place of employment.

C. An individual's subscription to professional journals.

D. Custodial fees for a brokerage account.

10. The Browns borrowed $20,000, secured by their home, to pay their son's college tuition. At the time of the loan, the fair market value of their home was $400,000, and it was unencumbered by other debt. The interest on the loan qualifies as

A. Deductible personal interest.
B. Deductible qualified residence interest.
C. Nondeductible interest.
D. Investment interest expense.

MULTIPLE-CHOICE WORK SPACE—This information will **not** be graded. Only answers recorded on the Objective Answer Sheet will be graded.

11. On January 2, 1990, the Philips paid $50,000 cash and obtained a $200,000 mortgage to purchase a home. In 1993 they borrowed $15,000 secured by their home, and used the cash to add a new room to their residence. That same year they took out a $5,000 auto loan.

The following information pertains to interest paid in 1993:

Mortgage interest	$17,000
Interest on room construction loan	1,500
Auto loan interest	500

For 1993, how much interest is deductible, prior to any itemized deduction limitations?

A. $17,000
B. $17,500
C. $18,500
D. $19,000

12. For 1993, Dole's adjusted gross income exceeds $500,000. After the application of any other limitation, itemized deductions are reduced by

A. The *lesser* of 3% of the excess of adjusted gross income over the applicable amount or 80% of *certain* itemized deductions.
B. The *lesser* of 3% of the excess of adjusted gross income over the applicable amount or 80% of *all* itemized deductions.
C. The *greater* of 3% of the excess of adjusted gross income over the applicable amount or 80% of *certain* itemized deductions.
D. The *greater* of 3% of the excess of adjusted gross income over the applicable amount or 80% of *all* itemized deductions.

13. In 1993, Wells paid the following expenses:

Premiums on an insurance policy against loss of earnings due to sickness or accident	$3,000
Physical therapy after spinal surgery	2,000
Premium on an insurance policy that covers reimbursement for the cost of prescription drugs	500

In 1993, Wells recovered $1,500 of the $2,000 that she paid for physical therapy through insurance reimbursement from a group medical policy paid for by her employer. Disregarding the adjusted gross income percentage threshold, what amount could be claimed on Wells' 1993 income tax return for medical expenses?

A. $4,000
B. $3,500
C. $1,000
D. $ 500

14. Jim and Kay Ross contributed to the support of their two children, Dale and Kim, and Jim's widowed parent, Grant. For 1993, Dale, a 19-year old full-time college student, earned $4,500 as a baby-sitter. Kim, a 23-year old bank teller, earned $12,000. Grant received $5,000 in dividend income and $4,000 in nontaxable social security benefits. Grant, Dale, and Kim are U.S. citizens and were over one-half supported by Jim and Kay. How many exemptions can Jim and Kay claim on their 1993 joint income tax return?

A. Two
B. Three
C. Four
D. Five

MULTIPLE-CHOICE WORK SPACE—This information will **not** be graded. Only answers recorded on the Objective Answer Sheet will be graded.

15. On December 1, 1992, Michaels, a self-employed cash basis taxpayer, borrowed $100,000 to use in her business. The loan was to be repaid on November 30, 1993. Michaels paid the entire interest of $12,000 on December 1, 1992. What amount of interest was deductible on Michaels' 1993 income tax return?
   A. $12,000
   B. $11,000
   C. $ 1,000
   D. $0

16. The credit for prior year alternative minimum tax liability may be carried
   A. Forward for a maximum of 5 years.
   B. Back to the 3 preceding years or carried forward for a maximum of 5 years.
   C. Back to the 3 preceding years.
   D. Forward indefinitely.

17. Which of the following credits can result in a refund even if the individual had **no** income tax liability?
   A. Credit for prior year minimum tax.
   B. Elderly and permanently and totally disabled credit.
   C. Earned income credit.
   D. Child and dependent care credit.

18. A calendar-year taxpayer files an individual tax return for 1992 on March 20, 1993. The taxpayer neither committed fraud nor omitted amounts in excess of 25% of gross income on the tax return. What is the latest date that the Internal Revenue Service can assess tax and assert a notice of deficiency?
   A. March 20, 1996.
   B. March 20, 1995.
   C. April 15, 1996.
   D. April 15, 1995.

19. A tax return preparer may disclose or use tax return information without the taxpayer's consent to
   A. Facilitate a supplier's or lender's credit evaluation of the taxpayer.
   B. Accommodate the request of a financial institution that needs to determine the amount of taxpayer's debt to it, to be forgiven.
   C. Be evaluated by a quality or peer review.
   D. Solicit additional nontax business.

20. Which, if any, of the following could result in penalties against an income tax return preparer?

I. Knowing or reckless disclosure or use of tax information obtained in preparing a return.

II. A willful attempt to understate any client's tax liability on a return or claim for refund.

   A. Neither I nor II.
   B. I only.
   C. II only.
   D. Both I and II.

21. An S Corporation has 30,000 shares of voting common stock and 20,000 shares of non-voting common stock issued and outstanding. The S election can be revoked voluntarily with the consent of the shareholders holding, on the day of the revocation,

	Shares of voting stock	Shares of nonvoting stock
A.	0	20,000
B.	7,500	5,000
C.	10,000	16,000
D.	20,000	0

MULTIPLE-CHOICE WORK SPACE—This information will **not** be graded. Only answers recorded on the Objective Answer Sheet will be graded.

22. The Haas Corp., a calendar year S corporation, has two equal shareholders. For the year ended December 31, 1993, Haas had taxable income and current earnings and profits of $60,000, which included $50,000 from operations and $10,000 from investment interest income. There were no other transactions that year. Each shareholder's basis in the stock of Haas will increase by
  A. $50,000
  B. $30,000
  C. $25,000
  D. $0

23. Tech Corp. files a consolidated return with its wholly-owned subsidiary, Dow Corp. During 1993, Dow paid a cash dividend of $20,000 to Tech. What amount of this dividend is taxable on the 1993 consolidated return?
  A. $20,000
  B. $14,000
  C. $ 6,000
  D. $0

24. Kisco Corp.'s taxable income for 1993 before taking the dividends received deduction was $70,000. This includes $10,000 in dividends from an unrelated taxable domestic corporation. Given the following tax rates, what would Kisco's income tax be before any credits?

Partial rate table	Tax rate
Up to $50,000	15%
Over $50,000 but not over $75,000	25%

  A. $10,000
  B. $10,750
  C. $12,500
  D. $15,750

25. On January 1, 1993, Kee Corp., a C corporation, had a $50,000 deficit in earnings and profits. For 1993 Kee had current earnings and profits of $10,000 and made a $30,000 cash distribution to its stockholders. What amount of the distribution is taxable as dividend income to Kee's stockholders?
  A. $30,000
  B. $20,000
  C. $10,000
  D. $0

26. On January 2, 1993, Black acquired a 50% interest in New Partnership by contributing property with an adjusted basis of $7,000 and a fair market value of $9,000, subject to a mortgage of $3,000. What was Black's basis in New at January 2, 1993?
  A. $3,500
  B. $4,000
  C. $5,500
  D. $7,500

27. Gray is a 50% partner in Fabco Partnership. Gray's tax basis in Fabco on January 1, 1993, was $5,000. Fabco made no distributions to the partners during 1993, and recorded the following:

Ordinary income	$20,000
Tax exempt income	8,000
Portfolio income	4,000

What is Gray's tax basis in Fabco on December 31, 1993?
  A. $21,000
  B. $16,000
  C. $12,000
  D. $10,000

MULTIPLE-CHOICE WORK SPACE—This information will **not** be graded. Only answers recorded on the Objective Answer Sheet will be graded.

28. On January 2, 1993, Arch and Bean contribute cash equally to form the JK Partnership. Arch and Bean share profits and losses in a ratio of 75% to 25%, respectively. For 1993, the partnership's ordinary income was $40,000. A distribution of $5,000 was made to Arch during 1993. What is Arch's share of taxable income for 1993?

   A. $ 5,000
   B. $10,000
   C. $20,000
   D. $30,000

29. Guaranteed payments made by a partnership to partners for services rendered to the partnership, that are deductible business expenses under the Internal Revenue Code, are

  I. Deductible expenses on the U.S. Partnership Return of Income, Form 1065, in order to arrive at partnership income (loss).

  II. Included on schedules K-1 to be taxed as ordinary income to the partners.

   A. I only.
   B. II only.
   C. Both I and II.
   D. Neither I nor II.

30. At the beginning of 1993, Paul owned a 25% interest in Associates partnership. During the year, a new partner was admitted and Paul's interest was reduced to 20%. The partnership liabilities at January 1, 1993, were $150,000, but decreased to $100,000 at December 31, 1993. Paul's and the other partners' capital accounts are in proportion to their respective interests. Disregarding any income, loss or drawings for 1993, the basis of Paul's partnership interest at December 31, 1993, compared to the basis of his interest at January 1, 1993 was

   A. Decreased by $37,500.
   B. Increased by $20,000.
   C. Decreased by $17,500.
   D. Decreased by $5,000.

31. Day's adjusted basis in LMN Partnership interest is $50,000. During the year Day received a nonliquidating distribution of $25,000 cash plus land with an adjusted basis of $15,000 to LMN, and a fair market value of $20,000. How much is Day's basis in the land?

   A. $10,000
   B. $15,000
   C. $20,000
   D. $25,000

32. On February 1, 1993, Hall learned that he was bequeathed 500 shares of common stock under his father's will. Hall's father had paid $2,500 for the stock in 1990. Fair market value of the stock on February 1, 1993, the date of his father's death, was $4,000 and had increased to $5,500 six months later. The executor of the estate elected the alternate valuation date for estate tax purposes. Hall sold the stock for $4,500 on June 1, 1993, the date that the executor distributed the stock to him. How much income should Hall include in his 1993 individual income tax return for the inheritance of the 500 shares of stock which he received from his father's estate?

   A. $5,500
   B. $4,000
   C. $2,500
   D. $0

33. In 1993, Sayers, who is single, gave an outright gift of $50,000 to a friend, Johnson, who needed the money to pay medical expenses. In filing the 1993 gift tax return, Sayers was entitled to a maximum exclusion of

   A. $0
   B. $ 3,000
   C. $10,000
   D. $20,000

MULTIPLE-CHOICE WORK SPACE—This information will **not** be graded. Only answers recorded on the Objective Answer Sheet will be graded.

34. To qualify as an exempt organization other than a church or an employees' qualified pension or profit-sharing trust, the applicant
   A. Cannot operate under the "lodge system" under which payments are made to its members for sick benefits.
   B. Need **not** be specifically identified as one of the classes on which exemption is conferred by the Internal Revenue Code, provided that the organization's purposes and activities are of a nonprofit nature.
   C. Is barred from incorporating and issuing capital stock.
   D. Must file a written application with the Internal Revenue Service.

35. Which of the following activities regularly carried out by an exempt organization will **not** result in unrelated business income?
   A. The sale of laundry services by an exempt hospital to other hospitals.
   B. The sale of heavy duty appliances to senior citizens by an exempt senior citizen's center.
   C. Accounting and tax services performed by a local chapter of a labor union for its members.
   D. The sale by a trade association of publications used as course materials for the association's seminars which are oriented towards its members.

Items 36 through 50 are in the area of managerial accounting.

36. Mat Co. estimated its material handling costs at two activity levels as follows:

Kilos handled	Cost
80,000	$160,000
60,000	132,000

What is Mat's estimated cost for handling 75,000 kilos?
   A. $150,000
   B. $153,000
   C. $157,500
   D. $165,000

37. A flexible budget is appropriate for a

	Marketing budget	Direct material usage budget
A.	No	No
B.	No	Yes
C.	Yes	Yes
D.	Yes	No

38. Para Co. is reviewing the following data relating to an energy saving investment proposal:

Cost	$50,000
Residual value at the end of 5 years	10,000
Present value of an annuity of 1 at 12% for 5 years	3.60
Present value of 1 due in 5 years at 12%	0.57

What would be the annual savings needed to make the investment realize a 12% yield?
   A. $ 8,189
   B. $11,111
   C. $12,306
   D. $13,889

MULTIPLE-CHOICE WORK SPACE—This information will **not** be graded. Only answers recorded on the Objective Answer Sheet will be graded.

39. During 1993, Thor Lab supplied hospitals with a comprehensive diagnostic kit for $120. At a volume of 80,000 kits, Thor had fixed costs of $1,000,000 and a profit before income taxes of $200,000. Due to an adverse legal decision, Thor's 1994 liability insurance increased by $1,200,000 over 1993. Assuming the volume and other costs are unchanged, what should the 1994 price be if Thor is to make the same $200,000 profit before income taxes?

    A. $120.00
    B. $135.00
    C. $150.00
    D. $240.00

40. The following information pertains to Lap Co.'s Palo Division for the month of April:

	Number of units	Cost of materials
Beginning work-in-process	15,000	$ 5,500
Started in April	40,000	18,000
Units completed	42,500	
Ending work-in-process	12,500	

All materials are added at the beginning of the process. Using the weighted-average method, the cost per equivalent unit for materials is

    A. $0.59
    B. $0.55
    C. $0.45
    D. $0.43

41. What is the normal effect on the numbers of cost pools and allocation bases when an activity-based cost (ABC) system replaces a traditional cost system?

	Cost pools	Allocation bases
A.	No effect	No effect
B.	Increase	No effect
C.	No effect	Increase
D.	Increase	Increase

42. Under Pick Co.'s job order costing system manufacturing overhead is applied to work in process using a predetermined annual overhead rate. During January 1994, Pick's transactions included the following:

Direct materials issued to production	$90,000
Indirect materials issued to production	8,000
Manufacturing overhead incurred	125,000
Manufacturing overhead applied	113,000
Direct labor costs	107,000

Pick had neither beginning nor ending work-in-process inventory. What was the cost of jobs completed in January 1994?

    A. $302,000
    B. $310,000
    C. $322,000
    D. $330,000

43. The following information pertains to Quest Co.'s Gold Division for 1993:

Sales	$311,000
Variable cost	250,000
Traceable fixed costs	50,000
Average invested capital	40,000
Imputed interest rate	10%

Quest's return on investment was

    A. 10.00%
    B. 13.33%
    C. 27.50%
    D. 30.00%

44. Brent Co. has intracompany service transfers from Division Core, a cost center, to Division Pro, a profit center. Under stable economic conditions, which of the following transfer prices is likely to be most conducive to evaluating whether both divisions have met their responsibilities?

    A. Actual cost.
    B. Standard variable cost.
    C. Actual cost plus mark-up.
    D. Negotiated price.

MULTIPLE-CHOICE WORK SPACE—This information will **not** be graded. Only answers recorded on the Objective Answer Sheet will be graded.

45. In a quality control program, which of the following is(are) categorized as internal failure costs?

I. Rework.

II. Responding to customer complaints.

III. Statistical quality control procedures.

    A. I only.
    B. II only.
    C. III only.
    D. I, II, and III.

46. As a consequence of finding a more dependable supplier, Dee Co. reduced its safety stock of raw materials by 80%. What is the effect of this safety stock reduction on Dee's economic order quantity?
    A. 80% decrease.
    B. 64% decrease.
    C. 20% increase.
    D. No effect.

47. Probability (risk) analysis is
    A. Used only for situations involving five or fewer possible outcomes.
    B. Used only for situations in which the summation of probability weights is greater than one.
    C. An extension of sensitivity analysis.
    D. Incompatible with sensitivity analysis.

48. Briar Co. signed a government construction contract providing for a formula price of actual cost plus 10%. In addition, Briar was to receive one-half of any savings resulting from the formula price being less than the target price of $2,200,000. Briar's actual costs incurred were $1,920,000. How much should Briar receive from the contract?
    A. $2,060,000
    B. $2,112,000
    C. $2,156,000
    D. $2,200,000

49. Clay Co. has considerable excess manufacturing capacity. A special job order's cost sheet includes the following applied manufacturing overhead costs:

Fixed costs	$21,000
Variable costs	33,000

The fixed costs include a normal $3,700 allocation for in-house design costs, although no in-house design will be done. Instead the job will require the use of external designers costing $7,750. What is the total amount to be included in the calculation to determine the minimum acceptable price for the job?
    A. $36,700
    B. $40,750
    C. $54,000
    D. $58,050

50. Bell Co. changed from a traditional manufacturing philosophy to a just-in-time philosophy. What are the expected effects of this change on Bell's inventory turnover and inventory as a percentage of total assets reported on Bell's balance sheet?

	Inventory turnover	Inventory percentage
A.	Decrease	Decrease
B.	Decrease	Increase
C.	Increase	Decrease
D.	Increase	Increase

Items 51 through 60 are in the area of accounting for governmental and not-for-profit organizations.

51. The primary emphasis in accounting and reporting for governmental funds is on
    A. Flow of financial resources.
    B. Income determination.
    C. Capital maintenance.
    D. Transfers relating to proprietary activities.

MULTIPLE-CHOICE WORK SPACE—This information will **not** be graded. Only answers recorded on the Objective Answer Sheet will be graded.

52. For which of the following governmental entities that use proprietary fund accounting should a statement of cash flows be presented?

	Public benefit corporations	Governmental utilities
A.	No	No
B.	No	Yes
C.	Yes	Yes
D.	Yes	No

53. The general purpose financial statements of a state government
   A. May **not** be issued separately from the comprehensive annual financial report.
   B. Are comprised of the combined financial statements and related notes.
   C. Are synonymous with the comprehensive annual financial report.
   D. Contain more detailed information regarding the state government's finances than is contained in the comprehensive annual financial report.

54. The operating statements of governmental units should embody the
   A. All-inclusive approach.
   B. Current performance approach.
   C. Prospective approach.
   D. Retroactive approach.

55. For governmental units, depreciation expense on assets acquired with capital grants externally restricted for capital acquisitions should be reported in which type of fund?

	Governmental fund	Proprietary fund
A.	Yes	No
B.	Yes	Yes
C.	No	No
D.	No	Yes

56. Shared revenues received by an enterprise fund of a local government for operating purposes should be recorded as
   A. Operating revenues.
   B. Nonoperating revenues.
   C. Other financing sources.
   D. Interfund transfers.

57. Taxes collected and held by Franklin County for a separate school district would be accounted for in which fund?
   A. Special revenue.
   B. Internal service.
   C. Trust.
   D. Agency.

58. A not-for-profit hospital issued long-term tax-exempt bonds for the hospital's benefit. The hospital is responsible for the liability. Which fund may the hospital use to account for this liability?
   A. Enterprise.
   B. Specific purpose.
   C. General.
   D. General long-term debt account group.

59. Which fund may account for a university's internally designated fund, the income from which will be used for a specified purpose?
   A. Endowment fund.
   B. Term endowment fund.
   C. Quasi-endowment fund.
   D. Restricted current fund.

60. Valley's community hospital normally includes proceeds from sale of cafeteria meals in
   A. Deductions from dietary service expenses.
   B. Ancillary service revenues.
   C. Patient service revenues.
   D. Other revenues.

MULTIPLE-CHOICE WORK SPACE—This information will **not** be graded. Only answers recorded on the Objective Answer Sheet will be graded.

Number 2 (Estimated time 25—40 minutes)

Number 2 consists of 25 items. Select the **best** answer for each item. Use a No. 2 pencil to blacken the appropriate ovals on the Objective Answer Sheet to indicate your answers. **Answer all items**. Your grade will be based on the total number of correct answers.

Kimberly Corp. is a calendar year accrual basis corporation that commenced operations on January 1, 1990. The following adjusted accounts appear on Kimberly's records for the year ended December 31, 1993. Kimberly is not subject to the uniform capitalization rules.

Revenues and gains

Gross sales	$2,000,000
Dividends:	
20%-owned domestic corporation	10,000
XYZ Corp.	10,000
Interest:	
U.S. treasury bonds	26,000
Municipal bonds	25,000
Insurance proceeds	40,000
Gain on sale:	
Unimproved lot (1)	20,000
XYZ stock (2)	5,000
State franchise tax refund	14,000
Total	2,150,000

Costs and expenses

Cost of goods sold	350,000
Salaries and wages	470,000
Depreciation:	
Real property	50,000
Personal property (3)	100,000
Bad debt (4)	10,000
State franchise tax	25,000
Vacation expense	10,000
Interest expense (5)	16,000
Life insurance premiums	20,000
Federal income taxes	200,000
Entertainment expense	20,000
Other expenses	29,000
Total	1,300,000
Net income	$ 850,000

NUMBER 2 CONTINUED ON PAGE 399

Additional information:

(1) Gain on the sale of unimproved lot—Purchased in 1991 for use in business for $50,000. Sold in 1993 for $70,000. Kimberly has never had any Sec. 1231 losses.

(2) Gain on sale of XYZ Stock—Purchased in 1991.

(3) Personal Property—The book depreciation is the same as tax depreciation for all the property that was placed in service before January 1, 1993. The book depreciation is straight line over the useful life, which is the same as class life. Company policy is to use half-year convention per books for personal property. Furniture and fixtures costing $56,000 were placed in service on January 1, 1993.

(4) Bad Debt—Represents the increase in the allowance for doubtful accounts based on an aging of accounts receivable. Actual bad debts written off were $7,000.

(5) Interest expense on:

Mortgage loan	$10,000
Loan obtained to purchase municipal bonds	4,000
Line of credit loan	2,000

Required:

For items 61 through 65, determine the amount that should be reported on Kimberly corporation's 1993 Federal income tax return. To record your answer, write the number in the boxes on the Objective Answer Sheet **and** blacken the corresponding oval below each box. Write zeros in any blank boxes preceding your numerical answer, and blacken the zero in the oval below the box. **You cannot receive credit for your answer if you fail to blacken the ovals.**

Items to be Answered:

61. What amount of interest income is taxable from the U.S. Treasury bonds?

62. Determine the tax depreciation expense under the Modified Accelerated Cost Recovery System (MACRS), for the furniture

and fixtures that were placed in service on January 1, 1993. Assume that no irrevocable depreciation election is made. Round the answer to the nearest thousand. Kimberly did **not** use the alternative depreciation system (ADS) or a straight-line method of depreciation. No election was made to expense part of the cost of the property.

63. Determine the amount of bad debt to be included as an expense item.

64. Determine Kimberly's net long-term capital gain.

65. What amount of interest expense is deductible?

Required:

For items 66 through 70, select whether the following expenses are Ⓕ fully deductible, Ⓟ partially deductible, or Ⓝ nondeductible, for regular tax purposes, on Kimberly's 1993 Federal income tax return. Blacken the corresponding oval on the Objective Answer Sheet to indicate your answer.

Items to be Answered:

66. Organization expense incurred at corporate inception in 1990 to draft the corporate charter. No deduction was taken for the organization expense in 1990.

67. Life insurance premiums paid by the corporation for its executives as part of their compensation for services rendered. The corporation is neither the direct nor the indirect beneficiary of the policy and the amount of compensation is reasonable.

68. Vacation pay earned by employees which vested under a plan by December 31, 1993, and was paid February 1, 1994.

69. State franchise tax liability that has accrued during the year and was paid on March 15, 1994.

70. Entertainment expense to lease a luxury skybox during football season to entertain clients. A bona fide business discussion precedes each game. The cost of regular seats would have been one half the amount paid.

NUMBER 2 CONTINUED ON PAGE 400

Required:

For items 71 through 75, select whether the following revenue items are Ⓕ fully taxable, Ⓟ partially taxable, or Ⓝ nontaxable on Kimberly Corp.'s 1993 Federal income tax return for regular tax purposes. Blacken the corresponding oval on the Objective Answer Sheet to indicate your answer.

Items to be Answered:

71. Dividends from the 20%-owned domestic corporation. The taxable income limitation does not apply. Kimberly does not have the ability to exercise significant influence.

72. Recovery of an account from prior year's bad debts. Kimberly uses an estimate of uncollectibles based on an aging of accounts receivable for book purposes. The account was written off for tax purposes and reduced Kimberly's income tax liability.

73. Refund of state franchise tax overpayment, previously expensed on Kimberly's 1991 federal tax return, thereby reducing federal taxes that year.

74. Interest income from municipal bonds purchased by Kimberly in 1992 on the open market.

75. Proceeds paid to Kimberly by reason of death, under a life insurance policy that Kimberly had purchased on the life of one of its vice-presidents. Kimberly was the beneficiary and used the proceeds to pay the premium charges for the group term insurance policy for its other employees.

Required:

Items 76 through 85 refer to Kimberly's need to determine if it will be subject to the alternative minimum tax. Determine whether the statement is true Ⓣ or false Ⓕ. Blacken the corresponding oval on the Objective Answer Sheet.

Items to be Answered:

76. The method of depreciation for commercial real property to arrive at alternative minimum taxable income before the adjusted current earnings (ACE) adjustment, is the straight-line method.

77. The corporate exemption amount reduces the alternative minimum taxable income.

78. The ACE adjustment can be a positive or negative amount.

79. Depreciation on personal property to arrive at alternative minimum taxable income before the ACE adjustment is straight-line over the MACRS recovery period.

80. The alternative minimum tax is the excess of the tentative minimum tax over the regular tax liability.

81. Municipal bond interest, other than from private activity bonds, is includible income to arrive at alternative minimum taxable income before the ACE adjustment.

82. The maximum corporate exemption amount for minimum tax purposes is $150,000.

83. The 70% dividends received deduction is available to determine ACE.

84. Municipal bond interest is includible income to determine ACE.

85. The method of depreciation for personal property placed in service after 1989 for determining ACE is the sum-of-the-years'-digits method.

OTHER OBJECTIVE ANSWER FORMAT WORK SPACE—This information will **not** be graded. Only answers recorded on the Objective Answer Sheet will be graded.

Number 3 (Estimated time—25 to 40 minutes)

Number 3 consists of 40 items. Select the **best** answer for each item. Use a No. 2 pencil to blacken the appropriate ovals on the Objective Answer Sheet to indicate your answers. **Answer all items.** Your grade will be based on the total number of correct answers.

The Wayne City Council approved and adopted its budget for 1993. The budget contained the following amounts:

Estimated revenues	$700,000
Appropriations	660,000
Authorized operating transfer to the Library debt service fund	30,000

During 1993, various transactions and events occurred which affected the general fund.

Required:

For items **86 through 125,** select whether the item Ⓓ should be debited, Ⓒ should be credited, or Ⓝ is not affected. Blacken the corresponding oval on the Objective Answer Sheet to indicate your answer.

Items 86 through 90 involve recording the adopted budget in the general fund.

86. Estimated revenues
87. Budgetary fund balance
88. Appropriations
89. Appropriations—Operating transfers out
90. Expenditures

Items 91 through 95 involve recording the 1993 property tax levy in the general fund. It was estimated that $5,000 would be uncollectible.

91. Property tax receivable.
92. Bad debt expense.
93. Allowance for uncollectibles—current.
94. Revenues.
95. Estimated revenues.

Items 96 through 100 involve recording, in the general fund, encumbrances at the time purchase orders are issued.

96. Encumbrances.
97. Budgetary fund balance reserved for encumbrances.
98. Expenditures.
99. Vouchers payable.
100. Purchases.

Items 101 through 105 involve recording, in the general fund, expenditures which had been previously encumbered in the current year.

101. Encumbrances.
102. Budgetary fund balance reserved for encumbrances.
103. Expenditures.
104. Vouchers payable.
105. Purchases.

Items 106 through 110 involve recording, in the general fund, the operating transfer of $30,000 made to the Library debt service fund. (No previous entries were made regarding this transaction.)

106. Residual equity transfer out.
107. Due from Library debt service fund.
108. Cash.
109. Other financial uses—operating transfers out.
110. Encumbrances.

Items 111 through 121 involve recording, in the general fund, the closing entries (other than encumbrances) for 1993.

111. Estimated revenues.
112. Budgetary fund balance.
113. Appropriations.
114. Appropriations—Operating transfers out.
115. Expenditures.
116. Revenues.
117. Other financial uses—Operating transfers out.
118. Allowance for uncollectibles—current.
119. Bad debt expense.
120. Depreciation expense.
121. Residual equity transfer out.

Items 122 through 125 involve recording, in the general fund, the closing entry relating to the $12,000 of outstanding encumbrances at the end of 1993 and an adjusting entry to reflect the intent to honor these commitments in 1994.

122. Encumbrances.
123. Budgetary fund balance reserved for encumbrances.
124. Unreserved fund balance.
125. Fund balance reserved for encumbrances.

CUT ALONG DOTTED LINE

UNOFFICIAL OBJECTIVE EARLY ANSWERS — ORDER FORM

To obtain at an early date the objective answers to the May 1994 Uniform CPA Examination, complete this form. The answers will provide the correct response without narrative explanation and are intended to be used for self-grading of objective answers.

MAILING ADDRESS

NAME _____

ADDRESS _____

CITY_____

STATE   ZIP

Early answers will be mailed beginning June 1, 1994. The complete examination questions and unofficial answers for all sections will be available from the AICPA after August 1, 1994, and cannot be ordered on this form.

• The price of a complete set of early answers for all sections is $9.00.

• Early answers to individual sections are not sold separately.

Make checks payable to AICPA.

Price includes appropriate Sales Tax.

Mail Order and Check to — AICPA — P.O. Box 2207 — Jersey City, NJ 07303-2207

EXAMINATION QUESTION BOOKLET

CANDIDATE NUMBER

Record your 7-digit candidate number in the boxes.

Q - FARE

FINANCIAL ACCOUNTING & REPORTING— BUSINESS ENTERPRISES

May 5, 1994; 1:30 P.M. to 6:00 P.M.

The point values for each question, and estimated time allotments based primarily on point value, are as follows:

	Point Value	Estimated Minutes Minimum	Estimated Minutes Maximum
No. 1	60	130	140
No. 2	10	15	25
No. 3	10	15	25
No. 4	10	30	40
No. 5	10	30	40
Totals	100	220	270

INSTRUCTIONS TO CANDIDATES *Failure to follow these instructions may have an adverse effect on your Examination grade.*

1. Record your 7-digit candidate number in the boxes provided at the upper right-hand corner of this page.

2. Question numbers 1, 2, and 3 should be answered on the *Objective Answer Sheet,* which is pages 11 and 12 of your *Examination Answer Booklet.* You should attempt to answer all objective items. There is no penalty for incorrect responses. Work space to solve the objective questions is provided in this *Examination Question Booklet* on pages 3 through 14. Since the objective items are computer-graded, your comments and calculations associated with them are not considered. Be certain that you have entered your answers on the *Objective Answer Sheet* before the examination time is up. The objective portion of your examination will not be graded if you fail to record your answers on the *Objective Answer Sheet.* You will not be given additional time to record your answers.

3. Question numbers 4 and 5 should be answered beginning on page 3 of the *Examination Answer Booklet.* Support **all** answers with properly labeled and legible calculations that can be identified as sources of amounts used to derive your final answer. If you have not completed answering a question on a page, fill in the appropriate spaces in the wording on the bottom of the page **"QUESTION NUMBER ___ CONTINUES ON PAGE ___"** If you have completed answering a question, fill in the appropriate space in the wording on the bottom of the page **"QUESTION NUMBER ___ ENDS ON THIS PAGE."** Always

begin the start of an answer to a question on the top of a new page (which may be the back side of a sheet of paper). Use the entire width of the page to answer requirements of a noncomputational nature. To answer requirements of a computational nature, you may wish to use the three vertical columns provided on the right side of each page.

4. Record your 7-digit candidate number, state, and question number where indicated on pages 3 through 10 of the *Examination Answer Booklet.*

5. Although the primary purpose of the examination is to test your knowledge and application of the subject matter, selected essay responses will be graded for writing skills.

6. You are required to turn in by the end of each session:

   a. Attendance Record and Calculator Sign-off Record Form, front page of *Examination Answer Booklet;*
   b. *Objective Answer Sheet,* pages 11 and 12 of *Examination Answer Booklet;*
   c. Remaining Portion of *Examination Answer Booklet;*
   d. *Examination Question Booklet;*
   e. Calculator; and
   f. All unused examination materials.

   Your examination will not be graded unless the above listed items are handed in before leaving the examination room.

Prepared by the Board of Examiners of the American Institute of Certified Public Accountants and adopted by the examining boards of all states, the District of Columbia, Guam, Puerto Rico, and the Virgin Islands of the United States.

7. Unless otherwise instructed, if you want your *Examination Question Booklet* mailed to you, write your name and address in both places indicated on the back cover and place 52 cents postage in the space provided. *Examination Question Booklets* will be distributed no sooner than the day following the administration of this examination.

8. To turn the calculator on press ⊂CA⊃. Display will read "0". The calculator automatically turns itself off approximately 8 minutes after the last entry. All data in the calculator will be lost once the calculator is off. We recommend that when you press ⊂=⊃ , you press ⊂CA⊃ before beginning a new calculation. The basic key descriptions are as follows:

⊂CA⊃ **On and Clear** — Clears the calculator of all entries, including entries in memory, once calculator is on.

⊂C.CE⊃ **Clear Calculation** — Clears the Display.

⊂0⊃ ... ⊂9⊃ **Numericals** — Inputs that number.

⊂·⊃ **Decimal** — Indicates that all numbers to follow are decimals.

⊂+/−⊃ **Change sign** — Changes plus (minus) to minus (plus).

⊂+⊃ & ⊂−⊃ **Add & Subtract** — Adds the next number entered to, or subtracts the next number entered from, the displayed number.

⊂x⊃ & ⊂÷⊃ **Multiply & Divide** — Multiplies or divides the displayed number by the next number entered.

⊂=⊃ **Equal** — Displays the results of all previously entered operations.

⊂√⊃ **Square Root** — Calculates the square root of the displayed number. It is unlikely that you will need to use this key during the exam.

⊂%⊃ **Percentage** — Converts the displayed number to a percentage (i.e., divides it by 100) and completes all previously entered operations. It is unlikely that you will need to use this key during the exam.

⊂M+⊃ **Memory Add** — Adds the displayed number to the balance in memory.

⊂M−⊃ **Memory Subtract** — Subtracts the displayed number from the balance in memory.

⊂R.CM⊃ **Recall Memory** — Pressed once, displays the balance in memory. Pressed twice in a row, eliminates the balance in memory but not the displayed number.

> **If your calculator does not work or malfunctions, a replacement calculator will be available from the proctor.**

Number 1 (Estimated time—130 to 140 minutes)

Instructions

Select the **best** answer for each of the following items. Use a No. 2 pencil to blacken the appropriate ovals on the Objective Answer Sheet to indicate your answers. **Mark only one answer for each item. Answer all items.** Your grade will be based on the total number of correct answers.

1. According to the FASB conceptual framework, the process of reporting an item in the financial statements of an entity is
   A. Allocation.
   B. Matching.
   C. Realization.
   D. Recognition.

2. What are the Statements of Financial Accounting Concepts intended to establish?
   A. Generally accepted accounting principles in financial reporting by business enterprises.
   B. The meaning of "Present fairly in accordance with generally accepted accounting principles."
   C. The objectives and concepts for use in developing standards of financial accounting and reporting.
   D. The hierarchy of sources of generally accepted accounting principles.

3. Reporting inventory at the lower of cost or market is a departure from the accounting principle of
   A. Historical cost.
   B. Consistency.
   C. Conservatism.
   D. Full disclosure.

4. During a period when an enterprise is under the direction of a particular management, its financial statements will directly provide information about
   A. Both enterprise performance and management performance.
   B. Management performance but **not** directly provide information about enterprise performance.
   C. Enterprise performance but **not** directly provide information about **management** performance.
   D. Neither enterprise performance nor management performance.

5. The primary purpose of a statement of cash flows is to provide relevant information about
   A. Differences between net income and associated cash receipts and disbursements.
   B. An enterprise's ability to generate future positive net cash flows.
   C. The cash receipts and cash disbursements of an enterprise during a period.
   D. An enterprise's ability to meet cash operating needs.

6. What is the purpose of information presented in notes to the financial statements?
   A. To provide disclosures required by generally accepted accounting principles.
   B. To correct improper presentation in the financial statements.
   C. To provide recognition of amounts **not** included in the totals of the financial statements.
   D. To present management's responses to auditor comments.

MULTIPLE-CHOICE WORK SPACE—This information will **not** be graded. Only answers recorded on the Objective Answer Sheet will be graded.

7. Consolidated financial statements are typically prepared when one company has a controlling financial interest in another **unless**
   A. The subsidiary is a finance company.
   B. The fiscal year-ends of the two companies are more than three months apart.
   C. Such control is likely to be temporary.
   D. The two companies are in unrelated industries, such as manufacturing and real estate.

8. At December 31, 1992 and 1993, Apex Co. had 3,000 shares of $100 par, 5% cumulative preferred stock outstanding. No dividends were in arrears as of December 31, 1991. Apex did not declare a dividend during 1992. During 1993, Apex paid a cash dividend of $10,000 on its preferred stock. Apex should report dividends in arrears in its 1993 financial statements as a(an)
   A. Accrued liability of $15,000.
   B. Disclosure of $15,000.
   C. Accrued liability of $20,000.
   D. Disclosure of $20,000.

Items 9 and 10 are based on the following:

Vane Co.'s trial balance of income statement accounts for the year ended December 31, 1993, included the following:

	Debit	Credit
Sales		$575,000
Cost of sales	$240,000	
Administrative expenses	70,000	
Loss on sale of equipment	10,000	
Sales commissions	50,000	
Interest revenue		25,000
Freight out	15,000	
Loss on early retirement of long-term debt	20,000	
Uncollectible accounts expense	15,000	
Totals	$420,000	$600,000

Other information

Finished goods inventory:

January 1, 1993	$400,000
December 31, 1993	360,000

Vane's income tax rate is 30%. In Vane's 1993 multiple-step income statement,

9. What amount should Vane report as the cost of goods manufactured?
   A. $200,000
   B. $215,000
   C. $280,000
   D. $295,000

10. What amount should Vane report as income after income taxes from continuing operations?
   A. $126,000
   B. $129,500
   C. $140,000
   D. $147,000

MULTIPLE-CHOICE WORK SPACE—This information will **not** be graded. Only answers recorded on the Objective Answer Sheet will be graded.

11. Brite Corp. had the following liabilities at December 31, 1993:

Accounts payable	$ 55,000
Unsecured notes, 8%, due 7-1-94	400,000
Accrued expenses	35,000
Contingent liability	450,000
Deferred income tax liability	25,000
Senior bonds, 7%, due 3-31-94	1,000,000

The contingent liability is an accrual for possible losses on a $1,000,000 lawsuit filed against Brite. Brite's legal counsel expects the suit to be settled in 1995, and has estimated that Brite will be liable for damages in the range of $450,000 to $750,000.

The deferred income tax liability is not related to an asset for financial reporting and is expected to reverse in 1995.

What amount should Brite report in its December 31, 1993, balance sheet for current liabilities?
- A. $ 515,000
- B. $ 940,000
- C. $1,490,000
- D. $1,515,000

12. The following information pertains to Grey Co. at December 31, 1993:

Checkbook balance	$12,000
Bank statement balance	16,000
Check drawn on Grey's account, payable to a vendor, dated and recorded 12/31/93 but not mailed until 1/10/94	1,800

On Grey's December 31, 1993, balance sheet, what amount should be reported as cash?
- A. $12,000
- B. $13,800
- C. $14,200
- D. $16,000

13. At December 31, 1993, Kale Co. had the following balances in the accounts it maintains at First State Bank:

Checking account #101	$175,000
Checking account #201	(10,000)
Money market account	25,000
90-day certificate of deposit, due 2-28-94	50,000
180-day certificate of deposit, due 3-15-94	80,000

Kale classifies investments with original maturities of three months or less as cash equivalents. In its December 31, 1993, balance sheet, what amount should Kale report as cash and cash equivalents?
- A. $190,000
- B. $200,000
- C. $240,000
- D. $320,000

14. Nola Co. has adopted Statement of Financial Accounting Standards No. 115, *Accounting for Certain Investments in Debt and Equity Securities*. Nola has a portfolio of marketable equity securities which it does not intend to sell in the near term. How should Nola classify these securities, and how should it report unrealized gains and losses from these securities?

	Classify as	Report as a
A.	Trading securities	Component of income from continuing operations
B.	Available-for-sale securities	Separate component of stockholders' equity
C.	Trading securities	Separate component of stockholders' equity
D.	Available-for-sale securities	Component of income from continuing operations

15. Delta, Inc. sells to wholesalers on terms of 2/15, net 30. Delta has no cash sales but 50% of Delta's customers take advantage of the discount. Delta uses the gross method of recording sales and trade receivables. An analysis of Delta's trade receivables balances at December 31, 1993, revealed the following:

Age	Amount	Collectible
0 - 15 days	$100,000	100%
16 - 30 days	60,000	95%
31 - 60 days	5,000	90%
Over 60 days	2,500	$500
	$167,500	

In its December 31, 1993, balance sheet, what amount should Delta report for allowance for discounts?

   A. $1,000
   B. $1,620
   C. $1,675
   D. $2,000

16. In its financial statements, Pare, Inc. uses the cost method of accounting for its 15% ownership of Sabe Co. At December 31, 1993, Pare has a receivable from Sabe. How should the receivable be reported in Pare's December 31, 1993, balance sheet?

   A. The total receivable should be reported separately.
   B. The total receivable should be included as part of the investment in Sabe, without separate disclosure.
   C. Eighty-five percent of the receivable should be reported separately, with the balance offset against Sabe's payable to Pare.
   D. The total receivable should be offset against Sabe's payable to Pare, without separate disclosure.

17. Cole Co. began constructing a building for its own use in January 1993. During 1993, Cole incurred interest of $50,000 on specific construction debt, and $20,000 on other borrowings. Interest computed on the weighted-average amount of accumulated expenditures for the building during 1993 was $40,000. What amount of interest cost should Cole capitalize?

   A. $20,000
   B. $40,000
   C. $50,000
   D. $70,000

18. Turtle Co. purchased equipment on January 2, 1991, for $50,000. The equipment had an estimated five-year service life. Turtle's policy for five-year assets is to use the 200% double-declining depreciation method for the first two years of the asset's life, and then switch to the straight-line depreciation method. In its December 31, 1993, balance sheet, what amount should Turtle report as accumulated depreciation for equipment?

   A. $30,000
   B. $38,000
   C. $39,200
   D. $42,000

19. On January 2, 1993, Kean Co. purchased a 30% interest in Pod Co. for $250,000. On this date, Pod's stockholders' equity was $500,000. The carrying amounts of Pod's identifiable net assets approximated their fair values, except for land whose fair value exceeded its carrying amount by $200,000. Pod reported net income of $100,000 for 1993, and paid no dividends. Kean accounts for this investment using the equity method and amortizes goodwill over ten years. In its December 31, 1993, balance sheet, what amount should Kean report as investment in subsidiary?

   A. $210,000
   B. $220,000
   C. $270,000
   D. $276,000

MULTIPLE-CHOICE WORK SPACE—This information will **not** be graded. Only answers recorded on the Objective Answer Sheet will be graded.

20. On January 2, 1993, Rafa Co. purchased a franchise with a useful life of ten years for $50,000. An additional franchise fee of 3% of franchise operation revenues must be paid each year to the franchisor. Revenues from franchise operations amounted to $400,000 during 1993. In its December 31, 1993, balance sheet, what amount should Rafa report as an intangible asset-franchise?

   A. $33,000
   B $43,800
   C. $45,000
   D. $50,000

21. Hudson Hotel collects 15% in city sales taxes on room rentals, in addition to a $2 per room, per night, occupancy tax. Sales taxes for each month are due at the end of the following month, and occupancy taxes are due 15 days after the end of each calendar quarter. On January 3, 1994, Hudson paid its November 1993 sales taxes and its fourth quarter 1993 occupancy taxes. Additional information pertaining to Hudson's operations is:

1993	Room rentals	Room nights
October	$100,000	1,100
November	110,000	1,200
December	150,000	1,800

What amounts should Hudson report as sales taxes payable and occupancy taxes payable in its December 31, 1993, balance sheet?

	Sales taxes	Occupancy taxes
A.	$39,000	$6,000
B.	$39,000	$8,200
C.	$54,000	$6,000
D.	$54,000	$8,200

22. Under state law, Acme may pay 3% of eligible gross wages or it may reimburse the state directly for actual unemployment claims. Acme believes that actual unemployment claims will be 2% of eligible gross wages and has chosen to reimburse the state. Eligible gross wages are defined as the first $10,000 of gross wages paid to each employee. Acme had five employees each of whom earned $20,000 during 1993. In its December 31, 1993, balance sheet, what amount should Acme report as accrued liability for unemployment claims?

   A. $1,000
   B. $1,500
   C. $2,000
   D. $3,000

23. Since there is no reasonable basis for estimating the degree of collectibility, Astor Co. uses the installment method of revenue recognition for the following sales:

	1993	1992
Sales	$900,000	$600,000
Collections from:		
1992 sales	100,000	200,000
1993 sales	300,000	—
Accounts written off:		
1992 sales	150,000	50,000
1993 sales	50,000	—
Gross profit percentage	40%	30%

What amount should Astor report as deferred gross profit in its December 31, 1993, balance sheet for the 1992 and 1993 sales?

   A. $150,000
   B. $160,000
   C. $225,000
   D. $250,000

MULTIPLE-CHOICE WORK SPACE—This information will **not be graded**. Only answers recorded on the Objective Answer Sheet will be graded.

24. Because Jab Co. uses different methods to depreciate equipment for financial statement and income tax purposes, Jab has temporary differences that will reverse during the next year and add to taxable income. Deferred income taxes that are based on these temporary differences should be classified in Jab's balance sheet as a
   A. Contra account to current assets.
   B. Contra account to noncurrent assets.
   C. Current liability.
   D. Noncurrent liability.

25. In the long-term liabilities section of its balance sheet at December 31, 1992, Mene Co. reported a capital lease obligation of $75,000, net of current portion of $1,364. Payments of $9,000 were made on both January 2, 1993, and January 2, 1994. Mene's incremental borrowing rate on the date of the lease was 11% and the lessor's implicit rate, which was known to Mene, was 10%. In its December 31, 1993, balance sheet, what amount should Mene report as capital lease obligation, net of current portion?
   A. $66,000
   B. $73,500
   C. $73,636
   D. $74,250

26. One criterion for a capital lease is that the term of the lease must equal a minimum percentage of the leased property's estimated economic life at the inception of the lease. What is this minimum percentage?
   A. 51%
   B. 75%
   C. 80%
   D. 90%

27. An employer's obligation for postretirement health benefits that are expected to be provided to or for an employee must be fully accrued by the date the
   A. Employee is fully eligible for benefits.
   B. Employee retires.
   C. Benefits are utilized.
   D. Benefits are paid.

28. Payne, Inc. implemented a defined-benefit pension plan for its employees on January 2, 1993. The following data are provided for 1993, as of December 31, 1993:

Accumulated benefit obligation	$103,000
Plan assets at fair value	78,000
Net periodic pension cost	90,000
Employer's contribution	70,000

What amount should Payne record as additional minimum pension liability at December 31, 1993?
   A. $0
   B. $ 5,000
   C. $20,000
   D. $45,000

29. On January 1, 1994, Oak Co. issued 400 of its 8%, $1,000 bonds at 97 plus accrued interest. The bonds are dated October 1, 1993, and mature on October 1, 2003. Interest is payable semiannually on April 1 and October 1. Accrued interest for the period October 1, 1993, to January 1, 1994, amounted to $8,000. On January 1, 1994, what amount should Oak report as bonds payable, net of discount?
   A. $380,300
   B. $388,000
   C. $388,300
   D. $392,000

30. The discount resulting from the determination of a note payable's present value should be reported on the balance sheet as a(an)
   A. Addition to the face amount of the note.
   B. Deferred charge separate from the note.
   C. Deferred credit separate from the note.
   D. Direct reduction from the face amount of the note.

MULTIPLE-CHOICE WORK SPACE—This information will **not** be graded. Only answers recorded on the Objective Answer Sheet will be graded.

31. East Corp., a calendar-year company, had sufficient retained earnings in 1993 as a basis for dividends, but was temporarily short of cash. East declared a dividend of $100,000 on April 1, 1993, and issued promissory notes to its stockholders in lieu of cash. The notes, which were dated April 1, 1993, had a maturity date of March 31, 1994, and a 10% interest rate. How should East account for the scrip dividend and related interest?

    A. Debit retained earnings for $110,000 on April 1, 1993.

    B. Debit retained earnings for $110,000 on March 31, 1994.

    C. Debit retained earnings for $100,000 on April 1, 1993, and debit interest expense for $10,000 on March 31, 1994.

    D. Debit retained earnings for $100,000 on April 1, 1993, and debit interest expense for $7,500 on December 31, 1993.

32. On January 2, 1994, Lake Mining Co.'s board of directors declared a cash dividend of $400,000 to stockholders of record on January 18, 1994, payable on February 10, 1994. The dividend is permissible under law in Lake's state of incorporation. Selected data from Lake's December 31, 1993, balance sheet are as follows:

Accumulated depletion	$100,000
Capital stock	500,000
Additional paid-in capital	150,000
Retained earnings	300,000

The $400,000 dividend includes a liquidating dividend of

    A. $0

    B. $100,000

    C. $150,000

    D. $300,000

33. On January 2, 1993, Kine Co. granted Morgan, its president, compensatory stock options to buy 1,000 shares of Kine's $10 par common stock. The options call for a price of $20 per share and are exercisable for 3 years following the grant date. Morgan exercised the options on December 31, 1993. The market price of the stock was $50 on January 2, 1993, and $70 on December 31, 1993. By what net amount should stockholders' equity increase as a result of the grant and exercise of the options?

    A. $20,000

    B. $30,000

    C. $50,000

    D. $70,000

34. On December 31, 1993, Moss Co. issued $1,000,000 of 11% bonds at 109. Each $1,000 bond was issued with 50 detachable stock warrants, each of which entitled the bondholder to purchase one share of $5 par common stock for $25. Immediately after issuance, the market value of each warrant was $4. On December 31, 1993, what amount should Moss record as discount or premium on issuance of bonds?

    A. $ 40,000 premium.

    B. $ 90,000 premium.

    C. $110,000 discount.

    D. $200,000 discount.

35. When property other than cash is invested in a partnership, at what amount should the non-cash property be credited to the contributing partner's capital account?

    A. Fair value at the date of contribution.

    B. Contributing partner's original cost.

    C. Assessed valuation for property tax purposes.

    D. Contributing partner's tax basis.

MULTIPLE-CHOICE WORK SPACE—This information will **not** be graded. Only answers recorded on the Objective Answer Sheet will be graded.

36. Red and White formed a partnership in 1992. The partnership agreement provides for annual salary allowances of $55,000 for Red and $45,000 for White. The partners share profits equally and losses in a 60/40 ratio. The partnership had earnings of $80,000 for 1993 before any allowance to partners. What amount of these earnings should be credited to each partner's capital account?

	Red	White
A.	$40,000	$40,000
B.	$43,000	$37,000
C.	$44,000	$36,000
D.	$45,000	$35,000

37. The following condensed balance sheet is presented for the partnership of Smith and Jones, who share profits and losses in the ratio of 60:40, respectively:

Other assets	$450,000
Smith, loan	20,000
	$470,000
Accounts payable	$120,000
Smith, capital	195,000
Jones, capital	155,000
	$470,000

The partners have decided to liquidate the partnership. If the other assets are sold for $385,000, what amount of the available cash should be distributed to Smith?
A. $136,000
B. $156,000
C. $159,000
D. $195,000

38. Which of the following statements is correct regarding the provision for income taxes in the financial statements of a sole proprietorship?
A. The provision for income taxes should be based on business income using individual tax rates.
B. The provision for income taxes should be based on business income using corporate tax rates.
C. The provision for income taxes should be based on the proprietor's total taxable income, allocated to the proprietorship at the percentage that business income bears to the proprietor's total income.
D. No provision for income taxes is required.

39. Which of the following statements is correct regarding accounting changes that result in financial statements that are, in effect, the statements of a different reporting entity?
A. Cumulative-effect adjustments should be reported as separate items on the financial statements pertaining to the year of change.
B. No restatements or adjustments are required if the changes involve consolidated methods of accounting for subsidiaries.
C. No restatements or adjustments are required if the changes involve the cost or equity methods of accounting for investments.
D. The financial statements of all prior periods presented should be restated.

MULTIPLE-CHOICE WORK SPACE—This information will **not** be graded. Only answers recorded on the Objective Answer Sheet will be graded.

40. The effect of a material transaction that is infrequent in occurrence but **not** unusual in nature should be presented separately as a component of income from continuing operations when the transaction results in a

	Gain	*Loss*
A.	Yes	Yes
B.	Yes	No
C.	No	No
D.	No	Yes

41. Wren Co. sells equipment on installment contracts. Which of the following statements best justifies Wren's use of the cost recovery method of revenue recognition to account for these installment sales?

- A. The sales contract provides that title to the equipment only passes to the purchaser when all payments have been made.
- B. No cash payments are due until one year from the date of sale.
- C. Sales are subject to a high rate of return.
- D. There is **no** reasonable basis for estimating collectibility.

42. Compared to the accrual basis of accounting, the cash basis of accounting understates income by the net decrease during the accounting period of

	Accounts receivable	*Accrued expenses*
A.	Yes	Yes
B.	Yes	No
C.	No	No
D.	No	Yes

43. Jent Corp. purchased bonds at a discount of $10,000. Subsequently, Jent sold these bonds at a premium of $14,000. During the period that Jent held this investment, amortization of the discount amounted to $2,000. What amount should Jent report as gain on the sale of bonds?

- A. $12,000
- B. $22,000
- C. $24,000
- D. $26,000

44. In 1993, Gar Corp. collected $300,000 as beneficiary of a keyman life insurance policy carried on the life of Gar's controller, who had died in 1993. The life insurance proceeds are not subject to income tax. At the date of the controller's death, the policy's cash surrender value was $90,000. What amount should Gar report as revenue in its 1993 income statement?

- A. $0
- B. $ 90,000
- C. $210,000
- D. $300,000

45. On January 2, 1993, Lem Corp. bought machinery under a contract that required a down payment of $10,000, plus 24 monthly payments of $5,000 each, for total cash payments of $130,000. The cash equivalent price of the machinery was $110,000. The machinery has an estimated useful life of ten years and estimated salvage value of $5,000. Lem uses straight-line depreciation. In its 1993 income statement, what amount should Lem report as depreciation for this machinery?

- A. $10,500
- B. $11,000
- C. $12,500
- D. $13,000

MULTIPLE-CHOICE WORK SPACE—This information will **not** be graded. Only answers recorded on the Objective Answer Sheet will be graded.

46. A bond issued on June 1, 1993, has interest payment dates of April 1 and October 1. Bond interest expense for the year ended December 31, 1993, is for a period of
  A. Three months.
  B. Four months.
  C. Six months.
  D. Seven months.

47. For the year ended December 31, 1993, Grim Co.'s pretax financial statement income was $200,000 and its taxable income was $150,000. The difference is due to the following:

Interest on municipal bonds	$ 70,000
Premium expense on keyman life insurance	(20,000)
Total	$ 50,000

Grim's enacted income tax rate is 30%. In its 1993 income statement, what amount should Grim report as current provision for income tax expense?
  A. $45,000
  B. $51,000
  C. $60,000
  D. $66,000

48. An extraordinary item should be reported separately on the income statement as a component of income

	Net of income taxes	*Before discontinued operations of a segment of a business*
A.	Yes	Yes
B.	Yes	No
C.	No	No
D.	No	Yes

49. On December 1, 1993, Clay Co. declared and issued a 6% stock dividend on its 100,000 shares of outstanding common stock. There was no other common stock activity during 1993. What number of shares should Clay use in determining earnings per share for 1993?
  A. 100,000
  B. 100,500
  C. 103,000
  D. 106,000

50. Fara Co. reported bonds payable of $47,000 at December 31, 1992, and $50,000 at December 31, 1993. During 1993, Fara issued $20,000 of bonds payable in exchange for equipment. There was no amortization of bond premium or discount during the year. What amount should Fara report in its 1993 statement of cash flows for redemption of bonds payable?
  A. $ 3,000
  B. $17,000
  C. $20,000
  D. $23,000

51. Kiwi, Inc.'s planned combination with Mori Co. on January 1, 1994, can be structured either as a purchase or a pooling of interests. In a purchase, Kiwi would acquire Mori's identifiable net assets for more than their book values. These book values approximate fair values. Mori's assets consist of current assets and depreciable noncurrent assets. Ignoring costs required to effect the combination and income tax expense, how would the combined entity's 1994 net income under purchase accounting compare to that under pooling of interests accounting?
  A. Less than pooling.
  B. Equal to pooling.
  C. Greater than pooling.
  D. Not determinable from information given.

MULTIPLE-CHOICE WORK SPACE—This information will **not** be graded. Only answers recorded on the Objective Answer Sheet will be graded.

52. A business combination occurs in the middle of the year. Results of operations for the year of combination would include the combined results of operations of the separate companies for the entire year if the business combination is a

	Purchase	Pooling of interests
A.	Yes	Yes
B.	Yes	No
C.	No	No
D.	No	Yes

53. For the purpose of estimating income taxes to be reported in personal financial statements, assets and liabilities measured at their tax bases should be compared to assets and liabilities measured at their

	Assets	Liabilities
A.	Estimated current value	Estimated current amount
B.	Historical cost	Historical cost
C.	Estimated current value	Historical cost
D.	Historical cost	Estimated current amount

54. Which of the following accounting bases may be used to prepare financial statements in conformity with a comprehensive basis of accounting other than generally accepted accounting principles?

I. Basis of accounting used by an entity to file its income tax return.
II. Cash receipts and disbursements basis of accounting.

A. I only.
B. II only.
C. Both I and II.
D. Neither I nor II.

Items 55 and 56 are based on the following:

On January 1, 1993, Owen Corp. purchased all of Sharp Corp.'s common stock for $1,200,000. On that date, the fair values of Sharp's assets and liabilities equaled their carrying amounts of $1,320,000 and $320,000, respectively. Owen's policy is to amortize intangibles over 10 years. During 1993, Sharp paid cash dividends of $20,000.

Selected information from the separate balance sheets and income statements of Owen and Sharp as of December 31, 1993, and for the year then ended follows:

	Owen	Sharp
Balance sheet accounts		
Investment in subsidiary	$1,300,000	—
Retained earnings	1,240,000	560,000
Total stockholders' equity	2,620,000	1,120,000
Income statement accounts		
Operating income	420,000	200,000
Equity in earnings of Sharp	120,000	—
Net income	400,000	140,000

55. In Owen's 1993 consolidated income statement, what amount should be reported for amortization of goodwill?
A. $0
B. $12,000
C. $18,000
D. $20,000

56. In Owen's December 31, 1993, consolidated balance sheet, what amount should be reported as total retained earnings?
A. $1,240,000
B. $1,360,000
C. $1,380,000
D. $1,800,000

MULTIPLE-CHOICE WORK SPACE—This information will **not** be graded. Only answers recorded on the Objective Answer Sheet will be graded.

57. During 1993, Smith Co. filed suit against West, Inc. seeking damages for patent infringement. At December 31, 1993, Smith's legal counsel believed that it was probable that Smith would be successful against West for an estimated amount in the range of $75,000 to $150,000, with all amounts in the range considered equally likely. In March 1994, Smith was awarded $100,000 and received full payment thereof. In its 1993 financial statements, issued in February 1994, how should this award be reported?
   A. As a receivable and revenue of $100,000.
   B. As a receivable and deferred revenue of $100,000.
   C. As a disclosure of a contingent gain of $100,000.
   D. As a disclosure of a contingent gain of an undetermined amount in the range of $75,000 to $150,000.

58. In its financial statements, Hila Co. discloses supplemental information on the effects of changing prices in accordance with Statement of Financial Accounting Standards No. 89, *Financial Reporting and Changing Prices*. Hila computed the increase in current cost of inventory as follows:

Increase in current
   cost (nominal dollars) $15,000
Increase in current
   cost (constant dollars) $12,000

What amount should Hila disclose as the inflation component of the increase in current cost of inventories?
   A. $ 3,000
   B. $12,000
   C. $15,000
   D. $27,000

59. During a period of inflation in which an asset account remains constant, which of the following occurs?
   A. A purchasing power gain, if the item is a monetary asset.
   B. A purchasing power gain, if the item is a nonmonetary asset.
   C. A purchasing power loss, if the item is a monetary asset.
   D. A purchasing power loss, if the item is a nonmonetary asset.

60. At December 30, 1993, Vida Co. had cash of $200,000, a current ratio of 1.5:1 and a quick ratio of .5:1. On December 31, 1993, all cash was used to reduce accounts payable. How did these cash payments affect the ratios?

	Current ratio	*Quick ratio*
A.	Increased	Decreased
B.	Increased	No effect
C.	Decreased	Increased
D.	Decreased	No effect

QUESTION NUMBER 2 BEGINS ON PAGE 419.

MULTIPLE-CHOICE WORK SPACE—This information will **not** be graded. Only answers recorded on the Objective Answer Sheet will be graded.

Number 2 (Estimated time 15—25 minutes)

Question 2 consists of 10 items. Select the **best** answer for each item. Use a No. 2 pencil to blacken the appropriate ovals on the Objective Answer Sheet to indicate your answers. **Answer all items.** Your grade will be based on the total number of correct answers.

On January 2, 1993, Quo, Inc. hired Reed to be its controller. During the year, Reed, working closely with Quo's president and outside accountants, made changes in accounting policies, corrected several errors dating from 1992 and before, and instituted new accounting policies.

Quo's 1993 financial statements will be presented in comparative form with its 1992 financial statements.

Required:

Items 61 through 70 represent Quo's transactions. List A represents possible classifications of these transactions as: a change in accounting principle, a change in accounting estimate, a correction of an error in previously presented financial statements, or neither an accounting change nor an accounting error.

List B represents the general accounting treatment required for these transactions. These treatments are:

- Cumulative effect approach—Include the cumulative effect of the adjustment resulting from the accounting change or error correction in the 1993 financial statements, and do **not** restate the 1992 financial statements.
- Retroactive restatement approach—Restate the 1992 financial statements and adjust 1992 beginning retained earnings if the error or change affects a period prior to 1992.
- Prospective approach—Report 1993 and future financial statements on the new basis, but do **not** restate 1992 financial statements.

For each item, select one from List A and one from List B and blacken the corresponding ovals on the Objective Answer Sheet.

List A (Select one)	List B (Select one)
A. Change in accounting principle.	X. Cumulative effect approach.
B. Change in accounting estimate.	Y. Retroactive restatement approach.
C. Correction of an error in previously presented financial statements.	Z. Prospective approach.
D. Neither an accounting change nor an accounting error.	

Items to be answered:

61. Quo manufactures heavy equipment to customer specifications on a contract basis. On the basis that it is preferable, accounting for these long-term contracts was switched from the completed-contract method to the percentage-of-completion method.

62. As a result of a production breakthrough, Quo determined that manufacturing equipment previously depreciated over 15 years should be depreciated over 20 years.

63. The equipment that Quo manufactures is sold with a five-year warranty. Because of a production breakthrough, Quo reduced its computation of warranty costs from 3% of sales to 1% of sales.

64. Quo changed from LIFO to FIFO to account for its finished goods inventory.

65. Quo changed from FIFO to average cost to account for its raw materials and work in process inventories.

66. Quo sells extended service contracts on its products. Because related services are performed over several years, in 1993 Quo changed from the cash method to the accrual method of recognizing income from these service contracts.

67. During 1993, Quo determined that an insurance premium paid and entirely expensed in 1992 was for the period January 1, 1992, through January 1, 1994.

68. Quo changed its method of depreciating office equipment from an accelerated method to the straight-line method to more closely reflect costs in later years.

69. Quo instituted a pension plan for all employees in 1993 and adopted Statement of Financial Accounting Standards No. 87, *Employers' Accounting for Pensions*. Quo had not previously had a pension plan.

70. During 1993, Quo increased its investment in Worth, Inc. from a 10% interest, purchased in 1992, to 30%, and acquired a seat on Worth's board of directors. As a result of its increased investment, Quo changed its method of accounting for investment in subsidiary from the cost method to the equity method.

Number 3 (Estimated time 15—25 minutes)

Question 3 consists of 12 items. Select the **best** answer for each item. Use a No. 2 pencil to blacken the appropriate ovals on the Objective Answer Sheet to indicate your answers. **Answer all items.** Your grade will be based on the total number of correct answers.

Edge Co., a toy manufacturer, is in the process of preparing its financial statements for the year ended December 31, 1993. Edge expects to issue its 1993 financial statements on March 1, 1994.

Required:
   Items 71 through 82 represent various information that has not been reflected in the financial statements. For each item, the following two responses are required:
   a. Determine if an adjustment is required and select the appropriate amount, if any, from the list below.
   b. Determine (Yes/No) if additional disclosure is **required,** either on the face of the financial statements or in the notes to the financial statements.
   Blacken the corresponding ovals on the Objective Answer Sheet.

Adjustment amounts

A. No adjustment is required
B. $100,000
C. $150,000
D. $250,000
E. $400,000
F. $500,000

Items to be answered:

71. Edge owns a small warehouse located on the banks of a river in which it stores inventory worth approximately $500,000. Edge is not insured against flood losses. The river last overflowed its banks twenty years ago.

72. During 1993, Edge began offering certain health care benefits to its eligible retired employees. Edge's actuaries have determined that the discounted expected cost of these benefits for current employees is $150,000.

73. Edge offers an unconditional warranty on its toys. Based on past experience, Edge estimates its warranty expense to be 1% of sales. Sales during 1993 were $10,000,000.

74. On October 30, 1993, a safety hazard related to one of Edge's toy products was discovered. It is considered probable that Edge will be liable for an amount in the range of $100,000 to $500,000.

75. On November 22, 1993, Edge initiated a lawsuit seeking $250,000 in damages from patent infringement.

76. On December 17, 1993, a former employee filed a lawsuit seeking $100,000 for unlawful dismissal. Edge's attorneys believe the suit is without merit. No court date has been set.

77. On December 15, 1993, Edge guaranteed a bank loan of $100,000 for its president's personal use.

78. On December 31, 1993, Edge's board of directors voted to discontinue the operations of its computer games division and sell all the assets of the division. The division was sold on February 15, 1994. On December 31, 1993, Edge estimated that losses from operations, net of tax, for the period January 1, 1994, through February 15, 1994, would be $400,000 and that the gain from the sale of the division's assets, net of tax, would be $250,000. These estimates were materially correct.

79. On January 5, 1994, a warehouse containing a substantial portion of Edge's inventory was destroyed by fire. Edge expects to recover the entire loss, except for a $250,000 deductible, from insurance.

80. On January 24, 1994, inventory purchased FOB shipping point from a foreign country was detained at that country's border because of political unrest. The shipment is valued at $150,000. Edge's attorneys have stated that it is probable that Edge will be able to obtain the shipment.

81. On January 30, 1994, Edge issued $10,000,000 bonds at a premium of $500,000.

82. On February 4, 1994, the IRS assessed Edge an additional $400,000 for the 1992 tax year. Edge's tax attorneys and tax accountants have stated that it is likely that the IRS will agree to a $100,000 settlement.

Number 4 (Estimated time 30—40 minutes)

York Co. sells one product, which it purchases from various suppliers. York's trial balance at December 31, 1993, included the following accounts:

Sales (33,000 units @ $16)	$528,000
Sales discounts	7,500
Purchases	368,900
Purchase discounts	18,000
Freight-in	5,000
Freight-out	11,000

York Co.'s inventory purchases during 1993 were as follows:

	Units	Cost per unit	Total cost
Beginning inventory, January 1	8,000	$8.20	$ 65,600
Purchases, quarter ended March 31	12,000	8.25	99,000
Purchases, quarter ended June 30	15,000	7.90	118,500
Purchases, quarter ended September 30	13,000	7.50	97,500
Purchases, quarter ended December 31	7,000	7.70	53,900
	55,000		$434,500

Additional information:

York's accounting policy is to report inventory in its financial statements at the lower of cost or market, applied to total inventory. Cost is determined under the last-in, first-out (LIFO) method.

York has determined that, at December 31, 1993, the replacement cost of its inventory was $8 per unit and the net realizable value was $8.80 per unit. York's normal profit margin is $1.05 per unit.

Required:

   a. Prepare York's schedule of cost of goods sold, with a supporting schedule of ending inventory. York uses the direct method of reporting losses from market decline of inventory.

   b. Explain the rule of lower of cost or market and its application in this situation.

Number 5 (Estimated time 30—40 minutes)

Chris Green, CPA, is auditing Rayne Co.'s 1993 financial statements. The controller, Dunn, has provided Green with the following information:

- At December 31, 1992, Rayne had a note payable to Federal Bank with a balance of $90,000. The annual principal payment of $10,000, plus 8% interest on the unpaid balance, was paid when due on March 31, 1993.

- On January 2, 1993, Rayne leased two automobiles for executive use under a capital lease. Five annual lease payments of $15,000 are due beginning January 3, 1993. Rayne's incremental borrowing rate on the date of the lease was 11% and the lessor's implicit rate, which was known by Rayne, was 10%. The lease was properly recorded at $62,500, before the first payment was made.

- On July 1, 1993, Rayne received proceeds of $538,000 from a $500,000 bond issuance. The bonds mature in 15 years and interest of 11% is payable semiannually on June 30 and December 31. The bonds were issued at a price to yield investors 10%. Rayne uses the effective interest method to amortize bond premium.

- For the year ended December 31, 1993, Rayne has adopted Statement of Financial Accounting Standards No. 109, *Accounting for Income Taxes*. Dunn has prepared a schedule of all differences between financial statement and income tax return income. Dunn believes that as a result of pending legislation, the enacted tax rate at December 31, 1993, will be increased for 1994. Dunn is uncertain which differences to include and which rates to apply in computing deferred taxes under FASB 109. Dunn has requested an overview of FAS 109 from Green.

Required:
- **a.** Prepare a schedule of interest expense for the year ended December 31, 1993.
- **b.** Prepare a brief memo to Dunn from Green:

    - identifying the objectives of accounting for income taxes,
    - defining temporary differences,
    - explaining how to measure deferred tax assets and liabilities, and
    - explaining how to measure deferred income tax expense or benefit.

ANSWER KEY
FOUR-OPTION MULTIPLE-CHOICE QUESTIONS

Be sure to read "Chapter 6—Chart Your Progress and Plan Your Course of Action." It will help you analyze your test and plan your study program.

Business Law & Professional Responsibilities (LPR)

QUESTION #	ANSWER	TOPICAL AREA
1	C	Professional Responsibilities
2	A	Professional Responsibilities
3	A	Professional Responsibilities
4	B	Professional Responsibilities
5	D	Professional Responsibilities
6	D	Professional Responsibilities
7	B	Professional Responsibilities
8	C	Professional Responsibilities
9	B	Accountants' Legal Responsibility
10	B	Accountants' Legal Responsibility
11	D	Corporations
12	B	Corporations
13	C	Corporations
14	C	Corporations
15	A	Estates and Trusts
16	C	Estates and Trusts
17	C	Estates and Trusts
18	A	Estates and Trusts
19	C	Estates and Trusts
20	B	Estates and Trusts
21	A	Suretyship and Creditor's Rights
22	D	Suretyship and Creditor's Rights
23	D	Suretyship and Creditor's Rights
24	B	Suretyship and Creditor's Rights
25	B	Suretyship and Creditor's Rights
26	A	Employment Regulations
27	B	Employment Regulations
28	B	Employment Regulations
29	A	Employment Regulations
30	D	Employment Regulations

QUESTION #	ANSWER	TOPICAL AREA
31	A	Federal Securities Regulations
32	D	Federal Securities Regulations
33	D	Federal Securities Regulations
34	B	Federal Securities Regulations
35	A	Federal Securities Regulations
36	C	Federal Securities Regulations
37	B	Federal Securities Regulations
38	D	Federal Securities Regulations
39	A	Federal Securities Regulations
40	B	Federal Securities Regulations
41	D	Sales
42	A	Sales
43	A	Sales
44	D	Sales
45	D	Sales
46	A	Sales
47	B	Sales
48	C	Secured Transactions
49	A	Secured Transactions
50	B	Secured Transactions
51	C	Secured Transactions
52	C	Secured Transactions
53	C	Secured Transactions
54	A	Secured Transactions
55	C	Secured Transactions
56	C	Property
57	D	Property
58	A	Property
59	A	Property
60	D	Property

Auditing (AUDIT)

QUESTION #	ANSWER	TOPICAL AREA
1	B	Audit Planning
2	C	Audit Planning
3	B	Auditing Concepts and Standards
4	D	Audit Planning
5	A	Audit Planning

QUESTION #	ANSWER	TOPICAL AREA
6	A	Audit Evidence
7	D	Audit Evidence
8	D	Audit Evidence
9	A	Other Reporting Areas
10	A	Other Reporting Areas
11	C	Audit Evidence
12	B	Other Reporting Areas
13	C	Other Reporting Areas
14	C	Other Reporting Areas
15	C	Auditing Concepts and Standards
16	B	Electronic Data Processing (EDP)
17	D	Statistical Sampling
18	D	Internal Control
19	C	Internal Control
20	B	Internal Control
21	B	Internal Control
22	A	Internal Control
23	C	Internal Control
24	D	Audit Planning
25	A	Internal Control
26	B	Internal Control
27	B	Internal Control
28	A	Internal Control
29	C	Internal Control
30	B	Internal Control
31	C	Electronic Data Processing (EDP)
32	C	Internal Control
33	D	Internal Control
34	A	Internal Control
35	A	Internal Control
36	D	Internal Control
37	A	Internal Control
38	B	Audit Evidence
39	A	Audit Evidence
40	B	Audit Evidence
41	B	Audit Evidence
42	B	Audit Evidence
43	C	Statistical Sampling
44	D	Statistical Sampling
45	D	Audit Evidence
46	D	Other Reporting Areas
47	A	Audit Evidence
48	A	Audit Evidence
49	C	Audit Evidence
50	D	Audit Evidence
51	B	Audit Planning
52	B	Audit Planning
53	D	Audit Reporting Standards
54	A	Audit Evidence

QUESTION #	ANSWER	TOPICAL AREA
55	B	Audit Evidence
56	D	Electronic Data Processing (EDP)
57	C	Audit Evidence
58	C	Audit Evidence
59	D	Other Reporting Areas
60	C	Other Reporting Areas
61	B	Other Reporting Areas
62	B	Audit Evidence
63	A	Audit Reporting Standards
64	A	Other Reporting Areas
65	A	Audit Reporting Standards
66	C	Audit Reporting Standards
67	A	Audit Reporting Standards
68	D	Other Reporting Areas
69	D	Audit Reporting Standards
70	B	Audit Reporting Standards
71	D	Audit Reporting Standards
72	A	Audit Reporting Standards
73	C	Audit Reporting Standards
74	D	Audit Reporting Standards
75	A	Audit Reporting Standards
76	B	Audit Reporting Standards
77	C	Audit Reporting Standards
78	C	Other Reporting Areas
79	C	Other Reporting Areas
80	B	Other Reporting Areas
81	D	Other Reporting Areas
82	C	Audit Reporting Standards
83	D	Other Reporting Areas
84	A	Other Reporting Areas
85	B	Other Reporting Areas
86	C	Audit Reporting Standards
87	C	Audit Reporting Standards
88	D	Audit Reporting Standards
89	D	Audit Reporting Standards
90	D	Audit Reporting Standards

Accounting & Reporting— Taxation, Managerial, and Governmental and Not-for-Profit Organizations (ARE)

QUESTION #	ANSWER	TOPICAL AREA
1	D	Federal Income Taxes— Capital Gains & Losses
2	C	Federal Income Taxes— Individuals

Question #	Answer	Topical Area	Question #	Answer	Topical Area
3	A	Federal Income Taxes—Individuals	29	C	Federal Income Taxes—Partnerships
4	C	Federal Income Taxes—Individuals	30	C	Federal Income Taxes—Partnerships
5	A	Federal Income Taxes—Individuals	31	B	Federal Income Taxes—Partnerships
6	C	Federal Income Taxes—Individuals	32	D	Federal Income Taxes—Individuals
7	A	Federal Income Taxes—Individuals	33	C	Federal Income Taxes—Estates & Trusts
8	C	Federal Income Taxes—Individuals	34	D	Federal Income Taxes—Exempt Organizations
9	B	Federal Income Taxes—Individuals	35	D	Federal Income Taxes—Exempt Organizations
10	B	Federal Income Taxes—Individuals	36	B	Managerial Accounting and Quantitative Methods
11	C	Federal Income Taxes—Individuals	37	C	Managerial Accounting and Quantitative Methods
12	A	Federal Income Taxes—Individuals	38	C	Managerial Accounting and Quantitative Methods
13	C	Federal Income Taxes—Individuals	39	B	Managerial Accounting and Quantitative Methods
14	B	Federal Income Taxes—Individuals	40	D	Cost Accounting
15	B	Federal Income Taxes—Miscellaneous Topics	41	D	Managerial Accounting and Quantitative Methods
16	D	Federal Income Taxes—Individuals	42	B	Cost Accounting
17	C	Federal Income Taxes—Individuals	43	C	Managerial Accounting and Quantitative Methods
18	C	Federal Income Taxes—Miscellaneous Topics	44	B	Managerial Accounting and Quantitative Methods
19	C	Federal Income Taxes—Miscellaneous Topics	45	A	Managerial Accounting and Quantitative Methods
20	D	Federal Income Taxes—Miscellaneous Topics	46	D	Managerial Accounting and Quantitative Methods
21	C	Federal Income Taxes—Corporations	47	C	Managerial Accounting and Quantitative Methods
22	B	Federal Income Taxes—Corporations	48	C	Managerial Accounting and Quantitative Methods
23	D	Federal Income Taxes—Corporations	49	B	Managerial Accounting and Quantitative Methods
24	B	Federal Income Taxes—Corporations	50	C	Managerial Accounting and Quantitative Methods
25	C	Federal Income Taxes—Corporations	51	A	Not-for-Profit Accounting—Governmental Units
26	C	Federal Income Taxes—Partnerships	52	C	Not-for-Profit Accounting—Governmental Units
27	A	Federal Income Taxes—Partnerships	53	B	Not-for-Profit Accounting—Governmental Units
28	D	Federal Income Taxes—Partnerships	54	A	Not-for-Profit Accounting—Governmental Units
			55	D	Not-for-Profit Accounting—Governmental Units

Question #	Answer	Topical Area
56	B	Not-for-Profit Accounting—Governmental Units
57	D	Not-for-Profit Accounting—Governmental Units
58	C	Not-for-Profit Accounting—Other Than Governmental Units
59	C	Not-for-Profit Accounting—Other Than Governmental Units
60	D	Not-for-Profit Accounting—Other Than Governmental Units

Financial Accounting & Reporting—Business Enterprises (FARE)

Question #	Answer	Topical Area
1	D	Accounting Concepts
2	C	Accounting Concepts
3	A	Accounting Concepts
4	C	Financial Statements
5	C	Cash Flows
6	A	Financial Statements
7	C	Consolidation
8	D	Stockholders' Equity
9	A	Financial Statements
10	C	Financial Statements
11	C	Liabilities
12	B	Cash
13	C	Cash
14	B	Investments
15	A	Receivables
16	A	Investments
17	B	Fixed Assets
18	B	Fixed Assets
19	D	Investments
20	C	Intangibles
21	B	Liabilities
22	A	Liabilities
23	D	Installment Sales
24	D	Income Taxes, Accounting for
25	B	Leases
26	B	Leases
27	A	Pension Costs
28	B	Pension Costs
29	B	Bonds, Accounting for
30	D	Liabilities

Question #	Answer	Topical Area
31	D	Stockholders' Equity
32	B	Stockholders' Equity
33	A	Stockholders' Equity
34	C	Bonds, Accounting for
35	A	Partnerships
36	B	Partnerships
37	A	Partnerships
38	D	Financial Statements
39	D	Financial Statements
40	A	Financial Statements
41	D	Installment Sales
42	D	Accounting Concepts
43	B	Bonds, Accounting for
44	A	Investments
45	A	Fixed Assets
46	D	Bonds, Accounting for
47	A	Income Taxes, Accounting for
48	B	Financial Statements
49	D	Stockholders' Equity
50	B	Cash Flows
51	A	Consolidation
52	D	Consolidation
53	A	Financial Statements
54	C	Financial Statements
55	D	Consolidation
56	A	Consolidation
57	D	Accounting Concepts
58	A	Inflation Accounting
59	C	Inflation Accounting
60	A	Financial Statement Analysis

SOLUTIONS AND EXPLAINED ANSWERS

Business Law & Professional Responsibilities (LPR)

FOUR-OPTION MULTIPLE-CHOICE QUESTIONS

Answer 1

1.   C   Rule 501 of the Code of Professional Conduct states that a CPA should not commit an act in his or her personal or professional life that discredits the profession. AICPA ethics Interpretation 501-1 requires the CPA to surrender working papers that constitute books and records upon request by the client, regardless of whether or not the fee is paid. A CPA <u>retaining</u> <u>client</u> <u>records</u> <u>after</u> <u>the</u> <u>client</u> <u>has</u> <u>demanded</u> <u>their</u> <u>return</u> most likely violates the profession's ethical standards.

   Answer choice "A" is incorrect because, when a CPA makes arrangements with a bank to collect notes issued by a client in payment of fees due, and so advises the client, no violation of any provision of the Code has occurred.

   Answer choice "B" is incorrect because the performance of bookkeeping services would not necessarily impair the CPA's independence if done by the CPA himself or herself. Similar functions performed by the CPA's spouse would also not necessarily constitute a violation of the Code. Furthermore, it should be noted that a CPA does not have to remain independent while performing compilation services.

   Answer choice "D" is incorrect because actuarial and administrative services performed in connection with employee benefit plans are proper functions of CPAs and are not incompatible with the practice of public accounting.

2.   A   A "profession" is distinguishable from other occupations because it has the following characteristics: (1) general and systematic knowledge, (2) orientation to community interests, (3) self monitoring via a code of ethics, and (4) recognition of excellent work and technical accomplishments. The statement that <u>a</u> <u>distinguishing</u> <u>mark</u> <u>of</u> <u>a</u> <u>profession</u> <u>is</u> <u>its</u> <u>acceptance</u> <u>of</u> <u>responsibility</u> <u>to</u> <u>the</u> <u>public</u> best explains why the CPA profession has found it essential to promulgate ethical standards and to establish means for ensuring their observance.

   Answer choice "B" is incorrect because no requirements exist for a group to qualify as a profession. Further, one of the characteristics of a profession is the orientation to the interests of the community, rather than to the primacy of responsibility to clients and colleagues.

Answer choices "C and "D" are incorrect because they are not recognized characteristics of a profession.

3.   A   When an accountant examines prospective financial statements, the accountant should:
1. Be independent.
2. Have adequate technical training and proficiency.
3. Adequately plan the engagement.
4. Adequately supervise the work of assistants, if any.
5. Obtain sufficient evidence to provide a reasonable basis for the examination report.

A standard report on an examination of a financial forecast may be issued only by an accountant who is independent of a client.

Answer choice "B" is incorrect because an accountant who issues a report on consulting services must maintain integrity and objectivity, but need not be independent of a client. The principle of objectivity imposes the obligation to be impartial, intellectually honest, and free of conflicts of interest, while independence precludes relationships that may appear to impair the accountant's objectivity in an attestation engagement.

Answer choices "C" and "D" are incorrect because an accountant may compile historical financial statements and prospective financial statements (including a financial projection) for a client even if the accountant lacks independence.

4.   B   Rule 101 of the Code of Professional Conduct provides that a CPA shall be independent in the performance of professional services rendered. Independence shall be considered impaired if the CPA (1) has a direct or material indirect financial interest in the client, (2) was a trustee of a trust, or an executor or an administrator of an estate having a direct or material indirect financial interest in the client, (3) has any joint or closely-held business investment with the client, or (4) has any loan to or from the client, with the exceptions of grandfathered or certain permitted loans.

An auditor would be considered independent where the auditor's checking account that is fully insured by a federal agency, is held at a client financial institution. The federal insurance eliminates the risk that the CPA might lose his/her money and thus eliminates the CPA's financial interest in the client.

Answer choice "A" is incorrect because the auditor would have an indirect financial interest in the client (i.e., receiving commissions from the stock transactions) and would, therefore, not be independent.

Answer choice "C" is incorrect because the auditor would be in the position of having extended a loan to the audit client and, therefore, would not be independent.

Answer choice "D" is incorrect because the auditor would have a material indirect financial interest in the client, since the client is the only tenant in the commercial building owned by the auditor; independence would be lacking.

5.   D   Consulting services employ the CPA's technical skills, education, observations, and experience. Consulting services consist of:
1. Consultations.
2. Advisory services.
3. Implementation services.
4. Transaction services.
5. Staff and other supporting services.
6. Product services.

In carrying out a consulting service for a client, a CPA may perform (1) <u>analysis of the client's accounting system</u> (i.e., an advisory service), (2) <u>review of the client's prepared business plan</u> (i.e., a consultation), and (3) <u>preparation of information for obtaining financing</u> (i.e., a transaction service).

Answer choices other than "D" are based on incorrect assumptions and/or combinations.

6.   D   A CPA who, after completing an audit, provides technical assistance to the same client for the purpose of implementing a new EDP system is engaged in providing consulting services. The AICPA's Statement on <u>Standards for Consulting Services</u> establishes guidelines for providing such nonaudit and nontax engagements.

Answer choices other than "D" are based on incorrect assumptions.

7.   B   When preparing a tax return, a CPA may, in good faith, rely on information furnished by the client or third parties. However, the CPA should make inquiries if the furnished information appears to be incorrect, incomplete, or inconsistent, either on its face or with other facts known to the CPA. A CPA preparing a client's tax return may rely on unsupported information furnished by the client, without examining underlying information, unless the information <u>appears to be incomplete on its face</u>.

Answer choices other than "B" are based on incorrect assumptions and/or interpretations of the CPA's responsibilities in tax practice.

8.   C   A CPA should not knowingly perform any act or prepare any tax return or related document that the CPA has reason to believe is false or misleading, or that the CPA does not have sufficient competence to handle. Further, a CPA should advise the client promptly upon learning of an error in a previously filed tax return, or of a client's failure to file a required return. However, a CPA will not incur an IRS penalty for <u>understating a client's tax liability as a result of an error in calculation</u>.

Answer choices other than "C" are incorrect because they represent acts by a CPA that will result in a CPA incurring an IRS penalty.

9.   B   Where a CPA engages in constructive fraud, the CPA will be liable to the client, third parties that the CPA knows to be relying on his or her work product, and to reasonably foreseeable third parties (i.e., parties belonging to a class of individuals whom the accountant could expect to rely on his or her report). An action for constructive fraud requires the plaintiff to prove the following elements:
1.   A material, false statement or omission.
2.   Made recklessly or in a grossly negligent manner.
3.   Justifiable reliance.
4.   Damages caused by the reliance.

If a CPA recklessly departs from the standards of due care when conducting an audit, the CPA will be liable to third parties who are unknown to the CPA based on <u>gross</u> <u>negligence</u>.

Answer choice "A" is incorrect because a CPA who is negligent when conducting an audit is not liable to third parties who are unknown to the CPA. The CPA is merely liable to the client and known third parties.

Answer choice "C" is incorrect because strict liability is not a legal theory which is applied to CPAs in the performance of audit services. Strict liability is normally only applied in product liability cases where the product is inherently dangerous.

Answer choice "D" is incorrect because criminal deceit in the conduct of an audit will not render a CPA liable to unknown third parties. Criminal deceit will render the CPA liable to the government for criminal prosecution.

10.   B   Working papers consist of notes, memoranda, audit plans, copies of client documents, and other miscellaneous materials compiled in connection with an engagement. Unless otherwise agreed, they are the property of the CPA, and need not be given to the client. A CPA may not disclose the contents of working papers unless the client consents, a court orders disclosure, or the disclosure is in accordance with AICPA or state society requirements. As a result of the confidential nature of the contents of the CPA's working papers, <u>working</u> <u>papers</u> <u>are</u> <u>not</u> <u>transferable</u> <u>to</u> <u>a</u> <u>purchaser</u> <u>of</u> <u>a</u> <u>CPA</u> <u>practice</u> <u>unless</u> <u>the</u> <u>client</u> <u>consents</u>.

Answer choice "A" is incorrect because a CPA firm's working papers may be obtained by a third party without the client's consent where the third party obtains a valid court order for the working papers.

Answer choice "C" is incorrect because the accountant-client privilege does not prevent third parties from gaining access to a CPA's working papers. The accountant-client privilege is not recognized by most jurisdictions, but where it is recognized, it authorizes the client to prevent the accountant from testifying in court regarding communications between the client and the CPA. Thus, the accountant-client privilege prevents certain testimony by the CPA from occurring in a court proceeding. In contrast, the CPA's ethical rules of confidentiality protect the contents of a CPA's working papers and prevent third-party access to such.

Answer choice "D" is incorrect because a CPA's working papers belong to the CPA, rather than to the CPA's client.

11.   D   The articles of incorporation are the basic governing document for a corporation. Under the Revised Model Business Corporation Act, the articles must include:
1.   Corporate name.
2.   The number of shares the corporation is authorized to issue.
3.   Name and address of each incorporator.
4.   The street address of the initial registered office, and the name of the initial registered agent at that office.

Answer choices other than "D" are based on incorrect assumptions and/or interpretations of the law.

12.   B   Corporate officers manage the corporation in its daily operations. Under the Revised Model Business Corporation Act, a corporation may indemnify a director or an officer who is made a party to a proceeding because of his or her corporate position against liability incurred in the proceeding if:
1.   The officer conducted himself or herself in good faith.
2.   The officer reasonably believed, in cases of conduct in his or her official capacity with the corporation, that the conduct was in the corporation's best interests and, in all other cases, that his or her conduct was at least not opposed to its best interests.
3.   In the case of any criminal proceeding, the officer had no reasonable cause to believe the conduct was unlawful.

Under the Revised Model Business Corporation Act, a corporation may be authorized to indemnify its officers for liability incurred in a suit by stockholders.

Answer choice "A" is incorrect because the Revised Model Business Corporation Act does permit the same individual to simultaneously hold more than one office in the corporation. Thus, an officer may simultaneously serve as a director.

Answer choice "C" is incorrect because the Revised Model Business Corporation Act allows a duly appointed officer to appoint one or more officers if authorized by the bylaws or the board of directors. Stockholders do not always have the right to elect a corporation's officers. However, it should be noted that, in most states, the board of directors is responsible for appointing corporate officers.

Answer choice "D" is incorrect because the Revised Model Business Corporation Act does not require that an officer own at least one share of the corporation's stock. Stock ownership is optional for a corporate officer.

13. C   Preferred stock normally has contractually superior rights with regard to dividends, assets upon liquidation, or both. These special rights must be expressed in the articles of incorporation. A holder of a public corporation's cumulative preferred stock is always entitled to <u>dividend</u> <u>carryovers</u> <u>from</u> <u>years</u> <u>in</u> <u>which</u> <u>dividends</u> <u>were</u> <u>not</u> <u>paid,</u> <u>to</u> <u>future</u> <u>years</u>.

Answer choice "A" is incorrect because a holder of a public corporation's cumulative preferred stock would not always be entitled to conversion of the preferred stock into common stock. The special rights, if any, of preferred stock must be expressed in the articles of incorporation.

Answer choice "B" is incorrect because a holder of a public corporation's cumulative preferred stock would not always be entitled to voting rights. The Revised Model Business Corporation Act requires that the articles of incorporation authorize at least one class of stock with unlimited voting rights. The Act also permits the authorization of classes of stock without voting rights.

Answer choice "D" is incorrect because a holder of a public corporation's cumulative preferred stock would not always be entitled to guaranteed dividends. The board of directors determines whether, and in what amount, to declare a dividend. All states restrict the funds from which a dividend may be paid and prohibit the payment of dividends that would render the corporation insolvent.

14. C   A merger occurs when one corporation absorbs another corporation, such that the survivor corporation holds title to their combined assets and is liable for the absorbed corporation's debts. Under the Revised Model Business Corporation Act, a merger of two public corporations requires:
1. Approval of a formal plan of merger by the board of directors of each corporation.
2. Approval of the holders of a majority of the shares of stock of each corporation entitled to vote.
3. Granting of an appraisal remedy to dissenting shareholders.
4. Filing of articles of merger with the Secretary of State of the state in which the surviving corporation was chartered.

The merger is effective when the articles of merger are filed.

The Revised Model Business Corporation Act does not require <u>receipt</u> <u>of</u> <u>voting</u> <u>stock</u> <u>by</u> <u>all</u> <u>stockholders</u> <u>of</u> <u>the</u> <u>original</u> <u>corporations</u>.

Answer choices other than "C" are based on incorrect assumptions and/or interpretations of the law.

15. A   An express trust exists where the creator's intent to create a trust is evidenced by a written document, an oral statement by the creator, or the conduct of the creator. The elements of a valid express trust are:
1. A creator, trustee and beneficiary.
2. A corpus.
3. A lawful purpose.
4. Legal capacity of the creator.
5. Transfer of the trust corpus with intent to create a trust.

A <u>successor</u> <u>trustee</u> is not necessary for the creation of an express trust.

Answer choices other than "A" are based on incorrect assumptions and/or interpretations of the law.

16. C   A trustee is bound to allocate trust revenues and expenditures between income and principal. Where the trust agreement does not specify how such items are to be allocated, the Uniform Principal and Income Act provides that changes in the form of the trust property and extraordinary expenses are chargeable against the trust principal, while proceeds from the use of the trust property and ordinary expenses are chargeable against trust income.

<u>Sidewalk</u> <u>assessments</u> resulting from a trust's ownership of commercial real estate should be allocated to the trust's principal because they constitute extraordinary expenses.

Answer choices other than "C" are based on incorrect assumptions and/or interpretations of the law.

17. C   A trustee's powers are express if they are granted in the trust agreement, by statute, or by a court decree. The trustee's powers are implied if they are not express but are necessary or convenient to the accomplishment of the trust purpose. A trustee has a statutory duty to manage the trust as a reasonably prudent investor by balancing the desire for a steady flow of income with the desire for the safety of the principal. In a written trust containing no specific powers, the trustee will not have the implied power to <u>accumulate</u> <u>income</u>.

Answer choices other than "C" are based on incorrect assumptions and/or interpretations of the law.

18. A   A trustee is a fiduciary who owes duties to both the trust beneficiaries and the trust creditors. The duty of loyalty is owed by the trustee to the beneficiaries and requires the trustee to act exclusively in the interests of the beneficiaries. Thus, a trustee will violate the <u>duty</u> <u>of</u> <u>loyalty</u> by borrowing money from the trust because such a loan creates a conflict of interest for the trustee. As a lender, the trustee should charge the highest rate of interest the market will bear. However, as a borrower, the trustee should seek out the lowest interest rate the market will provide.

Answer choice "B" is incorrect because the duty to properly account requires the trustee to keep accurate and thorough records and would not necessarily be violated by the trustee borrowing money from the trust.

Answer choice "C" is incorrect because the duty to safeguard the trust res (i.e., corpus) is part of the trustee's duty to manage and invest the trust assets with the care of a reasonably prudent investor. This duty would not necessarily be violated by the trustee borrowing money from the trust.

Answer choice "D" is incorrect because the duty to properly manage the trust refers to the trustee's duty to carry out the trust according to the terms of the trust agreement and to do so with reasonable skill, prudence, and diligence. This duty would not necessarily be violated by the trustee borrowing money from the trust.

19.   C   A trust will terminate upon the happening of one of the following events:
1. Merger of equitable and legal title of the trust corpus.
2. Revocation of the trust corpus by the creator.
3. Failure of the trust purpose.
4. Achievement of the trust purpose or expiration of the trust term.

This trust will automatically end on the death of Hardy. Per the terms of the trust agreement, both legal and equitable title in the trust corpus will merge with King upon Hardy's death, thereby terminating the trust.

Answer choices other than "C" are based on incorrect assumptions and/or interpretations of the law.

20.   B   A spendthrift trust is used where the creator is concerned that the beneficiary may squander the right to future income from the trust by attempting to transfer the income to third parties, such as creditors. The spendthrift trust includes a provision that prohibits the beneficiary from transferring the right to future payments of income or principal.

A spendthrift trust will terminate upon the happening of one of the following events:
1. Merger of equitable and legal title of the trust corpus.
2. Revocation of the trust corpus by the creator.
3. Failure of the trust purpose.
4. Achievement of the trust purpose or expiration of the trust term.

An irrevocable spendthrift trust established for a period of five years will terminate when the <u>income beneficiaries die</u> because of a failure of the trust purpose (i.e., it is no longer possible to pay the trust income to the spendthrift trust's beneficiaries for the remainder of the five-year trust term).

Answer choice "A" is incorrect because the death of the grantor of the trust corpus does not terminate the trust. (The grantor of a trust is also known as the creator of the trust.)

Answer choice "C" is incorrect because the grantor of a trust may not unilaterally terminate a trust that is irrevocable.

Answer choice "D" is incorrect because most courts will not terminate a trust as long as any of its purposes remain unfulfilled. This is true even where all the income beneficiaries agree to and request the trust's termination.

21. A   A fraudulent conveyance is a transfer of property by a debtor to a third party, in an attempt to defraud the debtor's creditors, which makes the property unavailable to the debtor's creditors. Fraudulent conveyances are voidable at the option of the debtor's creditors. A debtor remaining in possession after conveyance, a secret conveyance, and/or a debtor retaining an equitable benefit in the property conveyed will be considered indications of fraudulent conveyance.

Answer choices other than "A" are based on incorrect assumptions and/or interpretations of the law.

22. D   Most states exempt certain real and personal property from the claims of creditors seeking to enforce a judgment against the debtor. A homestead exemption permits a debtor to retain his or her residence in its entirety, or at least to retain up to a specified dollar amount of the equity in the residence. However, certain debts are not subject to the debtor's homestead exemption, including tax liens, liens for labor and/or materials to improve the premises, and obligations contracted to purchase the premises. A homestead exemption will not apply to either a valid home mortgage lien or a valid IRS Tax lien.

Answer choices other than "D" are based on incorrect assumptions and/or interpretations of the law.

23. D   A writ of garnishment is a postjudgment remedy that directs the garnishee (often the debtor's employer) to take specified action against property belonging to the debtor, but that is in the possession of the garnishee (often to pay some portion of the debtor's wages to a creditor). A writ of garnishment will allow a creditor to collect money from a debtor's wages.

Answer choice "A" is incorrect because a debtor may not be arrested to assist a creditor in forcing a debtor to honor his or her debt.

Answer choice "B" is incorrect because a mechanic's lien is a remedy that provides a lien for a contractor or laborer who has provided services and/or materials for the improvement of real property. The lien is against the improved real property and not the debtor's wages. Thus, a mechanic's lien would not allow a creditor to collect money from a debtor's wages.

Answer choice "C" is incorrect because receivership is an equitable remedy that will not be granted where an adequate legal remedy exits. Legal remedies exist to allow a creditor to collect money from the debtor's wages; thus, receivership is not available.

24.   B   When a party contracts to guaranty the collection of the debts of another, the guarantor's liability is secondary. This means that the guarantor is liable only if the debtor defaults, and the creditor has attempted unsuccessfully to collect the debt from the debtor. A contract to guaranty the collection of a debt is otherwise the same as a surety contract. Like a surety contract, <u>the guaranty must be in writing</u>, as indicated by the Statute of Frauds.

Answer choice "A" is incorrect because the liability of a guaranty of collection is secondary. This means that the creditor must first attempt to collect from the debtor and, if unsuccessful, may then proceed against the guarantor.

Answer choice "C" is incorrect because some defenses that are available to the debtor are not available to the guarantor (i.e., debtor's minority or insanity).

Answer choice "D" is incorrect because a guarantor of collection is not required to notify the creditor of the debtor's default. The creditor is in a better position, relatively, to know that the debtor has defaulted and the creditor is expected to be vigilant to protect his or her interests.

25.   B   A noncompensated surety is a party who acts as a surety for the debt of another without compensation, while a compensated surety assumes the surety obligation in return for compensation. The liability of a noncompensated and a compensated surety is basically the same. A surety is released from liability to the creditor as a result of any of the following:
1.   Most ordinary contract defenses (i.e., failure of consideration, mutual mistake, undue influence, fraud by the creditor; but not fraud by the debtor against the surety or the minority, bankruptcy, insolvency, or death of the debtor).
2.   The creditor's failure to inform the surety of a material increase in risk.
3.   Material modification of the original contract without the consent of the surety.
4.   Release of the debtor by the creditor without the consent of the surety and without a reservation of the creditor's rights against the surety.
5.   Release of collateral or a co-surety by the creditor without the consent of the surety.

<u>Modification by the principal debtor and creditor of their contract that materially increases the surety's risk of loss</u> will release a noncompensated surety from liability.

Answer choice "A" is incorrect because the release of the principal debtor's obligation by the creditor with the reservation of the creditor's rights against the surety does not deprive the surety of his or her rights to seek reimbursement from the debtor. As a result, the surety does not lose any legal protection and therefore is not entitled to a release.

Answer choice "C" is incorrect because the filing of an involuntary petition in bankruptcy against the principal debtor will result in a release of the debtor only. While, in general, the surety is released from liability by the contractual defenses that result in a release of the debtor, some ordinary contract defenses that release the debtor do not also release the surety. The death or incapacity of the debtor, minority of the debtor, and bankruptcy or insolvency of the debtor do not provide a basis for release of the surety. Instead, these defenses provide a basis for release of the debtor only.

Answer choice "D" is incorrect because the insanity or other lack of capacity of the principal debtor at the time the contract was entered into with the creditor does not result in a release from liability for the surety. This is another example of an ordinary contract defense of the debtor, which results in a release of the debtor only.

26. A An employer may deduct social security and medicare taxes actually paid to the IRS. Where Syl, an employer, fails to withhold the employees' portion of FICA taxes, and subsequently voluntarily pays the entire FICA tax for its share and the amounts that it could have withheld from the employees, the employees' share of the FICA taxes paid to the IRS is <u>deductible</u> <u>by</u> <u>Syl</u> <u>as</u> <u>additional</u> <u>compensation</u> <u>that</u> <u>is</u> <u>included</u> <u>in</u> <u>the</u> <u>employees'</u> <u>taxable</u> <u>income</u>.

Answer choice "B" is incorrect because the employees' share of the FICA taxes paid by Syl was an ordinary and necessary business expense and therefore meets the deductibility requirements of the IRS for business expenses. An employer must pay FICA taxes to the IRS whether or not the employer withholds the employees' portion.

Answer choice "C" is incorrect because Syl's payment of the employees' share of the FICA taxes will not be considered a nontaxable gift, regardless of the annual amount paid per employee.

Answer choice "D" is incorrect because the employer paid the FICA taxes in a timely manner. It should be noted that the employer has an equitable right to reimbursement by the employees for their share of the FICA taxes that the employer paid for the employees.

27. B The federal Occupational Safety and Health Act (OSHA) imposes a general duty on employers to provide a workplace "free from recognized hazards that are causing or are likely to cause death or serious physical harm" to employees. Liability exists only where the employer actually knew or should have known of the danger. The Act

Solutions and Explained Answers/LPR *439*

applies to virtually all private employers, but exempts federal, state, and local governments, as well as certain regulated industries such as railroads and coal mining.

In order to encourage employees to report workplace hazards, <u>OSHA prohibits an employer from discharging an employee for revealing OSHA violations</u> to the Department of Labor, which is the federal agency authorized to administer and enforce the act.

Answer choice "A" is incorrect because OSHA does not require an employer to provide employees a workplace free from risk, but only a workplace that is "free from recognized hazards that are causing or are likely to cause death or serious physical harm" to employees. OSHA does not require an employer to provide a workplace that is free from unknown risks, free from risks unlikely to cause death, or free from risks that are inconsequential.

Answer choice "C" is incorrect because OSHA inspections are subject to constitutional safeguards. When an employer objects to an inspection of its workplace, OSHA must obtain a search warrant based upon probable cause before it may engage in an inspection.

Answer choice "D" is incorrect because OSHA does not preempt state regulation of workplace safety. Instead, OSHA establishes minimum workplace standards and permits states to enact more stringent standards.

28. B Title VII of the 1964 Civil Rights Act prohibits employers from discriminating against employees on the basis of race, color, religion, gender, or national origin. The act <u>does not prohibit discrimination based upon age</u>. The federal Age Discrimination in Employment Act prohibits employers from discriminating against employees solely on the basis of age.

Answer choices other than "B" are based on incorrect assumptions and/or interpretations of the law.

29. A The Fair Labor Standards Act (FLSA) establishes minimum wage, overtime pay, and child labor standards. Congress has gradually removed exemptions from the Act and broadened its coverage. Some workers are exempt from both the minimum wage and the overtime requirements of the Act, including outside sales personnel, and administrative, executive, and professional employees. In addition, <u>some workers may be included within the minimum wage provisions but exempt from the overtime provisions</u>. Examples include taxi drivers, news editors, farmers, and employees of railroads and airlines.

Answer choice "B" is incorrect because there are no workers included within the FLSA's overtime provisions who are also exempt from the minimum wage provisions.

Answer choice "C" is incorrect because some categories of workers are exempt from the Fair Labor Standards Act's minimum wage provisions and some groups of workers are exempt from its overtime provisions. Thus, not all workers are required to be included within both provisions.

Answer choice "D" is incorrect because no exemptions from the minimum wage and the overtime provisions of the Fair Labor Standards Act exist for union contracts.

30.   D   The Comprehensive Omnibus Budget Reconciliation Act of 1985 (COBRA) was an amendment to the Employee Retirement and Income Security Act (ERISA) and requires employers with twenty or more employees to permit employees terminated from their jobs, other than for misconduct, to continue their group health insurance coverage for at least 18 and no more than 36 months following termination of employment. The terminated employee must pay his or her insurance premiums.

The Act also extends protection to qualified dependents, such as a spouse or dependent child who was covered by the plan on the day before termination.

The Act was subsequently amended to provide coverage to employees who become disabled.

When an employee voluntarily resigns from a job, the former employee's group health insurance coverage that was in effect during the period of employment with the company may be retained for the former employee and spouse at the former employee's expense for at least 18 months after leaving the company.

Answer choice "A" is incorrect because, under the Act, an employee's group health insurance coverage does not automatically cease if the employee resigns before normal retirement age. The Act provides employees who resign before normal retirement age the option to continue, at their own expense, group health insurance for themselves and qualified dependents for at least 18 months but no more than 36 months.

Answer choice "B" is incorrect because, under the Act, an employee's group health insurance coverage does not automatically cease if the employee voluntarily resigns, nor does the group health coverage automatically continue for such an employee's spouse. The Act provides such employees the option to continue, at their own expense, group health insurance for themselves and for qualified dependents, such as a spouse, for at least 18 months but no more than 36 months.

Answer choice "C" is incorrect because the Act does not require that the group health insurance coverage of the spouse of a former employee be terminated. The Act provides that the former employee, as well as his or her qualified dependents, must be provided with the option to continue, at their own expense, group health insurance coverage for at least 18 months but no more than 36 months.

31.   A   The Securities Act of 1933 requires that all new issues of securities to be sold in interstate commerce must be registered with the Securities and Exchange Commission (SEC) before sale, unless an exemption applies. The registration statement filed with the SEC consists of two parts: (1) part one is the prospectus that must be given to each purchaser, either before or concurrently with the sale, and (2) part two must contain accurate, detailed information about the issuer, including certified financial statements, a description of the significant provisions of the securities being offered for sale and their relationship to the issuer's other securities, the principal purposes for which the offerings' proceeds will be used, the issuer's business, and the issuer's management. Thus, <u>the prospectus is a part of the registration statement</u>.

Answer choice "B" is incorrect because the SEC does not rule on the merits of registered securities. The SEC merely certifies that the information required by law has been provided for prospective securities purchasers.

Answer choice "C" is incorrect because the registration statement, including the prospectus, must be filed before, rather than after, an offer to sell the securities has been made. Before filing the registration statement, it is illegal to sell, offer to sell, or to buy securities, but the issuer may give notice of its intent to publicly offer the securities. After the registration statement has been filed, but before it is effective, the issuer may make oral offers to sell the securities and may publicize the pending availability of the securities by means of a preliminary prospectus (called a "red herring" prospectus because it contains a statement in red ink to the effect that the registration statement has not yet become effective), and/or a "tombstone ad" (a notice that is customarily surrounded by black borders).

Answer choice "D" is incorrect because the SEC does not approve the accuracy of the information contained in the registration statement nor does it evaluate the merits of the securities. Also, the registration statement, including the prospectus, becomes public information immediately upon filing with the SEC.

32.   D   After the registration statement has been filed with the SEC, but before it is effective, the issuer may publicize the pending availability of the securities by means of a preliminary prospectus known as a <u>"red-herring" prospectus</u>. This document contains information substantially similar to the information in the final prospectus but must contain a legend in red ink stating that the registration statement has not yet become effective.

Answer choices other than "D" are based on incorrect assumptions and/or interpretations of the law.

33. D   After a registration statement has been filed with the SEC, but before it becomes effective, the issuer may publicize the pending availability of the securities by means of a tombstone advertisement. This advertisement identifies the security, its price, the party to whom orders should be sent, and <u>makes</u> <u>known</u> <u>the</u> <u>availability</u> <u>of</u> a <u>prospectus</u>.

Answer choice "A" is incorrect because a tombstone advertisement may not be substituted for a prospectus under any circumstances.

Answer choice "B" is incorrect because a tombstone advertisement may not offer to sell the securities but may merely identify the security, its price, the party to whom orders should be sent, and make known the availability of a prospectus.

Answer choice "C" is incorrect because a tombstone advertisement does not notify prospective investors that a previously offered security has been withdrawn from the market. Instead, it notifies prospective investors of the pending availability of a new security or issuance thereof.

34. B   The Securities Exchange Act of 1934 imposes registration and reporting requirements on all publicly-held companies. A company is considered publicly-held if:
1. A class of its securities is listed on a national exchange, or
2. It has at least 500 shareholders and at least $5 million in assets.

<u>Shares</u> <u>listed</u> <u>on</u> <u>a</u> <u>national</u> <u>securities</u> <u>exchange</u>, by itself, require a corporation to comply with the reporting requirements of the Securities Exchange Act of 1934.

Answer choice "A" is incorrect because the number of employees of a corporation is not controlling as to whether a corporation must comply with the reporting requirements of the Securities Exchange Act of 1934.

Answer choice "C" is incorrect because total assets alone are not controlling as to whether a corporation must comply with the reporting requirements of the Securities Exchange Act of 1934.

Answer choice "D" is incorrect because the number of holders of equity securities alone is not controlling as to whether a corporation must comply with the reporting requirements of the Securities Exchange Act of 1934.

35. A   The Securities Exchange Act of 1934 requires reporting companies to make significant disclosures to the SEC in order to preserve the integrity of the securities markets. The required disclosures include:
1. A disclosure statement to both the SEC and to the target company where a person or group acquires or makes a tender offer for a 5 percent or more interest in a reporting company.

2. A report by each insider (i.e., director, officer, or owner of 10 percent or more, of an equity security) for any month during which changes in ownership of equity securities of the issuer occurred. This report helps the SEC to monitor insider trading.
3. Preliminary copies of proposed proxy statements at least 10 days before the statements are to be distributed to shareholders of a reporting company.

The reporting provisions of the Securities Exchange Act of 1934 require that <u>tender offers</u>, <u>insider trading</u>, <u>and soliciting proxies</u> be reported to the SEC.

Answer choices other than "A" are based on incorrect assumptions and/or interpretations of the law.

36. C The SEC has attempted to integrate the disclosure requirements of the Securities Exchange Act of 1934 with the registration requirements of the Securities Act of 1933. Thus, where a public issuer of securities has made a registered offering under the Securities Act of 1933, <u>the issuer must file an annual report (Form 10-K) with the SEC</u>. This requirement reduces the redundancy and overlap that can exist when separate disclosures are made under the Securities Act of 1933 and the Securities Exchange Act of 1934.

Answer choice "A" is incorrect because a public issuer of securities who has made a registered offering under the Securities Act of 1933 is not required to distribute an annual report to its stockholders. It is required to file annual (Form 10-K), quarterly (Form 10-Q), and periodic (Form 8-K) reports with the SEC with respect to any security registered under the Securities Act of 1933.

Answer choice "B" is incorrect because the Securities Exchange Act of 1934, rather than the Securities Act of 1933, regulates the proxy solicitation process.

Answer choice "D" is incorrect because a public issuer of securities who has made a registered offering is required to file a quarterly report (Form 10-Q), whether or not a material event occurs.

37. B Regulation A does not provide a complete exemption from the registration requirements of the Securities Act of 1933. Instead, Regulation A provides an appropriate registration process for offerings of up to $1.5 million that are completed within a 12-month period. Under Regulation A, an offering circular may be substituted for a full prospectus, and audited financial statements are not required. <u>All offerings made under Regulation A</u> will be exempt from the full registration requirements of the Securities Act of 1933.

Answer choice "A" is incorrect because the intrastate offerings exemption is interpreted narrowly and only applies where all offerees and securities purchasers are residents of the state in which the issuer derives 80 percent of its earnings. Therefore, intrastate offerings in states where the issuer derives less than 80 percent of its earnings are not exempt from registration. All intrastate offerings will not be exempt from full registration under the Securities Act of 1933.

Answer choice "C" is incorrect because securities purchased under a Regulation D offering are "restricted securities" that may not be resold for two years unless they are first registered with the SEC. Some resales of securities purchased under Regulation D will not be exempt from the full registration requirements of the Securities Act of 1933 (i.e., those resales held for less than two years).

Answer choice "D" is incorrect because resales within two years of purchase of restricted securities purchased under Regulation D, and unrestricted sales by parties under control of the issuer, must be registered with the SEC. A stockbroker may be under the control of the issuer and, thus, any stockbroker transaction will not be exempt from the full registration requirements of the Securities Act of 1933. The only exempt stockbroker transactions are those by stockbrokers who are not under the direct or indirect control of the issuer of the involved securities.

38. D A security under the Securities Exchange Act of 1934 is defined broadly to include not only traditional investment mechanisms, such as stocks and bonds, but to include any investment of money involving the receipt of an ownership interest in a common enterprise, the aim of which is a return on investment primarily through the managerial efforts of others. <u>Certificates</u> <u>of</u> <u>deposit</u> are excluded from the definition of "securities."

Answer choices other than "D" are based on incorrect assumptions and/or interpretations of the law.

39. A Section 10b and Rule 10b-5 condemn any device, scheme, or artifice to defraud by using the mail or other instrument of interstate commerce for the purchase or sale of a security. This section is applied broadly and applies whether or not the traded securities were exempt from registration under the Securities Act of 1933. Thus, where securities are exempt from the registration provisions of the Securities Act of 1933, any fraud committed in the course of selling such securities <u>can</u> <u>be</u> <u>challenged</u> <u>by</u> the <u>SEC</u> and the <u>person</u> <u>defrauded</u>. The SEC can bring a criminal action, and the person defrauded can bring a civil action for damages.

Answer choices other than "A" are based on incorrect assumptions and/or interpretations of the law.

40. B Regulation D of the Securities Act of 1933 provides an exemption from registration. In general, Regulation D requires (1) a private placement, (2) reporting of the first sale of any unregistered securities to the SEC within 15 days, and (3) completion of the sale within a 12-month period. However, all purchases of securities issued under Regulation D result in "restricted securities." Since the securities issued under the Regulation D exemption were never

registered, they may not be resold for at least two years. Earlier resales must be registered with the SEC. Securities issued under Regulation D <u>cannot</u> <u>be</u> <u>the</u> <u>subject</u> <u>of</u> <u>an</u> <u>immediate</u> <u>unregistered</u> <u>reoffering</u> <u>to</u> <u>the</u> <u>public</u>.

Answer choice "A" is incorrect because Regulation D permits the sale of an unregistered offering over a period of as long as 12 months.

Answer choice "C" is incorrect because Regulation D permits, but does not require that, the unregistered securities be sold to accredited institutional investors.

Answer choice "D" is incorrect because no version of Regulation D (i.e., Rules 504, 505, or 506) requires that the unregistered securities be sold to fewer than 20 nonaccredited investors. Rule 504 permits the unregistered securities to be sold to an unlimited number of investors, whether accredited or nonaccredited, while Rules 505 and 506 permit the unregistered securities to be sold to up to 35 nonaccredited investors.

41. D   The Uniform Commercial Code (UCC) Sales Article (i.e., Article 2) recognizes the existence of a contract, despite missing terms, if a reasonable basis exists for granting a remedy in case of a breach of contract. Accordingly, a contract for the sale of goods may exist even though one or more terms have been omitted, and various sections of Article 2 act as "gap fillers" to supply missing terms. However, an <u>open</u> <u>acceptance</u> will prevent the formation of an enforceable sale of goods contract.

Answer choice "A" is incorrect because an enforceable sale of goods contract will not be prevented by an open price term. Where the price term is open, Article 2 mandates a reasonable price at the time of delivery.

Answer choice "B" is incorrect because an enforceable sale of goods contract will not be prevented by an open delivery term. Where the term for delivery is open, Article 2 mandates that the place of delivery shall be the seller's place of business.

Answer choice "C" is incorrect because an enforceable sale of goods contract will not always be prevented by an open quantity term. Output and requirements contracts do not specify an exact quantity of goods, yet Article 2 recognizes both as enforceable, with the quantity based on the good faith of the parties.

42. A   The Uniform Commercial Code (UCC) Sales Article governs contracts for the sale of goods. Goods are defined as tangible personal property. The UCC Sales Article contains numerous provisions that hold a merchant of specific goods to a different standard than a non-merchant of those same goods. A merchant is defined as a party who regularly deals in goods of the kind called for in the contract at hand. In a contract involving a merchant seller and a non-merchant buyer, <u>whether</u> <u>the</u> <u>UCC</u> <u>Sales</u> <u>Article</u> <u>is</u> <u>applicable</u> <u>does</u> <u>not</u>

depend <u>on the price of the goods involved</u>, but depends on whether or not the subject matter of the contract is goods or something else.

Answer choice "B" is incorrect because the UCC Sales Article imposes an obligation to perform in good faith on both the seller and the buyer in all contracts for the sale of goods.

Answer choice "C" is incorrect because whether a contract is a sale or return or sale on approval is not determined by the status of the seller and buyer as either a merchant or non-merchant. A sale or return is a trial sale of goods where the goods are delivered primarily for resale by the buyer. In contrast, a sale on approval is a type of trial sale where the goods are delivered primarily for the buyer's use. Whether or not a contract is a sale on approval or a sale or return depends on the primary purpose for which the goods were delivered by the seller to the buyer, rather than the status of the seller and buyer as merchants or non-merchants.

Answer choice "D" is incorrect because under the UCC Sales Article, a contract between a merchant seller and a non-merchant buyer may involve the sale of personal property with a price of $500 or more.

43. A   In general, all implied warranties may be excluded by the seller as long as the disclaimer is set forth in clear, conspicuous language. The implied warranties of merchantability and fitness for a particular purpose may be disclaimed by expressions such as "as is," "with all faults," or other language that calls the buyer's attention to the fact that the seller is providing no guarantees of quality for the goods. However, the implied warranty of title may only be disclaimed by specific language or circumstances that give the buyer reason to know that the person selling the goods does not claim title and that he or she is purporting to sell only such right or title as he or she has. A statement disclaiming "any and all warranties" does not give the buyer reason to know that the seller does not claim title. <u>Vick</u> is likely to prevail against Ocean <u>because the implied warranty of title has been breached</u>. (Note: The implied warranty of title and the implied warranty against encumbrances are often merged and treated as a single implied warranty of title and against encumbrances.)

Answer choice "B" is incorrect because a merchant is able to disclaim implied warranties. The status of merchant or non-merchant is not relevant in determining whether or not a seller can disclaim a particular implied warranty.

Answer choice "C" is incorrect because the language of this disclaimer is not sufficient to give the buyer reason to know that Ocean does not claim ownership of the used boat; Ocean will not prevail in this lawsuit against Vick.

Answer choice "D" is incorrect because Vick did not forgo the right to sue Ocean for breach of the implied warranty of title by surrendering the boat to Kidd when confronted with proof that the boat was stolen from Kidd.

44.   D   Under the UCC Sales Article, a contract, or part thereof, which is unconscionable (i.e., grossly unfair) is unenforceable. A disclaimer of liability for personal injury in a contract for the sale of consumer goods has been held unconscionable and, thus, unenforceable by the courts. Larch <u>will be liable because liability for personal injury cannot be disclaimed</u>. (Note that such a disclaimer in a contract involving commercial goods would not be considered unconscionable.)

Answer choice "A" is incorrect because the UCC warranty provisions have abandoned the privity requirement and have extended the right to sue to third parties who are members of the buyer's family or household and even to guests in the buyer's home, if it is reasonable to expect that such persons may use, consume, or be affected by the goods and who are personally injured by the breach of warranty.

Answer choice "B" is incorrect because Larch was notified within a reasonable time after the stove exploded and the breach of warranty occurred. Accordingly, there was no failure to give Larch, the seller of the stove, proper notice of the injuries to Oak's spouse.

Answer choice "C" is incorrect because liability for personal injury cannot be disclaimed. Such disclaimers are unconscionable and unenforceable.

45.   D   The term "F.O.B." is a shipping term that determines the seller's obligations to physically deliver goods by utilizing a common carrier. Where the term is F.O.B. point of shipment, the risk of loss and title to the goods pass from the seller to the buyer upon delivery of the goods to the common carrier. Where the term is F.O.B. point of destination, the risk of loss and title to the goods pass from the seller to the buyer upon tender of the goods at the agreed destination. In this question, the F.O.B. term is point of shipment since the seller has agreed to deliver the typewriters to the common carrier at the seller's loading dock. Thus, <u>Quick</u> bears the risk of loss for the typewriters during shipment <u>because the risk of loss passes when the typewriters are delivered to the carrier</u>.

Answer choice "A" is incorrect because the risk of loss passes when the typewriters are delivered to the carrier, rather than when Quick receives the typewriters.

Answer choice "B" is incorrect because the F.O.B. term determines when the risk of loss passes from the seller to the buyer; their status as merchants is not determinative of when risk of losses passes.

Answer choice "C" is incorrect because risk of loss under the UCC passes independently of title. Thus, the timing of the passage of title is not necessarily determinative of the timing for passage of risk of loss. In this question, title passed to Quick at the time the typewriters were delivered to the carrier, rather than when they were shipped.

46. A   The Statute of Frauds requires written evidence for certain contracts to be enforceable. The UCC Statute of Frauds provision requires contracts for the sale of goods to be evidenced by a writing where the contract price of the goods is $500 or more. The UCC recognizes certain exceptions to this rule. If a merchant seller and a merchant buyer orally agree to a contract for the sale of goods for a price of $500 or more, either party may satisfy the Statute of Frauds requirement by sending, within a reasonable time, a signed, written confirmation of the terms of the oral contract to the other party. If that other party does not object either to the confirmation itself or to the express terms of the confirmation within ten days after it was received, the Statute of Frauds may not be successfully raised against a suit to enforce the contract per the terms of the written confirmation.

Here, Webstar's claim that the purchase order did not satisfy the UCC Statute of Frauds because it was not signed by Webstar is <u>incorrect</u>, <u>because</u> <u>it</u> <u>failed</u> <u>to</u> <u>object</u> <u>to</u> <u>Northco's</u> <u>purchase</u> <u>order</u>. The merchant's confirmation provision permits either party to sign the written confirmation and then to enforce such against the other party. Thus, this provision deviates from the normal rule that the writing that satisfies the Statute of Frauds must be signed by the party against whom enforcement of the contract is sought.

Answer choice "B" is incorrect because the party who must sign a contract for the sale of goods is the party against whom enforcement of the contract is sought. That could be either the buyer or the seller. The UCC does not provide that only the buyer must sign the contract in a sale-of-goods transaction.

Answer choice "C" is incorrect because the merchant's confirmation rule specifies that either party may sign and send a written confirmation of an oral contract between two merchants. This rule deviates from the normal rule that the writing must be signed by the party against whom enforcement is sought. A written confirmation between merchants may be enforceable against a party, such as Webstar, who did not sign the written confirmation.

Answer choice "D" is incorrect because a signed writing did exist to satisfy the Statute of Frauds. The Statute of Frauds requires a signed writing for all contracts involving the sale of goods where the contract price is $500 or more. This writing is valid and enforceable, despite the fact it was developed and executed after the contract was orally agreed upon and was signed by Northco rather than Webstar.

47. B   The UCC does not address the issue of punitive damages. Where the UCC is silent on an issue, it is supplemented by the relevant principles of law and equity established by the courts. The courts do not grant punitive damages in breach of contract cases. This is

true despite the fact that a breach may have been intentional and/or malicious. A buyer would not have the remedy of a <u>suit</u> <u>for</u> <u>punitive</u> <u>damages</u> when a seller fails to transfer and deliver goods identified to the contract.

Answer choices other than "B" are based on incorrect assumptions and/or interpretations of the law.

48. C   Attachment occurs when all three of the following have taken place:
1. Secured party has possession of the collateral pursuant to an agreement with the debtor, or the debtor has signed a security agreement describing the collateral.
2. Creditor gives value.
3. Debtor has property rights in the collateral.

<u>Failure</u> <u>of</u> <u>the</u> <u>debtor</u> <u>to</u> <u>have</u> <u>rights</u> <u>in</u> <u>the</u> <u>collateral</u> will always prevent a security interest from attaching.

Answer choice "A" is incorrect because attachment may occur without a written security agreement. This may occur where the secured party has possession of the collateral pursuant to a verbal security agreement with the debtor.

Answer choice "B" is incorrect because the creditor need not have possession of the collateral for attachment to occur. Attachment may occur where the debtor retains possession of the collateral but has provided the creditor with a signed security agreement describing the collateral.

Answer choice "D" is incorrect because attachment may occur where the creditor has given value but has not presented consideration for the security interest. Value differs from consideration, in that value is broader and includes the taking of property as security for a preexisting claim. Thus, under the UCC's Secured Transactions Article, the value necessary for attachment need not be exchanged simultaneously (i.e., presently) in return for the security interest from the debtor.

49. A   A security agreement may provide that collateral, whenever acquired, shall secure all obligations secured by the security agreement. Thus, the debtor and creditor may agree to the creation of a floating lien by means of an after-acquired property clause. <u>Both</u> <u>inventory</u> <u>and</u> <u>equipment</u> are types of after-acquired property that may be attached to a security agreement given to a secured lender.

Answer choices other than "A" are based on incorrect assumptions and/or interpretations of the law.

50. B   Perfection is the process whereby a creditor establishes the priority of his or her claim against a debtor's property. Perfection may be accomplished by:
1. Filing a financing statement.
2. Taking possession of the collateral.

3. Attachment of the security interest (without filing) where the secured party has a purchase money security interest in consumer goods.

Since taking possession of negotiable instruments is the only acceptable method for perfection of negotiable instruments, then taking possession of the instrument will best perfect a security interest in a negotiable instrument against any other party.

Answer choices other than "B" are based on incorrect assumptions and/or interpretations of the law.

51. C   As against subsequent creditors and most other third parties, a secured party who has perfected his or her security interest will be protected against the claims of most other parties. However, a buyer in the ordinary course of business takes free of a security interest created by his or her seller even though the security interest was perfected and the buyer knew of its existence. A buyer in the ordinary course of business is a person who buys in good faith and without knowledge that the sale is in violation of a security interest. This situation commonly occurs where inventory is pledged as collateral. A buyer in the ordinary course of business is not affected by perfection of a security interest.

Answer choice "A" is incorrect because a prospective creditor's claim will not defeat the claims of a secured creditor whose claim is perfected. A prospective creditor has no legal claim against the debtor's property, including the collateral pledged by the debtor to secure his or her debt.

Answer choice "B" is incorrect because a trustee in bankruptcy will not defeat the claims of a secured creditor whose claim is perfected.

Answer choice "D" is incorrect because a subsequent personal injury judgment creditor will not defeat the claims of secured creditors whose claims are perfected. Perfection provides the creditor with priority of claim against the collateral pledged by the debtor to secure his or her debt over the claims of subsequent creditors and most other parties.

52. C   A secured party perfects his or her security interest to protect and prioritize his or her interest against the claims of other third parties. The UCC Secured Transactions Article establishes priorities among conflicting interests in the same collateral as follows:
1. If no interests are perfected, priority is determined by the order of attachment of the interests.
2. If some interests are perfected and some are not, the perfected interests prevail over the unperfected interests.
3. If all of the interests are perfected, priority is generally determined by the chronological order in which perfection of the interests occurred. Since most claims are perfected by filing a

financing statement, the order of filing often determines priority.

4. The holder of a purchase money security interest in noninventory collateral who perfects by filing a financing statement will be treated as having perfected on the date the interest was created (as opposed to the date the filing occurred), if the creditor perfects his or her interest within ten days of receiving possession of the collateral.

5. The holder of a purchase money security interest (PMSI) in inventory has priority over conflicting security interests if:
   a. The holder of the PMSI perfected the interest in the inventory at the time the debtor received it.
   b. The holder gave written notice of the acquisition of the interest and a description of the secured inventory to all holders of conflicting security interests who had filed a financing statement covering the same type of inventory.

In the question, the security interests are in store equipment and will have the following order of priority: the purchase money security interest attached April 11, 1994, and perfected by filing on April 20, 1994 (III); the security interest perfected by filing on April 15, 1994 (I); and the security interest attached on April 1, 1994 (II).

Answer choices other than "C" are based on incorrect assumptions and/or interpretations of the law.

53.   C   Where the secured party files a financing statement to perfect his or her security interest and the underlying debt is due within five years from the date of the filing, the filing is effective for the entire period of the debt. If the debt is not due within five years, the filing must be renewed, whereby the secured party files a continuation statement within six months prior to the expiration of the original financing statement.

While an intrastate change in the location of the collateral does not affect the validity of the filing, an interstate change in either the location of the collateral or the debtor's place of business or residence requires the debtor to file another financing statement in the new state. However, the original filing continues to be valid for the remaining term of the original filing or four months from the date the collateral entered the new state, whichever occurs first.

Larkin's security interest is superior even though at the time of Elk's default Larkin had not perfected its security interest in the state of Blackacre.

Answer choice "A" is incorrect because Quarry's interest is not superior to Larkins's interest, and because Larkin's time to file a financing statement in Blackacre had not yet expired. Larkin's filing in Whiteacre was valid in Blackacre for a total of four months, only two of which had expired when Elk went into default.

Thus, Larkin had two additional months within which to file a new financing statement in Blackacre. In the interim, Larkin's security interest was superior to the security interest of Quarry since it was perfected before Quarry's.

Answer choice "B" is incorrect because Quarry's interest is not superior to Larkin's. Larkin's filing in Whiteacre protected him in Blackacre for four months from the time the computers entered Whiteacre. At the time Elk went into default, only two months of this four-month period had expired. Thus, Larkin's interest is superior to Quarry's interest, even if Quarry did not have actual notice of Larkin's interest.

Answer choice "D" is incorrect because the superiority of Larkin's interest is not dependent upon Larkin repossessing the computers before Quarry does. Larkin's security interest is superior to Quarry's because Larkin filed in Whiteacre before Quarry filed in Blackacre. Larkin's Whiteacre filing was valid for four months from the date the computers first arrived in Blackacre. Elk's default occurred only two months after the computers arrived in Blackacre and, thus, Larkin's claim against the computers is superior to Quarry's.

54. A   Upon default by the debtor, the UCC Secured Transactions Article permits a secured party to sell the debtor's collateral and then apply the proceeds first to the costs of repossessing and selling the collateral and then to the outstanding debt. If the proceeds from the sale of the collateral are insufficient to pay the debt in full, the debtor is liable for the deficiency. Hale may <u>obtain a deficiency judgment against Drew for the amount owed</u>.

Answer choice "B" is incorrect because a secured party who sells collateral following the debtor's default must account to the debtor for any surplus.

Answer choice "C" is incorrect because a secured party whose debtor has defaulted may not retain the collateral over the objection of the debtor where the debtor has paid at least 60 percent of the price of the collateral and has not signed a default statement renouncing or modifying his or her rights. Instead, the secured party must sell the collateral and account to the debtor for any surplus.

Answer choice "D" is incorrect because the secured party whose debtor has defaulted and who opts to sell the collateral must notify the debtor of the time and place of the sale, except where the collateral is perishable or is otherwise likely to quickly decline in value.

55. C   The UCC Secured Transactions Article permits a debtor who has paid at least 60 percent of the price of the collateral, and who has not signed a default statement renouncing or modifying his or her rights, to force the secured party to sell the collateral and apply

the proceeds to the debt. The debtor remains liable for any deficiency and is entitled to any surplus. Drew has the right to force Hale to sell the computer.

Answer choice "A" is incorrect because the debtor's right to redeem the collateral expires when the secured party sells the collateral.

Answer choice "B" is incorrect because a secured party who sells collateral following the debtor's default is entitled to apply the proceeds of the sale first to the reasonable expenses of repossessing the collateral and selling it and then to the unpaid debt.

Answer choice "D" is incorrect because a debtor who defaults may not prevent the secured party from peacefully repossessing the collateral, selling it, and applying the net proceeds to the debtor's unpaid debt.

56.   C   A joint tenancy is a type of concurrent ownership of property with the distinguishing characteristic that the co-owners have the right of survivorship (i.e., when a co-owner dies, the survivors automatically inherit the interest of the deceased co-tenant). A joint tenant may convey his or her interest to a third party and thus terminate his or her joint tenancy rights. The new co-owner becomes a tenant in common with the remaining joint tenants. As a result of the sale from Court to Plank, Plank owns one-third of the land as a tenant in common.

Answer choice "A" is incorrect because the new tenant, Plank, will not be a joint tenant with Fell and Miles. Plank will be a tenant in common with both Fell and Miles because the sale by Court to Plank terminates the joint tenancy and renders Plank a tenant in common with Fell and Miles. In order for Plank to be a joint tenant with Fell and Miles, Plank must acquire his or her interest at the same time as the other joint tenants. This did not occur; therefore, no joint tenancy was created between Plank, Fell, and Miles.

Answer choice "B" is incorrect because the transfer of one joint tenant's interest to a third party does not destroy the joint tenancy relationship between the remaining joint tenants. Fell and Miles will continue to own their respective interests as joint tenants with survivorship and not as tenants in common.

Answer choice "D" is incorrect because the transfer by Court to Plank destroys the joint tenancy. Plank, the new owner, will be a tenant in common with Fell and Miles, rather than a joint tenant. In order to be a joint tenant with Fell and Miles, Plank must acquire his or her interest at the same time that the other joint tenants acquire their interests. Since Plank acquired his or her interest after Fell and Miles acquired their interests, Plank is not a joint tenant with Fell and Miles.

57. D A contract for the sale of real property contains the implied obligation for the seller to deliver marketable title for the real property to the buyer at closing. Marketable title is a title that is free from encumbrances, defects in the chain of title that appear in the public records, and impairments to the seller's ownership rights, such as adverse possession. Therefore, an <u>unrecorded easement</u> is a defect in marketable title to real property.

Answer choice "A" is incorrect because most states do not define marketable title to include the obligation to convey a title free from recorded zoning restrictions.

Answer choice "B" is incorrect because most states do not define marketable title to include the obligation to convey a title free from easements or rights of way of which the buyer is or should be aware. A buyer should be aware of a recorded easement that is referred to in the contract of sale.

Answer choice "C" is incorrect because marketable title does not include the obligation to convey a title free from unrecorded lawsuits against the seller. A lawsuit constitutes a contingent claim against the seller's real property. This claim must be recorded in order to follow the real property into the hands of a good-faith purchaser of the real property.

58. A A mortgage creates an encumbrance upon real property and is typically given by a mortgagor to a mortgagee to secure a loan from the mortgagee that enables the mortgagor to purchase the real property. A mortgage must be written, contain an adequate description of the mortgaged property, be executed by the mortgagor, and delivered to the mortgagee with the intent to create a mortgage obligation. In order to create an enforceable mortgage, <u>an accurate description of the property must be included in the mortgage</u>.

Answer choice "B" is incorrect because an enforceable mortgage may be created without an accompanying negotiable promissory note. The note is a separate document from the mortgage, although it may be merged with and included in the mortgage.

Answer choice "C" is incorrect because an enforceable mortgage may be created without the exchange of present consideration for the mortgage. A mortgage is not a contract and may be given for present consideration, for an antecedent debt, or for a debt to arise in the future.

Answer choice "D" is incorrect because an enforceable mortgage may be created without stating the amount of the debt and/or the interest rate for the debt. These terms are commonly contained in the promissory note that accompanies the mortgage, rather than in the mortgage itself.

59. A Under both the Clean Air Act and the Clean Water Act, states are the primary enforcement parties. However, individual citizens may bring

suits for damages against violators and/or against the EPA to force it to act to enforce these environmental protection laws. The remedies available to a real property owner who seeks to enforce the provisions of federal acts regulating air and water pollution include: <u>citizen suits against the Environmental Protection Agency to enforce compliance with the laws, state suits against violators, and citizen suits against violators</u>.

Answer choices other than "A" are based on incorrect assumptions and/or interpretations of the law.

60.   D   A bailment exits whenever possession of personal property is temporarily transferred from one party (the bailor) to another party (the bailee). A bailment requires:
1. The delivery of possession (rather than title) of personal property from a bailor to a bailee.
2. Possession by the bailee for a determinable period of time.
3. An absolute duty by the bailee to return the property to the bailor or to dispose of it according to the bailor's instructions.

The following requirements must be met to create a bailment: <u>delivery of personal property to the intended bailee (I), possession by the intended bailee (II), and an absolute duty on the intended bailee to return or dispose of the property according to the bailor's directions (III)</u>.

Answer choices other than "D" are based on incorrect assumptions and/or interpretations of the law.

OTHER OBJECTIVE FORMATS/ESSAY QUESTIONS

Answer 2

Part 2(a)

61.   C   Under the Securities Act of 1933, the plaintiff must prove that (1) the security was purchased, (2) a material misstatement or omission occurred, and (3) a loss was incurred. Under the Securities Exchange Act of 1934, the plaintiff must prove (1) a material misstatement or omission of fact, (2) knowledge of the falsity or omission (i.e., scienter), (3) defendant's intention that plaintiff rely on the misstatement or omission, (4) justifiable reliance by plaintiff, and (5) damages caused by the plaintiff's reliance. Thus, <u>under both statutes</u>, the plaintiff security purchaser must allege or prove that material misstatements were included in a filed document.

62.   C   <u>Under both</u> the Securities Act of 1933 and the Securities Exchange Act of 1934, one of the elements that a plaintiff security purchaser must allege or prove is that a monetary loss occurred.

63.   D   Due diligence is an affirmative defense for a defendant CPA being sued under the Securities Act of 1933. A plaintiff security

purchaser <u>need</u> <u>not</u> <u>allege</u> or prove lack of due diligence by the CPA <u>under</u> <u>either</u> the Securities Act of 1933 or the Securities Exchange Act of 1934.

64.   D   Privity refers to a contractual relationship existing between a plaintiff and a defendant. The requirement of privity has been abandoned for suits brought under the federal securities acts. A plaintiff security purchaser <u>need</u> <u>not</u> allege or prove privity with the CPA <u>under</u> <u>either</u> the Securities Act of 1933 or the Securities Exchange Act of 1934.

65.   B   Reliance upon the material misstatement or omission by the defendant is an element of fraud and a plaintiff security purchaser <u>must</u> <u>prove</u> reliance on the document to prevail <u>under</u> the Securities Exchange <u>Act</u> <u>of</u> <u>1934</u>. However, reliance is not an element that a plaintiff security purchaser must allege or prove under the Securities Act of 1933.

66.   B   Scienter is an element of fraud; thus, a plaintiff security purchaser <u>must</u> allege or <u>prove</u> that the CPA acted with scienter <u>under</u> the Securities Exchange <u>Act</u> <u>of</u> <u>1934</u>. However, scienter is not an element that a plaintiff securities purchaser must prove under the Securities Act of 1933.

Part 2(b)

67.   T   Chapter 7 of the Federal Bankruptcy Code provides for voluntary or involuntary liquidation of a debtor's nonexempt assets, as well as the discharge of most of the debtor's debts. Chapter 7 is available to all debtors (including corporations and partnerships) except railroads, insurance companies, banks, savings and loans, homestead associations, and credit unions. <u>Able</u> <u>can</u> <u>file</u> <u>a</u> <u>voluntary</u> <u>petition</u> <u>for</u> <u>bankruptcy</u>. (Note that Able's solvency is not relevant to Able's eligibility to file for voluntary bankruptcy.)

68.   F   An involuntary bankruptcy petition is filed by the debtor's creditors. If the debtor has 12 or more creditors, at least three petitioning creditors are required. If the debtor has less than 12 creditors, only one creditor need file the petition. In either case, the petition must allege in good faith that the debtor owes at least $5,000 in unsecured debts to the petitioning creditors. <u>Lake</u>, <u>Young</u>, <u>and</u> <u>Thorn</u> <u>cannot</u> <u>file</u> <u>a</u> <u>valid</u> <u>involuntary</u> <u>petition</u> because the total of the unsecured claims owed to them by Able is only $4,500.

69.   T   <u>Cole</u> <u>alone</u> <u>can</u> <u>file</u> <u>a</u> <u>valid</u> <u>involuntary</u> <u>petition</u> because only one (out of the total of four) of Able's creditors must sign the petition and that creditor is owed $5,000 in unsecured debt. Cole alone satisfies the criteria for filing a valid involuntary bankruptcy petition.

70.   F   A preferential transfer has five elements:
1. Made to or for the benefit of a creditor.
2. Enables a creditor to obtain a preference over the other creditors.

3. Made in connection with an antecedent debt.
4. Made within 90 days of the filing of the petition (one year for an insider; i.e., one with whom the debtor has close ties).
5. Made while the debtor is insolvent (in the balance sheet sense).

The payment to Vista Bank would not be set aside as a preferential transfer because it was not made within 90 days of the filing of the involuntary petition for bankruptcy for Able Corp.

71. T   The payment to Owen (who was an insider because he was an officer of Able Corp.) that was made for the benefit of a creditor, for an antecedent debt, was made within one year of the filing of the petition and while the debtor was insolvent (i.e., presumed to have been insolvent during the 90 days immediately preceding the date that the petition was filed). Accordingly, the payment to Owen would be set aside as a preferential transfer.

72. F   Certain transfers are not deemed preferential, including cash purchases (no antecedent debt). The purchase from Core Computer Co. would not be set aside as a preferential transfer.

Answer 3

Part 3(a)

73. F   A promissory note is commercial paper with an unconditional promise by the maker to pay a definite sum of money at a fixed or determinable future time, or on demand, to the order of a named payee or to bearer. Document I is a promissory note.

74. C   A draft is a written document containing an unconditional order by the drawer to the payee to pay on demand, or at a fixed or determinable future time, a sum certain in money to a named payee or to bearer. Document II is a type of draft.

75. D   In order to be negotiable, an instrument must satisfy all of the following criteria:
1. Be payable at a fixed or determinable future time or on demand.
2. Be in writing.
3. Be payable to order or bearer.
4. Be signed by the maker or drawer.
5. Contain an unconditional promise or order.
6. Be payable in money only.
7. Be for a sum certain.

Document I is negotiable.

76. D   In order to be negotiable, an instrument must satisfy all of the following criteria:
1. Be payable at a fixed or determinable future time or on demand.
2. Be in writing.
3. Be payable to order or bearer.
4. Be signed by the maker or drawer.

5. Contain an unconditional promise or order.
6. Be payable in money only.
7. Be for a sum certain.

Document II is <u>negotiable</u>.

77. A   Every endorsement is (1) blank or special, (2) qualified or unqualified, and (3) restrictive or unrestrictive. A blank endorsement names no endorsee, while a special endorsement specifically names the endorsee of the instrument. The endorsement by Mark Eden is a <u>blank</u> endorsement.

78. G   Every endorsement is (1) blank or special, (2) qualified or unqualified, and (3) restrictive or unrestrictive. A qualified endorsement is a blank endorsement accompanied by wording that disclaims the endorser's contractual liability (i.e., without recourse), while an unqualified endorsement contains no such wording. The endorsement by Nancy Ferry is a <u>qualified</u> endorsement.

Part 3(b)

79. T   An insurable interest is an interest such that, upon the happening of the insured against peril, a pecuniary loss will be suffered by the insured. As of January 12, 1994, Frank had equitable title to the factory building owned by Henderson, because Frank had contracted to purchase the building. Both the Unity and the Imperial policies were taken out on January 15, 1994. Thus, <u>Frank had an insurable interest at the time the Unity and Imperial policies were taken out</u>.

80. F   An insurable interest is an interest such that, upon the happening of the insured against peril, a pecuniary loss will be suffered by the insured. With property insurance, the insurable interest must exist at the time of the loss. Since Frank and Henderson had consummated the sale of the factory building on March 15, 1994, and the fire occurred on March 16, 1994, <u>Henderson did not have an insurable interest at the time of the fire</u> (i.e., the loss) because Henderson no longer owned the factory building.

81. F   A coinsurance clause requires the insured to maintain insurance on his or her property up to a certain percentage value of the property. Frank's policies with Unity and Imperial both had 80 percent coinsurance clauses. Frank's aggregate insurance coverage for the building was $210,000 and the value of the building at the time of the fire was $250,000. Thus, Frank's property insurance coverage was for 84 percent (i.e., $210,000/$250,000) of the insured property's value and, <u>assuming Frank had an insurable interest, Frank's coverage would be sufficient under the Unity and Imperial coinsurance clauses</u>.

82. T   A coinsurance clause requires the insured to maintain insurance on his or her property up to a certain percentage value of the property. Henderson's policy with Summit had an 80 percent

coinsurance clause. Henderson's policy with Summit was for $180,000 while the value of the building at the time of the fire was $250,000. As a result, Henderson's coverage was only 72 percent (i.e., $180,000/$250,000) of the insured property's value. Assuming Henderson had an insurable interest, Henderson's coverage would be insufficient under the Summit coinsurance clause.

83. T Where a property insurance policy contains a coinsurance clause and the policy holder insures his or her property for less than the required amount, the insurer is liable for only its appropriate share of the amount of insurance that was required to be carried. The following formula must be applied to determine the recovery:

$$\text{Recovery} = \text{Loss} \times \frac{\text{Face amount of policy}}{\text{Coinsurance \% } \times \text{ Value at time of loss}}$$

$$\text{Recovery} = \$150,000 \times \frac{\$210,000}{.80 \times \$250,000}$$

Recovery = $157,500

However, the amount of recovery is limited to the amount of the loss, or $150,000.

Where more than one insurer has issued a policy on the property, recovery is normally limited by "other insurance" clauses which require pro-rata distribution of the loss among the various insurers based on their respective policy limits, as follows:

$$\text{Unity} = \frac{\$140,000}{\$210,000} \times \$150,000 \qquad \text{Imperial} = \frac{\$70,000}{\$210,000} \times \$150,000$$

Unity = $100,000   Imperial = $50,000

Assuming only Frank had an insurable interest, Frank will recover $100,000 from Unity and $50,000 from Imperial.

84. T Where a property insurance policy contains a coinsurance clause and the policyholder insures his or her property for less than the required amount, the insurer is liable only for its appropriate share of the amount of insurance that was required to be carried. The following formula must be applied to determine the recovery:

$$\text{Recovery} = \text{Loss} \times \frac{\text{Face amount of policy}}{\text{Coinsurance \% } \times \text{ Value at time of loss}}$$

$$\text{Recovery} = \$150,000 \times \frac{\$180,000}{.80 \times \$250,000}$$

Recovery = $135,000

> Assuming <u>only</u> <u>Henderson</u> <u>had</u> <u>an</u> <u>insurable</u> <u>interest</u>, <u>Henderson</u> <u>will</u>
> <u>recover</u> <u>$135,000</u> <u>from</u> <u>Summit</u>.

Answer 4

Part 4(a)
<u>Jackson's Assertion</u> - <u>Correct</u>

An agent who acts for an undisclosed principal is personally liable on
contracts entered into on behalf of the undisclosed principal. Here, Baker was
contracting on behalf of an undisclosed principal (i.e., Best Aviation), since
Baker contracted with Jackson without disclosing that the aircraft was being
purchased for Best. The contract provided that Jackson would deliver the
airplane to Baker on January 2, 1994, and that the purchase price would be paid
at that time. When Jackson attempted to deliver the airplane, Baker, acting on
Martin's instructions, refused to either accept delivery or pay the purchase
price. Thus, Jackson can hold Baker responsible for any damages incurred as a
result of this breach of contract. (Note: If Jackson obtains a judgment against
Baker and collects on such, Baker has the right to be reimbursed by Best.)

Part 4(b)
<u>Martin's Assertion #1</u> - <u>Correct</u>

A partner may assign his/her partnership interest to a third party. However,
the assignee does not automatically become a partner because admission as a
partner requires the unanimous approval of all partners. The assignee merely
becomes entitled to the assigning partner's share of partnership profits plus
the assigning partner's share of any surplus that exists upon liquidation of
the firm. Thus, Green is not entitled to inspect the partnership books or to
participate in the management of the partnership, since Green is not a partner
in Best Aviation.

<u>Martin's Assertion #2</u> - <u>Incorrect</u>

Each partner in a general partnership has unlimited personal responsibility for
the debts of the firm. A creditor of the firm must first look to the partnership
assets to satisfy its claim before looking to the personal assets of the general
partners. Thus, Martin is incorrect in asserting that only the partnership is
liable for the debt to Laco. Laco can look to Martin's personal assets to
satisfy its claim if Best's assets are insufficient. Martin is also incorrect in
asserting that Martin's personal liability is limited to 50 percent of the total
of the unpaid bills. Martin has unlimited personal liability for the Laco debt
that could exceed 50 percent of the total unpaid bill.

Part 4(c)
<u>Kent's Assertion #1</u> - <u>Incorrect</u>

When a partner assigns his/her partnership interest, the assignor remains a
partner with all the rights (except the right to profits that has been
assigned) and responsibilities of a partner. Thus, Kent's assertion that only
Martin is liable for the 1993 operating loss is incorrect. Both Kent and Martin
are liable for the operating loss since they are both general partners, and
general partners have unlimited personal liability for partnership debts.

Kent's Assertion #2 - Incorrect

In the absence of a contrary agreement, general partners share losses in the same proportion in which they share profits (in this case, equally, rather than in proportion to their financial contributions). Since the partners had no agreement as to how they would share losses, the losses will also be shared equally. Thus, Kent's assertion that the 1993 operating loss should be allocated between them on the basis of their original capital contributions is incorrect.

Answer 5

Assertion #1 - Correct

A lease is a contract wherein the landlord promises to provide possession and control of real property to the tenant for the period as specified in the lease. Leases of real property are governed by the common-law rule, which requires that contract modifications be supported by new or additional consideration in order to be enforceable. Here, Suburban did not receive any new or additional consideration in return for its agreement to modify the lease and share the proposed utility costs equally with Bridge Hardware. Thus, Suburban is correct in its assertion that the agreement to share equally the utility costs with Bridge is not binding.

Assertion #2 - Incorrect

In contract negotiations where the subject of the proposed contract is real property, an offeror is free to revoke his/her offer at any time prior to its acceptance. Here, Dart offered to purchase a shopping center (i.e., real property) from Suburban; therefore, Dart was free to revoke its offer at any time prior to Suburban's acceptance of the offer. Because Dart withdrew its offer to purchase the shopping center before Suburban accepted Dart's purchase offer, Dart is not obligated to purchase the shopping center. Dart's offer is not an irrevocable firm offer because the subject matter was not goods and thus is not governed by Article 2 of the U.C.C. Suburban did not pay consideration to Dart to obtain an option that would have made Dart's offer irrevocable for a stated time. Also, Suburban's acceptance was not effective when mailed because Dart specified in the offer that an acceptance must be received by Dart to be effective.

Assertion #3 - Correct

At common-law, a landlord has no obligation to maintain and repair leased premises once the lease period begins. This rule applies to both residential and commercial leases. While most states now recognize by statute the duty of a landlord in a residential lease to make all repairs and do whatever is necessary to keep the leased premises in a habitable condition, no such duty exists by statute in commercial leases. The lease between Surburban and World was a commercial lease because it was for space in a shopping center and, as such, the lease would be governed by the common-law rule. Thus, Suburban is not liable to World for World's losses resulting from the fire.

Auditing (AUDIT)

FOUR-OPTION MULTIPLE-CHOICE QUESTIONS

Answer 1

1. B When a change in auditors is contemplated by an entity, communication should take place between the predecessor auditor and his or her designated successor before the successor accepts the engagement. The communication should be designed to assist the designated successor in obtaining information that will assist in determining whether to accept the engagement. Accordingly, the primary purpose of the communication is to identify the predecessor's understanding as to the reasons for the change of auditors.

    The successor's inquiries should include specific questions concerning such items as facts that might bear on the integrity of management, disagreements the predecessor had with the client concerning auditing procedures, accounting principles, or other similarly significant matters.

    Answer choices other than "B" are incorrect because they do not represent items the successor auditor would ask of the predecessor auditor in determining whether to accept the audit.

2. C A CPA firm has a responsibility to establish quality control policies and procedures to assure itself of compliance with GAAS in conducting an audit. One area of concern is the acceptance and/or continuation of client relationships. It obviously is not in a CPA firm's interest to be associated with a client whose management lacks integrity.

    In considering whether to accept a new client engagement, a CPA firm should (1) review the financial statements of the potential client, (2) inquire of bankers and lawyers as to the reputation of the proposed client, (3) inquire of the predecessor auditor, if any, and (4) determine that the CPA firm has the expertise and professional staff to properly serve the potential client.

    Answer choices other than "C" are incorrect because although they represent concerns of the auditor, they would be of little consequence to the CPA firm in pursuing its quality control objectives with respect to acceptance of a new audit engagement.

3. B The first standard of field work under GAAS indicates that the audit work is to be adequately planned, and assistants, if any, are to be properly supervised. Thus, planning the engagement must be supplemented by determining whether the audit plan is being executed as designed. Supervision involves the review of the audit effort and related audit judgments made by assistants to ascertain whether these judgments are appropriate.

The work performed by each assistant should be reviewed to determine whether it was adequately performed and to evaluate whether the <u>results</u> <u>are</u> <u>consistent</u> <u>with</u> <u>the</u> <u>conclusions</u> <u>to</u> <u>be</u> <u>presented</u> <u>in</u> <u>the</u> <u>auditor's</u> <u>report</u>.

Answer choice "A" is incorrect because quality control relates to the conduct of the audit firm itself and does not relate to the conduct of a particular audit engagement.

Answer choice "C" is incorrect because audit procedures performed are a matter of the auditor's professional judgment.

Answer choice "D" is incorrect because it relates to the first general standard under GAAS and not to the first standard of field work under GAAS.

4.   D   The first standard of field work under GAAS indicates that the audit is to be adequately planned and assistants, if any, are to be properly supervised.

Planning of the audit involves developing an overall strategy for the expected conduct and scope of the audit. Adequate planning includes the auditor's acquiring an understanding of the client's business, its organization, the location of its facilities, the products sold or services rendered, its financial structure, etc.

To acquire the requisite level of knowledge, the auditor makes use of any prior experience with the client or the industry, including the review of prior years' audit work papers, financial statements, and auditor's reports.

Discussions on matters that potentially could influence the audit should be held with audit and nonaudit personnel. Discussions with management personnel will prove to be an important source of information, as will a review of interim financial statements. The auditor should coordinate the assistance of client personnel, including the internal auditor and any anticipated use of consultants.

All planning should be well documented and should include an audit program. The auditor should obtain a level of knowledge of the entity's business to enable him or her to obtain an <u>understanding</u> <u>of</u> <u>the</u> <u>events</u>, <u>transactions</u>, and practices <u>that</u>, in his or her judgment, <u>may</u> <u>have</u> <u>a</u> <u>significant</u> <u>effect</u> <u>on</u> <u>the</u> <u>financial</u> <u>statements</u>.

Answer choice "A" is incorrect because making constructive suggestions about the internal control structure is not even a requirement in an audit.

Answer choice "B" is incorrect because an attitude of professional skepticism is maintained during audit planning and performance because of the risk of material misstatement.

Answer choice "C" is incorrect because the evaluation of material misstatements relates to financial statement assertions and not to the knowledge of the client's business and industry.

5.   A   The purpose of applying analytical procedures in planning the audit is to assist in planning the nature, timing, and extent of auditing procedures that will be used to obtain evidential matter for specific account balances or classes of transactions.

Analytical procedures used in planning the audit should focus on (1) enhancing the auditor's understanding of the client's business and the transactions and events that have occurred since the last audit date, and (2) identifying areas that may represent specific risks relevant to the audit.

As such, the objective of the procedures is to identify such things as the <u>existence of unusual transactions and events</u>, and the amounts, ratios, and trends that might indicate matters having financial statement and audit planning ramifications.

Answer choices other than "A" are incorrect because, although they represent concerns to the auditor, they would not necessarily be identified by applying analytical procedures during the planning phase of an audit.

6.   A   Illegal acts refer to violations of laws or governmental regulations by the audited entity, its management, or its employees acting on behalf of the entity.

The auditor's responsibility to detect and report misstatements resulting from illegal acts having a direct and material effect on the financial statements (e.g., tax laws affecting accruals and the amounts recognized as expense in the accounting period) is the same as that for material errors and irregularities. The auditor should assess the risk that such illegal acts may cause the financial statements to contain material misstatements.

Based on that assessment, the auditor should design the audit to provide <u>reasonable assurance of detecting direct effect illegal acts</u> that are material to the financial statements.

The auditor should be aware of the possibility of <u>illegal acts having</u> an <u>indirect effect</u> on financial statements (e.g., those related to securities trading, occupational safety and health, food and drug administration, etc.). These acts relate more to an entity's operating aspects than to its financial and accounting aspects. As such, the auditor ordinarily does not have sufficient basis for recognizing possible violations of such laws and regulations. Accordingly, an audit made in accordance with GAAS provides <u>no assurance</u> that these illegal acts will be detected or that any contingent liabilities that may result will be disclosed.

It should be noted that if specific information comes to the auditor's attention that provides evidence concerning the existence of possible illegal acts that could have a material indirect effect on the financial statements, the auditor should apply audit procedures specifically directed to ascertaining whether an illegal act has occurred.

Answer choices other than "A" are based on incorrect assumptions and/or combinations.

7.   D   Illegal acts refer to violations of laws or governmental regulations by the audited entity, its management, or employees acting on behalf of the entity.

When the auditor becomes aware of information concerning a possible illegal act, the auditor should inquire of management at a level above those involved.

If the auditor concludes that an illegal act has, or is likely to have, occurred, the auditor should:
1.   Consider the effects on the financial statement.
2.   Consider the implications for other aspects of the audit, particularly the reliability of management representations.
3.   Inform the audit committee, or others with equivalent authority, about all but clearly inconsequential illegal acts. Oral communication is permissible but should be documented in the work papers.

The auditor should:
1.   Express a qualified or adverse opinion if an illegal act has a material effect on the financial statements and has not been properly accounted for or disclosed.
2.   Disclaim an opinion if the auditor is precluded by the client from obtaining sufficient competent evidential matter needed to evaluate whether an illegal act that could be material has, or is likely to have, occurred.
3.   <u>Withdraw</u> <u>from</u> <u>the</u> <u>engagement</u> <u>if</u> <u>the</u> <u>client</u>:
     a.   <u>Refuses</u> <u>to</u> <u>accept</u> <u>the</u> <u>auditor's</u> <u>report</u> <u>as</u> <u>modified</u> <u>for</u> <u>the</u> <u>illegal</u> <u>act</u>.
     b.   Does not take the remedial action the auditor considers necessary in the circumstances, even when the illegal act is not material to the financial statements.

Answer choice "A" is incorrect because the auditor should disclaim an opinion, rather than withdraw from the engagement, if precluded from obtaining sufficient competent evidential matter.

Answer choices "B" and "C" are incorrect because the auditor would express a qualified or adverse opinion, rather than withdraw from the engagement, if the illegal act has not been properly accounted for or disclosed.

8.   D   In planning the audit, the auditor should consider the nature, extent, and timing of work to be performed and should prepare a

written audit program (or a set of written audit programs). An audit program aids in instructing assistants in the work to be done. It should set forth in reasonable detail the audit procedures that the auditor believes are necessary to accomplish the objectives of the audit.

The auditor develops specific audit objectives in the light of <u>financial statement assertions</u>. In developing the audit objectives of a particular engagement, the auditor should consider the specific circumstances of the entity, including the nature of its economic activity and the accounting practices unique to its industry.

Answer choices other than "D" are incorrect because the specific audit procedures depend on or relate to the specific audit objectives selected.

9.   A   The Accounting and Review Services Committee is designated to issue pronouncements in connection with unaudited financial statements of nonpublic entities. Its pronouncements take the form of Statements on Standards for Accounting and Review Services (SSARS), which have established the concept of compilation and review.

The accountant should not submit unaudited financial statements of a nonpublic entity to a client or others unless, at a minimum, the CPA <u>complies with the provisions of Statements on Standards for Accounting and Review Services</u>.

Answer choice "B" is incorrect because such statements are nonexistent.

Answer choice "C" is incorrect because Statements on Standards for Consulting Services outline a CPA's responsibilities when performing consulting services.

Answer choice "D" is incorrect because Statements on Standards for Attestation Engagements provide guidance, and establish a broad framework, for a variety of attest services beyond historical financial statements.

10. A   Statements on Standards for Attestation Engagements provide guidance, and <u>establish a broad framework, for a variety of attest services beyond historical financial statements</u>.

An attestation engagement is an engagement wherein a CPA is requested to issue, or does issue, a written communication containing the expression of a conclusion as to the reliability of a written assertion that is the responsibility of another party. Standards for attestation engagements are:
1.   <u>General</u>
     a.   Training in the attest function.
     b.   Knowledge in the subject matter.
     c.   Acceptance of engagement only if:

        (1) Reasonable criteria exist against which the assertion can be evaluated.

        (2) There is reasonable consistent estimation or measurement.

   d. Mental independence.

   e. Due care.

2. <u>Standards of field work</u>

   a. Planning work adequately.

   b. Evidence sufficient to support conclusion expressed.

3. <u>Standards of reporting</u>

   a. Identification of assertion and character of engagement.

   b. Conclusion as to conformity with established or stated criteria.

   c. Significant reservations as to the engagement and presentation of assertion.

   d. Limit the report's use, when prepared in conformity with agreed-upon criteria or when the engagement is based upon agreed-upon procedures, to the parties who have agreed upon such criteria or procedures.

Answer choice "B" is incorrect because mental independence is both an attestation and an auditing standard.

Answer choice "C" is incorrect because business acquisition or feasibility studies could involve an attestation engagement.

Answer choice "D" is incorrect because attestation standards include standards relating to planning and evidence, both of which are part of the standards of field work under GAAS.

11.   C   The audit should be planned and performed with an <u>attitude of professional skepticism</u>. The auditor does not assume that management is dishonest, nor does he or she assume unquestioned honesty. Accordingly, objective evaluation is needed to determine whether the financial statements are free of material misstatement.

         The auditor should assess the risk that errors and irregularities may cause the financial statements to contain a material misstatement. Based on that assessment, the auditor should design the audit to provide reasonable assurance of detecting errors and irregularities that are material to the financial statements.

         Answer choices other than "C" are based on incorrect assumptions.

12.   B   An accountant who has been engaged to audit the financial statements of a nonpublic entity in accordance with GAAS may, before the completion of the audit, be requested to change the engagement to a review or compilation of financial statements. A request to change the engagement may result from a change in circumstances affecting the entity's requirement for an audit, a misunderstanding as to the nature of an audit or the alternative review or compilation services originally available, or a restriction on the scope of the audit.

The accountant should consider the following before agreeing to a change in the engagement:

1. <u>Client's reason for request</u>.
2. Implications of a restriction, whether imposed by circumstances or by the client.
3. <u>Additional audit</u> (or review) <u>effort</u>, and cost <u>required to complete the engagement</u>.

Changes in circumstances or misunderstandings concerning the nature of the original engagement are ordinarily reasonable bases for changing the engagement.

If the auditor concludes, based on professional judgment, that there is reasonable justification for the change, he or she should honor the client's request and accept a change in the engagement. In doing so, the auditor should issue an appropriate review or compilation report but should not include any reference to the original engagement, any auditing procedures that may have been performed, or any scope limitations that resulted in the revised engagement.

Answer choices other than "B" are based on incorrect assumptions and/or combinations.

13. C The accountant is required to issue a report whenever he or she completes a compilation or review of financial statements of a nonpublic entity. An accountant may issue a review report on one financial statement (such as a balance sheet) and not on other related financial statements (such as the statements of income, retained earnings, and cash flows), <u>if the scope of the accountant's inquiry and analytical procedures is not restricted</u>.

Answer choice "A" is incorrect because a compilation report on the other financial statements is not required.

Answer choice "B" is incorrect because during the review of the balance sheet, Smith may become aware of material modifications needed for the balance sheet to conform with GAAP. Smith would then be required to modify the review report issued.

Answer choice "D" is incorrect because the timing of the review engagement in not a factor.

14. C Prospective financial statements include financial forecasts and financial projections.

A financial forecast presents, to the best of the responsible party's (usually management's) knowledge and belief, an entity's expected financial position, results of operations, and cash flows. A financial forecast is based on assumptions reflecting conditions expected to exist and the course of action expected to be taken.

A financial projection presents, to the best of the responsible party's (usually management's) knowledge and belief, given one or more hypothetical assumptions (i.e., assumptions used to present a condition or course of action that is not necessarily expected to occur), an entity's expected financial position, results of operations, and cash flows. A financial projection is therefore based on "what if" assumptions.

Prospective financial statements are for either "general use" or "limited use."

"General use" refers to the use of prospective financial statements by persons with whom the responsible party is not negotiating directly. It should be understood that because recipients of prospective financial statements distributed for "general use" are unable to ask the responsible party directly about the presentation, the presentation most useful to them is one that portrays, to the best of the responsible party's knowledge and belief, the expected results. Thus, only a financial forecast is appropriate for general use.

"Limited use" refers to the use of prospective financial statements by the responsible party alone, or by the responsible party and third parties with whom the responsible party is negotiating directly. Both financial forecasts and projections are appropriate for "limited use."

Since the question involves an engagement to examine a financial projection, its use would appropriately be for "limited use" only. Hence, <u>distributing the projection to a bank with which the entity is negotiating a loan would</u> imply "limited use," and would therefore <u>be appropriate</u>.

Answer choices other than "C" relate to "general use"; hence, it would not be appropriate to accept an engagement to examine an entity's financial projection if the projection were to be distributed to the parties mentioned.

15.   C   Reasonable assurance of achieving the basic objective of providing professional services that conform to professional standards can be accomplished through adherence to prescribed <u>standards of quality control</u>.

The four basic elements of quality control for a CPA firm are (1) personnel, (2) independence, (3) acceptance and continuance of clients, and (4) inspection. Further, the personnel-related element concerns hiring, supervision, <u>assigning personnel to engagements</u>, advancement, professional development, and consultation.

Answer choices other than "C" are incorrect because they are not elements of quality control.

16.   B   Microcomputers are self-contained computers in which both the machines and files are maintained independently from a larger control processing device.

Two unique characteristics of microcomputer-prepared data files vs. manually prepared files are (1) the relative ease in accessing the computer and the related files, and (2) storage of information on disks (diskettes), which can be removed from the hardware component. These characteristics may lead to potential control problems for a business.

Given the nature of microcomputers, it may be readily concluded that it is usually easier for unauthorized persons to access and alter the files.

Answer choice "A" is incorrect because the accuracy of the programming process would represent a control feature implemented to eliminate potential problems and would not be a disadvantage of microcomputer-prepared files.

Answer choice "C" is incorrect because random error associated with processing similar transactions in different ways is usually less in a computerized system.

Answer choice "D" is incorrect because when using computer-generated files, it is usually easier, and not more difficult, to compare recorded accountability with physical count of assets.

17. D The definitions of sampling plans are as follows:

Variable sampling - useful in auditing where the purpose is to perform substantive testing, such as determining aggregate dollar amounts of accounting data within a prescribed range of precision and confidence. Because it provides an answer in dollars, it is also referred to as dollar-value estimation.

Attribute sampling - useful in auditing where the purpose is to perform tests of controls. In using this sampling plan, it is necessary to define the attributes sought. Each item in the population does or does not possess the given attributes. The distribution of the population is specified by knowing how many, or what percentage of, items in the population have the attributes.

In light of the definitions provided, the auditor should use attribute sampling when performing a test of controls such as inspecting employee time cards for proper approval by supervisors.

Answer choices other than "D" are incorrect because they refer to situations related to variable sampling or estimation for substantive testing.

18. D A flowchart of internal control is a symbolic, diagrammatic representation of the client's documents and their sequential flow in the organization. An adequate flowchart shows the origin of each document and record in the accounting system, the subsequent processing, and the final disposition of any document or record included in the chart. In addition, it is possible for the flowchart

to show the separation of duties, authorizations, approvals, and internal verifications that take place within the system.

Flowcharting is advantageous primarily because it can provide a concise picture of the client's system that is useful as an analytical tool in an evaluation. A well-prepared flowchart aids in identifying inadequacies by facilitating a clear <u>understanding of the system</u>.

Answer choices other than "D" are incorrect because they involve the exercise of auditor judgment or other auditor actions subsequent to obtaining an understanding of the accounting system, which is part of the internal control structure.

19. C   For purposes of an audit of financial statements, an entity's internal control structure consists of (1) the control environment, (2) the accounting system, and (3) control procedures.

The "control environment" reflects the overall attitude, awareness, and actions of the board of directors, management, owners, and others concerning the importance of control and its emphasis in the entity.

Specific control environment factors concern:
1. Management's philosophy and operating style.
2. Organizational structure.
3. Functioning of the board of directors and its audit committee.
4. Methods of assigning authority and responsibility.
5. Management control methods, including use of internal auditors.
6. Personnel policies and practices.
7. External influences.

Management's philosophy and operating style encompasses a broad range of characteristics. Such characteristics may include management's approach to taking and monitoring business risks, management's attitudes and actions toward financial reporting, and management's emphasis on meeting budget, profit, and other financial and operating goals. These characteristics have significant influence on the control environment, <u>particularly</u> <u>when</u> <u>management</u> <u>is</u> <u>dominated</u> <u>by</u> <u>one</u> <u>or</u> <u>a</u> <u>few</u> <u>individuals</u>, regardless of the consideration given to the other control environment factors.

Answer choices other than "C" are incorrect because they reflect conditions that would tend to offset the influence of management's attitude toward aggressive financial reporting and emphasis on meeting projected profit goals.

20. B   The auditor should obtain a sufficient understanding of each of the three elements of the entity's internal control structure (i.e., control environment, accounting system, and control procedures) to plan the audit of the entity's financial statements. The understanding should include knowledge about the design of relevant policies, procedures, and records, and whether they have been placed in operation by the client.

The auditor should obtain sufficient knowledge of the accounting system to understand the following:
1. The classes of transactions in the entity's operations that are significant to the financial statements.
2. How those transactions are initiated.
3. The accounting records, supporting documents, machine-readable information, and specific accounts in the financial statements involved in the processing and reporting of transactions.
4. The accounting process involved from the initiation of a transaction to its inclusion in the financial statements, including how the computer is used to process data.
5. The financial reporting process used to prepare the entity's financial statements, including <u>the process to prepare significant accounting estimates</u> and disclosures.

Answer choices other than "B" are incorrect because they represent aspects of elements of the internal control structure other than the accounting system.

21. B In obtaining knowledge about whether policies, procedures, or records have been placed in operation, the auditor must determine if the client is using them.

The auditor should concentrate on the <u>substance</u> of management's policies, procedures, and related actions, rather than their form (i.e., substance over form) because <u>management may establish appropriate policies and procedures</u>, but may <u>not act on them</u>. For example, management may establish a budgetary reporting system, but the reports may not be analyzed and acted upon.

Answer choice "A" is incorrect because the auditor determines operating effectiveness subsequent to obtaining an understanding of the internal control structure.

Answer choice "C" is incorrect because the auditor determines reliance on the internal control structure subsequent to obtaining an understanding of the internal control structure.

Answer choice "D" is incorrect because the cost of management's procedures is unrelated to the substance of the procedures.

22. A The following are the general considerations of an internal control structure:
1. Management has the basic responsibility for the establishment and maintenance of an internal control structure.
2. The concept of reasonable assurance recognizes that an entity's internal control structure will accomplish its objectives within the framework of a reasonable cost/benefit equation.
3. Limitations are inherent in any internal control structure. Errors may be caused by misunderstandings, mistakes in judgment, individual carelessness, fatigue, etc. The structure may also be ineffective because of collusion among personnel, both within and outside the entity, and by management's override of certain policies and procedures.

In light of point "3," <u>incompatible</u> <u>duties</u> <u>are</u> <u>not</u> <u>an</u> <u>inherent</u> <u>limitation</u>. Internal control procedures should be designed to eliminate incompatible duties.

Answer choices other than "A" are incorrect because they all represent inherent limitations of the potential effectiveness of an internal control structure.

23.　C　The second standard of field work indicates that a sufficient understanding of the internal control structure is to be obtained to plan the audit and to determine the nature, timing, and extent of the substantive tests to be performed.

An auditor uses the knowledge provided by the understanding of the internal control structure and the assessed level of control risk primarily to determine the nature, timing, and extent of substantive tests for financial statement assertions. The substantive tests that the auditor performs consist of tests of details of transactions, tests of account balances, and analytical procedures. As the assessed level of control risk increases, because certain control procedures were determined to be ineffective, the acceptable level of detection risk should decrease, therefore necessitating an increase in the <u>extent</u> <u>of</u> <u>tests</u> <u>of</u> <u>details</u> in order to gain audit satisfaction.

Answer choice "A" is incorrect because the extent of tests of controls would not increase when the auditor has assessed control risk at a level higher than planned. At this point, the auditor has decided that the control cannot be relied upon and that substantive testing should be increased.

Answer choice "B" is incorrect because the level of detection risk would most likely decrease.

Answer choice "D" is incorrect because the level of inherent risk would remain unchanged.

24.　D　Audit risk and materiality affect the application of GAAS, in particular the standards of field work and reporting.

<u>Audit Risk</u> - The risk that the auditor may unknowingly fail to modify his or her opinion on financial statements that are materially misstated. Inherent, control, and detection risks are the constituent parts of audit risk as follows:
1. <u>Inherent Risk</u> - The susceptibility of an assertion to a material misstatement assuming there are no related internal control structure policies or procedures.
2. <u>Control Risk</u> - Risk that a material misstatement that could occur in an assertion will not be prevented or detected on a timely basis by an entity's internal control structure policies or procedures.
3. <u>Detection Risk</u> - Risk that the auditor will not detect a material misstatement that exists in an assertion.

Inherent and control risks exist independently of the audit of financial statements. Detection risk relates to the auditor's procedures and can be altered at his or her discretion.

An auditor uses the knowledge provided by the understanding of the internal control structure and the assessed level of control risk primarily to determine the nature, timing, and extent of substantive tests for financial statement assertions. The substantive tests that the auditor performs reduce detection risk. The auditor uses the assessed level of control risk (together with the assessed level of inherent risk) to determine the acceptable level of detection risk.

Answer choice "A" is incorrect because the evaluation of the entity's internal control policies and procedures leads to the assessment of control risk.

Answer choice "B" is incorrect because the assessment of inherent risk is independent of the assessment of control risk. Further, inherent risk does not relate to account balances and transactions; rather, inherent risk relates to particular assertions.

Answer choice "C" is incorrect because materiality levels are established prior to assessment of control risk. In subsequent stages of the audit, the auditor may lower materiality levels because of audit findings.

25. A Assessing control risk is the process of evaluating the effectiveness of an entity's internal control structure policies and procedures in preventing or detecting material misstatements in the financial statements.

Control risk is the risk that a material misstatement that could occur in an assertion will not be prevented or detected on a timely basis by an entity's internal control structure.

The auditor may assess control risk at the maximum level (i.e., 100 percent, which is the greatest probability that a material misstatement in a financial statement assertion will not be prevented or detected by an entity's internal control structure) for some or all assertions because the auditor believes that:
1. Policies and procedures are unlikely to pertain to an assertion.
2. Policies and procedures are unlikely to be effective.
3. Evaluating the effectiveness of the policies and procedures would be inefficient.

Hence, after obtaining an understanding of the internal control structure and in assessing control risk of an entity, an auditor may decide not to perform additional tests of controls. This is so because the auditor most likely decided that it would be inefficient to perform tests of controls that would result in a reduction in planned substantive tests; that is, additional evidence to support a further reduction in control risk was not cost-beneficial to obtain.

Answer choices other than "A" are based on incorrect assumptions.

26.   B   The nature of the particular policies and procedures that pertain to an assertion influences the type of evidential matter that is available to evaluate the effectiveness of the design or operation of these policies and procedures.

For some policies and procedures, documentation of design or operation may exist. As such, the auditor may decide to inspect the documentation to obtain evidential matter.

However, for other policies and procedures, such documentation may not be available. For example, documentation may not exist for some factors, such as assignment of authority and/or responsibility, or segregation of functions for cash disbursements. In such circumstances, the auditor most likely will test the procedures by <u>observation</u> <u>and</u> <u>inquiry</u>.

Answer choices other than "B" are incorrect because confirmations and analytical procedures are used in substantive testing and are not relevant to tests of controls.

27.   B   Audit procedures for management's assertion concerning completeness of sales transactions should be designed to determine whether all sales that have occurred are properly recorded in the accounts.

The essential source documents in executing sales transactions include the customer order, sales order, shipping document (bill of lading), sales invoice, and a daily sales summary. To achieve maximum accountability, sales orders, shipping documents, and sales invoices should be prenumbered and subsequently accounted for in sequence.

There are numerous opportunities for independent internal verification in executing sales transactions. For example, the shipping department is generally required to compare the goods received from the warehouse with the sales order before shipping the merchandise. Likewise, in the billing department, the sales orders are matched with shipping documents before invoices are prepared.

Furthermore, to help ensure that all credit sales transactions of an entity are recorded (i.e., complete), the billing department supervisor, who is not otherwise involved in the sales stream, <u>should</u> <u>match</u> <u>prenumbered</u> <u>shipping</u> <u>documents</u> <u>with</u> <u>entries</u> <u>in</u> <u>the</u> <u>sales</u> <u>journal</u>. <u>Shipping</u> <u>documents</u> <u>that</u> <u>have</u> <u>not</u> <u>been</u> <u>recorded</u> <u>should</u> <u>be</u> <u>investigated</u>.

Answer choices other than "B" are incorrect because they would not ensure that all sales transactions have been properly recorded.

28.   A   The essential source documents in executing sales transactions include the customer order, sales order, shipping document (bill of lading), sales invoice, and a daily sales summary.

Comparing <u>daily sales summaries</u> <u>with</u> <u>the daily postings of credit sales</u> (<u>based on the sales invoice</u>) <u>in the accounts receivable ledger</u> would provide assurance that all billed (i.e., credit) sales have been correctly posted.

Answer choices other than "A" are incorrect because, although they represent sound procedures, they would not ensure that all billed sales transactions have been correctly posted to the accounts receivable ledger.

29. C   For proper functioning of internal controls, there must be a separation of:
          1. The custody of, or access to, assets from the accounting or recordkeeping for those assets.
          2. The proper authorization of transactions from the custody of, or access to, the related assets.
          3. Duties within the accounting function.
          4. Operational responsibility from recordkeeping responsibility.

          Proper segregation of duties in the payroll cycle is essential. The personnel department, which has authorizing responsibilities, should inform timekeeping and the payroll department of new hires, pay rate changes, and terminations. Timekeeping and the payroll department perform the recordkeeping functions and should be separate from personnel, payroll payment, and payroll distribution. Specifically, anyone responsible for check preparation should not have responsibility for signing or distributing checks. The treasurer's office should have the custodial responsibilities for signing and distributing paychecks.

          A weakness in the internal control structure for the payroll cycle exists when <u>the payroll department supervisor is also responsible for authorizing payroll rate changes for all employees</u>. As a result, the custody of or access to assets and the authorization functions do not remain segregated. Therefore, the auditor would most likely assess control risk at the maximum.

          Answer choices other than "C" are incorrect because they represent proper responsibilities for the payroll department supervisor.

30. B   In a properly designed internal control structure, documentation is necessary for each of the major steps in the purchasing and cash disbursement functions. The documents in ordering goods and services begin with a two-part purchase requisition and a multi-part purchase order.

          One copy of the purchase requisition is sent to the accounts (vouchers) payable department and the other copy to the purchasing department.

          Upon receipt of the purchase requisition, the purchasing department prepares a purchase order, with the original and a copy going to the vendor, and copies distributed internally to receiving, accounts (vouchers) payable, and the department that made the request. On the receiving department copy, the quantity ordered is generally blacked out so that receiving clerks will take a blind count of the goods received.

Upon receipt of the merchandise by the receiving department, the receiving clerk should match the goods with the vendor's shipping document and the copy of the approved purchase order on file.

In turn, an independent count of the merchandise is made and a three-part receiving report is prepared, indicating the quantity, description of goods, and vendor name and address. Copies of the receiving report are distributed to the initiating, purchasing, and accounts (vouchers) payable departments.

Typically, upon <u>receipt of a vendor's invoice</u> (which includes an attached remittance advice), <u>the invoice is checked for mathematical accuracy by the accounts (vouchers) payable department, and then matched against copies of the receiving report, inspection report, purchase order, and purchase requisition</u>. The accounting department is then in a position to approve the invoice, and a voucher (i.e., a request for payment) is prepared. The entire voucher package is then checked and approved by a responsible individual in the accounts (vouchers) payable department, and the amount is posted to the expense ledger.

Answer choices "A" and "C" are incorrect because these procedures would allow the same person to handle the documents for the authorization of payment and participate in the recordkeeping function.

Answer choice "D" is incorrect because it would allow the same person to execute the authorization for payment and validate that payments were made.

31. C   The objective of using the test data (sometimes referred to as test decks) approach is to determine whether the client's computer programs can correctly handle valid and invalid transactions as they arise. To fulfill this objective, the auditor develops input for different types of transactions, which are then processed under the auditor's control, using the client's computer programs and equipment.

The auditor's test data must include both valid and <u>invalid</u> transactions in order to determine whether the client's computer programs will react properly to the different kinds of data, such as <u>employee ID numbers</u>. By using test data, which the auditor controls and which has a known output, the auditor is able to gain certain assurances relating to the procedures contained within the program.

If the general and application controls are functioning properly, the client's program should detect all of the exceptions planted in the test data by the auditor. Thus, to be an effective and useful audit tool, test data must specifically test each control in which the auditor is interested.

Although answer choices "A," "B," and "D" are of concern to the auditor, they involve "unauthorized," rather than "invalid," situations and would not be tested by the use of the test data method.

32.   C   Where direct and indirect labor represent a significant portion of inventory valuation, as in the case of manufacturing and construction companies, the improper account classification of payroll can significantly affect this asset valuation. For example, the overhead charged to inventory at the balance sheet date can be misstated if administrative salaries are charged to indirect manufacturing costs, or direct labor is charged to manufacturing overhead.

The <u>use of time tickets to record actual labor worked on production orders</u> would most likely prevent direct labor hours from being charged to manufacturing overhead.

Answer choice "A" is incorrect because independent counts of work in process (i.e., inventory quantities) for comparison to recorded amounts would not prevent direct labor hours from being charged (i.e., recorded) to manufacturing overhead.

Answer choice "B" is incorrect because comparison of daily journal entries with factory labor summaries, and not with approved production orders, would prevent direct labor hours from being charged to manufacturing overhead. (A factory labor summary is a report showing total direct labor and indirect labor costs charged to specific jobs. As such, these amounts can be compared with the daily journal entries that form the basis for the recorded amount of the inventory.)

Answer choice "D" is incorrect because the reconciliation of work-in-process inventory with periodic cost budgets would not preclude actual direct labor hours from being charged to manufacturing overhead.

33.   D   Control procedures are those policies and procedures in addition to the control environment and accounting system that management has established to provide reasonable assurance that an entity's established objectives will be achieved.
Control procedures include:
1. <u>Segregation of functions</u> - to avoid a position that can both perpetrate and conceal an error, etc.
2. <u>Proper authorization of transactions and activities</u> - need for independent evidence that authorizations are issued by personnel acting within the scope of their authority, and that transactions conform to such authorization.
3. <u>Adequate safeguards</u> over access to and use of assets and records.

4. <u>Recording of transactions</u> - design and use of adequate documents and records to help ensure proper recording of transactions and events; e.g., use of prenumbered invoices.
5. <u>Checks on performance</u> and proper valuation of recorded amounts; e.g., clerical checks, reconciliations, comparison of assets with recorded amounts.

In light of item "5," <u>use of periodic inventory counts to adjust perpetual inventory records</u> would be the internal control procedure most likely used to maintain accurate inventory records.

Answer choice "A" is incorrect because the comparison of perpetual inventory records with the current cost of individual items may result in accurate pricing but would not result in accurate inventory records.

Answer choice "B" is incorrect because a just-in-time inventory system to maintain minimum inventory levels does not, in and of itself, result in accurate inventory records.

Answer choice "C" is incorrect because the payment for goods does not relate to the maintenance of inventory records.

34. A   Proper safeguarding against the loss of marketable securities through concealment of fraud requires segregation of:
1. The custody of, or access to, marketable securities from the accounting or recordkeeping responsibility for the securities.
2. The proper authorization of transactions from the custody of, or access to, the marketable securities.
3. Operational responsibility from recordkeeping responsibility.

In light of item "2" above, separation of the custody of marketable securities from the recordkeeping responsibility to reduce the possibility of concealing fraud is ensured when <u>an independent trust company, as custodian of the marketable securities, has no direct contact with the entity's employees responsible for maintaining investment accounting records</u>. The trust company would release the securities only on receipt of proper authorization from the entity. The individual responsible for recordkeeping has no direct contact with the trust company, thereby minimizing the opportunity for loss.

Answer choice "B" is incorrect because the registration of securities in the name of the trust company would increase the possibility of concealing fraud.

Answer choice "C" is incorrect because the mailing of interest and dividend checks directly to an entity employee authorized to sell securities would increase the possibility of concealing fraud.

Answer choice "D" is incorrect because the placing of securities in a safe-deposit vault under the trust company's exclusive control, as custodian, would increase the possibility of concealing fraud.

35.   A   Assertions are representations by management that are embodied in financial statement components. They can be classified as to:

1.   Existence or occurrence - deals with whether assets or liabilities of the entity exist at a given date, or whether recorded transactions have occurred during a given period.
2.   Completeness - deals with whether all transactions and accounts that should be presented in the financial statements are so included.
3.   Rights and obligations - deals with whether assets are the rights of the entity (i.e., owned) at a given time.
4.   Valuation and allocation - deals with whether asset, liability, revenue, or expense components have been included in the financial statements at the appropriate amounts.
5.   Presentation and disclosure - deals with whether particular components of the financial statements are properly classified, described, and disclosed.

In light of item "4," an entity's policy of obtaining credit approval before shipping goods to customers helps ensure that customers can pay for credit sales and thus, accounts receivable are properly valued. Accordingly, an auditor tests this policy in support of management's financial statement assertion of valuation or allocation.

Answer choices other than "A" are incorrect because the policy of obtaining credit approval before shipment is not relevant to the assertions listed.

36.   D   An entity may use services of other organizations to process significant transactions or to handle significant assets or liabilities. Examples of service organizations include EDP service centers and bank trust departments. The internal control structure of the service organization may be considered part of the user organization's internal control structure and thus be subject to audit planning and control risk assessment considerations by the auditor of the user organization.

In planning the audit, the user auditor should consider available information about the service organization's internal control structure, including reports issued by the service auditor. In assessing control risk below the maximum level for assertions related to controls at the service organization, the user auditor should obtain from the service auditor a report on the operating effectiveness of the controls at the service organization. The user auditor should gain satisfaction concerning the service auditor's professional reputation as a basis for reliance on the report. If a service auditor's report is not available, it may be necessary for the user auditor or the service auditor to perform tests of controls at the service organization. If the user auditor is unable to obtain sufficient evidence concerning his or her audit objectives, the user auditor should qualify or disclaim the opinion on the financial statements due to a scope limitation.

The <u>user</u> <u>auditor</u> <u>should</u> <u>not</u> <u>make</u> <u>reference</u> <u>to</u> <u>the</u> <u>report</u> <u>of</u> <u>the</u> <u>service</u> <u>auditor</u> <u>as</u> <u>a</u> <u>basis,</u> <u>in</u> <u>part,</u> <u>for</u> <u>his</u> <u>or</u> <u>her</u> <u>own</u> <u>opinion</u> <u>on</u> <u>the</u> <u>user</u> <u>organization's</u> <u>financial</u> <u>statements</u>. The service auditor's report is used in the audit, but the service auditor is not responsible for examining any portion of the financial statements as of any specific date or for any specified period. Thus, there cannot be a division of responsibility for the audit of the financial statements.

Answer choices other than "D" are incorrect because the user auditor may not refer to the report of the service auditor as a basis, in part, for the user auditor's opinion.

37.   A   SSAE #2, "Reporting on an Entity's Internal Control Structure over Financial Reporting," provides guidance when performing attestation engagements to examine and report on management's written assertion about the effectiveness of an entity's internal control structure as of a point in time or during a period of time.

Management may present its written assertion about the effectiveness of the entity's internal control structure as a separate report that will accompany the practitioner's report, or as a representation letter to the practitioner.

The practitioner's objective in an <u>attestation</u> <u>engagement</u> <u>to</u> <u>examine</u> <u>and</u> <u>report</u> <u>on</u> <u>management's</u> <u>assertions</u> <u>about</u> <u>the</u> <u>effectiveness</u> <u>of</u> <u>the</u> <u>entity's</u> <u>internal</u> <u>control</u> <u>structure</u> is to express an opinion about whether management's assertions regarding the effectiveness of the entity's internal control structure are fairly stated, in all material respects, based upon the control criteria used.

Answer choices other than "A" are incorrect because they do not represent attestation engagements to report on an entity's internal control structure over financial reporting.

38.   B   The gathering of evidential matter from which the auditor can form an opinion as to the fairness of financial statements is mandated under GAAS and is covered by the third standard of field work. To be useful for this purpose, evidence must be (1) competent; that is, it must be both valid (true) and relevant (pertaining to the matter under review), and (2) sufficient enough to form a conclusion.

The following presumptions about the validity of evidential matter should be considered:
1. Evidential matter obtained from independent sources outside an entity provides greater assurance of reliability than evidence obtained solely from within the organization.
2. When accounting data and financial statements are developed under strong internal controls, reliability is enhanced.
3. The auditor's direct personal knowledge, obtained through physical examination, observation, computation, and inspection, is more persuasive than information obtained indirectly from independent outside sources.

In light of the above, a presumption that <u>an auditor's opinion, to be economically useful, is formed within reasonable time and based on evidence obtained at a reasonable cost</u>, does not relate to the competence of audit evidence.

Answer choices other than "B" are incorrect because they all are presumptions that relate to the competence of audit evidence.

39.   A   Assertions are representations by management that are embodied in financial statement components. They can be classified as to:
1.   <u>Existence or occurrence</u> - deals with whether assets or liabilities of the entity exist at a given date, or whether recorded transactions have occurred during a given period.
2.   <u>Completeness</u> - deals with whether all transactions and accounts that should be presented in the financial statements are so included.
3.   <u>Rights and obligations</u> - deals with whether assets are the rights of the entity (i.e., owned) at a given time.
4.   <u>Valuation and allocation</u> - deals with whether asset, liability, revenue, or expense components have been included in the financial statements at the appropriate amounts.
5.   <u>Presentation and disclosure</u> - deals with whether particular components of the financial statements are properly classified, described, and disclosed.

In light of item "4," an auditor's conclusion that no excessive costs for idle plant were charged to inventory most likely related to the auditor's objective of obtaining evidence related to the <u>valuation</u> <u>and</u> <u>allocation</u> assertion.

Answer choices other than "A" are incorrect because they do not represent assertions concerning the auditor's conclusion that no excessive costs for idle plant were charged to inventory.

40.   B   As higher levels of assurance are desired from analytical procedures, more predictable relationships are required to develop the expectation.

Relationships in a stable environment are usually more predictable than relationships in a dynamic, or unstable, environment. Relationships involving income statement accounts that are not subject to management discretion, such as <u>interest</u> <u>expense</u>, tend to be more predictable than relationships involving only balance sheet accounts, since income statement accounts represent transactions over a period of time, whereas balance sheet accounts represent amounts as of a particular point in time.

Answer choices "A" and "C" are incorrect because they represent balance sheet accounts and are less predictable.

Answer choice "D" is incorrect because relationships involving transactions subject to management's discretion (e.g., travel and entertainment expense) are sometimes less predictable.

41.   B   Assertions are representations by management that are embodied in financial statement components. They can be classified as to:

1.   <u>Existence or occurrence</u> - deals with whether assets or liabilities of the entity exist at a given date, or whether recorded transactions have occurred during a given period.

2.   <u>Completeness</u> - deals with whether all transactions and accounts that should be presented in the financial statements are so included.

3.   <u>Rights and obligations</u> - deals with whether assets are the rights of the entity (i.e., owned) at a given time.

4.   <u>Valuation and allocation</u> - deals with whether asset, liability, revenue, or expense components have been included in the financial statements at the appropriate amounts.

5.   <u>Presentation and disclosure</u> - deals with whether particular components of the financial statements areproperly classified, described, and disclosed.

In light of item "2," selecting test counts and tracing them to the client's inventory listing would most likely obtain evidence that inventory that should be presented in the financial statements is so included; i.e., the <u>completeness</u> of inventory.

Answer choices other than "B" are incorrect because they represent assertions for which evidence is not provided when tracing test counts to the client's inventory listing.

42.   B   Assertions are representations by management that are embodied in financial statement components. They can be classified as to:

1.   <u>Existence or occurrence</u> - deals with whether assets or liabilities of the entity exist at a given date, or whether recorded transactions have occurred during a given period.

2.   <u>Completeness</u> - deals with whether all transactions and accounts that should be presented in the financial statements are so included.

3.   <u>Rights and obligations</u> - deals with whether assets are the rights of the entity (i.e., owned) at a given time.

4.   <u>Valuation and allocation</u> - deals with whether asset, liability, revenue, or expense components have been included in the financial statements at the appropriate amounts.

5.   <u>Presentation and disclosure</u> - deals with whether particular components of the financial statements are properly classified, described, and disclosed.

In light of item "1," an auditor's examination of new additions that are listed on an analysis of plant and equipment provides evidence of <u>existence</u>; i.e., that the new additions reflected in plant and equipment balances actually exist.

Answer choices other than "B" are incorrect because they represent assertions for which evidence is not provided when examining new additions that are listed on an analysis of plant and equipment.

43.   C   Sampling risk arises from the possibility that, when a test of controls or a substantive test is limited to a sample, the auditor's conclusions may be different from the conclusions that would have been drawn had the test been applied to all of the items in the population.

The auditor is concerned with two aspects of sampling risk in conducting tests of controls:
1.   Risk of assessing control risk too low - the risk that the sample supports the auditor's planned control risk when, in fact, the true occurrence rate does not justify such an assessed level of control risk.
2.   Risk of assessing control risk too high - the risk that the sample does not support the auditor's planned control risk when, in fact, the true occurrence rate does support such an assessed level of control risk.

The two aspects of sampling risk with which the auditor is concerned in conducting substantive test of details are:

1.   The risk of incorrect acceptance - the risk that the sample supports the conclusion that the recorded account balances are not materially misstated when, in fact, they are.
2.   The risk of incorrect rejection - the risk that the sample supports the conclusion that the recorded account balances are materially misstated when, in fact, they are not.

Answer choices "A" and "B" are incorrect because they relate to tests of controls, and not to tests of details.

Answer choice "D" is incorrect because it represents the risk of accepting a sample when it should be rejected.

44.   D   The objective in determining the sample size in a test of controls is to obtain a sample that will meet desired statistical objectives for each control being tested. The factors that affect the determination of sample size are (1) tolerable rate, (2) risk of assessing control risk too low, and (3) the expected population deviation rate.

The expected population deviation rate has a significant and direct effect on sample size. These effects recognize that, as the expected population deviation rate increases, more exact information is required and a larger sample size results. Conversely, a smaller sample size would result as the expected population deviation rate decreases.

On the other hand, the tolerable rate and risk of assessing control risk too low are inversely related to sample size. Accordingly, as these two parameters increase, a decrease in sample size will result.

Answer choices other than "D" are based on incorrect assumptions and/or illogical combinations.

45.   D   The auditor is responsible for evaluating the reasonableness of accounting estimates made by management (e.g., allowance for doubtful accounts, warranty expenses, etc.). When planning and performing procedures to evaluate accounting estimates, the auditor should consider, with an attitude of professional skepticism, both the subjective and objective factors.

When evaluating accounting estimates, the auditor's objective is to obtain sufficient competent evidential matter to provide reasonable assurance that:
1.   All accounting estimates that could be material to the financial statements have been developed.
2.   The accounting estimates are reasonable in the circumstances.
3.   The accounting estimates are presented in conformity with GAAP and are properly disclosed.

Answer choices other than "D" are incorrect because they do not represent objectives of the auditor in evaluating accounting estimates.

46.   D   SSARS #1, "Compilation and Review of Financial Statements," provides guidance in connection with unaudited statements of a nonpublic entity.

For a compilation of financial statements, the accountant should possess a level of knowledge of the accounting principles and practices of the industry in which the entity operates and an understanding of the entity's business that will enable him or her to compile financial statements that are appropriate in form for an entity operating in that industry. This standard does not prevent an accountant from accepting a compilation engagement for an entity in an industry with which the accountant has no previous experience. It does, however, place upon the accountant a responsibility to obtain the required level of knowledge.

Similarly, for a review of financial statements, the accountant should possess a level of knowledge of the accounting principles and practices of the industry in which the entity operates and an understanding of the entity's business. This does not prevent an accountant from accepting a review engagement for an entity in an industry with which the accountant has no previous experience. It does, however, place upon the accountant a responsibility to obtain the required level of knowledge.

Answer choices other than "D" are based on incorrect assumptions and/or combinations.

47.   A   The best audit procedure that could assist in determining the existence of unrecorded trade accounts payable, is to review a sample of cash disbursements in the period subsequent to year-end

since the disbursements clearly indicate the liquidation of liabilities. The auditor seeks to ascertain in which time period the liability arose; i.e., the period under audit or the period subsequent thereto.

Answer choice "B" is incorrect because it incorporates the investigation of payables recorded prior to, as well as subsequent to, year-end and a determination of whether they are supported by receiving reports. The examination of the former will not necessarily detect unrecorded liabilities. Rather, it might reveal liabilities recorded in the period under audit that belong in the subsequent period.

Answer choice "C" is incorrect because it relates to recorded cash payments and not to unrecorded liabilities.

Answer choice "D" is incorrect because reconciling vendors' statements to receiving reports just prior to year-end may not detect unrecorded liabilities due to the fact that vendor statements may be missing, nonexistent, or received at a later date.

48.　A　Audit procedures to test for unrecorded retirements of equipment would relate to management's assertion of existence; i.e., whether assets of the entity exist. An audit procedure to <u>select items of equipment</u> <u>from</u> <u>the</u> <u>accounting</u> <u>records</u> <u>and</u> <u>then</u> <u>locate</u> <u>them</u> <u>during the</u> <u>plant</u> <u>tour</u> would provide evidence that assets had been retired but not removed from the accounting records.

Answer choice "B" is incorrect because the comparison of depreciation journal entries with similar prior-year entries in search of fully depreciated equipment would not indicate whether such assets were removed from the accounting records.

Answer choice "C" is incorrect because inspecting items observed during the plant tour and tracing them to the equipment subsidiary ledger provides evidence of unrecorded equipment additions, and not retirements.

Answer choice "D" is incorrect because scanning the general journal would not aid in the identification of unrecorded retirements.

49.　C　An auditor performs substantive tests of details on payroll transactions and balances based on the assessed level of control risk for payroll. Substantive tests may be performed when payroll has a significant effect on manufactured inventory, or when the internal control structure for payroll is weak. An auditor most likely would extend substantive tests of payroll when <u>overpayments</u> <u>are</u> <u>discovered</u> <u>in</u> <u>performing</u> <u>tests</u> <u>of</u> <u>details.</u>

Answer choice "A" is incorrect because the extensive audit by the state government would not result in the auditor extending his or her own substantive testing of details.

Answer choice "B" is incorrect because the auditor would utilize the level of payroll expense to determine the initial test of details based on the assessed level of control risk.

Answer choice "D" is incorrect because the amount of overtime would be utilized to determine the initial test of details based on the assessed level of control risk.

50.   D   To determine that investments exist, auditors typically will physically inspect the securities. Generally, security counts should be made as of the balance sheet date because securities may be negotiable, and evidence that they exist on another date does not necessarily provide evidence that they also existed as of the balance sheet date.

If counts cannot be made on the same day, frequently the auditor will place a seal over the boxes containing the securities so that the securities cannot be removed without the auditor's knowledge. This precaution also prevents the entity from transferring assets from one account to another.

Accordingly, if the securities are kept in a bank safe deposit box, and the auditor is unable to count the securities at the balance sheet date, the auditor most likely will request the client to have the bank seal the safe deposit box until the auditor can count the securities at a subsequent date.

Answer choices "A" and "C" are incorrect because the bank is not the custodian of the securities in a safe deposit box.

Answer choice "B" is incorrect because examining supporting evidence for transactions occurring during the year does not provide evidence concerning existence of securities at the balance sheet date.

51.   B   The first standard of field work indicates that the audit work is to be adequately planned, and assistants, if any, are to be properly supervised. Thus, planning the engagement must be supplemented by determining whether the audit plan is being executed as designed. Supervision involves the review of the audit effort and related audit judgments made by assistants to ascertain whether these judgments are appropriate.

In planning his or her audit, the auditor should consider the nature, extent, and timing of work to be done and should prepare a written audit program describing the necessary procedures to be performed. An audit program aids in instructing assistants in the work to be done. It should set forth in reasonable detail the audit procedures that the auditor believes are necessary to accomplish the objectives of the audit.

Answer choices other than "B" are incorrect because although they represent forms of documentation that are generally recommended in the conduct of an audit, they are not specifically required by GAAS.

52.   B   In accordance with SAS #11, "Using The Work of a Specialist," a specialist is one who possesses special skill or knowledge in a field other than accounting or auditing; i.e., an actuary, appraiser, engineer, etc.

When expressing an unqualified opinion, the auditor generally should not refer to the work or findings of a specialist. Such reference might be construed as a qualification of the auditor's opinion or a division of responsibility, neither of which is intended.

If the <u>auditor</u>, <u>as a result of the</u> report or <u>findings of the specialist</u> decides to (1) add an explanatory paragraph describing an uncertainty, (2) add an explanatory paragraph describing his or her substantial doubt about the entity's ability to continue as a going concern, (3) <u>add an explanatory paragraph to emphasize a matter regarding the financial statements</u>, or (4) depart from an unqualified opinion, reference to, and identification of, the specialist may be made in the auditor's report if the auditor believes such reference will facilitate an understanding of the reason for the explanatory paragraph or the departure from the unqualified opinion.

Answer choices other than "B" are incorrect because none of the circumstances support making a reference to the specialist's findings in the auditor's report.

53.   D   Subsequent events are those events that have a material effect and occur after the balance sheet date but before the issuance of the financial statements and the auditor's report.

<u>Type I subsequent events</u> - provide additional information about conditions that actually existed at the balance sheet date. Financial statements should be adjusted.
<u>Type II subsequent events</u> - provide information about conditions that did not exist at the balance sheet date but arose thereafter. Financial statements should not be adjusted. However, they may require disclosure in order to prevent the financial statements from being misleading. Such events include:
1. Sale of a debt or equity issue.
2. Purchase of a business.
3. Loss of assets in a flood or fire.
4. Loss on receivables from conditions arising subsequent to the balance sheet date.

The auditor's standard report implies that the auditor is satisfied that there have been no material changes in GAAP affecting comparability. When there is a material change in accounting principles, the auditor's report should indicate a lack of consistency.

In this question, a type II subsequent event occurred. Accordingly, <u>the financial statements should not be adjusted</u> and <u>the event should be disclosed</u>. Since a subsequent event is not a change in accounting

principle, <u>the</u> <u>auditor's</u> <u>report</u> <u>should</u> <u>not</u> <u>be</u> <u>modified</u> <u>for</u> <u>a</u> <u>lack</u> <u>of</u>
<u>consistency</u>.

Answer choices other than "D" are based on incorrect assumptions
and/or incorrect combinations of responses.

54.   A   As part of an audit performed under GAAS, the independent auditor is
          required to obtain certain written representations from management.
          Such representations are part of the evidential matter the
          independent auditor obtains, but they are not a substitute for the
          application of other auditing procedures necessary to afford a
          reasonable basis for an opinion on the financial statements.
          Representations cover such matters as:
          1. Acknowledgment of management's responsibility for the financial
              statements.
          2. Completeness and availability of the accounting records and
              minutes of meetings of stockholders, directors and audit
              committees.
          3. The absence of unrecorded transactions and errors and
              irregularities in the financial statements.
          4. Noncompliance with aspects of contractual agreements that may
              affect the financial statements.
          5. Information concerning related-party transactions and related
              amounts receivable or payable.
          6. Information concerning subsequent events.
          7. Management's plans or intentions that may affect the carrying
              value or classification of assets or liabilities.
          8. <u>Disclosure</u> <u>of</u> <u>compensating</u> <u>balances</u> <u>or</u> <u>other</u> <u>arrangements</u>
              <u>involving</u> <u>restrictions</u> <u>on</u> <u>cash</u> <u>balances</u>.
          9. Irregularities involving management or employees.

          Answer choice "B" is incorrect because it would be unlikely that
          management could acknowledge responsibility for illegal actions
          committed by employees, since management may not be aware of such
          illegal acts.

          Answer choice "C" is incorrect because obtaining sufficient
          evidential matter is a matter of the auditor's professional judgment
          and is not acknowledged in the client representation letter.

          Answer choice "D" is incorrect because management's acknowledgment
          that there are no material weaknesses in the internal control
          structure is not included in the client representation letter.

55.   B   The auditor must evaluate whether there is substantial doubt
          concerning the entity's ability to continue as a going concern for a
          reasonable time period, not to exceed one year beyond the date of
          the audited financial statements.

          The following might indicate substantial doubt concerning the
          entity's ability to continue as a going concern:
          1. Negative trends, such as recurring operating losses.

2. Other indications of possible financial difficulties, such as default on loan or similar difficulties.
3. Internal matters, such as work stoppages/labor difficulties.
4. External matters, such as legal proceedings and/or legislative matters jeopardizing entity's ability to operate, uninsured catastrophes, and loss of key customers/suppliers.

Accordingly, an audit procedure that <u>confirms with third parties the details of arrangements to maintain financial support</u> would likely assist an auditor in identifying conditions and events that may indicate substantial doubt about an entity's ability to continue as a going concern.

Answer choices other than "B" are incorrect because they represent procedures that would not likely assist an auditor in identifying conditions and events that may indicate substantial doubt about an entity's ability to continue as a going concern.

56. D Many microcomputer applications are useful for auditing. Some of these are specifically designed to perform audit tasks. Common types of applications include electronic spreadsheets, word processing, database management, text database software, communications software, graphics software, and practice management software.

Reviewing the work of staff assistants may be affected by microcomputers because <u>working paper documentation may not contain readily observable details of calculations</u>. For example, accounting transactions, such as discounts and interest calculations, may be generated by computer programs with no visible authorization of individual transactions. In addition, a printed report may only contain summary totals while supporting details are retained in computer files.

Answer choice "A" is incorrect because the audit field work standard for supervision (i.e., the first standard) does not differ for staff assistants using microcomputer methods instead of manual methods.

Answer choice "B" is incorrect because, although the assistance of consultants or specialists may be necessary when using microcomputers in auditing, documenting the supervisory review will generally not require the assistance of consulting services personnel.

Answer choice "C" is incorrect because supervisory personnel must have sufficient computer-related knowledge to review the work of staff assistants using microcomputers.

57. C A related party relationship exists when one party, directly or indirectly, has the ability to influence the management or operating policies of another party so significantly that one of the parties might be prevented from fully pursuing its own separate interests. Audit procedures to identify related party transactions include:

1. Emphasizing the auditing of material transactions with known related parties.
2. Reviewing minutes, proxy material, and management conflict-of-interest statements.
3. Considering whether transactions are occurring and are not being given accounting recognition; e.g., services at no charge.
4. Examining unusual or large transactions.
5. Reviewing confirmations of compensating balance arrangements, and loans receivable and payable for guarantees.

Accordingly, <u>reviewing accounting records for nonrecurring transactions recognized near the balance sheet date</u> most likely would assist an auditor in identifying related party transactions. In these situations, an auditor might question the existence of a valid business purpose for such one-time transactions.

Answer choice "A" is incorrect because retesting ineffective internal control procedures previously reported to the audit committee would not identify related party transactions.

Answer choice "B" is incorrect because sending second requests for unanswered positive confirmations of accounts receivable would not identify the debtor as a related party.

Answer choice "D" is incorrect because inspecting communications with law firms for evidence of unreported contingent liabilities would not likely assist an auditor in identifying related party transactions.

58. C Interim testing increases the risk that misstatements may exist at year-end and not be detected. The greater the time remaining to year-end, the greater the risk.

Difficulty in controlling incremental audit risk should be judged by:
1. The existence of rapidly changing business circumstances that might cause management-misstatement in the remaining period.
2. <u>Whether account balances are reasonably predictable as to amount, composition, and relative significance</u>.
3. Whether the accounting system will permit investigation of unusual transactions, fluctuations, or changes in composition.
4. Whether the entity's procedures for analyzing and adjusting accounts at interim dates and establishing proper cutoffs are appropriate.

Answer choice "A" is incorrect because assessing control risk at below the maximum is not required in order to have a reasonable basis for extending audit conclusions from an interim date to the balance-sheet date; however, if the auditor assesses control risk at the maximum during the remaining period, he or she should consider whether the effectiveness of the substantive tests to cover that period will be impaired.

Answer choice "B" is incorrect because the auditor deals only with accounts that are material to the financial statements.

Answer choice "D" is incorrect because the auditor, at the conclusion of the audit, should obtain written representation from management that all financial records and related data were made available.

59.   D   <u>During</u> <u>a</u> <u>compilation</u>, <u>the</u> <u>accountant</u> <u>is</u> <u>not</u> <u>required</u> <u>to</u> make inquiries or <u>perform</u> other procedures (including <u>analytical</u> <u>procedures</u> designed to identify relationships that appear to be unusual) to verify, corroborate, or review information supplied by the entity.

<u>In</u> <u>performing</u> <u>a</u> <u>review</u>, <u>the</u> <u>accountant</u> makes inquiries of the entity's personnel and <u>performs</u> <u>analytical</u> <u>procedures</u>. Specific review procedures include the following:
1.   Inquiries concerning the entity's accounting principles and practices and the methods followed in applying them.
2.   Inquiries concerning the entity's procedures for recording, classifying, and summarizing transactions.
3.   Analytical procedures designed to identify relationships and individual items that appear to be unusual.
4.   Inquiries concerning actions taken at meetings of stockholders and the board of directors that may affect the financial statements.
5.   Reading the financial statements to consider whether they appear to be in conformity with GAAP.
6.   Inquiries concerning consistency in application of GAAP, changes in business activities or accounting principles and practices, and subsequent events.

Answer choices other than "D" are based on incorrect assumptions and/or combinations.

60.   C   The purpose of a review is to provide the accountant with a basis for expressing limited assurance that the financial statements conform to GAAP or to a comprehensive basis of accounting other than GAAP.

In performing a review, the accountant makes inquiries of the entity's personnel and performs analytical procedures. Specific review procedures include the following:
1.   Inquiries concerning the entity's accounting principles and practices and the methods followed in applying them.
2.   Inquiries concerning the entity's procedures for recording, classifying, and summarizing transactions.
3.   Analytical procedures designed to identify relationships and individual items that appear to be unusual.
4.   Inquiries concerning actions taken at meetings of stockholders and the board of directors that may affect the financial statements.
5.   Reading the financial statements to consider whether they appear to be in conformity with GAAP.

6. Inquiries concerning consistency in application of GAAP, changes in business activities or accounting principles and practices, and subsequent events.

A representation letter must be obtained from members of management whom the accountant believes are responsible for and knowledgeable about, directly or through others in the organization, the matters covered in the representation letter. Normally, the chief executive officer and chief financial officer should sign the representation letter.

A review, unlike an audit, does not contemplate assessing an entity's internal control structure. Therefore, assessing control risk would not be an appropriate procedure in a review.

Answer choices other than "C" are incorrect because they represent procedures normally performed during a review engagement.

61.   B   When an accountant is associated with the financial statements of a publicly held entity, but has not audited or reviewed them, he or she must disclaim an opinion on them. In this situation, the accountant has no responsibility for the application of procedures other than reading the financial statements for obvious material misstatements. In this context, the term "misstatements" refers to mistakes in the preparation of financial statements, including arithmetical or clerical mistakes, and mistakes in the application of accounting principles, including inadequate disclosure.

Answer choice "A" is incorrect because it refers to a procedure that is not relevant to preparing financial statements.

Answer choice "C" is incorrect because ascertaining conformity with GAAP would require the use of audit or review procedures, which are not part of the engagement to prepare financial statements.

Answer choice "D" is incorrect because the omission of substantially all required disclosures is but one example of an obvious material misstatement.

62.   B   During the course of an audit, an auditor may become aware of events that seriously threaten the client's continued existence. Questions of continued existence usually hinge upon a company's ability to meet its financial obligations, but may also involve such factors as loss of key employees or major customers.

After considering evidence contrary to the assumption of a going concern, and after considering any mitigating factors (which may include management's plans), the auditor may conclude that substantial doubt remains about the client's ability to continue in operation. Such a conclusion significantly affects the financial statements; accordingly, it is generally appropriate to issue an unqualified opinion with an additional explanatory paragraph (following the opinion paragraph) that refers to the disclosures concerning the client's ability to continue as a going concern. Inadequate disclosure pertaining to the entity's ability to continue as a going concern represents a departure from GAAP and would generally result in the issuance of an "except for" qualified opinion or an adverse opinion.

However, it should be pointed out that an auditor is not precluded from declining to express an opinion in cases involving uncertainties. If the auditor decides to disclaim an opinion, the uncertainties and their possible effects on the financial statements should be disclosed in the appropriate manner, and the auditor's report should give all the substantive reasons for the disclaimer of opinion.

Therefore, in the circumstances, the auditor's responsibility is to <u>consider the adequacy of disclosure about the entity's possible inability to continue as a going concern</u>.

Answer choice "A" is incorrect because the issuance of a qualified or adverse opinion would generally result from inadequate disclosure.

Answer choice "C" is incorrect because the auditor's conclusion that there is substantial doubt about the client's ability to continue as a going concern would not require communication with the audit committee regarding adjustments to accounting estimates.

Answer choice "D" is incorrect because modification of the prior year's audit report is not appropriate.

63.   A   When an auditor submits, to a client or others, a document containing the basic financial statements and other accompanying information, he or she must report on all of the client representations in the document. Examples of such representations are (1) additional details or explanations of items related to the financial statements, (2) consolidating information, (3) historical summaries, and (4) statistical data.

When such additional information is submitted, the auditor is required by the fourth standard of reporting to indicate the degree of responsibility he or she is taking. The auditor should either express an opinion as to the fairness of the additional information in relation to the financial statements taken as a whole, or disclaim an opinion, depending on whether the information has been subjected to the auditing procedures applied in the audit of the basic financial statements. When reporting in this manner, the measurement of materiality is the <u>same as that used in forming an opinion on the basic financial statements taken as a whole</u>.

Answer choices other than "A" are incorrect because they all reflect inappropriate measures of materiality for additional information accompanying basic financial statements in an auditor-submitted document.

64.   A   Ordinarily, when an independent accountant's report is included in registration statements, proxy statements, or periodic reports filed under the federal securities statutes, the accountant's responsibility generally is no different from that involved in other types of reporting.

The investing public must be provided a prospectus that includes information submitted to the SEC in a registration statement. The Securities Act of 1933 indicates that a statement should be made in the prospectus that certain information is included in the registration statements in reliance upon the report of certain named experts, inclusive of accountants, engineers, appraisers, etc. Furthermore, the Act states that an expert may be held liable by any purchaser of securities for any false and/or misleading statements of material facts or material omissions from that portion of the financial statements that is "expertised" (i.e., for accountants, the portion of the financial statements covered by the CPA's opinion).

In general, a report based on a review of interim financial information of a public entity is not considered to be a report governed by federal securities statutes.

Furthermore, the SEC requires that when an independent accountant's report based on a review of interim financial information is incorporated by reference in a registration statement, the prospectus must clarify that the accountant's report is not a part of the registration statement within the meaning of the Securities Act of 1933.

Answer choice "B" is incorrect because it is not an appropriate statement for a prospectus.

Answer choice "C" is incorrect because the accountant's review should be performed in accordance with the appropriate standards issued by the American Institute of Certified Public Accountants.

Answer choice "D" is incorrect because it is not appropriate for a prospectus or a review report.

65.   A   When part of the audit is performed by another auditor, the principal auditor must be able to gain satisfaction as to the independence and professional reputation of the other CPA, as well as to the quality of the audit. Having done so, the principal auditor must then decide whether he or she is willing to express an opinion on the financial statements taken as a whole without referring to the audit of the other auditor. If the auditor decides to do so, it should not be stated that part of the audit was performed by another auditor, because to do so may cause a reader to misinterpret the degree of responsibility being assumed. As such, a standard audit report is issued when the principal auditor decides not to make reference to the other auditor.

Generally, no reference to the other auditor is necessary when:
1. The other auditor is associated with the principal auditor.
2. The principal auditor retained, supervised, or guided and controlled the other auditor.
3. The principal auditor becomes satisfied as to the work of the other auditor.
4. The work of the other auditor is not material in relation to the financial statements.

When the auditor's report is based in part on the opinion of another auditor, and the principal auditor decides to make reference to the audit of the other auditor, he or she should indicate the division of responsibility in the introductory, scope, and opinion paragraphs of the report.

Answer choice "B" is incorrect because no reference to the other auditor is generally made for work that is immaterial to the financial statements.

Answer choice "C" is incorrect because the principal auditor must become satisfied as to the independence and professional reputation of the other auditor, regardless of the decision of whether or not to make reference to the other auditor.

Answer choice "D" is incorrect because the type of opinion expressed by the other auditor may be included in the report of the principal auditor (i.e., in the introductory paragraph) as part of the indication of divided responsibility.

66.   C   An auditor may reissue a previously issued report at the request of the client. It is important that the auditor, in the reissued report, use the original report date. This removes any implication that records, transactions, or events after that date have been examined or reviewed. In such cases, the auditor has no responsibility to make further investigation or inquiry as to events that may have occurred during the period between the original report date and the release date of the reissued report.

Answer choices other than "C" are incorrect because they reflect inappropriate report dates.

67.   A   Management, accountants, and intermediaries (i.e., attorneys, investment bankers) often consult with professionals, including other accountants, on the application of accounting principles (GAAP and other comprehensive bases of accounting) to specific transactions or to increase their knowledge of specific financial reporting issues. Such consultations are meaningful in that they may provide information and insights not otherwise available.

When an accountant is asked to prepare a written report on the application of accounting principles to a specific transaction, the report should ordinarily include the following:

1. A brief description of the nature of the engagement and a statement that the engagement was performed in accordance with applicable AICPA standards.
2. A description of the transaction(s), a statement of the relevant facts, circumstances, and assumptions, and a statement about the source of the information. Principals to specific transactions should be identified, and hypothetical transactions should be described as involving nonspecific principals (for example, Company A and Company B).
3. A statement describing the appropriate accounting principle(s) to be applied or the type of opinion that may be rendered on the entity's financial statements and, if appropriate, a description of the reasons for the reporting accountant's conclusion.
4. A statement that the responsibility for the proper accounting treatment rests with the preparers of the financial statements, who should consult with their continuing accountants.
5. A <u>statement</u> <u>that</u> <u>any</u> <u>difference</u> <u>in</u> <u>the</u> <u>facts</u>, <u>circumstances</u>, <u>or</u> <u>assumptions</u> <u>presented</u> <u>may</u> <u>change</u> <u>the</u> <u>report</u>.

Answer choices other than "A" are incorrect because they represent statements that are not appropriate for inclusion in reports on the application of accounting principles.

68.   D   The objective of pro forma financial information is to show what the significant effects on historical financial information might have been had a consummated or proposed transaction (or event) occurred at an earlier date. Pro forma financial information is commonly used to show the effects of transactions such as business combination, changes in capitalization, disposition of a significant portion of business, or changes in the form of business organization or status as an autonomous entity.

An accountant's report on pro forma financial information should include:
1. An identification of the pro forma financial information.
2. A <u>reference</u> <u>to</u> <u>the</u> <u>financial</u> <u>statements</u> <u>from</u> <u>which</u> <u>the</u> <u>historical</u> <u>financial</u> <u>information</u> <u>is</u> <u>derived</u>, and a statement as to whether such financial statements were audited or reviewed.
3. A statement that the examination or review of the pro forma financial information was made in accordance with standards established by the American Institute of Certified Public Accountants. If a review is performed, the report should include the following statement:

> "A review is substantially less in scope than an examination, the objective of which is the expression of an opinion on the pro forma financial information. Accordingly, we do not express such an opinion."

4. A separate paragraph explaining the objective of pro forma financial information and its limitations.

Answer choices other than "D" are incorrect because they refer to statements that are inappropriate for a report on a review of pro forma financial information.

69. D   In some situations, the auditor may wish to emphasize a matter regarding the financial statements. Such information should be presented in an additional paragraph of the audit report, the inclusion of which <u>is appropriate</u> and <u>would</u> <u>not</u> <u>negate</u> <u>the</u> <u>unqualified</u> <u>opinion</u>. Emphasis that the entity being reported on had significant transactions with related parties is a situation that may be presented in an additional paragraph.

   Answer choice "A" is incorrect because emphasis of a matter, by itself, does not call for an "except for" qualified opinion.

   Answer choice "B" is incorrect because it is acceptable for the auditor to emphasize, in his or her report, a matter that has already been disclosed in the notes to the financial statements.

   Answer choice "C" is incorrect because the auditor should not refer, in the opinion paragraph, to the matter being emphasized, and a phrase such as "with the foregoing explanation" could be misconstrued as a qualification of the opinion.

70. B   If, after issuing his or her report, the independent auditor concludes that an auditing procedure considered necessary at the time of the audit was omitted from such audit, the auditor should first assess the importance of the omitted procedure to his or her present ability to support the opinion previously expressed on the financial statements taken as a whole.

   To accomplish this, the auditor should review the working papers, make necessary inquiries, and reevaluate the overall scope of the audit. For example, the results of other procedures that were applied may tend to compensate for the one omitted, or make its omission less important. Also, subsequent audits may provide audit evidence in support of the previously expressed opinion.

   If the auditor concludes that his or her present ability to support the previously expressed opinion is impaired, he or she should promptly <u>undertake</u> <u>to</u> <u>apply</u> the omitted procedure or apply <u>alternative</u> <u>procedures</u> <u>that</u> <u>would</u> <u>provide</u> <u>a</u> <u>satisfactory</u> <u>basis</u> <u>for</u> <u>the</u> <u>unqualified</u> <u>opinion</u>.

   Answer choice "A" is incorrect because it refers to an action that would be necessary only if alternative procedures cannot be undertaken to provide a satisfactory basis for the opinion.

   Answer choice "C" is incorrect because a reissued report is inappropriate. Further, the departure from GAAS would result in a qualified opinion or disclaimer of opinion.

Answer choice "D" is incorrect because the need for the omitted procedure or alternative procedures (i.e., substantive tests) would not be eliminated by performing tests of controls.

71.   D   The auditor's standard report includes the following elements and paragraphs:
1.   <u>Title</u> - The report must contain a title that includes the word "independent."
2.   <u>Addressee</u> - The report should be addressed to the company, its board of directors, or the stockholders.
3.   <u>Introductory paragraph</u> - Includes statements that the financial statements:
   a.   Were audited.
   b.   Are the responsibility of management and that the auditor's responsibility is to express an opinion on the audited financial statements.
4.   <u>Scope paragraph</u> - Includes statements that:
   a.   The audit was conducted in accordance with GAAS.
   b.   GAAS requires that the auditor plan and perform the audit to obtain reasonable assurance about whether the financial statements are free of material misstatements.
   c.   An audit includes:
      (1)   Examining, on a test basis, evidence supporting the amounts and disclosures in the financial statements.
      (2)   Assessing the accounting principles used and significant estimates made by management.
      (3)   Evaluating the overall financial statement presentation.
   d.   The auditor believes that his or her audit provides a reasonable basis for an opinion.
5.   <u>Opinion paragraph</u> - An opinion as to whether the financial statements are presented fairly, in all material respects, in conformity with GAAP.
6.   <u>Signature</u> - Manual or printed signature of the auditor.
7.   <u>Date</u> - Usually the completion of field work.

By contrast, an auditor performing an audit in accordance with Government Auditing Standards is required to report on compliance with laws and regulations and on the internal control structure, in addition to fulfilling the reporting responsibilities under GAAS.

An entity that does not receive governmental financial assistance would not require an audit in accordance with Government Auditing Standards. Thus, the standard audit report would ordinarily be used and would <u>not</u> <u>refer</u> <u>to</u> <u>the</u> <u>entity's</u> <u>internal</u> <u>control</u> <u>structure</u>.

Answer choices other than "D" are incorrect because they represent statements that would be included in the standard auditor's report.

72.   A   An auditor may be engaged to provide reports expressing an opinion on specified elements, accounts, or items of financial statements. GAAP may or may not apply, and such an engagement may be undertaken as a separate engagement or in conjunction with an audit of financial statements.

However, no report should be given on specified elements when the auditor has expressed either an adverse opinion or a disclaimer of opinion, when such reporting could be taken as tantamount to a piecemeal opinion. A piecemeal opinion should not be expressed when the auditor has disclaimed an opinion or has expressed an adverse opinion on the financial statements taken as a whole because a piecemeal opinion tends to overshadow or contradict a disclaimer of opinion or an adverse opinion.

Answer choice "B" is incorrect because an auditor is not prohibited from reporting on only one basic financial statement.

Answer choices "C" and "D" are incorrect because the auditor's report is not appropriate in the situation given.

73.　C　The auditor's standard report implies that the auditor is satisfied that there have been no material changes in GAAP affecting comparability.

When there is a material change in accounting principle, the auditor's report should include an explanatory paragraph (following the opinion paragraph). For example:

> "As discussed in note Z to the financial statements, the company changed its method of computing depreciation in 19XX."

The auditor's concurrence with such a change is implicit unless he or she takes exception to the change. Although the report is modified, it is still unqualified.

In the circumstances, because the effect of the change is not material, the auditor should not refer to consistency in the auditor's report.

Answer choice "A" is incorrect because the effect of the change is not material.

Answer choice "B" is incorrect because the auditor does not concur explicitly with the change in accounting principle.

Answer choice "D" is incorrect because, if required, a change in accounting principle is referred to in an explanatory paragraph following the opinion paragraph.

74.　D　When single-year financial statements are presented, an auditor ordinarily would express an unqualified opinion in an unmodified report if the prior year's financial statements were audited by another CPA whose report, which expressed an unqualified opinion, is not presented. Accordingly, the single-year statements are not affected.

For reports on comparative financial statements, when the financial statements of a prior period have been audited by a predecessor auditor whose report is not presented, the successor auditor should indicate in the introductory paragraph of his or her report (a) that the financial statements of the prior period were audited by another auditor, (b) the date of the report, (c) the type of report issued by the predecessor auditor, and (d) if the report was other than a standard report, the substantive reasons therefor.

Answer choice "A" is incorrect because the inability to obtain audited financial statements to support the entity's investment in a foreign affiliate constitutes a scope limitation that would require a qualified opinion or disclaimer of opinion and modification of the report.

Answer choice "B" is incorrect because the absence of a statement of cash flows constitutes incomplete presentation, necessitating a qualified opinion and a modified report.

Answer choice "C" is incorrect because the emphasis of a matter would require an additional paragraph that modifies the report, even though the opinion is still unqualified.

75. A   The independent auditor is generally precluded from expressing an opinion that the financial statements are presented in conformity with GAAP if these statements contain any material departures. This would ordinarily lead to an "except for" qualified opinion or an adverse opinion. However, when the independent auditor can demonstrate that, due to unusual circumstances, the financial statements presented in accordance with a FASB Standard would otherwise be misleading, an unqualified opinion would be warranted. In this case, the auditor's report must describe the departure, the approximate effects, if practicable, and the reasons why compliance with the principle would result in a misleading statement.

Answer choices other than "A" are incorrect because they refer to opinions that would not be appropriate in the circumstances given.

76. B   The auditor's report is customarily issued in connection with an entity's basic financial statements (i.e., balance sheet, statement of income, statement of retained earnings and statement of cash flows). Each financial statement audited should be specifically identified in the introductory paragraph of the auditor's report.

The objective of the fourth standard of reporting is to prevent misinterpretation of the degree of responsibility the auditor is assuming when his or her name is associated with financial statements. The auditor may express an unqualified opinion on one of the financial statements and express a qualified or adverse opinion, or disclaim an opinion, on another if the circumstances warrant.

A disclaimer of opinion is issued whenever the auditor has been unable to satisfy himself or herself that the financial statement is fairly presented. The necessity for disclaiming an opinion may arise because of a severe limitation on the scope of the audit.

In the question situation, sufficient audit evidence exists for the expression of an <u>unqualified</u> <u>opinion</u> <u>on</u> Tech's 1993 <u>balance</u> <u>sheet</u>. The lack of evidence for the opening inventory would most likely lead to <u>a</u> <u>disclaimer</u> <u>of</u> <u>opinion</u> <u>on</u> Tech's 1993 <u>income</u> <u>statement</u> because the opening inventory is an important component of Tech's cost of goods sold.

Answer choices other than "B" are based on incorrect assumptions and/or illogical combinations.

77. C The auditor's standard report consists of the following elements and paragraphs:
1. <u>Title</u> - The report must contain a title that includes the word "independent."
2. <u>Addressee</u> - The report should be addressed to the company, its board of directors, or the stockholders.
3. <u>Introductory paragraph</u> - Includes statements that the financial statements:
    a. Were audited.
    b. Are the responsibility of management and that the auditor's responsibility is to express an opinion on the audited financial statements.
4. <u>Scope paragraph</u> - Includes statements that:
    a. <u>The</u> <u>audit</u> <u>was</u> <u>conducted</u> <u>in</u> <u>accordance</u> <u>with</u> <u>GAAS</u>.
    b. GAAS requires that the auditor plan and perform the audit to obtain reasonable assurance about whether the financial statements are free of material misstatements.
    c. An audit includes:
        (1) Examining, on a test basis, evidence supporting the amounts and disclosures in the financial statements.
        (2) Assessing the accounting principles used and significant estimates made by management.
        (3) Evaluating the overall financial statement presentation.
    d. The auditor believes that his or her audit provides a reasonable basis for an opinion.
5. <u>Opinion paragraph</u> - An opinion as to whether the financial statements are presented fairly, in all material respects, <u>in</u> <u>conformity</u> <u>with</u> <u>GAAP</u>.
6. <u>Signature</u> - Manual or printed signature of the auditor.
7. <u>Date</u> - Usually the completion of field work.

Answer choices other than "C" are based on incorrect assumptions and/or illogical combinations.

78. C A compilation of financial statements is an accounting service, provided to a nonpublic entity, in which an accountant prepares or assists in preparing financial statements without expressing any assurance that the statements are accurate, complete, or in conformity with GAAP.

The accountant's compilation report, which should accompany the financial statements, should state that:

1. A compilation was performed in accordance with Statements on Standards for Accounting and Review Services issued by the AICPA.

2. A <u>compilation</u> <u>is</u> <u>limited</u> <u>to</u> <u>presenting</u> <u>in</u> <u>the</u> <u>form</u> <u>of</u> <u>financial</u> <u>statements</u> <u>information</u> <u>that</u> <u>is</u> <u>the</u> <u>representation</u> <u>of</u> <u>management</u>.

3. No audit or review has taken place and the accountant does not express an opinion or any other form of assurance on the statements.

4. The report date is the date on which the compilation was completed.

Furthermore, each page of the financial statements should be marked, "See Accountant's Compilation Report."

Answer choice "A" is incorrect because it represents a statement that is not appropriate for inclusion in a compilation report.

Answer choice "B" is incorrect because the accountant does not express limited assurance or any other form of assurance in a compilation report.

Answer choice "D" is incorrect because the accountant compiles financial statements in accordance with standards established by the Accounting and Review Services Committee of the AICPA. The AICPA Auditing Standards Board promulgates standards and procedures that are applicable to audits of financial statements.

79. C   Compiled financial statements that omit substantially all of the disclosures required by GAAP are not comparable to financial statements that include such disclosures. Therefore, an accountant should not issue a report on comparative financial statements when statements for one or more, but not all, of the periods presented omit substantially all of the disclosure required by GAAP.

The accountant's standard compilation report should be modified when the accountant has compiled a nonpublic entity's financial statements that omit substantially all the disclosures required by GAAP.

The compilation report should be modified by adding the following paragraph:

> "Management has elected to omit substantially all of the disclosures required by generally accepted accounting principles. If the omitted disclosures were included in the financial statements, they might influence the user's conclusions about the company's financial position, results of operations, and cash flows. Accordingly, these financial statements are not designed for those who are not informed about such matters."

Therefore, the accountant may compile such financial statements provided that the <u>omission</u> of substantially all disclosures <u>is</u> <u>clearly indicated in the accountant's report and is not</u>, to the accountant's knowledge, <u>undertaken with the intention of misleading those who might reasonably be expected to use such financial statements</u>.

Answer choices other than "C" are based on incorrect assumptions and/or illogical combinations.

80.   B   A review engagement is substantially less in scope than an audit conducted in conformity with GAAS and does not provide a basis for expressing an opinion on the fairness of the financial statements.

The purpose of a review is to provide the accountant with a basis for expressing limited assurance that the financial statements conform either to GAAP or to a comprehensive basis of accounting other than GAAP.

A standard review report should state that:
1.   A review was performed in accordance with Statements on Standards for Accounting and Review Services issued by the American Institute of Certified Public Accountants.
2.   All information included in the financial statements is the representation of the management (owners) of the entity.
3.   A review consists principally of inquiries of company personnel and analytical procedures applied to financial data.
4.   A review is substantially less in scope than an audit, the objective of which is the expression of an opinion regarding the financial statements taken as a whole and, accordingly, no such opinion is expressed.
5.   The accountant is <u>not aware of any material modifications that should be made to the financial statements in order for them to be in conformity with GAAP</u>.

Answer choices other than "B" are incorrect because they represent statements that are not appropriate for inclusion in a report on a review of financial statements.

81.   D   An accountant <u>may issue a review report</u> on one financial statement (such as a balance sheet) and not on the other related financial statements (such as the statements of income, retained earnings, and cash flows), <u>if the scope of the accountant's inquiry and analytical procedures has not been restricted</u>.

Answer choice "A" is incorrect because compliance with the request would not a result in a violation of the ethical standards of the profession.

Answer choice "B" is incorrect because an engagement to review one financial statement is a limited reporting engagement and can be accepted.

Answer choice "C" is incorrect because the existence of material departures from GAAP would affect the review report but not the undertaking of the review itself.

82. C Supplementary information required by the FASB or the GASB is not considered a required part of basic financial statements and need not be audited.

Because supplementary information is not a required part of the basic financial statements, the auditor should apply only certain limited procedures. The following procedures would be considered appropriate:
1. Inquiring of management regarding the methods of preparing the information.
2. Comparing the information for consistency.
3. Considering whether representations concerning the information should be included in a client representation letter.
4. Making additional inquiries if the information is not presented within applicable guidelines.

The auditor need not refer to the information except if it is omitted, departs from FASB or GASB guidelines, or the auditor cannot complete the limited procedures relating to the method of preparation and consistency.

The supplementary information does not change the standards of financial accounting or reporting. The omission of certain supplementary information that is required by the FASB or GASB does not affect the auditor's opinion on the fairness of the presentation of the financial statements in conformity with GAAP.

The auditor need not present the omitted supplementary information, but must identify it in a separate paragraph, the result of which is still an unqualified opinion.

Answer choice "A" is incorrect because the auditor does have a responsibility to apply certain limited procedures to the required supplementary information.

Answer choice "B" is incorrect because the auditor is also required to report deficiencies in, or omissions of, supplementary information.

Answer choice "D" is incorrect because only limited procedures apply to supplementary information. Substantive testing is not required, and the auditor's opinion is not affected.

83. D A special report is required when financial statements are prepared in accordance with a comprehensive basis of accounting other than GAAP, such as a basis used in filing an income tax return.

A report on financial statements prepared on a comprehensive basis of accounting other than GAAP should include a paragraph that states that the audit was conducted in accordance with GAAS.

The auditor's report should also include a separate paragraph indicating the basis of presentation and a reference to the note to the financial statements that describes the basis. This paragraph should include a statement indicating that the basis of presentation is a comprehensive basis of accounting other than GAAP.

Answer choice "A" is incorrect because financial statements prepared on an entity's income tax basis may be examined (i.e., audited) in accordance with generally accepted auditing standards.

Answer choice "B" is incorrect because the auditor should express such an opinion as part of a special report.

Answer choice "C" is incorrect because the auditor's special report should not include an explanation of how the results of operations differ from the cash receipts and disbursements basis of accounting.

84.   A   An auditor performing an audit in accordance with Government Auditing Standards is required to report on compliance with laws and regulations and on the internal control structure in addition to fulfilling the reporting responsibilities under GAAS.

A governmental entity may provide financial assistance to other governmental and/or nongovernmental entities. The recipient entities may be subject to laws and regulations that have a direct and material effect on the financial statements.

The auditor should document both the understanding of the internal control structure as it pertains to compliance with laws and regulations and the procedures performed to evaluate compliance with laws and regulations.

As part of the audit, the auditor should obtain, in part, written management representations acknowledging responsibility for compliance with applicable laws and regulations and that all laws and regulations that have a direct and material effect on the financial statements have been identified and disclosed.

Answer choice "B" is incorrect because management would not represent that its internal control would be designed to detect all illegal acts.

Answer choice "C" is incorrect because management does not express positive or negative assurance to the auditor.

Answer choice "D" is incorrect because it does not reflect a management representation made to the auditor.

85.   B   Government Auditing Standards require a written report on the internal control structure in all audits, regardless of the circumstances. The report should include:
     1. References to the audit of the financial statements and the auditor's report thereon.

2. References to GAAS and Government Auditing Standards issued by the Comptroller General of the U.S.

3. A statement that the audit included consideration of the internal control structure to determine audit procedures as a basis for an opinion on the financial statements and not to provide assurance on the internal control structure.

4. A statement that the internal control structure is the responsibility of management.

5. An explanation of the broad objectives and inherent limitations of any internal control structure.

6. A description of significant internal control structure policies and procedures.

7. A description of the scope of the work to obtain an understanding of the internal control structure and to assess control risk.

8. The definition of reportable conditions, if applicable.

9. A description of any reportable conditions noted, if applicable.

10. The definition of material weaknesses, if applicable.

11. A description of any material weaknesses noted, if applicable.

12. A reference that "nonreportable conditions" (i.e., deficiencies not considered significant enough to be reportable conditions) were separately communicated to management, if applicable.

13. The intended distribution of the report (e.g., audit committee, management, regulatory bodies and, if a matter of public record, that limited distribution is not intended).

Answer choices other than "B" are incorrect because they represent items that would not be included in the auditor's report on the internal control structure.

86. C   The term "uncertainties" refers to financial statement matters that, prior to the issuance of the financial statements, are not susceptible to reasonable estimation. On the basis of the evidence available, the auditor has the responsibility of determining whether the uncertainties are properly accounted for and disclosed.

The effects of uncertainties on the auditor's report depend on professional judgment. When the auditor concludes that there is a minimal likelihood that the resolution of an uncertainty will have a material effect on the financial statements, an unqualified opinion would be issued. However, when the auditor believes that the effect of the uncertainty may be material, the report should be appropriately modified. Accordingly, the uncertainty should be described in a separate explanatory paragraph following the opinion paragraph of the auditor's report. Although the report is modified, the opinion is still unqualified.

Answer choice "A" is incorrect because a qualified opinion is not appropriate.

Answer choice "B" is incorrect because a departure from GAAP, necessitating a qualified opinion, does not exist.

Answer choice "D" is incorrect because the addition of the explanatory paragraph results in modification of the auditor's standard report.

87. C An adverse opinion states that the auditor believes that the financial statements are not fairly presented in accordance with generally accepted accounting principles. In rendering an adverse opinion, the auditor must clearly disclose, in a separate explanatory paragraph, all the reasons therefor and the effects on the financial statements, if reasonably determinable.

It should be understood that the auditor must decide whether the statements taken as a whole are fairly presented except for certain items, or are not fairly presented (and thus misleading) because of them. In the former case, a qualified opinion is rendered; in the latter, an adverse opinion is warranted.

Accordingly, the auditor would be most likely to express an adverse opinion if the financial statements are not in conformity with the FASB Statements regarding the capitalization of leases.

Answer choice "A" is incorrect because it describes a significant client-imposed scope limitation that would result in a disclaimer of an opinion. If a scope limitation is not material enough to overshadow the opinion on fairness, the auditor may express a qualified opinion.

Answer choice "B" is incorrect because the type of opinion to be issued by the auditor cannot be ascertained from the mere fact that tests of controls indicate that the entity's internal control structure cannot be relied upon. In such circumstances, the auditor would increase substantive testing in order to arrive at an informed opinion as to whether the financial statements are fairly presented in conformity with GAAP.

Answer choice "D" is incorrect because it describes circumstances that would result in either an unqualified opinion or a disclaimer of opinion.

88. D When restrictions on the scope of the audit exist, the auditor should express an "except for" qualified opinion or issue a disclaimer of opinion, depending on his or her judgment as to the significance of the restrictions.

A scope limitation may result from restrictions imposed by the client or from circumstances of the engagement, such as the timing of the work, inadequacies in the accounting records, and the inability to obtain sufficient competent evidential matter.

When an "except for" qualified opinion results from a scope limitation, the auditor should describe the situation in an explanatory paragraph preceding the opinion paragraph and should refer to the situation in both the scope and opinion paragraphs. The opening (introductory) paragraph is unaffected.

Answer choices other than "D" are based on incorrect assumptions and/or illogical combinations.

89.   D   When unaudited financial statements <u>of</u> <u>a</u> <u>nonpublic</u> <u>entity</u> for the prior year are presented in comparative form with audited financial statements for the current year, the financial statements should be clearly marked to indicate their status and either (a) <u>the</u> <u>report</u> <u>on</u> <u>the</u> <u>prior</u> <u>period</u> <u>should</u> <u>be</u> <u>reissued</u> <u>or</u> (b) <u>the</u> <u>report</u> <u>on</u> <u>the</u> <u>current</u> <u>period</u> should <u>include</u> <u>a</u> <u>separate</u> <u>paragraph</u> <u>describing</u> <u>the</u> <u>responsibility</u> <u>assumed</u> <u>for</u> <u>the</u> <u>unaudited</u> <u>financial</u> <u>statements</u> of the prior period.

Answer choices other than "D" are based on incorrect assumptions and/or illogical combinations.

90.   D   If an auditor has previously qualified his or her opinion on the financial statements of a prior period because of a departure from GAAP, and the prior period financial statements are restated in the current period to conform with GAAP, the auditor's updated report on the financial statements of the prior period should indicate that the statements have been restated, and should <u>express</u> <u>an</u> <u>unqualified</u> <u>opinion</u> <u>concerning</u> <u>the</u> <u>restated</u> <u>financial</u> <u>statements</u>.

In the updated report, the auditor should discuss in a separate paragraph(s), preceding the opinion paragraph of his or her report:
1.   The date of the auditor's previous report.
2.   The type of opinion previously expressed.
3.   The circumstances that caused the auditor to express a different opinion.
4.   That the auditor's updated opinion on the financial statements of the prior period is different from his or her previous opinion on these statements.

Answer choice "A" is incorrect because the updated report need not be accompanied by the auditor's original report.

Answer choice "B" is incorrect because such qualification would not be appropriate.

Answer choice "C" is incorrect because the previous opinion, as well as the circumstances causing the different opinion, should be referred to in the updated report.

OTHER OBJECTIVE FORMATS/ESSAY QUESTIONS

Answer 2

91.   I   The report correctly references the audit; i.e., "<u>In</u> <u>planning</u> <u>and</u> <u>performing</u> <u>our</u> <u>audit</u> <u>of</u> <u>the</u> <u>financial</u> <u>statements</u> of Stone Co. for the year ended December 31, 1993,...."

92.   C   The report should state "...we considered its internal control structure in order to determine our auditing procedures for the

purpose of expressing our opinion on the financial statements <u>and not to provide assurance on the internal control structure</u>."

93. C   The first paragraph of the report should end with the phrase "...report financial data consistent with <u>the assertions of management in the financial statements</u>."

94. I   The report should contain <u>no reference</u> to generally accepted accounting principles.

95. I   The report correctly included a paragraph <u>to describe the reportable conditions noted</u>.

96. I   The report <u>should not include a description of the assessed level of control risk</u>.

97. C   By definition, <u>a material weakness is a reportable condition</u>.

98. I   The report <u>should not indicate</u> that the auditor assumes no responsibility for errors or irregularities resulting from reportable conditions noted.

99. C   The third paragraph of the report should end with the phrase "...and not be detected <u>within a timely period by employees in the normal course of performing their assigned functions</u>."

100. I   The report <u>should not indicate</u> that consideration of the internal control structure is expected to disclose all reportable conditions.

101. I   The report may <u>indicate</u> that the auditor concluded that none of the reportable conditions described is believed to be a material weakness.

102. C   The report <u>should</u> state that "this report is intended solely for the information and use of the audit committee (board of directors, board of trustees, or owners in owner-managed enterprises), <u>management</u>, and others within the organization (or specified regulatory agency or other specified third party)."

103. I   The report should <u>not</u> make reference to the opinion expressed on the financial statements.

104. I   The report should <u>not</u> indicate that the auditor is not responsible for updating the report.

105. I   The auditor <u>may</u> choose to <u>communicate significant matters during the course of the audit</u> rather than after the audit is concluded.

Answer 3

106. D   Operating at a profit would most likely reduce the motivation of management to misstate the financial statements and therefore <u>decrease</u> audit risk.

107.   I   Management operating and financing decisions dominated by a single individual <u>increases</u> audit risk.

108.   I   The lack of objectivity caused by the internal auditor reporting directly to the controller <u>increases</u> audit risk.

109.   I   High management turnover, particularly senior accounting personnel, <u>increases</u> audit risk.

110.   D   Outside monitoring by major creditors would tend to <u>decrease</u> audit risk.

111.   N   At the financial statement level, audit risk would most likely <u>not be affected</u> by payroll transactions, as such transactions are normally routine.

112.   D   Prior audit history; i.e., the fact that Bond has audited TWD for five years, would most likely <u>decrease</u> audit risk.

113.   I   Changing the method of financial statement presentation may create significant difficult-to-audit transactions or balances, thereby <u>increasing</u> audit risk.

114.   I   Significant related party transactions would most likely <u>increase</u> audit risk.

115.   D   The elimination of an accounting issue, such as contingent liabilities, would most likely <u>decrease</u> audit risk.

116.   I   Significant related party transactions would most likely <u>increase</u> audit risk.

117.   I   Significant difficult-to-audit transactions or balances would most likely <u>increase</u> audit risk.

118.   N   Increasing casualty insurance coverage, by itself, would not affect the likelihood of material misstatements in the financial statements, and most likely would <u>not affect</u> audit risk.

119.   I   Significant difficult-to-audit transactions and contentious accounting issues <u>increase</u> audit risk.

120.   I   An initial public offering for 1994 may motivate management to place undue emphasis on meeting earnings projections in 1993 and thereby <u>increases</u> audit risk.

Answer 4

Part 4(a)
Relevant activities of the internal audit function are those that provide evidence about the design and effectiveness of internal control structure policies and procedures that pertain to the entity's ability to record, process, summarize, and report financial data consistent with the assertions

embodied in the financial statements or that provide direct evidence about potential misstatements of such data.

Part 4(b)
In deciding whether to use the work of internal auditors, the auditor should obtain an understanding of the internal audit function. The auditor ordinarily should make inquiries of appropriate management and internal audit personnel about the internal auditors':
1. Organizational status within the entity.
2. Application of professional standards.
3. Audit plan, including the nature, timing, and extent of audit work.
4. Access to records and whether there are limitations on the scope of their activities.

In addition, the auditor might inquire about the internal audit function's charter, mission statement, or similar directive from management or the board of directors.

If the auditor decides that it would be efficient to consider how the internal auditors' work might affect the nature, timing, and extent of audit procedures, the auditor should assess the competence and objectivity of the internal audit function. In making this assessment, the auditor should:
1. Inquire about qualifications of the internal audit staff, including education, professional experience, and/or certification.
2. Consider audit policies, programs, and procedures.
3. Inquire about assignments, supervision, and review.
4. Consider the organizational level to which the internal auditor reports:
    a. Generally, results of the internal auditor's work should be reported to an officer of sufficient status to ensure broad coverage and consideration.
    b. Inquire whether they have direct access and report regularly to the audit committee or its equivalent.

Answer 5
Part 5(a)
Circumstances that would justify omitting confirmation of accounts receivable as an auditing procedure include the following:
1. Accounts receivable are immaterial to the financial statements.
2. The use of confirmations would be ineffective.
3. The auditor's combined assessed level of inherent and control risk is low, and the assessed level, in conjunction with the evidence expected to be provided by analytical procedures or other substantive tests of details, is sufficient to reduce audit risk to an acceptably low level for financial statement assertions about accounts receivable.

Part 5(b)

Confirmation requests should be tailored to the specific audit objectives. When designing the confirmation requests, the auditor should consider factors that are likely to affect the reliability of the confirmations, such as:

1. The form of the confirmation request; i.e., whether to use the positive or negative form.
2. Prior experience on the audit or similar engagements.
3. The nature of the information being confirmed.
4. The intended respondent (i.e., recipient).

Part 5(c)

When the auditor has not received replies to positive confirmation requests, alternative procedures to reduce audit risk to an acceptably low level would include the following:

1. Examination of subsequent cash receipts and matching such receipts with the actual items being paid.
2. Examination of shipping documents.
3. Examination of other documentation concerning the existence of accounts receivable, such as correspondence with debtors.

Accounting & Reporting—Taxation, Managerial, and Governmental and Not-for-Profit Organizations (ARE)

FOUR-OPTION MULTIPLE-CHOICE QUESTIONS

Answer 1

1. D While gain may be realized from the sale or exchange of a residence, if an individual sells his or her principal residence and buys and occupies another residence 24 months before or after the sale, gain is recognized only to the extent that the adjusted sales price of the old residence exceeds the cost of the new residence. The gain not recognized is postponed, not forgiven. Any untaxed gain is subtracted from the cost of the new residence, reducing its basis.

   A loss is not deductible and has no effect on the basis of the new residence.

   The adjusted sales price is the amount realized, reduced by any fixing-up expenses necessary to make the house saleable.

   The amount realized is the selling price reduced by selling expenses such as sales commissions, advertising, legal fees, etc.

   In view of the above, it should be obvious that <u>the amount of gain recognized from the sale of the former residence on Davis' 1993 tax return is $0</u>, because the cost of Davis' new residence (i.e., $200,000) was in excess of the adjusted sales price of the old residence (i.e., $80,000 less $5,000 commission, or $75,000).

   It should be noted that the gain realized (and postponed) on the sale of Davis' residence is determined as follows:

Sales price		$80,000
Less: Commission paid to realtor		5,000
Adjusted sales price		75,000
Less: Adjusted basis of old residence		
Original cost	$65,000	
Bathroom added	5,000	70,000
Gain realized (postponed)		$ 5,000

   Further, the basis of Davis' new residence is equal to the $200,000 cost of the new residence reduced by the $5,000 postponed gain, or $195,000.

   Answer choice "A" is incorrect because it fails to consider (1) the commission paid to the realtor in determining the adjusted sales price and (2) the cost of the bathroom, which must be added to the basis of the old residence. In any event, any gain realized in 1993 will not be recognized since it must be postponed because the cost of the new residence exceeds the adjusted sales price of the old residence.

Answer choice "B" is incorrect because, in determining the gain realized, it fails to consider either the commission paid to the realtor or the cost of the bathroom. In any event, any gain realized in 1993 will not be recognized; rather, it must be postponed.

Answer choice "C" is incorrect because it reflects the gain realized, which will not be recognized in 1993. The recognition of gain will be postponed because the cost of Davis' new residence exceeds the adjusted sales price of his old residence.

2.　C　Interest on U.S. obligations is generally not exempt from federal income tax, except for an available exclusion on U.S. Series EE Savings Bonds. To qualify for the exclusion, (1) the bonds must have been issued after 1989 in the name of the taxpayer (and/or his/her spouse), (2) the taxpayer must have attained the age of 24 at the time of the bonds' issuance, and (3) the redemption proceeds must be used for the qualified higher education expenses of the taxpayer, the taxpayer's spouse, or the taxpayer's dependents.

Qualified higher education expenses include tuition and fees paid to a college, a junior college, university, or a technical or vocational school. "Otherwise qualified higher education expenses" must be reduced by qualified scholarships not includible in gross income.

The exclusion is not allowed if the taxpayer's filing status is married filing separately. Furthermore, the exclusion may be partially or totally disallowed when adjusted gross income exceeds certain threshold amounts, which change annually based on inflation.

Answer choices other than "C" are based on incorrect assumptions and/or combinations.

3.　A　Generally, all interest received, including interest on tax refunds and federal obligations, is fully taxable, except for interest received on state or municipal obligations.

Since both of the items presented are taxable, the total amount of interest subject to tax in Kay's 1993 tax return is $4,500.

Answer choice "B" is incorrect because it fails to include the interest on the refund of 1991 federal income tax.

Answer choice "C" is incorrect because it fails to include the interest on U.S. Treasury certificates, which is fully taxable.

Answer choice "D" is incorrect because it treats the interest on both the U.S. Treasury certificates and the refund of 1991 federal income tax as nontaxable when, in fact, both interest items are taxable.

4.　C　Social security and railroad retirement benefits are includible as income if the taxpayer's "modified adjusted gross income" and 50

percent of the benefits received exceed the following "base amounts":
1. $32,000 in the case of a joint return.
2. Zero in the case of a married taxpayer who has lived with his or her spouse during the entire year but is not filing a joint return.
3. $25,000 for a single taxpayer.

Modified adjusted gross income (MAGI) equals adjusted gross income (prior to inclusion of any social security and railroad retirement benefits) plus any of the following:
1. Tax-exempt interest (whether received or accrued).
2. Income from U.S. possessions and Puerto Rico.
3. Foreign source income (under certain circumstances).

If the base is exceeded, one-half of each dollar of such excess up to the amount of one-half of the benefits received is includible in the recipient's gross income.

Beginning in 1994, a second gross income inclusion tier is created. The rate of inclusion is increased to 85 percent but only if "provisional income" is in excess of the following "adjusted base amounts":
1. $44,000 in the case of a joint return.
2. Zero in the case of married taxpayers filing separately.
3. $34,000 for a single taxpayer.

"Provisional income" is generally adjusted gross income plus (1) tax-exempt income and (2) one-half of the benefits received.

Accordingly, for those taxpayers with provisional income in excess of the applicable adjusted base amounts, the taxable portion of the benefits is the lesser of:
1. 85 percent of the benefits received, or
2. The sum of the following:
   a. The smaller of
      (1) the amount includible under pre-1994 law (i.e., the first tier), or
      (2) $6,000 if married filing jointly, or $4,500 if single.
   b. 85 percent of the excess of provisional income over the applicable adjusted base amount.

In summary, for the 1993 tax year, one-half of the social security benefits is the maximum amount of benefits to be included in gross income.

Answer choices other than "C" are clearly based on assumptions and calculations that are not valid under current tax law.

5.   A   Net earnings from self-employment are (1) the gross income derived from any trade or business, less allowable deductions attributable to the trade or business, and (2) the distributive share of partnership ordinary income or loss derived by a partnership from

carrying on a trade or business, except for the rental of real estate. (Directors' fees are considered to be income from self-employment.)

Rich should report net self-employment income in the amount of $15,100, determined as follows:

Gross business receipts		$20,000
Less: Air conditioning parts	$2,500	
Yellow Pages listing	2,000	
Business long-distance telephone calls	400	4,900
Net self-employment income		$15,100

The estimated federal income taxes on self-employment income are not deductible in arriving at either net self-employment income or taxable income. The charitable contributions are not deducted in determining net self-employment income since they are not allowable deductions attributable to a trade or business; rather, charitable contributions may be claimed as an itemized deduction.

Answer choice "B" is incorrect because it includes a deduction for the charitable contributions.

Answer choice "C" is incorrect because it includes a deduction for the estimated federal income taxes on self-employment income.

Answer choice "D" is incorrect because it includes deductions for the estimated federal income taxes on self-employment income and the charitable contributions.

6. C In arriving at adjusted gross income, a deduction is allowed for one-half of the self-employment tax owed by a self-employed individual.

When calculating the amount of self-employment tax owed, a deduction is allowed for one-half of the self-employment tax. Accordingly, the self-employment tax is based on 92.35 percent of the self-employment income (before deduction for self-employment tax), which in turn is multiplied by the rate of tax (i.e., 15.3 percent).

Answer choice "A" is incorrect because the self-employment tax is never deductible as an itemized deduction.

Answer choice "B" is incorrect because the self-employment tax is not deductible in determining net income from self-employment.

Answer choice "D" is incorrect because, as noted, when calculating the amount of self-employment tax owed, a deduction is allowed for one-half of the self-employment tax.

7. A In arriving at adjusted gross income, a deduction may be available for contributions to an individual retirement account (IRA).

With respect to taxpayers who are not active participants in another retirement plan, annual contributions in cash equal to 100 percent of earned income (including taxable alimony) up to $2,000 may be made to an individual retirement account, annuity, or bond program and be excluded from the employee's gross income.

If both a husband and wife are employed, each qualifies for the maximum deduction.

With respect to taxpayers who are active participants in another retirement plan, a full deduction is available if adjusted gross income (AGI) is less than $25,000 ($40,000 for a married couple filing a joint return, and $0 for a married couple filing separate returns). A partial deduction is available if AGI is between $25,000 and $35,000 (between $40,000 and $50,000 for a married couple filing a joint return; between $0 and $10,000 for a married couple filing separate returns). As AGI increases within the $10,000 phase-out range, the deduction is reduced proportionately. Regardless of the phase-out provisions, a taxpayer will be permitted to deduct $200 if AGI does not exceed the phase-out range.

It should be noted that to be bound by the AGI limitations, only one spouse need be an active participant in another retirement plan.

Since Val was covered by his employer's qualified pension plan, both Val and Pat are bound by the AGI limitations. Further, the alimony received by Pat, which is fully taxable, is considered earned income for the purpose of computing the IRA deduction. Accordingly, the White's AGI was $35,000 + $5,000, or $40,000. The allowable IRA deduction on the White's 1993 joint tax return is $4,000, since their AGI was exactly $40,000 and both Val and Pat had earned income of at least $2,000.

Answer choice "B" is incorrect because it reflects a $250 deduction for a spousal IRA, which is available only when one spouse has no earned income, and because it fails to consider Pat's taxable alimony as earned income, which entitles Pat to a $2,000 IRA deduction.

Answer choice "C" is incorrect because it fails to consider Pat's taxable alimony as earned income, which entitles Pat to a $2,000 IRA deduction.

Answer choice "D" is clearly incorrect because the Whites did not exceed the $50,000 AGI threshold, which results in the complete disallowance of the IRA deduction.

8.   C   Interest on investment indebtedness is deductible as an itemized deduction, but only to the extent of net investment income.

Interest deductions that are disallowed under this rule may be carried over indefinitely and may be deducted in future years, subject to the annual limit.

Net investment income is the amount by which investment income exceeds investment expenses. Investment income generally includes interest, dividends, royalties, net capital gains from investment property (but only if an election is made to tax the net capital gains as ordinary income), and amounts recaptured as ordinary income subject to the provisions of Sections 1245, 1250 and 1254. Investment expenses are those deductions directly connected with the production of investment income.

Answer choice "A" is incorrect because the deduction for interest on investment indebtedness is not necessarily limited to the investment interest paid during the tax year; the deduction could also include a carryover that is available from prior years.

Answer choice "B" is incorrect because the deduction for interest on investment indebtedness is limited to net investment income, which may include income other than interest.

Answer choice "D" is incorrect because it presumes that interest on investment indebtedness is fully deductible regardless of whether the taxpayer had any net investment income.

9. B   In general, miscellaneous expenses are deductible only if the aggregate amount of such expenses exceeds 2 percent of AGI. Included in this category of expenses are tax return preparation fees, subscriptions to professional journals, and custodial fees for a brokerage account.

Ordinary and necessary educational expenses qualify if incurred for education that:
1. Maintains or improves skills required by employment, trade, or business.
2. Is expressly required by an employer or the requirements of law or regulations for maintaining employment status.

Education expenses are not deductible if incurred in order to meet the minimum educational requirements for qualification in a trade, business, or particular employment situation.

Answer choices other than "B" are incorrect because they represent allowable miscellaneous itemized deductions which are subject to the 2 percent of AGI floor.

10. B   Qualified residence (mortgage) interest includes interest on up to $1,000,000 of acquisition indebtedness (i.e., debt pertaining to acquiring, constructing, or substantially improving the taxpayer's principal and/or second residence, and that is secured by the residence), and interest on up to $100,000 of a home equity loan. The deduction for interest on a home equity loan is allowable even if the loan proceeds are used for personal purposes, such as payment of college tuition.

The $20,000 borrowed by the Browns clearly qualifies as a home equity loan because the equity in their home (i.e., $400,000) was more than the amount borrowed, and the loan was secured by their home. It should then be obvious that the interest on the loan qualifies as <u>deductible</u> <u>qualified</u> <u>residence</u> <u>interest</u>.

Answer choice "A" is incorrect primarily because personal interest is never deductible.

Answer choice "C" is clearly incorrect because interest on up to $100,000 of a home equity loan is deductible. Nondeductible interest includes interest on loans to invest in tax-exempt securities, as well as personal interest. Personal interest includes interest on bank, insurance, and auto loans, credit cards, and tax deficiencies.

Answer choice "D" is incorrect because interest on a loan secured by a residence is not considered to be investment interest expense.

11. C Qualified residence (mortgage) interest includes interest on up to $1,000,000 of acquisition indebtedness (i.e., debt pertaining to acquiring, constructing, or substantially improving the taxpayer's principal and/or second residence, and that is secured by the residence), and interest on up to $100,000 of a home equity loan. The deduction for interest on a home equity loan is allowable even if the loan proceeds are used for personal purposes.

Nondeductible interest includes interest on loans to invest in tax-exempt securities, as well as personal interest. Personal interest includes interest on bank, insurance, and auto loans, credit cards, and tax deficiencies.

In view of the above, the $17,000 mortgage interest and the $1,500 interest on the room construction loan represent deductible qualified residence interest. The auto loan interest, however, is not deductible. Accordingly, <u>the</u> <u>total</u> <u>interest</u> <u>that</u> <u>is</u> <u>deductible</u> <u>in 1993, prior</u> <u>to</u> <u>any</u> <u>itemized</u> <u>deduction</u> <u>limitations, is</u> $17,000 + $1,500, or <u>$18,500</u>.

Answer choice "A" is incorrect because it fails to include the $1,500 interest on the room construction loan, which is deductible as qualified residence interest.

Answer choice "B" is incorrect because it (1) includes the $500 auto loan interest, which is not deductible, and (2) does not include the $1,500 interest on the room construction loan, which is deductible.

Answer choice "D" is incorrect because it includes the $500 auto loan interest, which is not deductible.

12. A <u>Itemized</u> <u>deductions</u> (<u>other</u> <u>than</u> <u>medical</u> <u>expenses, investment</u> <u>interest, and</u> <u>casualty</u> <u>and</u> <u>theft</u> <u>losses</u>) <u>must</u> <u>be</u> <u>reduced</u> <u>by</u> <u>3</u> <u>percent</u> <u>of</u> <u>adjusted</u> <u>gross</u> <u>income</u> (<u>AGI</u>) <u>in</u> <u>excess</u> <u>of</u> <u>an</u> "<u>applicable</u> <u>amount</u>". The "applicable amount" is based on the taxpayer's filing

status and is adjusted annually for inflation. It should be noted that in no event may the reduction exceed 80 <u>percent</u>.

Answer choices "B" and "D" are easily eliminated because only certain itemized deductions must be reduced when AGI is in excess of the "applicable amount."

Answer choice "C" is based on assumptions not valid under current tax law.

13. C Qualifying medical expenses include:
1. Medical insurance premiums.
2. Prescription drugs and insulin.
3. Fees paid to doctors, dentists, hospitals, and laboratories.
4. Transportation expenses. (In lieu of actual automobile expenses, a taxpayer may deduct nine cents per mile plus parking and tolls.)
5. Fees for cosmetic surgery (e.g., face lift), or other similar procedure (e.g., hair transplant), if the surgery or procedure is necessary to correct or improve a physical deformity caused by a congenital abnormality, an accident or trauma-related personal injury, or a disfiguring disease. (Costs for cosmetic surgery incurred for the sole purpose of improving physical appearance and self-esteem do not qualify.)
6. Expenses for lodging while away from home primarily for and essential to medical care provided by a physician in a licensed hospital or its equivalent. A maximum of $50 per day, per individual (including a person accompanying the patient), is allowed and cannot include the cost of meals or any pleasure element.
7. Tuition for schooling at a special school for the physically or mentally handicapped. If an individual is in the educational facility primarily for the availability of medical care, the cost of meals and lodging, incident to that care, is also deductible.
8. The costs to purchase, repair, and maintain special equipment (e.g., wheelchairs and hearing aids) used to alleviate the effects of a medical condition.

A deduction for medical expenses of a child paid for by a legally divorced or separated parent is available even though the dependency exemption cannot be claimed by the payor. Thus, each parent can include in his or her medical expense deduction those payments attributable to their child.

The deduction for medical expenses includes expenses paid by the taxpayer for the benefit of dependents. Furthermore, the deduction includes those expenses paid for a person who would have qualified as a dependent except for the fact that they (1) had gross income from sources not exempt from tax equal to or greater than the exemption amount or (2) filed a joint return.

Logically, disregarding the adjusted gross income percentage threshold, the amount that could be claimed on Wells' 1993 income tax return for medical expenses is $1,000 (i.e., the $2,000 paid for physical therapy after spinal surgery, reduced by the $1,500 recovered through insurance reimbursement, plus the $500 premium on an insurance policy that covers reimbursement for the cost of prescription drugs).

Answer choice "A" is incorrect because it includes the premiums (i.e., $3000) on an insurance policy against loss of earnings due to sickness or accident; such premiums are not deductible.

Answer choice "B" is incorrect because it includes the nondeductible premiums (i.e., $3,000) on an insurance policy against loss of earnings due to sickness or accident, and does not include the $500 premium on an insurance policy that covers reimbursement for the cost of prescriptions drugs, which is deductible.

Answer choice "D" is incorrect because it does not include the $500 premium on an insurance policy that covers reimbursement for the cost of prescription drugs.

14.   B   There are five tests that must be met to permit a deduction for dependency exemptions. These are the tests for (1) support, (2) gross income, (3) relationship, (4) citizenship, and (5) whether or not dependent and spouse filed a joint return, as explained below.

1. The support test generally means that more than one-half of the dependent's total support must be provided by the taxpayer. (Social Security payments, like other nontaxable income used for support, are considered as having been contributed by the recipient for his or her support.)

2. The gross income test generally means that the dependent's gross income from sources not exempt from tax is less than the appropriate exemption amount ($2,350 for 1993), except for a child under 19, or a child under the age of 24 who is a full-time student for 5 months of the calendar year.

3. The relationship test generally provides that a person who is a relative in any of the following ways does not have to live with the taxpayer in order for the exemption to be claimed: a child, grandchild, great-grandchild, stepchild, brother, sister, half brother, half sister, stepbrother, stepsister, parent, grandparent or other direct ancestor, stepfather or stepmother, aunt or uncle, niece or nephew, father-in-law, mother-in-law, son-in-law, daughter-in-law, brother-in-law, or sister-in-law. Any other person would have to live with the taxpayer to qualify as a dependent.

    A custodial parent (i.e., one who has custody of a child or stepchild, pursuant to a decree of divorce or agreement of separate maintenance) is entitled to the exemption for his or her child unless he or she elects not to claim it.

4. The citizenship test requires that the dependent be a U.S. citizen, resident or national, or a resident of Canada or Mexico for some part of the tax year.

5. The joint return test precludes dependency status for a person who files a joint return. However, if the sole purpose of filing a joint return is to obtain a refund, even though no return is required to be filed, the joint return test is considered satisfied.

No exemption is allowed to a taxpayer who is claimed as a dependent on another taxpayer's return.

In light of the preceding discussion, only Dale may be claimed as a dependent. Since Kim (1) is over the age of 19, (2) is not a full-time student, and (3) had income from sources not exempt from tax greater than the appropriate exemption amount (i.e., $2,350 for 1993), Kim does not satisfy the "gross income" test and may not be claimed as a dependent. Since Grant received $5,000 in dividend income, which is subject to tax, he does not satisfy the "gross income" test. Consequently, Grant may not be claimed as a dependent.

Accordingly, the number of exemptions that Jim and Kay can claim on their 1993 joint income tax return is three (i.e., one each for Jim, Kay, and Dale).

Answer choice "A" is incorrect because it fails to include the exemption for the Ross' child, Dale.

Answer choice "C" is incorrect because it includes an exemption for either the Ross' child, Kim, or Jim's widowed parent, Grant, neither of whom qualifies as a dependent.

Answer choice "D" is incorrect because it includes exemptions for the Ross' child, Kim, and Jim's widowed parent, Grant, neither of whom qualifies as a dependent.

15. B   Under the cash (cash receipts and disbursements) method of accounting, taxable income is determined by (1) including all items of gross income (whether in the form of cash, property, or services) in the tax year in which they are actually or constructively received, and (2) deducting all expenses in the year in which they are actually paid. (An exception exists for interest, which is limited to the amount that accrued for the year.)

It should be noted that under the doctrine of constructive receipt, income that has not actually been received by the taxpayer will be taxed as if it had been received if (1) it is readily available to the taxpayer, and (2) actual receipt is not subject to substantial limitations or restrictions.

In view of the above, on her 1992 income tax return, Michaels' deduction for interest was limited to the interest for the month of December 1992 (i.e., 1/12 of $12,000, or $1,000). Accordingly, interest <u>in the amount of $11,000,</u> which represents the balance of the prepaid interest, and which covers the period January 1, 1993, to December 1, 1993, <u>is deductible on Michaels' 1993 income tax return.</u>

Answer choice "A" is incorrect because the $12,000 interest paid in 1992 is partially deductible in both 1992 and 1993.

Answer choice "C" is incorrect because it reflects the interest deductible in 1992.

Answer choice "D" is incorrect because it presumes that the interest paid in 1992 was fully deductible in that year.

16. D   In effect, if an individual's tentative minimum tax exceeds the regular tax, the excess amount is payable in addition to the regular tax.

Technically referred to as the "alternative minimum tax" (AMT), the minimum tax is equal to alternative minimum taxable income (in excess of the exemption amount) multiplied by the applicable AMT tax rate, reduced by the regular tax liability and the AMT foreign tax credit.

Alternative minimum taxable income is equal to taxable income, after certain adjustments, plus tax preference items.

Tax preference items may be classified as either exclusion preferences or deferral preferences. Exclusion preferences, which represent items that would never be taxed when computing an individual's regular tax liability, include tax-exempt interest. Deferral preferences represent items that are taxed for AMT purposes in one year and for regular tax purposes in a future year. Examples of deferral preferences include adjustments for depreciation, and the disallowance of passive activity loss deductions.

In order to prevent deferral preferences from being taxed twice (i.e., first under the AMT system and then in a future year under the regular tax system), a minimum tax credit is available. <u>The minimum tax credit,</u> which reduces the regular tax liability in a later year by the amount of AMT liability attributable to deferral preferences in the earlier year, <u>may be carried forward indefinitely.</u>

Answer choice "A" is incorrect because it refers to the carryforward period for capital losses of a corporation.

Answer choice "B" is incorrect because it refers to both the carryback and carryforward periods for corporate capital losses.

Answer choice "C" is incorrect because it refers to the carryback period of corporate capital losses and net operating losses.

17. C   An "earned income" credit is available to a low-income worker who maintains a household that is the principal place of abode of himself/herself and a child of his/hers who is under 19 or is a full-time student under the age of 24, or is disabled. (Beginning in 1994, the credit will be available to a childless low-income earner who is at least 25 years old, but less than 65 years old, and is not a dependent of another individual.)

An individual will be considered to have met the requirements for claiming the credit even though he or she may not be entitled to the dependency exemption (as a result of the application of the dependency exemption rules for custodial parents).

The credit is based on earned income - wages, salaries, or other regular compensation, plus earnings from self-employment and adjusted gross income.

Taxpayers eligible to claim the earned income credit include a married couple filing a joint return, a surviving spouse, and a head of household. Also, the credit may be claimed only for a full 12-month tax year, except in the case of death.

The earned income credit may reduce the tax below zero. The amount below zero is refundable to the taxpayer, even if the taxpayer had no tax withheld from wages.

Answer choices other than "C" are incorrect because they represent credits that cannot be claimed unless an income tax liability exists.

18. C   In its broadest terms, a "deficiency" is the difference between the correct tax liability and the tax liability as reported on the tax return as filed.

Once the Internal Revenue Service determines that a deficiency exists, it mails a "notice of deficiency," or "90-day letter," to the taxpayer. The taxpayer then has 90 days to either pay the tax or petition the Tax Court.

The Service must mail the "notice of deficiency" prior to the expiration of the statute of limitations.

The general rule is that the statute of limitations will expire three years after the later of either the due date of the return or the date the return was filed.

A major exception to the general rule relates to the "substantial omission of items" from the return. Simply stated, the three-year period will be extended to six years if the taxpayer omits from gross income an amount in excess of 25 percent of the amount of gross income as reported on the return (prior to the deduction for costs of goods sold).

Additionally, an assessment may be made at any time for filing a false or fraudulent return or for failing to file a tax return.

It should be obvious that the general rule is applicable to this question and that the latest date that the Internal Revenue Service can assess tax and assert a notice of deficiency is April 15, 1996, which is three years after the due date of the 1992 return (i.e., April 15, 1993).

Answer choices other than "C" are based on assumptions that are not valid under current tax law.

19.   C   The Internal Revenue Service may impose a $250 penalty on a tax return preparer for improper disclosure or use of tax return information.

In general, in order to avoid the imposition of the penalty, the tax return preparer must obtain the consent of the taxpayer to disclose or use tax return information. No consent, however, is necessary when the disclosure or use of the tax return information is in connection with the quality or peer review of the tax return preparer.

Answer choices other than "C" are incorrect because they represent situations that require the taxpayer's consent for disclosure or use.

20.   D   Some of the more common civil penalties that may be imposed on an income tax return preparer are:
1. $1,000 ($10,000 with respect to a corporate tax return) for knowingly aiding in the preparation of a tax return which results in an understatement of the taxpayer's liability.
2. $250 for claiming a position that (a) has no realistic possibility of being sustained, and (b) is not disclosed on the return, or is frivolous.
3. $1,000 for willful understatement of the taxpayer's liability on a return or claim for refund.
4. $500 for endorsing or negotiating a taxpayer's income tax refund check.
5. $250 for improper disclosure or use of tax return information.
6. $50 for failure to:
    a. Sign a return.
    b. Report the preparer's identification number on the return.
    c. Give a copy of the return to the taxpayer.
    d. Keep a copy (or a list) of the returns prepared.
    e. Keep a list of tax return preparers employed.

Federal statutes also provide that, in certain instances, a criminal action can be brought against the tax return preparer.

With respect to tax return preparers, prohibited conduct includes:
1. Willfully delivering documents that are known by the preparer to be fraudulent.

2. Fraudulently executing documents required by provisions of the Internal Revenue Code.

3. Removing or concealing goods with the intent to evade any tax imposed by the Internal Revenue Code.

Answer choices other than "D" are based on incorrect assumptions and/or combinations.

21. C   To be eligible for the Subchapter S election, a corporation must:
1. Be a domestic corporation.
2. Not be an active member of an affiliated group.
3. Have one class of stock. Differences in the voting power attached to shares of stock will not be deemed to create more than one class of stock.
4. Have no more than 35 shareholders who are individuals or estates (or trusts under certain circumstances). (All stockholdings, whether jointly or individually held, of a husband, wife, or their estates, are counted as one shareholder.)

Given proper election, there will be no federal tax except for the tax on "built-in" gains (which is beyond the scope of the CPA examination) and the tax on excessive passive investment income.

The election may be made at any time during the previous taxable year and at any time on or before the 15th day of the third month of the current taxable year.

An S Corporation election may be revoked or terminated if:
1. Shareholders owning more than 50 percent of the outstanding stock consent to revoke the election.
2. The corporation ceases to qualify.
3. The corporation has passive investment income in excess of 25 percent of its gross receipts for three consecutive tax years and the corporation has accumulated earnings and profits (derived from its days as a corporation not under the provisions of Subchapter S) at the end of each of these three years. Passive investment income is generally defined as interest, rents, dividends, etc.

Terminations and revocations are effective as of the date the election to terminate is made or the date that the revocation is mandatory. As such, the taxable year will be split into two short years that will require a proration of the tax due on non-S income (or "C Corporation" income).

It should be noted that after a corporation's status as an S Corporation is revoked or terminated, the corporation must wait five years before making a new S election, in the absence of IRS consent to an earlier election.

Since the S Corporation in the question has a total of 50,000 shares of common stock outstanding (i.e., 30,000 shares of voting common stock plus 20,000 shares of non-voting common stock), the S election can be revoked voluntarily only with the consent of the shareholders holding, on the day of the revocation, more than 25,000 shares (i.e., 50,000 shares × 50%) in total. Accordingly, the S election can be revoked voluntarily with the consent of shareholders holding 10,000 shares of voting stock and 16,000 shares of nonvoting stock.

Answer choices other than "C" are incorrect because they do not represent situations in which shareholders owning more than 50 percent of the outstanding stock consent to revoke the election.

22.   B   The basis of a shareholder's stock in an S corporation is increased by his or her ratable share of all items of corporate income that are passed through to him or her, whether or not separately stated.

His or her basis will be reduced by (1) all items of corporate loss and deduction, whether or not separately stated, (2) all nontaxable distributions that represent return of capital, and (3) all expenses not deducted in computing taxable income and not properly chargeable to the capital account.

Property distributions reduce the basis of the shareholder's stock by the fair market value of the property.

The reduction in basis is first applied against stock, and then against any indebtedness owed to the shareholder by the corporation.

Accordingly, each shareholder's basis in the stock of Haas will increase by one-half of the $60,000 taxable income and current earnings and profits, or $30,000.

Answer choice "A" is incorrect because the $50,000 income from operations is not prorated between the shareholders, and it fails to include a prorata share of the $10,000 investment interest income.

Answer choice "C" is incorrect because it does not include a pro rata share of the $10,000 investment interest income.

Answer choice "D" is clearly based on assumptions that are not valid under current tax law.

23.   D   A group of affiliated corporations may file consolidated tax returns for the period that they are affiliated, but only if all the corporations that were members of the affiliated group at any time during the tax year consent before the last day for filing the return.

An affiliated group may be defined as one or more chains of includible corporations connected through stock ownership with a common parent corporation that is an includible corporation, but only if (1) the common parent owns stock possessing at least 80 percent of the total voting power and at least 80 percent of the total value of the stock of at least one includible corporation, and (2) stock meeting the 80 percent requirement in each of the includible corporations (except the common parent) is owned directly by one or more of the other includible corporations.

An "includible corporation" means all corporations except: (1) exempt corporations, (2) life insurance or mutual insurance companies, (3) foreign corporations, (4) corporations with 80 percent income from U.S. possessions, (5) regulated investment companies, (6) real estate investment trusts, and (7) certain domestic international sales corporations (DISCS).

Logically, <u>affiliated</u> <u>corporations</u> that <u>file</u> a <u>consolidated</u> <u>tax</u> <u>return</u> <u>will</u> <u>not</u> <u>be</u> <u>taxed</u> <u>on</u> <u>dividends</u> <u>paid</u> <u>from</u> <u>one</u> <u>includible</u> <u>corporation</u> to <u>another.</u> (Practically, this is a result of the intercompany eliminations necessary to prevent double taxation.)

(Affiliated corporations that do not file a consolidated tax return similarly are entitled to a 100-percent-dividends-received deduction for qualifying dividends received from members of the affiliated group.)

Answer choices other than "D" are based on assumptions that are not valid under current tax law.

24.   B   The graduated tax rates applicable to a C Corporation are as follows:

First $50,000	15%
$50,001 to $75,000	25%
$75,001 to $10,000,000	34%
$10,000,001 and above	35%

All personal service corporations eligible to use the cash basis of accounting cannot avail themselves of the lower graduated rates; rather, they are subject to taxation at a flat 35 percent.

A corporation that has taxable income in excess of $100,000 must pay an additional tax equal to the smaller of (1) 5 percent of such excess, or (2) $11,750.

A corporation that has taxable income in excess of $15,000,000 must pay a second additional tax equal to the smaller of (1) 3 percent of such excess, or (2) $100,000.

In the case of a controlled group of corporations, only one of each of the income tax brackets, with rates below the maximum rate, is allowed to the group.

A controlled group of corporations must divide each of these preferential bracket amounts equally among all members of the group unless all members of the group elect to an apportionment plan. An apportionment of the additional tax is also necessary, and is made in the same manner as the allocation of the preferential bracket amounts.

For this purpose, there are two types of controlled groups. One type is the parent-subsidiary group. In addition, there is a brother-sister controlled group when (1) five or fewer persons (individuals, estates, and trusts) own at least 80 percent of the voting stock or value of shares of each of two or more corporations, and (2) these five or fewer persons own more than 50 percent of the voting power or value of shares of each corporation, considering a particular person's stock only to the extent that it is owned identically with regard to each corporation.

The dividends-received deduction is generally 70 percent (80 percent as to dividends received from a 20 percent-or-more-owned corporation) of dividends received from taxable domestic corporations limited to 70 percent (80 percent as noted) of the corporation's taxable income computed without regard to the dividends-received deduction and net operating loss deduction.

If a corporation sustains a net operating loss for the year, the limitation of 70 percent (80 percent as noted) of taxable income does not apply.

The 70 percent (80 percent as noted) of taxable income limitation will not apply if the full dividends-received deduction results in a net operating loss.

Dividends-received deductions for "affiliated corporations" are subject to different rules. Under certain circumstances, 100 percent of such dividends may be excluded.

In view of the above, Kisco's taxable income is $70,000 reduced by the dividends-received deduction of $7,000 (i.e., 70% × $10,000), or $63,000.

Kisco's 1993 income tax before any credits would be $10,750; i.e., $7,500 (15% × $50,000) plus $3,250 ([$63,000 - $50,000] × 25%).

Answer choice "A" is incorrect because it is based on taxable income of $60,000, which assumes that 100 percent of the dividends, or $10,000, is deductible.

Answer choice "C" is incorrect because it is based on taxable income of $70,000, which assumes that no part of the dividends received is deductible.

Answer choice "D" is incorrect because it presumes that the tax rates are not graduated. Instead, it applies a 25 percent tax rate to the $63,000 taxable income.

25. C Generally, any distribution made by a corporation to its shareholders is considered a dividend to the extent of earnings and profits, both accumulated and for the current year. In determining the source of a distribution, current-year earnings and profits are considered before accumulated earnings and profits. In the event

that a corporation has current-year earnings and profits but has a deficit in accumulated earnings and profits at the beginning of the year, the distribution will be considered a dividend, but only to the extent of the current-year earnings and profits.

Any distribution that is not taxed as a dividend will first reduce the shareholders' basis in the stock, and then result in a capital gain.

It should be noted that, in general, the amount of dividend income resulting from a property distribution received by a shareholder is the fair market value of the property received.

Accordingly, <u>the amount of the distribution made by Kee that is taxable as dividend income to Kee's shareholders is</u> limited to the current earnings and profits of $10,000.

Answer choice "A" is incorrect because it treats the entire distribution as a taxable dividend. As such, it ignores the effect of earnings and profits on the taxability of the distribution.

Answer choice "B" is incorrect because, in determining the taxable portion of the distribution, it presumes that the $30,000 cash distribution is reduced by the current earnings and profits of $10,000.

Answer choice "D" is incorrect because it assumes that no portion of the distribution is taxable since there is still a deficit in earnings and profits at the end of the year, after taking into account the current-year earnings and profits.

26. C   The original basis of a partner's interest includes the amount of money paid, plus the adjusted basis of any contributed property, reduced by the portion of any indebtedness on such property assumed by the other partners.

The adjusted basis of Black's partnership interest is <u>$5,500:</u>

Adjusted basis of property contributed	$7,000
Less: Portion of mortgage assumed by other partners;	
50% × $3,000	1,500
<u>Black's basis in New:</u> January 2, 1993	<u>$5,500</u>

Answer choice "A" is incorrect because it assumes that Black's basis in New is equal to one-half of the adjusted basis of the property contributed (i.e., 1/2 × $7,000, or $3,500); therefore, it fails to consider the effect of the mortgage assumed by the partnership.

Answer choice "B" is incorrect because it assumes that Black's basis in New is equal to Black's adjusted basis of the property contributed (i.e., $7,000) reduced by the full amount of the mortgage (i.e., $3,000) assumed by the partnership.

Answer choice "D" is incorrect because it reduces the fair market value of the contributed property (i.e., $9,000), rather than reducing Black's adjusted basis of the contributed property (i.e., $7,000) by the portion of the mortgage assumed by the other partners (i.e., 50% × $3,000, or $1,500). This results in the incorrect answer choice of $7,500.

27. A   The basis of a partner's interest in a partnership is the original basis and subsequent adjustments thereto.

When one receives a partnership interest in exchange for services, the value of the interest is ordinary income and the basis is its fair market value.

The original basis equals the amount of money paid plus the adjusted basis of any contributed property, reduced by the portion of indebtedness on such property, if any, assumed by the other partners. (In general, no gain or loss is recognized either to the partnership or any partner upon a contribution of property in exchange for a partnership interest.)

Subsequent increases to a partner's basis in a partnership result from further contributions, the sum of the partner's distributive shares of partnership income (whether or not taxable), and increases in partnership liabilities that increase each partner's share of the liabilities.

Subsequent decreases in basis result from the amount of money and the adjusted basis of property distributed, the sum of distributive shares of partnership losses, and nondeductible, noncapital expenditures. The adjusted basis for an interest in a partnership can never be less than zero.

Accordingly, Gray's tax basis in Fabco on December 31, 1993, must reflect Gray's distributive share of all partnership items of income for 1993; Gray's tax basis in Fabco on December 31, 1993, is therefore equal to $5,000 plus $16,000 (i.e., 50% × [$20,000 + $8,000 + $4,000]), or $21,000.

Answer choice "B" is incorrect because it fails to include Gray's $5,000 tax basis on January 1, 1993.

Answer choice "C" is incorrect because it fails to include both Gray's $5,000 tax basis on January 1, 1993, and Gray's 50 percent share of Fabco's tax exempt income (i.e., 50% × 8,000, or $4,000).

Answer choice "D" is incorrect because it fails to include (1) Gray's $5,000 tax basis on January 1, 1993, (2) Gray's share of Fabco's tax exempt income (i.e., 50% × $8,000, or $4,000) and (3) portfolio income (i.e., 50% × $4,000, or $2,000).

28. D   Even though partnership profits are not taxed to the partnership, the partnership must file an information return on Form 1065 showing

the results of the partnership's operations for its tax year and the items of income, gain, loss, deduction, or credit affecting its partners' individual income tax returns.

Each partner, in determining his or her income for the year, must take into account, separately, his or her distributive share (whether or not distributed) of various items, including, of course, ordinary income.

Income or loss, etc., will be allocable to a partner only for the portion of the year he or she is a member of the partnership.

When money is withdrawn by a partner, it must be included in income only to the extent that it exceeds the adjusted basis of the partner's interest.

Arch's share of taxable income from the partnership is therefore equal to 75 percent of its $40,000 ordinary income, or $30,000.

Answer choice "A" is incorrect because it (1) treats the distribution to Arch as taxable income and (2) fails to consider Arch's distributive share of the partnership's ordinary income.

Answer choice "B" is incorrect because it reflects Bean's 25 percent distributive share, instead of Arch's 75 percent distributive share, of the partnership's ordinary income.

Answer choice "C" is incorrect because it is based on Arch and Bean sharing profits and losses equally, which is clearly not the case.

29.   C   A partnership may deduct fixed salaries, determined without regard to the income of the partnership, paid to partners for services.

Similarly, a partnership may deduct fixed payments, determined without regard to the income of the partnership, paid to partners for the use of their capital. Such payments, frequently called "guaranteed payments," merely alter the manner in which respective partners share profits.

Thus, guaranteed payments are deductible expenses on the U.S. Partnership Return of Income, Form 1065, in order to arrive at partnership income (loss), and are included on schedules K-1 to be taxed as ordinary income to the partners.

Answer choices other than "C" are based on incorrect assumptions and/or combinations.

30.   C   The basis of a partner's interest in a partnership is the original basis and subsequent adjustments thereto.

When one receives a partnership interest in exchange for services, the value of the interest is ordinary income and the basis is its fair value.

The original basis equals the amount of money paid plus the adjusted basis of any contributed property reduced by the portion of indebtedness on such property, if any, assumed by the other partners. (In general, no gain or loss is recognized either to the partnership or any partner upon a contribution of property in exchange for a partnership interest.)

Subsequent increases result from further contributions, the sum of the partner's distributive share of partnership income, and increases in partnership liabilities that increase each partner's share of the liabilities.

Subsequent decreases in basis result from the amount of money and the adjusted basis of property distributed, the sum of distributive shares of partnership losses, and nondeductible, noncapital expenditures. Basis is further reduced by decreases in partnership liabilities that decrease each partner's share of the liabilities. The adjusted basis for an interest in a partnership can never be less than zero.

Accordingly, as a result of the $50,000 decrease in partnership liabilities, the basis of Paul's partnership interest was decreased by $17,500, which is the difference between his $37,500 (i.e., 25% × $150,000) share of partnership liabilities at January 1, 1993, and his $20,000 (i.e., 20% × $100,000) share of partnership liabilities at December 31, 1993.

Answer choice "A" is incorrect because it only reflects Paul's $37,500 share (i.e., 25% × $150,000) of the partnership's liabilities at January 1, 1993.

Answer choice "B" is incorrect because it merely reflects Paul's $20,000 share (i.e., 20% × $100,000) of the partnership's liabilities at December 31, 1993.

Answer choice "D" is incorrect because it is based on applying Paul's 5 percent decrease in ownership to the partnership's liabilities at December 31, 1993 (i.e., $100,000).

31. B The basis of property distributed as a current nonliquidating distribution is equal to the lower of (1) the adjusted basis of the property in the hands of the partnership immediately prior to the distribution, or (2) the adjusted basis of the partner's partnership interest immediately prior to the distribution, reduced by any money distributed simultaneously.

Day's basis in the distributed property is $15,000, which is the lower of (1) $15,000, the adjusted basis of the property to the partnership, or (2) $25,000, the adjusted basis of Day's partnership interest ($50,000) reduced by the cash ($25,000) distributed in the same transaction.

Answer choices other than "B" are based on assumptions that are not valid under current tax law.

32.   D   Property received as a gift, bequest, or inheritance is excluded from gross income. Income generated from such property, however, is generally taxable.

It should therefore be obvious that <u>Hall</u> <u>should</u> <u>include</u> <u>$0</u> <u>in</u> <u>his</u> <u>individual</u> <u>income</u> <u>tax</u> <u>return</u> for the inheritance of the 500 shares of stock that he received from his father's estate.

Answer choice "A" is incorrect because it refers to Hall's basis in the inherited stock, which is the stock's $5,500 fair market value at the estate's alternate valuation date.

Answer choice "B" is incorrect because it refers to the fair market value of the stock at the date of death, which would have been Hall's basis in the stock had the alternate valuation date not been elected.

Answer choice "C" is incorrect because it reflects the basis of the stock to Hall's father, which is clearly irrelevant.

33.   C   To be taxable, gifts have to exceed an annual exclusion of $10,000 ($20,000 in the case of joint gifts) per recipient.

All gifts between spouses are tax-free with no limitation.

Gifts are also unlimited if they are made for educational or medical purposes. The payment, however, must be made directly to the educational institution or the provider of the medical services.

In view of the above, since <u>Sayers</u>, who is single, gave an outright gift to a friend, instead of making payments directly to the provider of medical services, he <u>was</u> <u>only</u> <u>entitled</u> <u>to</u> <u>a</u> <u>maximum</u> <u>exclusion</u> <u>of</u> <u>$10,000</u>.

Answer choice "A" is incorrect because it refers to the annual exclusion (i.e., $0) for gift tax purposes applicable to a gift of a future interest, whereby the donee is to receive possession of a gift at some future time.

Answer choice "B" is incorrect because it refers to the maximum capital loss deduction available on an individual income tax return.

Answer choice "D" is incorrect because it refers to the maximum annual gift tax exclusion applicable to a gift made jointly by a taxpayer and his or her spouse.

34.   D   To be eligible as an exempt organization, and therefore not subject to income tax, the following conditions must be satisfied.
1. The entity must file a written application with the Internal Revenue Service, even when no official forms are provided.
2. Organization and operation of the entity must be exclusively for exempt purposes.
3. The operation of the entity must serve a public interest.

4. The organization may not devote a "substantial part" of its activities on propaganda, attempting to influence legislation, or intervening in political campaigns.

5. The entity's articles of organization must (a) state that the purpose of organization is limited to one or more exempt purposes, (b) specify the exempt purposes(s) and (c) state that all of the organization's assets will be utilized for the exempt purposes.

In light of point #1 above, to qualify as an exempt organization, the <u>applicant</u> <u>must</u> <u>file</u> <u>a</u> <u>written</u> <u>application</u> <u>with</u> <u>the</u> <u>Internal Revenue Service</u>.

Answer choice "A" is incorrect because an exempt organization may operate under the "lodge system," under which payments are made to its members for sick benefits.

Answer choice "B" is incorrect because an exempt organization must be of a type specifically identified as one of the classes on which exemption is conferred by the Code.

Answer choice "C" is incorrect because an exempt organization may incorporate and issue capital stock. However, as a practical matter, the stock in an exempt organization is generally not issued.

35.   D   Exempt organizations are liable for income tax on unrelated business income in excess of a $1,000 exemption and allowable deductions for ordinary and necessary expenses.

If the entity is a trust, the regular trust income tax rates will prevail. If an exempt organization is a corporation, the tax on unrelated business taxable income is computed at rates applicable to corporations.

Unrelated business income is any income derived from a trade or business regularly carried on by the exempt organization that is not substantially related to the purpose giving rise to the exempt status. Specifically excluded from the category of an unrelated trade or business are (1) any activities where substantially all work is performed for the organization without compensation (i.e., by volunteers), (2) any activities carried on for the convenience of its members, students, patients or employees, or (3) any activities involving the selling of merchandise, substantially all of which have been received by the organization as gifts or contributions, (4) any activity involving games of chance (e.g., bingo) if such games are (a) conducted in accordance with local laws and (b) confined to nonprofit organizations (i.e., do not compete with profit-motivated business).

If carried out regularly by an exempt organization, <u>the</u> <u>sale</u> <u>by</u> <u>a</u> <u>trade</u> <u>association</u> <u>of</u> <u>publications</u> <u>used</u> <u>as</u> <u>course</u> <u>materials</u> <u>for</u> <u>the</u> <u>association's</u> <u>seminars</u> <u>that</u> <u>are</u> <u>oriented</u> <u>towards</u> <u>its</u> <u>members</u> will not result in unrelated business income, since the sale involves an activity carried on for the convenience of the organization's members.

Answer choices other than "D" are incorrect because they represent activities which will result in unrelated business income.

36.   B   Generally, total cost contains both fixed and variable elements. Given total costs and a measure of activity (such as kilos handled), it is possible to separate the fixed and variable elements of total cost. A simple technique to accomplish this is known as the "high-low point" method.

1. The first step is to determine the variable cost per unit of activity.

	Kilos Handled	Cost
High	80,000	$160,000
Low	60,000	132,000
Difference	20,000	$ 28,000

Therefore, the variable rate is $28,000/20,000 kilos, or $1.40 per kilo handled.

2. The second step is to determine the total fixed costs.

Total cost	$160,000
Variable cost; 80,000 kilos × $1.40 per kilo	112,000
Fixed cost for material handling	$ 48,000

3. The third step is to compute total cost at the 75,000 kilos level.

Variable cost; 75,000 kilos × $1.40 per kilo	$105,000
Fixed cost	48,000
Total estimated cost for handling 75,000 kilos	$153,000

Answer choice "A" is incorrect because it uses the total rate at the high point of $2 (i.e., $160,000/80,000) multiplied by 75,000 kilos. As such, it erroneously treats all costs as variable costs.

Answer choice "C" is incorrect because it uses an average total rate for the high and low point of $2.10 (which is the average of $2 and $2.20 [i.e., $132,000/60,000]) multiplied by 75,000 kilos. As such, it erroneously treats all costs as variable costs.

Answer choice "D" is incorrect because it uses the total rate at the low point of $2.20 (i.e. $132,000/60,000) multiplied by 75,000 kilos. As such, it erroneously treats all costs as variable costs.

37.   C   Flexible budgets relate to the breakeven analysis concept. They require the separation of fixed and variable costs; once this is accomplished, it is possible to compare actual and budgeted results at virtually any level of activity bounded by the relevant range.

The following definitions should be noted:

1. <u>Relevant range</u> - The range of activity in which revenue/cost behavior patterns are valid.
2. <u>Fixed costs</u> - Within the relevant range, these will not change in response to changes in volume. They are incurred as a function of time. Examples, such as rent and property taxes, remain the same in total, but vary on a unit basis with the level of production.
3. <u>Variable costs</u> - These change proportionately in response to changes in volume. Examples, such as direct materials and direct labor, remain constant per unit, but vary in total based on the level of production.

While flexible budgets are generally associated with the control of overhead factors, they may also be used to control the cost of direct materials (as in a <u>direct material usage budget</u>), direct labor costs, and nonmanufacturing costs (as in a <u>marketing budget</u>).

Answer choices other than "C" are based on incorrect assumptions and/or combinations.

38. C   The net present value method of capital budgeting holds that at a desired rate of return, the discounted cash flow generated is equal to the original investment. Discounted cash flows are generated by annual savings (i.e., additional revenue and/or decreased costs) plus the anticipated residual value of the investment, if any. Any excess of the discounted cash flow over the original investment is positive net present value, which indicates a rate of return higher than the desired rate; any excess of the original investment over the discounted cash flow indicates negative net present value and a lesser return. (The desired rate of return is built into the tables that are used.)

Discounted cash flow is determined by applying the desired rate of return to cash inflows for each period. When the inflows are uniform for each period, an annuity table is used. When the cash inflows are not uniform, they must be discounted separately by using the present value of $1.

As such, the difference between the investment and the discounted cash flows of the residual value would yield the total discounted cash flows of the annual savings.

Investment	$50,000
Discounted cash flow of residual value; $10,000 × 0.57	5,700
Discounted cash flows of total annual cash savings	$44,300
Annual savings needed: $44,300/$3.60	$12,306

Answer choice "A" is not logical based on the facts presented.

Answer choice "B" is incorrect because the residual value is subtracted from the cost at the actual amount of $10,000, rather than the related discounted cash flow of $5,700 (i.e., [$50,000 - $10,000]/3.60 equals $11,111).

Answer choice "D" is incorrect because it completely ignores the residual value. The annual savings is therefore erroneously determined to be $50,000/3.60, or $13,889.

39.   B   Pricing decisions are among the most challenging decisions facing managers. Factors that influence pricing decisions include customers, competitors, costs, volume, and profits.

A properly priced product will recover all costs and provide for anticipated profits.

Given the fact that all costs, volume, and profits remain constant for both 1993 and 1994, with the exception of an increase in the 1994 liability insurance of $1,200,000, the 1994 selling price would be the 1993 selling price of $120 plus an increase of $15 (i.e., $1,200,000/80,000), to allow for the increase in liability insurance, or $135.

Answer choice "A" is incorrect because the 1994 increase in liability insurance is not considered, and should be.

Answer choices "C" and "D" are not logical based on the facts presented.

40.   D   Equivalent units of production in process cost accounting may be computed under either the first-in, first-out method, or the weighted-average method (as in this question).

To calculate the cost per equivalent unit, using the weighted-average method, divide the total of the beginning inventory and current costs by the equivalent production for the period.

Under the weighted-average method, there are two components of equivalent production: units completed (transferred), and units in the ending inventory of work-in-process, multiplied by the percentage of completion for each cost element (i.e., 100 percent when costs are added at beginning of process).

Accordingly, the answer is $0.43:

Total of beginning inventory and current costs;		
$5,500 + $18,000		$23,500
Equivalent production:		
Units completed	42,500	
Ending work-in-process	12,500	55,000
Cost per equivalent unit; $23,500/55,000		$0.43

Answer choices "A" and "C" are not logical based on the facts presented.

Answer choice "B" is incorrect because the ending inventory is ignored in the calculation of equivalent units (i.e., $23,500/42 equals $0.55).

41. D Activity-based costing (ABC) assigns costs to products on the basis of the types and quantities of activities that must be performed to produce those products.

The following relevant background should be understood:
1. Costs are assigned on the basis of activities performed to produce, distribute, or support products (i.e., purchasing, administrative, and engineering functions). In this sense, costs are not accumulated by department or function, as they are in traditional systems such as job order costing or process costing, etc. In a traditional cost system, the basis for cost allocation is usually direct labor hours, direct labor costs, or machine hours, etc.
2. Cost drivers are actions or conditions that directly influence and create costs; they are used as a basis for cost allocation. (For example, cost drivers for the purchasing activity would include the number of purchase orders, the number of supplier contracts, and the number of shipments received.)
3. Activity-based costing allows management to identify value-adding and nonvalue-adding activities. Clearly, a value-adding activity increases the worth (i.e., "value") of a product, while a nonvalue-adding activity increases the time spent on a product or service, but does not increase its worth. The objective therefore is to ensure that activities that do not add value to the product are identified and reduced to the extent possible.

Thus, when an activity-based cost (ABC) system replaces a traditional cost system, the numbers of <u>cost pools</u> <u>and allocation bases increase</u>.

Answer choices other than "D" are based on incorrect assumptions and/or combinations.

42. B The cost of goods (i.e., jobs) manufactured (i.e., completed) for a period is equal to costs placed into production reduced by the ending inventory of work-in-process. Costs placed into production are the total of beginning work-in-process and the costs of direct material, direct labor, and factory (i.e., manufacturing) overhead applied. Logically, when beginning and/or ending work-in-process does not exist, it shall be ignored.

The cost of jobs completed is <u>$310,000</u>:

Direct materials issued to production	$ 90,000
Direct labor costs	107,000
Manufacturing overhead applied	113,000
<u>Cost of jobs completed: January 1994</u>	<u>$310,000</u>

(The indirect materials of $8,000 is included as an element of overhead. Furthermore, the $125,000 manufacturing overhead incurred should be ignored; it is a consideration of variance analysis.)

Answer choice "A" is incorrect because the $90,000 direct materials is reduced by the $8,000 indirect materials issued to production, and should not be.

Answer choice "C" is incorrect because it includes the $125,000 manufacturing overhead incurred, rather than the $113,000 of manufacturing overhead applied.

Answer choice "D" is incorrect because it includes the $125,000 manufacturing overhead incurred, rather than the $113,000 of manufacturing overhead applied. In addition, the indirect materials issued to production of $8,000 is erroneously included and should not be, as it is already included as an element of overhead.

43.   C   Return on investment is equal to earnings (operating income) divided by investment in assets; in this case, the denominator would be average invested capital.

Operating income must be determined from the facts provided; it is equal to sales (i.e., $311,000) less the sum of variable cost (i.e., $250,000) and traceable fixed costs (i.e., $50,000), or $11,000.

Return on investment was therefore $11,000 divided by $40,000, or 27.50 percent.

Answer choice "A" is incorrect because 10.00 percent is the imputed interest rate (i.e., desired rate) and not the actual return on investment.

Answer choice "B" is not logical based on the facts given. It is arrived at by dividing the average invested capital by the sum of the variable and traceable fixed costs (i.e., $40,000/[$250,000 + $50,000]).

Answer choice "D" is not logical based on the facts given. It is arrived at by dividing the sum of the average invested capital plus the traceable fixed costs divided by total costs [i.e., ($40,000 + $50,000)/($250,000 + $50,000)].

44.   B   Transfer pricing refers to the unit price assigned to goods or services that one segment transfers to another segment. The appropriate price used for transferring goods and services from one organizational segment to another is important because it affects the reported income of both the selling segment and the buying segment. The basic method for establishing transfer prices involves some form of cost (i.e., standard variable cost, differential cost, full cost, or full cost plus a markup), market price, or a negotiated price.

Generally, transfers are priced at cost if the transferring division is viewed as a cost center (where the manager is responsible for costs only). However, if the transferor is a profit center (where the manager is responsible for cost and revenue), the transfer price may include a profit factor, thus approximating outside market prices.

Responsibility accounting relates income, costs, and expenses to positions and people in the organizational structure who control and are directly responsible for creating them; it fixes responsibility for performance.

Since the transferor is a cost center and the transferee is a profit center, the use of a <u>standard</u> <u>variable</u> <u>cost</u> would be most conducive in evaluating whether both divisions have met their responsibilities.

Answer choice "A" is incorrect because a transfer price using actual costs would be appropriate if the company treats both segments as cost centers, rather than one as a cost center and the other as a profit center.

Answer choice "C" is incorrect because the transferor is a cost center; as such, it would be inappropriate to use actual cost plus mark-up as the transfer price since cost center managers are responsible for costs only.

Answer choice "D" is incorrect because negotiated price, as the transfer price, would be appropriate if both segments were considered profit centers.

45.   A   The manufacturing and delivery of high-quality products is often guided by an entity's quality control program.

Four categories of costs associated with product quality programs include:
1. <u>Prevention costs</u> - Useful in preventing production of products that do not conform to specifications, including supplier evaluations, employee training, machine tooling calibration, and preventive maintenance.
2. <u>Appraisal costs</u> - Useful in detecting which individual products do not conform to specifications, including inspection and testing programs for materials, work-in-process and finished goods, and engineering programs, such as statistical quality control procedures.
3. <u>Internal failure costs</u> - Costs useful in detecting nonconforming products before shipment to customers, including rework costs, storage costs for rework and scrap, tooling changes, and downtime costs.
4. <u>External failure costs</u> - Useful in detecting nonconforming products after shipment to customers, including the costs of returned products, warranty work, product liability, and responding to customer complaints.

Based on point 3, internal failure costs, only <u>rework</u> costs would be categorized as internal failure costs in a quality control program.

Answer choice "B" is incorrect because responding to customer complaints is an external failure cost and not an internal failure cost.

Answer choice "C" is incorrect because statistical quality control procedures are appraisal costs and not internal failure costs.

Answer choice "D" is based on incorrect assumptions and/or combinations.

46. D   The economic order quantity (EOQ) formula addresses the question of how much to order. It is equal to the square root of:

$$\frac{2 \times \text{Cost to place one order} \times \text{Demand per period}}{\text{Cost to hold one unit for one period}}$$

On the other hand, safety stock reduction is a consideration of when to re-order, and has no effect on the EOQ formula.

Answer choices other than "D" are incorrect because safety stock reduction has no effect on EOQ.

47. C   Probability (risk) analysis is a mathematical technique to evaluate the chance of the happening of an event. If a situation has only one possible outcome, it is said to be certain. If a situation has more than one possible outcome, it is said to be uncertain. The sum of the probabilities of all possible outcomes must always equal one. Since probability analysis is able to quantify the likelihood of an event, it is an extension of sensitivity analysis, which is a technique used to measure the effects of changes made to certain data.

Answer choice "A" is incorrect because probability analysis can be used with any amount of possible outcomes.

Answer choice "B" is incorrect because the summation of probability weights must always equal one.

Answer choice "D" is incorrect because probability analysis is compatible (as an extension) with sensitivity analysis.

48. C   Firms may decide not to seek a profit-maximizing price but, rather, work with alternative rules, such as pricing with a set relationship to a competitor's pricing, or using an add-on percentage formula to costs, which is generally referred to as cost-plus pricing.

Cost-plus pricing, which yields approximately average returns on investment, gains positive acceptance among customers and establishes good relations among fellow competitors.

Government contracts are often based on a cost-plus pricing formula, with incentives to the seller if actual costs are less than targeted amounts.

Thus, the amount Briar should receive from the government contract would be $2,156,000:

Actual costs	$1,920,000
Additional 10%	192,000
Cost plus 10%	2,112,000
Savings incentive; ($2,200,000 - $2,112,000)/2	44,000
Amount to be received by Briar	$2,156,000

Answer choice "A" is incorrect because it includes the original cost of $1,920,000 plus an erroneous savings incentive of $140,000 (i.e., [$2,200,000 - 1,920,000]/2), and ignores the additional $192,000 (i.e., 10% × $1,920,000).

Answer choice "B" is incorrect because it only considers the cost of $1,920,000, and the additional 10 percent (i.e., $192,000); it ignores the savings incentive of $44,000.

Answer choice "D" is incorrect because it includes the cost of $1,920,000, the additional 10 percent (i.e., $192,000), and the entire savings of $88,000, instead of one-half, or $44,000.

49. B   A special order decision requires that management compute a reasonable sales price for production or service jobs outside the company's normal realm of operations. Special order situations include jobs that require a bid, those taken during slack periods, or those that are made to a particular buyer's specifications.

Typically, the sales price quoted on special order jobs should be high enough to cover the job's variable and incremental fixed costs and to generate a profit. The fixed manufacturing costs are irrelevant; they will not change in total if the order is accepted.

As such, the total amount to be included in the determination of the minimum acceptable price for the job would be the job's $33,000 overhead variable costs and the $7,750 incremental fixed costs of the external designers, or a total of $40,750.

Answer choice "A" is incorrect because it is the sum of the variable costs of $33,000 and the fixed costs of $3,700 for in-house design. The fixed costs for in-house design should not be included; instead, the additional costs of $7,750 for external designers should be included.

Answer choice "C" is incorrect because it is the sum of the fixed costs of $21,000 and the variable costs of $33,000. The fixed costs should not be included; instead, the additional costs of $7,750 for external designers should be and are not.

Answer choice "D" is incorrect because, while it correctly includes the variable costs of $33,000 and the additional costs of $7,750 for external designers, it erroneously includes the $17,300 (i.e., $21,000 - $3,700) component for fixed costs.

50. C The basic principle of a "just-in-time" production system is to receive raw materials as needed, rather than building up inventories. Fewer goods on hand requires less warehouse space and storage equipment, resulting in cost savings.

Inventory turnover is calculated by dividing the cost of goods sold by the average inventory.

Since inventory levels would be greatly reduced or eliminated entirely if Bell changed from a traditional manufacturing philosophy to a just-in-time philosophy, the <u>inventory</u> <u>turnover</u> <u>would</u> <u>increase</u>, whereas <u>inventory</u> as a <u>percentage</u> of total assets <u>would</u> <u>decrease</u>.

Answer choices other than "C" are based on incorrect assumptions and/or combinations.

51. A The nature of fund accounting lies in its nonprofit orientation. There is no profit motive and what is measured is accountability, rather than profitability. The main objective is stewardship of financial resources received and expended in compliance with legal requirements; i.e., <u>flow</u> <u>of</u> <u>financial</u> <u>resources</u>.

Fund accounting concepts are a feature of accounting for governmental units (as well as other not-for-profit institutions, such as hospitals, universities, and voluntary health and welfare organizations). These concepts adhere to generally accepted principles as applicable to not-for-profit institutions. Legal/contractual compliance, if at odds with GAAP, would be reported in supplementary information.

Answer choice "B" is incorrect because fund accounting measures accountability rather than profitability; i.e. income determination.

Answer choice "C" is incorrect because the focus is on financial resources rather than economic resources; i.e., capital maintenance is not a primary concern of fund accounting and reporting.

Answer choice "D" is incorrect because transfers between funds, although part of fund accounting and reporting, are not the primary emphasis.

52. C Cash flow statements should be presented for proprietary and nonexpendable trust funds and governmental entities that use proprietary fund accounting, including <u>public</u> <u>benefit</u> <u>corporations</u> <u>and</u> authorities, <u>governmental</u> <u>utilities</u>, as well as governmental hospitals and other health care providers.

Answer choices other than "C" are based on incorrect assumptions and/or illogical combinations.

53. B General purpose financial reporting for governmental entities includes "general purpose financial statements" (GPFS), "popular reports," and "comprehensive annual financial reports" (CAFRs).

These are the principal means of communicating financial information to external users.

1. "Popular reports" are less detailed than GPFS and are intended for users whose needs are met through condensed information.
2. "Comprehensive annual financial reports" (CAFRs) are more detailed than GPFS and are intended for users who need a broad range of information.
3. Both popular reports and CAFRs may include nonfinancial information such as statistical, analytical, and demographic data.

The comprehensive annual financial report (CAFR) is a government's official annual report, covering all funds and account groups of a governmental unit. In addition to the CAFR, government units may issue, as general purpose financial statements (GPFS), combined financial statements with columns for each fund type and account group, accompanied by related notes. These statements constitute the basic financial statements necessary for fair presentation in accordance with GAAP as follows:

1. Combined Balance Sheet - All fund types and account groups.
2. Combined Statement of Revenues, Expenditures, and Changes in Fund Balance - All governmental fund types.
3. Combined Statement of Revenues, Expenditures, and Changes in Fund Balance, Budget and Actual - General and special revenue fund types.
4. Combined Statement of Revenues, Expenses, and Changes in Retained Earnings - All proprietary fund types.
5. Combined Statement of Cash Flows - All proprietary fund types and nonexpendable trust funds.
6. Notes to the financial statements.
7. Required supplementary information.

Answer choice "A" is incorrect because the general purpose financial statements (GPFS) may be issued separately from the comprehensive annual financial report (CAFR).

Answer choice "C" is incorrect because the comprehensive annual report (CAFR) not only includes GPFS but also is more detailed and is intended for users who need a broad range of information; hence, it is not synonymous.

Answer choice "D" is incorrect because the general purpose financial statements (GPFS) contain less detailed information than does the comprehensive annual financial report (CAFR).

54.   A   Governmental units present operating statements encompassing all revenues, expenditures, or expenses (as appropriate), and other changes in fund balance or other equity for all funds. Such statements:

1. Provide similar operating statement format for all funds - both for governmental and proprietary funds and for combined, combining, and individual fund statements.

2. Present all changes in the fund balance or retained earnings (or equity) during the period, thus providing (a) an understandable summary of such changes and (b) a reconciliation of the beginning and ending balance sheets. Further, such statements may readily be related to more detailed statements and schedules.

3. Embody the all-inclusive approach, thus clarifying questions as to whether certain changes in fund balances or other equity should be reported directly in a statement of changes in equity while other changes are shown in the operating statement (e.g., transfers). The all-inclusive format eliminates the need for separate statements of changes in fund balance and retained earnings or equity in most cases, because such changes usually are set forth clearly under this approach.

Answer choice "B" is inappropriate for governmental units; the current performance approach would not present all changes in the fund balance or other equity in the operating statement.

Answer choices "C" and "D" are incorrect, as these approaches relate to reporting changes in accounting principle.

55. D In governmental accounting, there are three broad types of funds and two "account groups." The three broad types of funds are governmental funds, proprietary funds, and fiduciary funds. The two account groups are the general fixed assets account group and the general long-term debt account group. Governmental-type funds include general funds, special revenue funds, capital projects funds, and debt service funds.

Proprietary funds include enterprise funds and internal service funds. Fiduciary funds include trust and agency funds. The two account groups are self-balancing sets of accounts and not "funds" in the strict sense.

In governmental accounting, the general fixed assets account group is used to account for all fixed assets other than those of a proprietary fund or a trust fund (e.g., a governmental fund). No depreciation is required to be reported on general fixed assets (i.e., including those of a governmental fund).

Proprietary funds and trust funds account for their own fixed assets; depreciation is reported in proprietary funds and certain trust funds.

It should be noted that while there is no requirement that depreciation should be recognized on general fixed assets, it may be recorded as an optional procedure. (When this option is exercised, depreciation is not an expense; it is recorded as a debit to the "investment in fixed assets" account and, of course, a credit to accumulated depreciation.)

Answer choices other than "D" are based on incorrect assumptions and/or illogical combinations.

56. B Recording of shared revenues received by a local government for operating purposes depends on the fund receiving the shared revenues. Shared revenues recorded in governmental funds should be recognized as revenue in the accounting period in which they become susceptible to accrual; that is, both measurable and available. Such resources should be recorded as revenues at the time of receipt, or earlier if the criteria are met.

Shared revenues received for proprietary fund operating purposes, or for either operations or capital expenditures at the discretion of the recipient government, should be recognized as "nonoperating" revenues in the accounting period in which they are earned and become measurable.

Accordingly, the enterprise fund of a local government entity should record shared revenues as <u>nonoperating revenues</u>, even though received for operating purposes.

Answer choice "A" is incorrect because the enterprise fund would not record shared revenues as operating revenues.

Answer choice "C" is incorrect because the enterprise fund does not use the "other financing sources" classification.

Answer choice "D" is incorrect because shared revenues would be received from another government unit, rather than from another fund within the same government unit, and therefore would not be recorded as interfund transfers.

57. D Background information with respect to the various funds and account groups in governmental accounting follows:
1. <u>Fund</u> - A fund is defined as a fiscal and accounting entity with a self-balancing set of accounts including cash and other financial resources, together with all related liabilities and residual equities or balances, and changes therein, which are segregated for the purpose of carrying on specific activities or attaining certain objectives in accordance with special regulations, restrictions, or limitations.
There can be as many as seven different types of funds, and two account groups. Each fund has its own self-contained double-entry set of accounts. Some governmental units often need several funds of a single type, such as special revenue or capital projects funds. On the other hand, many governmental units do not need funds of all types at any given time. For example, many small governmental units do not require internal service funds.
2. <u>Governmental funds</u>
   a. <u>General fund</u> - used to account for all financial resources, except those required to be accounted for in another fund.
   b. <u>Special revenue fund</u> - similar to a general fund, except

that it is used to account for the proceeds of specific revenue sources (other than expendable trusts or for major capital projects) that are legally restricted to expenditures for specified purposes. Examples of special revenue funds are those established for the purpose of financing schools, parks, or libraries.

    c. <u>Capital projects fund</u> - used to account for financial resources to be expended for the acquisition or construction of major capital facilities (other than those financed by proprietary funds and trust funds).

    d. <u>Debt service fund</u> - used to account for the accumulation of resources for, and the payment of, general long-term debt principal and interest.

3. <u>Proprietary funds</u>

    a. <u>Enterprise fund</u> - used to account for operations that are financed and conducted in a manner similar to private business enterprises, such as utilities. These funds have profit and loss attributes and will record depreciation.

    b. <u>Internal service fund</u> (also called "intragovernmental service fund" or "working capital fund") - used to account for goods or services performed by one department for another on a cost-reimbursement basis. These funds have profit and loss attributes and will record depreciation.

4. <u>Fiduciary funds</u>

<u>Trust and agency fund</u> - used to account for assets held by a governmental unit as trustee or agent. These include expendable and nonexpendable trust funds, pension, and agency funds.

    a. The distinction between "trust" and "agency" is that agency transactions wash out, while a trust implies custody over assets in a more permanent sense.

    b. In general, a "nonexpendable" trust fund requires that principal be maintained while income may be available to support a specific activity. In the case of an "expendable" trust, principal need not be maintained.

    c. A trust fund may be referred to as an "endowment" fund.

5. <u>Account groups</u> - These are self-balancing sets of accounts and not "funds" in the strict sense. The two types of account groups that may exist are:

    a. <u>General fixed assets account group</u> - used to account for all fixed assets other than those specifically associated with and carried in a proprietary fund or certain trust funds. Other than for proprietary funds, and in certain trust funds in which income is measured, there is no recording of depreciation. (This account group has no assets other than fixed assets.)

    b. <u>General long-term debt account group</u> - used to account for the principal on all unmatured long-term debt (inclusive of lease-purchase agreements, etc.) except debt payable from a proprietary fund or trust fund.

All other unmatured general long-term liabilities of the governmental unit, which include special assessment debts for which the government is obligated in some manner, should be accounted for through this account group.

The long-term debt account group has only two assets. One is the "amount available in debt service funds," and the second is termed "amount to be provided for retirement of general long-term debt."

As assets available in debt service funds increase, the "amount to be provided" decreases, since fewer resources must be raised in the future.

<u>Taxes</u> <u>collected</u> <u>and</u> <u>held</u> <u>by</u> one governmental entity (e.g., <u>Franklin County</u>) <u>for</u> another (e.g., <u>a school</u> <u>district</u>) <u>would</u> <u>be</u> <u>accounted</u> <u>for</u> <u>in</u> <u>an</u> <u>agency</u> <u>fund</u>. Such taxes would be held only for a short time.

Answer choices "A" and "B" are incorrect because the funds identified are not agency funds, and would generally not collect and hold taxes for another fund.

Answer choice "C" is incorrect because a trust fund implies custody over assets in a more permanent sense than is implied in an agency transaction, which involves almost immediate transfer.

58. C The fund groups of a hospital are summarized as follows:
1. <u>General (unrestricted) funds</u>
   a. <u>Operating funds</u>
      For routine hospital activities (includes plant assets and related long-term debt).
   b. <u>Board-designated funds</u>
      Resources set aside by action of the board for special uses.
2. <u>Temporarily or permanently restricted funds</u>
   a. <u>Specific-purpose</u>
      Resources restricted by donors for specific operating purposes.
   b. <u>Endowment</u>
      Principal is kept intact by donor restrictions. Earnings may or may not be available subject to donor restrictions.
   c. <u>Plant replacement and expansion</u>
      Resources restricted by donors for plant and equipment acquisition.

Long-term debt issued for the hospital's benefit is <u>reported</u> <u>in</u> <u>a</u> <u>general</u> <u>fund</u>.

Answer choice "A" is incorrect because a not-for-profit hospital would not use an enterprise fund.

Answer choice "B" is incorrect because resources restricted for specific purposes by donors would be accounted for in a specific purpose fund. Debt is not provided by donors.

Answer choice "D" is incorrect because a not-for-profit hospital would not use a general long-term debt account group.

59. C   The following summarizes the main fund groups of colleges and
         universities:
         1. Current funds - Resources available for use in carrying out the
             primary educational objectives of the institution. Classified as
             unrestricted or temporarily restricted (if restricted to a
             specific primary objective by reason of gift, grant, etc.).
         2. Loan funds - Repayment of principal and interest are returned to
             the fund and made available for further loans to students,
             faculty, or staff. May be unrestricted, temporarily restricted,
             or permanently restricted.
         3. Endowment funds - Principal may be unrestricted (i.e., "quasi"
             endowment), temporarily restricted (i.e., "term" endowment), or
             permanently restricted (i.e., "pure" endowment).
         4. Annuity and life income funds - Restricted funds that provide
             for repayment to the donor of a portion of fund income.
         5. Agency funds - Resources managed by the institution as an agent
             on behalf of others. These funds are not available for the
             organization's own use and therefore appear as assets and
             offsetting liabilities.
         6. Plant funds - These funds include the plant assets and related
             debt, along with assets to be used for future
             acquisitions/replacements. They can be unrestricted, temporarily
             restricted, or permanently restricted.

         As the fund is internally designated, only the quasi-endowment fund
         may be used to account for the fund. The specific purpose for use
         of the income is from action of the university, rather than a donor.
         Thus, there is no temporary or permanent restriction on the net
         assets of the fund imposed by donors.

         Answer choice "A" is incorrect because an endowment fund accounts
         for funds restricted by a donor, rather than an internal action of
         an institution.

         Answer choice "B" is incorrect because a term endowment fund is one
         for which donors have specified a specific date or event, after
         which the principal balance of the funds may be expended. No such
         condition is indicated.

         Answer choice "D" is incorrect because a restricted current fund
         would be used to account for external restrictions (i.e., "use for a
         specified purpose"), and not internally designated restrictions.

60. D   In a hospital, operating revenues are those earned as part of the
         ongoing functions of the institution. They are further classified as
         "patient service revenues" and "other operating revenues."

         "Other operating revenues" are associated with sources indirectly
         related to providing patient services; e.g., tuition from an
         educational program, cafeteria revenues, parking fees, or gift shop
         revenue.

Proceeds <u>from</u> <u>the</u> <u>sale</u> <u>of</u> <u>cafeteria</u> <u>meals</u> <u>would</u> <u>appropriately</u> <u>be</u>
<u>reported</u> <u>as</u> <u>other</u> <u>operating</u> <u>revenues</u>.

Answer choice "A" is incorrect because, as a general rule, revenues
should not be reported as deductions from expenses.

Answer choice "B" is incorrect because "ancillary" service revenues,
which include laboratory tests, X-rays, and similar services
provided to patients, are part of patient service revenue.

Answer choice "C" is incorrect because the sale of cafeteria meals
is not directly related to providing patient services.

OTHER OBJECTIVE FORMATS/ESSAY QUESTIONS

Answer 2

61. $26,000   The amount of interest income that is taxable from the U.S.
             Treasury Bonds is $26,000, because interest on U.S. obligations
             is generally not exempt from federal income tax.

62. $8,000   The tax depreciation expense under the Modified Accelerated Cost
             Recovery System (MACRS) for the furniture and fixtures is
             $8,000. Under MACRS, furniture and fixtures are depreciated
             utilizing the 200 percent declining-balance method, with a
             switch to the straight-line method in the middle of the recovery
             period which, in this case, is seven years. Further, since the
             property was placed into service on January 1, 1993, the general
             rule (i.e., half-year convention) is applicable. Kimberly's tax
             depreciation expense is therefore $8,000 (i.e., $56,000 × 1/7
             × 200% × 1/2).

63. $7,000   The amount of bad debt to be included as an expense item is
             $7,000, which represents the actual bad debts written off.

             With respect to business bad debts, the specific (direct)
             charge-off method must be used. Under this method, an ordinary
             deduction is available only for those debts that become
             partially or totally worthless during the year. The "allowance
             for doubtful accounts" (i.e., "reserve") method may not be used
             for tax purposes.

64. $25,000   Kimberly's net long-term capital gain is $25,000, which consists
             of $20,000 gain on the sale of the unimproved lot and $5,000
             gain on the sale of the XYZ stock.

             While the gain on the sale of the unimproved lot (which
             satisfies the long-term holding period) is initially considered
             to be a Section 1231 gain, it will be treated as a long-term
             capital gain since Kimberly has never had any Section 1231
             losses, which might have required recapture as ordinary income.

The sale of the XYZ stock obviously results in long-term capital gain because it was held for more than one year.

65. $12,000 Kimberly may deduct $12,000 of interest, which consists of mortgage loan interest in the amount of $10,000 and $2,000 interest on a line of credit loan.

Interest on indebtedness to purchase municipal bonds is not deductible because the interest income derived from these bonds is not taxable.

66. N Kimberly's organization expenses for 1993 are nondeductible.

A corporation's organization expenses may be amortized over a period of not less than 60 months by a newly organized corporation that elects to do so. Failing the election, as in the question situation, the amount is deductible only upon liquidation. Organization expenses do not include expenses for the sale or issuance of stock or securities.

67. F The life insurance premiums paid by Kimberly for its executives as part of their compensation for services rendered are fully deductible, because the corporation is neither the direct nor indirect beneficiary of the policy and the amount of compensation is reasonable.

(Such premiums are referred to as "keyman" insurance premiums.)

68. F The vacation pay earned by employees which, vested under a plan by December 31, 1993, and which was paid on February 1, 1994, is fully deductible.

An accrual-basis corporation may accrue and deduct salaries (including bonuses and vacation pay) for nonshareholder-employees if paid on or before the due date of the corporation's tax return (which is generally the 15th day of the third month following the close of the taxable year).

69. F The $25,000 state franchise tax liability that has accrued during the year and that was paid on March 15, 1994 (i.e., the due date of the corporation's tax return), is fully deductible.

It should be noted that federal income taxes are not deductible.

70. P The entertainment expense to lease a luxury skybox during the football season to entertain clients is partially deductible.

Deductions for the use of skyboxes used for entertainment are limited to the cost of nonluxury box seats. Further, for 1993, only 80 percent of the cost of meals and entertainment is deductible. Beginning in 1994, only 50 percent of the cost of meals and entertainment is deductible.

71. P The dividends received from the 20-percent-owned domestic corporation are <u>partially</u> <u>taxable</u> because an 80 percent dividends-received deduction is available.

It should be noted that the dividends-received deduction is generally limited to 70 percent of the dividends received from less-than-20-percent-owned corporations. Further, the deduction is generally limited to 70 percent (80 percent in the case of a 20-percent-or-more-owned corporation) of the corporation's taxable income computed without regard to the dividends-received deduction and net operating loss deduction. The operation of this general rule is such that the full dividends-received deduction does not create a net operating loss for the year.

72. F Kimberly's recovery of an account from the prior year's bad debts is <u>fully</u> <u>taxable</u> under the tax benefit rule.

Under the tax benefit rule, the recovery of an account is taxable to the extent that (1) the account had been previously written off for tax purposes, and (2) the taxpayer's income tax liability had been reduced in a previous year.

73. F Under the tax benefit rule (as discussed in the answer to #72), the refund of Kimberly's state franchise tax overpayment, previously expensed on Kimberly's 1991 federal tax return, thereby reducing federal taxes that year, is <u>fully</u> <u>taxable</u>.

74. N Interest income from municipal bonds is <u>nontaxable</u>.

It should be noted, however, that interest on obligations of the United States is generally fully taxable.

75. N The proceeds paid to Kimberly by reason of death, under a life insurance policy that Kimberly had purchased on the life of one of its vice-presidents, is <u>nontaxable</u>.

It should be noted that premiums for keyman life insurance policies are not deductible if the corporation is the beneficiary. On the other hand, premiums for group-term life insurance policies are deductible if the corporation is not the beneficiary.

76. T In determining alternative minimum taxable income before the adjusted current earnings (ACE) adjustment, a depreciation adjustment may be necessary because the Alternative Depreciation System must be utilized. Accordingly, commercial real property, as well as residential rental property, must be depreciated using the <u>straight-line</u> <u>method</u>, over a 40-year recovery period.

77. T A corporation's alternative minimum tax is equal to 20 percent of alternative minimum taxable income (in excess of the exemption amount) reduced by the corporation's regular tax liability. <u>The corporate exemption amount</u>, which therefore <u>reduces the alternative minimum taxable income</u> (AMTI), is equal to $40,000, but must be reduced by 25 percent of the excess of AMTI over $150,000.

78. T   In determining alternative minimum taxable income (AMTI) of a corporation, it may be necessary to include an adjusted current earnings (ACE) adjustment. The ACE adjustment is generally equal to 75 percent of the amount by which adjusted current earnings exceed AMTI. However, if AMTI exceeds adjusted current earnings, a reduction in AMTI equal to 75 percent of the difference is allowed. Accordingly, the ACE adjustment can be a positive or negative amount.

           Adjusted current earnings is equal to AMTI (before the ACE adjustment and the AMTI net operating loss deduction) plus or minus certain adjustments. The calculation of adjusted current earnings is based on tax concepts similar to those used in determining earnings and profits (i.e., E&P) for regular tax purposes. Accordingly, adjustments may be necessary for (1) depreciation, (2) certain items excluded from gross income but that are properly includible in E&P, and (3) items of deduction that are allowed in arriving at regular taxable income, but that are not allowed in arriving at E&P.

79. F   Depreciation on personal property to arrive at alternative minimum taxable income before the ACE adjustment is computed under the Alternative Depreciation System, except that personal property is depreciated using the 150 percent declining-balance method. Further, under the Alternative Depreciation System, recovery periods are longer than those utilized for deductions under the Modified Accelerated Cost Recovery System.

80. T   The alternative minimum tax (AMT) is the excess of the tentative minimum tax over the regular tax liability. Accordingly, if a corporation is liable for the AMT, the excess amount is payable in addition to the regular tax.

81. F   Municipal bond interest, other than from private activity bonds, is not includible income to arrive at alternative minimum taxable income before the ACE adjustment.

82. F   The maximum corporate exemption amount for minimum tax purposes is $40,000. However, the exemption must be reduced by 25 percent of the excess of AMTI over $150,000.

83. F   In general, in computing adjusted current earnings (ACE), no deduction is allowed for any item that is not deductible for the purpose of computing earnings and profits. As a result, the 70 percent dividends received deduction is not available to determine ACE.

           It should be noted, however, that the 80 percent dividends received deduction will be allowed. The 80% dividends received deduction is applicable to 20-percent-or-more-owned corporations.

84. T   All municipal bond interest is includible income to determine adjusted current earnings (ACE).

It should then be obvious that all costs to purchase and carry such municipal bonds would be deductible to determine ACE.

85. F   The method of depreciation for personal property placed in service after 1989 for determining adjusted current earnings (ACE) is governed by the Alternative Depreciation System. Accordingly, the straight-line method must be used.

Answer 3

86. D   In this situation, the journal entry to record the adoption of the budget is as follows:

Dr. Estimated revenues   700,000
    Cr. Appropriations   660,000
    Cr. Appropriations-Operating transfers out   30,000
    Cr. Budgetary fund balance   10,000
Accordingly, estimated revenues is debited.

Parenthetically, it should be noted that appropriations for operating transfers out may alternately be classified as a credit to "estimated other financing uses."

87. C   As indicated by the answer to #86, the budgetary fund balance account is used to balance the entry.

The difference between estimated revenues and appropriations will determine whether the budgetary fund balance is decreased or increased. In this case, since estimated revenues exceed authorizations for spending and operating transfers, the budgetary fund balance is increased (i.e., credited).

88. C   As indicated by the answer to #86, appropriations represent the authority to spend; this account is credited upon adoption of the budget.

89. C   Since the operating transfer was specifically authorized by action of the governmental unit, appropriations—operating transfers out would be credited as indicated in the answer to #86.

90. N   The expenditures account is not affected by the adoption of the budget.

91. D   The typical journal entry to record the property tax levy is as follows:

Dr. Property tax receivable
    Cr. Allowance for uncollectibles-current
    Cr. Revenues

92. N   In accounting for a general fund, revenues are recorded net of estimated uncollectibles. As such, there is no bad debt expense.

93.   C   As indicated in the answer to #91, revenues are recorded net of the estimated amounts that will be uncollectible. Accordingly, the allowance for uncollectibles—current is credited in this situation to reflect the estimate.

94.   C   As indicated in the answer to #91, revenues are credited. In the general fund, revenues are credited when susceptible to accrual; i.e., when measurable and available. This is considered to be the date on which the taxes are levied.

95.   N   The estimated revenues account is not affected by the recording of the property tax levy. It is initially debited as a nominal account when the budget is recorded (see answer to #86) and is closed at the end of the period (see answer to #111).

96.   D   Encumbrance accounting is peculiar to governmental accounting, particularly with respect to governmental-type funds. It is an integral part of budgetary accountability.

        Encumbrances represent commitments related to unfilled contracts for goods and services. (It should be noted that unpaid wages and salaries, a significant expenditure by governmental units, represent a known, incurred liability and, hence, are not encumbered.) The purpose of encumbrance accounting is to prevent further expenditures of funds in light of commitments already made.

        When an estimated contractual liability is entered into, the entry made is as follows:

        Dr. Encumbrances
             Cr. Budgetary fund balance reserved for encumbrances

        (It should be noted that the terms "reserve for encumbrances" and "budgetary fund balance reserved for encumbrances" are interchangeable.)

97.   C   As indicated in the answer to #96, the reserve for encumbrances sets aside a portion of the budgetary fund balance to ensure that authorized amounts are available to pay for goods and services when received. Consequently, the budgetary fund balance reserved for encumbrances should be credited.

98.   N   Governmental units utilize the modified accrual basis to account for expenditures. As such, they are recorded when the liability for the expenditure is incurred. As an encumbrance is only a commitment, no liability exists. Therefore, no expenditure is recorded at the time the encumbrance is recorded.

99.   N   As indicated in the answer to #98, no liability is incurred at the time the encumbrance is initially recorded. Hence, the vouchers payable account is not affected.

100. N   Accounting for the general fund <u>does</u> <u>not</u> generally <u>utilize</u> <u>a</u> <u>purchase</u> <u>account</u>.

101. C   When the actual expenditure of an amount previously encumbered in the current year is known, two entries are made. One entry reverses the original encumbrance and the second records the expenditure.

     1. Dr. Budgetary fund balance reserved for encumbrances
             Cr. <u>Encumbrances</u>
     2. Dr. Expenditures
             Cr. Vouchers payable

102. D   As indicated in the answer to #101, when expenditures that had previously been encumbered are recorded, the <u>budgetary fund balance reserved for encumbrances is debited</u>.

103. D   Accounting for the general fund uses the modified accrual basis. <u>Expenditures are</u> recognized (i.e., <u>debited</u>) when the liability is incurred, as shown by entry "2" in the answer to #101.

104. C   As indicated by entry "2" in the answer to #101, and the explanation in the answer to #103, <u>vouchers payable is credited</u> when the liability for expenditures is recognized.

105. N   Accounting for the general fund <u>does</u> <u>not</u> <u>utilize</u> <u>a</u> "<u>purchases</u>" <u>account</u>.

106. N   As the budget authorized an operating transfer to the Library debt service fund, <u>no entry would be made</u> to the residual equity transfer out account. Residual equity transfers are nonrecurring or nonroutine transfers of equity between funds and are generally used to establish or disestablish funds.

107. N   In this situation, the action of the governmental unit established an authorized transfer to the Library debt service fund. Therefore, the general fund has <u>no receivable from</u> (i.e., "due from") the Library debt service fund. Obviously, transfers are not temporary shifts of resources, as are receivables/payables.

108. C   The operating transfer of resources from the general fund to the Library debt service fund would result in a decrease of cash in the general fund as follows:

     Dr. Other financing uses-operating transfers out
         Cr. <u>Cash</u>

109. D   As indicated in the answer to #108, the transfer of cash to the Library debt service fund would be recorded as a <u>debit</u> to "<u>other financial uses-operating transfers out</u>." This account is a nominal account that will be closed at the end of the year. (See answer to #117.)

110. N   The encumbrances account is used to account for commitments made to acquire goods and services. Therefore, it is <u>not affected</u> by transfers to the Library debt service fund.

111. C   The closing process in a general fund involves a reversal of the entry to record the budget at the beginning of the year (see answer to #86) as follows:

   Dr. Appropriations
   Dr. Appropriations-Operating transfers out
   Dr. Budgetary fund balance
       Cr. <u>Estimated</u> <u>revenues</u>

112. D   See the illustrative entry in the answer to #111. Accordingly, <u>budgetary fund balance should be debited</u>.

113. D   See illustrative entry in the answer to #111. <u>Appropriations should</u>, therefore, <u>be debited</u>.

114. D   See illustrative entry in the answer to #111. Therefore, there should be a <u>debit</u> to <u>appropriations—operating transfers out</u>.

115. C   Closing entries in the general fund include a decrease in the unreserved fund balance for actual expenditures incurred during the year as follows:

   Dr. Unreserved fund balance
       Cr. <u>Expenditures</u>

116. D   Closing entries in the general fund include an increase in the unreserved fund balance for actual revenues recorded during the year as follows:

   <u>Dr.</u> <u>Revenues</u>
       Cr. Unreserved fund balance

117. C   Other financial uses-operating transfers out was debited when the cash was transferred out of the general fund. As part of the closing process, <u>this nominal account is credited</u>.

118. D   At the end of the current year, any property taxes receivable established as part of the tax levy estimated to be uncollectible may be reclassified from current to delinquent. Accordingly, the allowance for uncollectibles account would also be reclassified from current to delinquent, resulting in a <u>debit</u> to <u>the current account</u>.

119. N   This account is <u>not</u> <u>used</u> in accounting for the general fund (see answer to #92).

120. N   This <u>account</u> <u>is</u> <u>not</u> <u>used</u> in accounting for the general fund. Depreciation is not recorded in governmental funds such as the general fund (except as an optional disclosure).

121. N Residual equity transfer out was <u>not affected</u> by the operations of the general fund for the situation given. (See answer to #106.)

122. C Encumbrances open at year-end (i.e., the commitment to acquire goods and services remained outstanding) would be closed as follows:

Dr. Budgetary fund balance reserved for encumbrances
    <u>Cr</u>. <u>Encumbrances</u>

Note that this is simply a reversal of the entry made to establish the encumbrance during the year (as noted in the answer to #96).

123. D See the illustrative entry in the answer to #122. Budgetary fund balance reserved for encumbrances is accordingly <u>debited</u>.

124. D When the "budgetary fund balance" account is used, as indicated in the question, it is closed out to "unreserved fund balance" at year-end. Thus, setting aside resources to reflect the intent to honor commitments made in 1993 when the invoices are received in 1994 would be indicated by the following entry:

<u>Dr</u>. <u>Unreserved fund balance</u>
    Cr. Fund balance reserved for encumbrances

<u>Parenthetically, apart from this question, procedures in the</u>
<u>following year would involve</u>:

1. The encumbrance would be reinstated at the beginning of the year:
Dr. Encumbrances
    Cr. Unreserved fund balance

2. Upon actual expenditure, the encumbrance would be closed out against the fund balance reserved for encumbrances in the usual manner. Thus, any effect on unreserved fund balance in the following year would only be the difference between the original encumbrance and the actual expenditure.

125. C See illustrative entry in the answer to #124. Accordingly, a <u>credit</u> must be made to <u>fund balance reserved for encumbrances</u>.

Financial Accounting & Reporting—Business Enterprises (FARE)

FOUR-OPTION MULTIPLE-CHOICE QUESTIONS

Answer 1

1.   D   According to the FASB's conceptual framework, the process of reporting an item in the financial statements of an entity is <u>recognition</u>. Recognition occurs when a business event is recorded in the accounting records.

Answer choice "A" is incorrect because allocation applies to the systematic reduction of an asset into an expense over the periods of benefit.

Answer choice "B" is incorrect because matching applies to charging an expense against the related revenue in the same accounting period.

Answer choice "C" is incorrect because realization refers to the recognition of revenue at the time of sale or rendering of a service.

2.   C   According to FASB Concepts Statement #1, "Objectives of Financial Reporting by Business Enterprises," the Statements of Financial Accounting Concepts are intended to establish <u>the objectives and concepts for use in developing standards of financial accounting and reporting</u>.

Answer choice "A" is incorrect because generally accepted accounting principles are established through Statements of Financial Accounting Standards.

Answer choice "B" is incorrect because the meaning of "Present fairly in accordance with generally accepted accounting principles" is established through Statements on Auditing Standards.

Answer choice "D" is incorrect because the hierarchy of sources of generally accepted accounting principles is established through Statements on Auditing Standards.

3.   A   Generally, assets are recognized on the balance sheet at historical cost. However, when the utility of an asset has been impaired, it should be written down to the lower of cost or market under the constraint of conservatism. This represents a departure from the accounting principle of <u>historical cost</u>.

Answer choice "B" is incorrect because consistency refers to the conformity in application of accounting principles over time.

Answer choice "C" is incorrect because conservatism is the reason for reporting inventory at the lower of cost or market.

Answer choice "D" is incorrect because according to full disclosure, all relevant material information is to be disclosed in the financial statements or the notes thereto.

4.   C   According to FASB Concepts Statement #1, "Objectives of Financial Reporting by Business Enterprises," financial reporting should provide information about an enterprise's financial performance during a period. Investors and creditors often use information about the past to help in assessing the prospects of an enterprise.

Financial reporting provides information about an enterprise during a period in which it was under the direction of a particular management, but does not directly provide information about that management's performance.

Because financial reporting usually cannot, and does not, separate management performance from enterprise performance, the information is limited for purposes of assessment.

Given the above, financial statements will directly provide information about <u>enterprise performance but not directly provide information about management performance</u>.

Answer choices other than "C" are inconsistent with the information provided.

5.   C   Under FASB Statement #95, "Statement of Cash Flows," the primary purpose of a statement of cash flows is to provide relevant information about <u>the cash receipts and cash disbursements of an enterprise during a period</u>.

Such information should help investors, creditors, and others to assess the (1) enterprise's ability to generate positive future net cash flows, (2) enterprise's ability to meet its obligations, its ability to pay dividends, and its need for external financing, (3) reasons for differences between net income and associated cash receipts and payments, and (4) effects on an enterprise's financial position of both its cash and noncash investing and financing transactions during the period.

Answer choices other than "C" are inconsistent with the explanation provided. Each of the incorrect answer choices are ways the users of financial information might utilize cash flow information, but they do not represent the primary purpose of the statement.

6.   A   The purpose of information disclosed in notes or parenthetically on the face of financial statements is to amplify or explain information recognized in the financial statements. This sort of information is essential in understanding the information recognized in the financial statements, and has long been viewed as a means of <u>providing disclosures required by generally accepted accounting principles</u>.

Answer choice "B" is incorrect because supplemental disclosure cannot correct improper presentation in the financial statements, and cannot contradict representations in the financial statements.

Answer choice "C" is incorrect because supplemental disclosure cannot, by definition, provide recognition. Recognition is the process of formally recording or incorporating an item (such as an asset, a liability, a revenue or expense amount, etc.) into the financial statements of an entity.

Answer choice "D" is incorrect because financial reporting is not the appropriate place for management to respond to auditor comments.

7. C As per FASB Statement #94, "Consolidation of all Majority-Owned Subsidiaries," consolidation is appropriate in all circumstances except for (1) <u>subsidiaries</u> <u>under</u> <u>temporary</u> <u>control</u>, and (2) subsidiaries whose control does not rest with the majority owner (subsidiary in legal reorganization or bankruptcy).

Answer choices "A" and "D" are incorrect because consolidation is required even if the parent and subsidiary are in entirely different lines of business.

Answer choice "B" is incorrect because consolidation is required even if the parent and subsidiary have different fiscal years. If the fiscal years are more than three months apart, the subsidiary should prepare financial statements that correspond to the parent's fiscal period.

8. D A dividend is a distribution of the earnings of a corporation to shareholders; it is a liability only when declared by the board of directors. When dividends are in arrears on cumulative preferred stock, the total amount in arrears, and the current year's dividend on the preferred stock, must be paid before common shareholders may receive a dividend.

Apex has had 3,000 shares of 5 percent, $100 par value, cumulative preferred stock outstanding since, at least, January 1, 1992, with no dividends in arrears as of December 31, 1992. No dividends were declared in 1992, and dividends of $10,000 were paid in 1993. Here, the annual preferred dividend requirement is $15,000 (i.e., 5% × $100 × 3,000 shares). Accordingly, at December 31, 1993, Apex should <u>disclose</u> (but not accrue) a dividend arrearage of <u>$20,000</u>; i.e., the remaining arrearage for 1992 ($5,000) plus the arrearage for 1993 ($15,000).

Answer choice "A" is incorrect because a liability does not exist for a dividend in arrears, and the amount of the arrearage is incorrect.

Answer choice "B" is incorrect because it reflects the wrong amount of the arrearage.

Answer choice "C" is incorrect because no liability for dividends in arrears exists at December 31, 1993; there is no liability until a dividend is declared.

9.   A   Simply stated, the cost of goods manufactured is the equivalent of purchases to a nonmanufacturing business. Thus, the beginning inventory of finished goods plus the cost of goods manufactured is equal to the cost of goods available for sale. In turn, the cost of goods available for sale reduced by the ending inventory of finished goods equals the cost of sales.

In light of the preceding, the cost of goods manufactured can be determined from the facts given by reversing the process, as follows:

Cost of sales	$240,000
Add: Ending inventory, finished goods	360,000
Less: Beginning inventory, finished goods	(400,000)
Cost of goods manufactured, 1993	$200,000

Answer choice "B" is incorrect because $15,000 of freight out is included and should not be; freight out is a selling expense, and not a component of the cost of sales.

Answer choice "C" is incorrect because the $400,000 beginning inventory is added to the cost of sales and should be subtracted, and the $360,000 ending inventory is subtracted from the cost of sales, and should be added.

Answer choice "D" is incorrect because the $400,000 beginning inventory is added to the cost of sales and should be subtracted, and the $360,000 ending inventory is subtracted from the cost of sales, and should be added. In addition, the $15,000 of freight out is included and should not be; freight out is a selling expense, and not a component of the cost of sales.

10.   C   In the multiple-step format, in arriving at income from continuing operations, there are sections, or "steps," for sales, cost of sales, gross margin (profit), operating expenses, operating income, other revenue and expense items, and the provision for income taxes on continuing operations. (The alternative to a multiple-step format is a statement listing all revenue items, from which is subtracted a listing of all costs and expenses, etc.; this is referred to as a "single-step" income statement.)

Additionally, regardless of whether the income statement is multiple-step or single-step, the results of discontinued operations (net of tax), extraordinary items (net of tax), and cumulative effects of changes in accounting principles (net of tax) must be presented separately; these all follow the results of continuing operations, and in the order indicated.

Obviously, the last item on the income statement is "net income," which includes all the captions indicated, and is after income taxes.

For the year ended December 31, 1993, Vane should report income after income taxes from continuing operations of $140,000:

Total revenue ($575,000 + $25,000)		$600,000
Total expenses and losses	$420,000	
Less: Extraordinary item - loss on early retirement of long-term debt	(20,000)	(400,000)
Income from continuing operations before tax		200,000
Income tax expense; $200,000 × 30%		(60,000)
__Income from continuing operations__ __after tax, 1993__		$140,000

It should be noted that gains and losses from the extinguishment of debt, if material, are always extraordinary.

Answer choice "A" is incorrect because the extraordinary loss is included as a component of income from continuing operations (i.e., [$600,000 - $420,000] - 30% × [$600,000 - $420,000] equals $126,000).

Answer choices "B" and "D" are not logical in view of the explanation provided for answer choice "C."

11. C Generally, liabilities due within one year are classified as current.

Accordingly, current liabilities total $1,490,000:

Accounts payable	$ 55,000
Unsecured notes, 8%, due 7-1-94	400,000
Accrued expenses	35,000
Senior bonds, 7%, due 3-31-94	1,000,000
Total current liabilities, December 31, 1993	$1,490,000

The following should be noted.
1. In accordance with FASB Statement #109, "Accounting for Income Taxes," a deferred income tax liability may be either current or noncurrent. The deferred tax liability is not related to an asset but will reverse in more than one year (1995); therefore, it should be classified as a noncurrent liability.
2. Since the 7 percent senior bonds payable and the 8 percent unsecured notes are due within one year of the balance sheet, they are current liabilities.
3. The contingent liability should be accrued only if it is probable that it will be incurred and if it is reasonably estimated. The facts of the question indicate that the loss is only possible; therefore, it should not be accrued.

Answer choice "A" is incorrect because it excludes the 7 percent senior bonds, which should be included, and incorrectly includes the deferred income tax liability.

Answer choice "B" is incorrect because it excludes the 7 percent senior bonds, which should be included, and incorrectly includes the contingent liability.

Answer choice "D" is incorrect because it inappropriately includes the deferred income taxes.

12. B Cash is legally disbursed only when it has been delivered, or mailed, to the payee. The check drawn on Grey's account and recorded on 12/31/93, but not mailed to the vendor until 1/10/94, was not legally disbursed at December 31, 1993.

On Grey's December 31, 1993, balance sheet, cash should be reported as $13,800; i.e., the $12,000 checkbook balance plus the $1,800 unmailed check.

Answer choice "A" is incorrect because it does not add back the check that was not mailed.

Answer choice "C" is incorrect because the unmailed check is subtracted from the bank statement balance; the result does not represent the book balance that should be reported on the balance sheet.

Answer choice "D" is incorrect because it represents the bank balance, and does not consider the check not mailed or other reconciling items.

13. C Cash and cash equivalents include cash that is generally unrestricted and available for use, and/or short-term, highly liquid investments that have original maturities of three months or less (e.g., treasury bills, commercial paper, money-market funds, etc.). Further, accounts with positive and negative balances on deposit in the same bank may be netted together because the bank generally has the right of offset.

As such, Kale should report cash and cash equivalents in its December 31, 1993, balance sheet as $240,000:

Checking account #101	$175,000
Checking account #201	(10,000)
Money market account	25,000
90-day certificate of deposit, due 2-28-94	50,000
Cash and cash equivalents, December 31, 1993	$240,000

Answer choice "A" is incorrect because the 90-day certificate of deposit, due 2/28/94 (i.e., $50,000), is not included, and should be.

Answer choice "B" is incorrect because neither the account with the negative balance nor the 90-day certificate of deposit is considered, and both should be (i.e., $175,000 + $25,000 equals $200,000).

Answer choice "D" is incorrect because the $80,000, 180-day certificate of deposit, due 3-15-94, is included, and should not be, since its original maturity was in excess of three months.

14.   B   This question is based on FASB Statement #115, "Accounting for Certain Investments in Debt and Equity Securities." Under this Statement, investments in both trading debt and equity securities and available-for-sale debt and equity securities are reported on the balance sheet at market value at the date of the financial statements. The only difference between the two categories of securities is the placement of the unrealized holding gains and losses in the financial statements. For trading securities, such gains and losses are recognized in earnings; for available-for-sale securities, such gains and losses are included as a separate component of shareholders' equity.

Trading securities are those that are bought and held principally for the purposes of selling them in the near future. Held-to-maturity debt securities are those that the entity has the positive intent and ability to hold to maturity. Available-for-sale securities are those that are not classified as trading or held-to-maturity securities.

Nola should classify these equity securities as available-for-sale securities, with unrealized gains and losses reported as a separate component of stockholders' equity.

Answer choices other than "B" are based upon incorrect assumptions and/or combinations.

15.   A   Accounts receivables should be stated at their net realizable value, which requires a provision for amounts of gross receivables that are not expected to be realized. This will require provisions for both uncollectible receivables and for discounts that will be taken.

Since receivables paid within 15 days are eligible for the 2 percent cash discount, the amount of the allowance for discounts that Delta should report at December 31, 1993, is $1,000 (i.e., $100,000 × 50% × .02), which takes into consideration the fact that only 50 percent of the customers take advantage of the discount.

Answer choice "B" is not logical in view of the facts presented.

Answer choice "C" is incorrect because it is based upon total receivables; only those in the "0-15 days" classification are eligible for the discount (i.e., $167,500 × 1% equals $1,675).

Answer choice "D" is incorrect because it provides for discounts on all the receivables in the "0-15 days" classification, when only 50% of the customers are expected to take advantage of the discount.

16.   A   A receivable from a party in which there is a material equity investment may involve a related party transaction that requires separate disclosure. Under FASB Statement #57, "Related Party Disclosures," related parties are affiliates of an enterprise, including: (1) its management and their immediate families, (2) its principal owners and their immediate families, (3) its investments accounted for by the equity method, (4) beneficial employee trusts that are managed by the management of the enterprise, and (5) any party that may, or does, deal with the enterprise, and has ownership of, control over, or can significantly influence the management or operating policies of another party to the extent that an arm's-length transaction may not be achieved.

It is not clear from the information provided that this situation requires separate disclosure; however, the total receivable should be reported separately because that is the only feasible answer.

Answer choice "B" is incorrect because there is no basis to include a receivable as part of an investment, without separate disclosure.

Answer choice "C" is incorrect because there is no basis for the treatment indicated.

Answer choice "D" is incorrect because it is not appropriate to offset receivables and payables when the ownership is 15 percent. Such offset would be appropriate in consolidation, or where the equity method (20 percent ownership, generally) applies.

17.   B   While this question nominally deals with interest expense, it is related to FASB Statement #34, "Capitalization of Interest Cost." The following should be noted:
1. In accordance with that Statement, interest capitalization is appropriate when a period of time is required to make assets ready for their intended use. Interest capitalization is required for those assets if its effect, compared with the effect of expensing interest, is material.
2. In general, interest should be capitalized for (a) assets constructed or produced for a company's own use, and (b) assets intended for sale or lease that are constructed or produced as discrete projects (e.g., ships or real estate developments).
3. Interest should not be capitalized for:
   a. Inventory items routinely manufactured in large quantities on a repetitive basis.
   b. Assets already in use or ready for use.
   c. Assets not used in the earning activities of the enterprise.
4. The amount of interest capitalized is based on the average amount of accumulated expenditures for the asset during the period.
5. The interest rate used shall be either (a) the weighted-average rate on the company's outstanding debt, or (b) the rate on specific borrowing associated with the debt.

Cole should capitalize interest of $40,000, which was the interest computed on the weighted-average amount of accumulated expenditures during 1993.

Answer choices other than "B" are inconsistent with the information provided.

18.   B   Under the declining-balance method of depreciation, salvage value is ignored and depreciation is based on the declining book value of the asset. When it is the policy to change to the straight-line method after a period of time, the remaining book value of the asset (i.e., cost less accumulated depreciation) is depreciated over its remaining useful life by the straight-line method.

It should be noted that the switch after two years does not represent a change in accounting method because, in fact, it is a matter of policy in establishing the method used.

Accumulated depreciation at December 31, 1993, is determined as follows:

	Accumulated Depreciation
Depreciation for 1991; $50,000 × 40%	$20,000
Depreciation for 1992; ($50,000 - $20,000) × 40%	12,000
Depreciation for 1993; ($50,000 - $32,000)/3 years	6,000
Accumulated depreciation for equipment, December 31, 1993	$38,000

Answer choice "A" is incorrect because it is the amount of accumulated depreciation at 12/31/93 that Turtle would have reported had it changed retroactively to the straight-line method (i.e., $50,000 × 3/5).

Answer choice "C" is incorrect because it is the amount of accumulated depreciation at 12/31/93 that Turtle would have reported had it continued to use the double-declining balance method.

Answer choice "D" is not logical in view of the explanation provided for answer choice "B."

19.   D   This question is based on APB Opinion #18, "The Equity Method of Accounting for Investments in Common Stock."

Generally, when an investor owns at least 20 percent of an investee company, there is a presumption that the equity method is to be used.

When the stock interest is less than 20 percent, the equity method is used only if it can be determined that operating control has been achieved.

If there is a difference between the purchase price and the equity (net assets) acquired, such excess is first allocated to specific assets and/or liabilities (and amortized or depreciated as appropriate). Any excess that is not so identified is goodwill, to be amortized in accordance with APB Opinion #17, which provides for an amortization period not to exceed 40 years.

The investor includes its share of investee income, net of amortization of goodwill, if any, in the investment account. (Depreciation and/or amortization of any differences between cost and equity acquired is treated in the same manner as goodwill amortization.) Any dividends received are a reduction of the investment account. Therefore, the recorded balance (carrying amount) in the investment account will always be at original cost adjusted to equity.

If the investment (or any portion thereof) is sold, the gain or loss is based on the carrying amount at the time of sale.

In its December 31, 1993, balance sheet, Kean should report its investment in Pod in the amount of $276,000:

Cost of investment			$250,000
Kean's share of Pod's earnings:			
$100,000 × 30%		$30,000	
Amortization of goodwill:			
Cost of investment	$250,000		
Less: Equity acquired:			
$500,000 × 30%	(150,000)		
Difference	$100,000		
Kean's share of undervalued land:			
$200,000 × 30%	(60,000)		
Goodwill	$ 40,000		
Amortization of goodwill: $40,000/10		(4,000)	26,000
Investment in subsidiary, December 31, 1993			$276,000

It should be noted that since land is not depreciated, the portion of the difference attributed to the undervalued land is not amortized.

Answer choices other than "D" are not logical in view of the explanation provided.

20. C An intangible asset is recorded at its acquisition cost, measured by the amount of cash disbursed to acquire it. The cost is amortized by the straight-line method over the shortest of the economic life, legal life, or forty (40) years.

The original cost of the franchise to be capitalized is $50,000. The additional franchise fee is charged to operations as incurred and does not affect the carrying value of the intangible asset.

At December 31, 1993, Rafa should report the intangible asset-franchise at $45,000:

Cost	$50,000
Less: Amortization; $50,000/10	(5,000)
Carrying value; December 31, 1993	$45,000

Answer choice "A" is incorrect because, while the $5,000 amortization of the $50,000 acquisition cost (i.e., $50,000/10) is appropriately deducted, the continuing franchise fee of $12,000 (i.e., 3% × $400,000) is also deducted, and should not be. Franchise fees are expensed as incurred.

Answer choice "B" is incorrect because, while the $5,000 amortization of the $50,000 acquisition cost (i.e., $50,000/10) is appropriately deducted, the continuing franchise fee of $12,000 (i.e., 3% × $400,000) is amortized over ten years (i.e., $12,000/10 equals $1,200) and is also deducted, and should not be. Franchise fees are expensed as incurred.

Answer choice "D" is incorrect because it is the $50,000 acquisition cost of the franchise, which should be amortized over its ten-year useful life, and is not.

21. B   Based on the facts presented, Hudson's liability for sales taxes at December 31, 1993, would relate to sales made in November (paid in January) and December (to be paid in February). Further, the liability for occupancy taxes would relate to sales for the fourth quarter of 1993 (due to be paid in January). As such, the respective amounts are $39,000 and $8,200:

Room rentals - November	$110,000
Room rentals - December	150,000
Total	260,000
Sales tax rate	× .15
Sales taxes payable, December 31, 1993	$ 39,000

Room nights - October	1,100
Room nights - November	1,200
Room nights - December	1,800
Total room nights for fourth quarter	4,100
Tax rate	× $ 2
Occupancy taxes payable, December 31, 1993	$ 8,200

Answer choices other than "B" are based on incorrect assumptions and/or combinations.

22. A   The amount that should be reported as accrued liability for unemployment claims should be the best estimate of the amounts that will actually be paid for claims.

As stated in the question, Acme has elected to reimburse the state directly for actual unemployment claims, which are estimated to amount to 2 percent of eligible gross wages (defined as the first $10,000 of gross wages paid to each employee).

At December 31, 1993, Acme should report an accrued liability for unemployment claims in the amount of $1,000:

Eligible wages; $10,000 × 5 employees	$50,000
Estimated cost	× 2%
Accrued liability, December 31, 1993	$ 1,000

Answer choice "B" is incorrect because it is the amount that would be paid had Acme elected to pay the tax at 3 percent, rather than reimburse the state for actual claims (i.e., 3% × $10,000 × 5).

Answer choice "C" is incorrect because it represents 2 percent of actual wages, rather than 2 percent of eligible wages.

Answer choice "D" is incorrect because it represents 3 percent of actual wages, rather than 2 percent of eligible wages.

23.   D   The question indicates that use of the installment sales method is appropriate. The installment sales method should be used for financial accounting purposes only when there is a significant risk of not collecting the sales price, and where the degree of collectibility cannot be estimated.

Under the installment sales method, gross profit is realized only as cash is collected.

Revenue realized under the installment method is equal to the cash collected multiplied by the applicable gross profit percentage for the year in which the sale was made. Any gross profit not collected is "deferred" on the balance sheet pending collection. When collections are subsequently made, realized gross profit is increased via debit to the deferred gross profit account. At any point, the amount of the deferred gross profit on installment sales will be the installment receivable multiplied by the appropriate gross profit percentage.

The installment accounts receivable is arrived at by subtracting both cash collections and accounts written off, attributable to a specific year's sales, from the amount of installment sales for that year.

Astor should report deferred gross profit in its December 31, 1993, balance sheet in the amount of $250,000:

	1993	1992
Sales	$900,000	$600,000
Less: Collections		
Year of sale	(300,000)	(200,000)
Year following year of sale		(100,000)
Less: Accounts written off		
Year of sale	(50,000)	(50,000)
Year following year of sale		(150,000)
Installment accounts receivable at 12/31/93	550,000	100,000
Gross profit percentage	× _____ 40%	× _____ 30%
Deferred gross profit at 12/31/93	$220,000	$ 30,000

<u>Total deferred gross profit</u>,
December 31, 1993: $220,000 + $30,000 $250,000

Answer choices other than "D" are not logical in view of the explanation provided.

24. D With respect to FASB Statement #109, "Accounting for Income Taxes," the following background material should be noted:

1. <u>Temporary differences in general</u>
   A temporary difference is the difference between the tax basis of an asset or liability and its basis as reported in the financial statements (i.e., book basis). Thus, if the asset is sold (recovered), or the liability settled at its financial accounting carrying value, taxable income (or a deduction) will result in a future period.

   The difference between the tax basis and the financial statement basis can be expressed in income statement relationships as well. Thus, for example, a warranty liability would be recorded for financial statement (book) purposes but would not enter into taxable income until a future year; the effect in the future year is the reversal of a temporary difference.

   The concept of permanent differences (i.e., an inherent difference between what is considered an accounting event vs. what is considered a taxable event), such as tax-exempt interest and nondeductible expenses, is not defined in FASB Statement #109. As under prior standards, deferred taxes are not provided for permanent differences; rather, they are simply adjustments to pretax book income to arrive at taxable income.

2. <u>Deferred tax liabilities</u>
   Deferred tax liabilities arise when the financial statement (book) basis of an asset exceeds its tax basis (e.g., accelerated depreciation), or when the financial statement (book) basis of a liability is less than its tax basis. This will give rise to a taxable temporary difference, since future taxable income will exceed future pretax accounting income when the difference reverses.

The amount of the deferred tax liability is measured by multiplying the amount of the taxable temporary difference by the tax rate scheduled to be in effect when the difference reverses.

3. Deferred tax assets
    A deferred tax asset arises when the financial statement (book) basis of an asset is less than its tax basis (e.g., market value for securities), or when the financial statement (book) basis of a liability is greater than its tax basis (e.g., as in the case of product warranties). This will give rise to a deductible temporary difference, since future taxable income will be less than future pretax accounting income.

    The amount of a deferred tax asset is measured by multiplying the amount of the deductible temporary difference by the tax rate scheduled to be in effect when the difference reverses.

4. Balance sheet classification
    a. The net current and the net noncurrent deferred tax assets and liabilities are presented separately. Such assets and liabilities are classified as current or noncurrent based upon the classification of the related asset or liability for financial reporting. That is, a liability resulting from using accelerated depreciation for tax purposes will result in a noncurrent deferred tax liability, since the depreciable asset is a noncurrent asset; an asset resulting from accruing a warranty liability for book purposes will result in a current deferred tax asset, since the warranty liability is a current liability.

        It should be noted that while a current deferred tax asset can be offset by a current deferred tax liability, a current deferred tax asset cannot be offset by a noncurrent deferred tax liability, etc.

    b. Deferred tax assets or liabilities that are not related to an asset or liability for financial reporting, such as a deferred tax asset related to a loss carryforward, are classified according to their expected reversal dates; those expected to be realized within one year are current, while those expected to reverse in more than one year are noncurrent.

In accordance with the background provided, there would clearly be a deferred tax liability since there was a taxable temporary difference (i.e., future taxable income will be higher).

Further, since the situation relates to depreciable assets, which are noncurrent assets, the related deferred tax liability would be noncurrent. As such, the temporary difference arising from the excess of the accelerated depreciation over the straight-line method will result in a noncurrent deferred tax liability.

Answer choices "A" and "B" are incorrect because temporary differences do not result in contra asset accounts. However, where a deferred tax asset has been recognized, and it is more likely than not that some or all of the asset will not be realized, a valuation allowance (contra account) to the deferred tax asset should be established.

Answer choice "C" is incorrect because the liability is noncurrent.

25.   B   While the facts indicate a capital lease, it should be noted that there are four criteria to determine if a lease is a capital lease. If one or more of the criteria are met, the lease is a capital lease; otherwise, it is an operating lease. The criteria are:
1. Property ownership transfers to the lessee by the end of the lease term.
2. The lease contains a bargain purchase option.
3. The lease term is at least 75 percent of the estimated life of the property.
4. The present value of minimum lease payments at the inception of the lease (excluding such executory costs as property taxes, maintenance, insurance, etc.) equals or exceeds 90 percent of the fair value of the property.

Under a capital lease, the lessee (buyer) records the asset at the capitalized present value of minimum lease payments, plus the present value of any bargain purchase option. This is the amount the lessor would record as the selling price. The lessee's obligation is recorded at the gross amount due and is reduced by unamortized discount (interest) on the obligation, which is the difference between the gross obligation and the present value thereof.

The unamortized discount is amortized over the life of the lease. To determine the periodic expense, the implicit rate on the transaction is applied to the present value of the lease obligation outstanding for the period; this is known as the "interest method."

The interest rate used is the lessee's incremental borrowing rate. If, however, it is practicable for the lessee to learn the implicit rate computed by the lessor, and such rate is less than the lessee's incremental borrowing rate, the lessor's rate should be used.

Every gross lease payment contains two elements: interest expense, and a reduction of the lease liability. It should be noted that at any date, the balance in the capital lease liability (obligation) account would be equal to the original capitalized present value reduced by gross lease payments, net of amounts representing amortized interest. In effect, therefore, the liability is equal to the gross unpaid obligation less the balance of unamortized discount.

Since Mene knows that the interest rate implicit in the lease is 10 percent, and that rate is less than the 11 percent incremental borrowing rate, 10 percent should be used to compute the present value of the minimum lease payments and the interest component of each payment.

The capital lease liability, net of current portion, at December 31, 1993, is $73,500:

Noncurrent lease liability at December 31, 1992		$75,000
Scheduled payment, January 2, 1993	$9,000	
Applied to interest; $75,000 × 10%	(7,500)	(1,500)
Noncurrent capital lease obligation:		
December 31, 1993		$73,500

Answer choice "A" is incorrect because the entire payment on January 2, 1993, is treated as a repayment of principal; a portion is interest.

Answer choice "C" is incorrect because it is the difference between the $75,000 noncurrent liability at December 31, 1992, and the $1,364 current portion at that date.

Answer choice "D" is incorrect because the 11 percent interest rate is used to allocate the payments between interest and principal, and the 10 percent rate should be used. (The result is an interest allocation of $75,000 × 11%, or $8,250, and a principal balance of $75,000 - ($9,000 - $8,250), or $74,250.)

26. B   There are four criteria to determine if a lease is a capital lease. If one or more criteria are met, the lease is a capital lease; otherwise, it is an operating lease. The criteria are:
1. Property ownership transfers to the lessee by the end of the lease term.
2. The lease contains a bargain purchase option.
3. The lease term is at least 75 percent of the estimated life of the property.
4. The present value of minimum lease payments at the inception of the lease (excluding such executory costs as property taxes, maintenance, insurance, etc.) equals or exceeds 90 percent of the fair value of the property.

As indicated, one condition for a lease to be classified as a capital lease is that the lease term must be 75 percent or more of the leased property's useful life.

Answer choices other than "B" are inconsistent with the information presented.

27. A   Under FASB Statement #105, "Employers' Accounting for Postretirement Benefits Other than Pensions," postretirement costs are accounted for on the accrual basis arising out of actuarial considerations; benefits are allocated over the service periods of employees who will receive them. Such benefits shall be fully accrued by the date the employee attains full eligibility for the benefits expected to

be received, even if the employee is expected to render additional services beyond that date.

Answer choice "B" is incorrect because it represents terminal funding, which is not generally accepted because it does not recognize costs when the benefits are earned by the employee.

Answer choices "C" and "D" are incorrect because they are pay-as-you-go methods, which are not generally accepted because they are not based upon accrual accounting.

28.   B   The minimum liability is a consideration in addition to the periodic pension cost and is intended to present a liability on the balance sheet when a pension plan is "significantly underfunded." No additional cost element results.

Immediate recognition of a minimum liability is required if the accumulated benefit obligation exceeds the fair value of plan assets. This is also known as the "unfunded accumulated benefit obligation."

The minimum liability is a combination of any existing pension asset or liability and any additional liability required to reach the minimum amount, as follows:

1. Accrued pension liability - When an accrued pension liability (accrued amounts exceed funding) exists, the additional liability required is equal to the unfunded accumulated benefit obligation less the accrued pension liability.
2. Prepaid pension cost - When an asset exists (amounts funded exceed amounts accrued), the additional liability required is equal to the unfunded accumulated benefit obligation plus the prepaid asset.

At December 31, 1993, Payne reported an accrued pension cost of $20,000, which is the excess of the $90,000 net periodic pension cost and the $70,000 employer's contribution for the first year of the pension. Therefore, the minimum liability is $5,000:

Accumulated benefit obligation	$103,000
Fair value of plan assets	78,000
Minimum pension liability	25,000
Less: Accrued pension cost	20,000
Additional minimum pension liability, December 31, 1993	$ 5,000

Answer choices other than "B" are incorrect in light of the explanation provided.

29.   B   The amount that Oak should report as bonds payable, net of discount, at January 1, 1994, is the amount received from the purchasers of the bonds for the bonds only, without regard to the amount of accrued interest. Accrued interest will be classified as a current liability and will be reported separately from the related bonds.

On <u>January 1, 1994, the bonds payable, net of discount, would be</u> equal to the issuance price; i.e., $400,000 × 97%, or <u>$388,000</u>.

It should be noted that subsequent to January 1, 1994, the bond discount would be amortized as an increase in interest expense over the period during which the bonds would be outstanding.

Answer choices "A" and "C" are not logical in view of the explanation provided for answer choice "B."

Answer choice "D" is incorrect because the $12,000 discount (i.e., 3% × $400,000) is not subtracted, and should be, and because the accrued interest of $8,000 is subtracted, and should not be (i.e., $400,000 - $8,000 equals $392,000).

30.   D   Notes receivable and payable should be presented on the balance sheet at the present value of the future cash flows discounted at the market rate of interest at the date the note was issued. Any premium or discount resulting from differences between the market rate of interest and the note's stated rate of interest should be amortized using the effective interest method.

A discount on a note payable is the result of the market rate of interest exceeding the note's stated rate of interest. Accordingly, a discount should be reported on the balance sheet as a <u>direct reduction from the face amount of the note</u>, so that the note may be reported at its present value.

Answer choice "A" is incorrect because a discount is subtracted from, not added to, the face amount of the note.

Answer choice "B" is incorrect because the discount does not represent a deferred charge (an asset) but, rather, is a contra-liability.

Answer choice "C" is incorrect because the discount has a debit (not a credit) balance, and because it is not accounted for separately from the note.

31.   D   A scrip dividend is declared in the form of an interest bearing note that is a legal liability of the corporation; the interest on the note is an expense.

During 1993, East should account for the scrip dividend with a <u>debit to retained earnings for $100,000 on April 1, 1993, and a debit to interest expense for $7,500</u> (i.e., $100,000 × 10% × 9/12) <u>on December 31, 1993</u>.

Answer choice "A" is incorrect because the amount of the dividend is only $100,000. The interest that will accrue on the dividend is not part of the dividend.

Answer choice "B" is incorrect because both the date and the amount of the dividend are incorrect. A legal liability for the scrip dividend has been incurred on April 1, 1993, the date on which it was declared. The dividend is $100,000 and, in any event, the interest expense is $7,500 (i.e., $100,000 × 10% × 9/12).

Answer choice "C" is incorrect because interest expense should be accrued for the period during which the note was outstanding in 1993 (April 1 through December 31). Thus, interest expense would be $100,000 × 10% × 9/12, or $7,500 for 1993, and not $10,000 on March 31, 1994.

32. B In general, a liquidating dividend is a dividend that is not derived from earnings but, rather, represents a return of capital to the stockholders.

Since retained earnings was only $300,000, and the dividend was $400,000, the $100,000 difference is the amount of the liquidating dividend.

Answer choices other than "B" are based on incorrect assumptions.

33. A In accordance with APB Opinion #25, "Accounting for Stock Issued to Employees," the measurement date for determining compensation cost under a compensatory stock option plan is the earliest date on which both the number of shares to be issued and the option price are known. The date is therefore January 2, 1993.

Compensation for services is measured by the quoted market price of the stock at the measurement date less the amount that the employee is required to pay.

Further, APB Opinion #25 indicates that compensation involved in a compensatory employee stock option plan should be expensed in the periods in which the related services are performed. This is consistent with the application of costs or expenses to periods benefiting therefrom. Since the options were exercisable immediately, the total expense for the options should be recognized in 1993.

Since the market price exceeds the option price by $30 (i.e., $50 - $20) on January 1, 1993, there is total compensation of 1,000 shares × $30, or $30,000.

Parenthetically, the following journal entries should be made in 1993:

1/2/93	Compensation expense	30,000	
	Paid-in capital - stock options		30,000
12/31/93	Cash	20,000	
	Paid-in capital - stock options	30,000	
	Common stock, $10 par value		10,000
	Additional paid-in capital		40,000

The amount of the net increase in stockholders' equity as a result of the grant and exercise of the options is $20,000, the cash received upon exercise. Note that compensation expense reduces earnings and, thus, shareholders' equity, which reduces the $40,000 of additional paid-in capital.

Answer choice "B" is incorrect because it is the amount of compensation expense, and not the increase in shareholders' equity in 1993.

Answer choice "C" is incorrect because it is the fair value of the stock on the measurement date, and not the increase in shareholders' equity in 1993.

Answer choice "D" is incorrect because it is the fair value of the stock on the date of exercise. Changes in the fair value of the stock after the measurement date are not given accounting recognition.

34. C In accordance with APB Opinion #14, "Accounting for Convertible Debt and Debt Issued with Stock Purchase Warrants," when bonds are issued with detachable stock purchase warrants, the warrants have a value that is accounted for separately from the related debt, as an element of additional paid-in capital (shareholders' equity).

The proceeds of issuance to be accounted for as stockholders' equity and bonds should be based on the relative values of the bonds and the warrants at the time of issuance. (In this connection, the market value given for the stock is not relevant.)

In the question, the market value of each stock warrant is indicated to be $4. Therefore, on December 31, 1993, Moss should record a discount on issuance of bonds in the amount of $110,000:

Total proceeds; $1,000,000 × 1.09	$1,090,000
Less: Amount allocated to warrants;	
($1,000,000/$1,000) × 50 × $4	(200,000)
Amount applicable to bonds	890,000
Less: Maturity value of bonds	(1,000,000)
Discount on issuance of bonds, December 31, 1993	$ 110,000

Answer choice "A" is incorrect because it only allocates $50,000 to the warrants, rather than $200,000.

Answer choice "B" is incorrect because no portion of the proceeds is allocated to the warrants. (It should be noted that had the warrants been nondetachable, rather than detachable, no portion of the proceeds would have been allocated to the warrants and the bond issue would have been accounted for as convertible debt.)

Answer choice "D" is incorrect because it represents the amount of the total warrants that are allocated to the proceeds, and not the related premium or discount, as explained in the answer to choice "C."

35.   A   Upon admission to a partnership, the transfer of property other than cash would be recorded at the <u>fair value at the date of contribution</u>.

A change in the composition of the partners results in the creation of a new entity; from a financial accounting standpoint, this requires a new basis of accountability.

Answer choice "B" is incorrect because the contributing partner's original cost is not relevant to the partnership.

Answer choice "C" is incorrect because the assessed valuation for property tax purposes does not represent a measure of value.

Answer choice "D" is incorrect because tax basis is never a basis for recognition for financial accounting purposes.

36.   B   The division of partnership profits and/or losses is based on the partnership agreement. If the agreement is silent as to the manner of division, then all partners share equally.

In dividing profits, a partnership may consider bonuses, salary provisions, and interest on capital balances (which may be based on beginning balances, ending balances, or weighted-average balances). These are a manner of dividing profits based on unequal time devoted and/or capital invested. Any remainder not specifically allocated is divided in accordance with the profit and loss ratios.

Finally, a partnership cannot divide more or less than its total profit or loss. Therefore, if bonus, interest, and/or salary provisions are in excess of the total profit, a "loss" created by such division will be allocated in the profit and loss ratios.

Based on the preceding discussion, and as noted following, <u>Red's capital account</u> should be credited for <u>$43,000</u> and <u>White's capital account</u> should be credited for <u>$37,000</u>:

	Red	White	Total
Salary	$55,000	$45,000	$100,000
Residual loss (allocated 60/40)	(12,000)	(8,000)	(20,000)
Earnings credited to partners' capital accounts	$ 43,000	$37,000	$ 80,000

It should be noted that the "residual loss" is equal to the $100,000 salary distributions less the 1993 earnings of $80,000.

Answer choices other than "B" are not logical in view of the explanation provided.

37.   A   Upon the liquidation of a partnership, assets are sold and any gains or losses are divided among the partners according to their profit-sharing ratios.

Any available cash is first used to pay off liabilities. Before cash may be distributed to any partner, his or her capital account (net of loans, if any) must first have been reduced by losses realized upon liquidation.

If, in the process of assigning liquidation losses, a debit balance exists in any partner's account, that deficiency must be eliminated by a charge to the remaining partner(s) in their respective profit and loss ratios.

With the foregoing as background, cash in the amount of $136,000, if available, should be distributed to Smith:

	Smith	Jones	Total
Capital balance before liquidation	$195,000	$155,000	$350,000
Reclassification of Smith loan	(20,000)		(20,000)
Allocation of loss on assets sold (60/40); $450,000 - $385,000, or $65,000	(39,000)	(26,000)	(65,000)
Available cash to be distributed	$136,000	$129,000	$265,000

Answer choice "B" is incorrect because it does not offset the loan to Smith against Smith's capital account.

Answer choices "C" and "D" are not logical in view of the explanation provided for answer choice "A."

38.   D   Under the Internal Revenue Code, a sole proprietorship is exempt from federal income taxes because income of the business is taxable to the owner of the business. In this way, the sole proprietor avoids double taxation that is imposed on most corporations. As such, no provision for income taxes is required in the financial statements of a sole proprietorship.

Answer choices other than "D" are inconsistent with the explanation provided.

39.   D   APB Opinion #20, "Accounting Changes," provides for the treatment of certain types of accounting changes, inclusive of the following:

1.   Change in accounting principle
    A change in accounting principle (which includes a change in accounting method) is generally reported as a "cumulative effect" type item. Not only is the new principle to be used in current and future periods, there is additional disclosure of the "cumulative effect," the measure of which is the difference between beginning retained earnings and the retained earnings balance had the method been retroactively applied. Such items appear on the income statement (net of tax effect) as a separate

component after extraordinary items (i.e., in between extra-ordinary items and net income).

In addition to the presentation indicated for the year of change, footnote disclosure of the pro forma effects of retroactive application is required.

2. Change in reporting entity
   A change in reporting entity, such as a change in the composition of subsidiaries in consolidated financial statements, requires the restatement of the financial statements of all periods presented.

3. Change in accounting estimate
   A change in accounting estimate is presented only in current and future periods, if the change affects both. It appears within the results of continuing operations on a before-tax basis.

Keeping in mind the background provided, the accounting change resulting from the inclusion in consolidated financial statements of a previously excluded subsidiary should be reported by restating the financial statements of all prior periods presented.

Answer choice "A" is incorrect because it represents the appropriate treatment for most changes in accounting principle, but not for a change in reporting entity.

Answer choice "B" is incorrect because a change in reporting entity does require restatement if the change involves consolidated methods of accounting.

Answer choice "C" is incorrect because a change in reporting entity involving the cost or equity methods does require restatement.

40.   A   In accordance with APB Opinion #30, "Reporting the Results of Operations," material transactions that are both infrequent in occurrence and unusual in nature are presented separately, net of income tax, as extraordinary items (before the cumulative effect of accounting changes, net of tax, and after discontinued operations, net of tax).

A material transaction that results in either a gain or a loss and has one characteristic, but not both, is presented separately as a component of income from continuing operations.

Answer choices other than "A" are based on incorrect assumptions and/or combinations.

41.   D   Generally, revenue is recognized at the time of sale. However, when exchange value is not susceptible of objective measurement with reasonable accuracy, or significant expenses related to the event likewise cannot be estimated with reasonable accuracy, revenue should be recognized upon collection of the proceeds.

There are two methods that could be used if there is no reasonable basis for estimating collectibility:
1. Under the installment sales method, revenue is recognized as the cash is collected, with the gross profit on uncollected receivables deferred.
2. Under the cost recovery method, revenue is recognized only when the cost of the asset sold is recovered; all collections, inclusive of interest income, are deferred until that time.

Wren is best justified in using the cost recovery method when <u>there is no reasonable basis for estimating collectibility</u>.

Answer choice "A" is incorrect because the recognition of an asset, not the passage of title, is typically the critical event in the earnings process.

Answer choice "B" is incorrect because revenue should be recognized when a valid, collectible receivable is recognized, without regard to the timing of the collection.

Answer choice "C" is incorrect because FASB Statement #48, "Revenue Recognition When Right of Return Exists," states that revenue should be recognized at the point of sale unless returns cannot be reasonably estimated; revenue should then be recognized when the right of return substantially expires.

42. D Under the cash basis of accounting, which is not appropriate under generally accepted accounting principles, net income is affected by the inflows and outflows of cash rather than by appropriate accrual basis considerations.

Under the accrual basis, a net decrease in accounts receivable would result in cash basis income exceeding accrual basis income; a net decrease in accrued expenses payable would result in cash basis income being less than accrual basis net income.

Consequently, as compared to the accrual basis, under the cash basis, <u>a decrease in accounts receivable would overstate, not understate, income</u>, since cash received would exceed accrual basis revenue. On the other hand, <u>a decrease in accrued expenses would understate income</u>, since cash paid for expenses would exceed expenses incurred.

Answer choices other than "D" are based on incorrect assumptions and/or combinations.

43. B When a bond is purchased at a discount, the acquisition price is less that its maturity value. When the bond is sold at a premium, the proceeds received are greater than its maturity value; thus, a gain is realized on the sale.

In the absence of a known maturity value, <u>the gain that Jent should report is</u> simply equal to the $8,000 of unamortized discount (i.e., $10,000 - $2,000) plus the $14,000 premium received, or <u>$22,000</u>.

Answer choice "A" is incorrect because it represents the premium of $14,000 less the $2,000 of amortized discount, which has no logical basis.

Answer choice "C" is incorrect because it does not consider the $2,000 amortization of the discount as a reduction.

Answer choice "D" is incorrect because it is the sum of the original $10,000 discount, plus the $2,000 amortization of the discount, plus the $14,000 premium on sale. The amortization of the discount should reduce the gain, not increase it.

44. A When a corporation purchases life insurance on an officer or employee where the corporation is the beneficiary of the policy, the annual premium payments must be allocated between expense and an increase in the cash surrender value of the policy.

Cash surrender value is classified as an investment because it represents the amount of cash that can be realized if the policy is canceled. When the insured party dies, the corporation will recognize a gain equal to the difference between the face amount of the policy and its cash surrender value.

In 1993, Gar should report $0 as revenue because the $210,000 excess of the $300,000 face amount of the policy over its $90,000 cash surrender value will be classified as a gain, not as revenue.

According to FASB Concepts Statement #6, "Elements of Financial Statements," revenues are inflows or other enhancements of assets of an entity or settlements of liabilities from delivering or producing goods or rendering services or other activities that constitute the entity's ongoing major or central operations. Gains are increases in equity from peripheral or incidental transactions and events. Certainly, the death of an employee is not part of major or central operations but, rather, is an incidental event.

Answer choice "B" is incorrect because it is the amount of the policy's cash surrender value at the date of death of the employee and does not relate to revenue.

Answer choice "C" is incorrect because it is the amount of gain, and not revenue, that should be recognized on the settlement of the life insurance policy, as explained in answer choice "A."

Answer choice "D" is incorrect because it does not consider the recovery of the cash surrender value of the policy, and because, in any event, the net insurance proceeds represent a gain, not revenue.

45. A Under the straight-line method, equal annual depreciation is computed by dividing the difference between the original cost of an asset and its estimated salvage value by its estimated useful life. The cost of an asset includes all costs necessary to be incurred to make the asset ready for its intended end use.

When a fixed asset is purchased on a deferred payment basis, it should be recorded at its current fair (cash) value at the date of acquisition. (Fair value is equal to the present value of the deferred payments using an appropriate discount rate as provided by APB Opinion #21, "Interest on Receivables and Payables.")

In its 1993 income statement, Lem should report depreciation for this machinery in the amount of $10,500:

Cost (cash equivalent price)	$110,000
Less: Estimated salvage value	(5,000)
Amount subject to depreciation	$105,000
Depreciation, 1993; $105,000/10	$ 10,500

Answer choice "B" is incorrect because it ignores estimated salvage value.

Answer choice "C" is incorrect because the cost of the machinery is erroneously assumed to be the total cash payments of $130,000 (i.e., [$130,000 - $5,000]/10 equals $12,500).

Answer choice "D" is incorrect because it improperly assumes the cost of the machinery to be the total of the cash payments to be made, or $130,000, and it ignores estimated salvage value (i.e., $130,000/10 equals $13,000).

46. D   When bonds are issued between interest dates, the purchaser of the bonds must pay accrued interest for the period of time that has elapsed between the last payment date and the date of issuance. This payment will effectively reduce the issuer's interest expense, so that the amount of interest expense for a year will be related to the period of time that the bonds will be outstanding during that year.

The bond will be outstanding for the period June 1, 1993, through December 31, 1993, or seven months, which is the period to which the interest expense should relate for the year ended December 31, 1993.

Answer choices other than "D" are not logical in view of the explanation provided.

47. A   Rather simply, the current portion of income tax expense is based on taxable income of $150,000, and a current tax rate of 30 percent; the current provision for income tax expense is therefore $45,000 (i.e., $150,000 × 30%).

Answer choice "B" is incorrect because it is equal to 30 percent of taxable income increased by the premium expense on keyman life insurance (i.e., [$150,000 + $20,000] × 30% equals $51,000). It should be noted that in general, keyman life insurance is deductible (unless the corporation is the beneficiary, which is not indicated).

Answer choice "C" is incorrect because it represents financial statement income at the current tax rate (i.e., $200,000 × 30%, or $60,000).

Answer choice "D" is incorrect because it is equal to 30 percent of the sum of $150,000 of taxable income and $70,000 of interest on municipal bonds (i.e., [$150,000 + $70,000] × 30% equals $66,000); municipal bond interest is not subject to tax.

48.　B　Under APB Opinion #30, "Reporting the Results of Operations," a gain or loss that is both unusual in nature and that occurs infrequently should be reported as an extraordinary item.

An extraordinary item should be reported net of income taxes, and as a separate component of income after discontinued operations of a segment of a business, but before the cumulative effect of a change in accounting principle.

Answer choices other than "B" are inconsistent with the explanation provided.

49.　D　When computing earnings per share, stock splits and stock dividends are assumed to have occurred at the beginning of the year, regardless of when they actually occurred.

Thus, Clay should use 106,000 shares (i.e., 100,000 × 106%) in determining 1993 earnings per share.

Answer choices other than "D" are incorrect in view of the explanation provided.

50.　B　Under FASB Statement #95, "Statement of Cash Flows," all operating, investing, and financing transactions actually involving cash should be included in the statement of cash flows. Information about investing and financing activities not resulting in cash receipts and payments, such as issuing bonds for equipment, should be reported separately and not included in the body of the statement. Further, it is assumed that the gross cash flow information is more useful than the net cash flow information.

Accordingly, Fara should report cash outflows for the redemption of bonds payable in its 1993 statement of cash flows in the amount of $17,000:

Bonds payable, December 31, 1992	$47,000
Bonds issued in exchange for equipment, 1993	20,000
Subtotal	67,000
Bonds payable, December 31, 1993	(50,000)
Cash paid for redemption of bonds; 1993	$17,000

Answer choice "A" is incorrect because it is only the net change in bonds payable, and does not reflect all the transactions affecting bonds payable.

Answer choice "C" is incorrect because it is the amount of the bonds issued in exchange for equipment, and does not represent a transaction affecting cash.

Answer choice "D" is incorrect because the $3,000 net increase in bonds payable is added to the $20,000 of bonds issued in exchange for equipment; it should be subtracted in order to arrive at cash flows for redemption of bonds payable.

51. A The following should be noted for background relative to this question:
1. In a pooling of interests, assets and liabilities of the combined companies go forward based on the recorded (book) values.
2. In a purchase transaction, assets and liabilities are recognized at their fair market values on the date of acquisition; new accounting bases result. Any excess of cost over net assets (i.e., book value) acquired is first allocated to identifiable assets and liabilities based on fair values. Any excess that remains after such allocation is recorded as goodwill, which is amortized over a period not to exceed forty (40) years.

If the business combination of Kiwi and Mori were accounted for as a purchase, goodwill would result since Kiwi would acquire Mori's identifiable assets at more than book value, and book values approximate fair values. Thus, goodwill acquired would be amortized through a charge to earnings.

Accordingly, the combined entity's 1994 net income under purchase accounting would be <u>less</u> <u>than</u> <u>net</u> <u>income</u> <u>under</u> <u>pooling</u> because of the amortization of goodwill.

Answer choices other than "A" are inconsistent with the explanation provided.

52. D A business combination accounted for by the pooling of interests method is assumed to be a combination of shareholders' equity and, as such, a new basis of accounting is not recognized. It is assumed, for purposes of preparing consolidated financial statements, that the entities had always been a single entity. In a <u>pooling of interests, the income of the previously separate entities should be combined for the entire year</u>, regardless of when the business combination actually occurred, and the retained earnings of the two previously separate entities should also be combined.

A business combination accounted for by the <u>purchase method</u> is considered to be a simple asset acquisition, rather than a combination of shareholders' equity. Thus, a new basis of accounting is recognized. The operating results of the subsidiary would only be consolidated with those of the parent from the date of the combination to the end of the year, <u>not</u> <u>for</u> <u>the</u> <u>entire</u> <u>year</u>.

Answer choices other than "D" are based upon incorrect assumptions and/or combinations.

53.   A   In a personal statement of financial condition, estimated income taxes (at appropriate tax rates) must be provided on the difference between the tax basis and <u>estimated</u> <u>current</u> <u>value</u> <u>of</u> <u>assets</u>, and the difference between the tax basis and <u>estimated</u> <u>current</u> <u>amount</u> <u>of</u> <u>liabilities</u>.

Answer choices other than "A" are based on incorrect assumptions and/or combinations.

54.   C   While financial statements are normally prepared in accordance with generally accepted accounting principles, financial statements are sometimes prepared in conformity with a comprehensive basis of accounting other than generally accepted accounting principles. According to Statement on Auditing Standards #62, "Special Reports," other comprehensive bases are restricted to the following:
   1.   A basis of accounting that the reporting entity uses to comply with requirements or financial reporting provisions of a governmental regulatory agency to whose jurisdiction the entity is subject.
   2.   A <u>basis</u> <u>of</u> <u>accounting</u> <u>used</u> <u>by</u> <u>the</u> <u>entity</u> <u>to</u> <u>file</u> <u>its</u> <u>income</u> <u>tax</u> <u>return</u>.
   3.   The <u>cash</u> <u>receipts</u> <u>and</u> <u>disbursements</u> <u>basis</u> <u>of</u> <u>accounting</u>, and modifications of the cash basis having substantial support, such as recording depreciation on fixed assets or accruing income taxes.
   4.   A definite set of criteria having substantial support that is applied to all material items appearing in financial statements, such as the price-level basis of accounting.

Answer choices other than "C" are based on incorrect assumptions and/or combinations.

55.   D   In a purchase business combination, assets acquired are presented in the consolidated balance sheet based upon their fair values at the date of the combination. Any excess of the purchase price over the fair value of net identifiable assets acquired is allocated to goodwill. Goodwill is amortized by the straight-line method over a period not to exceed 40 years (in this case the amortization period is 10 years).

The amortization of goodwill is <u>$20,000</u>:

Cost of investment	$1,200,000
Fair value of net assets acquired;	
$1,320,000 - $320,000	<u>1,000,000</u>
Goodwill	<u>$ 200,000</u>
<u>Amortization of goodwill, 1993</u>; $200,000/10	<u>$ 20,000</u>

Answer choices other than "D" are based on incorrect assumptions.

56. A   In a consolidation by purchase, the parent is not entitled to any pre-acquisition retained earnings of the subsidiary; indeed, such earnings will be eliminated against the investment account in the preparation of a consolidated balance sheet.

Therefore, the consolidated balance sheet will include the parent's retained earnings plus the parent's share of subsidiary retained earnings subsequent to the date of acquisition.

Accordingly, since it is obvious that the equity method is used on the parent's balance sheet, and the acquisition took place on January 1, 1993, the parent's retained earnings already include the increase since acquisition.

Apart from the background provided, the answer to this question is a simple matter of examining the balance sheets given; total retained earnings is the parent's retained earnings, or $1,240,000.

(It should be noted that whether the parent uses the cost method or equity method in carrying its investment, for purposes of consolidated financial statements, cost is adjusted to equity. Therefore, in any event, the parent's retained earnings become consolidated retained earnings.)

Answer choice "B" is incorrect because the parent's equity in earnings of Sharp (i.e., $120,000) has been added to Owen's $1,240,000 retained earnings; that amount has already been included in consolidated income and retained earnings.

Answer choice "C" is incorrect because the subsidiary's 1993 net income of $140,000 is included, and should not be, since it is already included in the parent's retained earnings under the equity method.

Answer choice "D" is incorrect because the subsidiary's retained earnings of $560,000 are included, and should not be.

57. D   This question deals with a gain contingency, rather than a loss contingency.

While accrual of a loss contingency is appropriate under certain conditions (i.e., when the loss is probable and can be reasonably estimated), accrual of a gain contingency is not appropriate. (Footnote disclosure of the gain contingency would be appropriate.)

Generally speaking, revenue is recognized when an earnings process is virtually complete and an exchange has taken place. Since neither event has occurred, Smith should not recognize a receivable or revenue. However, Smith should disclose in the footnotes a contingent gain of an undetermined amount in the range of $75,000 to $150,000. Obviously, the settlement of the lawsuit after the issuance of the financial statements could not affect the statements.

Answer choice "A" is incorrect because neither a receivable nor revenue should be recognized.

Answer choice "B" is incorrect because neither a receivable nor deferred revenue should be recognized.

Answer choice "C" is incorrect because the range of the contingent gain should be disclosed.

58.　A　Under FASB Statement #89, "Financial Reporting and Changing Prices, "entities that voluntarily disclose information on the effects of changing prices are required to disclose the increase or decrease in the current cost, or lower recoverable amount, of inventory and property, plant and equipment, net of inflation. By definition, the inflation component of the increase in current cost is the difference between the nominal dollar and constant dollar measures.

Thus, the inflation component of Hila's increase in the current cost of inventories is $15,000 - $12,000, or $3,000.

Answer choice "B" is incorrect because it is the increase in current cost (constant dollars), and not the inflation component.

Answer choice "C" is incorrect because it is the increase in current cost (nominal dollars), and not the inflation component.

Answer choice "D" is incorrect because it is the sum of the two components, and not the difference.

59.　C　Monetary items are assets and liabilities with amounts that are fixed or determinable without reference to future prices of specific goods or services. Monetary assets include cash and claims to cash (i.e., receivables [including related allowances for uncollectibles], deposits with suppliers, and investments in nonconvertible securities, etc.). Monetary liabilities include obligations payable in cash (i.e., accounts payable, bonds payable, etc.).

Nonmonetary items are all items that are not monetary. They are items stated in older dollars and require adjustment in supplementary price level financial statements. Nonmonetary assets include land and other plant assets, along with related allowances for depreciation, and equity investments in unconsolidated subsidiaries. Nonmonetary liabilities include liabilities not payable in cash, such as obligations under warranties.

During a period of inflation, a purchasing power gain will be recognized from the holding (i.e., "the account balance remains constant") of net monetary liabilities, and a purchasing power loss will be recognized from the holding of net monetary assets. This relationship occurs because in a period of inflation (rising prices), liabilities will be settled with cheaper dollars (gain), and assets will be settled with more expensive dollars (loss).

Consequently, during a period of inflation, if an asset account remains constant, <u>a purchasing power loss will result if the item is a monetary asset</u>.

Answer choice "A" is incorrect because a loss, not a gain, results from holding a monetary asset during a period of inflation.

Answer choices "B" and "D" are incorrect because purchasing power gains and losses result from holding monetary items, not nonmonetary items.

60.   A   The current ratio is equal to current assets divided by current liabilities.

The quick (acid test) ratio is equal to the sum of cash, receivables, and marketable equity securities, divided by current liabilities.

In general, if cash is used to reduce accounts payable, the dollar amount of working capital would remain unchanged since current assets and current liabilities decreased by the same amount.

This question deals with the effect of cash payments on ratios. Thus, if all the cash were used to reduce accounts payable, <u>the current ratio would increase, and the quick ratio would decrease</u>.

This result occurs because the question notes that the ratios were not the same. Presumably, therefore, there would have been more current assets for purposes of the current ratio than for the quick ratio. This operates by reason of the definitions above; the most significant current asset not included in the quick ratio is inventory.

<u>Parenthetically, the following example (based on assumed numbers)</u> should be noted:

	Current Ratio	Quick Ratio
Before payment of cash		
Cash	$ 200,000	$ 200,000
Inventories	1,000,000	—
Accounts receivable	300,000	300,000
Total current assets	$1,500,000	—
Total quick assets	—	$ 500,000
Total current liabilities	$1,000,000	$1,000,000
Ratio	1.5:1	.5:1

After payment of cash
Current ratio;
    ($1,500,000 - $200,000)/
       ($1,000,000 - $200,000)   1.625:1

Quick ratio;
    ($500,000 - $200,000)/
       ($1,000,000 - $200,000)   .375:1

Answer choices other than "A" are based on incorrect assumptions and/or combinations.

OTHER OBJECTIVE FORMATS/ESSAY QUESTIONS

Answer 2

This question is based on APB Opinion #20, "Accounting Changes," and FASB Statement #16, "Prior Period Adjustments."

The following selected background information should be noted:

1. "Cumulative effect" type items
   The "cumulative effect of an accounting change" is a separate income statement item provided for in APB Opinion #20. Such items appear on the income statement (net of tax effect) after extraordinary items.

   In accordance with APB Opinion #20, "cumulative effect" items arise from changes in accounting principles (including changes in accounting methods). Not only is the new principle to be used in current and future periods, there is additional disclosure of the "cumulative effect," the measure of which is the difference between beginning retained earnings and the retained earnings balance had the method been retroactively applied.

2. Special changes in accounting principle
   Two changes in accounting principle are accounted for by a restating of the financial statements of all prior periods, rather than by the "cumulative effect" approach.
   a. A change from LIFO to another inventory method.
   b. A change in accounting for long-term construction contracts; i.e., a change to or from the completed-contract or percentage-of-completion methods.

3. Changes in accounting estimate
   Such changes require presentation within "income from continuing operations" on a before-tax basis. They are accounted for prospectively and affect income in the current and future years; if the change affects both, there is no "cumulative effect" involved.

4. Prior period adjustments
   For all practical exam purposes, the only prior period adjustments of which candidates should be aware are corrections of errors. The correction of an error (net of tax effect) is appropriately reported on the retained earnings statement as an adjustment of the beginning balance. This, of course, represents a retroactive adjustment.

   (While there are other items that are treated as prior period adjustments, they are beyond the scope of the CPA exam.)

   Corrections of errors may be broadly classified into two categories:
   a. Those resulting from corrections of mathematical mistakes,

mistakes in the application of accounting principles, or oversight or misuse of facts that existed at the time the financial statements were prepared. (The last type of error should not be confused with an appropriate change in estimate, which is not a prior period adjustment.)

b. Those resulting from a change from an accounting principle that is not generally accepted to one that is generally accepted.

61. A Y   A change from the completed-contract to the percentage-of-completion method is a <u>change</u> in <u>accounting principle</u> because both methods are generally accepted. However, it is one of the changes in principle that requires the <u>retroactive restatement approach</u>.

62. B Z   A change in the estimated useful life of a depreciable asset is a <u>change in accounting estimate</u> that is accounted for by the <u>prospective approach</u>; that is, the effect of the change in estimate is taken into income over the remaining useful life of the asset.

63. B Z   A change in estimated warranty costs is a <u>change in accounting estimate</u> that is accounted for by the <u>prospective approach</u>; the effect of the change in estimate is taken into income in the year of change.

64. A Y   A change from LIFO to FIFO is a <u>change in accounting principle</u> because both methods are generally accepted. However, it is one of the changes in principle that requires the <u>retroactive restatement approach</u>.

65. A X   A change from FIFO to average cost is a <u>change in accounting principle</u> because both methods are generally accepted. Like most changes in accounting principle, it is accounted for by the <u>cumulative effect approach</u>.

66. C Y   A change from the cash method of accounting for service contracts to the accrual method is a <u>correction of an error in previously presented financial statements</u> because the cash method is not generally accepted. Like all corrections of errors, the <u>retroactive restatement approach</u> is used.

67. C Y   Insurance premiums should be charged to operations over the policy period; it is inappropriate to expense a premium when it is paid. The discovery of this error will result in a <u>correction of an error in previously presented financial statements</u> that will require the <u>retroactive restatement approach</u>.

68. A X   A change from an accelerated depreciation method to the straight-line method for existing assets is a <u>change in accounting principle</u> because both methods are generally accepted. Like most changes in principle, it is accounted for by the <u>cumulative effect approach</u>.

69. D Z   The initiation of a pension plan for employees is <u>neither an accounting change nor an accounting error</u>; rather, it will result in

the initial adoption of the accounting requirement under generally accepted accounting principles. The effect of the adoption of the pension plan will be accounted for by the prospective approach.

70.   D Y   A change from the cost method of accounting for an investment to the equity method of accounting because of an increase in ownership is neither an accounting change nor an accounting error; rather, it is an initial adoption of an accounting principle due to a change in circumstance. According to APB Opinion #18, "The Equity Method of Accounting for Investments in Common Stock," the adoption of the equity method requires the retroactive restatement approach.

Answer 3

These questions relate primarily to FASB Statement #5, "Accounting for Contingencies," which provides the following:

1.   In order for an estimated loss to be accrued as a charge against income, the loss must be probable at the date of the financial statements, and the amount of the loss must be reasonably estimated.
2.   Where a range of estimates is involved, the best estimate within the range should be used. When no amount within the range is a better estimate than any other amount, the minimum amount should be accrued with supplemental disclosure of the range of possible loss.
3.   When a loss contingency is reasonably possible, but not probable, footnote disclosure is required. The disclosure shall indicate the nature of the contingency and give an estimate of the possible loss, or range of loss, or state that an estimate cannot be made.
4.   Where the probability of loss is remote, an accrual is not appropriate and it is not necessary to provide supplementary disclosure.
5.   This statement is concerned with the accrual of loss contingencies; gain contingencies should not be recognized until they are realized.

71.   A N   Since no loss has been incurred, no adjustment is required; further, additional disclosure is not required because it is not reasonably possible that a loss has been incurred.

72.   C Y   Under FASB Statement #106, "Employers' Accounting for Postretirement Benefits Other than Pensions," the cost of postretirement health care benefits must be accrued as the rights to those benefits are earned. Accordingly, the $150,000 discounted expected cost of these benefits must be accrued. Further, supplemental disclosure of the status of the plan is required in the notes to the financial statements.

73.   B N   Since the payment of the warranties is probable and reasonably estimated, adjustment is required in the amount of $100,000 ($10,000,000 × 1%). Supplemental disclosure is not required in the

notes to the financial statements because the necessary information about the warranty program is disclosed in the actual financial statements.

74.   B Y   Since it is probable that Edge will be held liable for the safety hazard and the amount can be reasonably estimated in the range of $100,000 to $500,000, an adjustment in the amount of $100,000, the minimum amount within the range, is required. Further, supplemental disclosure in the notes to the financial statements is required for the additional possible loss up to $500,000.

75.   A N   This item involves a gain contingency. No adjustment is required for a gain contingency; rather, any gain will be recognized when realized. No disclosure in the notes to the financial statements is required because such disclosure might lead to misleading implications as to the likelihood of realization.

76.   A N   The facts indicate that Edge's attorneys believe the suit is without merit; thus, the chance of loss is remote. Accordingly, no adjustment is required and disclosure is not required in the notes to the financial statements.

77.   A Y   There is no evidence to suggest that the president is likely to default on the loan; therefore, no adjustment is required because, at best, a loss is only reasonably possible. Additional disclosure in the notes to the financial statements is required for all material guarantees and commitments that have not been recognized in the financial statements.

78.   C Y   Under APB Opinion #30, "Reporting the Results of Operations," when a loss is expected on the disposal of a segment of a business, the loss should be accrued on the measurement date (i.e., the date management committed to a formal plan of action, and the proceeds from the sale are reasonably estimated along with the operating losses during the phaseout period). Accordingly, adjustment is required in the amount of $150,000 (i.e., the $400,000 estimated losses from operations during the phaseout period less the $250,000 expected gain on disposal). Additional disclosure is required in the notes to the financial statements to provide the details of the plan of disposal.

79.   A Y   The fire that destroyed the warehouse occurred after the balance sheet date; therefore, no adjustment is required because no loss had been incurred at the balance sheet date. However, additional disclosure in the notes to the financial statements is required for material post-balance sheet events, such as the loss of major facilities.

80.   A N   Since Edge's attorneys have stated that Edge will probably be able to obtain the shipment, the chances of loss are remote; therefore, no adjustment is required. No additional disclosure is required in the notes to the financial statements because the likelihood of loss is remote.

81. A Y The issuance of the bonds occurred after the balance sheet date; therefore, <u>no adjustment is required</u>. However, <u>additional disclosure is required in the notes to the financial statements</u> for post-balance sheet events, such as material investment or financing transactions.

82. B Y Edge's attorneys and tax accountants have stated that it is likely (i.e., probable) that the IRS will agree to a $100,000 settlement; thus, Edge should accrue a loss in the amount of <u>$100,000</u>, which is a reasonable estimate of the loss. <u>Additional disclosure in the notes to the financial statements is required</u> for the details of the assessment and the additional possible liability up to $400,000.

Answer 4

Part 4(a)

<u>York Co.</u>
<u>Schedule of the Cost of Goods Sold</u>
<u>Year ended December 31, 1993</u>

Beginning inventory; 8,000 units at $8.20		$ 65,600
Purchases:		
Gross (47,000 units)	$368,900	
Less purchase discounts	18,000	350,900
Freight-in		5,000
Cost of goods available for sale		421,500
Less ending inventory (see schedule #1)		176,000
Cost of goods sold, year ended		
<u>December 31, 1993</u>		$245,500

<u>Schedule #1</u>
<u>Supporting Schedule - Ending Inventory</u>

Inventory at historical cost:		
8,000 at $8.20	$ 65,600	
12,000 at $8.25	99,000	
2,000 at $7.90	15,800	
Total inventory at historical cost		$180,400
Replacement cost; 22,000 × $8		$176,000
Net realizable value; 22,000 × $8.80		$193,600
"Floor" value; 22,000 × ($8.80 - $1.05)		$170,500

Note: Based on the calculations indicated, the lower-of-cost-or-market valuation is replacement cost of $176,000. In effect, there is a valuation allowance of $4,400 (i.e., $180,400 - $176,000).

Part 4(b)

The lower-of-cost-or-market rule follows the constraint of conservatism; that is, losses are recognized in the period in which a loss of utility occurs, while gains are not recognized until realized at the time of sale.

As used in the term "lower-of-cost-or-market," market means "replacement by purchase or reproduction, except that market should never be more than net realizable value (i.e., selling price reduced by costs of completion and disposal) nor less than net realizable value reduced by an allowance for an approximate normal profit margin." (The limits referred to are defined as the "ceiling" and the "floor.")

(Once the valuation for a particular item is at an amount below cost, the lower amount becomes the new cost.)

The limits indicated provide that inventory is never reported at more than net realizable value so as to ensure a write-down in the period that the utility of the inventory has been impaired. Also, the "floor" limit ensures that the recognized loss in one period is not offset by an abnormal profit in a future period.

In this situation, replacement cost (i.e., $176,000) is between the ceiling (i.e., $193,600) and the floor (i.e., $170,500); thus, market is represented by replacement cost. Since market is less than the $180,400 historical cost of the ending inventory, the ending inventory under LIFO must be reduced by $4,400.

Under the direct method, this write-down is effectively included as an increase in the cost of goods sold since the ending inventory is lower than historical cost. Under the indirect method, the ending inventory is presented at historical cost, and the write-down is presented below gross profit (labeled as "loss due to market decline," etc.).

Answer 5

Part 5(a)

Note payable, Federal Bank:		
1/1/93 - 3/31/93; $90,000 × 3/12 × 8%		$ 1,800
4/1/93 - 12/31/93; ($90,000 - $10,000) × 9/12 × 8%		4,800
		6,600
Capital leases, automobile:		
Lease balance, 1/2/93	$62,500	
Payment, 1/3/93	15,000	
Balance outstanding, year ended 12/31/93	$47,500	
Interest at 10%		4,750
Bonds payable; $538,000 × 6/12 × 10%		26,900
Interest expense, year ended December 31, 1993		$38,250

Part 5(b)

```
TO:   Controller, Rayne Co.
FROM: Chris Green, CPA
DATE: May 5, 1994
RE:   FASB Statement #109, "Accounting for Income Taxes"
```

I am pleased to provide you with the information you requested on the above-referenced matter. Under Statement #109, the objectives of accounting for income taxes are to (1) recognize in the financial statements the amount of taxes payable or refundable for the current year, and (2) recognize deferred tax assets and liabilities for the future tax consequences of events that have been recognized in the financial statements or tax returns.

A temporary difference is the difference between the tax basis of an asset or liability and its basis as reported in the financial statements (book basis). Thus, if an asset is sold (recovered), or the liability settled at its accounting carrying value, taxable income (or a deduction) will result in a future period. For example, a warranty liability would be recorded for book purposes, but would not enter into taxable income until a future year.

Deferred tax liabilities arise when the financial statement (book) basis of an asset exceeds its tax basis or when the book basis of a liability is less than its tax basis. This will give rise to a taxable temporary difference since future taxable income will exceed future pretax accounting income when the difference reverses.

A deferred tax asset arises when the financial statement (book) basis of an asset is less than its tax basis, or when the book basis of a liability is greater than its tax basis.

Regardless of whether the deferred tax is an asset or liability, it is measured using the enacted tax rate scheduled to be in effect when the difference is scheduled to reverse. The fact that tax rates may increase in the future should not be given accounting recognition until they are enacted. Accordingly, the amount of the deferred tax asset or liability is equal to the difference in basis of the related asset or liability multiplied by the appropriate tax rate.

For deferred tax assets, a valuation allowance is required if it is more likely than not that some or all of the deferred tax assets will not be realized.

The deferred income tax expense or benefit is measured by the amount of the change in the deferred tax asset (net of the valuation allowance, if any) and liability accounts from the beginning of the period to the date of the financial statements.

I hope this information will be of assistance in the preparation of the 1993 income tax accrual. Please do not hesitate to contact me if you need further information on this matter.

10. At the Exam...General Suggestions

The attributes of successful candidates were identified in Chapter 3. They consist of being highly motivated, well-prepared, and confident. By examination day the first two have been accomplished. Confidence remains and must be sustained through the two days of the examination. As we have noted previously, the CPA exam is as much a test of a candidate's ability to cope with pressure as it is of his academic preparation.

Approaching the exam with confidence comes from knowing that you have done your homework and are ready to compete. You know what is likely to be covered on the exam and you know how to handle the pressures of time and concentration. Like any successful competitor, you have studied the situation, rehearsed your strategy, and have developed the mental discipline that separates winners from losers. Discipline is essential. A candidate must not only have a plan but must have the self-discipline to stick with it, both before and during the CPA exam. Ideally, the candidate approaches examination day at the peak of his readiness. If his review program has been sound, and if his belief in himself is true, he will have every reason to expect success on the CPA exam.

Since the fifteen and one-half hours of test-taking represent the culmination of many weeks of hard work and mounting hope, the concern of the candidate during the days of the exam is to not lose the readiness achieved because of factors peculiar to the exam environment. That possibility can be minimized by becoming as familiar as possible with the situations likely to be faced at the exam site.

THE EXAM SITE ENVIRONMENT

In many parts of the country, contending with the physical limitations of the site selected for administration of the test is one of the chief obstacles to be overcome by the candidate. Because of the large number of candidates sitting for the exam, a site is selected more on the basis of its ability to hold a large number of people than its suitability for concentrated intellectual effort.

There are no permanent examination centers since the CPA exam is administered only twice annually. Consequently, each administrative body must scramble to line up a facility in time for the dates scheduled by the AICPA. In large states with thousands of candidates, this means the use of exposition centers, athletic arenas, national guard armories, etc. Many veterans of the CPA exam are fond of recalling the distractions endured while taking the examination: poor lighting, rickety tables, strange aromas, jarring noises, etc. Frequently, they sat for the exam amid the paraphernalia of circuses, trade shows, or military units.

In the end, of course, the candidate has no choice about where he will be sitting for the exam. The best that he can do is to expect the distractions or inconveniences that are likely to occur and to regard them as minor impediments to achieving his objective of becoming a CPA. Like those before him, he will one day view those peculiarities of the exam site as amusing nostalgia.

If possible, the candidate should reconnoiter the exam site some time in advance of arrival for LPR on Wednesday morning. The locations of eating facilities, restrooms, parking places, etc., should be noted. Lighting and room temperature should also be noted so as to try to ensure sitting in a desirable area and dressing comfortably while taking the examination. Since the exam poses an arduous physical, as well as intellectual, challenge—requiring, as it does, sitting for long periods of time, bent in concentration—it is wise to avoid sitting in areas where there are drafts, glares, temperature changes, distracting activity, etc. Do not sit near doorways, drinking fountains, windows, proctors' tables, etc.

Determine what rules exist for bringing snacks into the examination room. Common sense should be exercised, of course. Select foods that are easily digestible and that will not distract neighboring candidates with noisy wrappers. Liquids should be drunk in moderate amounts so as to minimize trips to the restroom. In sum, snacks should be light and energizing, not a hindrance to working efficiently.

ACCOMMODATIONS

One of the concerns of candidates who live more than a half-hour's drive from the exam site is the advisability of securing overnight accommodations near the site. Nightmares of transportation breakdowns or delays causing one to arrive late can cause anxiety to the diligent candidate as he makes his final preparation. The last thing he needs as he travels forth is a blown radiator hose or snarled train system. For those who live more than three hours away, the solution is obvious: stay near the exam site. For others, it is a question of willingness to assume some risk that travel will be uneventful.

The primary concern should be to preserve the concentration that presumably has peaked just at the right time. Continuity and stability are important. The candidate needs to approach the competition of the CPA exam poised and confident. There will be enough anxiety over the content of the exam itself without the added anxiety over the logistics of room, board, and travel.

Whether the candidate stays at home or stays in a motel, his final hours before the exam should be relaxed. His preparation program should have been concluded by the weekend preceding the exam so that all that needs to be done is to give a quick once-over to subjects most likely to appear. By Monday of exam week, he should be able to say, with optimism and confidence, "If I don't know it now, I'll never know it." Any last-minute cramming will probably succumb to the law of diminishing returns. Whatever accommodations are arranged, they should ensure that nothing will dissipate the readiness the candidate has worked so hard to achieve.

ARRIVAL AT THE EXAMINATION

Finally the day of expectation dawns! The candidate arrives at the end of his arduous preparation journey, travel-weary but ready to contend with the only remaining obstacle between him and professional stature. Once again, familiarity with what is about to take place will minimize the possibility of disturbing the confidence and concentration that have been achieved.

You should arrive early and be adequately supplied. Plan to arrive an hour before the designated starting time. Filing into the testing room will usually begin about a half-hour before starting time. This will give you an additional half-hour to stretch your legs, breathe some fresh air, and relax your mind. Make sure that all the necessary implements of test-taking are on hand: *pencils, erasers, watches. Be like Noah: bring two of everything!* Fine-lead mechanical pencils are excellent for essay writing and computational problems, but bring two! You wouldn't want the day to be lost because of a broken spring. The standard, wood, No. 2 lead pencil is necessary for entering answers to objective questions on machine-scored answer sheets. Bring three or four. Bring one rectangular eraser and one pencil-style eraser. Bring two watches! (Suppose a gear jams or the battery dies on your new LCD special!) Rulers are usually prohibited (too easy to write useful information on them), so plan on constructing a straightedge at the exam by carefully folding a sheet of scrap paper. Items that should *not* be brought are any study materials you have been using during your review program. They will not be permitted inside the testing room, and you risk losing them by having to pile them along with everybody else's outside the door.

Once seated at your designated spot, arrange yourself comfortably and prepare to begin answering questions. There usually will be fifteen or twenty minutes of idle time while you wait for the rest of the candidates to get seated and for the proctors to get things organized. This time can be used constructively by doing two things: (1) unburdening your mind by jotting down on the scrap paper provided all of the key concepts, memory aids, etc., that you have been studying over the previous weeks, and (2) heading up the blank essay and computational answer sheets provided. Make sure, of course, that such activity is permitted by the proctors at your test site. Generally it is, but in some places there may be rules against writing anything other than headings before the examinations are distributed. Even if you are not permitted activity (1), it is still advisable to make such notations as soon as you are able. Very likely they will prove to be time-saving notes later on during the exam.

All answer sheets are intended to be anonymous as far as the grader is concerned. The only identifying information is (1) candidate number, (2) date, (3) state, (4) subject, (5) question number, and (6) page number. Do not write your name anywhere on the pages you turn in. While having your name replaced by a number may seem impersonal, that very impersonality will ensure that the grader will not be influenced by any of the factors of sex, race, religion, or nationality that can often be suggested by a surname. Once you have completed the exam, arrange your answer sheets in their proper sequence. Paper clips or staples, if permitted, are useful for grouping papers by individual questions.

READING DIRECTIONS

As was noted in our discussion of how to answer CPA exam questions (Chapter 5), the examination is a test of reading comprehension as much as any other skill. The need for reading directions carefully, therefore, should be obvious. Nevertheless, many candidates, in their haste to get started, neglect to read the set of directions printed on the cover page of each exam section and on the computer-graded answer sheet for the objective questions. The AICPA attempts to minimize the hazards of careless attention to directions by including the following instructions for the exam in Appendix B of its publication "Information for CPA Candidates" (eleventh edition):

Instructions for the Uniform Certified Public Accountant Examination

1. The only aids you are allowed to take to the examination tables are pens, pencils, and erasers.

2. You will be furnished a prenumbered identification card (or admission notice) with your seven-digit candidate number on it. The prenumbered identification card must be available for inspection by the proctors throughout the examination.

3. Any reference during the examination to books or other materials or the exchange of information with other persons shall be considered misconduct sufficient to bar you from further participation in the examination.

4. You must observe the fixed time for each session. It is your responsibility to be ready at the start of the session and to stop writing when told to do so.

5. The following is an example of point values and estimated time allotments for each examination question in the Business Law & Professional Responsibilities section as it might appear in its Examination Question Booklet.

   The point values for each question and estimated time allotments, based primarily on point value, are as follows:

	Point Value	Estimated Minutes Minimum	Maximum
No. 1	60	90	100
No. 2	10	10	15
No. 3	10	10	15
No. 4	10	15	25
No. 5	10	15	25
Total	100	140	180

6. An Examination Question Booklet will be distributed shortly before each session begins. You are not permitted to open the Examination Question Booklet until the starting signal is given by the proctor. Prior to the start of the examination you are permitted to record your seven-digit candidate number in the boxes provided at the upper right-hand corner of the front cover of the Examination Question Booklet. For the Accounting & Reporting (ARE) section, you are permitted to blacken the corresponding oval below each box on the front and back covers and complete the Attendance Record Form on the front cover.

7. For the Business Law & Professional Responsibilities (LPR), Auditing (AUDIT), and Financial Accounting & Reporting (FARE) sections, an Examination Answer Booklet will be distributed shortly before each session begins. Answers must be written on the paper provided in the Examination Answer Booklet as follows:

   a. Prior to the start of the examination you are permitted to record your seven-digit candidate number and blacken the corresponding oval below each box on the front and back covers and complete the Attendance Record Form on the front cover.

   b. After the start of the examination you should record your seven-digit candidate number, state, and question number where indicated.

8. For the ARE and FARE examination sections you will be provided with a calculator. You should test the calculator in accordance with the instructions on the cover page of the Examination Question Booklet. Inform your proctor if your calculator is defective.

9. All amounts given in objective items or essay/problem-type questions are to be considered material unless otherwise stated.

10. Answer all objective items on the Objective Answer Sheet provided. Use a No. 2 pencil only. You should attempt to answer all objective items.

There is no penalty for incorrect responses. Since the objective items are computer-graded, your comments and calculations associated with them are not considered.

11. The Objective Answer Sheet may vary for each section of the examination. It is important to pay strict attention to the manner in which your Objective Answer Sheet is structured. As you proceed with the examination, be absolutely certain that the space in which you have indicated your answer corresponds directly in number with the item in your Examination Question Booklet. If you mark your answers on the Examination Question Booklet, be certain that you transfer them to the Objective Answer Sheet before the session ends. Your examination papers cannot be graded properly if you fail to blacken the ovals correctly. Extra time is not allowed for this at the end of the session.

.2. Answer all essay/problem-type questions on the paper provided. Always begin the start of an answer to a question at the top of a new page.

13. Include all computations to the problem-type questions in the FARE section. This may assist the examiners in understanding your answers.

14. **You are required to turn in separately by the end of each session:**
    a. Attendance Record Form;
    b. Objective Answer Sheet;
    c. Remaining Portion of Examination Answer Booklet (for LPR, AUDIT, and FARE);
    d. Examination Question Booklet;
    e. Calculator (for ARE and FARE);
    f. All other examination materials;
    g. Prenumbered Identification Card at the last examination section for which you sit (if required by your examining jurisdiction).

    Your examination will not be graded unless the above-listed items are handed in before leaving the examination room.

15. Unless otherwise instructed, if you want your Examination Question Booklet mailed to you, write your name and address in both places indicated on the back cover, and place 52 cents postage in the space provided.

16. Penalties will be imposed on any candidate who is caught cheating before or during the examination. These penalties may include expulsion from this and future examination sessions.

The specific directions for each exam section, as printed on the cover page for each, are essentially an abridged version of the rules enumerated above. They should be reviewed, of course, for particular items, and because, in the words of the examiners, "failure to follow these instructions may have an adverse effect on your examination grade."

SCANNING AND PLANNING

Once the examination booklets have been distributed and the directions noted, the candidate must progress with all due speed through the exam questions. But before he forges ahead, he should take time to plan his attack. Answering the questions in straight numerical sequence is not always the best approach. First, all of the questions should be scanned, and then an order for answering them decided upon.

Usually, working from easiest to most difficult is the best way to handle questions. This is because the question or two that at the start seemed most intimidating seem less so after the candidate has been answering questions effectively for the past two or three hours. It's true. In the course of answering perhaps sixty (or ninety) four-option multiple-choice questions and two to four essay, computational, and other objective formats questions, a great deal of knowledge has been brought to the forefront of the mind. The candidate knows more by the end of the exam than he did at the beginning.

One of the decisions to make regarding question sequence is whether to do the four-option multiple-choice questions first. Most candidates do. There are several reasons for this. One is that all of the four-option multiple-choice questions taken together represent the largest block of credit available and also the longest question in terms of budgeted time. Second is that, as individual items, they represent a series of brief, manageable tasks that provide a warm-up for the more extended problems and/or essays to follow. Third is that, in the course of handling all of the four-option multiple-choice questions, most of the relevant body of information for that exam section will have been reviewed, thus preparing the way for the in-depth questions that follow. Fourth is that four-option multiple-choice questions are usually answerable in less time than the budget suggests—90–100 minutes for LPR, 140–150 minutes for AUDIT, 120–130 minutes for ARE, and 130–140 minutes for FARE—so that the candidate often has a time surplus that can be allocated among the remaining other objective formats, essay or computational questions.

Another approach to dealing with exam sections having essay questions is the following:

Step 1: Analyze essay questions one by one and sketch, in outline form, a tentative answer to each.

Step 2: Answer objective questions, adding information to essay outlines as it occurs while answering objective questions.

Step 3: Write essay answers based on outlines generated.

Such an approach is systematic and logical, but the candidate must be careful about controlling his use of time. It will be more difficult to keep a time budget under control for a particular essay if it is handled in two separate stages as suggested above. The great danger in not using time efficiently is that the candidate will find himself out of time, but with answers still to be written. If *that* occurs, chances for passing the examination are not good.

GOING THE DISTANCE

For the candidate taking all four sections, the two days of examinations will be especially arduous. He will experience unparalleled physical, emotional, and mental strain. At 6:00 P.M. Wednesday afternoon, after completing three hours of LPR and/or four and one-half hours of AUDIT, the candidate's emotional state will run from grim pessimism to ebullient optimism, depending upon how he feels he performed earlier in the day. A candidate should *not* give up at this point because he has no real way of determining how his test will be graded.

Further, the ability of the candidate to shift smoothly from one subject to another is important to his success. Confidence and concentration—question by question, section by section—must be maintained throughout the two days. This is particularly true when Thursday afternoon rolls around and the candidate is relieved to face his final obstacle, FARE. The tendency for many—whether because of assumptions about past performance on other sections, fatigue, or overconfidence—is to let up on FARE. The candidate must discipline himself to be no less conscientious on Thursday afternoon than he was on Wednesday.

One thing that should be avoided is rehashing an exam section with other candidates before the entire exam is over. While it is difficult not to discuss and compare answers, the end result of such conversations usually is to make everyone less confident about how he

did. Wednesday evening should be spent in quiet relaxation, far from the pressures and concerns of the CPA exam.

The CPA exam should be a once-in-a-lifetime experience. Unfortunately, for many candidates it is experienced more than once. As we have seen elsewhere in this book, success on the CPA exam stems from preparation and commitment. Preparation must be thorough, both in terms of topical review and examsmanship skills. Nothing that can be prepared for should be ignored. Every situation should be anticipated so far as possible. The CPA exam is a crucible—a test of what a candidate is made of.

There are few satisfactions in life that can match knowing you have achieved a goal through your own hard work. For many candidates the two days of the CPA exam, and the months of preparation preceding it, represent the most demanding test they will ever experience. It is a measure of their abilities and their character. The satisfaction that comes from passing the CPA exam is all the more sweet because it has been earned.

More selected BARRON'S titles:

ACCOUNTING HANDBOOK, Joel G. Siegel and Jae K. Shim
Provides accounting rules, guidelines, formulas and techniques etc. to help
students and business professionals work out accounting problems. Hardcover:
$29.95, Canada $38.95/ISBN 6176-4, 832 pages

REAL ESTATE HANDBOOK, 3rd EDITION
Jack P. Freidman and Jack C. Harris
A dictionary/reference for everyone in real estate. Defines over 1500 legal,
financial, and architectural terms. Hardcover, $29.95, Canada $39.95
ISBN 6330-9, 810 pages

**HOW TO PREPARE FOR THE REAL ESTATE LICENSING
EXAMINATIONS-SALESPERSON AND BROKER, 4th EDITION**
Bruce Lindeman and Jack P. Freidman
Reviews current exam topics and features updated model exams and supplemental
exams, all with explained answers.
Paperback, $11.95, Canada $15.95/ISBN 4355-3, 340 pages

BARRON'S FINANCE AND INVESTMENT HANDBOOK,
3rd EDITION, John Downes and Jordan Goodman
This hard-working handbook of essential information defines more than 3000 key
terms, and explores 30 basic investment opportunities. The investment
information is thoroughly up-to-date. Hardcover $29.95, Canada $38.95
ISBN 6188-8, approx. 1152 pages

FINANCIAL TABLES FOR MONEY MANAGEMENT
Stephen S. Solomon, Dr. Clifford Marshall, Martin Pepper,
Jack P. Freidman and Jack C. Harris
Pocket-sized handbooks of interest and investment rate tables used easily by
average investors and mortgage holders. Paperback
Real Estate Loans, 2nd Ed., $6.95, Canada $8.95/ISBN 1618-1, 336 pages
Mortgage Payments, 2nd Ed., $5.95, Canada $7.95/ISBN 1386-7, 304 pages
Bonds, 2nd, Ed., $5.95, Canada $7.50/ISBN 4995-0, 256 pages
Canadian Mortgage Payments, 2nd Ed., Canada $8.95/ISBN 1617-3, 336 pages
Adjustable Rate Mortgages, 2nd Ed., $6.95, Canada $8.50/ISBN 1529-0, 288 pages

All prices are in U.S. and Canadian dollars and subject to change without notice. At your
local bookseller, or order direct adding 10% postage (minimum charge $3.75, Canada $4.00),
N.Y. residents add sales tax.   ISBN PREFIX 0-8120

Barron's Educational Series, Inc.
250 Wireless Boulevard, Hauppauge, NY 11788
In Canada: Georgetown Book Warehouse
34 Armstrong Ave., Georgetown, Ontario L7G 4R9   R 10/94

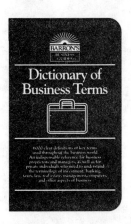
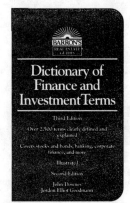